STUDIES IN MEDIEVAL AND RENAISSANCE HISTORY

STUDIES IN MEDIEVAL AND RENAISSANCE HISTORY

Edited by Roger Dahood and Peter E. Medine

THIRD SERIES, VOLUME XI
(Old Series Volume XXXVI, New Series Volume XXVI)

AMS Press, Inc.

New York

Studies in Medieval and Renaissance History

ISSN 0081-8224

Studies in Medieval and Renaissance History is published under the auspices of the Arizona Center for Medieval and Renaissance Studies

International Standard Book Numbers
ISBN-10: 0-404-64550-X (Set)
ISBN-13: 978-0-404-64550-2 (Set)

ISBN-10: 0-404-64561-5 (Series III.11)
ISBN-13: 978-0-404-64561-8 (Series III.11)

Library of Congress Card Number 63-22098

All AMS books are printed on acid-free paper that meets the guidelines for performance and durability of the Committee on Production Guidelines for Book Longevity of the Council on Library Resources.

AMS PRESS, INC.
Brooklyn Navy Yard, 63 Flushing Avenue-Unit #221
Brooklyn, NY 11205-1073, USA
www.amspressinc.com

Manufactured in the United States of America

Table of Contents

Abstracts

Uroscopy in Middle English: A Guide to Texts and Manuscripts

M. Teresa Tavormina

DESPITE THE IMPORTANCE of uroscopic diagnosis and prognosis in medieval medicine, the wide array of Middle English treatises on the subject remains an exceptionally challenging genre to navigate. To ameliorate some of those challenges, this article provides a comprehensive survey of Middle English uroscopic writings, organized in an analytical taxonomy of approximately 130 distinct works. The taxonomy describes these works and their principal variant forms, lists their witnesses, and comments briefly on selected individual witnesses. Six appendices complement the taxonomy:

1. a list of selected non-uroscopic texts regularly associated with specific uroscopies;
2. an index of manuscripts containing Middle English uroscopy texts;
3. a list of Middle English uroscopies with more than five witnesses;
4. defining uroscopic signs in major uroscopic token lists;
5. a list of the Latin texts cited in the taxonomy;
6. linguistic perspectives on Middle English uroscopy texts.

Paris to Rome and Back Again: The Nuns of Longchamp and Leo X's 1521 Bull *Piis omnium*
Sean L. Field

AROUND 1517 THE Franciscan nuns of Longchamp launched an effort to secure papal permission for the celebration of a newly-composed office in honor of their founder, Isabelle of France (1225–1270). The request was approved by Pope Leo X and promulgated by his legate, Cardinal Adrien de Boisy, by the end of 1521. The present article first unpacks the networks of influence involved in the effort to obtain recognition for Isabelle's cult, and edits the Latin texts of the pope's response and the cardinal's promulgation. But under the leadership of Abbess Catherine Le Picart the nuns also quickly recorded their own triumphant narrative of their success and produced their own French translations of the two Latin texts. This article edits these French texts as well, and highlights the rhetorical moves involved in their creation.

Between Aristotle and Augustine: Peter Martyr Vermigli and the Development of Protestant Ethics
Simon J. G. Burton

PETER MARTYR VERMIGLI (1499–1562), the Italian Reformer, is now widely acknowledged as one of the pioneering figures in the development of Protestant ethics. This article examines the scholastic contours of his unfinished Commentary on Aristotle's Nicomachean Ethics and its relation to his Protestant convictions. In doing so it demonstrates the innovative way in Vermigli reconfigured, and even transfigured, Aristotelian notions of virtue in light of his distinctive Thomist and late medieval Augustinian synthesis, and in opposition to what he saw as a dangerous Neo-Pelagianism, as epitomised by his Catholic opponent Albert Pighius (c. 1490–1542). In this way Vermigli's ethics emerge as profoundly shaped not only by the Reformation sola scriptura, but also by the renewed Augustinian scholasticism of the late Middle Ages.

"And openly I profes myself/ of the *Arminian* sect": Arminianism in *Sir John van Oldenbarnavelt* (1619) and Two Seventeenth Century English Political Prints, ca. 1628–41
Christina M. Carlson

THIS ESSAY USES Nicholas Tyacke's historical argument about the rise of Arminianism in England, as well as the anti-Tyacke camp, to present a new reading of John Fletcher and Philip Massinger's topical political drama, Sir John Van Oldenbarnavelt. It compares the play's emphasis on political and polemic appropriations of Arminianism, with two visual satires from the late 1620s, "Arminius Between Truth and Heresie" (1628) and the fold-out engraving that accompanies John Russell's *The Spy* (1628). This essay argues that, while theological concerns are certainly described in these more "popular" materials, more often such issues are translated into such "political" issues, including debates over censorship, the international situation in the United Provinces, and an anti-Arminian bias (in England) that connects the "religious" question (of Arminian vs. Calvinist) to a more generalized anti-Catholicism.

"It's good to talk: conversations between gods, men and beasts in Early Modern English versions of Lucian's 'Dialogues'"
Paul Hartle

THIS ESSAY TRACES the reception and transmission of Lucian's works to English readers in the sixteenth and seventeenth centuries. It assesses the Humanist response to Lucian and his influence on the work of More and Erasmus, before examining his literary and moral reputation in Elizabethan and Stuart writing. It focusses on the texts in which Lucian is introduced to English readers without either Greek or Latin, especially the versions of Francis Hickes (1634), Thomas Heywood (1637), Jasper Mayne (1663), and Ferrand Spence (1684–85). It analyzes the ways in which those versions engage with the social, religious and political contexts into which they were published, and draws attention to other texts which claim paternity from Lucian (and sometimes parody the arch-parodist). Finally, it speculates on the contributory impact of Lucian to the topsy-turvy experience of civil war and interregnum and subsequently to the growing intellectual climate of rationalism and atheism after the Restoration.

Peter Heylyn's Seventeenth-Century English Worldview
Peter Craft

PETER HEYLYN'S *COSMOGRAPHIE* (1652) summarizes the collective observations of dozens of European voyagers over a century and averaged more than one new edition per decade between 1652 and 1700. As such it reflects English readers' "common sense" or general knowledge about the world until at least the publication of John Dryden's Aureng-Zebe in 1676. Heylyn's work therefore forms a general template of a historically specific worldview in which India's economic prosperity and immense armies make England appear insignificant by comparison. At the same time, Heylyn's work, like other contemporary voyage collections, downplays the role of disease in the European conquest of the New World during the fifteenth and sixteenth centuries. This perspective in turn led to an inflated sense of English power in relation to West "Indians." Heylyn invokes religion and ethics both to excuse England's economic frailty in relation to India and to justify the exploitation of Amerindian peoples. This essay aims to pave the way for studies of popular and canonical works of English fiction during the mid-seventeenth century to suggest how voyage collection editors influenced the bestselling literature of the ensuing decades.

Diamond Jubilee: A History of the New England Renaissance Conference, 1939–2014
Christopher Carlsmith

FOUNDED IN THE SPRING of 1939, the New England Renaissance Conference (NERC) was the first scholarly association in the United States dedicated to study of the Renaissance. The purpose of NERC, then and now, was to promote and disseminate Renaissance Studies in the northeast through an annual meeting. Initially an enclave of senior scholars from prestigious universities, with a narrow focus on high culture, NERC has evolved during the past seventy-five years to include broader membership and more diverse fields of study. Unlike its sister organizations in other regions of the country, and unlike the national Renaissance Society of America (RSA), NERC has deliberately avoided any kind of permanent structure—it has no constitution, no minutes, no membership fees, no publications, and no fixed office. Drawing from conference programs, professional correspondence, oral interviews, and personal papers, this essay traces the development of NERC from 1939 to 2014.

Uroscopy in Middle English: A Guide to the Texts and Manuscripts

M. Teresa Tavormina
Michigan State University

> "This were a wikkede wey, but whoso hadde a gyde."
> *Piers Plowman* **B.6.1**

INTRODUCTION

AMONG THE MANY areas of Middle English medical writing in need of more extensive scholarly and editorial work, one of the most textually challenging is the wide array of uroscopic treatises. The diagnostic centrality of uroscopy in medieval medicine led to the inclusion of urine

The work reported in the following pages would have been impossible without the assistance of many colleagues and staff members of many manuscript repositories and other libraries. Thanks are owed, first and foremost, to Lister M. Matheson and Linda Ehrsam Voigts, who have both provided unfailing expert advice and personal support throughout this project. Personal thanks are also due to Paul Acker, Javier Calle Martín, Margaret Connolly, Roger Dahood, A. S. G. Edwards, Monica H. Green, Carrie Griffin, Ralph Hanna, E. Ruth Harvey, Patrick J. Horner, Tony Hunt, George R. Keiser, Patricia Deery Kurtz, Kirsten Jungersen, Laurence Moulinier-Brogi, Laura Nuvoloni, Kari Anne Rand, E. G. Stanley, Toshiyuki Takamiya, Jake Walsh Morrissey, and Stefanie Zaun. Errors that remain are my own.

I am also grateful for the assistance of librarians at all the institutions holding manuscripts and scholarly resources on which this article is based, in particular at the Michigan State University Libraries, especially Collections Librarian Agnes Haigh Widder and the Interlibrary Loan staff; Susan L'Engle and the Vatican Film Library at St. Louis University; Marcia Bailey and the

texts in most medical compendia, often but not always relatively short works;[1] assemblages of several uroscopies as booklets or parts of larger medical manuscripts are not uncommon; more than twenty scribes undertook to copy the massive *Liber Uricrisiarum* by Henry Daniel, with another dozen or so copying abridgments and excerpts of that text. Over 200 manuscripts contain one or more Middle English uroscopic treatises; the revised Voigts-Kurtz database of scientific and medical texts subject-tags almost 500 records as dealing with urine or uroscopy.[2] A more detailed reading of the manuscripts and further searches of manuscript

---

University of Michigan Serials and Microforms Department; the British Library, the Bodleian Library, Cambridge University Library, the Wellcome Library, Glasgow University Special Collections, the National Library of Medicine, and the Huntington Library; the libraries of Trinity College, Gonville and Caius College, St. John's College, Jesus College, Magdalene College, Corpus Christi College, and Emmanuel College, Cambridge; and of Magdalen College, All Souls College, and Corpus Christi College, Oxford: all of them institutions that have extended access to their collections and other resources to me on multiple occasions. Financial support for some of the research travel involved in the project was provided by the National Endowment for the Humanities through the Vatican Film Library and by the internal grant programs of Michigan State University.

[1]   As George R. Keiser observes, "The great majority of medical miscellanies contain at least one treatise on uroscopy" ("Works of Science and Information," *A Manual of the Writings in Middle English 1050-1500*, vol. 10 [New Haven, 1998], 3661). A general review of medieval and early modern uroscopy is not within the scope of this essay, but interested readers will find good starting points for that history in the recent work of Laurence Moulinier-Brogi and Michael Stolberg. See Moulinier-Brogi, "L'Uroscopie en vulgaire dans l'occident médiéval: Un tour d'horizon," in *Science Translated: Latin and Vernacular Translations of Scientific Treatises in Medieval Europe*, ed. Michèle Goyens et al., Mediaevalia Lovaniensia ser. 1, 40 (Leuven, 2008), 221–41; eadem, *L'Uroscopie au Moyen Âge: Lire dans un verre la nature de l'homme* (Paris, 2012); Stolberg, *Die Harnschau: Eine Kultur- und Alltagsgeschichte* (Köln, 2009), focused on the early modern period but with partial applicability to the later Middle Ages.

[2]   Linda Ehrsam Voigts and Patricia Deery Kurtz, *Scientific and Medical Writings in Old and Middle English: An Electronic Reference* (Ann Arbor, 2000), CD. Rev. online edition 2011 (cited henceforth as eVK2). (The 2014 update to eVK2 appeared after production of this essay had begun; constraints of time have precluded a complete collation of eVK2 references with the 2014 revisions, but spot checks suggest that few if any of the references in this essay are affected by the update.) The online edition of Lynn Thorndike and Pearl Kibre, *A Catalogue of Incipits of Mediaeval Scientific Writings in Latin*, rev. and augmented ed. (Cambridge, MA, 1963) will be cited henceforth as eTK. Both works are available through the Medieval Academy of America's Digital Tools website: http://www.medievalacademy. org/?page=DigitalTools.

catalogues allow many other witnesses and a number of additional texts to be added to those tallied by Voigts and Kurtz.

If incipits were all one needed to sort out the various surviving uroscopy treatises, it might be reasonably easy, albeit time-consuming, to provide a comprehensive index to the genre. Unfortunately, several factors combine to complicate the picture and perplex readers, indexers, and editors:

(1) distinct texts can have very similar openings, such as the standard definition of urine as a "cleansing of the blood,"[3] the number of urinary colors (most often twenty, echoing "bis deni" in Giles of Corbeil's *Carmen de urinis*, line 19),[4] the characteristics to examine in a uroscopic sample, and so on;

(2) the texts often contain easily rearranged modules (e.g., colors, contents, women's urines, humoral traits, etc.), so two witnesses to what is essentially the same work might begin at different points and simply order the content differently, yielding different incipits for fundamentally identical texts;

---

[3] This definition, usually expressed in Latin as *colamentum sanguinis* ('filtrate of the blood'), originates in Theophilus Protospatharius's *De urinis* (*Peri ouron*), translated into Latin in the early twelfth century and included among the core texts of the medical textbook known as the *Ars medicine*, later called the *Articella*; see Cornelius O'Boyle, *The Art of Medicine: Medical Teaching at the University of Paris, 1250–1400* (Leiden, 1998), 92–94.

The same definition appears in Constantine the African's Latin translation of Isaac Israeli's *Liber de urinis* (*Kitab al-Baul*), ed. Johannes Peine, *Die Harnschrift des Isaac Judaeus* (diss. Borna-Leipzig, 1919); rpt. in *Isḥāq ibn Sulaymān al-Isrā'īlī (d. c. 325/935): Texts and Studies*, Islamic Medicine 35, ed. Fuat Sezgin (Frankfurt am Main, 1996), 52. Other occurrences include but are not limited to the *Regule urinarum* of Johannes Platearius, Maurus of Salerno's *Regule urinarum* (citing both Theophilus and Isaac), and Bernard de Gordon's *De urinis*, chap. 1. See Salvatore De Renzi, *Collectio Salernitana*, 5 vols. (Naples, 1852–59), 4:409 and 3:2; Bernard de Gordon, *Lilium medicinae* (Lyons, 1574), 730. By far the most common Middle English translation of the phrase is "cleansing of (the) blood." Cf. *The Middle English Dictionary* (henceforth *MED*), s.vv. *clensen* (v.), senses 1(a) and 1(b) [of grain: 'sift, winnow'; of liquids: 'clarify, strain'], and *clensing* (ger.), senses 1(a) [including 'sifting, straining'] and 1(b) [phr. ~ *sive*, 'cleansing sieve']. The *MED* entries do not include uses of *clensen/clensing* in uroscopic contexts. The sifting/winnowing and straining/clarifying senses do not appear to have carried over very far into Modern English: the *Oxford English Dictionary* does not include any of these narrower senses in its entries for *cleanse*, v., or *cleansing*, n.

[4] Giles of Corbeil, *Carmen de urinis*, ed. and trans. Camille Vieillard, *L'Urologie et les médecins urologues dans la médecine ancienne: Gilles de Corbeil, sa vie, ses oeuvres, son poème des urines* (Paris, 1903), 267–301, at 273. Also in a critical edition by Ludwig Choulant, *Liber de urinis metrice compositus*, in *Aegidii Corboliensis Carmina medica* (Leipzig, 1826), 1–18.

(3) the modularity of the texts makes it easy for scribes to omit sections deliberately or inadvertently;

(4) the practical purpose of the texts may have given scribes greater license to abridge the texts or expand them with useful materials from other sources.

Aside from the variability of incipits and plasticity of structure, many of these treatises are fairly short, often less than three folios long, and scribes frequently embed them in longer texts with little or no signaling of incipits and desinits—factors that make them easy to overlook and complicated to identify.

The following taxonomy of Middle English uroscopy treatises is thus offered as a finding and identifying aid for future editors and scholars of these texts and for indexers of Middle English prose and vernacular medicine more generally. It grows out of a survey project that sought to locate and to examine directly as many Middle English uroscopic texts as possible, in libraries throughout the United Kingdom, Ireland, and the United States, with microfilm copies from collections in other countries where available.[5]

---

[5]   As indicated by the tag **NOT SEEN** in the entries below, I have been unable to examine the following manuscripts, either directly or in reproductions: Copenhagen Royal n.c. 314, GC 609/340, and the erstwhile Brussels Bibliothèque Royale MS IV 249 now in private hands, affecting the witness lists for items 1.1.2, 8.5, and 15.2. I base my inclusion of these manuscripts in those witness lists on eVK2 and on published descriptions of the manuscripts, as reported in footnotes under the relevant items.

Following the lead of the Voigts-Kurtz database, I have included witnesses preserved in sixteenth-century manuscripts and printed texts, if those texts are attested in earlier, Middle English copies. However, I have not attempted to locate all sixteenth-century manuscripts with medical content, and I exclude printed texts that appear to be new compositions (though with largely familiar content), such as the uroscopy at the end of *The Great Herbal* (1526), titled "The Knowledge of the Diversities and Colors of All Manner of Urines"; the uroscopic section of Thomas Elyot's *Castle of Health* (bk. 4, chaps. 8–9; 1539); Robert Record's *Urinal of Physick* (1547); Humphrey Llwyd's translation of Jean Vassès's *De iudiciis urinarum* (1553); and John Fletcher's *The Differences, Causes, and Judgements of Urine* (1598). After some deliberation, I have chosen to omit the short uroscopic chapter in Bartholomaeus Anglicus's *On the Properties of Things* (5.45), the passing mentions of uroscopic *tokenes* of illness in Gilbertus Anglicus's *Compendium medicine* and the Middle English *Secreta Mulierum*, and similar passages in other comprehensive scientific and medical treatises. As Bartholomaeus observes, after a brief overview of etymology, uses, regions, and colors of urine, "It longiþ nouȝt to þis work to determyne and rekene þe particulers circumstaunces of þise coloures" (*On the Properties of Things;*

I begin by dividing the texts into two very broad groups: anonymous works and works with known or attributed authorship. Within each group, the listings start with the most widely disseminated texts and move (broadly speaking) to those with the fewest witnesses. I occasionally modify the general principle of decreasing frequency in order to group similar texts together or to reflect other relationships. An outline of classification headings and a table of libraries and collections containing Middle English uroscopies precede the taxonomy proper. Headnotes for the different texts vary in length, depending on the complexity of textual variation, source relationships, and content. The total number of distinct works listed below comes in somewhere between 125 to 150, depending on how one counts embedded and compendious texts. The witness lists for individual works are roughly arranged from more to less complete versions of the text, with notably similar copies placed together or near each other where possible.[6]

A word on title format is in order: wherever possible, I have sought to provide titles based on manuscript titles or explicits, rubrics and headings, internal self-references, or incipits. More specifically:

(1) titles that originate in scribal or authorial titles for prose works, as reflected in headings, rubrics, or internal references, or that have been assigned by modern editors, are given in italics;

(2) titles drawn from incipits,[7] in the absence of headings and other indicators, are given in quotation marks, as are titles for the handful of short versified works;

(3) titles of sections within longer works, whether in English or Latin, are in small caps;

(4) category labels and other descriptors created for this taxonomy appear in roman font without quotation marks, except for descriptors that include identifying words or phrases set off in quotes.

John Trevisa's Translation of Bartholomaeus Anglicus De Proprietatibus Rerum, 3 vols., gen. ed. M. C. Seymour [Oxford, 1975–88], 1:258).

[6] Although an alphabetical listing of witnesses by city and library might be more transparent, it would limit the taxonomy's indications of relative completeness and textual similarity; for a complete list of manuscripts containing Middle English uroscopies organized alphabetically by city, library, and shelfmark, see Appendix B.

[7] Like Voigts and Kurtz, I normalize incipits to modern spelling for ease of reference; for texts with multiple witnesses, I have tried to use the most common or the most general incipit. Other quotations of Middle English material are left in the original spelling.

Where a witness is included (in whole or in part) in the Voigts-Kurtz database, I have placed the relevant eVK2 number(s) to the right of the shelfmark and folio/page numbers in the list of manuscript witnesses.[8] I have also noted co-occurrences of selected works, where such recurring associations may shed light on the textual relationships among those works. Several appendices at the end of the taxonomy provide additional information that may prove useful to students of Middle English medical writing.

A number of texts and textual components are cross-referenced often enough to warrant abbreviations, given in bold and signalled in the classification headings and on first reference. Cross-references within the taxonomy are frequent but not exhaustive. The subgrouping of texts that take on multiple forms is more pragmatic than stemmatic, usually based on variations at the structural level, such as the order of parts, differing prologues or starting points, selected key features, and so on. I leave closer analysis of textual relationships at the word and sentence level to future editors of individual texts. The taxonomy seeks to err on the side of distinguishing rather than conflating texts, though it does treat prologues as part of the work they introduce. I have aimed at a broadly coherent map of the genre, but rigid organizational consistency and equal depth of annotation from one section to the next are neither desirable nor possible, given the differences in purpose, form, and content between texts.

Although it is likely that other witnesses and perhaps even other texts remain to be discovered, the taxonomic overview provided here should make it easier to place such discoveries in the larger framework of the genre as a whole, and, where necessary, to correct or refine the classifications, source identifications, and other information given below. In addition to the potential usefulness of the survey itself, the project has enabled a handful of editions already in print and several others in progress by the present writer. I hope that others will be encouraged by the information presented below to undertake their own editions and studies of Middle English uroscopic writings and would be grateful to learn of any addenda or corrigenda that might be noted in future publications.

---

[8] When an eVK entry shares an incipit but differs in the folio or page extent from a witness listed below, I indicate the difference with an asterisk (e.g., "eVK2 *1234.00"); when eVK does not record the incipit for a particular witness, I use a dash ("eVK2 – "). I include prologues in texts without distinguishing them, aside from indicating distinct eVK2 numbers for the prologue and the main text.

CLASSIFICATION HEADINGS

I. Anonymous Works
1.0 *The Twenty-Jordan Series* (**20J**, comprising **20Col**, **20Sick**, **20Med**, and **Cir** as described in **20J** entry below)
  1.1 Karapos incipit
    1.1.1 Sloane 7 type (**S**)
    1.1.2 Digby 75 type (**D**)
      1.1.2a Digby 75 – Livida subtype (**Da**)
  1.2 Rubea incipit
  1.3 Rufus incipit
  1.4 Albus/Lacteus incipits
  1.5 Miscellaneous incipits
2.0 *The Dome of Uryne* Compendium (**DU**; selected components and their abbreviations also included in headings below; abbreviations for all components listed in **DU** entry below)
  2.1 Core Version
  2.2 Expanded Version
  2.3 Abbreviated Version
  2.4 Hybrid Version
  2.5 Peculiar Versions and Singleton Components
    2.5a Peculiar Versions
    2.5b Singleton Components
3.0 Vade Mecum Suite
  3.1 *Twenty Colors by Digestion Groups* (**20Col-Dig**)
    3.1.1 Unillustrated Texts
      3.1.1a "Crocus orientalis/occidentalis" simile
      3.1.1b "Saffron d'orte/belynger" simile
      3.1.1c Idiosyncratic Texts
    3.1.2 Illustrated Texts (*Ring of Urines*)
      3.1.2a One-Ring Versions
      3.1.2b Three-Ring Version
      3.1.2c Derivative Texts
  3.2 *Urina Rufa*
    3.2.1 "Good Disposition" Texts
      3.2.1a Citrine "with a middle substance"
      3.2.1b Citrine "with a mean substance"
      3.2.1c Citrine with no reference to substance
    3.2.2 "Good Digestion" Texts
    3.2.3 Idiosyncratic Texts
  3.3 *Cleansing of Blood*
    3.3.1 Complete
      3.3.1a "Each urine" incipit
      3.3.1b "Every urine" incipit
      3.3.1c "All urine" or no-modifier incipit

II. Attributed Works

COLLECTIONS CONTAINING MIDDLE ENGLISH UROSCOPIC TEXTS

The following table lists all libraries and collections known to me that hold manuscripts in which Middle English uroscopies are preserved. The abbreviations and short-form references in parentheses after the library and collection names are used in the witness-lists for individual texts below, to save space and reduce repetition; some fuller forms appear in running text for ease of reading.[9]

Collection and Abbreviation	Collection and Abbreviation
Aberystwyth, National Library of Wales (NLW)	London
Bethesda, National Library of Medicine (NLM)	Royal College of Physicians (RCP)
Boston	Society of Antiquaries (SAL)
Harvard Medical School, Countway Library of Medicine (Countway)	Wellcome Library (Wellcome)
Massachusetts Historical Society (MassHS)	Manchester, John Rylands Library (Rylands)
Brussels, Bibliothèque Royale (Br Roy)	New Haven, Yale Medical School, Cushing-Whitney Library (Yale)
Cambridge	New York
Corpus Christi College (CCCC)	Columbia University Library, Plimpton (Plimpton)
Emmanuel College (Emm)	Jewish Theological Seminary of America (JTSA)
Gonville and Caius College (GC)	Pierpont Morgan Library (PML)

---

[9] Abbreviations for biographical reference works cited in the taxonomy are as follows: DB = Ernest Wickersheimer, *Dictionnaire biographique des médecins en France au moyen âge*, 2 vols. (Geneva, 1936); DB/S1 = Danielle Jacquart, *Supplément: Ernest Wickersheimer, Dictionnaire biographique des médecins en France au moyen âge* (Geneva, 1979); DB/S2 = Danielle Jacquart, *Le milieu médical en France du XIIᵉ au XVᵉ siècle, en annexe 2ᵉ supplément au* Dictionnaire *d'Ernest Wickersheimer* (Geneva, 1981); MPME = C. H. Talbot and E. A. Hammond, *The Medical Practitioners in Medieval England: A Biographical Register* (London, 1965); MPME/S = the supplement to MPME by Faye Getz, "Medical Practitioners in Medieval England," *Social History of Medicine* 3 (1990): 245-83.

Jesus College (Jesus)	Oxford
Magdalene College, Pepys (Pepys)	All Souls College (All Souls)
St. John's College (StJC)	Bodleian Library
Trinity College (TCC)	Additional (Bodl Add)
University Library (CUL)	Ashmole (Ashmole)
Copenhagen, Royal Library, MS (Cop Roy)	Bodley (Bodley)
Dublin, Trinity College (TCD)	Digby (Digby)
Durham, University Library, Cosin (Cosin)	Douce (Douce)
Exeter, Cathedral Library (ExCathL)	e Musaeo (e Mus)
Glasgow, University Library	Hatton (Hatton)
Ferguson (Ferguson)	lat. misc. (Bodl lat misc)
Hunterian (Hunter)	Laud misc. (Laud misc)
Gloucester, Cathedral Library (GlCathL)	Rawlinson (Rawl)
London	Selden (Selden)
British Library	Corpus Christi College (CCCO)
Additional (BL Add)	Magdalen College (MagdO)
Arundel (Arun)	San Marino, Huntington Library (Huntington)
Egerton (Eger)	Sheffield, Central Library, Jackson (Jackson)
Harley (Harl)	Stockholm, Royal Library (St Roy)
Lansdowne (Lansdowne)	Tokyo, Takamiya (Takamiya)*
Royal (BL Roy)	Warminster, Longleat House (Longleat)
Sloane (Sloane)	Woking, Surrey Historical Society (SurreyHS)
Lambeth Palace Library (Lambeth)	York, York Minster Library (YkMinL)

* The Takamiya collection is presently on deposit in New Haven, at the Beinecke Rare Book and Manuscript Library, Yale University.

TAXONOMY

I. ANONYMOUS WORKS

1.0 *The Twenty-Jordan Series* (or *The Twenty Jordans*) (69 manuscript witnesses, 4 prints)

A description of the twenty colors of urine (**20Col**) and associated sicknesses (**20Sick**) for each color, usually accompanied by recommended medicines (**20Med**) for each color and ten descriptions of urinary circles and other contents (**Cir**). The color-descriptions typically give a color term and a descriptive simile (e.g., "Albus as clear water of the well"). Often illustrated with flasks, sometimes colored. Some witnesses belong to the "Sloane Group" of related medical manuscripts identified by Voigts.[10]

The Twenty Jordans (**20J**) appears in several forms, distinguishable in part by the color or color-pair with which they begin and in part by the order of subsequent colors. The most common ordering of the colors begins with Karapos, the color of camel hair or camel skin, with some thirty-one witnesses to this version and its variants. Other relatively common versions begin with Rubea, Rufus, Albus or Lacteus, Subrufus, and Niger.[11]

The Karapos texts can be further divided into three subtypes. The first (**S**) begins with the colors Karapos-Pallidus-Subpallidus-Plumbeus-Viridis-Subviridis and ends in Kyanos-Inopos-Lacteus-Albus-Niger-Glaucus, with eight reddish and yellowish colors in the middle; the text in Sloane 7 exemplifies this type. The underlying principle of the Sloane 7 type is the pairing of colors and their subcolors where possible (with the dark red or purplish Kyanos and Inopos possibly seen as a pair despite the lack of a "sub-" prefix on either). A second type (**D**) begins

---

[10] Linda Ehrsam Voigts, "The 'Sloane Group': Related Scientific and Medical Manuscripts from the Fifteenth Century in the Sloane Collection," *British Library Journal* 16 (1990): 26–57.

[11] For a critical edition of the Karapos version, see M. Teresa Tavormina, "The Twenty-Jordan Series: An Illustrated Middle English Uroscopy Text," *ANQ* 18, no. 3 (Summer 2005): 40-64. The Rubea version has been edited from Harvard MS Countway 19 by Marta Powell Harley, "The Middle English Contents of a Fifteenth-Century Medical Handbook," *Mediaevalia* 8 (1985 for 1982): 171–88, at 180–82. Variation between masculine and feminine endings in Latin color terms depends on the explicit or implicit noun modified: *color* (m.) or *urina* (f.).

Karapos-Pallidus-Plumbeus-Viridis-Inopos-Subpallidus and ends with Kyanos-Lacteus-Subviridis-Albus-Niger-Glaucus; it is exemplified by Digby 75. The **D** type pulls Inopos nearer the front of the list, while moving Subviridis near the end; other colors in the middle of the series are no longer in primary and subcolor pairs.[12] The third type of Karapos text (**Da**) occurs only in three related manuscripts; these witnesses resemble the Digby 75 type except that they substitute Livida for Subrubicunda, thereby creating a list with two kinds of lead-colored urine, Plumbea and Livida, and one less option among the reddish colors.

By and large, the actual texts of the color-descriptions, lists of associated illnesses, and so on remain reasonably stable no matter how the colors are rearranged, although some witnesses extract parts of the series (such as the lists of medicines or descriptions of the circles and contents) and present them separately from the rest of the text. In the "Manuscript Witnesses" lists here and elsewhere below, the significance of special symbols (such as asterisks and daggers) is particular to the list in which the symbol appears. In the headnote to each list I indicate as necessary the significance of the symbols.

MANUSCRIPT WITNESSES

In the following list of witnesses, asterisks indicate illustrated texts; daggers indicate texts that are blended with the Twenty Colors component of the *Dome of Uryne* or inserted integrally into the *Dome of Uryne*.

1.1 Karapos incipit

1.1.1 Sloane 7 type (S; 19 witnesses)

*Sloane 7, 58^r–60^r	[eVK2 3294.00]
*Sloane 297, 104^r–106^r	[eVK2 3289.00]
*Eger 2433, 19^v–22^r (in Karapos **S** order, except that Rufus/Subrufus are moved to the end of the series)	[eVK2 3292.00]
*Wellcome 564, 128^v–130^v	[eVK2 3290.00]
*Wellcome 8004, 57^v–60^r (58^v–61^r in eVK2)[13]	[eVK2 *2403.00, *3291.50]
*GC 451/392, pp. 58–67	[eVK2 3290.00]

---

[12]   In classifying Karapos group witnesses under **S** and **D** types, I generally ignore minor transpositions of adjacent colors.

[13]   Folio numbers for Wellcome 8004 in eVK2 differ by +1 from the foliation indicated in the digitized images of the manuscript that can be accessed at the UK Web Archive: http://www.webarchive.org.uk/wayback/archive/20040929120000/ http://library.wellcome.ac.uk/physicianshandbook.html.

*Cosin V.IV.7, 50^r–59^v [eVK2 3291.00]
NLW Sotheby C.2, pp. 144–150   [eVK2 –]
*Cosin V.III.10, 9^r–13^v (preceded by *Dome of Uryne*;
  see 2.1 below)   [eVK2 3290.00]
*Ashmole 1447, pp. 166–185 (followed by *Dome of Uryne*;
  see 2.1 below)   [eVK2 3298.00]
*Sloane 433, 60^r–64^r (acephalous, omitting Karapos and
  Plumbeus signs)   [eVK2 *2638.00]
*Sloane 5, 187^v–190^r (a reworked and somewhat disorganized
  text, with Kyanos/Inopos switching place with Rubeus/
  Subrub[eus])   [eVK2 3287.00]
*NLM 30, 12^v–15^r (incomplete; fourteen flasks and color names,
  with some material from omitted colors assigned to those
  remaining; interspersed with material from several other texts,
  most notably *Urina Rufa,* item 3.2.3 below, along with other
  token lists)   [eVK2 3288.00]
Bodl Add C.246, 93^v–94^v (incomplete, with fourteen
  colors in a modified Karapos **S** order but omitting most
  subcolors and two primary colors)   [eVK2 2847.00]
Rawl C.299, 2^r (incomplete; the first three colors and then
  the first five colors in **S** type Karapos text)   [eVK2 0542.00]
*Ashmole 1393, 62^v–63^r (incomplete; possible **S** type; flasks
  and text in lower margins, numbered [1] –4 and 20)   [eVK2 *0300.00]
*TCC O.1.65, 265^v–266^v, 266a verso–269^v (**Cir** given first,
  in Karapos order; after intervening brief texts,
  20Col/20Sick/20Med follow in an idiosyncratic order,
  beginning with Glaucus and grouping the subcolors
  together at the end)   [eVK2 *3779.00]
MagdO 221, 29^v–30^v (**Cir** only, in a modified Karapos
  S order)   [eVK2 5428.00]
Harl 2375, 32^v (**Cir** only, in a modified Karapos **S** order)   [eVK2 –]

1.1.2 Digby 75 type (D; 9 witnesses)

*Digby 75, 108$^{r–v}$, 109^v–110^v (**20Col/20Sick/Cir** on 108$^{r–v}$;
  20Med on 109^v–110^v, embedded within *Urina Rufa* in a
  Vade Mecum suite, item 3.2.1a below)   [eVK2 3299.00, –]
Harl 3383, 37^r–40^r (unillustrated, but with annotation
  "vas urinale depictum addendum erat" in later hand
  on fol. 37^r)   [eVK2 *3282.00]
*Ashmole 1413, pp. 3–12   [eVK2 *3295.00]
Bodl lat misc c.66, 88^v–89^r (much of this s. xvi text faded
  or illegible; ends with a reference to "Magistrum R.")   [eVK2 3300.00]

Wellcome 537, 17^r–23^v, 36^r–40$^{v\,14}$ (begins with **20Col/20Sick**,
  followed by **Cir** given separately; **20Med** on 36^r–40^v;
  incorporates some material from Rubea Group below)   [eVK2 *3286.00]
BL Add 4698, 15^v–16^v (**20Med** only)   [eVK2 –]
Pepys 878, 184–187 (**20Med** only)   [eVK2 –]
†BL Roy 17 C.xv, 57^r, 61^v–62^r (the first four **D**-type colors
  and sicknesses on 57^r and four of the ten **Cir** signs on
  61^v–62^r, also in an order consistent with type **D**, inserted
  integrally into a highly idiosyncratic blend of *Dome of
  Uryne* components, excerpts from *Urine White and Red*
  and *Rufus Subrufus,* and other unidentified token lists)   [eVK2 –]
*Cop Roy n.c. 314, 6^v (incomplete; only Subrufus and Rubeus,
  with their Sicknesses and Medicines, and one Circle;
  acephalous and atelous, but textually related to other
  D type texts; NOT SEEN)^{15} [eVK2 0578.00]

1.1.2a Digby 75 – Livida subtype (Da; 3 witnesses)

These three witnesses all incorporate **20Med** in a larger collection of uroscopic texts, with the Vade Mecum suite preceding and a version of the Walter Agilon *Craft of Urines* text following **20Med** (items 3.1-3.3 and 16.1 below).

Sloane 121, 40^v–41^v (**20Med** only, except for Karapos
  sicknesses)   [eVK2 –]
Sloane 706, 3^v–4^v (**20Med** only, except for Karapos
  sicknesses)   [eVK2 3561.00]
TCC R.14.32, 69^r–70^r (**20Med** only, except for Karapos
  sicknesses)   [eVK2 –]

1.2 Rubea incipit (6 witnesses)

This variant only appears in Sloane Group manuscripts. All witnesses that I have seen are very close textually; all follow the *Practica Urinarum* text on inspection of urines, item 11.2 below. They do not include **20Med**; their version of **Cir** has only seven separate "circles" (i.e., circles or contents), combining and modifying some of the ten normally found in the Karapos group. They are always followed by a brief Latin list of fifteen

---

[14] *Recte* 39^v: foliation erroneously jumps from 37 to 39, though there is no missing leaf or loss of text between fol. 37 and fol. 39. Wellcome 537, 15^r–40^v appears to have been conceived as a compendium of several uroscopic texts, titled "þe practise of þe sighte of vrynes" on fol. 15^r and "practif of fisike" in the explicit (40^v), and composed of **20J**, the Vade Mecum suite, and JUDICIUM PERFECTUM from the *Dome of Uryne*, the latter texts noted in their respective entries below.

[15] Transcribed in full by Irma Taavitsainen, *The Index of Middle English Prose X: Manuscripts in Scandinavian Collections* (Cambridge, 1994), 15.

uroscopic colors with descriptive similes, titled "Exposiciones urinarum in ordine" in the list's rubricated heading.

*Sloane 2320, 4ᵛ–9ᵛ	[eVK2 4401.00]
*Sloane 3566, 28ᵛ–33ᵛ	[eVK2 –]
*Countway Ballard 19, 16ʳ–19ᵛ	[eVK2 –]
*GC 336/725, 137ᵛ–139ᵛ	[eVK2 –]
*Takamiya 33, 35ᵛ–37ᵛ (corresponds to text in GC 336/725)[16]	[eVK2 –]
*TCC O.1.77, 24ᵛ–29ᵛ (with **Cir** moved to end of text)	[eVK2 –]

1.3 Rufus incipit (4 witnesses)[17]

Aside from TCC R.14.52 and its copy Wellcome 7117, none of the witnesses below has exactly the same order of colors or of circles/contents, but they all follow a similar general principle of placing reddish colors first, dim and dark colors in the middle, and pale to light colors at the end. The yellow colors Citrine/Subcitrine are the most mobile in these texts, appearing at the end, in the middle and end, and near the beginning in the three distinct orders. The reddish to dark to light pattern derives from the metabolic order of colors discussed in the Vade Mecum suite headnotes below, a derivation most obvious in the Trinity manuscript, which provides rubrics in scrolls on each page identifying the digestion group to which the colors on that page belong (Perfect Digestion, Excess Digestion, Much Adustion, Death, Indigestion, Beginning of Digestion, and Mediate Digestion). In Oxford, Magdalen 221, a later hand or hands has added similar but much less carefully written labels to the groups of flasks. The **Cir** texts resemble those in the Karapos group, with approximately ten circle/contents but somewhat different color-correspondences.

    *MagdO 221, 57ʳ–60ʳ (same order as next two manuscripts
    for the first eleven colors, with some subsequent
    variation)[18]   [eVK2 4406.00, 3284.00]

---

[16] See Voigts, "The 'Sloane Group'" (n. 10 above), where Takamiya 33 and GC 336/725, fols. 104–57, are described as "twin manuscripts" and "twin codices" (27, 33, 50–51).

[17] A possible (but very incomplete) fifth witness is Sloane 1100, 118ᵛ–121ᵛ, which contains drawings of twenty urine flasks after a copy of the *Liber Uricrisiarum*. The flasks appear in groups of four, four, four, three, three, and two, with Latin color names written in the mouths of the first eight flasks but no other text. The first four colors are Rufus/Subrufus/Citrinus/Subcitrinus, while the second are Rubeus/Subrubeus/Rubicundus/Subrubicundus, an ordering most similar to that in the non-illustrated CUL Ii.6.17.

[18] The foliation of Magdalen 221 is late, intermittent, and sometimes inaccurate, as here, where the manuscript numbers fol. 57ʳ as "56." More generally, foliations in the manuscript (whether original or corrected), in eVK2, and in Sarah

*TCC R.14.52, 173a verso—173d verso (appended to a
version of the *Practica urinarum* text found with the
Rubea/Sloane Group texts above, and incorporated
into an abbreviated redaction of the medical
compendium translated by the cleric "Austin" for the
London barber-surgeon Thomas Plawdon; that
compendium survives nearly complete in GC 196/97
[see item 17.0 below])[19]   [eVK2 7314.00]
*Wellcome 7117, 119ʳ–122ʳ (s. xvi copy of TCC R.14.52)   [eVK2 7312.00]
CUL Ii.6.17, 25ᵛ–29ʳ (**20Col/20Sick/20Med**; no **Cir**)   [eVK2 7750.50]

1.4 Albus/Lacteus incipits[20] (7 witnesses)

*Sloane 120, 79ᵛ–83ʳ (begins with Albus; separates the **20Col**
descriptions from the flasks and **20Sick/20Med/Cir** texts,
presenting them on fol. 83ʳ, in an incomplete list of sixteen
colors, of which only eleven offer their descriptive similes)   [eVK2 7492.00]
Ashmole 1393, 58ʳ–60ʳ (begins with Albus; incomplete,
omitting Subrubicundus, Subviridis, and Niger; **Cir** texts
in Karapos S order extracted and placed at end of series)   [eVK2 8107.00]
†Ashmole 1405, pp. 78–84 (begins with Albus; inserted in a
Dome of Uryne text; **20Col/20Sick/20Med**, with some **Cir** items
added in margins and interlinearly by a later hand)   [eVK2 1431.00]
*†Huntington HM 64, 38ᵛ–47ᵛ (begins with Albus, but wants
part of Albus and all of Lacteus due to loss of one leaf; **20Col/
20Sick/20Med** blended with **20C** list from *Dome of Uryne*;
also notes digestion groups associated with colors, as in the
TCC R.14.52 version of **20J** above [item 1.3] and **20Col-Dig**
text below [item 3.1])   [eVK2 *6707.00]
CUL Dd.10.44, 134ᵛ, 140ʳ–143ʳ (**Cir** extracted from rest
of text and included in a treatise *De urinis* on 134ᵛ,
beginning and ending like the **Cir** texts in the Karapos

Ogilvie-Thomson's *Index of Middle English Prose VIII: Oxford College Libraries* (Cambridge, 1991) and H. O. Coxe's *Catalogus codicum MSS qui in Collegiis Aulisque Oxoniensibus hodie adservantur*, 2 vols. (Oxford, 1852) diverge from each other at various points. My own calculations of folio numbers for the uroscopy texts usually match eVK2, except near the end of the manuscript. I indicate the divergence from eVK2 but not from other reference works.

[19] On the "Austin"/Plawdon compendium, see Linda E. Voigts and Michael R. McVaugh, *A Latin Technical Phlebotomy and Its Middle English Translation*, Transactions of the American Philosophical Society 74, no. 2 (Philadelphia, 1984), 14–18. Voigts and McVaugh suggest Plawdon's identity with Thomas Plouden (d. 1413), barber-surgeon dwelling in the parish of All Hallows the Great (15).

[20] Several texts beginning with Albus are included in the Miscellaneous incipits group in order to keep manuscripts and editions with related copies of **20J** together.

group but with different internal order; **20Col/20Sick/20Med**
laid out in a table of three-cell columns on 140^r–143^r, with
one column per color, beginning with Albus)　　　[eVK2 – , *7387.00]
Sloane 340, 73^v–74^r (begins with Lactea; only ten colors,
with their descriptions and sicknesses; association of some
colors and sicknesses varies from usual correspondences;
20Med and **Cir** texts omitted entirely)　　　[eVK2 –]
GC 336/725, 95^v–96^r (begins with Lactea; same material
and order as Sloane 340)　　　[eVK2 3320.00]

1.5 Miscellaneous incipits (21 witnesses)

*Hatton 29, 68^v–72^r (only sixteen flasks, omitting Subcitrinus,
Subviridis, Rufus, Rubicundus; begins like **S** type with
Karapos, but order diverges from both **S** and **D** types after
Plumbeus)　　　[eVK2 3296.00]
*Sloane 635, 88^r–92^v (begins and ends like **S** type, pairing
colors and subcolors, but rearranges order of internal
colors)　　　[eVK2 3293.00]
CUL Ee.1.15, 75^r–77^r (begins with Karapos, but with
idiosyncratic subsequent order, with the six red
colors at the end; **20Col/20Sick/Cir** given first, followed
by the first sixteen remedies in **20Med** and then **20Med**
repeated in full)　　　[eVK2 3297.00]
*Sloane 963, 2^r–3^r (fragments at the beginning of the
manuscript; six flasks, possibly from an acephalous
Karapos-based series, starting now in Viridis and ending
in Albus-Niger-Glaucus)　　　[eVK2 7877.00]
†Sloane 382, 19^r–23^v (begins with Albus; blends **20C** of
Dome of Uryne with **20Med** in a *Dome of Uryne* hybrid
text)　　　[eVK2 –]
Sloane 382, 33^r–36^v (begins with Subrufus; contains
20Sick/20Med/Cir, but omits most of the **20Col** color
descriptions; similar to Sloane 1388, 45^v–46^r below)　　　[eVK2 4631.00]
Sloane 1388, 38^r (acephalous; six colors, beginning part
way through Kyanos and running to Glauca; probably
the conclusion to a **D** type Karapos text, with **20Col/20Sick/**
20Med/Cir elements for the surviving colors)　　　[eVK2 0375.00]
†Sloane 1388, 43^v–44^v (begins with Albus, and blends **20C**
text from *Dome of Uryne* with **20Med** in a *Dome of Uryne*
hybrid text)　　　[eVK2 –]
Sloane 1388, 45^v–46^r (acephalous; begins partway through
Citrinus and omits Subrufus, Rubeus, and Subrubicundus,
probably from a position at the beginning as in Sloane
382, 33^r–36^v above; omits **20Col** and **20Med**, but contains
most of **20Sick/Cir**)　　　[eVK2 –]
*Sloane 3160, 87^r–89^v (begins with Subrubea/Rufa; contains

20Col/20Sick/Cir but not 20Med; concludes by repeating
the last four colors with their Col/Sick/Med/Cir
elements)   [eVK2 *4628.00]

*Wellcome 7, 2ʳ–3ᵛ (begins with Subruffa/ Subrubicunda;
contains 20Col/20Sick/Cir; some medicines omitted,
others possibly added by later hand)   [eVK2 4630.00]

*TCC O.1.13, 23ᵛ–25ᵛ (begins with Rubius/Subrubius;
20Col/20Sick/20Med/Cir, but only eighteen flasks,
omitting Niger and Glaucus)   [eVK2 0580.00]

*GC 457/395, 57ᵛ–58ᵛ (incomplete, beginning with
Rubicunda; twelve flasks, eleven with color descriptions
and illnesses inside the flask, ten of those with circles/
contents and medicines outside the flask)   [eVK2 4402.00]

*Ashmole 1477, III, 11ʳ–12ᵛ (begins with Subviridis;
20Col/20Sick/20Med, no Cir)   [eVK2 –]

Rawl D.1221, 50ʳ–62ᵛ (material taken from 20Col/20Sick
and Cir, in the margins of a text based on Henry
Daniel, *Liber Uricrisiarum,* book 2, item 15.4 below, and
following its color-order, beginning with Niger)   [eVK2 1430.00]

*Hunter 328, 1ᵛ–25ᵛ (begins with Niger; incorporated into
John Arderon's commentary on the *Carmen de urinis* of
Giles of Corbeil, item 21.0 below, following order of colors
in Giles)   [eVK2 –]

Rylands Eng 1310, 1ʳ–13ᵛ (begins with Niger; incorporated
into Arderon's commentary)   [eVK2 –]

*Sloane 357, 30ʳ–39ᵛ (begins with Niger, proceeds through
dark, reddish, yellow, pale, white colors)   [eVK2 0579.00]

†NLM 49, 38ᵛ–42ʳ (begins with Subrufus; inserted integrally
in *Dome of Uryne* in Robert Denham's manuscript, copied
1586/87 from the 1540 Wyer reprint of *The Seynge of
Uryns* [STC2 22153b]; cf. also Sloane 382, 33ʳ–36ᵛ, and
Sloane 1388, 45ᵛ–46ʳ)   [eVK2 –]

NLM 49, 58ʳ–60ᵛ (20Med only; like its print source,
the 1540 *Seynge of Uryns,* begins with Karapos but does
not follow either type S or D order)   [eVK2 2330.00]

*Sloane 783B, 221ʳ–224ᵛ (incomplete, begins with Citrine;
20Col/20Sick/Cir; illustrated with sixteen flasks; interspersed
with material from *Urina Rufa* and other as yet unidentified
sources)   [eVK2 0345.00]

PRINT WITNESSES

1.5 Miscellaneous incipits (4 witnesses)

*†*The Seynge of Uryns* (London: J. Rastell for Richard Banckes, 1525; STC
22153), sigs. A2ʳ–A4ᵛ (begins with Albus, and blends 20C text from *Dome
of Uryne* with 20Med; multiple editions in subsequent years)   —

*†*The Seynge of Uryns*, sigs. B1ʳ–B3ᵛ (**20Col/20Sick/20Med/Cir**; inserted
integrally in *Dome of Uryne* after blended **20C/20Med**; begins with
Subrufus and shares the same order and some unusual errors and
variants with Sloane MSS 382 and 1388 and NLM 49)   —

The Seynge of Uryns, sigs. H2ᵛ–H3ᵛ (**20Med** only; begins with Karapos but
does not follow either type **S** or **D** order)   —

The Judgement of All Urynes (London: Robert Wyer, 1555; STC 14834), sigs.
I1ᵛ–I3ᵛ (**20Med** only, as in *Seynge of Uryns* Karapos text)   —

2.0 *The Dome of Uryne* Compendium (DU; 55 manuscript witnesses,
2 prints)

A very widely disseminated compendium of up to seventeen short texts,
with over fifty manuscripts and two distinct printed editions containing
some or all of the assemblage. A full set of components contains the following segments, listed here in the order found in the longest (i.e., the
Expanded) version of the text and with abbreviations for convenience of
further reference:

FOUR THINGS THAT BELONG TO THE DOOM OF URINE (**4Th**; describes the characteristics to consider in judging urine and gives a brief overview of thick,
mean, and thin substance)

THE TWENTY COLORS (**20C**; compare other twenty-color lists below: items
6.2–6.8)[21]

URINE THAT HAS GREAT CONTENTS (**GrCon**; see item 10.1 below)

DE GRADIBUS (*gra*; usually Latin)[22]

DE ETATE LUNE (*lun*; usually Latin)

DE SIGNIS (*sig*; usually Latin)

TO KNOW THE PULSE (**Pul**)

THE COMPLEXIONS OF URINE (**CplU**; see item 8.1 below)

WHERE THE COMPLEXIONS ARE GENERATED (**CplG**; see item 8.1 below)

URINES OF MAN, WOMAN, AND BEAST (**MWB**; see item 7.3.1 below)

THE FIRST AND SECOND URINES (**1&2U**; see item 11.1 below)

JUDICIUM PERFECTUM OMNIUM URINARUM (**JP**; see item 5.1 below)

URINA MULIERIS (**UMul**; see item 7.2.1 below)

AD COGNOSCENDUM PREGNANTES (**CogPr**; see item 7.2.2 below)

URINA MORTIS TAM HOMINUM QUAM MULIERUM (**UMort**; see item 7.1.1 below)

THE THIRD KNOWLEDGE OF URINES: THE REGIONS (**3Reg**; see item 9.1 below)

ON THE [FOUR] CONTENTS OF URINES (**4Con**; see item 10.1 below)

---

[21] Many of the **DU** segments are similar in content to other uroscopic text
types; I describe them individually and list their witnesses under the items cross-
referenced here (see also n. 38 below).

[22] An English translation of *gra, lun, sig* occurs in BL Additional 10440 and
Ashmole 1477, X.

The compendium occurs in several structurally distinct forms: a Core Version, an Expanded Version, an Abbreviated Version, a Hybridized Version that blends the *Dome of Uryne* with the Twenty-Jordan Series (items 1.4 and 1.5 above), various Peculiar Versions (idiosyncratic orders, plus excerpts and fragments too short to identify as belonging to the four main Versions), and singleton instances of individual segments.[23]

The Core Version begins with **4Th**, an introductory paragraph that outlines the four most important qualities of urine to examine: "substance" (density or opacity), color, content, and the regions of the urine flask. The **4Th** paragraph also includes a brief description of different types of substance and how to distinguish them. From this opening, the treatise proceeds to the **20C** component, followed by **UMort, 3Reg, 4Con**, and **GrCon**. Most notably, this Core Version order puts **GrCon** in the medically logical position *after* **4Con**: the Four Contents component treats the four highest contents in a urine flask: froth and bubbles, clouds ('sky'), circles, grains; Great Contents begins with the fifth content, pus, and carries on to the hypostasis in the bottom of the flask. **GrCon** concludes, in all versions, with what may have been the original explicit: "Now have I showed the substance of the urine, the colors, the regions, and the contents that longeth to the doom of urine. Explicit." In the extant witnesses, the Core Version usually omits the brief Latin texts, and follows **GrCon** with the two complexion-related texts, several "specialty" urine texts, and a general list of uroscopic tokens and their significance, most often in the order **CplU, CplG, MWB, 1&2U, JP, UMul, CogPr**, though the positioning of some of these latter segments may vary.

In the Expanded Version, whose order appears above, **GrCon** has come unmoored from its natural position after **4Con** and moved forward in the compendium to follow **20C**. The Latin texts (*gra, lun, sig*) typically occur in Expanded Version witnesses, where they are usually followed by **Pul**; this expansion is most often inserted between GrCon and the two complexions texts. After **CplU** and **CplG**, the Expanded Version proceeds with the segments from **MWB** to **CogPr**, and concludes with **UMort, 3Reg**, and **4Con** (dislocated from their probable original position between **20C** and **GrCon**).

---

[23] In earlier conference papers on the *Dome of Uryne*, I have labelled the first four of these versions as Type A, Type B, Abbreviated B (or Abbreviated Long Version), and Hybrid Type B respectively, labels that have been incorporated in eVK2. The revised labels are meant to be more descriptive, especially for types A and B, and to allow for abbreviation or hybridization of the Core Version (Type A).

The Abbreviated Version truncates the Expanded Version: in the manuscript witnesses, it omits the sequence from **4Th** to **CplG**, to begin with **MWB** and carry on to **4Con**. The printed edition of 1555 (*The Judgement of Urynes*) applies a similar truncation to the 1525 edition of a Hybrid Version, but leaves **CplG** at the beginning of the sequence. Such truncation may have been intended to resolve the dislocation in the Expanded version by dropping **GrCon** entirely.

The Hybrid Version is essentially the Expanded Version of the text with the **20C** segment further enlarged to include the **20Med** recipes from the *Twenty Jordan Series* (**20J**; see above) or, in one witness (Huntington HM 64), **20Med** and **20Sick** from that series. **Pul**, *gra*, and *lun* appear after **4Con** in two Hybrid Version witnesses; the full *Twenty Jordans* treatise is itself inserted after the **20C/20Med** hybrid in the 1525 *Seynge of Uryns* edition, which is later copied in a 1586 manuscript based partly on a reprint (1540) of that edition. In **HM 64**, the Latin texts and **Pul** float freely some twenty-odd leaves before an excerpted Hybrid Version consisting of **4Th**, the **20C/20Med/20Sick** hybrid, **GrCon**, and (after more intervening texts) **CogPr**.[24]

MANUSCRIPT WITNESSES[25]

2.1 Core Version ("Type A"; 12 witnesses)

MagdO 221, 94ʳ–101ʳ — [eVK2 2895.00, 7763.00, 0999.00, 7809.00]
Cosin V.III.10, 4ʳ–8ʳ (acephalous? missing **4Th, 20C** components) — [eVK2 7765.00, 1994.00, 7810.00]
Wellcome 564, 193ᵛ–194ᵛ (acephalous? missing **4Th, 20C** components) — [eVK2 7761.00]
Ashmole 1447, pp. 186–192 — [eVK2 *2878.00]
Cosin V.V.13, 29ʳ–41ʳ (incomplete owing to loss of leaves) — [eVK2 0500.00, 7762.00, 1995.00, 2675.00, 3324.00]
Harl 2274, 47ʳ–50ᵛ (atelous) — [eVK2 *2878.00, 7764.00]
Digby 95, 101ᵛ–103ᵛ (atelous) — [eVK2 2871.00, 7770.00]
Digby 29, 127ʳ–128ᵛ, 114ᵛ–116ʳ (misbound; atelous) — [eVK2 *2871.00, 7837.00]
Hatton 29, 60ʳ–67ᵛ (acephalous) — [eVK2 *0288.00, 2765.00]

---

[24] I am currently in the process of editing *The Dome of Uryne*, along with the Vade Mecum suite, *Urine White and Red, Urine White and Brown, Rufus Subrufus,* and *Ten Cold Ten Hot* (items 2.0, 3.0, 4.2, 5.2, 6.2, 6.3 below). Further details of the textual relationships for each of these uroscopies will be found in that edition.

[25] Because of the plasticity of the **DU** compendium and the potential for deliberate selection and omission of its components, I indicate incompleteness only for clearly acephalous or atelous texts or those wanting internal material as the result of lost leaves.

Sloane 1388 (b), 48^v–50^v (a different text from that on fols.
43^v–45^r of the same manuscript) [eVK2 –]
Rawl C.81, 6^v–12$^{v\,26}$ [eVK2 2879.00, *7836.00]
Ashmole 1477, X, 16^r–24^r (a late text with components
significantly rearranged, though still with **GrCon** directly
after **4Con**) [eVK2 *7776.00, 8233.00, 6793.00, 6789.00,
3327.00, 2867.00, 7839.00, 7771.00, 3741.00, *6645.00]

2.2 Expanded Version ("Type B"; 9 witnesses)

Sloane 374, 5^v–13^v [eVK2 2878.00, 3330.00, 3699.00, 2745.00,
7535.00, 5424.00, 7834.00, 7813.00, 7768.00]
Harl 3407, 43^v–48^r (incomplete owing to
loss of leaves) [eVK2 2878.00, 5424.00, 7834.00,
7767.00, 7536.00, 3739.00]
BL Add 10440, 50^r–55^v [eVK2 2878.00, 6753.00, 6690.00, 3328.00,
3700.00, 2725.00, 7513.00, 5426.00,
7834.00, 7812.00, 7769.00, 7514.00]
Wellcome 409, 55^r–66^r [eVK2 2872.00, 1676.00]
StJC K.49, 68^r–79^v [eVK2 2875.50, 7839.50, 6299.50, 7762.50]
BL Add 30338, 151^v–160^r, 185^r, 186^v, 187^r [eVK2 2879.00, 7535.00,
5425.00, 7840.00, 7812.00, 6087.00, 7769.00,
7514.00, 3740.00, 1423.00, 2079.00, 3325.00]
Selden Supra 73, 107^r–112a recto (incomplete
owing to lost leaf) [eVK2 3698.00, 2880.00, 7821.00, 7534.00,
5425.00, 7844.00, 7812.00, 993.00, 7769.00]
Rawl C.506, 41^v, 54^r–60^r (incomplete owing to loss
of leaves) [eVK2 – , 0347.00, 7840.00, 7808.00,
4916.00, 7766.00, 1996.00]
Ashmole 1405, pp. 71-88 (with a copy of **20J** inserted
after **GrCon**; see item 1.4 above)[27] [eVK2 2677.00, 1431.00,
7825.00, *7774.00]

2.3 Abbreviated Version ("Abbreviated B"; 5 witnesses)

TCC O.8.35, 52^v–57^r (same scribe and manuscript
layout as Bodl Add B.60) [eVK2 *7534.00]
Bodl Add B.60, 52^v–57^r (same scribe and manuscript
layout as TCC O.8.35) [eVK2 7534.00, 7840.00, 7812.00, 7773.00, 1996.00]

---

[26] Ed. Javier Calle Martín, "A Late Middle English Version of the *Doom of Urines* in Oxford, MS Rawlinson C.81, ff. 6r–12v," *Analecta Malacitana* (Universidad de Málaga) 35, nos. 1–2 (2012): 243–73.

[27] This insertion of **20J** within a **DU** array of texts could be seen as a step on the way to the Hybrid type. Other **DU** manuscripts in which the two texts travel together without actually blending **20J** and **20Col** are Cosin V.III.10, Wellcome 564, Ashmole 1447; Hatton 29 and Sloane 1388 (b) (Core texts); and NLW Sotheby C.2, CUL Dd.10.44, BL Royal 17 C.xv, and Wellcome 7 (Peculiar texts).

Lambeth 444, 157^r–158^r [eVK2 7534.00, 7838.00]
Sloane 297, 113^r–115^r (acephalous) [eVK2 0371.00]
Pepys 1307, 59^r–62^r [eVK2 2690.00, 5425.00,
7807.00, 7536.00, *3738.00]

2.4 Hybrid Version ("Hybrid B"; 4 witnesses)

Sloane 382, 19^r–33^r [eVK2 7524.00, 3326.00]
Sloane 1388 (a), 43^v–45^v (a different text from that on
fols. 48^v–50^v of the same manuscript) [eVK2 2873.00, *1675.00]
Huntington HM 64, 14^v, 16^v–17^r, 38^v–48^v, 51^v [eVK2 – , 3329.00, *2879.00,
6707.00, 7820.00, 6087.00]
NLM 49, 38^v–48^v (copied by Robert Denham from Robert Wyer's
1540 reprint of *The Seynge of Uryns*, noted below; Denham omits
the blended **20C/20Med** text in his exemplar but retains the full
20J text inserted integrally after the blended text in Wyer's edition.
Folios 49^r–58^r contain another English uroscopic text from *Seynge
of Uryns*, but not one that I have found in any manuscripts
["Diverse and Many Colors of Urine"]; the material from *Seynge
of Uryns* ends with **20Med** on fols. 58^r–60^v) [eVK2 *2868.00, 8069.00]

2.5 Peculiar Versions and Singleton Components (25 witnesses)

2.5a Peculiar Versions: Excerpts, Fragments, Idiosyncratic Arrangements

Rawl D.1221, 47^v–49^v (possibly an excerpted and rearranged
Core Version, with segments ordered **JP**-[intervening texts]-**Pul-
4Con-GrCon-CplU-1&2U**) [eVK2 7845.00, 3329.00, 4614.00]
Harl 5401, 93^r–94^v (possibly a fragmentary Expanded Version, ordered
4Th-20C-GrCon atelous [ends in Hypostasis]) [eVK2 2874.00]
CCCO 291, 116^v–120^r (possibly a fragmentary Expanded Version,
ordered **4Th-20C-GrCon** atelous [ends in Gravel]) [eVK2 2881.00, 1674.00]
Harl 3810, 101^r–104^v (possibly a fragmentary Expanded Version,
ordered **4Th-20C-GrCon** atelous [ends in Blood]) [eVK2 *2876.00]

— —

Harl 218, 154^v–155^v (**4Th**-abridged **20C**; adds short notes on
moisture, dryness, quantity, and tastes of urine to **4Th**; omits
Subrufus, Viridis, and Niger as raven's feather) [eVK2 2883.00]
CUL Dd.5.76, 28^r–29^v (**4Th-20C** atelous, ending in Kyanos, the
sixteenth color) [eVK2 2877.00]
Hunter 328, 44^{r-v} (abridged **4Th-UMort**, appended to a
commentary on Giles of Corbeil's *Carmen de urinis* and
followed by seven signs from "Urine Troubly with Clouds"
[7.1.2 below]) [eVK2 –]
Rylands Eng 1310, 20^v–21^r (abridged **4Th-UMort**, appended
to a commentary on Giles of Corbeil and followed by signs from
"Urine Troubly with Clouds," as in Hunter 328) [eVK2 –]

St Roy X.90, pp. 123–127 (**UMort-MWB-JP-UMul-CogPr**)   [eVK2 7769.00, 5355.00]

Wellcome 7, 3ᵛ (**MWB-1&2U-JP** atelous)   [eVK2 – , 7534.00, –]

PML Bühler 21, 16ʳ⁻ᵛ (signs excerpted from each of
JP-UMul-[*Urine White and Brown*]-**UMort**)   [eVK2 7841.00]

Ashmole 1438, II, pp. 79–80 (signs excerpted from each
of **UMort-3Reg-4Con**)   [eVK2 7772.00]

NLW Sotheby C.2, pp. 135–144 (idiosyncratic: **JP**-[excerpted
Urine White and Brown]-**UMul**-[excerpted
Urine White and Brown]-abridged **UMort**-abridged
4Con-MWB-1&2U-CogP-3Reg-abridged **4Con**)   [eVK2 *7845.50]

CUL Dd.10.44, 143ᵛ–144ᵛ (idiosyncratic:
3Reg-CplU-CplG-abridged **GrCon**)   [eVK2 – , 1243.00, –]

Jackson 1302, 14ᵛ (idiosyncratic: **4Th-MWB-1&2U-CplU**)   [eVK2 3087.00, 2674.50]

BL Roy 18 A.vi, 26ʳ, 29ʳ–31ᵛ (idiosyncratic: **4Con-GrCon**
atelous [ends in Motes]-**4Th-20C-UMort**; leaves disordered)   [eVK2 –]

Harl 2558, 168ᵛ, 170ʳ, 172ʳ (idiosyncratic: selected signs from
MWB-UMul, 4Th-1&2U-JP, UMort)[28]   [eVK2 – , 2676.00, 7760.00]

BL Roy 17 C.xv, 55ʳ–61ʳ (idiosyncratic: **MWB** atelous-**UMul**
atelous-[other text]-abridged and rearranged **4Con**-[incomplete
20J]-**GrCon**-abridged and rearranged **JP**, interwoven with
material from several other token lists, continuing to fol.
64ʳ)   [eVK2 0286.00, 0709.00, *6779.00]

2.5b Singleton Components

Harl 1735, 43ʳ–44ʳ (incomplete and modified **20C**, adding
remedies for the ailments signified by the thirteen colors
covered; the remedies differ from those in **20Med** and may
be those of the practitioner-owner of the manuscript, John
Crophill)[29]   [eVK2 3119.00]

---

[28]   Harley 2558 was owned and partly written by the early fifteenth-century physician Thomas Fayreford. It has been studied in several articles by Peter Murray Jones: "Harley MS 2558: A Fifteenth-Century Medical Commonplace Book," in *Manuscript Sources of Medieval Medicine*, ed. M. R. Schleissner (New York, 1995), 35–54; "Thomas Fayreford: An English Fifteenth-Century Medical Practitioner," in *Medicine from the Black Death to the French Disease*, ed. R. French et al. (Aldershot, 1998), 156–83; and "Witnesses to Medieval Medical Practice in the Harley Collection," *eBLJ* (2008), article 8 http://www.bl.uk/eblj/2008articles/article8.html.

[29]   Ed. Lois Jean Ayoub, "John Crophill's Books: An Edition of British Library MS Harley 1735" (Ph.D. diss., University of Toronto, 1994), 239–45, ProQuest Order No. NN97155. Jones compares Fayreford's and Crophill's books and practices in

TCC O.7.20, II, 45ʳ–46ʳ (**JP**)   [eVK2 –]
Wellcome 537, 25ᵛ–28ᵛ (**JP**; included in compendium titled
Practice of the Sight of Urines)   [eVK2 –]
BL Roy 17 C.xxiv, 12ʳ⁻ᵛ (**UMort**; an excerpt of some half dozen
signs, plus two non-**UMort** tokens)   [eVK2 –]
TCC R.14.39, III, 105ʳ (**UMort**; included in a compendium of
other uroscopies)   [eVK2 –]
All Souls 81, 174ᵛ (acephalous **4Con**)   [eVK2 0570.00]
Rawl D.248, 11ᵛ (last four signs of **UMul**, somewhat
confused)   [eVK2 0955.00]

PRINT WITNESSES

2.3 Abbreviated Version (1 witness)
The Judgement of Urynes (1555), sigs. A1ᵛ–C1ᵛ   —

2.4 Hybrid Version (1 witness)
The Seynge of Uryns (1525, with later reprints), sigs. A2ʳ–D3ᵛ   —

3.0 Vade Mecum Suite (59 witnesses, in 52 manuscripts)
Three texts translated from a set of Latin originals widely disseminated
throughout Europe.[30] The first, *Twenty Colors by Digestion Groups*
(**20Col-Dig**; cf. eTK 1366L), lists the canonical twenty colors of urine,

---

"Witnesses to Medieval Medical Practice" (n. 28 above). For biographies of Fayreford and Crophill, see Jones's entries on them in the *Oxford Dictionary of National
Biography*, online at http://www.oxforddnb.com/view/article/45762 and http://www.
oxforddnb.com/view/article/6780.

[30] For studies of the Latin and some of the continental vernacular versions of
this set of texts, see Gundolf Keil, "Die mittellateinische Übersetzung vom Harntraktat des 'Bartholomäus': Untersuchungen zur Wirkung der frühen deutschen
Rezeptliteratur," *Sudhoffs Archiv* 47 (1963): 417–55; "Der 'kurze Harntraktat' des
Breslauer 'Codex Salernitanus' und seine Sippe," Inaugural Dissertation, Rhein-
ische Friedrich-Wilhelms-Universität (Bonn, 1969); *Die urognostische Praxis in vor-
und frühsalernitanischer Zeit*, Freiburg-im-Breisgau Habilitationsschrift (Freiburg,
1970); Karl Sudhoff, "Eine Pariser 'Ketham'-Handschrift aus der Zeit König Karls
VI. (1380–1422)," *Archiv für Geschichte der Medizin* 2 (1909): 84–100 and Tafel IV;
"Neue Beiträge zur Vorgeschichte des 'Ketham'," *Archiv für Geschichte der Medizin*
5 (1912): 280–301 and Tafel III–VI; Albert Kadner, "Ein *Liber de urinis* des Breslauer
Codex Salernitanus," Inaugural Dissertation, Universität Leipzig (Leipzig, 1919);
Karl Wentzlau, "Frühmittelalterliche und salernitanische Harntraktate (teilweise in
deutscher Sprache)," Inaugural Dissertation, Universität Leipzig (Leipzig, 1923); Karl
Sudhoff, introd., and Charles Singer, trans., *The "Fasciculus medicinae" of Johannes
de Ketham alemanus: Facsimile of the first (Venetian) edition of 1491*, Monumenta
Medica 1 (Milan, 1924). The Sudhoff-Singer facsimile has been reprinted with an
English translation of the Latin text by Luke Demaitre, in the Classics of Medicine
series (Birmingham, AL, 1988).

based ultimately on Giles of Corbeil's *Carmen de urinis*, along with simple similes describing the colors and classified according to the stage of digestion (from lack of digestion to mortification) that they signify.[31] Some versions appear as unillustrated tabular lists, which can be grouped into textual families based on the similes given for the colors and other characteristics; others are presented in circular diagrams. The second text, *Urina Rufa* (incipit "Urina rufa signifies health and good disposition [*var.* digestion]"; cf. *e*TK 1610B), is a loosely organized series of some forty-odd uroscopic signs, or tokens, and the state of health or illness that they signify. The third text, *Cleansing of Blood* (incipit "All/Each/Every urine is a cleansing of blood"; cf. *e*TK 1004G, 1608C-E), presents a compact, clearly structured summary of the humoral, qualitative, and anatomical correspondences of urine. Because the sections on the individual subtopics in *Cleansing of Blood* are clearly distinguished from each other, the text truncates easily and occurs in several abridged forms.

In England, Latin versions of these texts sometimes occur in the "physician's handbooks" or *vade mecum* compendia that began appearing in the late fourteenth century, along with texts on bloodletting, illustrations of zodiac men and vein men, and calendric and astronomical material.[32]

For discussions of early printed translations of the "Ketham" version of the text, see Maria Teresa Herrera, ed., *Compendio de la Humana Salud: Estudio y edición* (Madrid, 1990); Tiziana Pesenti, ed., *Fasiculo de Medicina in Volgare* (2 vols.: facsimile and study; Padua, 2001); Chris Coppens, *De vele levens van een boek: De "Fasciculus medicinae" opnieuw bekeken* (Brussels, 2009); Stephanie Zaun, "Die Harnfarbbezeichnungen im *Fasciculus medicine* und ihre italienischen und spanischen Übersetzungen," in *Farbe im Mittelalter: Materialität – Medialität – Semantik*, ed. Ingrid Bennewitz and Andrea Schindler (Berlin, 2011), 2: 969–85. A digital facsimile of the Italian translation of the *Fasciculus medicine*, the *Fasiculo de Medicina*, is available from the National Library of Medicine, at http://archive.nlm.nih.gov/proj/ttp/flash/ketham/ketham.html.

[31] These stages are essentially metabolic in nature, reflecting the degree of coction of food and drink: indigestion (i.e., lack of digestion), beginning of digestion, mediate digestion (sometimes omitted), perfect or completed digestion, excess digestion, adustion, and mortification. The further coction proceeds, the darker the urine becomes. The metabolic digestion groups are to be distinguished from the first, second, and third digestions of medieval physiology, referring to the processing of nutriment in the stomach and intestines, the liver and kidney, and the limbs.

[32] C. H. Talbot discusses and transcribes one of these English manuscripts of the Latin *vade mecum* (the Dickson Wright manuscript) in "A Mediaeval Physician's Vade Mecum," *Journal of the History of Medicine and Allied Sciences* 16 (1961): 213–33; Talbot reproduces the uroscopic texts on 225–27 and in Fig. 4. See also Cornelius O'Boyle,

The Middle English versions usually translate the Anglo-Latin texts quite closely, and probably began to emerge by the late fourteenth or early fifteenth century. In sixteen manuscripts, all three of the Middle English texts occur together; combinations of two of them occur in twelve witnesses (in eleven manuscripts), with *Urina Rufa* and *Cleansing of Blood* the most common pairing, in nine witnesses. Twenty-six witnesses (in twenty-five manuscripts) present only one of the three English texts, most often *Cleansing of Blood*.

A more detailed analysis of the textual families outlined below will be provided in my edition-in-progress of the Vade Mecum suite.

MANUSCRIPT WITNESSES

3.1 *Twenty Colors by Digestion Groups* (29 witnesses)

3.1.1 Unillustrated Texts (21 witnesses)

3.1.1a Colors Rubeus/Subrubeus compared to **"crocus oriental(is)"/ "crocus occidental(is)"**; Citrina compared to "color of a pome (orange)"

Laud misc 553, 30^v–31^r	[eVK2 –]
Sloane 2584, 9^v	[eVK2 –]
Harl 3383, 40^{r-v}	[eVK2 –]
GC 457/395, 58^v–59^r	[eVK2 *7749.00]

3.1.1b Colors Rubeus/Subrubeus compared to **"saffron d'ort(e)"/ "saffron belyng(er)"**('saffron of the garden'/?'rustic saffron'); Citrina compared to "(a) pome orange" or "appel of orynge"

Wellcome 537, 28^v–30^r	[eVK2 –]
Digby 75, 108^v	[eVK2 *7750.00]
Sloane 121, 38^v–39^r	[eVK2 –]
Sloane 706, 2^r (acephalous)	[eVK2 *7315.00]
TCC R.14.32, 67^v–68^r	[eVK2 –]
CUL Ee.1.15, 77^{r-v}	[eVK2 –]
Sloane 3160, 90^r (only eighteen colors)	[eVK2 –]

3.1.1c Idiosyncratic Texts (possibly independent translations of the Latin original)

Rawl D.1210, 119^v	[eVK2 4407.00]
Harl 2390, 119^{r-v} (mixed Latin/English, with similes and some color-names in English)[33]	[eVK2 4629.00]

"Astrology and Medicine in Later Medieval England: The Calendars of John Somer and Nicholas of Lynn," *Sudhoff's Archive* 89 (2005): 1–22, which notes the presence of uroscopic texts in some of the calendars discussed and a list of manuscripts containing calendars, urine charts, and urine wheels, *inter alia* (at 8 nn. 28–29, n. 31; Appendix, 20–22).

[33] For discussion of the contents of Harley 2390, including its advertisement of uroscopic services offered by a travelling physician, see Linda Ehrsam Voigts,

Sloane 135, 37^v–38^r [eVK2 1294.00]

Pepys 1661, pp. 27–28 (expanded to twenty-one colors by adding
  "tulye as smaragde stone" to the Mortification/Death
  digestion group; embedded in item 8.4 below and textually close
  to the copy in Wellcome 408) [eVK2 –]

Wellcome 408, 6^v (textually close to Pepys 1661 list; embedded
  in item 8.4) [eVK2 –]

Harl 1010, 1$^{r–v}$ (two lists in parallel columns, in English and Latin;
  reduced to nineteen colors by omission of Black/Niger as ink;
  preceded by a sentence defining urine as a cleansing of blood;
  no digestion groups named but colors still follow those
  groupings) [eVK2 *7799.00]

TCC R.14.39, III, 91^r (expanded to twenty-one colors by
  adding Subviridis after Viridis; no digestion groups
  named in this late copy, but the colors still follow those
  groupings) [eVK2 *0795.00]

Eger 2433, 22^v–23^r (incomplete, with only fifteen colors and
  their digestion groups, giving descriptive similes for only
  eight of the colors listed) [eVK2 –]

TCC O.7.20, II, 39^v–42^v (incomplete; conflated with *Urina
  Rufa*) [eVK2 –]

Sloane 340, 73$^{r–v}$ (a mixed Latin/English text, of which only
  the digestion-group labels are in English; adds "urina oleagina"
  at end) [eVK2 –]

3.1.2 Illustrated Texts (*Ring of Urines*) (8 witnesses)

3.1.2a One-Ring Versions

GC 336/725, 75^v–76^r [eVK2 8106.50]

Ashmole 1413, p. 1 [eVK2 7313.00]

YkMinL XVI.E.32, 167^r (new foliation; possibly an
  independent translation) [eVK2 –]

Wellcome 404, 30^r (only sixteen colors) [eVK2 –]

3.1.2b Three-Ring Version

BL Roy 18 A.vi, 27^r–28^r [eVK2 –]

Digby 29, 129^r–130^r [eVK2 *4405.00]

3.1.2c Derivative Texts (tabular lists related textually to the ring diagrams)

Sloane 1388, 55^r [eVK2 –]

Wellcome 404, 29$^{r–v}$ (sixteen colors; text similar to
  that in ring on 30^r) [eVK2 *4343.00]

"Fifteenth-Century English Banns Advertising the Services of an Itinerant Doctor,"
in Florence Eliza Glaze and Brian K. Nance, eds., *Between Text and Patient: The
Medical Enterprise in Medieval and Early Modern Europe,* Micrologus Library 39
(Florence, 2011), 245–77.

3.2 *Urina Rufa* (31 witnesses)

3.2.1 "Good Disposition" Texts: incipit as in headnote above, with "disposition" variant, following Latin original; approximately forty-five signs in complete copies (20 witnesses)

3.2.1a Token 3 = citrine urine "with a middle substance," translating *cum substancia mediocri*; other shared features later in the text allow inclusion of acephalous witnesses

Laud misc 553, 31ʳ–32ʳ	[eVK2 –]
Sloane 2584, 9ᵛ–11ᵛ	[eVK2 –]
Harl 3383, 40ᵛ–43ʳ	[eVK2 –]
GC 457/395, 59ʳ–60ʳ	[eVK2 –]
Wellcome 537, 30ʳ–35ᵛ	[eVK2 –]
Digby 75, 108ᵛ–109ᵛ, 110ᵛ (interrupted by **20Med**)	[eVK2 –]
Sloane 121, 39ʳ–40ᵛ	[eVK2 –]
Sloane 706, 2ʳ–3ᵛ	[eVK2 –]
TCC R.14.32, 68ʳ–69ʳ (slightly incomplete at end)	[eVK2 –]
Pepys 878, pp. 181–183 (urines of women only)	[eVK2 7811.00]
BL Add 4698, 15ʳ (approx. six of the women's urines signs; textually close to Pepys 878)	[eVK2 –]
Ashmole 1393, 63ʳ (acephalous owing to loss of leaves between fols. 62 and 63)	[eVK2 *0533.00]

3.2.1b Token 3 = citrine urine "with a mean substance"

Wellcome 408, 4ʳ–5ᵛ	[eVK2 *7751.00]
Wellcome 8004, 61ʳ–63ʳ (eVK2 62ʳ–64ᵛ)	[eVK2 *1648.00]
Pepys 1661, pp. 22–25	[eVK2 *7752.00]
GC 84/166, pp. 193–194	[eVK2 1647.00, 7854.00]
GC 84/166, pp. 331–333, 329 (women's urines moved up in the manuscript with women's urines from rearranged *Urine White and Brown*, item 5.2.2 below)	[eVK2 1652.00, *7855.00]

3.2.1c Token 3 omits reference to substance

CUL Ee.1.15, 77ᵛ (atelous)	[eVK2 –]
GC 336/725, 74ʳ⁻ᵛ (abridged)	[eVK2 7818.50, 7810.50]
Harl 2375, 31ᵛ–32ᵛ	[eVK2 –]

3.2.2 "Good Digestion" Texts: "digestion" substituted for "disposition" in incipit; number of signs reduced (4 witnesses)

Digby 29, 75ᵛ–76ᵛ (mixed Latin/English, mostly Latin; thirty-eight numbered signs)	[eVK2 –]
Huntington HM 64, 49ʳ–50ʳ (titled *The Kinds of Urine*; thirty-seven numbered signs)	[eVK2 6803.00]
Sloane 120, 76ᵛ–78ʳ (thirty-eight signs)	[eVK2 –]
Sloane 3542, 32ᵛ–33ʳ (thirty signs)	[eVK2 7759.00]

3.2.3 Idiosyncratic Texts: possible independent translations, blending with other texts, and abridgments (7 witnesses)

YkMinL XVI.E.32, 167ᵛ–169ʳ (new foliation; possible independent
   translation) [eVK2 *7818.00]
TCC R.14.39, III, 103ʳ–104ᵛ (moves women's urines to the
   beginning of the text) [eVK2 –]
Sloane 5, 183ᵛ–185ʳ (independent translation, including "brown"
   for "rufa") [eVK2 –]
Sloane 5, 185ᵛ–186ʳ (abridged) [eVK2 –]
NLM 30, 13ᵛ–15ᵛ (interspersed with material from **20J**, the **ST**
   series, *Urine White and Brown*, and other sources [items 1.1.1,
   4.1.3c, 5.2.1, and 7.5.6 above and below]) [eVK2 – , *7814.00]
Sloane 783B, 221ʳ–224ᵛ (incomplete; illustrated with sixteen
   flasks; interspersed with material from **20J** and other
   as yet unidentified sources) [eVK2 0345.00]
TCC O.7.20, II, 39ᵛ–42ᵛ (incomplete; conflated with
   20Col-Dig) [eVK2 –]

3.3 *Cleansing of Blood* (41 witnesses)

As noted above, this text falls into several easily demarcated short sections: 1) the definition of urine; 2) things to consider in judging urine; 3) the four elemental qualities in urine; 4) the four parts of urine (circle, body of air, *perforatio*, ground); 5) the three regions of urine (nethermost, middle, and overmost); and 6) contents in the regions.[34] Non-idiosyncratic witnesses that are complete or that appear to have been originally complete are listed first, followed by the various abridged forms of the text, with idiosyncratic witnesses given last.

3.3.1 Complete (or with only minor losses at head; 17 witnesses)

3.3.1a Incipit: "Each urine is a cleansing of blood" (for Latin "Omnis urina est colamentum sanguinis")

Laud misc 553, 32ʳ⁻ᵛ [eVK2 –]
Sloane 2584, 11ᵛ–12ʳ [eVK2 –]
Harl 3383, 43ʳ–44ʳ [eVK2 –]
GC 457/395, 60ʳ⁻ᵛ [eVK2 –]
Wellcome 537, 23ᵛ–25ᵛ [eVK2 –]
Sloane 121, 38ʳ⁻ᵛ [eVK2 *1520.00]
TCC R.14.32, 67ʳ⁻ᵛ [eVK2 *1520.00]
Pepys 878, pp. 183–184 [eVK2 *7801.00]
Ashmole 1393, 63ʳ⁻ᵛ [eVK2 –]

---

[34] Unlike the sections in **DU**, these divisions are generally not scribally marked with rubrics or other visual indicators; they are based simply on topical units that are useful for distinguishing broad textual groupings. However, in the discussion below, I have set my purely editorial titles for these units in small caps, for consistency with the policies laid out in the Introduction.

3.3.1b Incipit: "Every urine is a cleansing of blood"

Digby 75, 110^v–111^r (first of two copies)   [eVK2 –]
GC 336/725, 73^v–74^r [eVK2 1579.00]
Ashmole 1438, I, pp. 149–150 (variant CONTENTS section)   [eVK2 *1573.00]

3.3.1c Incipit: "All urine is a cleansing of blood" or no modifier for "urine"

Wellcome 408, 5^v–6^r (slightly acephalous; no modifier survives)   [eVK2 –]
Wellcome 8004, 63^{r-v} [eVK2 –]
Pepys 1661, pp. 25–26   [eVK2 –]
GC 84/166, pp. 194–195   [eVK2 *0843.00]
GC 84/166, pp. 328–329   [eVK2 0843.00]

3.3.2 Abridged or Abbreviated (13 witnesses)

3.3.2a Incipit: "Every urine is a cleansing of blood"

Jesus 43 (Q.D.1), 64^r (omits FOUR PARTS section and breaks
  off incomplete in THREE REGIONS)   [eVK2 1580.00]
Sloane 1388, 54^v (omits FOUR PARTS section; abridges
  CONTENTS section)   [eVK2 –]
Digby 29, 126^v–127^r, 129^r (abridges QUALITIES section and
  CONTENTS section)   [eVK2 –]
Ashmole 1444, pp. 226–227 (ends after THREE REGIONS
  section)   [eVK2 –]
GC 336/725, 70^r (ends after THREE REGIONS)   [eVK2 –]
Wellcome 7, 1^v (ends after THREE REGIONS)   [eVK2 1575.00]
Wellcome 784, 6^v–7^r (ends after THREE REGIONS)   [eVK2 1577.00, 7802.00]
MagdO 221, 68^v–69^v (ends after THREE REGIONS)   [eVK2 1574.00]
NLM 4, 59^v–60^r (ends after THREE REGIONS)   [eVK2 –]
NLM 30, 12^v (ends after FOUR PARTS)   [eVK2 –]
TCC R.14.52, 172^v–173^r (ends after FOUR PARTS)   [eVK2 1578.00]

3.3.2b Incipit: No modifier for "urine"

BL Roy 18 A.vi, 28^v, 26^r (folios out of order; abridges QUALITIES
  section and CONTENTS section)   [eVK2 –]
BL Add 4698, 15^{r-v} (omits DEFINITION, THINGS TO CONSIDER,
  and QUALITIES; textually close to full version in Pepys 878
  [item 3.3.1a])   [eVK2 –]

3.3.3 Idiosyncratic Texts (11 witnesses)

CUL Ee.1.15, 77^r (all sections; incipit with "Every")   [eVK2 *1576.00]
Sloane 5, 185^{r-v} (all sections; no modifier in incipit)   [eVK2 –]
YkMinL XVI.E.32, 169^r–170^r (new foliation; ends in
  CONTENTS section; no modifier in incipit)   [eVK2 –]
Sloane 635, 93^v (ends after DEFINITION section; incipit with "Euery")   [eVK2 –]
TCC O.1.65, 266^v–266a recto (omits "cleansing of blood" opening
  of DEFINITION; variant ending following the QUALITIES section,
  with color and substance typical of each humor, followed
  by a FOUR PARTS section)   [eVK2 –]

Bodl Add C.246, 47^v–48^r (omits "cleansing of blood" opening
of DEFINITION; THREE REGIONS moved after THINGS TO
CONSIDER; variant ending following the QUALITIES section,
with color and substance typical of each humor, followed by
signs of headache) [eVK2 1223.00]

Digby 75, 112^{r-v} (second of two copies; omits "cleansing of
blood" opening of DEFINITION; variant ending following the
QUALITIES section, with color and substance typical of each humor,
followed by signs of headache and fever) [eVK2 –]

Harl 2375, 30^r, 31^v, 32^v (DEFINITION omitted on 30^r, but inserted
on 31^v and again, with rest of opening paragraph, on 32^v,
between other texts; definition incipit "Every urine…") [eVK2 *2782.00]

TCC R.14.39, III, 98^v–99^r (DEFINITION omitted) [eVK2 –]

TCC O.7.20, II, 43^r–45^r (omits DEFINITION, THINGS TO
CONSIDER, and QUALITIES sections; expands CONTENTS
with humoral material and other contents) [eVK2 –]

Rylands Eng. 404, 42^v–43^r (a radical adaptation or possibly
a different text on similar topics, continuing to 43^v?) [eVK2 *7803.00]

4.0 White and Red Token-Lists

At least three distinct series of uroscopic tokens and their significance,
beginning with a description of healthy urine as "white in the morning
and red before meat (and white after meat)" (i.e., more dilute vs. more
concentrated/intense). Translations or adaptations of shorter and longer
versions of the Anglo-Norman or French *Lettre d'Hippocrate*.[35]

---

[35] For discussion and editions of the *Letter of Ipocras* and the *Fifteen Discretions
of Urine*, see M. Teresa Tavormina, "The Middle English *Letter of Ipocras*," *English
Studies* 88, no. 6 (2007): 632–52, with references to related AN and OF uroscopies in
nn. 2–3, 18–19, 21–24. See also Tony Hunt, *Old French Medical Texts* (Paris, 2011),
editing another witness to the French *Lettre d'Hippocrate* and a unique, incomplete
French translation of one of the standard commentaries on Giles of Corbeil's *Carmen de urinis*, both from Wellcome MS 546 (ca. 1340).

The White and Red texts do not comment on why the color of the urine lightens
after a meal, nor do the White and Brown texts (items 5.1–5.2 below) explain their
apparently contradictory assertion of a darker color after a meal. The quantity of
liquid intake can affect the color of urine—dehydration causes darker urine—but
there is no sign that the two groups of texts envision different quantities of drink at
meals. I have not yet found a satisfactory explication of this key difference between
the White and Brown texts on the one hand and the *Lettre d'Hippocrate* and White
and Red texts on the other.

4.1 *Letter of Ipocras* (38 witnesses)

A short compendium whose fullest versions comprise a brief (sometimes versified) prologue attributing the following material to Hippocrates (twenty-two witnesses; sometimes abridged in ways that omit the Hippocrates reference), a short overview of the "humors" (properly, the four qualities) found in "man beast and bird" (**MBB**; twenty-four witnesses), a list of six uroscopic tokens beginning with the white and red urine of a healthy man (*Six-Token List*, or **ST**; thirty-two witnesses), and one or another collection of medical recipes, often beginning with a headache recipe based on hillwort or puliol seethed in eisell (vinegar).

MANUSCRIPT WITNESSES

4.1.1 Texts with Verse Prologues (11 witnesses)

4.1.1a Ipocras and Caesar incipit

Laud misc 553, 30^v (with **MBB, ST**)	[eVK2 8204.00, 1549.00, *7320.00]
Sloane 2584, 9^{r-v} (with **MBB, ST**)	[eVK2 3108.00, *1560.00, –]
Bodl Add A.106, 139^{r-v} (with **MBB, ST**)	[eVK2 3111.00, 8187.00, 1552.00, 7775.00]
Wellcome 405, 21^v–23^v (with **MBB, ST**)	[eVK2 7426.00]

4.1.1b "Good leech" incipit

Harl 3383, 85^v–86^r (with **MBB, ST**)	[eVK2 8178.00, 1555.00, 6896.00]
Sloane 3285, 73^r–74^r (with **MBB, ST**)	[eVK2 8205.00, *1561.00, –]
Douce 84, 1^{r-v} (with **MBB, ST**)	[eVK2 8182.00, 1548.00, 7321.00]
StJC B.15 (37), II, 10^v–11^r (with **MBB, ST**)	[eVK2 8179.00, *1554.00, *3731.00]
Ferguson 147, 131^v–132^v (with **MBB, ST**)	[eVK2 7693.00, *1562.00, –]
Yale 27, 16^r–17^v (with **MBB, ST**)	[eVK2 *8175.00, 1550.00, 7319.00]

4.1.1c Tetrameter quatrain prologue

Ashmole 1438, II, p. 79 (with **MBB, ST** [with an added token on women's urine])	[eVK2 3791.00, 3495.00, 7805.00]

4.1.2 Texts with Prose Prologues (11 witnesses)

4.1.2a With verbal echoes of verse prologues

The last three witnesses in this section are textually very close and are all preceded by a Middle English hematoscopy text (eVK2 1909.00, 7181.00, 7149.00; also found in Sloane 3160, eVK2 7599.00).

Wellcome 409, 70^r–71^r (includes reference to Ipocras and Caesar; with **MBB, ST**)	[eVK2 3109.00, 1553.00, 6588.00]
Sloane 3217, 116^r–117^r (with **MBB, ST** [tokens #1–#4 only])	[eVK2 – , *1517.00, –]
BL Add 19674, 57^v (with **MBB, ST** [tokens #1–#4 only])	[eVK2 – , 1518.00, –]
Ashmole 1477, II, 43^{r-v} (with **MBB, ST** [tokens #1–#4 only])	[eVK2 – , 1517.00, 3818.00]

4.1.2b Treasure prologue (including asseveration "wit ye well it is good treasure")

CUL Dd.10.44, 114^{r-v} (with **MBB** and a longer white/red
    token-list; see item 4.2.2 below)   [eVK2 7346.00, 1556.00, 2555.00]
Jesus 43 (Q.D.1), 126^v–127^r (with **MBB**)   [eVK2 7354.00, *1558.00]
TCC R.14.32, 81^r (with **MBB**)   [eVK2 7353.00, *1558.00]
Sloane 706, 95^r (with **MBB**)   [eVK2 7353.00, *1559.00]

4.1.2c Unique prose prologues

Lansdowne 388, 371^r, 372^r (with **MBB**)   [eVK2 6630.00, 1557.00]
TCC O.5.32, 31^v (with **MBB**)   [eVK2 2095.00]
ExCathL 3521, p. 106 (with **ST**)   [eVK2 3110.00, 1563.00]

4.1.3 Texts without Prologues (16 witnesses)

4.1.3a "Man Beast and Bird" and *Six-Token List*

BL Add 4698, 66^r [eVK2 1546.00, 0613.00, 1565.00]
BL Add 34111, 68^{r-v} (variant texts, with expanded **MBB** and
    only a modified version of **ST** token #1)   [eVK2 3766.50, 2682.00]
Bodl Add A.106, 259^r (abbreviated **ST** token #1; "drovy"
    instead of "seemeth bloody" in token #2)[36]   [eVK2 0814.00, 7091.00]

4.1.3b "Man Beast and Bird" only

none found (but note the verbal echoes to **MBB** in the Rawlinson D.1210 Compendium, 125^r: shared references to bones, things through which we live, governance – item 14.1.4 below)

4.1.3c *Six-Token List* only

Eger 827, 53^v [eVK2 6592.00]
Wellcome 404, 2^v–3^r (rearranged and appended to a token list
    focused on white and pale urines, item 7.5.11 below)   [eVK2 –]
TCC R.14.52, 175^{r-v} (variant text appended to the *Approbate*
    Treatise for the Pestilence, a derivative of the John of
    Burgundy plague treatises)[37]   [eVK2 –]
BL Add 5467, 87^r (variant text appended to the *Approbate*
    Treatise for the Pestilence)   [eVK2 –]
Sloane 357, 26^r (abbreviated list, missing token #3; embedded
    in the *Book of Egidij*, item 29.0 below)   [eVK2 –]
Sloane 1317, 88^r (abbreviated list; missing token #3, for being
    with child; embedded in the "Urine as Snot" token list)   [eVK2 –]

---

[36] On this "drovy" variant, see Tavormina, "The Middle English *Letter of Ipocras*" (n. 35 above), 647 and 647 n. 30.

[37] Ed. in Lister M. Matheson, "John of Burgundy: Treatises on Plague," *Sex, Aging, and Death in a Medieval Medical Compendium: Trinity College Cambridge MS R.14.52, Its Texts, Language, and Scribe*, ed. M. Teresa Tavormina (Tempe, AZ, 2006), 569–602 (**ST**: lines 400–412, pp. 596–97 and nn.).

TCC R.14.39, III, 91^v (abbreviated list, missing token #1, and
  slightly reordered; embedded in a sixteenth-century copy of
  De Urinis Egrorum [item 16.5 below])	[eVK2 –]
CUL Dd.6.29, 32^v–33^r (abbreviated list: tokens #2–#3, #5; "drovy
  and white" instead of "seemeth bloody" in token #2)	[eVK2 7057.00]
YkMinL XVI.E.32, 170^v–171^r (new foliation; abbreviated list;
  signs #1, #5–#6, after **WBw** [item 5.2.1 below], which includes
  signs #2–#4)	[eVK2 –]
BL Roy 17 A.iii, 61^v (tokens #5 and #6 only, after **WBw**)	[eVK2 –]
TCC R.14.51, 18^v (token #5 only, after **WBw**)	[eVK2 –]
SurreyHS LM 1327/2, 47^v (token #5 only, after **WBw**)	[eVK2 –]
NLM 30, 15^r (token #5 only, in a collection of signs from
  several token-lists)	[eVK2 –]

4.2 *Urine White and Red* (14 witnesses)

A simple series of about twenty tokens, standing alone or in non-systematic associations with other urine texts, translating about two-thirds of the fullest version of the *Lettre d'Hippocrate* (found in Harl 2558). In half of the witnesses, a brief prologue introduces the text, listing the four parts of the body that "show the dwelling of" health and sickness (head, stomach, liver, and bladder). Of these witnesses, all but Hatton 29 are embedded in large recipe collections. In the fuller copies of the text, aside from a couple of rearranged versions, approximately the last third focuses on urines of women. The first four tokens from the *Six-Token List* in item 4.1 above appear in the fuller versions of this text, in the same order as in **ST**, but interspersed among other signs, not as a group in themselves. Individual witnesses occasionally add one or more extra signs, though not in any recurring pattern; over half of the copies abridge the series to a lesser or greater degree.

MANUSCRIPT WITNESSES
4.2.1 With Four-Parts Prologue (7 witnesses)
Sloane 3542, 69^v–70^v	[eVK2 2568.00]
Rawl C.299, 16^v–17^r (17^v–18^r in modern pencilled
  foliation)	[eVK2 3136.00, 2569.00]
Ashmole 1438, II, pp. 22–23	[eVK2 3192.00]
BL Add 4698, 57^{r-v} (omits about 9 tokens)	[eVK2 3138.00, 2568.00]
Hatton 29, 72^v (omits about 10 tokens)	[eVK2 3138.00]
Sloane 1388, 51^r (omits about 13 tokens)	[eVK2 –]
NLW Peniarth 388C, 3^r–4^r (slightly abridged, omitting about
  four tokens; with a possibly corrupt, variant form of the Four
  Parts prologue)	[eVK2 3503.00]

4.2.2 Other Versions (7 witnesses)

Bodl Add C.246, 48^v–49^r (rearranged, with women's urines first, and given the heading "Hearre Ipocras techeis to knowe þe vyryne of a woman"; several additional tokens for women's urines inserted, including the last two signs from **ST**)   [eVK2 3103.00, 2683.00]

BL Roy 17 C.xv, 60^r, 61^v, 62^r (rearranged, partially repeated, interspersed with other token-lists)   [eVK2 –]

Sloane 121, 58^v (substantially abridged, omitting about ten tokens)   [eVK2 –]

Sloane 3466, 64^v (same abridgment as Sloane 121)   [eVK2 7056.00]

CUL Dd.10.44, 114^{r-v} (substantially abridged, omitting women's urines and some other tokens; replaces the even shorter **ST** in a *Letter of Ipocras* text)   [eVK2 2555.00]

Ashmole 1438, I, pp. 164–165 (only the tokens for women's urines)   [eVK2 –]

TCC R.14.39, II, 69^r (acephalous, with only the final sign from the women's urines section, and a partial word from the penultimate sign)   [eVK2 –]

4.3 *Fifteen Discretions of Urine* (7 witnesses)

A list of uroscopic tokens, the first five of which coincide with the first five signs of **ST** in the *Letter of Ipocras* above (item 4.1). Incorporates more complex similes for the uroscopic colors than do most other token-lists (e.g., discretion 8, "urine yellow as amber and clear with a yellow gravel, as it were small sand falling easily on one side of the urinal").

MANUSCRIPT WITNESSES

Sloane 7, 57^{r-v} [eVK2 6589.00]

Sloane 297, 109^r [eVK2 6591.00]

Cosin V.III.10, 14^r–15^r [eVK2 1999.00, 6590.00]

Wellcome 564, 195^v [eVK2 1999.00]

Sloane 433, 59^{r-v} (incomplete, ends in discretion 12, owing to folio loss)   [eVK2 6587.00]

Hatton 29, 74^r–75^r (omits discretions 1 and 14, with variant discretion 10; rearranged in roughly reverse order)   [eVK2 –]

Sloane 1388, 51^{r-v} (similar to Hatton 29, with further rearrangement, omission of discretion 2, and additional variation in discretion 9)   [eVK2 –]

5.0 White and Brown Token-Lists

Somewhat less literal adaptations of the Anglo-Norman or French *Lettre d'Hippocrate*, translating the opening *blanche-rouge(-blanche)* sign of good health as "urine white in the morning, brown after meat." Three principal Middle English uroscopy texts begin with diagnoses involving white and brown urine: the JUDICIUM PERFECTUM text usually found in the *Dome of Uryne* (see above) and two similar but distinguishable variants of a different and probably earlier series of signs, whose earliest witness—and the earliest surviving Middle English uroscopy—occurs in the ca. 1320–30 manuscript Cambridge, Corpus Christi College 388. Of these three texts, the closest to the *Lettre d'Hippocrate* is *Urine White and Brown* (Woman variant), followed by the Phlegm variant of that text, with JUDICIUM PERFECTUM the furthest removed from the French original.

5.1 JUDICIUM PERFECTUM OMNIUM URINARUM (JP) in DU (35 manuscript witnesses, 2 prints)[38]

The most widespread uroscopy with a white/brown incipit, **JP** has at least thirty-seven witnesses, in thirty-three separate manuscripts and two distinct editions. In its full form, it contains twenty-six uroscopic signs; a few manuscripts number the signs to twenty-six, although a couple of the signs actually describe two kinds of urine. Distinguishing features in **JP** include its reference to the troubled urine signifying headache as being like horse piss, rather than the ass piss or ashes found in the next two White-Brown texts; the thin green or black circles that signify phthisic and "lust of kynde" (rather than "talent to woman"); and the contents like shavings of parchment or shives of flax signifying obstruction in the "pipes epatis."

MANUSCRIPT WITNESSES

Asterisks indicate the two copies that occur without any other **DU** components.

---

[38]   In the next seven sections (5.0-11.0), I analyze the components of the *Dome of Uryne* that are generically related to other types of uroscopy texts together with their congenerics (white and brown token-lists; other twenty-color lists; urines of death; women's urines and urines of pregnancy; urines of man, woman, and beast; complexions; regions; contents; and inspections of urines), so as to highlight their similarities to those texts. For most of these components, I group the witnesses by the **DU** version to which they belong, run in and without folio numbers to save space. Potential confusion with other white/brown incipits and the relatively complex variations in the text of **JP** warrant sorting it independently, but I have also indicated the **DU** version to which each **JP** witness belongs in parentheses after the folio or page numbers, using the short forms Core, Exp., Abb., Hyb., Pec., and Sing. for the six groups described in item 2.0 above.

5.1a Full text

Cosin V.III.10, 6ᵛ–7ʳ (Core)   [eVK2 *7810.00]
MagdO 221, 99ʳ–100ʳ (Core)   [eVK2 7809.00]
BL Add 10440, 53ᵛ–54ʳ (Exp.)   [eVK2 7834.00]
Sloane 374, 10ᵛ–11ᵛ (Exp.)   [eVK2 7834.00]
Sloane 1388 (b), 48ᵛ (Core; occurs in a set of **DU**
   components and other uroscopies that appear to
   be related to Hatton 29; text illegible in parts, and
   somewhat corrupt, repeating signs 6–8 after sign 13
   and omitting the end of sign 16b and beginning of 17)   [eVK2 –]
Wellcome 564, 194ᵛ (Core; closely related to Cosin V.III.10;
   also to MagdO 221 and [in **DU** overall] to Hatton 29)   [eVK2 –]
Wellcome 409, 61ᵛ–62ᵛ (Exp.)   [eVK2 –]
Rawl C.506, 56ʳ–57ᵛ (Exp.)   [eVK2 7840.00]
Selden Supra 73, 110ʳ–111ʳ (Exp.)   [eVK2 7844.00]

5.1b Slightly imperfect copies (three or fewer signs missing)

BL Add 30338, 156ʳ–157ʳ (Exp.). Conflates signs 9–10.   [eVK2 7840.00]
Digby 29, 114ᵛ–115ʳ (Core). Conflates signs 3–4.   [eVK2 *7837.00]
St Roy X.90, pp. 124–126 (Pec.). Omits sign 12b.   [eVK2 –]
Rawl D.1221, 47ᵛ–48ʳ (Pec.). Omits sign 12b, reverses signs
   23/24.   [eVK2 7845.00]
*Wellcome 537, 25ᵛ–28ᵛ (Sing.). Omits sign 22, reverses signs
   6/7, 23/24, 25/26. Idiosyncratic adaptation of usual text, with
   a number of unique readings and expansions, incorporated into
   a compilation of texts including **20J**, **20Col-Dig**, *Urina Rufa*,
   Cleansing of Blood, and *Practica Urinarum* (items 1.1.2, 3.1.1b,
   3.2.1a, 3.3.1a, and 11.2 above and below).   [eVK2 –]
StJC K.49, 75ʳ–76ᵛ (Exp.). Omits last half of sign 8 and all of
   sign 9.   [eVK2 7839.50]
Sloane 382, 27ᵛ–28ᵛ (Hyb.). Omits sign 1 and conflates signs
   2–3 and 21–22. Textually related to Sloane 1388, 45ʳ⁻ᵛ; print
   eds.; and NLM 49.   [eVK2 –]
NLM 49, 44ᵛ–46ʳ (Hyb.; omits sign 1, conflates signs 2–3 and
   21–22, reverses signs 23/24; in Robert Denham's book, copied in
   1586 from the 1540 ed. of *Seynge of Uryns* [London: Robert
   Redman])   [eVK2 –]
NLW Sotheby C.2, pp. 135–137 (Pec.). Omits signs 5, 17.   [eVK2 *7845.50]
Bodl Add B.60, 53ʳ–54ʳ (Abb.). Omits signs 17, 25.   [eVK2 7840.00]
TCC O.8.35, 53ʳ–54ʳ (Abb.). Omits signs 17, 25.   [eVK2 –]
Lambeth 444, 157ʳ (Abb.). Omits signs 17, 25.   [eVK2 *7838.00]
Rawl C.81, 9ʳ⁻ᵛ (Core). Omits end of sign 23, all of 24–25,
   and beginning of 26.   [eVK2 *7836.00]
Ashmole 1477, X, 16ᵛ–17ʳ (Core). Omits signs 6, 17, 19; inserts
   seven signs from **WBp** (item 5.2.2 below).   [eVK2 –]

5.1c Substantially imperfect copies (four or more signs missing)

Ashmole 1477, X, 22ʳ (Pec.). Omits 4 signs (2, 15, 22, 23)
and radically rearranges the rest (order of signs = 1, 5–8,
12b, 20, 10, 21, 4, 3, 25–26, 17, 9, 13–14, 16a–b, 24, 18–19,
11–12a), with a non-JP sign at the end.   [eVK2 *7839.00]

Pepys 1307, 59ʳ–60ʳ (Abb.). Omits signs 17–18, 20, 22, 26.   [eVK2 –]

*TCC O.7.20, II, 45ʳ–46ʳ (Sing.). Conflates signs 23–24; omits
signs 11, 12b, 16b, 18, 21, 25–26.   [eVK2 –]

Ashmole 1447, p. 192 (Core). Omits signs 12b and 16–26.   [eVK2 –]

Harl 2558, 170ʳ (Pec.). Omits signs 6, 8–18, 20, 24–25;
remaining signs rearranged: 26, 23–21, 19, 1–5, 7.   [eVK2 –]

PML Bühler 21, 16ʳ (Pec.). Omits signs 3–7, 11–15,
17–21, 23–26.   [eVK2 *7841.00]

5.1d Acephalous and atelous copies

Harl 3407, 46ʳ⁻ᵛ (Exp.). Breaks off incomplete in sign 22,
owing to a lost leaf between fol. 46 and fol. 47; textually
very close to Sloane 374.   [eVK2 *7834.00]

Sloane 1388 (a), 45ʳ⁻ᵛ (Hyb.). Acephalous; begins in sign
8 and omits some seven signs thereafter (9, 11, 13, 16,
18–19, 21). Text often faded, illegible in parts.   [eVK2 –]

Sloane 297, 113ʳ (Abb.). Acephalous due to lost leaves at
the beginning of the DU ensemble; JP begins partway
through sign 18.   [eVK2 *0371.00]

Hatton 29, 60ʳ (half of sign 25, sign 26), 67ʳ (rubricated
heading only) (Core). Acephalous; only the last one and
a half items and the dislocated heading remain.   [eVK2 *0288.00, –]

BL Roy 17 C.xv, 58ᵛ–61ʳ (Pec.) Acephalous or deliberately
excerpted; signs 18, 19, 24, 25, 26; 8, 2, ?9, 11, 12 interspersed
with signs from other token lists.   [eVK2 –]

Wellcome 7, 3ᵛ (Pec.). Atelous from loss of leaves; only sign
1 remains.   [eVK2 –]

PRINT WITNESSES

5.1b Slightly imperfect copies (three or fewer signs missing)

Both editions omit sign 1, conflate signs 2–3 and 21–22, and reverse signs
23 and 24.

The Seynge of Uryns, 1525, sigs. C1ᵛ–C3ʳ (Hyb.; London: J.
Rastell for Richard Banckes, with at least ten subsequent
printings by various printers)   —

The Judgement of All Urynes, 1555, sigs. A2ᵛ–A4ᵛ (Abb.; London:
Robert Wyer)   —

5.2 *Urine White and Brown*

5.2.1 *Urine White and Brown* (Woman variant: WBw; 28 witnesses)

The second most widely-distributed "White-Brown" text varies somewhat more than **JP**, though one can construct a full list of signs to serve as a notional source from which all the witnesses select items, usually in the same order (even if they omit a few signs here and there). Because its witnesses nearly always include the early sign "urine thin and black above betokens talent to woman" and many of its witnesses end with a group of women's urines, I have labelled this text *Urine White and Brown* (Woman variant), abbreviated **WBw**.

The full complement of signs in **WBw** runs to about two dozen, but most sets omit at least a couple. The series of women's urines at the end of the text overlaps to some extent with other urines-of-women lists (e.g., the subsets of women's urines in the White and Red Urine texts [4.1–4.3 above], in **WBp**, and several items in section 7.2 below, largely reflecting derivation from shared or related French antecedents).

In five manuscripts, the **WBw** list directly follows "The Doom of Urine Thou Shalt Cast in Four" (indicated by a dagger in the list of witnesses below) and, in three of those manuscripts, *Three Manners of Inspecting Urine* (indicated with an asterisk; see also items 7.4 and 11.3 below). About half a dozen witnesses have a form of the heading, "Here mayst thou know urines by colors" or "How thou shalt know urine" (indicated by ° below). Several copies end with a comment, sometimes truncated, about knowing the location of ailments in different parts of the body through inspection of the urine, and making diverse medicines for those ailments (indicated by a ‡ below).

MANUSCRIPT WITNESSES

°CCCC 388, 53ᵛ–54ʳ (earliest known Middle English
uroscopy, ca. 1320–30)³⁹   [eVK2 7835.00]

---

³⁹ Tony Hunt has studied the manuscript, in collaboration with Michael Benskin, in *Three Receptaria from Medieval England* (Oxford, 2001). He edits its medical recipe collections (fols. 3ʳ–35ᵛ, 36ʳ–48ᵛ; pp. 93–192) and a Latin and a French uroscopy (fols. 1ʳᵇ–2ᵛᵃ, 2ᵛᵃ–3ʳᵃ; pp. 89–93), but not the English uroscopy, which shares a number of signs with the French uroscopy.

An even earlier example of Middle English reference to uroscopy occurs in Lawman's *Brut* (ca. 1200), expanding on a passage in Wace's *Roman de Brut* (ca. 1155), in which King Aurelius is assassinated by a Saxon disguised as a physician. In Lawman's version, the false doctor examines the king's urine (a detail not in Wace)

*†BL Add 4898, 116^r–117^r (ends with signs of malady on
right or left side)   [eVK2 –]
*†Ashmole 1477, III, 10^v–11^r (ends with signs of malady on
right or left side)   [eVK2 –]
*†‡Plimpton 254, 27^{r-v} (ends with signs of malady on
right or left side)   [eVK2 –]
†CUL Ff.2.6, 128^{r-v} [eVK2 –]
°‡BL Roy 12 G.iv, 4^v, 185^r, 206^r (4^v and 206^r are copies
of 185^r)   [eVK2 7846.00, 8206.00]
°‡Sloane 963, 12^v–13^r, 54^r–55^r (copies of the same text)   [eVK2 7842.00]
‡Sloane 2584, 12^{r-v} [eVK2 7830.00]
°‡Hatton 29, 73^r–74^r [eVK2 *7832.00]
‡Ashmole 1438, I, p. 117   [eVK2 7831.00]
‡Ashmole 1438, II, pp. 71–72 (**ST** signs #5, #6 at end)   [eVK2 *7852.00]
‡YkMinL XVI.E.32, 170^{r-v} (new foliation; **ST** signs #1,
#5, #6 at end)   [eVK2 –]
Sloane 1388, 41^{r-v}, ‡51^r (different versions)   [eVK2 –]
°TCC R.14.51, 18^{r-v} (**ST** sign #5 at end)   [eVK2 7833.00]
°SurreyHS LM 1327/2, 47^{r-v} (**ST** sign #5 at end)   [eVK2 7843.00]
BL Roy 17 A.iii, 60^v–61^v (**ST** signs #5, #6 added at end) [eVK2 7850.00]
Sloane 357, 26^r–27^r (embedded in *Book of Egidij*, item 29.0
below; ends with signs of malady on right or left side)   [eVK2 –]
Sloane 5, 186^r–187^r (ends with signs of malady on right or
left side)   [eVK2 –]
Arun 42, 109^v (after "Urine as Snot," item 7.5.1 below, with
no indication of a textual break)   [eVK2 –]
Sloane 1317, 88^v–89^v (after "Urine as Snot" with no indication
of a textual break)   [eVK2 –]
†TCC R.14.39, III, 101^v, 104^v–105^r (part of a compendium of
several uroscopy and related treatises [item 14.1.5 below])   [eVK2 –]
Ashmole 1393, 61^v–62^r [eVK2 7853.00]
PML Bühler 21, 16^r (only one sign, "urine ray [OF *raie*] and
clear and shining as silver," inserted into abridged versions
of **JP** [5.1c above] and **UMul** from **DU** [7.2.1 below]; possibly
drawn from some other token list including women's urines
from the French tradition)   [eVK2 –]
NLM 30, 15^{r-v} (a few signs from **WBw** intermixed with several
more from *Urina Rufa*)   [eVK2 – , *7814.00]

---

and then administers a fatal potion under the guise of medicine. The scene has been analyzed in detail and against its medical-historical context by Gail Ivy Berlin, "Medicine in Lawman's *Brut*" (paper presented at the 49th International Medieval Congress, Kalamazoo, MI, 2014).

5.2.2 *Urine White and Brown* (Phlegm variant: WBp; 9 witnesses)

The third "White-Brown" text contains up to twenty-one signs, and most of the witnesses give all or nearly all the signs, aside from minor eye-skips and similar omissions. It shares a good deal of material with **WBw**, but distinguishes itself in the second sign, with the diagnosis "phlegm among/in the bowels [*var.* lights]" instead of "water in the bowels" as in **JP** and **WBw**. It also has the unique diagnoses of "headache from water between the filmen/felmyn ['membrane, *dura mater*'] and the brain" for the fourth sign (a great circle and changing colors) and "the stomach (is) (en)glaymed" for Glaucus urine later in the text. There are a couple other diagnoses focused on the stomach as well, which do not occur in the same phrasing in **JP** or **WBw**, and fewer women's urines at the end of the series. I have labelled this list *Urine White and Brown* (Phlegm variant), with the abbreviation **WBp**.

Several witnesses in the list below are introduced with versions of the heading "Here mayst thou know how thou shalt ken & disscrive [*varr.*: know, discern, deem, descry] all manner of sickness within mans body or womans by the sight of his [*var.*: their] water" (indicated by ° below). Witnesses marked with an asterisk directly precede or (in Sloane 635) follow a short text on the diagnostic correspondence between the "four regions of a man's body and the four parts of his water" (item 9.2 below), which I have not found separately from **WBp**, and which should probably be considered as creating a subvariant of **WBp**. The first four of these witnesses continue with English (Wellcome 8004, GC 84/166 twice) or Latin (Sloane 7) versions of *Urina Rufa* and *Cleansing of Blood*; the Ashmole 1413 copy of **WBp** follows a Latin *Urina Rufa* (acephalous) and *Cleansing of Blood*.

MANUSCRIPT WITNESSES

°*Wellcome 8004, 60ʳ–61ʳ (eVK2 61ʳ–62ʳ) [eVK2 *7847.00]
°*GC 84/166, p. 193 [eVK2 7851.00]
°GC 84/166, pp. 329–331 (textually close to the copy on p. 193 of the same manuscript, but rearranged so that the urines of women appear first, after the women's urines section from the end of *Urina Rufa*, item 3.2.1b above) [eVK2 – , 7851.00]
°*Sloane 7, 60ᵛ [eVK2 7848.00]
°*Ashmole 1413, pp. 151–154 [eVK2 7849.00]
*Sloane 635, 93ʳ⁻ᵛ (followed by an abbreviated version of *Cleansing of Blood* and *Ten Cold Ten Hot*) [eVK2 –]
Eger 2433, 22ᵛ (followed by a Latin list of women's urines, an incomplete **20Col-Dig,** and additional Latin uroscopy texts) [eVK2 *7829.00]

NLW Sotheby C.2, pp. 137–138, 139–140 (interspersed in this
late manuscript with the **JP** and the **UMul** sections of the
Dome of Uryne)   [eVK2 –]
Ashmole 1477, X, 16ᵛ. Signs 3–7, 10, 12 inserted in a version of
JP (item 5.1b above).   [eVK2 –]

6.0 Other Twenty-Color Lists

6.1 The Twenty Colors (20C) in DU (27 manuscript witnesses, 1 print)

MANUSCRIPT AND PRINT WITNESSES (by versions)

Core Version: MagdO 221; Ashmole 1447; Cosin V.V.13; Harl 2274; Digby 95;
Digby 29; Rawl C.81; Ashmole 1477, X

Expanded Version: Sloane 374; Harl 3407 (missing colors 3-18 owing to lost
leaf); BL Add 10440; Wellcome 409; StJC K.49; BL Add 30338; Selden Supra
73; Rawl C.506 (acephalous); Ashmole 1405

Abbreviated Versions: none, due to truncation

Hybrid Version (blended with **20Med**): Sloane 382; Sloane 1388 (a); *Seynge of
Uryns*; Huntington HM 64 (blended with **20Col/20Sick/20Med**)

Peculiar Versions: BL Roy 18 A.vi, CCCO 291; Harl 3810; Harl 5401; Harl 218
(abridged); CUL Dd.5.76 (atelous)

Singleton: Harl 1735 (abridged)

6.2 *Rufus Subrufus* (18 witnesses)

A list of twenty urinary colors and their diagnostic implications, followed
by a token list integrated with recipes for the indicated ailments; the text
thereby takes on a notably therapeutic orientation. Ends with a series
of women's urines similar to those in the *Urina Rufa* text and related
Latin-based treatises (including signs of the two-, three-, and four-month
stages of pregnancy). Some of the recipes occur in other Middle English
recipe collections, but the specific selection of recipes in *Rufus Subrufus* remains generally consistent and I have not found its combination of
materials elsewhere. Includes a number of particularly striking recipes:
the apple filled with saffron and ivory shavings used to cure yellow jaundice, a urine and cumin suffumigation followed by putting the patient
to bed in a "new pair of washed sheets," a plaster of sheep dung used
for excessive menstrual bleeding, the gladden roots and vinegar used to
stimulate the menses, and so on.

The text occurs with several related but distinguishable prologues or introductions: one asserts a royal commissioning of the text, either specifically by
Henry IV or Henry V or attributed to an unnamed English king and his lords;
another invokes the (ap)probation of Ipocras, Galen, Maurus, Egidius (Giles
of Corbeil), and other doctors; a third refers more generally to the declarations
of "doctors and authors" as justification for the subsequent text; and other

witnesses begin the text with only a brief reference to a circular color diagram ("as is showed hereafter in a circle") or are acephalous. Followed or preceded in about a dozen witnesses by *Cleansing of Blood* (3.3 above).

MANUSCRIPT WITNESSES

6.2a "Royal" prologue

GC 336/725, 67ʳ–70ʳ	[eVK2 2193.00, 1797.00]
Wellcome 784, 1ᵛ–7ʳ	[eVK2 2262.00, 8101.00]
MagdO 221, 63ʳ–68ᵛ	[eVK2 2263.00, 1796.00]
NLM 4, 57ᵛ–59ᵛ	[eVK2 2261.00, *4409.00]

6.2b "Ipocras" prologue

Digby 29, 125ʳ–126ᵛ	[eVK2 7619.00, *1194.00]
Jesus 43 (Q.D.1), 61ᵛ–64ʳ	[eVK2 0812.00]
BL Roy 18 A.vi, 23ʳ–25ᵛ, 26ᵛ, 28ᵛ	[eVK2 *7620.00]
Sloane 1388, 53ʳ–54ᵛ	[eVK2 –]

6.2c "Doctors and Authors" prologue

TCC R.14.52, 170ᵛ–172ᵛ	[eVK2 –]
Wellcome 7117, 122ᵛ (copying only the prologue and a couple more lines of TCC R.14.52 text)	[eVK2 –]
NLM 30, 11ʳ–12ᵛ	[eVK2 1616.00, *4410.00]
Rawl C.81, 1ʳ–3ᵛ (although the phrase "doctors and authors" does not appear, derivatives of "declaren" occur twice in the prologue here, with other similarities to the TCC, Wellcome, and NLM texts; atelous, breaking off near the end of the text)	[eVK2 7428.00, *5041.00]

6.2d "Circle" prologue

Ashmole 1438, I, pp. 150–156	[eVK2 *5992.00]
Ashmole 1444, pp. 219–226	[eVK2 *4408.00]

6.2e Acephalous copies

Ashmole 1413, p. 2 (acephalous and atelous, beginning in urines indicating excess digestion and ending in urines indicating adustion)	[eVK2 *3723.00, 5043.00]
BL Roy 17 C.xv, 62ʳ–64ᵛ (begins in urines indicating indigestion)	[eVK2 –]
Wellcome 7, 1ʳ⁻ᵛ (begins in recipe for shortness of breath, using crops of horehound and roots of milfoil)	[eVK2 0476.00]
BL Add 19674, 68ʳ (only 3 tokens from the end of the text, all involving women's urines, plus recipes for relief of *suffocatio matricis*, using inhalation and suffumigation with smoke from stinking and sweet substances respectively)	[eVK2 0331.00]

6.3 *Ten Cold Ten Hot* (14 witnesses)

A concise summary of information about colors, contents, humoral correspondences, astromedicine, and cosmology, suitable as an introduction to or quick-review reminder of the broad conceptual framework under-pinning more detailed and circumstantial treatises. Includes up to six textual components, which may be rearranged or excerpted: A) qualities, elements, the concentric cosmos, and complexions; B) the quarters of the year, day, world, and four ages of man; C) four parts of the body, four parts of the urine sample, and substances, quantities, and tastes of urine; D) ten cold and ten hot colors of urine; E) eighteen contents in urine; and F) the four principal limbs of the body (the "souled," "spiritual," "nour-ishing," and "gendring" limbs, i.e., the intellectual and cephalic sensory organs, the cardiac and respiratory organs, the digestive organs, and the reproductive and excretory organs).

MANUSCRIPT WITNESSES

Sloane 213, 117^r–118^v (one of the most coherent texts, ordered
ABCDEF; incorporated into a larger compendium of short
prognostic, medical, and astromedical treatises)   [eVK2 8176.00]
Sloane 2270, 11^r–12^v (ABCDEF; incorporated into a larger
compendium of short medical and astromedical treatises that
are closely related to those in Sloane 213 and Harl 1735;
manuscript copied by John Eames, 1530)   [eVK2 *0716.00]
Harl 1735, 33^r–35^v (ABCDE; incorporated into a larger
compendium of short medical and astromedical treatises
that are closely related to those in Sloane 213 and
2270; John Crophill's notebook)[40]   [eVK2 8190.00, *8096.00]
Sloane 5, 181^r–183^v (ABC-E-CD; slightly rearranged by the
insertion of segment E partway through segment C;
preceded by several lunaries and by planetary material
extracted and abbreviated from Henry Daniel's *Liber Uricrisiarum*,
book 2, and from the astromedical compendium containing
Ten Cold Ten Hot in Sloane 213 and 2270, Harl 1735, and other
manuscripts)   [eVK2 1539.00, *3086.00]
Cosin V.V.13, 41^v–44^v (BCDEF, incomplete in CD segments
owing to loss of leaves)   [eVK2 3046.00, 0997.00, 3869.00]
Rawl D.1210, 126^r–127^v (BCDEF, truncated at the start of B,
perhaps deliberately; part of a larger medical compendium,
item 14.1.4 below; textually close to GC 451/392)   [eVK2 –]
GC 451/392, pp. 27–29 (CDEF, with C acephalous, omitting some
material on parts of the body; textually close to Rawl D.1210)   [eVK2 2763.00]
Harl 1612, 1^r–2^r (CDEF)   [eVK2 1971.00]
CUL Ee.1.13, 97^r–100^v (DEFABC)   [eVK2 *3088.00, 1566.00]
Harl 2375, 30^r–31^v (ED BC, with a short text on correspondences
of urine and three stages of disease between D and B [item 14.2.3b

---

40   Ed. Ayoub (n. 29 above), 182–91.

below]; followed by a list of zodiacal signs and the parts of the
  body they govern; textually close to Sloane 635)   [eVK2 *2782.00]
Sloane 635, 94^r–95^r (D BC, with a short text on correspondences
  of urine and three stages of disease between D and B [item 14.2.3b
  below]; followed by a list of zodiacal signs and the parts of the body
  they govern; textually close to Harl 2375)   [eVK2 – , *3052.00]
NLM 49, 64^r–65^r (acephalous, with only the last sentence of D
  followed by EF; title in running head: "The buke of knawelage
  of thinges vnknawin")   [eVK2 1003.00]
Harl 218, 154^v (excerpts from C and D, inserted into a **DU**
  text between substances and colors)   [eVK2 –]
CUL Dd.10.44, 139^v, 143^v (excerpt from the end of C,
  rearranged; seventeen-content variant of E)   [eVK2 3169.00; –]

6.4 *The Knowing of Twenty Colors of Urines* (4 witnesses)

Primarily a series of uroscopic tokens, prefaced by a light-to-dark numbered list of twenty colors whose descriptions differ somewhat from those
given in *Twenty Colors by Digestions* (e.g., comparisons of two colors to
yellow cloth and fine red cloth respectively) and an overview of the relative heat, digestion groups, and regions of urines; always accompanied
by *Tokens of Ipocras*, usually directly after the *Knowing of Twenty Colors*.

MANUSCRIPT WITNESSES
Digby 29, 73^r–74^v (mixed Latin/English)   [eVK2 –]
CUL Dd.6.29, 26^r–30^r [eVK2 6708.00]
MagdO 221, 70^v–75^r [eVK2 6709.00]
Sloane 1388, 40^r–41^r (text rearranged and interspersed
  with material from **WBw**; slightly separated from *Tokens
  of Ipocras*)   [eVK2 *1783.00]

6.5 *The Knowledge and the Colors of All Manner Urines* (1 witness)

A dark-to-light list of the twenty colors and relatively detailed charac-
terizations of their diagnostic and prognostic significance, with several
rare or unique descriptive similes (e.g., "brown as slou ['sloe']," "lik tan-
wose ['tanning liquor']," "tewly [= *tuly*, 'vermilion, crimson'] red," "lik
Parys golde," "mousedon," "wȝete" ['wheat'?]) and psychological as well
as physical significations (e.g., nature "wastyd & consumyd awey þrow
þowt ['thought'] & anger"; being "ful of dremys as þow he were among
hyll & castell & spiritys").

MANUSCRIPT WITNESS
Pepys 1307, 62^r–64^r [eVK2 –]

6.6 *Colors and Digestions* (1 witness)

A paragraph summarizing the digestion groups and the colors associated with them, in a larger, s. xvi collection of uroscopies (item 14.1.5 below).

MANUSCRIPT WITNESS

TCC R.14.39, III, 104ᵛ   [eVK2 –]

6.7 "Colors of Waters Diverse There Be Twenty" (1 witness)

An incomplete text, with many signs for each of the colors it covers (only black and white, citing Giles of Corbeil to justify the starting point) before breaking off; may originally have been intended as a much longer text.

MANUSCRIPT WITNESS

Sloane 297, 110ʳ⁻ᵛ   [eVK2 1432.00]

6.8 "Aqua Alba ut Aqua Pura" (1 witness)

A mixed-language list of the twenty colors running from light to dark, using only Latin for the first ten colors and giving only the color and descriptive simile for the first four of these, followed by color, simile, and stage of digestion for the next six. The last ten (and more dangerous) colors are described in increasing detail, in Latin and English interspersed, with more specific diagnoses and distinctions. Spaces have been left between the first fourteen colors, probably for later expansion of the text.

MANUSCRIPT WITNESS

Sloane 1388, 46ᵛ–48ʳ   [eVK2 –]

7.0 Other Token Lists

7.1 Urines of Death

7.1.1 URINA MORTIS TAM HOMINUM QUAM MULIERUM (UMort) in DU (39 manuscript witnesses, 2 prints)

One of the most recognizable texts within the **DU** compendium, thanks partly to its striking incipit, "Urine in a hot access in one part red in another black in another green in another blue." **UMort** may also help to date at least part of the compendium, since it and the passage on substance in **4Th** are both appended to John Arderon's commentary on Giles (21.0 below), which is probably from the early fifteenth century.

MANUSCRIPT AND PRINT WITNESSES

Core Version: MagdO 221; Cosin V.III.10; Wellcome 564; Ashmole 1447; Cosin V.V.13; Harl 2274; Digby 95; Digby 29; Hatton 29; Sloane 1388 (b); Rawl C.81; Ashmole 1477, X

Expanded Version: Sloane 374; Harl 3407; BL Add 10440; Wellcome 409; StJC K.49; BL Add 30338; Selden Supra 73; Rawl C.506; Ashmole 1405

Abbreviated Versions: TCC O.8.35; Bodl Add B.60; Lambeth 444; Sloane 297;
Pepys 1307; *Judgement of Urynes*
Hybrid Version: Sloane 382; Sloane 1388 (a); *Seynge of Uryns*; NLM 49
Peculiar Versions: St Roy X.90; PML Bühler 21; Ashmole 1438, II; Hunter 328;
Rylands Eng 1310; NLW Sotheby C.2; BL Roy 18 A.vi; Harl 2558
Singletons: BL Roy 17 C.xxiv; TCC R.14.39, III

7.1.2 "Urine Troubly with Clouds" (8 witnesses)

A series with up to some thirty-odd uroscopic tokens, often including indications of the pulse and other symptoms; many of the signs prognosticate
impending death, peril, or long sickness. The word normalized as "clouds" in
the title appears both as *cloudes/clowdis* and *clod(de)s*, but the sense "clouds"
seems more likely, as a reflex of the Latin content terms *nebulae* and *nubes*.

MANUSCRIPT WITNESSES

CUL Dd.10.44, 133^v–134^v (the fullest list; approx. thirty-four
signs)   [eVK2 2681.00]
Harl 5401, 87^v–88^r (approx. thirty-three signs; titled "ffor to
knaw vrynes" in manuscript)   [eVK2 2680.00]
Ashmole 1438, I, pp. 163–164 (acephalous, probably owing to
loss of leaves; approx. twenty-eight signs survive, beginning in
the third sign)   [eVK2 *0391.00]
Sloane 1388, 52$^{r–v}$ (about thirty signs, substantially
rearranged)   [eVK2 –]
Harl 1602, 12^r–13^r (about twenty signs)   [eVK2 2678.00]
TCC R.14.51, 32$^{r–v}$ (about ten signs, including one or two not
found in other versions)[41]   [eVK2 2679.00]
Hunter 328, 44^v (seven signs, added after **UMort** at the end of
Arderon's commentary [item 21.0 below])   [eVK2 –]
Rylands Eng. 1310, 21^r (seven signs, as in Hunter 328) [eVK2 –]

7.1.3 Longleat Urines of Death (1 witness)

Two short, consecutive treatises, apparently unique, on tokens of death. The
first follows directly upon a list of traditional Hippocratic signs of death
(shrinking testicles, changes in facial appearance, chilling feet, rapid pulse,
etc.) and concentrates on red, livid, green, and black urines. The second
attributes its content to "the gret master Avicena . . . in the secound part of
his ffirst bok" (44^v; cf. *Canon* book 1, fen 2, doct. 3, summa 2, chap. 3), and
is similarly focused on abnormal urines of black, livid, or green hues.

---

[41]   Ed. Elaine M. Miller, "'In Hoote Somere': A Fifteenth-Century Medical
Manuscript" (Ph.D. diss., Princeton University, 1978), 72–73, ProQuest Diss. No.
7905635.

MANUSCRIPT WITNESS

Longleat 333, 44ʳ, 44ᵛ   [eVK2 7823.00, 6836.00]

7.2 Women's Urines

7.2.1 URINA MULIERIS (UMul) in DU (30 manuscript witnesses, 2 prints)

MANUSCRIPT AND PRINT WITNESSES

Core Version: MagdO 221; Cosin V.III.10; Wellcome 564; Digby 29; Hatton 29; Sloane 1388 (b); Rawl C.81; Ashmole 1477, X

Expanded Version: Sloane 374; BL Add 10440; Wellcome 409; StJC K.49; BL Add 30338; Selden Supra 73; Rawl C.506; Ashmole 1405

Abbreviated Versions: TCC O.8.35; Bodl Add B.60; Lambeth 444; Sloane 297; Pepys 1307; *Judgement of Urynes*

Hybrid Version: Sloane 382; Sloane 1388 (a); *Seynge of Uryns*; NLM 49

Peculiar Versions: NLW Sotheby C.2; Harl 2558; BL Roy 17 C.xv; St Roy X.90; PML Bühler 21

Singleton: Rawl D.248, 11ᵛ (the last four signs, somewhat confused, from the **UMul** component of **DU**)

7.2.2 AD COGNOSCENDUM PREGNANTES (CogPr) in DU (29 manuscript manuscript witnesses, 1 print)

MANUSCRIPT AND PRINT WITNESSES

Core Version: MagdO 221; Cosin V.III.10; Wellcome 564; Cosin V.V.13; Digby 29; Hatton 29; Sloane 1388 (b); Rawl C.81; Ashmole 1477, X

Expanded Version: Sloane 374; Harl 3407; BL Add 10440; Wellcome 409; StJC K.49; BL Add 30338; Selden Supra 73; Rawl C.506; Ashmole 1405

Abbreviated Version: TCC O.8.35; Bodl Add B.60; Lambeth 444; Sloane 297; Pepys 1307

Hybrid Version: Sloane 382; Sloane 1388 (a); *Seynge of Uryns*; NLM 49; Huntington HM 64

Peculiar Versions: NLW Sotheby C.2; St Roy X.90

7.2.3 Hatton-Sloane Insertions in DU (2 witnesses)

Two added passages in each of two manuscripts containing the *Dome of Uryne* (Core Version), pertaining largely though not entirely to women's urines. The Hatton text is better and fuller than that in the Sloane manuscript. In the Hatton copy of the first passage, the text includes signs for the first three months of pregnancy, the significance of motes in the urine (either gout in various parts of the body or conception and fetal sex), and branny contents. The second passage varies less between the two manuscripts, though Hatton remains the better text; it includes signs of pregnancy, headache, obstruction, windiness, and incurable illness.

MANUSCRIPT WITNESSES
Hatton 29, 60ᵛ–61ʳ (inserted between the **UMul** and **UMort**
components of **DU**), 67ᵛ–68ʳ (inserted between the **CogPr**
component of **DU** and an illustrated Twenty Jordans series;
copies of *Urine White and Red* and **WBw** follow **20J**)   [eVK2 –]
Sloane 1388 (b), 49ʳ (inserted between the **UMul** and **UMort**
components of **DU**, both atelous), 50ᵛ (inserted between the
CogPr component of **DU** and copies of *Urine White and Red*
and **WBw**)   [eVK2 –]

7.2.4 *Eleven Manners of Urine for a Woman* (1 witness)
An apparently unique series of numbered signs of women's urine. The
first seven signs are drawn from the women's urines section in *Urine
White and Red* or directly from the *Lettre d'Hippocrate*, the last four from
the women's urines section in the English *Urina Rufa* (a copy of which
occurs on fol. 74ʳ⁻ᵛ of the same manuscript) or from its Latin antecedent.
Because many uroscopies incorporate selected women's urines from these
two sources, the text as a whole shares signs with *Urine White and Brown*
(both variants, though overlapping more extensively with **WBw**), *Fifteen
Discretions,* the **ST** series in the *Letter of Ipocras*, *Rufus Subrufus*, and the
Urina Mulieris component in the *Dome of Uryne*, among others.

MANUSCRIPT WITNESS
GC 336/725, 103ʳ⁻ᵛ   [eVK2 7806.00]

7.2.5 *Whether She Will Conceive* (1 witness)
An apparently unique, mixed English/Latin series of signs in a late hand,
different from the main scribe of this Henry Daniel manuscript; focused
primarily on conception and pregnancy, with the opening rubric "Ad
sciendum vtrum concipiet an non." Also includes distinctions between
men's and women's urines, a few signs that apply to both women and
men, methods for determining fetal sex, and a recipe to prevent maternal
death before conception of a son and "myscary[ing] thowh sche wolde."

MANUSCRIPT WITNESS
CUL Ff.2.6, 127ᵛ–128ʳ   [eVK2 *6648.00]

7.2.6 *The Content of Woman's Urines* (1 witness)
Approximately twenty tokens relating to women's health and pregnancy, drawn from the French tradition behind the *Urine White and
Red* and *Urine White and Brown* texts; the title is that given by the
rubricator. Several signs occur more than once, albeit with somewhat
different phrasing, possibly reflecting a conflation of multiple series of

women's urines. Earlier in the manuscript, the scribe provides the non-gynecological portion of a *Urine White and Red* text, and he may have deliberately abbreviated that text in order to present a dedicated series of women's tokens here. (A number of uroscopic texts in the manuscript suggest a scribe who actively excerpted and rearranged source materials.) Preceded by excerpts from several **DU** components and a unique tabular presentation of the Twenty Jordans text; followed by a series of some fifty-plus signs labeled in the rubrics as *Other Contentes of Uryne* (item 7.5.4 below).

MANUSCRIPT WITNESS
CUL Dd.10.44, 144^v–145^v [eVK2 –]

7.2.7 Other Women's Urine Texts (4 texts, 1 witness each)
A number of short uroscopy texts focus mainly or entirely on the urines of women, often with a particular concern for issues related to pregnancy, gynecological ailments, or sexual behavior. Most derive from Latinate traditions, including commentaries on and expansions of Giles of Corbeil, the *Flos medicine* (*Regimen sanitatis salernitana*), and *Urina Rufa* (Latin or English versions). Additional discussions of women's urines often arise in longer treatises that include sections on the contents of urine, especially in paragraphs about motes (*atthomi*), thought to indicate conception and the sex of the fetus, and to a lesser extent those about sperm and ashes, associated with sexual activity and sicknesses in or near the lower organs. Among other examples, see Henry Daniel's *Liber Uricrisiarum*, book 3; the texts derived from Walter Agilon; *The Book of Narborough* 3.15–17; and the **GrCon** component of the *Dome of Uryne*.

MANUSCRIPT WITNESSES
Sloane 357, 27^{r-v}: Several signs relating to women's urines and signs of pregnancy and fetal sex, embedded in the *Book of Egidij* (item 29.0 below). Echoes of the Latin tradition include the phrases *sedemen in fundo* and *mala* [sic] *matricis*, as well as the misreading "a maydyn" for "amidoun" ('crushed wheat, grits'), to which the hypostasis of a pregnant woman is compared in Giles of Corbeil's *Carmen*, the *Flos medicine*, commentaries on Giles, and such writers as Henry Daniel, Walter Agilon, "Barton," and "Narborough" in items 15.0, 16.0, 20.0, and 22.0 below. Preceded by a variant form of **WBw** and followed by a non-**DU** Man-Woman-Beast text.   [eVK2 –]

Ashmole 1393, 61^{r-v}: Four signs from the *Urina Rufa* tradition: signs of intercourse, of the menses, of the second and third months

of pregnancy, and of the fourth month. Preceded by an inspection
of urines text, a non-**DU** Man-Woman-Beast text, and a note on
the four humors and four elements; followed by **WBw**.   [eVK2 –]

Harl 3383, 86^r: Four signs from the *Urina Rufa* tradition, similar
but not identical to those in Ashmole 1393, 61^{r-v}: signs of the
menses, of virginity, of the first three months of pregnancy, and
of the fourth month. Preceded by the *Letter of Ipocras*, which
concludes with the last sign of **ST**, the urine of a virgin; followed
by charms and recipes for childbirth and women's illnesses.   [eVK2 –]

Hunter 329, 11^v: Two uroscopic signs, for obstruction of the menses
("*termes*," read by eVK2 as "[travails]") and over-long "passe of [the
menses]," with remedies. Preceded by an acephalous list of seven
fevers; followed by *Seven Amber Colors*, item 7.5.13 below.   [eVK2 2573.00]

7.3 Urines of Man, Woman, and Beast

All very short texts, typically less than a page long. Although brief, they
invoke a recurrent theme in medical anecdotes and some learned uroscopic texts, concerning patients who deceive or test physicians by offering urine samples from another person or an animal.[42] Unrelated to the
humoral text "Man Beast and Bird" in the *Letter of Ipocras*.

7.3.1 URINES OF MAN, WOMAN, AND BEAST (MWB) in DU (29 man-
uscript witnesses, 2 prints)

MANUSCRIPT AND PRINT WITNESSES

Core Version: Ashmole 1477, X; Rawl C.81; Sloane 1388 (b); Hatton 29; Cosin
V.V.13; Ashmole 1447; Wellcome 564; Cosin V.III.10; MagdO 221

Expanded Version: Sloane 374; Harl 3407; BL Add 10440; Wellcome 409; StJC
K.49; BL Add 30338; Selden Supra 73; Ashmole 1405

Abbreviated Versions: TCC O.8.35; Bodl Add B.60; Lambeth 444; Pepys 1307;
Judgement of Urynes

Hybrid Version: Sloane 382; *Seynge of Uryns*; NLM 49

Peculiar Versions: Wellcome 7; BL Roy 17 C.xv; Harl 2558; Jackson 1302; NLW
Sotheby C.2; St Roy X.90

---

[42]   On tensions and possible deception in patient-doctor interactions surrounding the judgment of urine and their relation to the power-dynamic in that relationship, see Michael R. McVaugh, "Bedside Manners in the Middle Ages," *Bulletin of the
History of Medicine* 71, no. 2 (1997): 201–23.

Intentional deception aside, skilled uroscopists recognized the difficulties of correctly reading a patient's water: as Giles of Corbeil put it, "Saepius artificem deludit forma
coloris / Et fraudat plerumque fidem censura liquoris; / Est in contentis rata lex, discre-
tio certa, / Judicii constans regula, vera fides" (*Carmen de urinis* 208–11; Vieillard, 288).
Translated by Michael R. McVaugh in *Medieval Medicine: A Reader*, ed. Faith Wallis
(Toronto, 2010), thus: "The color of urine often misleads the physician in his assessment of
it; but there is an exact law, a definite rule for judgment, to be found in its contents" (257).

7.3.2 "A Man Hath Three Circles" (2 witnesses)

Five signs in the fuller and more reliable Sloane text, two distinguishing men's from women's urines and three distinguishing animal from human. The Magdalen copy only differentiates men's and women's urines, with a couple of semantically significant but probably erroneous variants (*colours* for *cerculus*; *foure* for *fome*), and is embedded in a longer set of uroscopic signs from multiple sources (7.5.9 below).

MANUSCRIPT WITNESSES

Sloane 357, 27ᵛ–28ʳ (embedded in the *Book of Egidij*, item 29.0 below)   [eVK2 –]
MagdO 221, 243ᵛ   [eVK2 –]

7.3.3 "The Beast's Water Will Be White" (2 witnesses)

One sign distinguishing human and animal urine, followed by several signs on distinguishing different kinds of animals through their urine (including male and female deer). The text does not indicate how one collects samples from wild animals.

The *Tractatus de Physica et Chirurgia* (item 14.2.3a below) occurs in close proximity to this text in both witnesses, but following the "Beast's Water" text and a list of medicines grouped by their elemental qualities (hot, cold, drying, moistening) in GC 336/725 and immediately preceding "Beast's Water" in Sloane 340, where the list of medicines appears a few leaves later.

MANUSCRIPT WITNESSES

GC 336/725, 96ʳ   [eVK2 6607.00]
Sloane 340, 65ʳ⁻ᵛ   [eVK2 6607.00]

7.3.4 Other Man, Woman, and Beast Texts (6 texts, 1 witness each)

Other short texts on the urines of man, woman, and beast share one or more of several different distinguishing features. Because the texts are quite short, I combine descriptive and comparative comments on them in the following paragraph.

The most common distinguishing feature in these texts is a sign that originates in a couplet from the Salernitan *Flos medicine*[43] (though

---

[43] "De prope spissa magis hominis minctura videtur; / non liquor est alius cui talis regula detur" ('Close up, human urine appears thicker; there is no other urine to which this rule applies'; lines 1367–68 in *Flos medicine* (*Regimen sanitatis Salernitanum*): *Estudio, edición crítica y traducción*, ed. Virginia de Frutos González (Valladolid, 2010), 316. See also the editions by Salvatore De Renzi, *Collectio Salernitana* (Naples, 1852 and 1859), 1:492 (lines 1438–39) and 5:65 (lines 2273–74), which were significantly expanded by the addition of extra lines from multiple manuscripts. For

the scribe of Sloane 2527 attributes it to Avicenna): the closer one holds human urine to the examining eye, the thicker it appears, while for animal urine, the closer one holds it, the clearer or thinner it appears (Sloane 1317, Sloane 2527, Rylands 404). Sloane 297 gives the same test but with opposite results: for human urine, nearer is clearer and further is thicker, and the contrary for animals. Other recurring distinctions include the brightness of human urine in contrast to the dullness and whitish or yellowish color in animals (Sloane 1317, Sloane 2527, and compare item 7.3.3 above); separation of human and animal urines if they are mixed in a single vessel (the animal urine gathers "all in plattes/ plottes" or sinks to the bottom of the flask: Sloane 1317, Sloane 2527; in the *Dome of Uryne*'s **MWB** text, item 7.3.1 above, the separable mixture is animal urine with wine); differences in the urines of infants, children, young men, old people, and crippled or bedridden individuals (Sloane 2527, Rylands 404); several signs that attend in different ways to the degree, shape, and position of turbidity or foam in the urines cast (sometimes after shaking), both as a way to tell men from women and animals from human beings (Sloane 1317, Sloane 297, Rylands 404, Wellcome 408, Ashmole 1393, and the **MWB** segment in the *Dome of Uryne*; cf. also item 7.3.2 above). Some texts also mention smell as a way to tell male, female, and different animal urines apart (Ashmole 1393, item 7.3.2, and the **MWB** segment).

MANUSCRIPT WITNESSES

Sloane 1317, 98^r	[eVK2 0647.00]
Sloane 2527, 196^v–197^r	[eVK2 2850.00]
Sloane 297, 106^v: Part of an incomplete inspection of urines text beginning on 106^v and possibly running to 108^v (see item 11.4 below).	[eVK2 *7748.00]
Wellcome 408, 10^v: Part of the *Tractatus de Urinis* compiled by William Bokynham, item 30.0 below.	[eVK2 –]

Rylands Eng 404, 44^v, 45^r: Two separate texts, the former a recipe added in originally blank space, distinguishing the urines of man and woman by whether earwax floats or sinks in the urine. The latter, described in the headnote above, is acephalous and notes the

---

discussion of the still imperfectly understood textual history of the *Flos medicine*, see Frutos González's introductory sections II and III (23–124) and Marilyn Nicoud, "Il *Regimen sanitatis Salernitanum*: Premessa ad un'edizione critica," in *La Scuola Medica Salernitana: Gli autori e i testi*, ed. Danielle Jacquart and Agostino Paravicini Bagliani (Florence, 2007), 365–84.

importance of having "rowlys ['rules'] to knowe þe dyuersyteis of
vrynis . . . for deseytys of the pepill."   [eVK2 – , 0508.00]
Ashmole 1393, 60ᵛ–61ʳ: Expresses concern about possible
"dysceyu[ing] þe leche yn cause of reprefe"; includes *differentiae*
between ass, goat, sheep, and horse waters as well as between
animal and human more generally; preceded by an inspection
of urines text and followed by a note on humors, a urines of women
text, and **WBw** (items 11.4 below, 7.2.7 and 5.2.1 above).   [eVK2 –]

7.4 "The Doom of Urine Thou Shalt Cast in Four" (6 witnesses)

A series of uroscopic signs, found in Latin as well as English; preceded
in three manuscripts by *Three Manners of Inspecting Urine* (item 11.3;
indicated by an asterisk below); followed by **WBw** in five manuscripts
(item 5.2.1; indicated by a dagger below). The introductory sentence of
the full text advises the practitioner to consider four things in examining
the substance of a urine sample: the height (i.e., the circle), the midregion,
the *founce* or depth, and the clouds that appear in different regions of the
urine flask, followed by some eight uroscopic tokens defined mainly by
the relative clarity, cloudy shapes, foaminess, and thickness of the urine
and the region of the urinal in which those features manifest themselves.
Colors play only a minimal role in this text, being limited to single mentions of "mirk and brownish" urine and of clouds that look like black or
white towers moving up and down in the sample.

Latin versions of the text may be translations from the vernacular
rather than sources: e.g., Sloane 1571, 10ʳ, followed by a Latin White-
Brown text and attributed in the explicit to "M. Galfridum Mydylton,
Doctorem"; St. John's Cambridge B.15, 20ʳ, followed by a Latin White-
Brown text; Sloane 783B, 194ᵛ, preceded by a Latin version of *Inspection
in Three Manners* and followed by a Latin White-Brown text.

MANUSCRIPT WITNESSES

*†Ashmole 1477, III, 10ᵛ   [eVK2 –]
*†BL Add 4898, 116ʳ⁻ᵛ   [eVK2 –]
*†Plimpton 254, 27ʳ   [eVK2 *6668.00]
†CUL Ff.2.6, 128ʳ (acephalous; begins after a single token
    labeled "Urina pestilencialis," with the first sign of the "Urine
    Cast in Four" text: "If the cloud hang on high by the circle
    of the urine and the circle be full of foam")   [eVK2 –]
†TCC R.14.39, III, 101ʳ⁻ᵛ (a fairly corrupt version, in a larger
    collection of uroscopic texts [item 14.1.5 below])   [eVK2 –]
Sloane 1101, 1ᵛ (incomplete, giving only the introductory sentence
    and the first three signs; written in a blank space after a passage
    marked for insertion in an incomplete *Liber Uricrisiarum* [item

15.2 below]; followed by a short paragraph on the inspection of
urines, item 11.4 below) [eVK2 3277.00]

7.5 Miscellaneous Token Lists

The texts included in this section consist of simple series of uroscopic
tokens, with little or no larger conceptual framework, interspersed in
some instances with recipes that offer cure or palliation of the patient's
condition. Given syntactically complete opening and closing signs, the
list structure can make it difficult to be sure if a particular text is complete or not. Except for the first item below, the works in this section are
all unique and some may have been compiled by scribes for their own
individual use.

7.5.1 "Urine as Snot"[44] (4 witnesses)

A series of eighteen tokens indicating a variety of ailments and conditions, based variously on colors, consistencies, and contents. Linguisti-
cally distinguished by its use of the word "ring" in several signs for the
much more common term "circle."

MANUSCRIPT WITNESSES

Arun 42, 109^v (followed by **WBw**; preceded by a Latin token list
with other signs. The two lists may have been seen or intended as
complementary pieces: the Latin list has an English heading, "ffor
to discerne wateres," the English text a Latin one, "Ad
cognoscendum vrinam hominis & femine.") [eVK2 7891.00]
Sloane 1317, 87^v–88^v (incipit reads "snevell in the glasse" in
place of the Arundel reading "snot in þe glas"; interrupted on
88^r by an imperfect copy of **ST** and followed by **WBw**, items
4.1.3c and 5.2.1 above) [eVK2 *6597.00]
MagdO 221, 245$^{r–v}$ (about a dozen signs from *Urine as Snot*,
accompanied by selected tokens and remedies from other texts
[see 7.5.9 below]; incipit reads "water of man þat is þik as þer were
put þe snof in þe glass") [eVK2 –]
Sloane 98, 1^r (only two signs, on determining fetal sex, from very
near the end of the text, given at the beginning of a collection of
recipes. An old foliation system indicates that the manuscript once
had another leaf preceding modern fol. 1, which could easily have

---

[44] "Snot" may have been intended as an English equivalent to Latin *sanies*
('pus'), one of the standard contents in urine; the interlinear glosses on Giles's versified Latin content-list (item 14.2.4 below) define *sanies* as 'snotte.' On the other hand,
the variant "snivel" in Sloane 1317's incipit suggests that at least one copyist intended
the sense 'nasal mucus' (see *MED*, s.vv. *snotte*, n., sense [a.], quotation from *Londs-
borough Nominale*; *snivel*, n., sense [a]).

held the full *Urine as Snot* text, though the omission of the two
final signs in *Urine as Snot* could imply that the extant signs are
a deliberate excerpt.)   [eVK2 *0546.00]

The remaining texts in this section are ordered by decreasing approximate length.

7.5.2 *The Chapter of Looking of Waters / Capitulum Inspectoris* (1 witness)

A lengthy token list, with more than a hundred signs, only loosely organized: series of tokens based on colors are periodically interrupted by sub-series based on substance, quantity, region, gender, selected contents, and so on. The titles are those given at the beginning and end of the text.

MANUSCRIPT WITNESS
Sloane 540A, 25^v–28^r [eVK2 7824.00]

7.5.3 "They That Know Water They Must Mark Four Thing" (1 witness)

A more general diagnostic text with several dozen signs, which begins with colors and contents, includes a passage of recipes and some non-uroscopic symptoms like vomit ('spewing'), and ends with signs of death and life.

MANUSCRIPT WITNESS
Ashmole 1447, pp. 192–196   [eVK2 –]

7.5.4 *Other Contents of Urine* (1 witness)

A series of over fifty kinds of urine and their significance, drawn from a number of other texts, including but not limited to *Urina Rufa, Urine White and Brown* (Woman), "The Doom of Urine Thou Shalt Cast in Four," and *Urine White and Red*. Title from the manuscript heading directly before the text.

MANUSCRIPT WITNESS
CUL Dd.10.44, 145^v–148^r [eVK2 –]

7.5.5 "In Six Manner Changes Urine" (1 witness)

A relatively long but not very systematic collection of uroscopic tokens, based both on colors and contents, interspersed with occasional etiological explanations; follows an excerpt from Henry Daniel's *Liber Uricrisiarum*, book 2.

MANUSCRIPT WITNESS
Sloane 1088, 94^r–98^v [eVK2 2855.00]

7.5.6 "He That Voids Blood and Gobbets" (1 witness)

An apparently unique set of tokens, interwoven with an incomplete text of the *Twenty Jordans* (beginning on fol. 12^v) and other signs drawn mainly from *Urina Rufa,* with a few others from *Urine White and Brown* [Woman] and a single token (#5) from the **ST** series (see items 1.1.1, 3.2.3, 5.2.1, 4.1.3c above).

MANUSCRIPT WITNESS
NLM 30, 13^r–15^v [eVK2 *7814.00]

7.5.7 *De Coloribus / Urina Generalis* (1 witness)

A late manuscript with lost and damaged leaves, written in a cramped and rapid hand, making exact description of this acephalous text difficult. It appears to comprise a pair of token lists, the first described in its explicit as "de coloribus," the next given the heading "Vrina generalis" and containing material on regions and contents. The second series concludes with the explicit "& sic fynis." After these two lists, the manuscript moves on to a form of the *Dome of Uryne* (Expanded Version, though with some unusual features; fols. 16^r–24^v). The two token lists may have been meant as add-ons to the **DU** text, though they are treated here as a separate item.

MANUSCRIPT WITNESS
Ashmole 1477, X, 14^r–16^r [eVK2 *7776.00]

7.5.8 *Colores Urinarum* (1 witness)

About three dozen uroscopic signs, beginning with white and other light colors, moving on to yellow, red, and dark colors, and ending with urines of death, urines of women, and a few tokens based on contents. Followed by several short Latin urinary and humoral texts: two color lists; urines of the four humors; urines of man, woman, and beast; correspondences of elements, qualities, humors, and seasons; and the four parts of the body. Described in the heading to the English (and possibly the Latin) material as the "colores vrinarum quibus magister Willelmus Kylinghale doctor phisice vsus fuit tempore suo" (see item 30.0 below).

MANUSCRIPT WITNESS
Wellcome 408, 1^v–3^r (or 4^r, if Latin material was intended as part
of the text)   [eVK2 7826.00]

7.5.9 Magdalen 221 Token List (1 witness)

A mixed bag of uroscopic tokens and tokens with remedies, some extracted from other texts, including five or six signs from the pregnancy tokens in Sloane 357 (7.2.7), 2 or 3 signs from the Man-Woman-Beast text in Sloane 357 (7.3.2), about a dozen signs from *Urine as Snot*, and a few signs parallel to items in **20J** and in *Urina Rufa*. Preceded by the four-line humoral text "All Red Waters and All High Colors" on 242^r (item 8.6 below).

MANUSCRIPT WITNESS
MagdO 221, 242^r–245^v (241^r–244^v in eVK2)   [eVK2 7819.00]

7.5.10 *Five Colors of Urine* (1 witness)

Some two dozen signs, roughly clustered in five color-based groups (red, white, black, yellow, and clear), interspersed with remedies for the sicknesses they signify, when those illnesses are not identified as mortal or as incurable. The list also notes differential diagnoses for the same color depending on the patient's complexion. Followed on fol. 3^v, with no sharp division between texts, by a series of recipes without uroscopic associations.

MANUSCRIPT WITNESS
Harl 3383, 1^r–3^v (acephalous, owing to minor damage at the tops
of fols. 1 and 2)   [eVK2 *0384.00]

7.5.11. "Urine Pale with White Small Thing Therein" (1 witness)

Around seventeen signs, four for pale urines and thirteen for white urines (with an internal heading "Howe thou schalt know why3tte watters"). Followed on fol. 2^v–3^r by a rearranged version of **ST** (item 4.1.3c above).

MANUSCRIPT WITNESS
Wellcome 404, 2^{r-v} (possibly acephalous, as the loss of a leaf
after fol. 1 and the heading for white urines may suggest similar
headings for other colors on the missing leaf)   [eVK2 *7815.00]

7.5.12 "Eight Colors" (1 witness)

Dietary advice and recipes for the eight hot colors (six reds and two citrines), gravel in the urinal, and for a "mann [who is] hot."

MANUSCRIPT WITNESS
MagdO 221, 42^r–43^r (possibly incomplete)   [eVK2 1527.00]

7.5.13 *Seven Amber Colors* (1 witness)

Four numbered amber-colored urines, possibly followed by an unnumbered fifth, and the numbers ".6.7." but no associated sixth or seventh tokens at the end of the short text. Three of the signs provide recipes for the ailments signified by the particular color. The opening rubric provides the title.

MANUSCRIPT WITNESS
Hunter 329, 11ᵛ   [eVK2 –]

7.5.14 "Urine Like Whey and Thin with a Circle Purple" (1 witness)
A few scribbled lines by a hand later than that of the manuscript's main scribe (the "Hammond Scribe"), indicating the significance of urine like whey, with a purple circle and a color like blood in the bottom, and approbation attributed to M[aster] Heryson.

MANUSCRIPT WITNESS
TCC R.14.52, iiʳ   [eVK2 7804.00]

8.0 Humors and Complexions

8.1 THE COMPLEXIONS OF URINE (CplU) and WHERE THE COMPLEXIONS ARE GENERATED (CplG) in DU (23, 21 witnesses respectively; 21 manuscripts, 2 prints)
Two very short texts, of which the first identifies the dominant humor in a patient by the color (white or red) and density (thick or thin) of the urine, and by taste (sweet, sour, savorless, salty). The second describes the organs in which the humors are generated (all in the liver) and those in which they "dwell" (the "coffer of the gall," veins, spleen, and no proper dwelling place).

The texts almost always occur together, and all known witnesses are accompanied by at least several other *Dome of Uryne* components. Given their brevity, however, undiscovered singleton witnesses may still remain to be found, embedded in some longer text.

MANUSCRIPT AND PRINT WITNESSES
Core Version: MagdO 221; Cosin V.III.10; Wellcome 564; Ashmole 1447; Cosin V.V.13; Hatton 29; Sloane 1388 (b); Rawl C.81; Ashmole 1477, X
Expanded Version: Sloane 374; BL Add 10440; Wellcome 409; StJC K.49; BL Add 30338; Selden Supra 73; Ashmole 1405
Abbreviated Version: *Judgement of Urynes* 1555 (**CplG** only)
Hybrid Version: Sloane 382; Sloane 1388 (a) (**CplU** only); *Seynge of Uryns*; NLM 49
Peculiar Versions: CUL Dd.10.44; Jackson 1302 (**CplU** only); Rawl D.1221 (**CplU** only)

8.2 *The Four Elements* (21 witnesses)

A treatise on the elements, humors, and urines, the complete form of which precedes, or probably once preceded, the Middle English translation of Gilbertus Anglicus's *Compendium Medicine* in six witnesses.[45] Uroscopic material occurs mainly in the latter half of the text (chaps. 5 and 6 in the numbering of Bodley 178). The humoral portion of the text frequently circulates on its own, usually ending after a section on the humoral correspondences of the four quarters of the day or (less commonly) after a mention of women's illnesses or the proper condition of the physician.

The treatise is well-marked by transition phrases between one topic and the next (e.g., "Now I have told of.... And now shall I tell of...."). Five witnesses (Bodley 178, Sloane 3486, SAL 338, Sloane 100, Ashmole 342) indicate chapter divisions in headings or marginal notes, sometimes in the original scribe's hand and sometimes in later hands, though these chapter numberings are not completely consistent. The principal point of discrepancy is the beginning of chapter 2: in Bodley 178 and Sloane 3486, the chapter begins before a discussion of correspondences between the four humors and the four ages of man, four seasons, four winds and parts of the world, and four quarters of the day; in SAL 338, Sloane 100, and Ashmole 342, chapter 2 starts after that discussion. All five witnesses end chapter 2 in the same place, after discussing abundance or excess in the various humors, and all agree on chapters 3, 4, and 5. A smaller difference in chapter divisions relates to the handling of chapter 6, a series of uroscopic signs organized from upper to lower members; one witness (Sloane 3486) divides that chapter into seven smaller chapters (numbered 6 to 12). The most common abbreviation of the treatise ends after the discussion of correspondences between the humors and other natural and human "fours," but that abbreviation is never divided into chapters.

---

[45] The *Compendium* has been edited from Wellcome MS 536 by Faye M. Getz, *Healing and Society in Medieval England: A Middle English Translation of the Pharmaceutical Writings of Gilbertus Anglicus* (Madison, 1991). Laura Esteban-Segura has recently edited *The Four Elements* and the *Compendium* from Hunter 509: *System of Physic (GUL MS Hunter 509, ff. 1r–167v): A Compendium of Mediaeval Medicine including the Middle English Gilbertus Anglicus*, Late Middle English Texts 3 (Bern, 2012). Although the *Compendium* itself does not focus on uroscopy in any systematic way, it does regularly include characteristics of the urine among the various tokens of individual diseases (see, for example, Getz, *Healing and Society*, 7/16–22, 11/1–12, 16/22–17/2, etc.).

In the following list, asterisks before shelfmarks indicate manuscripts that also contain Gilbertus Anglicus's *Compendium*.

MANUSCRIPT WITNESSES

8.2.1 Full Version (6 witnesses)

8.2.1a Complete copies

*Hunter 307, 1ʳ–13ʳ	[eVK2 3206.00]
*Hunter 509, 1ʳ–13ʳ	[eVK2 3206.00]
*Bodley 178, 44ʳ–51ᵛ (chapter numbering in a later, s. xvi hand)	[eVK2 3206.00]
*SAL 338, 1ʳ–7ᵛ (foliation disordered: should be 1-2-6-4-5-3-7; chapter numbering in a later hand)	[eVK2 3207.00]

8.2.1b Probable originally complete copies

*Sloane 3486, 86ʳ–90ᵛ (originally complete, based on table of contents to the *Compendium*, fols. 148ʳ–149ᵛ, which takes the Four Elements text as the first twelve chapters of Gilbertus's work. Chapter numbering occurs in both the text and the table of contents. Compilation or editing of the *Compendium* attributed in colophon to Thomas Betrisden.)   [eVK2 *3206.00]

*TCD 365, 34ʳ⁻ᵛ, 26ʳ–29ᵛ (acephalous, beginning in the description of phlegmatic complexion in chap. 1, and continuing to the end of the full treatise; disordered leaves; followed by an originally blank page [30ʳ] and on 30ᵛ by Gilbertus Anglicus's *Compendium*)   [eVK2 0559.00, 0895.00, *5115.00]

8.2.2 Abbreviated Versions (12 witnesses)

8.2.2a Abbreviated Version A (through day-quarters = end of chap. 1 in SAL 338, Sloane 100, Ashmole 342)

Lambeth 444, 159ʳ–160A recto (preceded by a text on the influence of the zodiac and moon on parts of the body [*The Governance of Signs*]; followed by a text on weights and measures, *The Manner of Writing of Bills for Receipts*)[46]   [eVK2 3210.00]

TCC O.8.35, 59ʳ–65ᵛ (preceded by *Governance of Signs*; followed by *The Manner of Writing of Bills for Receipts*; same scribe as Bodl Add B.60)   [eVK2 3211.00]

Bodl Add B.60, 59ʳ–65ᵛ (prec. by *Governance of Signs*; followed by *The Manner of Writing of Bills for Receipts*; same scribe as TCC O.8.35)   [eVK2 3208.00, 3704.00]

---

[46] As far as I have been able to determine, *The Governance of Signs* appears only in conjunction with *The Four Elements*, usually in the abbreviated version A (once with abbreviation C), although *The Four Elements* also appears without the zodiacal text. Oliver Pickering and Veronica O'Mara suggest that scribes of manuscripts containing the two texts together may have seen them as a single work, in the *Index of Middle English Prose XIII: Manuscripts in Lambeth Palace Library* (Cambridge, 1999), 20–21 and 34.

Sloane 297, 116ᵛ–121ʳ (preceded by *Governance of Signs*;
incomplete owing to damaged leaves, but probably ended
shortly after the last bit of text that can be matched with
other copies, at the beginning of the discussion of the four
day-quarters)   [eVK2 3211.00, –]
TCC O.7.2A, 8ᵛ–13ᵛ (preceded by *Governance of Signs*; *not*
followed by weights text)   [eVK2 3222.00]
Lambeth 306, 117ᵛ–121ʳ (occasional insertions of extraneous
material)   [eVK2 3206.00]
Ashmole 1444, pp. 61–67 (preceded by Latin "inspeccio
vrinarum" text on pp. 55–59, consisting of Latin texts of
Urina Rufa and *Cleansing of Blood*; followed by John of
Burgundy plague treatise in English)   [eVK2 3216.00]
Digby 95, 96ᵛ–101ʳ (titled *Donet of Fesike*; followed by a
Latin white/red urines text and an incomplete **DU**)   [eVK2 7452.00]
Sloane 3449, 1ᵛ–5ʳ   [eVK2 3212.00]

8.2.2b Abbreviated Version B (through chapter 3)

Ashmole 342, 115ʳ–126ᵛ (three chapters; mentions "Austin Leche" in
headings to chapters 2 and 3)   [eVK2 3210.00]

8.2.2c Abbreviated Version C (through most of chapter 4)

Sloane 100, 38ʳ–54ᵛ (four chapters; mentions "Austin Leche"
in headings to chaps. 2, 3, and 4; breaks off near the end of the
4th chapter, at "in his ocupacioun . and þat god wolde vouche."
Preceded by *Governance of Signs*; *The Manner of Writing of Bills*
occurs a few leaves before *Governance of Signs*)   [eVK2 3210.00]
GC 336/725, 45ʳ–52(bis) verso (ends incomplete near the end
of chapter 4, at "in his occupacioun"; no chapter headings
or references to "Austin," though various sections of the text
are marked by larger or smaller dropped caps, more or less
elaborately decorated)   [eVK2 3209.00, 2488.00]

8.2.3 Excerpts (3 witnesses)

*Wellcome 537, 45ʳ–46ʳ (the passage on ages, seasons, winds,
parts of the world, and day-quarters)   [eVK2 7166.00]
RCP 411, 51ʳ–53ʳ (chaps. 5–6 in Bodley 178, on inspection of
urine and urinary diagnoses organized by parts of the body,
respectively)   [eVK2 7930.00]
Bodley 591, 31ʳ–33ʳ (chaps. 5–6 in Bodley 178)   [eVK2 –]

8.3 *De Urinis Sanorum / The Four Complexions* (3 witnesses)

A short description of the urine of healthy men of each complexion: the
colors should be Rufus or Subrufus (as fine or french gold) for sanguine;
Citrine or Subcitrine (as pome orange or juice of celandine) for choleric; White or Pale for phlegmatic; White, Pale, or Glaucus (like lantern

horn) for melancholy. Substance should be clean and even (i.e., consistent throughout) and either thin (for choleric and melancholy complexions) or neither too thick nor too thin (for sanguine and phlegmatic). In Harley 1010 and TCC R.14.39, III, this text is followed by a token list based on the Walter Agilon uroscopies (*De Urinis Egrorum*; item 16.5 below).

MANUSCRIPT WITNESSES
Sloane 1388, 38ʳ (preceded by the Twenty Jordan series and followed
by a Latin version of the Vade Mecum suite) [eVK2 –]
Harl 1010, 1ᵛ–2ʳ [eVK2 –]
TCC R.14.39, III, 91ʳ [eVK2 –]

8.4 *Substances, Colors, and Phlegms* (2 witnesses)
Three short texts that follow *Urina Rufa* and *Cleansing of Blood* in the two witnesses, all simple summaries like those in *Cleansing of Blood*. The first defines five degrees of substance (density) in urine and how to distinguish each kind in terms of the ease or difficulty of seeing one's fingers or the degree of magnification seen when looking through the sample. The second lists twenty-one colors of urine, running from light to dark and grouped according to the degree of digestion they signify; the descriptions of the colors include several similes not found in the more common color lists ("milkish" urine as goat's whey, subcitrine "as fistulet," green as "herba violaria"), including the added color "tulye as smaragde stone." ("Tulye" normally refers to a deep red color, and "smaragde" to an emerald green, so the precise color or stone envisioned here is uncertain; the color is included in the group of urines that signify "deth of brennyng": tulye, green, livid, glossy black, dark [black].) The third summary covers five kinds of phlegm (*dulce, acetosum, vitreum, insipidum, salsum*) and five kinds of choler (*rubea*, citrine, vitelline, prassine, eruginous), with the characteristics of each, followed by the qualities of the four elements, four seasons, and (Wellcome 408 only) four complexions.

MANUSCRIPT WITNESSES
Pepys 1661, pp. 26–28 [eVK2 –]
Wellcome 408, 6ʳ–7ʳ [eVK2 –]

8.5 "Thou That Art a Physician" (2 witnesses)
A nuanced text on the diagnosis of and remedies for repletion or excess of humors, both generally and individually. Diagnostic signs include a wide range of symptoms (urine, pulse, spittle, feces, vomit, pain, sleep

and dreams, appearance of skin and eyes, etc.), taking up about a quarter of the text. Moves from diagnosis to considerations in giving medicines, including time of year, time of day, time of onset, temperament, age, sex, geography, and state of digestion; how to care for the sick; and descriptions of different simples, compound medicines, powders, opiates, oils and their qualitative degrees (e.g., hot in the third degree, etc.).

MANUSCRIPT WITNESSES

Sloane 121, 66ʳ–86ᵛ   [eVK2 7540.00]
GC 609/340, 47ʳ–50ᵛ (**NOT SEEN**;[47] incomplete, giving only
about a third of the text; preceded on 46ᵛ by a contents list
describing 107 topics covered)   [eVK2 7539.00]

8.6 Other Complexion Texts (9 texts, 1 witness each)
A number of other distinct texts, some no more than a few lines between other works, also lay out the relationships of urines to the four complexions from a variety of perspectives.

MANUSCRIPT WITNESSES

TCC O.7.20, II, 37ʳ–39ᵛ: *A Short Treatise to Know the
Four Complexions and to Discern Urine*: overview of the
elements, qualities, humors; correspondences among them
and with red or white, thick or thin urine; groupings of some
of the Aegidian colors under the four humors and the illnesses
that they signify.   [eVK2 *3194.00]
Ashmole 1477, X, 17ᵛ: *The Five Manner of Phlegms That Reign*:
a paragraph distinguishing among the five different kinds of
phlegm (natural, sweet, salt, sour, watery or glassy), embedded
in a version of **DU**.   [eVK2 6789.00]
Wellcome 564, 195ʳ: Four sentences describing uroscopic
color and substance for the complexions and their associated
primary qualities: red for heat, white for cold, thick for moisture,
thin for dryness; the same correspondence is laid out in *Cleansing
of Blood* and other general discussions of urines and
complexions.   [eVK2 7817.00]
StJC K.49, 79ᵛ–80ᵛ: Four sentences on colors and substances
associated with the complexions: red and meanly thick for

---

[47]   Described, with enough incipit and desinit to identify the equivalent material in Sloane 121, by Kari Anne Rand Schmidt, *Index of Middle English Prose XVII: Manuscripts in the Library of Gonville and Caius College, Cambridge* (Cambridge, 2001), 114. The copy in GC 609/340 was erroneously included in Carleton Brown and Rossell Hope Robbins, *Index of Middle English Verse* (New York, 1943), no. 3694, but has been dropped by Julia Boffey and A. S. G. Edwards from *A New Index of Middle English Verse* (London, 2005), 246, as a text in prose.

sanguine; red, subrufus, or citrine with thin substance for
choleric; white, pale, karapos, or milky with thin substance
(possibly an error for thick) for phlegmatic; white, yellow,
or pale with thin substance for melancholy. Followed by an
English version of the traditional Latin couplets[48] on the
complexions and their physiognomic traits.   [eVK2 4433.50, 4433.40]
CUL Dd.10.44, 143^r: Four sentences on the regions of the
body governed by the humors: choler in the animate or
"soulend" limbs from the breast up, blood in the spiritual
limbs from the midriff to the throat, phlegm in the nourishing
limbs from the kidneys to the midriff, and melancholy from
the kidneys down; laid out as a final column in a a unique
tabular presentation of **20J**, item 1.4 above. Compare *Ten Cold
Ten Hot*, section F, item 6.3 above.   [eVK2 –]
Sloane 357, 41^v–42^r: Material on the primary qualities of urines
and foam in urine, embedded in an astromedical text on the
influences of planets, signs, elements and qualities, phases of the
moon, quarter of the day, and so on.   [eVK2 –]
MagdO 221, 242^r [241^r in eVK2]: "All Red Waters and All High
Colors," four lines on the correspondences between the primary
qualities and the colors and substance of urine.   [eVK2 0816.00]
TCC R.14.39, III, 99^r–101^r: *The Contents*, a treatment of the
humors and humoral correspondences and their influence
on health and illness; despite the title, there is little direct
reference to urines in the text proper, but it is included in a larger
collection of mostly uroscopic texts (item 14.1.5 below).   [eVK2 –]
Sloane 1388, 41^v–42^r: "Man's Body Is Made of Four Humors,"
another overview of the humors, humoral correspondences, and
complexional types. Bears partial verbal resemblance to the
text in TCC R.14.39, III, but shorter and with fewer subtopics;
no direct reference to urines in the text proper, but is included
in a substantial collection of uroscopic texts.   [eVK2 3512.00]

9.0 Regions of Urines

Brief definitions and descriptions of the three or four layers in a urine
sample, whose characteristics were thought to reveal maladies proper
to analogous locations in the body. The general principle of head-to-toe

---

[48] Incipit: "(Sanguineus:) Largus amans hilaris ridens rubeique coloris"; eTK
0811N, 1374D–E. These verses are included in the *Flos medicine* (*Regimen sanitatis
salernitanum*), ed. Virginia de Frutos González (n. 43 above), 262, 264, 266, lines
951–52, 958–59, 966–67, 972–73 (= De Renzi, *Collectio Salernitana* [n. 3 above], 1: 484,
lines 1178–79, 1184–85, 1190–91, 1196–97; 5: 48–49, lines 1696–97, 1702–03, 1708–09,
1714–15). For a brief discussion of their appearance in various later manuscript contexts, see Lynn Thorndike, "Unde Versus," *Traditio* 11 (1955): 163–93, at 177–80.

diagnostic stratification can also be seen in the lists of contents derived from Giles of Corbeil's *Carmen de urinis*.

The **3Reg** text from the *Dome of Uryne* is widely disseminated, but it takes the relatively cursory approach of describing only three regions, defining them in a purely positional way (two fingers-breadth at the bottom, the "circle" at the top, and everything between), and not mentioning specific associations between each region and a portion of the body. In this, it corresponds to the brief description of three urinary regions given in *Cleansing of Blood*.

More useful from a diagnostic perspective are those texts that identify four regions of a urine sample and explicitly associate those regions with four principal regions of the body, usually defined as the head, the respiratory/circulatory organs, digestive organs, and the excretory and reproductive organs. In *Cleansing of Blood*, these layers and their corresponding members are referred to as "parts," a label that some other texts (e.g., *Barton's Urines*, item 20.0 below) also use.[49] However, many texts apply the term "regions" to the fourfold partition,[50] and I have adopted the word as the umbrella term for both stratificational schemes. The four regions/parts in the urine are typically identified as the circle, sometimes referred to as a "compass"; the *corpus aereum* or airy body, sometimes also called the *superficies*; the *perforacio* or *substancia*, by some authors simply called the middle; and the ground or *founce/fundus*. The circle was thought to reveal information concerning the head and brain; the *corpus aereum* gave information on the "spiritual" members such as the throat, lungs, heart, and diaphragm; the *perforacio* on the liver, stomach, spleen, and intestines (seen as "perforated members"); and the ground on

---

[49] Giles of Corbeil distinguishes the *summum, medium,* and *imum* sections of the urine, and refers to both *partes* and *regiones* (*Carmen de urinis* 97–102; Vieillard, 279). The well-attested commentary on Giles that begins "Liber iste quem legendum proponimus est novelle institutionis" (eTK 0821I; cf. eTK 0820G, 0821B, 0821J) expounds the lines in terms of four *regiones* of the body and of the urine (Sloane 282, 28ʳ). Laurence Moulinier attributes the four-region concept to Maurus of Salerno, in distinction to Giles's three regions, derived from Galen ("La science des urines de Maurus de Salerne et les *Sinthomata Magistri Mauri* inédits," in *La Scuola Medica Salernitana: Gli autori e i testi,* ed. Danielle Jacquart and Agostino Paravicini Bagliani [Florence, 2007], 261–81, at 268).

[50] Including the first three witnesses under item 9.3, Henry Daniel (item 15.0), and "Friar Narborough" (item 22.0). Item 9.2, *Four Regions and Four Parts,* speaks of the regions of the body and parts of the urine.

the kidneys, bladder, reproductive organs, and sometimes other members like the legs or joints.

9.1 THE THIRD KNOWLEDGE OF URINES: THE REGIONS (3Reg) in DU (27 manuscript witnesses, 2 prints)
MANUSCRIPT AND PRINT WITNESSES

> Core Version: MagdO 221; Cosin V.III.10; Wellcome 564; Ashmole 1447; Harl 2274; Digby 29; Digby 95; Hatton 29; Sloane 1388 (b); Rawl C.81; Ashmole 1477, X
>
> Expanded Version: Sloane 374; Harl 3407; BL Add 10440; Wellcome 409; StJC K.49; BL Add 30338
>
> Abbreviated Versions: TCC O.8.35; Bodl Add B.60; Lambeth 444; Sloane 297; Pepys 1307; *Judgement of Urynes*
>
> Hybrid Version: Sloane 382; *Seynge of Uryns*; NLM 49
>
> Peculiar Versions: NLW Sotheby C.2; CUL Dd.10.44; Ashmole 1438, II

9.2 *Four Regions and Four Parts* (5 witnesses)
A short description of the correspondences between the regions of the body and parts of the urine, always preceded or (in Sloane 635) followed by a copy of **WBp**, item 5.2.2 above; the two together should probably be considered as a variant of **WBp**.

MANUSCRIPT WITNESSES

GC 84/166, p. 193	[eVK2 –]
Wellcome 8004, 61ʳ	[eVK2 –]
Sloane 7, 60ᵛ	[eVK2 –]
Ashmole 1413, p. 154	[eVK2 –]
Sloane 635, 93ʳ (slightly acephalous)	[eVK2 *2935.00]

9.3 Other Four-Region Lists (4 texts, 1 witness each)
Additional brief summaries of the regions/parts of the urine sample.

MANUSCRIPT WITNESSES

> Wellcome 408, 7ʳ: A concise but clear presentation of the four regions, followed by similar summary paragraphs on substance, complexions, and quantity, proceeding to longer treatments of colors and contents; part of the *Tractatus de Urinis* compiled by William Bokynham, item 30.0 below. [eVK2 *2779.00]
>
> Rylands Eng 404, 43ᵛ–44ᵛ: Brief summary of the four regions and their anatomical correspondences, followed by several circle-based diagnoses and a general token-list. [eVK2 7800.00]

Douce 84, 32^v: Atelous; identifies the circle as the first region, followed by several circle-based diagnoses, and then breaks off in the middle of identifying the second region.   [eVK2 –]

BL Roy 17 C.xv, 55^v: A brief and somewhat corrupt passage listing the four regions (labelled "contents"), with the single instruction to see which region is "moost turbely or moost dyscolowryd" in order to determine where the malady lies, followed by causal correspondences between the four primary qualities and red, wan, watery (?), and white colors; replaces the **3Reg** text in an idiosyncratic and substantially abridged version of **DU**.   [eVK2 *6779.00]

10.0 Contents of Urines

This category focuses on texts based on the contents presented in Giles of Corbeil's *Carmen de urinis*, usually taken as running from eighteen to twenty items. Most treatments of contents in the uroscopy flask appear as part of a larger work, usually in concert with descriptions of the uroscopic colors and their significance, and often with other material as well.

Larger works with systematic discussion of uroscopic contents include the *Dome of Uryne* (**4Con** and **GrCon**, the only embedded texts whose witnesses are tallied here), *Ten Cold Ten Hot*; *Liber de Judiciis Urinarum*; "Urine Brown with a Black Ring"; Henry Daniel's *Liber Uricrisiarum*, book 3; the abridged form of the *Liber Uricrisiarum*, ch. 17; most of the texts associated with Walter Agilon; the original plan of *Barton's Urines*; Arderon's Commentary on Giles; and the *Book of Narborough*, book 3. See items 2.0, 6.3, 12.0, 15.0, 16.0, 20.0, 21.0, and 22.0 above and below. Manuscript witnesses for texts dealing only with contents in general or with only a few contents (e.g., *Cleansing of Blood*, *Practica Urinarum*, etc.) are not listed here, nor (with the exception of **4Con** and **GrCon**) the treatments of uroscopic contents in larger works.

10.1 On the [Four] Contents of Urines (4Con) and Urine That Has Great Contents (GrCon) in DU (36, 32 witnesses respectively; 39 manuscripts, 2 prints)

MANUSCRIPT AND PRINT WITNESSES

Core Version: MagdO 221; Cosin V.III.10; Wellcome 564; Ashmole 1447; Cosin V.V.13; Harl 2274; Digby 95 (**4Con** only); Digby 29; Hatton 29; Sloane 1388 (b); Rawl C.81; Ashmole 1477, X (**4Con** twice)

Expanded Version: Sloane 374; Harl 3407; BL Add 10440; Wellcome 409; StJC K.49; BL Add 30338; Selden Supra 73; Rawl C.506; Ashmole 1405 (**GrCon** only; see item 12.1 below)

Abbreviated Versions (**4Con** only): TCC O.8.35; Bodl Add B.60; Lambeth 444;
Sloane 297; Pepys 1307; *Judgement of Urynes*
Hybrid Version: Sloane 382; Sloane 1388 (a) (**GrCon** only); *Seynge of Uryns*;
NLM 49; Huntington HM 64 (**GrCon** only)
Peculiar Versions: NLW Sotheby C.2 (**4Con** only); CUL Dd.10.44 (**GrCon** only);
BL Roy 18 A.vi; BL Roy 17 C.xv; CCCO 291 (**GrCon** only); Harl 3810 (**GrCon**
only); Harl 5401 (**GrCon** only); Rawl D.1221; Ashmole 1438, II (**4Con** only)
Singleton: All Souls 81 (**4Con** only)

10.2 *De Contentis Urinarum* (1 witness)

Extensive discussion of the Aegidian contents, longer than those in *Ten
Cold Ten Hot,* the combined **4Con** and **GrCon** in *Dome of Uryne,* most
versions of Agilon's *Craft of Urines,* or "Urine Brown with a Black Ring,"
but shorter than those in the *Liber de Judiciis Urinarum,* Arderon's Commentary on Giles, and the encyclopedic treatments by Henry Daniel and
Friar Narborough. Preceded at the top of fol. 69^r by three lines of text
from the end of *Urine White and Red* (item 4.2.2 above), not part of the
recipe collection on fols. 1^v–68^v (eVK2 6520.00).

MANUSCRIPT WITNESS

TCC R.14.39, II, 69^r–73^v (probably slightly atelous, ending in
what appears to be an incomplete sentence, with the stub of
a missing folio visible after fol. 73^v; not necessarily acephalous,
pace eVK2; see item 4.2.2 above)   [eVK2 0328.00]

11.0 Inspection of Urines

In this group are included texts that provide some level of instruction on
how a practitioner goes about collecting and examining a sample of urine,
aside from the particular interpretation of the various uroscopic characteristics of the sample itself (which may or may not follow the instructions on
technique) and the additional questions to be asked of or about the patient,
analogous in some ways to modern medical histories.[51] Instructions for
inspection techniques and additional questions are also detailed in some of

---

[51]   Besides eliciting additional information useful for diagnostic and prognostic
purposes, some of these questions may have helped prevent the deception of physicians by patients, allowing practitioners to retain authority when interacting with
patients. Similar concerns are expressed more explicitly in the treatise *De cautelis
urinarum / Cautele medicorum* attributed variously (but probably spuriously) to
both Bernard de Gordon and Arnald of Villanova. See Luke Demaitre, *Doctor Bernard de Gordon: Professor and Practitioner,* Pontifical Institute Studies and Texts 51
(Toronto, 1980), 92–94. For a nuanced reading of the dynamics of these interactions,
see McVaugh, "Bedside Manners in the Middle Ages" (n. 42 above), 201–23.

the more comprehensive uroscopies, including Henry Daniel's *Liber Uricrisiarum* 1.4, the *Book of Narborough* 1.4, *Barton's Urines* chaps. 6-7, and Richard of England, *De Urinis* (items 15.0, 22.0, 20.0, and 25.0 below).

11.1 THE FIRST AND SECOND URINES (1&2U) in **DU** (28 manuscript witnesses, 2 prints)

A very brief (two-sentence) text describing differences in color-intensity between the first and second samples taken from a patient (he "that oweth ['owns'] the water"), depending on his dietary extravagance or moderation. Although not cast in the imperative syntax of most instructions, this **DU** segment does suggest a dual sampling procedure only occasionally mentioned in other inspection texts.

MANUSCRIPT AND PRINT WITNESSES

    Core Version: MagdO 221; Cosin V.III.10; Wellcome 564; Ashmole 1447; Cosin V.V.13; Hatton 29; Sloane 1388 (b); Rawl C.81; Ashmole 1477, X

    Expanded Version: Sloane 374; Harl 3407; BL Add 10440; Wellcome 409; StJC K.49; BL Add 30338; Selden Supra 73; Ashmole 1405

    Abbreviated Versions: Pepys 1307; rubric but no text in TCC O.8.35; Bodl Add B.60; Lambeth 444; *Judgement of Urynes*

    Hybrid Version: Sloane 382; *Seynge of Uryns*; NLM 49

    Peculiar Versions: NLW Sotheby C.2; Jackson 1302; Harl 2558; Rawl D.1221; Wellcome 7

11.2 *Practica Urinarum* (8 witnesses)

Instructions for inspecting urine, used as an introduction to the version of *Twenty Jordans* that begins with the color Rubea (six witnesses, asterisked below) and with two other **20J** texts beginning with Rufus and Karapos urines respectively. Factors to consider include the patient's age, length of illness, time of onset, and diet; the substance, quality, quantity, and contents of the urine; the region of the urinal, the type and stage of the illness, and the color and sedimen of the urine sample. The text ends with a summary of the relation between the elemental qualities and the colors, substance, and humoral associations of different urines.[52]

MANUSCRIPT WITNESSES

*Sloane 2320, 4^{r-v}	[eVK2 3229.00]
*Sloane 3566, 24^r–28^r	[eVK2 *3229.00]

---

[52]   Edited from Harvard MS Countway 19 by Harley, "Middle English Contents," 179–80 (n. 11 above); Countway 19 is among the manuscripts related to the Sloane Group identified by Voigts ("The 'Sloane Group'" [n. 10 above], 27, 32, 50–51).

*GC 336/725, 136ᵛ–137ʳ	[eVK2 *3229.00]
*Takamiya 33, 34ᵛ–35ʳ (corresponds to text in	
GC 336/725)	[eVK2 *3229.00]
*Countway Ballard 19, 14ʳ–16ʳ	[eVK2 *3229.00]
*TCC O.1.77, 21ʳ–24ʳ	[eVK2 *3229.00]
TCC R.14.52, 173ʳ⁻ᵛ (followed by **20J** with Rufus	
incipit)	[eVK2 3228.00]
Wellcome 537, 15ʳ–17ᵛ ("Practice of the Sight of Urines";	
followed by **20J** with Karapos incipit)	[eVK2 3225.00]

11.3 *Three Manners of Inspecting Urine* (4 witnesses)

Short text on external factors to consider in judging a patient's urine: the person's age, the length of the illness, and the time of day and season of the year when the sample was taken, with the dominant humor for those times and seasons. Followed by "The Doom of Urine Thou Shalt Cast in Four" in three manuscripts (asterisked below).

MANUSCRIPT WITNESSES

*BL Add 4898, 115ᵛ–116ʳ	[eVK2 *2112.75]
*Plimpton 254, 26ᵛ	[eVK2 –]
*Ashmole 1477, III, 10ᵛ (shorter version, omitting approx. the	
last third of the text, on specific maladies that arise at	
different times of the year)	[eVK2 *3082.00]
Harl 2375, 31ᵛ (only the opening sentence of the text, followed	
by a short explanation of the humoral relevance of "ages" of	
the patient, year, disease, planets, and signs for uroscopic diagnosis;	
embedded in a collection of other summary uroscopy materials,	
including *Cleansing of Blood, Ten Cold Ten Hot,* and *Urina Rufa*)	[eVK2 –]

11.4 Other Inspection Texts (5 texts, 1 witness each)

Several distinct but overlapping explanations of what to do and consider in examining urines.

MANUSCRIPT WITNESSES

GC 336/725, 70ᵛ–73ʳ: A relatively complex overview of
theoretical frameworks for uroscopy, starting with definitions
and etymology, the twenty colors and their digestive groups and
descriptive similes, complexions, qualities of colors, stages of acute
fevers, critical days, and so on, but not covering the twenty external
"conditions" for judging urine, the five substances, or eleven
pulses also mentioned in the opening paragraph as necessary
to all "men þat wolen be trewe iugis & domesmen of
vreynes." [eVK2 0839.00, 7798.00]
Sloane 297, 106ᵛ–108ᵛ: An incomplete text or collection of short
texts, atelous and probably missing a leaf or two between folios
106 and 107; begins with instructions on how to take, protect,

and inspect a urine sample, followed by a Man-Woman-Beast text
(item 7.3.4 above), and probably proceeding thereafter to the
interpretations of the different colors and densities of urine
(cf. 106^v, near the bottom: "thre prinspall thynges . . . the whych
been these . Colowre Substans. and the content"). A discussion
of urinary contents fills folios 106–107, beginning in foam near
the top and ending in the sediment near the bottom of the flask;
preceded by **20J** and followed by *Fifteen Discretions* (items
1.1.1 and 4.3 above).   [eVK2 1890.00, 7748.00]

Ashmole 1393, 60$^{r–v}$: External factors to consider in
judging urines, cleanness of the vessel, ambient light for
inspection, color, substance, circle, regions, hypostasis,
distinguishing pus from raw phlegm. Followed by
a Man-Woman-Beast text and a Women's Urines
text (items 7.3.4 and 7.2.7 above).   [eVK2 *0606.00]

Sloane 1101, 1^v: A brief text following an incomplete copy of
"The Doom of Urine Thou Shalt Cast in Four" (item 7.4 above),
detailing extrinsic factors, the kind of flask to use, and the
stages—hot, cold, and after shaking—at which to examine the
sample. Opening sentence somewhat similar to opening
of *Three Manners of Inspecting Urine* (item 11.3 above).   [eVK2 –]

Digby 75, 111^r–112^r: Identifies four extrinsic factors, followed
by a series of tokens and their interpretation.   [eVK2 –]

12.0 Colors and Contents Judicials

All of these treatises are relatively learned in their content and more or
less reflect the plan of Giles of Corbeil's *Carmen de urinis* and other Latin
texts that treat the colors and contents of urines in some detail. A number
of the attributed works in part II below also fit into this category: Henry
Daniel's *Liber Uricrisiarum*, John Arderon's Commentary on Giles, the
Book of Narborough, and *Barton's Urines*.

12.1 "Urine Brown with a Black Ring" (3 witnesses)

A general treatise on urines, beginning with discussion of colors, organized around embedded Latin verses from Giles of Corbeil's *Carmen de
urinis*, followed by discussion of the contents (numbered to nineteen) and
concluding in the two complete copies with a paragraph listing about
thirteen of the standard twenty colors and their digestion groups.

MANUSCRIPT WITNESSES

BL Add 4698, 8^r–14^v [eVK2 *7758.00]

Pepys 878, pp. 39–54   [eVK2 7758.00]

Ashmole 1405, pp. 89–96 (only the contents section,
appended to an Expanded Version of **DU** [item 2.2 above],
in lieu of **3Reg** and **4Con**)   [eVK2 –]

12.2 *Liber de Judiciis Urinarum* (2 witnesses)
A well-organized general treatise on urines, the translation of which is
attributed in Wellcome 784 to a 'John L.' (eVK2 suggests the possibility that "John L." may be John Lelamour, translator in 1373 of the *De
virtutibus herbarum*); title taken from Wellcome 784. After an opening
table of contents, the treatise proper begins with a discussion of twenty
colors, then of twenty contents, followed by four regions, seven kinds of
"residence" (the hypostasis or material that gathers in the bottom of the
urinal), and three concluding "notable rules" about the urines of women,
praiseworthy residence, and urines of death.

MANUSCRIPT WITNESSES
    Wellcome 784, 13^r–32^v [eVK2 *3927.00]
    NLM 4, 47^r–57^r [eVK2 7816.00, 3737.00, 3185.00,
                                                     6714.00, 3750.00, 6795.00]

12.3 "In Mankind Be Four Qualities" (1 witness)
A clearly organized exposition of the colors of urine (in a slightly atypi-
cal order beginning with light colors but with the dark red colors at the
end after green, black, and livid) and the contents from the circle to the
hypostasis, with a brief humoral prologue similar to the QUALITIES section of *Cleansing of Blood*. Relatively academic in tone, with references
to Gilbert, Avicenna, Constantine, Isaac, Galen, Theophilus, "doctors &
autores in phisike," "dyuers auctors," "th'apynions of dyuers doctours,"
and "the myndes of dyuers Doctors."

MANUSCRIPT WITNESS
    BL Roy 17 C.xxiv, 4^r–12^r [eVK2 *2815.00]

13.0 Verse Uroscopies[53]
13.1 "Urines for the Simple" (1 witness)
Unique fifty-line verse uroscopy, giving a definition of urine, a list of
nineteen uroscopic colors, and brief summary of the urines and complexions associated with the four qualities.

MANUSCRIPT WITNESS
    Sloane 120, 75^r–76^r [eVK2 2093.00]

---

   [53] I discuss these five versified (or quasi-versified, for item 13.4) texts, with editions of the first three of them, in "Three Middle English Verse Uroscopies," *English
Studies* 91 (2010): 591–622.

13.2 "Medicine for Every Manner Urine" (1 witness)

Unique thirty-line verse uroscopy followed by a short paragraph on the humors; the text touches briefly on the colors and their humoral associations, but recommends moderation in diet as the best medicine for all sicknesses.

MANUSCRIPT WITNESS
Sloane 120, 78^r–79^r [eVK2 2336.00]

13.3 "For to See Waters and Humors" (1 witness)

Unique 178-line verse uroscopy, with sections in prose or only roughly rhymed; longer and more sophisticated in its content than items 13.1 or 13.2, with a clear humoral framework underpinning its presentation of a relatively broad range of urines and the diseases they signify.

MANUSCRIPT WITNESS
BL Add 18216, 6^r–7^v [eVK2 7757.00]

13.4 *Manuale de Physica et Chirurgica* (1 witness)

Unique text, described in its prologue as a "tretys . . . of vrynes" that will "trete togydere boþe theorik & practyk"; included here because the prologue asserts that the text will be "in metir . . . raþer þan in prose / þat it be lustiere to lere & liȝtere to kunne" (65^v–66^r). The first two sections (prologue; qualities, elements, and humors) comprise some sixty lines. These lines are not right-justified and they are joined in pairs by brackets, suggesting verse, but they neither rhyme, alliterate, nor display any other obvious metrical features. After these lines, the text shifts to a combination of figures of division and right-justified prose, dealing again with the qualities and their effects on pulse and urine, the elements, and the humors and their effects on pulse and urine, leading up to Englished versions of three of the traditional Latin couplets on the complexions (sanguine, phlegmatic, choleric). It ends with more figures of division, on the quarters of the day, regions of the world, ages of man, seasons of the year, types of aposteme, spirit, fevers, and maladies of the head, eyes, and ears.

The *Manuale* follows the *Tractatus de Physica et Chirurgia* and a short paragraph on distinguishing the urines of man and beast, "The Beast's Water Will Be White" (both of them also found in GC 336/725, though in a different order). Followed immediately by the same list of medicines found in GC 336/725 between the "Beast's Water" text (item 7.3.3 above) and the *Tractatus de Physica et Chirurgia* (item 14.2.3a below).

MANUSCRIPT WITNESS
Sloane 340, 65^v–70^r ("Explicit manuale." is written after the
figures of division for "passiouns of yen" and "passyouns of
eryn" on fol. 70^r)   [eVK2 *3336.00]

13.5 Stanza on the Founders of Medicine, from John Lydgate, *Pageant of Knowledge*, st. 16 (2 manuscript witnesses, 1 print)
A single rhyme royal stanza attributing the establishment of medicine to Phebus and Esculapius, with a one-line reference to diagnosis by pulse and urine (*New Index of Middle English Verse* 2751, 3651).[54]

MANUSCRIPT WITNESSES
Huntington HU 1051, 49^v (1 stanza only)   [eVK2 4008.00]
TCC R.3.21, 288^r (in complete *Pageant of Knowledge*)   [eVK2 –]

PRINT WITNESS
"The fyrst fynders of the vii. scyences artyfycyall," in *The loue and complayntes bytwene Mars and Venus* (Westminster: Julian Notary, ca. 1500), sigs. B4^r-B5^r (reads "vayne" with TCC R.3.21)   —

14.0 Other Miscellaneous Texts
The texts in this section include several anonymous texts that do not fit neatly into earlier sections: compendious collections of shorter urine texts, with at least one component not found in any of the categories detailed above; short works on urines not seen and on urines and diet; brief summaries of the correspondences between urine and other medical entities such as humors, fevers, and parts of the body; and English notes, glosses, and definitions of Latin texts and terms. Collections of uroscopic texts whose elements are all classified elsewhere in this taxonomy (e.g., in Hatton 29, GC 336/725, Wellcome 537, Harley 2375, and others) are not listed here, although they too may have been deliberately compiled.

---

[54] Note 47 above; see also Alain Renoir and C. David Benson, "John Lydgate," *A Manual of the Writings in Middle English 1050-1500*, vol. 6, fasc. XVI (New Haven, 1980), 1883–85, 2141. The Huntington copy of the stanza is edited by Rossell Hope Robbins, "Doctrines of Temperate Diet," *Secular Lyrics of the XIVth and XVth Centuries* (Oxford, 1952), 76; the Trinity copy by Henry Noble MacCracken, *The Minor Poems of John Lydgate*, EETS e.s. 107, o.s. 192 (London, 1911, 1934), 2: 728. MacCracken's edition of the *Pageant* reads "touche of pounce, veyne, & inspeccions" rather than Robbins's "touche of poues & vryne Inspections."

14.1 Compendia

14.1.1 *A Short Treatise of Urines Which Is Good to Know* (1 witness)

A collection of texts in English and occasionally Latin, somewhat like a more extensive and more discursive version of *Ten Cold Ten Hot*, including material on humors, times of day and year, planets and signs, things to consider in judging urines, substance, parts, quantity, color and contents (with both English and Latin token lists), and the two uroscopic chapters of *The Four Elements* (8.2.3 above). Followed on 33^r–37^r by Latin texts, including what appears to be a charm for bloodletting, Latin versions of *Urina Rufa* and *Cleansing of Blood*, a vein-text, a text "de pueris saruandis," and another on the seasons, humors, day-quarters, and associated organs and regions of the body. On 37^r–40^r, there follow English texts on the humors, bloodletting, perilous days, thunder prognostics, and the calculation of movable feasts.

MANUSCRIPT WITNESS

Bodley 591, 26^r–33^r [eVK2 2637.00, 1522.00, 3101.00, 3511.00]

14.1.2 "Urine Awmery ['Amber'?] Color Tokens Good Hele and Being in Youth" (1 witness)

Several separately titled components, beginning with an untitled, color-based token list, followed by titled sections on regions; nineteen colors with their digestion groups and degrees of heat or cold; elemental qualities and quantity; five degrees of substance, including passages on women's urines and the relation of changing substance to stages of disease; and twenty contents in urine, ending incomplete after the eleventh content, Humor Crudus. Preceded by an illustrated copy of the *Twenty Jordans* series and a **20Col-Dig** text (items 1.5, 3.1.1b above); followed by a Latin-English herbal synonymy and an English *Agnus Castus* text.

MANUSCRIPT WITNESS

Sloane 3160, 91^r–96^v [eVK2 7753.00]

14.1.3 "Urine Is a Water Departed from the Blood" (1 witness)

A compendium with no title or explicit, but with rubricated headings for sections on the regions, twenty colors (classified by their digestion groups and by degrees of heat or cold), quality and quantity, substance (including differences between urines of man, woman, and beast and a passage on women's urines), twenty contents, and hypostasis; followed by the *Judicium Urinarum secundum Magistrum Galterium Agilon* (16.3 below).

MANUSCRIPT WITNESS
 CUL Dd.6.29, 110ʳ–118ᵛ   [eVK2 *7777.00]

14.1.4 "A Man's Body Is Governed by Four Qualities" (1 witness)

An untitled assemblage of several texts, including an embedded copy of *Ten Cold Ten Hot* (item 6.3 above). Other contents are an introductory section on the organs in the human body, with some echoes of the **MBB** text in the *Letter of Ipocras* (4.1 above); a section on the complexions in English followed by the traditional Latin couplets on the complexional traits; the three parts of the body where sickness arises and diets for those parts (head, stomach, and bladder); *Ten Cold Ten Hot*; the regions of the urine flask; short Latin paragraphs on sedimen, circles, and regions added to English passages on those subjects; and finally another colors and contents text titled "Exposition of All Urines," which includes a couple of short passages of Latin verse and ends incomplete in the content Hairs.

MANUSCRIPT WITNESS
 Rawl D.1210, 125ʳ–134ᵛ   [eVK2 0646.00, 2090.00]

14.1.5 *De Judicio Urinarum*[55] (1 witness)

A late (s. xvi) assemblage of short and medium-length uroscopies, with some alterations in vocabulary and omissions or rearrangements of material; much but not all of its content corresponds to texts listed elsewhere in this taxonomy. Includes a twenty-one color variant of **20Col-Dig**, the humoral overview *De Urinis Sanorum*, the Agilon-derived *De Urinis Egrorum*, an embedded abbreviation of **ST**, an abbreviated *Cleansing of Blood*, a humoral uroscopy titled *The Contents*, a corrupt version of "The Doom of Urine Thou Shalt Cast in Four," about eight signs from the beginning of *Urine White and Brown* (Woman), a still unidentified token list, a paragraph on conception and embryology, a rearranged *Urina Rufa* (with women's urines moved to the beginning), a summary of the colors and digestions, the rest of *Urine White and Brown*, additional women's urines, and **UMort** (which concludes at the foot of a page with the word "finis" in a later hand). Another urine text occurs a leaf and a half later (incipit "Without knowledge of the disease or infirmity it is impossible to help any manner of person"; fols. 106ʳ–107ᵛ), followed by a brief descriptive list of twelve colors of urine (Alba through Subrubea;

---

[55] The title on fol. 91ʳ may have been intended to refer only to the list of colors, but is applicable to the entire collection of texts and a useful label for the set.

fol. 107^v), repeating the descriptions and the title from the beginning of the compendium in a lighter ink. Cf. items 2.5b, 3.1.1c, 3.2.3, 3.3.3, 4.1.3c, 5.2.1, 6.6, 7.1.1, 7.4, 8.3, 8.6 above and 16.5 below.

MANUSCRIPT WITNESS
TCC R.14.39, III, 91^r–105^r, 106^r–107^v [eVK2 *0795.00]

14.1.6 *Tractatus de Urinis*, comp. William Bokynham (1 witness)
See item 30.0 below.

14.2 Other Texts
14.2.1 Urines Not Seen (anonymous)
Much simpler than William of England's *De Urina non Visa* (item 19.0 below), the astromedical texts in this section are based on the cosmic correspondences between celestial entities, the elements and qualities, and the complexions, urines, and parts of the human body.[56]

14.2.1a *Judgments of Urines Not Seen* (2 witnesses)
Two versions of a text that diagnoses illnesses from the planet ruling the day or the hour in which the sickness begins.[57] The Longleat version is

---

[56] References to "urine(s) not seen" in the scribal titles of the works in this category are analogous to, and possibly imitations of, William of England's Latin *De urina non visa* (1220), the Middle English translations of which appear below (item 19.0) Although texts on analyzing urines by consulting the stars instead of actual urine samples are relatively rare, they do hint at some level of distaste among at least some practitioners for dealing with bodily wastes, an attitude occasionally evidenced by passing comments in other medical and scientific texts, such as Bartholomaeus Anglicus's remark that "me schal not be squaymous of vryne ['people should not be squeamish about urine'; Lat. *vrina non est abhorrenda*], for in many thinges it is profitable and leef ['worthy, esteemed']" (*On the Properties of Things* 5.45, ed. Seymour, 1:258 [see n. 5 above]). Bartholomaeus's remark may have been influenced by Bernard de Gordon, who criticizes the "arrogantia & ignorantia quorundam qui dedignantur iudicia vrinarum & eam nauseant" ('the arrogance and ignorance of those who despise the judgments of urines and are nauseated by it'; *De urinis*, chap. 1, in *Lilium medicinae* 732 [see n. 3 above]). In *Barton's Urines Which He Treated at Tilney* (Sloane 280, fol. 271^r; item 20.0 below), the author defends uroscopy as being "fayrir & also muche certeynyr" than the examination of "þost" ('dung'). Fastidious disdain for uroscopy by non-medical medieval writers is perhaps most vigorously represented in Petrarch's *Invectives against a Physician*, ed. and trans. David Marsh, in *Francesco Petrarca: Invectives* (Cambridge, MA, 2003), 2–179, with at least a dozen scornful references to physicians' association with urine, latrines, chamber-pots, bedpans, sewers, and other excretory items and phenomena.

[57] This text may have a Latin source, but the eTK incipit (1517J: "Solis die in lecto qui ceciderit") that appears to be closest to the eVK2 incipit ("Sol if a man or

slightly fuller, adding the zodiacal position of the moon in the houses of the planet in question (e.g., Leo for Sol; Aries, Libra, and Taurus for Mars; Virgo, Libra, and Gemini for Mercury; etc.). The two versions present the planets in different orders: for Longleat, Sun-Moon-Mars-Mercury-Jupiter-Venus-Saturday (following the days of the week); for Ashmole, Sun-Venus-Mercury-Moon-Saturn-Jupiter-Mars.

MANUSCRIPT WITNESSES

Longleat 333, 44ᵛ–45ᵛ	[eVK2 4573.00]
Ashmole 210, 20ᵛ–21ʳ	[eVK2 2114.00]

14.2.1b *A Tract to Discern Urine What It Is Not Seen* (1 witness)
A treatise predicting the color, substance, and contents of urines and associated ailments from the zodiacal sign in the ascendant at the time of the judgment, translated from a Latin text *De iudicio urine* (incipit "Dixit Hermes pater philosophorum non est medicus"; eTK 0453C, 0919C).[58] Incomplete, covering only Aries through Libra and ending with "etc.," whereas the Latin original continues to the later zodiacal signs and the influence of the planets independent of the zodiac. Most of the sicknesses named in the English text correspond to the part of the body governed by the particular zodiacal sign. Fire signs (Aries, Leo) are linked to red colors, water and earth signs (Taurus, Cancer, Virgo) to white colors, air signs (Gemini, Libra) to citrine and "under-red" colors, as one would expect given the humoral associations of the elements.

MANUSCRIPT WITNESS

RCP 384, 27ʳ	[eVK2 2413.00, 8074.00]

14.2.2 Urines and Diet

Besides the two texts listed here, dietary recommendations also appear in other uroscopies (e.g., items 7.5.12, 14.1.4, 14.2.3a, and 23.0 above and below; texts that offer remedies may also include use of or abstinence from particular foods and drinks among their recommendations). The

---

woman begin to be sick upon the day of Sol") does not introduce a text on planets. I am very grateful to Dr. Susan L'Engle for sending me an image of eTK 1517J as found in Vatican Library, Vat. reg. lat. 1324, 66ʳ.

[58] Discussed by Danielle Jacquart, "L'opuscule sur le jugement des urines attribué a Hermès," in *Hermetism from Late Antiquity to Humanism,* ed. Paolo Lucentini et al. (Turnhout, 2003), 461–75, with comparisons to William of England's *De urina non visa*. See also Francis J. Carmody, *Arabic Astronomical and Astrological Sciences in Latin Translation: A Critical Bibliography* (Berkeley, 1956), 67.

two texts below simply focus more exclusively on diet than do other works and do not fit very well in other classifications.

14.2.2a *Of Colors and Medicines Thereto Longing* (1 witness)
Mixed-language text, beginning in English, continuing from p. 157 in Latin. Contains paragraphs on specific urines in groups of one to four colors, with the illnesses—mainly fevers—that they signify, other diagnostic signs for those ailments, dietary recommendations, and—for some urines—other remedies. Preceded by copies of *Cleansing of Blood, Rufus Subrufus,* and a list of colors in the order used by the Digby 75 variant of the Twenty Jordans; followed on pp. 159-160 by the Latin text of *Urina Rufa* and a Latin text on urines, humors, and circles in urine.

MANUSCRIPT WITNESS
Ashmole 1438, I, pp. 156–159   [eVK2 *3777.00]

14.2.2b *Dietary by the Twenty Colors* (1 witness)
A dietary by the twenty colors of urine, in digestion groups from light to dark colors.

MANUSCRIPT WITNESS
Sloane 122, 107^r–111^v [eVK2 2298.00, 3285.00]

14.2.3 Correspondences
14.2.3a *Tractatus de Physica et Chirurgia* (2 witnesses)
Four tables giving correspondences of months, zodiacal signs, and planets with a particular element, season, humor, and urine (e.g., months, signs, and planets that correspond to air, spring, blood, and hot moist urine, and so on for each of the other elements). Each table accompanied by a prose paragraph describing the sicknesses signified by such urine and recommended remedies, diet, and surgery for apostemes generated by the humor. In Sloane 340 but not GC 336/725, the *Tractatus* precedes a Man-Woman-Beast text and the *Manuale de Physica et Chirurgica*; in the Caius manuscript, the *Tractatus* follows the Man-Woman-Beast text and a list of medicines, but the *Manuale* does not appear (see items 7.3.3 and 13.4 above).

MANUSCRIPT WITNESSES
GC 336/725, 97(bis) recto–98^r [eVK2 7464.50]
Sloane 340, 63^v–65^r [eVK2 7464.00]

14.2.3b *A Good Consideration That a Man Shall Be Whole in Waters* (2 witnesses)

Three sentences on the urines that correspond to the stages of disease (incipit "If a man piss thin and the water hold him clear after"): the beginning (urine thin and clear), increase (urine thickening), and decline (urine clarifying); inserted into versions of *Ten Cold Ten Hot* in both witnesses. (See item 6.3 above.)

MANUSCRIPT WITNESSES

Harl 2375, 30ᵛ [eVK2 –]

Sloane 635, 94ᵛ (incipit partly damaged by cropping and wear) [eVK2 –]

14.2.3c Other Uroscopic Correspondences (4 texts, 1 witness each)
Miscellaneous individual texts, in some cases perhaps merely urine-related sections of some larger work.

MANUSCRIPT WITNESSES

Sloane 5, 185ᵛ: Brief overview of the generation of urine; its association with the liver, blood, and bladder; the relation of the four qualities to colors and substances; three regions of the urinal and the associated parts of the body (incipit "All urine is a matter that first was in the stomach defied"). Occurs between copies of *Cleansing of Blood* and *Urina Rufa*, within a collection of several uroscopic texts on fols. 181ʳ–190ʳ. [eVK2 –]

BL Sloane 120, 76ʳ⁻ᵛ: Brief summary of the relation between the four parts of the body and four parts of a urine sample; together with a copy of *Urina Rufa*, the text occurs between the two unique verse uroscopies in Sloane 120, items 13.1 and 13.2 above. [eVK2 *3510.00]

Wellcome 564, 193ʳ: Two sentences on the location of the illness on the right or left side of the body, depending on the color of the urine, no matter whether thick or thin: red for the right side where the liver is, white for the left side where the spleen is; followed by a short lunary text on when to give medicines based on the attractive, retentive, digestive, or expulsive purpose of the medicine in question. [eVK2 7822.00]

Sloane 357, 45ʳ: A paragraph on the three species of hectic fever and the urines that accompany them (incipit "There beth three kinds of a fever that is called *etica*"); embedded in a text on the virtues of herbs, following water of celandine, whose virtues are said to include "put[ting] awey the feuer etyke cotydian tercyan and quartan." [eVK2 –]

14.2.4 Glosses and Notes (6 texts, 1 witness each)
One glossary and five sets of interlinear or marginal notes and glosses on
Latin texts.

MANUSCRIPT WITNESSES

Wellcome 408, 71^r–75^r: *Nomina Infirmitatum Instrumentorum
& Medicinarum*, a series of medical terms with definitions,
including uroscopic and urological terms, names of diseases,
humoral terms, anatomical terms, kinds of fever, and
medicines of various sorts; incipit "Stranguria is when the
urine cometh dropping phlegmon is a bolning of the neck
of the vesica."   [eVK2 4624.00, 2595.00]

Rawl D.1221, 15^r: English and Latin glosses on fifteen
Latin verses *De coloribus urine*, listing nineteen colors
with descriptive similes. The Latin base text begins "Albus
aque lacteus sero glaucus quasi cornu"; it differs from the
descriptions of uroscopic colors given in the editions of the
Flos medicine, in Giles's *Carmen de urinis*, and in the
eighteen-line *Carmen de coloribus urinae* (eTK 0075H)
that accompanies an elaborate urine-wheel in Vat. pal.
lat. 1229, 5^r.   [eVK2 4031.00]

Rawl D.1221, 17^r–44^v: Marginal notes in Latin and English on
the standard Commentary on Giles of Corbeil's *Carmen de
urinis* (incipit "Liber iste quem legendum proponimus"
[eTK 0821I]); the English notes end on 42^v.   [eVK2 8082.00]

Ashmole 1477, X, 22^v: Inserted in a **DU** text, lines 216-19
from the *Carmen de urinis*, giving the eighteen Aegidian
contents, with glosses for all content names.   [eVK2 –]

Sloane 121, 59^r: Following the *Tractatus Magistri Bartholomei*
(item 16.1 below), a brief hematoscopy, and an abridged version
of *Urine White and Red* (item 4.2.2 above), lines 216–19 from
the *Carmen de urinis*, with interlinear English glosses on ten
of the eighteen contents.   [eVK2 –]

Sloane 706, 20^v: Following the *Tractatus Magistri Bartholomei*,
lines 216–19 from the *Carmen de urinis*, with interlinear English
glosses on ten of the eighteen contents; nine of the ten agree with
the Sloane 121 glosses.   [eVK2 –]

14.2.5 Leprosy Diagnostics (2 witnesses)
Two manuscripts contain a pair of diagnostic recipes for determining
if a person has leprosy, based on the reaction of burnt lead or a kale leaf
placed gently in a sample of the patient's urine. I have found this text
only in a collection of Englished versions of works principally by John of

Arderne, with extracts from Bernard de Gordon, anonymous works, and John of Burgundy's plague treatise.[59]

MANUSCRIPT WITNESSES

Emm 69, 198^v [eVK2 4042.00]

Sloane 776, 262^v–263^r (in an s. xvi copy or close relative of
Emm 69)   [eVK2 4043.00]

14.2.6 Unclassified Texts and Late Additions (2 witnesses)
MANUSCRIPT WITNESSES

Wellcome 8515, 19^r: Acephalous short text on uroscopic signs
of pestilence, with recommendations for bloodletting at
different points depending on the position of the bubo on
the body.   [eVK2 0257.25]

Wellcome, London Medical Society 136, 90^v: Three uroscopic
signs "to knaw waters of man or woman" embedded in a collection
of medical recipes.   [eVK2 –]

II. ATTRIBUTED WORKS

15.0 Henry Daniel, *Liber Uricrisiarum* (37 manuscript witnesses, 2 prints)[60]

The master work of Middle English uroscopic writing, encyclopedic in scope, and extant in several forms; at least some of the variation among the versions may stem from the author's own work of revision. Some copies open with a Latin or English prologue; some conclude with a Latin verse epilogue whose variants date the work to 1379, 1380, or 1382. The work is normally divided into three books, the first giving general information on urine, its production, and its inspection; the second dealing with the colors of urine; and the third with the contents of urine. Some versions add a section titled *Regule Isaac* at the end of book 3. Daniel frequently digresses on

---

[59]   At least two other kinds of prognostic recipe use urine as an ingredient, typically mixed with a drop of woman's milk or of blood, in order to determine fetal sex or whether a patient will live or die. The technique is broadly analogous to mixing a urine sample with human urine or with wine to determine whether the unknown sample is of human or animal origin (see item 7.3.4 above). However, these fetal sex and life vs. death recipes are usually embedded in recipe collections or other larger and non-uroscopic texts, which makes locating them more serendipitous than systematic, and they are not indexed in this taxonomy. Similarly, individual recipes that use urine as a therapeutic ingredient—for its astringent or mordant qualities—are passed over here.

[60]   MPME 79; MPME/S 260, 261 (see n. 9 above for abbreviations of biographical reference works).

a wide variety of non-uroscopic but related topics, including astronomy, computus, anatomy, humoral theory, physiognomy, and so on.

Some copies of the *Liber Uricrisiarum* divide the three books into relatively few long chapters, while others divide the books into many more, shorter chapters, notably in books 1 and 2; furthermore, chapter breaks are not always clearly marked or consistent, even among the more closely related copies. A full analysis of the manuscripts of the *Liber Uricrisiarum* and its variant forms has been undertaken by E. Ruth Harvey, with detailed attention to internal evidence (work in progress/forthcoming). The following basic outline derives from my own more general inspection of the manuscripts, but is also much indebted to Professor Harvey's generous sharing of her findings in advance of publication.[61]

The seventeen-chapter abridgment of the *Liber Uricrisiarum* devotes its first three chapters to the nature of urine, its generation and human anatomy, the considerations to apply and questions to ask in judging urines, and the complexions and elements; chapter 4 is a general discussion of the digestion groups and colors; chapters 5 through 16 deal with the individual colors, and chapter 17 addresses the regions and contents of the urine flask.

---

[61] The *Liber Uricrisiarum* has been edited by Joanne Jasin, "A Critical Edition of the Middle English Liber Uricrisiarum in Wellcome MS 225" (Ph.D. diss., Tulane University, 1983), ProQuest, Order No. 8400801. For a more recent partial edition from Huntington HM 505, see Ralph Hanna, ed., "Henry Daniel's *Liber Uricrisiarum*, Book I, Chapters 1–3," in *Popular and Practical Science of Medieval England*, ed. Lister M. Matheson (East Lansing, MI, 1994), 185–218. George R. Keiser discusses Daniel's herbal writings in "Through a Fourteenth-Century Gardener's Eyes: Henry Daniel's Herbal," *The Chaucer Review* 31 (1996): 58–75 and "Rosemary: Not Just for Remembrance," in *Health and Healing from the Medieval Garden*, ed. Peter Dendle and Alain Touwaide (Woodbridge, 2008), 180–204. The Latin prologue is recorded in eTK 0433B and (in early modern catalogues) 0089A, 0089B; eTK 0422D and 0422G, cited in eVK2 as eTK correspondences to several Henry Daniel witnesses, refer to Giles of Corbeil's *Carmen de urinis*, which Henry quotes at the beginning of the Middle English text ("Urine is as much for to say in English as one in the reins"). Further on Daniel, see Jake Walsh Morrissey, "Anxious Love and Disordered Urine: The Englishing of *Amor Hereos* in Henry Daniel's *Liber uricrisiarum*," *Chaucer Review* 49 (2014): 161–83; "An Unnoticed Fragment of *A Tretys of Diverse Herbis* in British Library, MS Sloane 2460, and the Middle English Career of Pseudo-Albertus Magnus," forthcoming in *Neuphilologische Mitteilungen* (2014), demonstrating Daniel's role as translator of the Pseudo-Albertine *De virtutibus herbarum* in BL Arundel 42.

A Latin version of the *Liber Uricrisiarum* is contained in Glasgow University Library, MS Hunter 362, 1^r–83^v.

MANUSCRIPT WITNESSES

15.1 Complete or nearly complete copies (15 witnesses; folio runs include Latin prologues and epilogues where present)

Sloane 1100, 3^r–118^r (Latin prologue and verse epilogue; *Regule Isaac*) [eVK2 7790.00]

Ashmole 1404, 3^r–184^v (Latin prologue and verse epilogue; *Regule Isaac*; followed on 185^r–206^r by Latin alphabetical index) [eVK2 7785.00]

GC 376/596, 1^r–169^v (Latin prologue and verse epilogue; *Regule Isaac*; followed by an alphabetical index on 170^r to the end of the manuscript) [eVK2 7792.00]

TCC O.10.21, 3^v–94^v (table of contents on 1^r–3^r; Latin prologue and verse epilogue; *Regule Isaac*) [eVK2 7784.00]

GlCathL 19, 1^r–189^v (*olim* 1^r–180^v, lacking seven leaves after old fol. 79 and with a stray leaf misbound in GlCathL 23, now rebound and renumbered, with the stray leaf reintegrated and seven blank but numbered leaves 82–88; Latin prologue and verse epilogue; *Regule Isaac*; Latin index on 190^r–195^r; two large, handsome color illustrations of physicians with flasks and a scroll or book on fols. 27^r and 134^v, at the beginnings of books 2 and 3) [eVK2 *7796.00]

e Mus 187, v recto – v verso, 1^r–78^v (English prologue; Latin/English table of contents; *Regule Isaac*; Latin verse epilogue) [eVK2 1986.00, 7755.00]

Eger 1624, 12^v–13^v, 16^r–108^v, 122^r–213^v (table of contents but no prologue; *Regule Isaac*; Latin verse epilogue reduced to a couplet; followed on 213^v–214^r by Latin index of diseases) [eVK2 *7754.00]

Wellcome 225, 5^r–143^v (no prologue; *Regule Isaac*; Latin verse epilogue reduced to a couplet) [eVK2 7783.00]

e Mus 116, 65^r–148^r (Latin prologue and verse epilogue) [eVK2 7779.00]

CUL Gg.3.29, 1^r–168^v (Latin prologue and verse epilogue) [eVK2 7792.00]

GC 180/213, 1^r–161^v (Latin prologue and verse epilogue) [eVK2 7780.00]

Huntington HM 505, 1^r–134^v (Latin prologue and verse epilogue) [eVK2 7781.00]

MassHS P-361 (*olim* 10.10), 3^v–140^v (Latin prologue and verse epilogue)[62] [eVK2 *7791.00]

CUL Ff.2.6, 1^r–127^v (Latin prologue; no epilogue) [eVK2 7781.00]

StJC B.16, 1^r–96^r (no prologue, no epilogue) [eVK2 7797.00]

---

[62] One of the earliest Middle English manuscripts to reach North America, donated to the Massachusetts Historical Society by Jeremy Belknap in 1791.

15.2 Imperfect copies (6 witnesses; chapter numbers are those of the individual witnesses)

BL Roy 17 D.i, 4ʳ–118ᵛ (English prologue; Latin/English table of
contents; some internal loss and mutilation of leaves; atelous, ending
in 3.20, in women's urines section of *Regule Isaac*)   [eVK2 1985.00, 7781.00]

Sloane 1721, 2ʳ–213ᵛ (Latin prologue; atelous, ending in 3.20.10,
in the section on turbid urines of *Regule Isaac*)   [eVK2 *7790.00]

Sloane 1101, 1ʳ⁻ᵛ, 2ʳ–166ᵛ (acephalous, beginning in 1.3 on
fol. 2ʳ; 1ʳ⁻ᵛ contains astronomical material marked for
insertion in 1.10, on fol. 17ʳ; atelous due to pages torn away
at end of manuscript, but reaches 3.22, on Hypostasis; no
Regule Isaac or epilogue survives)   [eVK2 0407.00]

Wellcome 226, 1ʳ–70ᵛ (no prologue; atelous, ending in
chapter on pale and subpale urines in book 2)   [eVK2 7789.00]

RCP 356, 1ʳ–64ᵛ (no prologue; atelous, ending in the
astronomy digression in book 2)   [eVK2 7782.00]

Charles W. Traylen, Guildford, catalogue 58 (1963), no. 331
(*olim* Br Roy IV 249⁶³); atelous, ending in 3.26⁶⁴ [**NOT SEEN**]   [eVK2 7781.00]

15.3 Seventeen-chapter abridgment (6 witnesses)

In the three stand-alone copies of the abridgment, most of the individual chapters are preceded by appropriate verses extracted from Giles of Corbeil's *Carmen de urinis*. See Rand Schmidt, *IMEP* 17:47, 66.⁶⁵

Sloane 340, 39ᵛ–62ᵛ (followed on 62ᵛ–63ᵛ by a short Latin text,
continuing discussion of hypostasis beyond that found in GC
336/725 and adding material on physician caution in answering
questions about urines)   [eVK2 *7787.00]

GC 336/725, 79ʳ–95ᵛ (Sloane 340 and GC 336/725 share a number
of uroscopic and other texts in addition to the abridged *Liber
Uricrisiarum*: see items 7.3.3, 14.2.3a above)   [eVK2 7788.00]

Bodl lat misc c.66, 75ʳ–83ʳ   [eVK2 0498.00, 7793.00]

GC 176/97, pp. 65–120 (incorporated as chaps. 5–22 in
the Plawdon Compendium compiled by "Austin," item
17.0 below, with chap. 5 of the original abridgment

⁶³ Thomas Kaeppeli, *Scriptores Ordinis Praedicatorum Medii Aevi* (Rome, 1975), 2:192.

⁶⁴ Hanna, "Henry Daniel's *Liber Uricrisiarum*" (n. 61 above), 190. See also Rand Schmidt, *IMEP* 17:47 (n. 47 above).

⁶⁵ The copy in GC 336/725 has been edited by Tom Arvid Johannessen, "The Liber Uricrisiarum in Gonville and Caius College, Cambridge, MS 336/725" (Master's Thesis, University of Oslo, 2005, available for download at https://www.duo.uio.no/handle/10852/25409) and the copy in Sloane 340 is currently being edited by José Francisco Martín del Pozo in a University of Málaga doctoral thesis. Johannessen provides a useful comparison between the abridgment and the full version of the *Liber Uricrisiarum*.

divided into two chapters numbered 9 and 10 in the
Compendium)[66]   [eVK2 1918.00, 7795.00]
TCC R.14.52, 170[r–v] (the first half of chap. 1 of the
seventeen-chapter abridgment; part of the incomplete
copy of the Plawdon Compendium, item 17.0 below)   [eVK2 *7794.00]
Wellcome 7117, 122[r–v] (the first half of chap. 1 of the
seventeen-chapter abridgment; Wellcome 7117 shares
a number of texts with TCC R.14.52)[67]   [eVK2 7623.00, 7778.00]

15.4 Modifications and excerpts (10 witnesses)

Sloane 2196, 3[r]–42[v] (book 1 rearranged, with some of the general
information from books 2 and 3 included; many of the astronomical,
calendric, anatomical, and other non-uroscopic digressions
omitted; ends incomplete in 3.16, on Motes)   [eVK2 1196.00]
Rawl D.1221, 50[r]–62[v] (book 2, abridged)   [eVK2 1430.00]
Sloane 1088, 61[r]–93[v] (extract from book 2 chapters on
Lacteus and Karapos, including a long "fates [*or* faces?] and
fortunes" digression on the influence of natal signs, otherwise
attested only in Ashmole 1404 and with significant differences
in Sloane 1101; breaks off incomplete at end of 93[v])   [eVK2 2934.00]
Sloane 2527, 178[r]–196[v] (appears to be an abridged version of
book 3, including the *Regule Isaac*;[68] Latin contents list on
177[v]; no epilogue, but the explicit on 196[v] gives date and
author/translator as follows: "Explicit tractatus translatus
.a. f. h. d. [*or* v.? {*so* eVK2}] ordinis predicatorum anno
domini m° ccc lxxix anno regn' Ricardi secundi secundo"
[196[v]]. "Translated by Frater Henry Daniel" seems a
reasonable expansion of "translatus .a. f. h. d.," if the reading
of the last letter is correct.[69])   [eVK2 8100.00]
Sloane 2527, 198[v]–201[v] (excerpts on critical days and fever
from book 2)   [eVK2 1450.00]
Sloane 134, 1[r]–3[v], 4[v]–20[v] (acephalous and atelous excerpt
on hypostasis and the *Regule Isaac* from the end of book 3;
excerpts on critical days, fevers, and astronomy from
book 2. Except for the astronomical passage, these texts are

---

[66] There is some evidence that the incorporation occurred at or very close to
the copying of GC 176/97: the chapter number "eyteþ" ('eighth') in the Caius manuscript has been corrected from "feerþe" ('fourth'), the number of the original chapter
in the seventeen-chapter abridgment.

[67] Patricia Deery Kurtz and Linda Ehrsam Voigts, "Contents, Unique
Treatises, and Related Manuscripts," in *Sex, Aging, and Death in a Medieval Medical
Compendium* (n. 37 above), 19–54, at 39–46.

[68] See Hanna: "a compendium drawn from Book 3" ("Henry Daniel's *Liber
Uricrisiarum*" [n. 61 above], 191).

[69] See MPME/S 260.

identical to what remains of the book 3 material and the two
excerpts from book 2 in Sloane 2527.)   [eVK2 *0400.00, 1451.00, 7730.00]
Sloane 1721, 214^r–216^v (titled *De urinis in genere*, a
precis of book 2.1–2, on colors in general and black
urine; partly in cipher on 216^{r-v})   [eVK2 7154.00]
Eger 1624, 214^v–215^r, 218^{r-v} (explanations of the names
of the zodiacal signs for the different times of the year, with
a cross-reference to book 2; an acephalous and atelous text
on the contents of urine, ending in mid-sentence with Blood as
the twelfth content)   [eVK2 6967.00, 0301.00]
Sloane 5, 179^v–181^r (seven paragraphs on the nature and
orbital periods of the planets, excerpted and abbreviated
from the astronomy section of book 2)   [eVK2 3817.00]
Pepys 1661, pp. 235–240 (a possible excerpt from book 2, on
astronomy and the calendar)[70]   [eVK2 4581.00]

Other excerpts probably still remain to be identified.

PRINT WITNESSES

15.1 Complete or nearly complete copies (2 witnesses)
The Iudycyall of Vryns (no prologue, no epilogue; STC
14836; Southwark: Peter Treveris, 1527?; repr. with
minor changes: STC 14836.3; Southwark: Peter Treveris, 1527?)[71]   —

16.0 Walter Agilon, *The Craft of Urines* (11 witnesses)[72]

A series of more than a hundred uroscopic tokens translated and expanded
from a Latin text, "Cum secundum auctores" (eTK 0338M), attributed in
manuscripts to various authors (Galterus/Galterius Agilon, "G.," "Rika."
or Rikardus, and so on) or left anonymous.[73] The "Cum secundum" is
related to another series of tokens attributed to Agilon, with the incipit
"Urina alba in colore tenuis in substantia" (eTK 1607A), and both of these
texts descend at least in part from Walter Agilon's *Summa* (or *Practica*)

---

[70]   As suggested by Laurel Means, "'Ffor as moche as yche man may not haue
þe astrolabe': Popular Middle English Variations on the Computus," *Speculum* 67
(1992): 596–623, at 604.

[71]   On the changes in the reprinted edition, see Hanna, "Henry Daniel's *Liber
Uricrisiarum*" (n. 61 above), 191.

[72]   DB 170–73, DB/S1 80–81.

[73]   Uncertainty about the authorship of the "Cum secundum auctores" is no
new thing: the prologue to the *Tractatus Magistri Bartholomei* version of the text
notes that "This booke þat we han nowe in hondes to turne in to englisshe is of þe
craft of vrinis but hwos werke it is we netith ['know not']. Gode neþeles we suppose
it is" (Sloane 2527, 295^r).

medicinalis (eTK 1480C, 1483G, 1499H).[74] The following descriptive remarks on these three Latin texts are no more than a preliminary sketch, in need of much more detailed study before a definitive picture of the precise textual relationships and authorship(s) can be drawn.

In Diepgen's edition, the *Summa medicinalis* consists of 142 chapters, most of which begin with a uroscopic token or *regula* and its diagnostic or prognostic significance, followed by other symptoms of the signified illnesses and remedies for those ailments. Humoral etiologies of diseases, especially fevers, occur *passim*. The chapters are ordered by urinary color, beginning with white urines, followed first by black, livid, and various red and pale urines with some lividity, and then by the remaining metabolic color spectrum, beginning with the other colors of indigestion and moving through the pale, citrine, and several red colors on to Inopos, Kyanos, and Viridis.

The "Urina alba" treatise extracts the uroscopic *regulae* from the *Summa*, more or less following the chapter order there, and drops the rest of each chapter (including the complete chapters that do not begin with a urinary sign). In at least one of the copies I have seen (Vat. pal. lat. 1243, 104^v–109^r), it proceeds with signs based on the Aegidian contents. "Cum secundum" also omits the non-uroscopic material in the *Summa*, but its colors follow the light-to-dark, metabolic order more closely, with livid and black urines placed at the end of the list along with green urines, followed by Giles's contents and their significance, from the circle to the hypostasis. Many but not all of the tokens in the *Summa medicinalis* can be matched up with those in "Urina alba," and from there to the "Cum secundum auctores," but each redaction modifies the list to a certain extent. "Cum secundum" also adds a short preface describing the six "operations" of nature (corresponding to the six digestion groups that organize the series of colors).[75]

---

[74] Ed. Paul Diepgen, *Gualteri Agilonis Summa medicinalis*, Studien zur Geschichte der Medizin Beiheft 3 (Leipzig, 1911). The text attributed to Agilon in some manuscripts and edited by Julius Pfeffer in an 1891 Berlin medical dissertation, "Das Compendium urinarum des Gualterus Agulinus (XIII. Jahrhundert)," is not by Agilon, but is rather a version of the anonymous "Harntraktat" noted under the Vade Mecum suite above (items 3.2-3.3); see Keil, "Der 'kurze Harntraktat'" (n. 30 above), 16–17.

[75] These operations differ from those described in the *Isagoge* of Johannitius in the *Ars medicine / Articella* (appetite for food, digestion, retention, expulsion, and the "composite" operations of *desiderium* and *deportatio*).

Most of the Middle English uroscopies with roots in Agilon's work are clear derivatives of the "Cum secundum" text, though usually with altered or expanded prefatory material and with internal digressions not in the Latin versions I have encountered. Middle English adaptations of "Cum secundum" occur in at least four, possibly five, distinct versions. The most common version begins with a long prologue discussing the six operations of nature, its own translating and commenting procedure, the battle between disease and nature, and the humors. Some versions of that prologue describe the text as a book "of the craft of urines," the phrase with which I have titled the collective versions of the text.[76] Like "Cum secundum," this most common version treats both colors and contents, but with substantial digressions into background information on such topics as the complexions, qualities, spirits, quarters of the year, fevers, crisis, and so on. In CUL Ii.6.17, uniquely, an opening rubric attributes the translation to Magister Bartholomeus, OFM, and the commissioning of the translation to Richard II and Queen Anne, "ad intelligenciam laicorum ad eos gubernandum prout placet altissimo" ('so that laypeople can understand how to govern themselves, in accordance with God's will'; fol. 2^r).[77] If accurate, the rubric implies a date of translation between 1382 and 1394, from Anne's marriage to Richard until her death. Witnesses

---

[76] The collective title is primarily one of convenience, to differentiate these texts from *The Dome of Uryne* and other texts titled with forms of the words *Judicium, Judiciale,* and so on. The phrase appears in the prologue in CUL Ii.6.17 (whose introductory rubric also labels the work "Tractatus Magistri Bartholomei") and Sloane 2527; three copies of the prologue offer the *lectio simplicior* "of the doom of urines" (TCC R.14.32, Sloane 121, Sloane 706); Harley 3810 abridges the prologue significantly, dropping the phrase entirely, but the text is preceded on the foregoing page by the underlined words "Iudiciale perfectum omnium urinarum," which might have been intended as a title or might belong with the atelous **DU** text on 101^r–104^v. The independent version in CUL Dd.6.29 is titled "Iudicium urinarum secundum Magistrum Galterium Agilon."

The eVK titles *Compendium urinarum* (also used in DB 170–73) and *Commentarium urinarum* are somewhat problematic, partly because the text is not a commentary and partly because the Latin text edited by Pfeffer under the title *Compendium urinarum* is not Agilon's work. See note 74 above. Identification of Agilon's authentic and spurious works remains a scholarly desideratum.

[77] None of the several Bartholomews in MPME and MPME/S, nor in A. B. Emden's biographical registers for Oxford and Cambridge, appears to be a likely Franciscan candidate for the authorship of the translation. See Emden, *Biographical Register of the University of Oxford to A.D. 1500,* 3 vols. (Oxford, 1957–59); *Biographical Register of the University of Cambridge to 1500* (Cambridge, 1963).

to this text can be further divided into two families, distinguished by phrasings peculiar to one or the other, marginal apparatus, and their explicits: the first family contains CUL Ii.6.17, Sloane 2527, and Harley 3810; the second Sloane 121, Sloane 706, and TCC R.14.32.

A second version lays out its material in figures of division, covering both colors and contents; it has a much briefer prologue listing the six operations of nature, translated closely from the prologue to "Cum secundum auctores," which is probably also the nucleus around which the much expanded prologue to the more common version developed. The third version is again in run-in prose, with a short prologue addressing the extrinsic conditions that a practitioner should attend to in judging urines. Compared to the first two versions, its signs are more loosely translated from the Latin original—"adapted" might be a better term. Those signs end at the color green, short of livid and black, which may imply an incomplete text.

The fourth version has no preface, is relatively loosely translated or adapted, and further modifies the underlying "Cum secundum" material by adding and subtracting signs at various points. It covers both colors and contents, ending with an overview of humoral correspondences. The fifth text below moves even farther from the other Walter Agilon treatises in this section, but still resembles them well enough to warrant classification here rather than in a miscellaneous category.

MANUSCRIPT WITNESSES

16.1 *Tractatus Magistri Bartholomei* (6 witnesses)

CUL Ii.6.17, 2^r–25^r	[eVK2 7361.00, 0788.00]
Sloane 2527, 295^r–306^v	[eVK2 7361.00, 0790.00]
Harl 3810, 104^v–120^r, 125^v–128^v (prologue adapted, text and folios disordered; ends incomplete after Rufa/Subrufa urines; humoral material within text	
also copied on 99^v–101^r)	[eVK2 *2876.00, 0789.00, 0658.00, 2099.00]
Sloane 121, 41^v–58^r	[eVK2 7362.00, 4559.00, 2380.50, 7297.50, 2380.00, 0787.00]
Sloane 706, 4^v–20^r	[eVK2 7362.00, 0787.00]
TCC R.14.32, 70^r–80^v	[eVK2 –]

16.2 "When That after Authors There Be Twenty Colors"[78] (1 witness)

Ashmole 1498, 89^r–94^v (presented in figures of division; followed by an English translation of another Agilon text,

---

[78] This incipit makes the relation to the "Cum secundum" text particularly clear; the explicits to the two sections of the text in Ashmole 1498 describe those sections as "þe coloures of urynes wiþ here substaunces" and "þe contentes and þe floures of urynes."

on pulse ["Cum decem sint genera pulsuum"; eTK 0291E],
also set out in figures of division)   [eVK2 7998.00, 1433.00]

16.3 *Judicium Urinarum secundum Magistrum Galterium Agilon* (1 witness)

CUL Dd.6.29, 119^r–125^v (preceded by a compendious treatment
of the regions, colors, quality and quantity, substance, content,
and hypostasis, fols. 110^r–118^v; item 14.1.3 above)   [eVK2 *7777.00]

16.4 *The Exposition of All Urines and Their Significations* (1 witness)

GC 451/392, pp. 29–44   [eVK2 7827.00]

16.5 *De Urinis Egrorum* (2 witnesses)

A colors-and-contents token list in its fuller version, preceded by the definition of urine as a cleansing of blood (only in Harley, citing Theophilus and Isaac), a listing of nineteen or twenty-one colors of urine in English (and Latin in Harley), and the healthy urines of each complexion (3.1.1c, 8.3 above). The token list proper supplements some of the diagnoses with additional, non-uroscopic symptoms. Although some of the signs given in this text are broadly analogous to those in the Middle English reflexes of "Cum secundum auctores," the *De Urinis Egrorum* (a title taken from the Harley copy) contains more signs than the "Cum secundum" texts described above, and its phrasing is not particularly close to the language of those texts.

Harl 1010, 2^r–23^v [eVK2 *7799.00]
TCC R.14.39, III, 91^r–98^v (ends in black urines, omitting the
contents series found in Harl 1010; contains a few embedded
passages from other uroscopic texts—e.g., an acephalous
ST series on 91^v—and is part of a larger compendium of
uroscopies [item 14.1.5 above])   [eVK2 –]

17.0 "Austin," *Compendium for Thomas Plawdon*, chaps. 5–22 (uroscopic chapters) (3 witnesses)[79]

The abridged version of Henry Daniel's *Liber Uricrisiarum*,[80] revised from seventeen to eighteen chapters by dividing chapter 5 of the abridgment in two (chaps. 9 and 10 of Austin's compendium, on black urine). The larger text containing these chapters was compiled by one "Austin," for Thomas Plawdon, "citiseyn & barbour of london" (GC 176/97, p. 39), probably the barber-surgeon of London whose will of 1413 survives.[81] The (nearly) full compendium begins with general materials on medicine, diseases, and

---

[79] MPME/S 279, s.n. 'Thomas Plawdon."
[80] Rand Schmidt, *IMEP* 17:45 (n. 47 above); see also item 15.3 above.
[81] Voigts and McVaugh, *Phlebotomy*, 15 n. 46 (n. 19 above).

the humors, then moves on to the chapters on uroscopy, followed by nine chapters on fevers, three chapters on simple and compound medicines, and finally eight chapters on particular maladies and remedies for them, organized *a capite ad calcem*. The concluding chapter ("þe 42 chapitre and þe laste," p. 226), on diseases of the kidneys, bladder, uterus, and joints, breaks off incomplete on p. 228.

MANUSCRIPT WITNESSES

GC 176/97, pp. 65–120 (compendium as a whole on
  pp. 37–228)   [eVK2 1918.00, 7795.00]
TCC R.14.52, 170^{r-v} (the end of an excerpt from the
compendium's opening chapters, which begins on fol.
159^r and ends about halfway through chap. 5, after the
definition and part of the etymology of the word "urine";
the excerpt omits the references to Austin and Plawdon
and occasionally drops short passages, possibly inadvertently,
but is otherwise textually close to the Caius manuscript,
including its chapter headings and almost all the original
marginal glosses and incorporating corrections indicated
in the longer version)   [eVK2 *7794.00]
Wellcome Library 7117, 122^{r-v} (first half of chap. 5
  only)   [eVK2 7623.00, 7778.00]

18.0 Bernard de Gordon, *Upon the Prognostics* (3 witnesses)[82]

A generally competent translation of Bernard de Gordon's *Tractatus de pronosticis* (also known as *Tractatus de crisi et de diebus creticis*; eTK 1428B–C [prologue]; 0692I, 0756D, 0960A),[83] incomplete in all three copies.

MANUSCRIPT WITNESSES

Takamiya 60, sigs. b1^r – h[3]^v (signed but unfoliated, acephalous,
beginning in *particula* 1, chap. 5; the uroscopic chapter, 4.10,
appears on sigs. e6^v–e8^r)[84]   [eVK2 0361.00]

---

[82] MPME 25; DB 75–76; DB/S1 43–44; DB/S2 437. Biographical treatments before 1980 are all superseded by Demaitre, *Doctor Bernard de Gordon* (n. 51 above).

[83] Ed. Alberto Alonso Guardo, *Los pronósticos médicos en la medicina medieval: El* Tractatus de crisi et de diebus creticis *de Bernardo de Gordonio* (Valladolid, 2003).

[84] Discussed in detail, including remarks on the other witnesses, by Voigts, "Takamiya MS 60 and the Middle English Text of Bernard of Gordon's *De pronosticis*," in *The Medieval Book and a Modern Collector: Essays in Honour of Toshiyuki Takamiya,* ed. Takami Matsuda, Richard A. Linenthal, and John Scahill (Cambridge and Tokyo, 2004), 149–60. I am most grateful to Professors Takamiya and Voigts for sharing digital scans of the manuscript with me, and to Professor Voigts for sharing her transcript of a portion of those scans.

Sloane 5, 61ʳ–63ʳ (atelous; Prologue and *particula* 1, chap. 1,
  incomplete)   [eVK2 0765.00, 7115.00]
TCC O.9.37, 31ʳ–32ᵛ (atelous; Prologue and *particula* 1, chap. 1,
  incomplete, ending slightly earlier than Sloane 5 copy)   [eVK2 0765.00,
                                                                7116.00]

19.0 William of England, *Of Urine Not Seen* (2 witnesses)[85]

A translation of William of England's *De urina non visa* (written in 1220;
eTK 0906G* [prologue], 0388B, and 0462C), an astrological treatise on
diagnosing and predicting the course of an illness without examining
either the patient or the patient's urine, based on astrological calculations. See also the anonymous Urines Not Seen texts above, items 14.2.1a,
14.2.1b.

MANUSCRIPT WITNESSES

TCC O.5.26, 39ᵛ–44ʳ[86]   [eVK2 3897.00, 2589.00]
Ashmole 210, 22ʳ–23ᵛ (approximately the last third
of the English version found in TCC O.5.26, and a
different translation from that copy)   [eVK2 1226.00]

A late version of the Latin text is printed in Bernard's *Lilium medicinae . . . una
cum aliquot aliis eius libellis* (Lyons, 1574), 993–1092, and the Latin text is analyzed
by Demaitre, *Doctor Bernard de Gordon* (n. 51 above), 40–43. Voigts and Demaitre
have a joint edition of the Latin and Middle English texts in progress.

[85] DB 224–25; DB/S1 99–100; MPME 381-82; MPME/S 281. For the most
recent treatments of William's works and dates, see Emmanuel Poulle, "William
the Englishman," *Complete Dictionary of Scientific Biography,* ed. Charles Coulston
Gillispie et al. (Detroit, 2008): http://www.encyclopedia.com/topic/William_the_
Englishman.aspx; Laurence Moulinier-Brogi, *Guillaume l'Anglais, le frondeur de
l'uroscopie médiévale (XIIIᵉ siècle): Édition commentée et traduction du "De urina
non visa"* (Geneva, 2011). Ralph Hoby's Latin treatise on astronomical medicine also
addresses determination of uroscopic qualities (color, substance, contents) of unseen
urines: see the tables of contents reproduced in Voigts, "Wolfenbüttel HAB Cod.
Guelf. 51.9.Aug. 4° and BL, Harley MS. 3542: Complementary Witnesses to Ralph
Hoby's 1437 Treatise on Astronomical Medicine," *eBLJ* 2008, article 10, figs. 1W,
1H, and Lynn Thorndike's summary of the text quoted on p. 1 (http://www.bl.uk/
eblj/2008articles/article10.html).

[86] Transcribed and discussed by Hilary M. Carey, "Medieval Latin Astrology
and the Cycles of Life: William English and English Medicine in Cambridge, Trinity College MS O.5.26," in *Astro-Medicine: Astrology and Medicine, East and West,*
ed. Anna Akasoy et al. (Florence, 2008), 33–74. Carey dates the manuscript to the
period from 1385–1405, which may be fairly close to the date of the Middle English translation, if it was undertaken more or less contemporaneously with the work
of such scientific and medical translators as Henry Daniel, "Master Bartholomew,"
John Trevisa, Geoffrey Chaucer, John Lelamour, et al.

20.0 "Barton," *Barton's Urines Which He Treated at Tilney* (2 witnesses)[87]

A general treatise on urine and uroscopy, with extensive digressions on astronomy, the calendar, humoral correspondences, anatomy, embryology and ensoulment, and so on. Incomplete in both copies, but the fuller and earlier copy contains an internal identification of "þis book . . . whos title is bartons vrynes wheche he treted at tilney," and a statement of intention to complete the treatise by discussing both colors and contents (fol. 280ʳ). The surviving chapters on colors in Sloane 280 are a relatively close prose translation of the lines on those colors in Giles of Corbeil's *Carmen de urinis*. Tilney is one of several villages (Tilney St. Lawrence, Tilney All Saints, etc.) in Norfolk, near Lynn.[88]

MANUSCRIPT WITNESSES

Sloane 280, 270ʳ–285ᵛ (incomplete, ending in chap. 14, on Pallidus, Subpallidus, Citrine, and Subcitrine colors)   [eVK2 1974.00]
StJC B.16, 97ʳ–106ᵛ (incomplete, ending in chap. 11, a discussion of andrology, conception, and embryology)   [eVK2 1973.00]

21.0 John Arderon, *De Judiciis Urinarum* (Commentary on Giles of Corbeil, *Carmen de urinis*) (2 witnesses)[89]

---

[87] Possibly the Johannes Barton *medicus* listed in MPME 121, who was purged of Lollardy in 1416.

[88] For further discussion of *Barton's Urines*, see Tavormina, "Practice, Theory and Authority in a Middle English Medical Text: 'Barton's Urines Which He Treated at Tilney'," *Journal of Nephrology* 22, Supplement 14 (2009): S33–S41. I am presently editing the text from the fuller Sloane copy, collated with the St. John's manuscript.

[89] The impersonal style, high degree of academic content, and date of composition all militate against identifying the author with the surgeon John Arderne responsible for the treatises *Practica de fistula in ano, Liber medicinalium, De arte phisicali et de cirurgia, De cura oculorum*, and others (MPME 111, MPME/S 263; DB/S 142; cf. eTK 0030M, 0085H, 0489F, 0631B, 1307G, 1331H). Getz notes a John Arderne the Younger who was pardoned for murder (MPME/S 263, citing the *Calendar of Patent Rolls* 1408–1413 [London, 1909], 269); this John Arderne had been indicted, with others, of having murdered and despoiled John Crophill of Annesley, Notts., in Burton Jorce, Notts. Given the self-proclaimed association of the surgical Arderne with Nottinghamshire and his possible associations with the grandfather of Henry IV (Henry duke of Lancaster), Arderne the Younger could have been at least a member of the same extended family, though the pardon makes no mention of his trade or profession. Other Ardernes, including other "John (de) Ardernes," can be found in contemporary and near-contemporary records, with a variety of name-spellings, county origins, and social levels, but as Peter Murray Jones notes, "[Arderne's] name is an extremely common one in the fourteenth century, and there

A commentary on the *Carmen de urinis* of Giles of Corbeil, incorporating color descriptions, diagnoses, medicines, and urinary contents information from *Twenty Jordans*; extensive citations of uroscopic authorities including Hippocrates, Galen, Theophilus, Isaac Israeli, Avicenna, Walter (Agilon?), Gilbertus, Bernard de Gordon, and Jean de Saint-Amand.

Attributed in the Latin prologue (Hunter 328 only) to "Ego Magister Johannes Arderoun," who describes himself, or possibly one of his authorities, as "medic[um] domini regis illustrissimi principis henrici quarti cuius anime propicietur deus," suggesting an s. xv$^{1/4}$ date of composition. The Hunterian copy includes the Latin text of Giles of Corbeil's *Carmen de urinis*. The Rylands copy is closely related to the earlier copy in Hunter 328 but omits the heading identifying author and sources, as well as the embedded quotations of Giles's Latin text and some of the marginal structural indicators.

In both manuscripts, the text concludes with two modified components of the *Dome of Uryne*: the four sentences on substance from **4Th**, presented in Hunter 328 as a (non-Aegidian) nineteenth "content" and followed by an equally non-canonical twentieth content, "Scintilla"; and **UMort**, followed by several signs of death from "Urine Troubly with Clouds."[90]

MANUSCRIPT WITNESSES

Hunter 328, 1^r–44^v (illustrated with flasks in the colors
  section of the text, all uncolored except for Albus)   [eVK2 0903.00]
Rylands Eng 1310, 1^r–21^r (illustrated with flasks in the
  colors section of the text, all uncolored)   [eVK2 1296.00, 7168.00]

22.0 "Friar Narborough," *The Book of Narborough* (2 witnesses)

An encyclopedic treatise similar in scope and often in content to Henry Daniel's *Liber Uricrisiarum,* but incomplete in both extant copies (one of which appears to be a deliberate excerpt). The author or compiler's identity is indicated by several "quod Narborough/Norborough" explicits

---

is no good reason for connecting him to any of the other John Ardernes found in contemporary documents, nor for linking him to any particular family of Ardernes" (*Oxford Dictionary of National Biography*, s.n. "John Arderne" [Oxford, 2004], http://www.oxforddnb.com/view/article/636).

[90] Relations between the two versions of the commentary have been discussed by Tavormina, "A Newly-Identified Copy of John Arderon's *De Judiciis Urinarum*," paper presented at the Annual Meeting of the Early Book Society, Salford, UK, July 2007. Javier Calle Martín has completed an edition of the Hunterian copy of the text, *The Middle English Version of Gilles of Corbeil's Treatise on Urines*, forthcoming from Liverpool University Press.

and captions in the Yale manuscript (fols. 11ʳ, 25ᵛ, 57ʳ, 59ᵛ); Narborough is a town about six miles southwest of Leicester. Several s. xvii¹ᐟ⁴ notes by Henry Fowler in Gloucester Cathedral Library 19 (a copy of the *Liber Uricrisiarum*) cite "Friar Narburg(h)," OFM, as a source for information on particular urinary colors (2ᵛ, 26ᵛ, 37ᵛ, 57ʳ, etc.), dating him to 1464 (37ʳ); the information cited often corresponds closely to discussion of those colors in the *Book of Narborough*.

Books 1 through 3 of the treatise deal with general medical information, colors, and contents respectively, parallel but not identical to the *Liber Uricrisiarum*. After book 3, the same scribe inserts an index to the preceding books, uroscopic and astromedical tables, and finally a fourth book devoted to "all sycknesses of mans body gevynge medycines competent, & most expert of auctours" (66ʳ).

MANUSCRIPT WITNESSES

Yale 45, 2ʳ–94ᵛ (acephalous and atelous; the text begins on p. 108 of a contemporary pagination, in book 1, chap. 3; it breaks off incomplete in book 4, chap. 10, with new acephalous material in another hand on fol. 95ʳ. Between books 3 and 4, fols. 57ᵛ–65ᵛ contain an index to the preceding material and several astromedical, humoral, and uroscopic tables and diagrams.) [eVK2 0334.00, 0762.00, 6883.00]

JTSA 2611, 1ʳ–4ʳ (excerpt: book 1, chap. 6, on critical days) [eVK2 6705.00]

23.0 Maurus of Salerno ("Magister Moras"), *Liber Urinarum* (also as *The Water[s] of Magister Moras*) (2 witnesses)[91]

An atelous, abridged translation of Maurus's *Liber urinarum* (eTK 0394A, 0394C, 1271I, 1272A; also known as *Regule urinarum, De urinis, Urine Mauri*, etc.). Begins by paraphrasing and citing Theophilus's and Isaac's definitions of urine, and proceeds with a series of summary paragraphs about the "issues" (excreta) of the body, complexions, qualities, humors, substance, and colors (counted as nineteen); the list of colors is followed by more detailed discussions of diseases and urines associated with the various kinds of phlegm (natural, sweet, acetous, sour, glassy) and medicines and dietary recommendations for the cure of the ailments. For the

---

[91] The most recent work on Maurus of Salerno, with further bibliography, is Moulinier's "La science des urines de Maurus de Salerne" (n. 49 above). The *Liber urinarum / Regule urinarum* is edited in De Renzi, *Collectio Salernitana* (n. 3 above), 3:2–51.

attention to types of phlegm as a classifying element, see items 8.4 above and 25.0 below.[92]

MANUSCRIPT WITNESSES

Rawl A.393, 100ʳ–102ᵛ (incomplete, breaking off in
mid-sentence in the section on salt phlegm;[93] a significantly
fuller and better written copy than BL Add 4698; author
identified as "Magister moras")   [eVK2 2306.00, 7756.00]
BL Add 4698, 3ʳ, 4ʳ (incomplete, ending near the beginning
of the section on phlegmatic urines; identifies the author
as "magister mores"; interrupted on fol. 3ᵛ by a Latin-English
herbal synonymy and a recipe)   [eVK2 7118.00]

24.0 Henry of Winchester, *Liber de Urinis* (1 witness)[94]

A learned treatise organized loosely around five (or, with taste and odor, seven) primary and thirteen secondary factors to consider in examining urines, including many individual uroscopic signs and some remedies for particular illnesses. Translated, with omissions and possibly additions, from Henry of Winchester's *De cognitione egritudinum per urinam et de cura earum* (as the text is rubricated in the sole copy recorded by Thorndike-Kibre, eTK 0222J, in GC 117/186).[95] Henry is also named as the author in the explicits of both the English and Latin versions: "Iam

---

[92] Discussion of phlegmatic and choleric humors, often in connection with the diagnosis and humoral etiology of fevers, is not uncommon in learned urine treatises, such as Richard of England's *De urinis* and Walter Agilon's *Summa medicinalis*. See also Moulinier, "La science des urines," 269–71.

[93] De Renzi, *Collectio Salernitana,* 3:14; for the end of the text in BL Additional 4698, see idem, 3:9, in the section on natural phlegm.

[94] MPME 87; MPME/S 261; DB 279; DB/S1 119–20. For more on Henry of Winchester and his work, see McVaugh, "An Early Discussion of Medicinal Degrees at Montpellier by Henry of Winchester," *Bulletin of the History of Medicine* 49 (1975): 57–71, and Voigts and McVaugh, *Phlebotomy,* 7, 36–52 (even pages) (n. 19 above).

[95] The reference in eTK to a "De urinis" in GC 117/186, pp. 221–223ᵛ, attributed to Henry of Winchester (eTK 0075J), should be corrected: the pages should be "pp. 221–223" and Henry is not the author. Rather, the "De urinis" on pp. 221–223 is made up of a list of twenty colors and and other parts of the *kurze Harntraktat* (e.g., "Sciendum est quod duarum rerum..."; *Urina rufa* signs) plus verses from the *Flos medicine* on moderation. Henry's actual work is on pp. 223–232. GC 117/186 is one of the manuscripts annotated and possibly owned by Roger Marchall, as noted by Voigts, "A Doctor and His Books: The Manuscripts of Roger Marchall (d. 1477)," in *New Science Out of Old Books: Studies in Manuscripts and Early Printed Books in Honour of A. I. Doyle,* ed. Richard Beadle and A. J. Piper (Aldershot, 1995), 249–314, at 271.

explicit de vrinis secundum Magistrum henricum montis pessilani' &c."
and "Et hec de urinis iuxta magistrum henricum sufficiant."

MANUSCRIPT WITNESS
Cosin V.IV.7, 11ʳ–31ʳ (missing leaf between fols. 26
and 27)   [eVK2 2781.00, *6651.00]

25.0 Richard of England, *De Urinis* (1 witness)[96]
A learned and relatively sophisticated treatise, translated freely from
Richard of England's *Regule de urinis* [eTK 0223A, 0223B, ?1100J, 1205G,
1247I, 1247J], the second text in his five-work compendium of medical
knowledge, the *Micrologus*. Titled "Judgment of Urines" in the unique
English witness, it begins with five general considerations for judging
urines (color, substance, quantity, contents, and equality) followed by
eight special considerations (age, complexion, sex, habit, time of the year
and of the illness, diet, region in the flask, and custom of the patient).
From this opening, the author turns to the four humors, subtypes of the
humors, and the kinds of fevers caused by different mixtures of humors
as revealed by the urine. The end of the surviving text addresses the four
regions of the flask but breaks off directly after introducing "aerea [*illeg.*]
vndir the serkill" as the second region.

MANUSCRIPT WITNESS
Douce 84, 25ʳ–32ᵛ (atelous)   [eVK2 7786.00]

26.0 Texts Derived from the Hippocratic *Prognostics*[97]
26.1 *Prognostics* with Anonymous Commentary (1 witness)
An ambitious but clumsy, unfinished translation of an as yet unidentified commentary on the *Prognostics*, including the Hippocratic text itself
and incorporating comments of Galen, Bartholomew of Salerno, Bernard
de Gordon, "the Cardynal" (probably Cardinalis of Montpellier, fl. ca.
1240), Richard of England, and Sernando de Pyonia. Extends to book 2,
chap. 45 of the medieval Latin text of the *Prognostics*; uroscopic material
is found *passim*, but is concentrated especially in book 2, chaps. 26–37.[98]

---

[96] MPME 270–72; MPME/S 274; DB 694–99; DB/S1 256–57.

[97] On the medieval Latin translations of and commentaries on the *Prognostics*,
see Pearl Kibre, *Hippocrates Latinus,* rev. ed. (New York, 1985), 199–221.

[98] Partial ed. by Tavormina, "Commentary on the Hippocratic *Prognostics*,
Part 1," in *Sex, Aging, and Death in a Medieval Medical Compendium* (n. 37 above),
373–454.

MANUSCRIPT WITNESS

TCC R.14.52, 62ʳ–104ʳ   [eVK2 3172.00, 0841.00, 0810.00]

26.2 "When the Sick Sleep by Day" (1 witness)

A series of prognostic tokens clearly adapted from but not completely identical to the signs treated in the Hippocratic *Prognostics*: sleep, feces, urine, vomit, sweat, nosebleed, quinsy, pain in the sides and breast, sputum, dropsy, but not the Hippocratic *facies*; concludes with several outcomes, mostly of recovery, for acute fevers; includes short explanatory comments on the reasons that particular signs are good or bad. Not the same text nor in the same order as that embedded in the *Prognostics* Commentary above, but possibly a translation of some brief Latin text derived from the *Prognostics*.

MANUSCRIPT WITNESS

Ashmole 1397, II, pp. 40–43   [eVK2 8054.00]

27.0 Valasco de Tharanta (Valescus of Tarenta), *Of Sharp Fevers after the* **Practice** *of Valassus* (1 witness)[99]

A translation of material from Valasco's *Practica*, book 7, chap. 6, "De acuta febre" (s. xivᵉˣ–xvⁱⁿ), probably translated from the Lyon 1490 or 1500 edition. Valasco includes uroscopic signs among his "Indicia" of acute fever, which are taken over in the Middle English text along with the numbering system in the printed editions. Followed on fols. 61ᵛ–62ᵛ and pp. 63–65 by material on ephemeral fever from chap. 5 of an as yet unidentified source (the English text does not seem to match Valasco's chapter 5 on ephemeral fever in either the 1490 or 1500 edition).

MANUSCRIPT WITNESS

Ashmole 1405, pp. 99–122, fols. 46ʳ–61ᵛ (pages misbound)   [eVK2 *0687.00]

28.0 *The Declaration of Urines after Isaac and Constantine* (1 witness)

A treatise on colors, humors, and diseases associated with particular colors of urine and several kinds of phlegm, described in its prologue as a "declaracioun of the same [i.e., of urines, the subject of the preceding text] . . . þat scheweth þe kynde & þe accidentes and þe cause of þe maledie and queche humor he is gendered" (p. 45). Possibly incomplete, if sections on diseases associated with the other three humors were part of the author's original intent. The attribution to Isaac and Constantine is probably a generic invocation of uroscopic and medical authority, with a

---

[99] DB 772; DB/S1 276.

broad reference to Isaac Israeli's *De urinis* in its translation by Constantine the African, rather than a citation of specific sources.

MANUSCRIPT WITNESS

GC 451/392, pp. 45–47 [eVK2 2242.00, 7132.00]

29.0 *Book of Egidij* (1 witness)

A mixed-language assortment of short uroscopic texts on several topics: a color-list in Latin and English (with nineteen colors and an acknowledgment that authors disagree on the number); white and green urines; women's urines (Latin); a slightly abridged version of **ST** from the *Letter of Ipocras* (4.1.3c above); an English token list mainly focused on women's urines, including signs also found in the *Urine White and Brown* texts (5.2.1 above); urines of pregnancy (7.2.7 above); and the distinctions between male, female, and animal urines (7.3.2 above). The Latin portion of the text is very similar to a Latin uroscopy in Sloane 1571 (fol. 11^{r-v}), attributed in its colophon to Master Galfridus Mydylton, Doctor. The identification of the work in its opening lines as the "boke of egidij þat sum tyme was a doctor of fesycke" may be a generic reference to Giles of Corbeil, though the text does not follow Giles's "bis deni" count of the colors of urines.

MANUSCRIPT WITNESS

Sloane 357, 23^r–28^r [eVK2 2225.00, 7828.00]

30.0 Kylinghale-Bokynham Compendium (1 witness)[100]

One manuscript associates a collection of uroscopies with two named Englishmen, though most texts included in that compilation are well attested elsewhere without attribution or association. The associations appear on fols. 1^v ("colores vrinarum quibus magister Willelmus Kylinghale doctor phisice vsus fuit tempore suo"), 4^r ("colores vrinarum per

---

[100] MPME 405, 386; ?MPME/S 282 (an entry for William of Kylingholme, scribe or owner of portions of York Minster Library XVI.E.32, but apparently identifying or associating him with the William Kylinghale entry on MPME 405, which refers to the name in Wellcome 408; however, Kylingholme and Kylinghale appear to be different places, possibly modern Killingholme, on the south side of the Humber estuary, in north Lincolnshire, and modern Killinghall, in the West Riding of Yorkshire.) Given the scribe's East Anglian *xal(t), xuln,* and *xulde* forms, it seems likely that the immediate provenance of the manuscript is closer to William Bokynham's monastic home in Norwich; Bokynham's own name may reflect family origins in the town now called Old Buckenham, Norfolk, the probable birthplace of the poet Osbern Bokenham.

Willelmum bokynham de bononia doctorem phisice ac [for ad?] cardi-
nalem Romane ecclesie"), 7ʳ ("tractatus de vrinis . compilatus per Willelmum Bokynham ecclesie Cath. Sancte trinitatis Norwici monachum"),
and 13ʳ ("tractatus de urinis compilatus per Willelmum Bokynham
Monachum . Testante R. G.").

    Texts in these collections include items 7.5.8 (*Colores Urinarum* asso-
ciated with Kylinghale); 3.2.1b, 3.3.1c, and 8.4 (*Urina Rufa* [attributed to
Bokynham as compiler under the title *Colores Urinarum*], *Cleansing of
Blood,* and *Substances, Colors, and Phlegms*); and the *Tractatus de Urinis*
attributed to Bokynham as compiler, containing items 9.3 (a Four-Region
List), 7.3.4 (a Man-Woman-Beast text), and sections on other topics, such
as four things to consider in judging urines; substance and relative opacity; uroscopic tokens running from white to black and green urines; and
differences between hypostasis, humor, and rottenness (pus). Although
the *Tractatus* is similar to other texts dealing with regions, colors, contents, and so on, some of the color and content terms and comparisons
are unusual or unique: Karapos "like bark of ginger," "faw" instead of
Glaucus, "fuske like brown green" as an extra color, Granules "like small
heads of saddlers' tackets," a suspension "like cotton that is carded" as
a sign of pregnancy, uroscopic signs of embryological stages, and so on.

MANUSCRIPT WITNESS
    Wellcome 408, 1ᵛ–3ʳ or 4ʳ (Kylinghale); 4ʳ–13ʳ
    (Bokynham)   [eVK2 7826.00, 7751.00, 2779.00]

Appendix A

Selected Non-Uroscopic Texts Frequently Associated with Individual Uroscopies

ALTHOUGH THE FOUR texts listed below do not contain any explicit uroscopic content, they frequently occur together with specific uroscopic texts, and are tied to those texts by shared concerns with diagnosis or prognosis, remedies, and/or astronomical and meteorological influences on health. They will be included in the Index of Manuscripts in Appendix B.

A.1 *Tokens of Ipocras*

A prognostic text listing non-uroscopic signs of death, drawn from the Hippocratic tradition, beginning with "dolor or aching in the head" and "swelling in the face." In the four asterisked witnesses below, it follows directly or very shortly after *The Knowing of Twenty Colors of Urines* (item 6.4 above); the two texts together may have been seen as a natural diagnostic/prognostic unit by some scribes.

*Digby 29, 74^v–75^v (mixed Latin/English)	[eVK2 –]
*CUL Dd.6.29, 30^r–32^v	[eVK2 2305.00, 1630.00]
*MagdO 221, 75^r–79^r	[eVK2 2260.00, 8123.00]
*Sloane 1388, 42^r–43^r	[eVK2 8126.00]
Huntington HM 64, 50^r–51^r (following a version of *Urina Rufa*)	[eVK2 8139.00]
GUL Hunter 513, 103^r–105^v (following several astromedical texts)	[eVK2 3107.00]

Sloane 405, 123^r–125^r (in a manuscript containing a rather mixed bag
of medical texts on ophthalmology, surgery, plague, recipes, Latin
Urina Rufa and *Urina Est Colamentum Sanguinis*, etc.)   [eVK2 8124.00]

A.2 *Dieta Ipocras*

An overview of correspondences between the seasons, elements, complexions, and qualities, with recommended food, drink, spices, and
other aspects of regimen for each season. Followed directly by *Four Parts
Where the Sicknesses of the Body Begin* in the first four witnesses below;
preceded directly by the *Letter of Ipocras* "treasure" prologue and **MBB**
(item 4.1.2b above) in the first three witnesses below and by the *Four
Parts* text in Harley 5401.

Sloane 706, 95^r–96^r	[eVK2 –]
Jesus 43 (Q.D.1), 127^r–128^r	[eVK2 –]
TCC R.14.32, 81^r–82^r	[eVK2 –]
Bodl Add C.246, 44^v–46^r	[eVK2 7167.00]
Harl 5401, 86^r–87^r	[eVK2 6823.00]

A.3 *Four Parts Where the Sicknesses of the Body Begin*

A discussion of non-uroscopic symptoms for ailments in the head, breast,
abdomen, and bladder, with recommended medicines for those maladies.
Follows directly on *Dieta Ipocras* in the first four witnesses, and occurs
close to the *Letter of Ipocras*, "Urine Troubly with Clouds," or a complete
or partial Vade Mecum suite (items 4.1, 7.1.2, and 3.0) in the witnesses I
have seen. In manuscripts where the *Letter of Ipocras* accompanies the
Four Parts text, the *Letter* has a prose prologue (either the "Treasure"
prologue or a unique prologue) and does not include the Six-Token series;
see items 4.1.2b and 4.1.2c above.

Sloane 706, 96^v–97^r (*Dieta Ipocras* and *Four Parts* follow the *Letter
of Ipocras*)   [eVK2 7273.00]
Jesus 43 (Q.D.1), 128^r–129^r (*Dieta Ipocras* and *Four Parts* follow the
Letter of Ipocras)   [eVK2 7274.00]
TCC R.14.32, 82^v–83^r (*Dieta Ipocras* and *Four Parts* follow the
Letter of Ipocras)   [eVK2 7272.00]
Bodl Add C.246, 46^r–47^r (*Dieta Ipocras* and *Four Parts* precede
Cleansing of Blood and *Urine White and Red*)   [eVK2 7269.00[1]]
Lansdowne 388, 370^v–372^r (interspersed with the
Letter of Ipocras)   [eVK2 2145.00, 8226.00]
Sloane 1388, 51^v–52^r (precedes "Urine Troubly with Clouds")   [eVK2 –]

---

[1]   The eVK2 reading "three parts" should be corrected to "four parts."

Harl 5401, 85ᵛ–86ʳ (precedes *Dieta Ipocras* and "Urine
Troubly with Clouds")   [eVK2 7938.00]
CUL Dd.10.44, 132ʳ–133ʳ (precedes "Urine Troubly with Clouds,"
with brief intervening material; several other uroscopy texts
appear on nearby leaves, including the *Letter of Ipocras*)   [eVK2 2311.00]
Pepys 878, pp. 178–181 (precedes an abridged Vade Mecum
suite)   [eVK2 2150.00]
GC 457/395, 61ᵛ–62ʳ (follows an incomplete *Twenty Jordans*
and the Vade Mecum suite; possibly a different text with similar
structure and content)   [eVK2 *6626.00]

A.4 *Governance of Signs*

On the influence of the zodiacal signs on health. Directly follows the
Abbreviated Version of the *Dome of Uryne* (item 2.3) in the first four witnesses below, and directly precedes an abbreviated version of the *Four
Elements* (item 8.2) in all six witnesses. Of the five manuscript witnesses
to the Abbreviated *Dome of Uryne*, only Pepys 1307 lacks the *Governance
of Signs* and the abbreviated *Four Elements*.

TCC O.8.35, 57ʳ–59ʳ   [eVK2 3137.00]
Bodl Add B.60, 57ʳ–59ʳ   [eVK2 3137.00, 0876.00]
Lambeth 444, 158ᵛ–159ʳ   [eVK2 *3137.00]
Sloane 297, 115ʳ–116ᵛ   [eVK2 *3137.00]
Sloane 100, 36ʳ–37ᵛ   [eVK2 3137.00]
TCC O.7.2A, 1ʳ–8ʳ   [eVK2 3213.00]

Appendix B

Index of Manuscripts Containing Middle English Uroscopies

THE FOLLOWING LIST includes all manuscripts known to me to contain Middle English uroscopies or the works listed in Appendix A, arranged alphabetically by city, library, and collection. For future editorial convenience, I have assigned each collection listed here a one-or two-letter sigil, depending on how many manuscripts with English uroscopic material are in the collection, except for the Bodleian Additional manuscripts, which are indicated by the letters "Add," in distinction from the British Library Additional manuscripts, signified by "Ad." For manuscripts within a given collection, the alphabetic part of the sigil is followed by arabic numerals that increase with the alphanumeric order of the shelfmarks, unless there is only one manuscript with Middle English uroscopic material in the collection, in which case no numeral is attached.

Texts classified above as belonging to the *Dome of Uryne* compendium (2.1–2.5a,b), the *Book of Egidij* (29.0), the Kylinghale-Bokynham compendium (30.0), or one of the compendia in section 14.1 are enclosed by parentheses following the item number for the particular compendium in question.

The vast majority of the manuscripts indexed below or the uroscopy texts they contain can be dated to the fifteenth century, with a handful from the fourteenth (mainly but not exclusively toward the end of the century) and a few more from the sixteenth. Dates provided here are based on a variety of reference sources, including the volumes of the *Index of Middle English Prose*, the catalogues of *Dated and Datable Manuscripts* in Oxford, London, and Cambridge by Andrew Watson and Pamela Robinson, George Keiser's volume in the *Manual of Writings in Middle English*, N. R. Ker's *Medieval Manuscripts in British Libraries*, the *Linguistic Atlas of Late Mediaeval English*, eVK2, and pertinent printed and online manuscript catalogues and other scholarly descriptions.[1] Although some manuscripts can be dated relatively precisely, the estimates for the majority are approximate at best and not always agreed on by these reference sources. In cases of disagreement, I have sought to make the best choice among alternatives. Where manuscripts contain hands or booklets of different dates, I have focused on the date(s) for the parts that include uroscopic texts, which may or may not match other parts of the manuscript. Similarly, dialect identifications apply to folios containing uroscopic texts, not necessarily the entire manuscript; they derive primarily from *The Linguistic Atlas*, occasionally from library catalogue descriptions and volumes in the *Index of Middle English Prose*, supplemented by other linguistic analyses where available. The phrase "Some [REGIONAL] features" is intended to suggest possible starting points for dialect analysis based on limited selections of forms (e.g., *xal-/xul-* for *shall/should*, *qw(h)-* for *wh-*, *mon* for *man*, *os* for *as*, etc.). More detailed examination of individual manuscripts will allow further refinement of these identifications and datings.

---

[1] Pamela Robinson, *Catalogue of Dated and Datable Manuscripts c. 737–1600 in Cambridge Libraries* (Cambridge, 1988); eadem, *Catalogue of Dated and Datable Manuscripts c. 888–1600 in London Libraries* (London, 2003); Andrew G. Watson, *Catalogue of Dated and Datable Manuscripts c. 700–1600 in the Department of Manuscripts, The British Library* (London, 1979); idem, *Catalogue of Dated and Datable Manuscripts c. 435–1600 in Oxford Libraries* (Oxford, 1984); N. R. Ker, *Medieval Manuscripts in British Libraries*, 5 vols. (Oxford, 1969–2002); Angus McIntosh, M. L. Samuels, and Michael Benskin, *A Linguistic Atlas of Late Mediaeval English*, 4 vols. (Aberdeen, 1985). For Keiser and eVK2, see nn. 1 and 2 on p. 2 above.

City, Library, Shelfmark	Sigil	Date	Dialect (when available)	Uroscopies Contained, by Taxonomy Item Number
Aberystwyth, National Library of Wales, MS Peniarth 388C	Nw1	s. xv^{med}	E Anglian	4.2.2
Aberystwyth, National Library of Wales, MS Sotheby C.2	Nw2	s. xvi$^{1/4}$–s. xvi^{med}	Some W Midland features	2.5a (5.1b, 7.1.1, 7.2.1, 7.2.2, 7.3.1, 9.1, 10.1, 11.1), 5.2.2, 1.1.1
Bethesda, National Library of Medicine, MS 4	Nm1	s. xiv^{ex}–s. xv$^{1/4}$		12.2, 6.2a, 3.3.2a
Bethesda, National Library of Medicine, MS 30	Nm2	s. xv		6.2c, 3.3.2a, 1.1.1, 7.5.6, 3.2.3, 5.2.1, 4.1.3c
Bethesda, National Library of Medicine, MS 49	Nm3	1586		2.4 (1.5, 5.1e, 7.1.1, 7.2.1, 7.2.2, 7.3.1, 8.1, 9.1, 10.1, 11.1), 6.3
Boston, Harvard University, Countway Library of Medicine, MS Ballard 19	Hv	s. xv (ante 1468)		1.2, 11.2
Boston, Massachusetts Historical Society, MS P-362 (olim 10.10)	Mh	s. xv$^{1/4}$		15.1
Brussels, Bibliothèque Royale, MS IV.249 (now in private hands)	Br	NOT SEEN		15.2
Cambridge, Corpus Christi College, MS 388	Cc	ca. 1320–30	Ely/West Norfolk	5.2.1
Cambridge, Emmanuel College, MS 69	Em	s. xv$^{1/4}$		14.2.5
Cambridge, Gonville and Caius College, MS 84/166	Gc1	s. xv^{med}	Derbys, probably Notts.	5.2.2 (2x), 9.2, 3.2.1b (2x), 3.3.1c (2x)
Cambridge, Gonville and Caius College, MS 176/97	Gc2	s. xv$^{1/2}$	Mixture of E Midland and Southern forms	17.0, 15.3

MS	Siglum	Date	Features	References
Cambridge, Gonville and Caius College, MS 180/213	Gc3	s. xv	Some northerly features	15.1
Cambridge, Gonville and Caius College, MS 336/725	Gc4	s. xv^{med} and s. xv$^{4/4}$		8.2.2c, 6.2a, 3.3.2a, 11.4, 3.3.1b, 3.2.1c, 3.1.2a, 15.3, 1.4, 7.3.3, 14.2.3a, 7.2.4, 11.2, 1.2
Cambridge, Gonville and Caius College, MS 376/596	Gc5	s. xv	Cambs.	15.1
Cambridge, Gonville and Caius College, MS 451/392	Gc6	s. xv	Cambs./Norfolk/ Suffolk border	6.3, 16.4, 28.0, 1.1.1
Cambridge, Gonville and Caius College, MS 457/395	Gc7	s. xv	Some E Anglian features	1.5, 3.1.1a, 3.2.1a, 3.3.1a, A.3
Cambridge, Gonville and Caius College, MS 609/340	Gc8	s. xv		8.5
Cambridge, Jesus College, MS 43 (Q.D.1)	Je	s. xv	Some E Anglian features	6.2b, 3.3.2a, 4.1.2b, A.2, A.3
Cambridge, Magdalene College, MS Pepys 878	Pe1	s. xv$^{1/2}$	Some E Anglian features	12.1, A.3, 3.2.1a, 3.3.1a, 1.1.2
Cambridge, Magdalene College, MS Pepys 1307	Pe2	s. xv$^{2/4}$	Norfolk	2.3 (5.1c, 7.1.1, 7.2.1, 7.2.2, 7.3.1, 9.1, 10.1, 11.1), 6.5
Cambridge, Magdalene College, MS Pepys 1661	Pe3	s. xv$^{1/2}$		3.2.1b, 3.3.1c, 8.4, 3.1.1c, 15.4
Cambridge, St. John's College, MS B.15	Sj1	s. xv	Norfolk, E Anglia	4.1.1b
Cambridge, St. John's College, MS B.16	Sj2	s. xvi$^{1/4}$		15.1, 20.0
Cambridge, St. John's College, MS K.49	Sj3	s. xv		2.2 (5.1b, 6.1, 7.1.1, 7.2.1, 7.2.2, 7.3.1, 9.1, 10.1, 11.1), 8.6

Cambridge, Trinity College, MS O.1.13	T1	s. XV		1.5
Cambridge, Trinity College, MS O.1.65	T2	s. XV	Some northerly features	1.1.1, 3.3.3
Cambridge, Trinity College, MS O.1.77	T3	1460		11.2, 1.2
Cambridge, Trinity College, MS O.5.26	T4	s. xiv^{ex}–s. xv^{in}		19.0
Cambridge, Trinity College, MS O.5.32, II	T5	s. xiv		4.1.2c
Cambridge, Trinity College, MS O.7.2A	T6	s. XV		A.4, 8.2.2a
Cambridge, Trinity College, MS O.7.20, II	T7	s. xv^{ex}		8.6, 3.1.1c, 3.2.3, 3.3.3, 2.5b (5.1c)
Cambridge, Trinity College, MS O.8.35	T8	s. xv$^{4/4}$		2.3 (5.1b, 7.1.1, 7.2.1, 7.2.2, 7.3.1, 9.1, 10.1, 11.1), A.4, 8.2.2a
Cambridge, Trinity College, MS O.9.37	T9	s. XV		18.0
Cambridge, Trinity College, MS O.10.21	T10	s. XV	Oxon.	15.1
Cambridge, Trinity College, MS R.14.32	T11	s. XV	Essex	3.3.1a, 3.1.1b, 3.2.1a, 1.1.2a, 16.1, 4.1.2b, A.2, A.3
Cambridge, Trinity College, MS R.14.39, II	T12	s. XV		4.2.2, 10.2
Cambridge, Trinity College, MS R.14.39, III	T13	s. xvi		14.1.5 (3.1.1c, 8.3, 16.5, 4.1.3c, 3.3.3, 8.6, 7.4, 5.2.1, 3.2.3, 6.6, 2.5b [7.1.1], etc.)
Cambridge, Trinity College, MS R.14.51	T14	s. XV		5.2.1, 4.1.3c, 7.1.2
Cambridge, Trinity College, MS R.14.52	T15	s. xv$^{3/4}$	NW Essex or SW Suffolk	7.5.14, 26.1, 17.0, 15.3, 6.2c, 3.3.2a, 11.2, 1.3, 4.1.3c

Manuscript	Siglum	Date	Region	References
Cambridge, University Library, MS Dd.5.76	Cu1	s. xv		2.5a (6.1)
Cambridge, University Library, MS Dd.6.29	Cu2	s. xiv^{ex}–s. xv^{in}	Herefords. (hand of fols. 110^r-124^v)	6.4, A.1, 4.1.3c, 14.1.3, 16.3
Cambridge, University Library, MS Dd.10.44	Cu3	s. xv		4.1.2b, 4.2.2, A.3, 7.1.2, 1.4, 8.6, 2.5a (8.1, 9.1, 10.1), 6.3, 7.2.6, 7.5.4
Cambridge, University Library, MS Ee.1.13	Cu4	s. xv	Suffolk, Norfolk	6.3
Cambridge, University Library, MS Ee.1.15	Cu5	s. xv^{med}		1.5, 3.3.3, 3.1.1b, 3.2.1c
Cambridge, University Library, MS Ff.2.6	Cu6	s. xv		15.1, 7.2.5, 7.4, 5.2.1
Cambridge, University Library, MS Gg.3.29	Cu7	s. xv		15.1
Cambridge, University Library, MS Ii.6.17	Cu8	s. xv^{ex}–s. xvi		16.1, 1.3
Copenhagen, Royal Library, MS n.c. 314	Cn	s. xv^{in}		1.1.2
Dublin, Trinity College, MS 365	Dt	s. xv		8.2.1b
Durham, University Library, MS Cosin V.III.10	Co1	s. xv^{med}		2.1 (5.1, 7.1.1, 7.2.1, 7.2.2, 7.3.1, 8.1, 9.1, 10.1, 11.1), 1.1.1, 4.3
Durham, University Library, MS Cosin V.IV.7	Co2	s. xv^{med}	Norfolk	24.0, 1.1.1
Durham, University Library, MS Cosin V.V.13	Co3	s. xv^{ex}		2.1 (6.1, 7.1.1, 7.2.2, 7.3.1, 8.1, 10.1, 11.1), 6.3
Exeter, Cathedral Library, MS 3521	Ex	s. xv$^{3/4}$		4.1.2c
Glasgow, University Library, MS Ferguson 147	Gw1	s. xv^{in}		4.1.1b
Glasgow, University Library, MS Hunter 307	Gw2	s. xv$^{1/2}$		8.2.1a
Glasgow, University Library, MS Hunter 328	Gw3	s. xv$^{4/4}$		21.0, 1.5, 2.5a (7.1.1), 7.1.2

Shelfmark	Siglum	Date	Provenance	References
Glasgow, University Library, MS Hunter 329	Gw4	s. xv		7.2.7, 7.5.13
Glasgow, University Library, MS Hunter 509	Gw5	ca. 1460	E Anglian	8.2.1a
Glasgow, University Library, MS Hunter 513	Gw6	s. xv^{med}		A.1
Gloucester, Cathedral Library, MS 19 (*olim* 19 and 23)	Go	s. xv^{med}		15.1
London, British Library, MS Additional 4698	Ad1	s. xv^{ex}–s. xvi^{in}	Herefords.	23.0, 12.1, 3.2.1a, 3.3.2b, 1.1.2, 4.2.1, 4.1.3a
London, British Library, MS Additional 4898	Ad2	s. xv	E Anglian	11.3, 7.4, 5.2.1
London, British Library, MS Additional 5467	Ad3	s. xv$^{3/4}$		4.1.3c
London, British Library, MS Additional 10440	Ad4	s. xv		2.2 (5.1a, 6.1, 7.1.1, 7.2.1, 7.2.2, 7.3.1, 8.1, 9.1, 10.1, 11.1)
London, British Library, MS Additional 18216	Ad5	s. xv	Kent	13.3
London, British Library, MS Additional 19674	Ad6	ca. 1475		4.1.2a, 6.2e
London, British Library, MS Additional 30338	Ad7	s. xv		2.2 (5.1b, 6.1, 7.1.1, 7.2.1, 7.2.2, 7.3.1, 8.1, 9.1, 10.1, 11.1)
London, British Library, MS Additional 34111	Ad8	s. xv		4.1.3a
London, British Library, MS Arundel 42	Ar	s. xv		5.2.1, 7.5.1
London, British Library, MS Egerton 827	Eg1	s. xiv		4.1.3c
London, British Library, MS Egerton 1624	Eg2	s. xv^{med}	Ely, Northern Middle English	15.1, 15.4
London, British Library, MS Egerton 2433	Eg3	s. xv$^{4/4}$		1.1.1, 5.2.2, 3.1.1c

London, British Library, MS Harley 218	H1	s. xv^{ex}–s. xvi^{in}		6.3, 2.5a (6.1)
London, British Library, MS Harley 1010	H2	s. xiv$^{2/2}$		3.1.1c, 8.3, 16.5
London, British Library, MS Harley 1602	H3	s. xv	Some northerly features	7.1.2
London, British Library, MS Harley 1612	H4	s. xv$^{1/4}$	Some northerly features	6.3
London, British Library, MS Harley 1735	H5	s. xv^{med}, s. xv$^{3/4}$	Norfolk, Suffolk	6.3, 2.5b (6.1)
London, British Library, MS Harley 2274	H6	s. xv		2.1 (6.1, 7.1.1, 9.1, 10.1)
London, British Library, MS Harley 2375	H7	s. xv	E Anglian	3.3.3, 6.3, 14.2.3b, 11.3, 3.2.1c, 1.1.1
London, British Library, MS Harley 2390	H8	s. xv	Norfolk	3.1.1c
London, British Library, MS Harley 2558	H9	s. xv		2.5a (5.1c, 7.1.1, 7.2.1, 7.3.1, 11.1)
London, British Library, MS Harley 3383	H10	ca. 1475		7.5.10, 1.1.2, 3.1.1a, 3.2.1a, 3.3.1a, 4.1.1b, 7.2.7
London, British Library, MS Harley 3407	H11	s. xv		2.2 (5.1d, 6.1, 7.1.1, 7.2.2, 7.3.1, 9.1, 10.1, 11.1)
London, British Library, MS Harley 3810	H12	s. xv		16.1, 2.5a (6.1, 10.1)
London, British Library, MS Harley 5401	H13	s. xv$^{2/2}$	NW Lincs. (hand of fols. 84^r–91^v)	A.3, A.2, 7.1.2, 2.5a (6.1, 10.1)
London, British Library, MS Lansdowne 388	Ln	s. xv		4.1.2c, A.3
London, British Library, MS Royal 12 G.iv	Ro1	s. xv	Warwicks.	5.2.1 (3x)
London, British Library, MS Royal 17 A.iii	Ro2	s. xiv		5.2.1, 4.1.3c

Shelfmark	Siglum	Date	Dialect	References
London, British Library, MS Royal 17 C.xv	Ro3	s. xv		2.5a (7.2.1, 7.3.1, 9.3, 10.1), 1.1.2, 5.1d, 4.2.2, 6.2e
London, British Library, MS Royal 17 C.xxiv	Ro4	s. xvi		12.3, 2.5b (7.1.1)
London, British Library, MS Royal 17 D.i	Ro5	ca. 1400		15.2
London, British Library, MS Royal 18 A.vi	Ro6	s. xv		6.2b, 2.5a (6.1, 7.1.1, 10.1), 3.1.2b, 3.3.2b
London, British Library, MS Sloane 5	S1	s. xv^{med}	Herefords.	18.0, 15.4, 6.3, 3.2.3 (2x), 3.3.3, 14.2.3c, 5.2.1, 1.1.1
London, British Library, MS Sloane 7	S2	s. xv	S Lincs. mixed with W Midland and more northerly features (Hand B: fols. 30^r–88^v, poss. 105^r–107^v, 108^v, 109^v–111^v)	4.3, 1.1.1, 5.2.2, 9.2
London, British Library, MS Sloane 98	S3	s. xvi		7.5.1
London, British Library, MS Sloane 100	S4	s. xv		A.4, 8.2.2c
London, British Library, MS Sloane 120	S5	ca. 1450	Mix of northerly and Midland features	13.1, 14.2.3c, 3.2.2, 13.2, 1.4
London, British Library, MS Sloane 121	S6	s. xv		3.3.1a, 3.1.1b, 3.2.1a, 1.1.2a, 16.1, 4.2.2, 14.2.4, 8.5
London, British Library, MS Sloane 122	S7	s. xv		14.2.2b
London, British Library, MS Sloane 134	S8	s. xv		15.4
London, British Library, MS Sloane 135	S9	s. xv		3.1.1c

Shelfmark	Siglum	Date	Dialect/Notes	Contents
London, British Library, MS Sloane 213	S10	s. xv	Notts. (Hand A: fols. 91^r–109^v, 111^r–123^r)	6.3
London, British Library, MS Sloane 280	S11	s. xv		20.0
London, British Library, MS Sloane 297	S12	s. xv		1.1.1, 7.3.4, 11.4, 4.3, 6.7, 2.3 (5.1d, 7.1.1, 7.2.1, 7.2.2, 9.1, 10.1), A.4, 8.2.2a
London, British Library, MS Sloane 340	S13	s. xv$^{3/4}$	Suffolk	15.3, 14.2.3a, 7.3.3, 13.4, 3.1.1c, 1.4
London, British Library, MS Sloane 357	S14	s. xv		29.0 (4.1.3c, 5.2.1, 7.2.7, 7.3.2), 1.5, 8.6, 14.2.3c
London, British Library, MS Sloane 374	S15	s. xv$^{2/4}$		2.2 (5.1a, 6.1, 7.1.1, 7.2.1, 7.2.2, 7.3.1, 8.1, 9.1, 10.1, 11.1)
London, British Library, MS Sloane 382	S16	s. xv		2.4 (5.1b, 6.1, 7.1.1, 7.2.1, 7.2.2, 7.3.1, 8.1, 9.1, 10.1, 11.1), 1.5
London, British Library, MS Sloane 405	S17	s. xv		A.1 (also a Latin *Urina Rufa*, Latin *Cleansing*, but no ME uroscopies)
London, British Library, MS Sloane 433	S18	s. xv		4.3, 1.1.1
London, British Library, MS Sloane 540A	S19	s. xv		7.5.2
London, British Library, MS Sloane 635	S20	s. xv		1.5, 9.2, 5.2.2, 3.3.3, 6.3, 14.2.3b
London, British Library, MS Sloane 706	S21	s. xv	Some E Anglian features	3.1.1b, 3.2.1a, 1.1.2a, 16.1, 14.2.4, 4.1.2b, A.2, A.3
London, British Library, MS Sloane 776	S22	1532/3		14.2.5
London, British Library, MS Sloane 783B	S23	s. xv		1.5, 3.2.3
London, British Library, MS Sloane 963	S24	s. xv		1.5, 5.2.1 (2x)

Shelfmark	Siglum	Date	Dialect	References
London, British Library, MS Sloane 1088	S25	s. xv		15.4, 7.5.5
London, British Library, MS Sloane 1100	S26	ca. 1450		15.1
London, British Library, MS Sloane 1101	S27	ca. 1450	Some northerly and some E Anglian features	15.2, 7.4, 11.4
London, British Library, MS Sloane 1317	S28	s. xvi^{med}		7.5.1, 4.1.3c, 5.2.1, 7.3.4
London, British Library, MS Sloane 1388	S29	ca. 1500		1.5, 8.3, 6.4, 5.2.1, A.1, 8.6, 2.4 (1.5, 5.1d, 6.1, 7.1.1, 7.2.1, 7.2.2, 8.1, 10.1), 1.5, 6.8, 2.1 (5.1a, 7.1.1, 7.2.1, 7.2.2, 7.2.3, 7.3.1, 8.1, 9.1, 10.1, 11.1), 4.2.1, 5.2.1, 4.3, A.3, 7.1.2, 6.2b, 3.3.2a, 3.1.2c
London, British Library, MS Sloane 1721	S30	ca. 1475		15.2, 15.4
London, British Library, MS Sloane 2196	S31	s. xv	Some northerly and Midland features	15.4
London, British Library, MS Sloane 2270	S32	1530		6.3
London, British Library, MS Sloane 2320	S33	1454		11.2, 1.2
London, British Library, MS Sloane 2527	S34	s. xv		15.4, 7.3.4, 16.1
London, British Library, MS Sloane 2584	S35	s. xiv		4.1.1a, 3.1.1a, 3.2.1a, 3.3.1a, 5.2.1
London, British Library, MS Sloane 3160	S36	s. xv	Derbys. or Cheshire (hand of fols. 91^r–96^v)	1.5, 3.1.1b, 14.1.2
London, British Library, MS Sloane 3217	S37	s. xv		4.1.2a

Manuscript	Siglum	Date	Origin	Items
London, British Library, MS Sloane 3285	S38	s. xv	Sussex	4.1.1b
London, British Library, MS Sloane 3449	S39	s. xv		8.2.2a
London, British Library, MS Sloane 3466	S40	s. xv		4.2.2
London, British Library, MS Sloane 3486	S41	s. xv^{med}		8.2.1b
London, British Library, MS Sloane 3542	S42	s. xv		3.2.2, 4.2.1
London, British Library, MS Sloane 3566	S43	s. xv		11.2, 1.2
London, Lambeth Palace Library, MS 306	Lm1	s. xv^{ex}–s. xvi^{in}		8.2.2a
London, Lambeth Palace Library, MS 444	Lm2	s. xv^{med}		2.3 (5.1b, 7.1.1, 7.2.1, 7.2.2, 7.3.1, 9.1, 10.1, 11.1), A.4, 8.2.2a
London, Royal College of Physicians, MS 356	Ph1	s. xvi^{in}		15.2
London, Royal College of Physicians, MS 384	Ph2	s. xv^{ex}–s. xvi^{in}		14.2.1b
London, Royal College of Physicians, MS 411	Ph3	s. xv^{ex}–s. xvi^{in}		8.2.3
London, Society of Antiquaries, MS 338	Sa	s. xv$^{1/2}$		8.2.1a
London, Wellcome Library, MS 7	W1	s. xv$^{1/4}$		6.2e, 3.3.2a, 1.5, 2.5a (5.1d, 7.3.1, 11.1)
London, Wellcome Library, MS 225	W2	ca. 1425	Northumberland	15.1
London, Wellcome Library, MS 226	W3	1425–1450	N Central Midlands	15.2
London, Wellcome Library, MS 404	W4	s. xv^{med}		7.5.11, 4.1.3c, 3.1.2c, 3.1.2a
London, Wellcome Library, MS 405	W5	s. xiv	Sussex	4.1.1a

Shelfmark	Siglum	Date	Localisation	Contents
London, Wellcome Library, MS 408	W6	s. xv^{med}, s. xv$^{4/4}$	E. Anglian	30.0 (7.5.8, 3.2.1b, 3.3.1c, 8.4, 3.1.1c, 9.3, 7.3.4, etc.), 14.2.4
London, Wellcome Library, MS 409	W7	s. xiv^{ex}–s. xv^{in}		2.2 (5.1a, 6.1, 7.1.1, 7.2.1, 7.2.2, 7.3.1, 8.1, 9.1, 10.1, 11.1), 4.1.2a
London, Wellcome Library, MS 537	W8	s. xv$^{3/4}$		11.2, 1.1.2, 3.3.1a, 2.5b (5.1b), 3.1.1b, 3.2.1a, 8.2.3
London, Wellcome Library, MS 564	W9	s. xvi^{med}		1.1.1, 14.2.3c, 2.1 (5.1a, 7.1.1, 7.2.1, 7.2.2, 7.3.1, 8.1, 9.1, 10.1, 11.1), 8.6, 4.3
London, Wellcome Library, MS 784	W10	s. xv^{med}		6.2a, 3.3.2a, 12.2
London, Wellcome Library, MS 7117	W11	s. xvi		1.3, 17.0, 15.3, 6.2c
London, Wellcome Library, MS 8004	W12	ca. 1454	Eastern part of England (Notts./ Lincs./ SE Yks./ poss. Norfolk)	1.1.1, 5.2.2, 9.2, 3.2.1b, 3.3.1c
London, Wellcome Library, MS 8515	W13	s. xv		14.2.6
London, Wellcome Library, Medical Society of London MS 136	W14	s. xv^{med}		14.2.6
Manchester, John Rylands Library, MS Eng. 404	Ry1	s. xv$^{2/2}$	Southerly, poss. with Kentish associations	3.3.3, 9.3, 7.3.4
Manchester, John Rylands Library, MS Eng. 1310	Ry2	s. xvi^{in}		21.0, 1.5, 2.5a (7.1.1), 7.1.2
New Haven, Yale Medical School, Cushing-Whitney Library, MS 27	Ya1	s. xv		4.1.1b

Shelfmark	Siglum	Date	Region / Hands	Codes
New Haven, Yale Medical School, Cushing-Whitney Library, MS 45[2]	Ya2	1551		22.0
New York, Columbia University Library, MS Plimpton 254	Cp	s. xv^{med}	SE Midlands	11.3, 7.4, 5.2.1
New York, Jewish Theological Seminary of America, MS 2611	Jt	s. xvi		22.0
New York, Pierpont Morgan Library, MS Bühler 21	Pm	s. xv^{med}	E Anglian, prob. Norwich	2.5a (5.1c, 7.1.1, 7.2.1), 5.2.1
Oxford, All Souls College, MS 81	Oa	s. xv (uroscopy s. xvi^{in}?)		2.5b (10.1)
Oxford, Bodleian Library, MS Additional A.106	Add1	s. xv	Several hands, mainly from diff. parts of Lincs., or mixed with other regional features	4.1.1a, 4.1.3a
Oxford, Bodleian Library, MS Additional B.60	Add2	s. $xv^{4/4}$		2.3 (5.1b, 7.1.1, 7.2.1, 7.2.2, 7.3.1, 9.1, 10.1, 11.1), A.4, 8.2.2a
Oxford, Bodleian Library, MS Additional C.246	Add3	s. xvi^{med}		A.2, A.3, 3.3.3, 4.2.2, 1.1.1
Oxford, Bodleian Library, MS Ashmole 210	A1	s. xvi^{in}		14.2.1a, 19.0
Oxford, Bodleian Library, MS Ashmole 342	A2	s. xv		8.2.2b
Oxford, Bodleian Library, MS Ashmole 1393	A3	s. xv		1.4, 11.4, 7.3.4, 7.2.7, 5.2.1, 1.1.1, 3.2.1a, 3.3.1a
Oxford, Bodleian Library, MS Ashmole 1397, II	A4	s. xiv or s. xv^{in}		26.2
Oxford, Bodleian Library, MS Ashmole 1404	A5	1400–1425		15.1

2 One entry in eVK2 with the subject tag "Urine and uroscopy," Yale Medical School, Cushing-Whitney MS 47, 114^v–116^r, is in fact a list of names and recipes for various flavored wines, and is not included here.

Manuscript	Siglum	Date	Notes	References
Oxford, Bodleian Library, MS Ashmole 1405	A6	s. xvi^{med}		2.2 (1.4, 6.1, 7.1.1, 7.2.1, 7.2.2, 7.3.1, 8.1, 10.1, 11.1), 12.1, 27.0
Oxford, Bodleian Library, MS Ashmole 1413	A7	s. xv		3.1.2a, 6.2e, 1.1.2, 5.2.2, 9.2
Oxford, Bodleian Library, MS Ashmole 1438, I	A8	s. xv		5.2.1, 3.3.1b, 6.2d, 14.2.2a, 7.1.2, 4.2.2
Oxford, Bodleian Library, MS Ashmole 1438, II	A9	s. xv	Multiple hands and dialects: southerly, W Midland, Staffs.	4.2.1, 5.2.1, 4.1.1c, 2.5a (7.1.1, 9.1, 10.1)
Oxford, Bodleian Library, MS Ashmole 1444	A10	s. xv$^{4/4}$, s. xv/xvi		8.2.2a, 6.2d, 3.3.2a
Oxford, Bodleian Library, MS Ashmole 1447	A11	s. xv		1.1.1, 2.1 (5.1c, 6.1, 7.1.1, 7.3.1, 8.1, 9.1, 10.1, 11.1), 7.5.3
Oxford, Bodleian Library, MS Ashmole 1477, II	A12	s. xv		4.1.2a
Oxford, Bodleian Library, MS Ashmole 1477, III	A13	ca. 1475		7.4, 11.3, 5.2.1, 1.5
Oxford, Bodleian Library, MS Ashmole 1477, X	A14	s. xvi		7.5.7, 2.1 (5.1b, 5.1c, 6.1, 7.1.1, 7.2.1, 7.2.2, 7.3.1, 8.1, 9.1, 10.1, 11.1), 5.2.2, 8.6, 14.2.4
Oxford, Bodleian Library, MS Ashmole 1498	A15	s. xv		16.2
Oxford, Bodleian Library, MS Bodley 178	Bo1	s. xv$^{2/2}$		8.2.1a
Oxford, Bodleian Library, MS Bodley 591	Bo2	s. xv		14.1.1 (8.2.3, etc.)
Oxford, Bodleian Library, MS Digby 29	Di1	s. xv$^{1/4\ or\ 1/2}$	Written mainly by Richard Stapilton, Master of Balliol in 1433; ME text added to fols. 125^r–128^v prob. SE Notts.	6.4, A.1, 3.2.2, 2.1 (5.1b, 6.1, 7.1.1, 7.2.1, 7.2.2, 9.1, 10.1), 6.2b, 3.3.2a, 3.1.2b

Shelfmark	Siglum	Date	Dialect	References
Oxford, Bodleian Library, MS Digby 75	Di2	ca. 1458		1.1.2, 3.2.1a, 3.1.1b, 3.3.1b, 11.4, 3.3.3
Oxford, Bodleian Library, MS Digby 95	Di3	s. xv^{ex}		8.2.2a, 2.1 (6.1, 7.1.1, 9.1, 10.1)
Oxford, Bodleian Library, MS Douce 84	Do	s. xv$^{1/4}$	Sussex (Hand A: fols. 1^r–24^r)	4.1.1b, 25.0, 9.3
Oxford, Bodleian Library, MS e Musaeo 116	Mu1	s. xv^{med}		15.1
Oxford, Bodleian Library, MS e Musaeo 187	Mu2	s. xv^{med}		15.1
Oxford, Bodleian Library, MS Hatton 29	Ht	s. xv$^{4/4}$		2.1 (5.1d, 7.1.1, 7.2.1, 7.2.2, 7.2.3, 7.3.1, 8.1, 9.1, 10.1, 11.1), 1.5, 4.2.1, 5.2.1, 4.3
Oxford, Bodleian Library, MS lat. misc. c.66	Lt	s. xv		15.3, 1.1.2
Oxford, Bodleian Library, MS Laud misc. 553	Ld	s. xv	Gloucs.	4.1.1a, 3.1.1a, 3.2.1a, 3.3.1a
Oxford, Bodleian Library, MS Rawlinson A.393	Ra1	ca. 1528	Northern English	23.0
Oxford, Bodleian Library, MS Rawlinson C.81	Ra2	s. xv	Worcs.	6.2c, 2.1 (5.1b, 6.1, 7.1.1, 7.2.1, 7.2.2, 7.3.1, 8.1, 9.1, 10.1, 11.1)
Oxford, Bodleian Library, MS Rawlinson C.299	Ra3	s. xv$^{4/4}$	Mainly Norfolk	1.1.1, 4.2.1
Oxford, Bodleian Library, MS Rawlinson C.506	Ra4	s. xv	Some E Anglian features	2.2 (5.1a, 6.1, 7.1.1, 7.2.1, 7.2.2, 10.1)
Oxford, Bodleian Library, MS Rawlinson D.248	Ra5	s. xv		2.5b (7.2.1)
Oxford, Bodleian Library, MS Rawlinson D.1210	Ra6	s. xv		3.1.1c, 14.1.4 (6.3, etc.)
Oxford, Bodleian Library, MS Rawlinson D.1221	Ra7	s. xv		14.2.4 (2x), 2.5a (5.1b, 8.1, 10.1, 11.1), 1.5, 15.4
Oxford, Bodleian Library, MS Selden Supra 73	Se	s. xv$^{4/4}$		2.2 (5.1a, 6.1, 7.1.1, 7.2.1, 7.2.2, 7.3.1, 8.1, 10.1, 11.1)

Manuscript	Siglum	Date	Provenance	References
Oxford, Corpus Christi College, MS 291	Oc	s. xv		2.5a (6.1, 10.1)
Oxford, Magdalen College, MS 221	Om	s. xv^{ex}–s. xvi		1.1.1, 7.5.12, 1.3, 6.2a, 3.3.2a, 6.4, A.1, 2.1 (5.1a, 6.1, 7.1.1, 7.2.1, 7.2.2, 7.3.1, 8.1, 9.1, 10.1, 11.1), 8.6, 7.5.9 (7.3.2, 7.5.1)
San Marino, Huntington Library, MS HM 64	Hg1	s. xv^{ex}		2.4 (1.4, 6.1, 7.2.2, 10.1), 3.2.2, A.1
San Marino, Huntington Library, MS HM 505	Hg2	s. xv$^{3/4}$		15.1
San Marino, Huntington Library, MS HU 1051	Hg3	s. xv$^{med/ex}$		13.5
Sheffield, Central Library, Jackson Collection MS 1302	Sh	s. xv^{ex}		2.5a (7.3.1, 8.1, 11.1)
Stockholm, Royal Library, MS X.90	St	s. xv	Norfolk	2.5a (5.1b, 7.1.1, 7.2.1, 7.2.2, 7.3.1)
Tokyo, Takamiya MS 33 (presently on deposit at the Beinecke Rare Book and Manuscript Library, New Haven CT)	Ta1	s. xv$^{4/4}$		11.2, 1.2
Tokyo, Takamiya MS 60 (presently on deposit at the Beinecke Rare Book and Manuscript Library, New Haven CT)	Ta2	s. xv$^{1/2}$, poss. s. xv$^{1/4}$		18.0
Warminster, Longleat House, MS 333	Lo	s. xvi$^{2/2}$		7.1.3, 14.2.1a
Woking, Surrey Historical Society, MS LM 1327/2	Su	s. xvi$^{1/4}$		5.2.1, 4.1.3c
York, York Minster Library, MS XVI.E.32	Yo	s. xiv^{ex}–s. xv^{in}	NW Norfolk	3.1.2a, 3.2.3, 3.3.3, 5.2.1, 4.1.3c

Appendix C

Uroscopies with More than Five Witnesses

UNLESS OTHERWISE NOTED, the number of manuscript witnesses refers to separate copies, occasionally with more than one copy in a single manuscript. Reprinted editions of print witnesses are not included.

Anonymous Works:

Item No.	Text
1.0	*The Twenty-Jordan Series* (69 manuscript witnesses, 4 prints)
2.0	*The Dome of Uryne* (components found in 55 manuscripts, 2 prints)
7.1.1	Urina Mortis Tam Hominum Quam Mulierum (39 manuscript, 2 print)
5.1	Judicium Perfectum Omnium Urinarum (35 manuscript, 2 print)
10.1	On the [Four] Contents of Urines (34 manuscript, 2 print)
10.1	Urine That Has Great Contents (30 manuscript, 2 print)
7.2.1	Urina Mulieris (30 manuscript, 2 print)
7.3.1	Urines of Man, Woman, and Beast (29 manuscript, 2 print)
7.2.2	Ad Cognoscendum Pregnantes (29 manuscript, 1 print)
11.1	The First and Second Urines (28 manuscript, 2 print)
6.1	The Twenty Colors (27 manuscript, 1 print)
9.1	The Third Knowledge of Urines: The Regions (27 manuscript, 2 print)

8.1	The Complexions of Urine (22 manuscript, 1 print)
8.1	Where the Complexions Are Generated (19 manuscript, 2 print)
3.0	Vade Mecum Suite (components found in 52 manuscripts; 16 manuscripts contain all three components)
3.3	*Cleansing of Blood* (41)
3.2	*Urina Rufa* (31)
3.1	*Twenty Colors by Digestion Groups* (29)
4.1	*Letter of Ipocras* (components found in 38 manuscripts; 15 manuscripts contain all three components)
4.1.1–4.1.2a, 4.1.2c, 4.1.3	*Six-Token List* (32)
4.1.1–4.1.3a	"Man Beast and Bird" (24)
4.1.1–4.1.2	Prologues (22)
5.2	*Urine White and Brown* (37)
5.2.1	Woman variant (28)
5.2.2	Phlegm variant (9)
6.2	*Rufus Subrufus* (18)
4.2	*Urine White and Red* (14)
6.3	*Ten Cold Ten Hot* (14)
7.1.2	"Urine Troubly with Clouds" (8)
8.2	*The Four Elements* (21 witnesses total, of which 8 contain the uroscopic chapters)
11.2	*Practica Urinarum* (8)
4.3	*Fifteen Discretions of Urine* (7)
7.4	"The Doom of Urine Thou Shalt Cast in Four" (6)

Attributed Works:

| 15.0 | Henry Daniel, *Liber Uricrisiarum* (37 manuscript witnesses, 2 prints) |
| 16.0 | Walter Agilon, *The Craft of Urines* (11; 6 of Friar Bartholomew's translation) |

Appendix D
Defining Uroscopic Signs in Major Token Lists

THE FOLLOWING TABLE gives the typical first three signs in the most common or substantial Middle English uroscopic token lists, i.e., texts that describe a series of urinary characteristics and provide diagnoses or prognoses based on those features.[1] In addition to the signs at the beginnings of the texts, I note other unique or unusual signs in the individual token lists and notable general characteristics of selected texts, to assist in future identifications of witnesses not included in this taxonomy.

---

[1] The challenges of distinguishing uroscopic token lists—which may begin with quite similar incipits but then diverge as they progress—are not unlike those of distinguishing recipe collections, which often begin with similar remedies (e.g., for headache) but may then go on to different groups of ailments and recipes. Using the first three tokens as a way to differentiate common token lists is analogous to Henry Hargreaves's suggestion of indexing recipe collections by transcribing "the first ten or twelve [words] of each of the first three recipes," in "Some Problems in Indexing Middle English Recipes," in *Middle English Prose: Essays on Bibliographical Problems,* ed. A. S. G. Edwards and Derek Pearsall (New York, 1981), 91–113, at 96.

3.2 *Urina Rufa* (31 witnesses)

Sign	Diagnosis/Prognosis
1: Urina rufa	Health and good disposition of man's body
2: Urina subrufa	Good health but not so perfect in all manner as rufa
3: Urina citrina with a middle substance and circle of the same color	Praisable / Laudable
Other: Urina rubea as blood in a glass	A fever of too much blood; the patient must be bled unless the moon is in the (middle) sign of Gemini

4.1.1–4.1.2a, 4.1.2c, 4.1.3 *Six-Token List* (32 witnesses)

Sign	Diagnosis/Prognosis
1: Urine white in the morning, red before meat, white after meat	The man is whole
2: Urine that seems bloody	The bladder is hurt with some filth that is within
3: Urine of a woman that is clear and fair and shines like silver, if she casts ('vomits') often and has no talent ('appetite') for meat	She is with child
Other: Urine of a man or woman with fever ague and a black gathering on one half of the urinal	Death

4.2 *Urine White and Red* (14 witnesses)

Sign	Diagnosis/Prognosis
1: Urine white in the morning, red before meat, white after meat	The man is whole
2: Urine fat, white, and troubled (or fat, thick, and strong)	Not good
Some witnesses add: Urine somewhat thick (or abundant, thin, not troubled)	Good
3: Urine fat and troubled as ass piss (or thick in the manner of ass piss/ashes)	Head ache (and fever)
Other: Woman's urine like "stable cleansing" / "steadfast purging" / the color of "meal spurging"	Quartan fever and death on the third day

4.3 *Fifteen Discretions* (7 witnesses)

Sign	Diagnosis/Prognosis
1: Urine white in the morning, red before meat, white after meat	The man is whole
2: Urine that seems bloody	The bladder is hurt with some filth within
3: Urine of a woman clear and fair, if it shines as crystal or silver, and she casts and has no talent to meat	She is with child
Other: Many unusually detailed signs, as noted in taxonomy entry for item 4.3 above; for the full list of signs, see Tavormina, "The Middle English *Letter of Ipocras*" (n. 35 above), 644-45.	

5.1 Judicium Perfectum Omnium Urinarum (35 manuscript, 2 print witnesses)

Sign	Diagnosis/Prognosis
1: Urine white in the morning, brown after meat	Health
2: Urine fat and troubly ('turbid')	Water in the bowels
3: Urine right red and clear	A burning fever of choler
Other: Urine clear with a black circle Black drests ('dregs') in the bottom like gobbets of coals	The patient will be *phthisicus* Worms in the body

5.2.1 *Urine White and Brown* (Woman variant) (28 witnesses)

Sign	Diagnosis/Prognosis
1: Urine white in the morning, brown after meat	Good hele
2: Urine fat and troubled/troubly	No good hele and water in the bowels
3: Urine thin and green above	Cold complexion
Other: Urine black and thin above when you cast it Urine in a feverous patient that turns red and then white (with a number of variations in the basic sign)	Talent ('desire, appetite') to woman/women Good hele except in hectic fever

5.2.2 *Urine White and Brown* (Phlegm variant) (9 witnesses)

Sign	Diagnosis/Prognosis
1: Urine white in the morning, brown after meat	Good hele/health
2: Urine fat and troubled/troubly	Phlegm among the bowels, beginning of digestion
3: Urine thin as water under the circle	Stomach fever and he should brake/cast ('vomit') all that is in his stomach
Other: Urine that has a great circle and changes colors (sometimes specified as green, blue, black, and red) Urine that shines like a lantern horn (= Glaucus)	Head ache on account of the water (and phlegm) between the filmen ('membrane, *dura mater*') and the brain No digestion; the stomach englaymed ('viscous; constipated')

6.2   *Rufus Subrufus* (18 witnesses; also characteristic of and possibly unique to this text are a number of the remedies supplied for various ailments, examples of which are provided in the taxonomy entry headnote)

Sign	Diagnosis/Prognosis
1: Rufus or subrufus	Perfect digestion, but few have it; no medicine is needed
2: Subrubeus, rubeus, subrubicundus, rubicundus	Excess of digestion; they need medicines which will be shown below
3: Inopos, kyanos, viridis	Much burning within (the body)
Other: Wan pale as lead, black as ink, black as black horn	Death or venomous matter going out by the water ways which betokens health; if death, then no medicine avails: *Contra vim mortis non est medicamen in ortis* (Latin line sometimes omitted)[2]

---

  [2] The phrase *in ortis* ('in gardens') refers metonymically to herbal medicine and, by further extension, to medicine more generally; the Latin line is the second half of a couplet about sage from the *Flos medicine,* also known as the *Regimen sanitatis Salernitanum* (ed. Frutos González [n. 43 above], lines 371–72).

6.3 *Ten Cold Ten Hot* (14 witnesses)

Sign	Diagnosis/Prognosis
1: Black as a dark coal, with livid color going before	Mortification
2: Livid like lead	Mortification
3: White as sheer water	Indigestion
Other: Karapos like grey russet or camel's hair	Indigestion
Yellow/sallow like fallow leaves falling off trees (for Glaucus)	Indigestion
Pale like sammen ('half') sodden flesh	Beginning of digestion

6.4   *Knowing of Twenty Colors of Urines* (4 witnesses)

Sign	Diagnosis/Prognosis
1: Urine red, thick, troubly without any clearness	Swelling of the sinews
2: Urine troubly and black throughout, or green also	Death is nigh
3: Urine red, partly evenly troubled above and pale	Sickness of great superfluity by the falling of blood in the veins (and rotting of all the body)
Other: Urine with the scum (foam) departed in three parts, with the first part full of grains in the manner of quicksilver and meanly thick	Rheum from the humors falling from the highest part of the body into the lowest, of which comes apostemes and phthisic and dry throat and other evils in the lowest part of the body

7.1.1 Urina Mortis (39 manuscript, 2 print witnesses)

Sign	Diagnosis/Prognosis
1: Urine in a hot access ('acute fever') part red, part black, part green, part blue	Death
2: Urine in a hot access black, little in quantity, fatty, stinking	Death
3: Urine colored overall as lead	Prolonging of death
Other: Urine black and thin, the sick person loathes ('feels great disgust, is nauseous?') when he goes to the privy, he speaks over-thwart ('confusedly') or does not understand correctly and this does not go away from him	Death

7.1.2 "Urine Troubly with Clouds" (8 witnesses)

Sign	Diagnosis/Prognosis
1: Urine troubly with clouds (or clods) floating above	Death is prolonged
2: Urine with drests ('dregs') in the bottom mixed with blood	Death
3: Urine that is white (= Albus 'clear') in a fever, if it turns into the semblance of milk (= Lacteus)	Death
Other: A great pulse with great dints ('beats') and swift, with urine white underneath	A fever with aching in the flanks
A steadfast pulse without stinting, clear urine, dry tongue, spewing/spitting "colorif" ('of diverse colors'?)	A burning fever
Urine black and thin, with stopping of the ears, without sleep and with clouds/clods	He has been long sick and his nose shall soon bleed

7.2.1 URINA MULIERIS (30 manuscript, 2 print witnesses)

Sign	Diagnosis/Prognosis
1: Urine of a woman with clear stripes, the most part troubly and the troubliness reddish like tanwose ('tanning liquor')	She is with child, and the token will not fail as soon as the child has life
2: Urine of a woman in which the troubliness hoves ('floats') thickest above	She is with a knave child
3: Urine of a woman in which the troubliness draws downward	She is with a maid child
Other: Urine of a woman red as gold with a watery circle above	She is with child

7.2.2 AD COGNOSCENDUM PREGNANTES (29 manuscript, 1 print witnesses)

Sign	Diagnosis/Prognosis
1: First water after dealing with a man is clear	She is with child
2: First water after dealing with a man is thick	She is not with child
3: The taste of a leek/garlic clove eaten at bedtime is/is not in a woman's mouth after her first sleep	She is not/is with child
Other: A woman's hand stinks, she has great pain about or above the navel, she goes ('walks') with difficulty and is evermore sitting still, her eyes are small	The child is dead within the woman

7.5.1 "Urine as Snot" (4 witnesses)

Sign	Diagnosis/Prognosis
1: Urine of a man thick like snot in the glass	He has lost his kind ('semen')
2: Urine of a woman thick like snot	She has the mother ('uterine displacement')
3: Urine clear before it is stirred and after	A cold taken
Other: Urine brown and blue	She is pregnant with a knave child
Urine right blue	She is pregnant with a maid child
Urine like gold with a white ring and blue above	She is with child

12.1 "Urine Brown with a Black Ring" (3 witnesses; one witness deals only with the contents. Also useful for identification is the fact that the text follows the order of Giles's *Carmen de urinis*; in the two complete witnesses, it includes brief apposite Latin quotations from the poem for many of the colors, as well as Giles's four-line list of urinary contents)

Sign	Diagnosis/Prognosis
1: Urine brown with a black ring	Death
2: Urine black or swart like a raven's feather	Mortification and extinction of kind heat
3: Urine black and thick	Wasting substantial moistness in the body

12.2 *Liber de Judiciis Urinarum* (2 witnesses; a particularly well-organized text, with clearly marked sections for twenty colors, twenty contents, four regions, seven hypostases, and concluding with three *regulae notabiles* dealing with urines of women, praiseworthy hypostasis, and urines of death)

Sign	Diagnosis/Prognosis
1: Urine red as saffron of the west with a thick substance, stinking and spumous	The jaundice
If the urine is clear	Ache in the right side
If the urine is thin	A tercian
2: Urine red as saffron of the east or as a red rose	Ephemeral or quotidian fever
If it has blood, in a woman	The woman has the *menstrua*
If it is crudded ('coagulated')	She is with child
If it is attred ('purulent'), thick, and blo ('livid') above like lead	An aposteme under the side
3: Urine red as flame of fire, not clear	Declination of the sickness and adustion of blood with choler

APPENDIX E
CITED eTK INCIPITS

THE FOLLOWING TABLE lists all eTK numbers cited in the taxonomy, most of them representing possible direct or indirect sources for the Middle English uroscopies classified above. It also indicates which eVK2 entries cite those Latin texts as potential sources or close parallels.

eTK Number	eTK Incipit, Author, Title	Cited in Item Number	eVK2 Number(s) Citing the eTK Incipit
0030M	"Ad cancrum in virga virili sive in umbilico": John Arderne, *Experimenta* (= *Liber receptarum ad fistulas, Liber medicinarum*)	21.0	—
0075H	"Albus aque similis est lacteus utpote serum": anon., *Carmen de coloribus urinae*	14.2.4	—
0075J	"Albus ut aqua lacteus ut lac glaucus": Henry of Winchester, *De urinis* (this text is actually a combination of material from **20Col-Dig**, *Urina Rufa*, and the *Flos medicine*; see n. 95 above)	24.0	6651.00 (= 24.0)
0085H	"Alopicia est infirmitas capillorum": John Arderne?, *Radix medicinarum*	21.0	Non-uroscopic texts, not in this taxonomy: 0871.00, 0872.00
0089A-B	"Amantissime socie pluries": Henry Daniel, *De iudiciis urinarum* / "Amantissime sodalis pluries et instanter": Henry Daniel, *Manipulus florum Gualtero Cateneo medicine doctori nuncupatus* (0089B probably the same as 0089A and 0433B)	15.0	—

0222J	"Circa urina quinque principaliter": Henry of Winchester, *De cognitione egritudinum per urinam et de cura earum*	24.0	—
0223A-B	"Circa urinas quinque attenduntur generalia et principalis": Richard of England, *De urinis* / "Circa urinas quinque sunt pensanda generalia": Richard of England, *De urinis*	25.0	—
0291E	"Cum decem sint genera pulsuum": Walter Agilon, *Liber de pulsibus*	16.2	—
0338M	"Cum secundum auctores viginti sunt urinarum colores": Walter Agilon, *Compendium urinarum* (also attrib. to other writers, e.g., Ricardus, Aegidius)	16.0	4559.00, 7361.00, 7362.00 (= 16.1); 1433.00 (= 16.2); 2225.00 (= 29.0, the *Book of Egidij*, but that text is not the same as the Agilon versions, despite an incipit similar to the main Agilon text)
0388B	"De quadruplici via speculationis astrologie": William of England, *De urina non visa*	19.0	—

0394A, C	"De urinarum scientia tractaturi earum notitiam": Maurus Salernitanus, *De urinis* (= *Regule urinarum Magistri Mauri, Liber urinarum*) "De urinis tractaturi quid sit urina": Maurus Salernitanus, *De urinis*	23.0	—
0422D, G	"Dicitur urina cum sit in renibus una": Giles of Corbeil, *De urinis* (verse) "Dicitur urina quoniam sit renibus una": Giles of Corbeil, *De urinis* (verse)	15.0	7780.00, 7788.00, 7790.00, 7791.00, 7792.00, 7796.00, 7797.00 (= 15.1-2, Henry Daniel, *Liber Uricrisiarum*); 7787.00, 7793.00, 7794.00, 7795.00 (= 15.3, *Liber Uricrisiarum*, 17-chapter abridgment)
0433B	"Dilecto socio in Christo magistro Waltero de Ketene": Henry Daniel, *Libri tres uricrisiarum*	15.0	—
0453C	"Dixit Hermes pater philosophorum non est medicus"): Hermes (attrib.), *De judicio urine*	14.2.1b	2413.00, 8074.00 (= 14.2.1b)
0462C	"Domicilia quoque corpus humanum sic distribuunt": William of England, *De urina non visa*	19.0	—
0489F	"Ego Iohannes predictus a prima pestilentia": John Arderne, *Practica chirurgiae* (= *Practica de fistula in ano*)	21.0	Non-uroscopic texts, not in this taxonomy: 0251.00, 0549.00, 1963.00, 2494.00, 2495.00, 2542.00

			Non-uroscopic texts, not in this taxonomy
0631B	"Hoc est speculum fleobothomie": John Arderne, *Libri sirurgie*	21.0	0402.00, 7410.00
0692I	"In morbis pronosticare non possumus nisi morbum cognoscamus": Bernard de Gordon, *Tractatus de pronosticis* [= *Liber pronosticorum*, *Compendium pronosticorum*]	18.0	7115.00, 7116.00 (= 18.0)
0756D	"Intelligendum est quod in cerebro sunt tres cellule": Bernard de Gordon, *Super pronostica* (a version of the *Liber pronosticorum* that is "incomplete or rearranged . . . open[ing] with the *inc.* of the *Liber pronosticorum* 4.1")[1]	18.0	—
0811N	"Largus amans hilaris ridens rubeique coloris": anon., *De quatuor complexionibus*	8.6	7750.50 (= 1.3; reporting Latin verses after **20J**) Other (non-uroscopic) texts: 1043.00; 2791.00, 2791.50, 3211.00; 3873.00, 3874.00, 3875.00, 3876.00; 4433.25, 4434.00; 4567.00
0820G	"Liber iste nove institutionis": Giles of Corbeil, *Carmen de urinis* (prol.)	9.0	—

---

1   Demaitre, *Doctor Bernard de Gordon*, 189 (n. 51 above).

0821B	"Liber iste liber est nove institutionis studiose": Gilbertus (?), Commentary on Giles of Corbeil, *Carmen de urinis*	9.0	—
0821I	"Liber iste quem legendum proponimus est novelle institutionis": anon., Commentary on Giles of Corbeil, *Carmen de urinis* (often erroneously attributed to Gentile de Foligno, but earliest manuscripts antedate Gentile by over a century; possible composition by Giles himself suggested by Sudhoff)[2]	9.0, 14.2.4	—
0821J	"Liber iste quem legendum proposimus nove institutionis et studiose": anon., Commentary on Giles of Corbeil, *Carmen de urinis*	9.0	—
0906G*	"Ne ignorantie vel potius invidie" / "De quadruplici via speculationis astrologie": William of England, *De urina non visa* (prol. /text)	19.0	3897.00 (= 19.0)
0919C	"Non est medicus sapiens in pronosticis signis": Hermes, *De judiciis urine*	14.2.1b	—
0960A	"Numerus et sufficientia dierum cretorum habetur": Bernard de Gordon, *De pronostico de Monte Pessulano* ("Probably identical with Bernard's *Liber pronosticorum* 5.6")[3]	18.0	—

---

[2] Karl Sudhoff, "Commentatoren der Harnverse des Gilles de Corbeil," *Archeion: Archivo di storia della scienza* 11 (1929): 129–35, at 132.

[3] Demaitre, *Bernard de Gordon*, 189.

ID	Incipit		
1004G	"Omnis urina est colamentum sanguinis": anon., *De urinis*	3.0	1520.00 (= 3.3.1a); 1573.00, 1579.00 (= 3.3.1b); 0843.00 (= 3.3.1c); 1574.00, 1577.00, 1578.00, 1580.00 (= 3.3.2a); 2879.00 (= 2.1, 2.2, 2.4); 7799.00 (= 3.1.1c, 8.3, 16.5); 7786.00 (= 25.0)
?1100J	"Primo de his que attenduntur in urina": Richard of England, *Regule urinarum*	25.0	—
1205G	"Qui cupit urinas mea per compendia scire": Richard of England, *Regule de urinis* [preceding verse]	25.0	—
12471-J	"Quinque attenduntur generalia et principalia": Richard of Salerno, *Libellus de urinis et febribus* / "Quinque circa urinam attenduntur": Richard of England, *Regule urinarum*	25.0	—
1271I	"Quoniam de urinarum differentia/ scientia tractaturi/ dicturi sumus": Maurus Salernitanus, *De urinis*	23.0	—
1272A	"Quoniam denique scientiam tractaturi sumus": Maurus Salernitanus, *De urinis*	23.0	—
1307G	"Quoniam ut ait Platearius in principio sue practice": John Arderne?, [*Radix medicinarum*] (prol.)	21.0	—

1331H	"Recipe ollam novam rudem": John Arderne, *Practica* [extract]	21.0	—
1366L	"Rufus subrufus significant perfectam digestionem": anon. (a colors and digestions list, but not a complete version of **20Col-Dig**, as it omits the descriptive similes; not a source for *Rufus Subrufus*, item 6.2)	3.0	8106.50 (= 3.1.2a); 7312.00, 7314.00 (= 1.3); 4408.00, 4409.00, 4410.00 (= 6.2)
1374D-E	"Sanguineus largus amans ridens rubeique coloris": anon., *De quatuor temperamentis (complexionibus)* "Sanguineus veluti Richardus de Florentino [sic] dicit in sequente largus amans": Anon., *De quatuor temperamentis*	8.6	Non-uroscopic texts: 2791.00, 2791.50; 3873.00, 3874.00, 3875.00, 3876.00; 4433.25, 4434.00; 4567.00
1428B-C	"Senectus domina oblivionis" / "Senectus est mater oblivionis nunc autem cum scientia": Bernard de Gordon, prol. to *Tractatus de pronosticis* [= *Liber pronosticorum, Compendium pronosticorum de crisi et criticis diebus*]	18.0	765.00 (= 18.0)
1480C	"Sicut ait Galienus in libro de interioribus circa curam egritudinis" / "Incipiamus ergo primo a colore": Walter Agilon, *Summa medicinalis* (prol. /text)	16.0	—
1483G	"Sicut dicit Galienus in libro de interioribus": Walter Agilon, *Practica* or *Summa*	16.0	—

1499H	"Sicut ut Galienus in libro de interioribus": Walter Agilon?, *Summula*	16.0	—
1517J	"Solis die in lecto qui ceciderit": Galen (attrib.), *Prognostica Galieni*; Hippocrates (attrib.), *Epitomia Ypocratis*	14.2.1a	—
1607A	"Urina alba in colore tenuis in substantia": Walter Agilon, *De urina*; anon.?, Comm. on Giles, *Carmen de urinis?*	16.0	787.00, 788.00, 789.00, 790.00 (= 16.1); 7827.00 (= 16.4); 7828.00? (= 29.0, the *Book of Egidij*, but that text is not the same as the Agilon versions, despite an incipit similar to the main Agilon text)
1608C-E	"Urina est colamentum sanguinis": Theophilus [*Liber urinarum*]; Isaac, *Liber Urinarum*; Comm. Egidius *De urina*; Bernard de Gordon [*De urinis*]; Ketham, *Fasc. Med.* (and in many manuscripts; see nn. 3, 30 above) / "Urina est colamentum sanguinis ut dicit Ysaac": Anon. / "Urina est liquamentum sanguinis et aliorum humorum colamentum": Aristotle (attrib.), *De urinis*; anon., *De urinis*	3.0	—
1610B	"Urina rufa significat salutem et bonam dispositionem": anon.; Ketham, *Fasc. Med.* (also in many manuscripts; see n. 30 above)	3.0	—

Appendix F
Linguistic Perspectives on Middle English Uroscopy

IMPORTANT DIRECTIONS OF future research on medieval uroscopy will include linguistic dimensions of uroscopic texts and the manuscripts in which they appear, editorial work on individual treatises, codicological analysis,[1] and integration with scholarship on medieval medical practices and practitioners.[2] Linguistic analysis will be of particular value, both for its own sake and for its contributions to the study of sources required in editing and of issues relating to readership, dissemination,

---

[1] For example, which uroscopies (whether in English, Latin, or French) tend to co-occur in manuscripts, or not to do so? What other kinds of medical, scientific, and non-scientific texts commonly accompany uroscopic texts? What kinds of ownership patterns, readerships, and uses can be determined for manuscripts containing uroscopic texts?

[2] For recent examples, see Linda Ehrsam Voigts, "Fifteenth-Century English Banns Advertising the Services of an Itinerant Doctor," in Florence Eliza Glaze and Brian K. Nance, eds., *Between Text and Patient: The Medical Enterprise in Medieval and Early Modern Europe,* Micrologus Library 39 (Florence, 2011), 245–77; and Peter Murray Jones's several articles on Thomas Fayreford's and John Crophill's books (Harley 2558 and 1735), including "Witnesses to Medieval Medical Practice in the Harley Collection," *eBLJ* (2008), article 8 <http://www.bl.uk/eblj/2008articles/article8.html> and earlier work cited there, and his "Mediating Collective Experience: The *Tabula Medicine* (1416–1425) as a Handbook for Medical Practice," in Glaze and Nance, eds., *Between Text and Patient,* 279–307.

and use of texts and manuscripts among different language communities. While the primarily taxonomic purpose of this essay precludes extended discussion of such perspectives, a sketch of possible starting points for more focused work on language and sources may be of use or interest to some readers, along with the briefer suggestions on codicological questions, readership, and medical practice in notes 1 and 2 of this Appendix.

1. Relations to sources and language-specific traditions

From the most general point of view, all medieval uroscopy is rooted in the learned tradition—Latinate learning most immediately, with a recognized genealogy tracing back through Arabic and Byzantine writers (most notably Isaac Israeli and Theophilus) to the ancient Greeks. However, the earliest surviving Middle English uroscopy, the *Urine White and Brown* token-list in Cambridge, Corpus Christi College 388 (item 5.2.1; MS ca. 1320–30), derives most immediately from an already thriving thirteenth-century tradition of Anglo-Norman and French medical writing, itself indebted to Latin texts. That French tradition, as far as I have been able to determine, seems to feed mainly into the White and Red and the White and Brown token lists above (items 4.1–4.3 and 5.1–5.2), along with the occasional excerpting of material from those texts in other token lists. It is certainly possible that other Middle English token lists or other texts in the taxonomy have French antecedents still to be identified; it would be particularly interesting if subgenres other than the token list could be traced back to a French source. Unfortunately, the very interesting albeit incomplete French translation of the standard commentary on Giles of Corbeil's *De urinis*[3] has no surviving English translation (and may never have had one), though a few of the items in the taxonomy above belong clearly or at least arguably to the commentary genre.

Middle English uroscopies with identifiable Latin sources begin appearing in the late fourteenth century, and include ambitious projects from early on, most notably the encyclopedic synthesis of Henry Daniel's *Liber Uricrisiarum* (self-dated in its earliest versions to 1377–79). By the end of the fifteenth century, Middle English uroscopies with direct

---

[3]   Ed. Tony Hunt, *Old French Medical Texts* (Paris, 2011), 119–47. Hunt points out the gap in scholarship and editions of Old French medical texts (preface, 7), which suggests that additional French sources for Middle English uroscopic texts may remain to be discovered.

or indirect Latin sources are not only more common than those with French sources, but also appear in a wider range of modes, including 1) close translations of learned treatises like Bernard de Gordon's *Tractatus de pronosticis* (item 18.0), William the Englishman's *De urina non visa* (19.0), and the anonymous commentary on the Hippocratic *Prognostics* (26.1); 2) adaptation/translations like the several versions of the already-simplified Latin abridgment(s) of Walter Agilon's *Summa medicinalis* (16.1–16.5) and the abbreviation of Maurus of Salerno's *Liber urinarum* (23.0); 3) multiple, more and less close translations of the simplified and schematized texts in the "kurze Harntraktat"/*Fasciculus medicine* tradition (3.1–3.3); 4) part of an apparent prose translation of Giles's *De urinis* embedded in *Barton's Urines* (20.0; internal dating to before 1400); and 5) the deep general debt to Giles, his commentators, and other Latin writers and commentators on urines for the twenty-color and eighteen- and nineteen-contents schemata (as in the *Twenty Jordans, Dome of Uryne,* other twenty-color lists, content lists, color and contents judicials), even in works that choose to disagree with the exact numbers and names for those colors or contents. The identifications of Latin originals in the pages above barely scratches the surface of the kinds of linguistic analyses that can and should be done for individual texts, including comparisons between different Middle English renderings (where such exist) of a given Latin original, close examination of the translation strategies of individual translators, more exact identification of versions of Latin originals that are closest to their English reflexes, and so on.

Finally, a striking number of Middle English uroscopies have no obvious direct source text in either Latin or French, though their overall content clearly draws on the broad general tradition. The synthesizing work of writers like Daniel, Barton, Arderon, and Narborough (15.1–15.4, 20.0, 21.0, 22.0), as well as the compilational efforts of "Austin" (17.0) and the *Isagoge*-like strategies of the anonymous *Ten Cold Ten Hot* (6.3), the somewhat fuller *Dome of Uryne* (2.1–2.5), and other entries in the taxonomy deserve detailed study both in their own right and in comparison with each other, with their Latin backgrounds, and with other contemporary medical and scientific English writing.

2. Technical vocabulary, definition, and explanation
Uroscopic texts offer an unusually rich domain for field-specific technical language, most obviously for the various colors to be seen in urine

samples, but also for other sensory characteristics of those samples, mainly but not purely visual, and names of illnesses signified by different kinds of urine. Color terms are notoriously difficult to define precisely in words alone, even within a single language, much less between languages and with terms whose meanings may be obscure or may change in the process of transmission, not only from Latin or French into English but also at earlier stages—Greek to Arabic or Latin, Arabic to Latin, Latin to French. Qualitative nuances among color-terms (e.g., the several reddish colors in the twenty-color scheme) and between different types of content (e.g., different degrees of oiliness, gradations of size or texture in flaky suspensions and bubbles, and so on) expand but hardly close off the lexical challenges faced by the translators of medieval uroscopic texts.[4]

Even in the source-language traditions, it was common to clarify color and content terms by way of similes to other substances: *albus ut aqua fontis, subrufus ut aurum impurum, [squame et furfure] sunt quasi petala que ex tritico fiunt, et modicis squamis piscium assimilantur* ('Albus like water of the well,' 'Subrufus like impure gold,' 'Scales and Bran are like the chaff that comes from wheat, and medium-sized Scales are similar to the scales of fish'). Besides making choices between direct borrowing or anglicization of particular words and phrases, Middle English translators and adapters may insert glosses, definitions, or similes of their own when the source texts or tradition are in some way insufficient or unfamiliar (comparison of *karapos* to a camel's skin or fleece may be one of the more egregious examples of unfamiliar referents, but even defining *[sub]citrine* by comparing it to an apple or a citrine apple—*pomum citrinum*—is problematized by differences in colors of apples, even from

---

    [4] Stephanie Zaun discusses urinary color-terms in Greek and Latin texts and their metamorphoses in selected vernacular translations of the 1491 edition of the *Fasciculus medicine,* in "Die Harnfarbbezeichnungen im *Fasciculus medicine* und ihre italienischen und spanischen Übersetzungen," in Ingrid Bennewitz, Andrea Schindler, et al., eds., *Farbe im Mittelalter: Materialität – Medialität – Semantik* (Berlin, 2011), 2:969–85 and plates 134–37 (pls. 134–36 in color). E. Ruth Harvey's work in progress on the *Liber Uricrisiarum* includes detailed and magisterial discussions of the semantic development of color and content terms from Greek through Latin and Arabic to Middle English (personal communication). For an analogous recent study of vernacular surgical vocabulary, see Chiara Benati, "*Dat Boek der Wundenartzstedye:* The Low German Translation of Hieronymus Brunschwig's *Buch der Cirurgia* and Its Rendering of Surgical Lexicon," in John Considine, ed., *Webs of Words: New Studies in Historical Lexicography* (Newcastle upon Tyne, 2010), 24–55.

the same variety or tree). A full inventory of borrowings, translations, glosses, definitions, and explanations of specialized uroscopic terminology in Middle English could simultaneously enrich our lexicographic understanding and provide an interesting case-study for larger questions of vernacularization in medieval scientific and medical texts.

3. Code-switching

Like other medieval English scientific and medical texts, Middle English uroscopies and the manuscripts in which they appear are very open to code-switching, at all levels. At the single-word level, one finds Latin (and occasionally French) words either left untranslated or glossed with synonyms from the same and other languages. On rare occasions, individual words are even switched to a ciphered form (sometimes including numbers, sometimes by reverse spelling),[5] perhaps from some scribal concern with decorum or secrecy. Some phrases seem to have a greater tendency than others to appear in Latin; this may be particularly true for assertions of a terminal diagnosis/prognosis, where "signat/significat mortem," "mortem est," and the like may conclude an otherwise English sign. As in other medical texts, certain diseases and anatomical terms may also retain Latin or French or mixed-language forms of their name, such as *colica passio* ('sharp abdominal pain, colic'), *ictericia(m)* ('jaundice'), *chaudepisse* ('strangury or other disease causing painful urination'), and "the pipes *epatis*" ('vessels of the liver'). Beyond these intrasentential forms of switching (i.e., switches within sentences), it is very common to find structural markers such as headings and subheadings in Latin; in longer works, tables of contents or indices may precede or follow a text, often in Latin though not always by the main scribe(s).

At the intertextual level, many compilers and scribes clearly moved easily between uroscopic and other texts in English, Latin, and to a lesser degree French, as has been well established by Voigts for scientific and medical texts and continues to be confirmed by subsequent studies of code-switching in late medieval England.[6] Though less common than

---

[5] See, for example, the reverse spellings that occur throughout Oxford, Magdalen College 221 and the ciphered words for sexual organs in the Huntington 64 version of *Urina Rufa* (3.2.2).

[6] Linda Ehrsam Voigts, "Scientific and Medical Books," in *Book Production and Publishing in Britain 1375–1475*, ed. Jeremy Griffiths and Derek Pearsall (Cambridge,

alternation of Latin and English in structural markers or between whole texts, some Middle English uroscopies also embed Latin passages within their "outermost" textual boundaries: noteworthy examples are the Latin prologue and verse epilogue of the *Liber Uricrisiarum* and Latin verses on complexions and the contents of urine embedded in some copies of the text (those verses also appear in humoral and contents sections of other uroscopies); the three brief Latin segments in the Expanded version of the *Dome of Uryne*; and the embedded text of Giles of Corbeil's *De urinis* in Arderon's Commentary on that text (in the Glasgow manuscript only; contrast the choice of the translator of the Commentary on the Hippocratic *Prognostics* to render—however awkwardly—his entire text, original lemmata and commentary together, in a single tongue).[7]

1989), 345–402; "What's the Word?: Bilingualism in Late-Medieval England," *Speculum* 71 (1996): 813–26. In the earlier study, Voigts tallied the monolingual and multilingual character of 178 manuscripts or discrete manuscript booklets of scientific and medical writing from late-medieval England (380–81). Her calculations indicate that of 101 manuscripts containing medical (or medical and scientific) texts, seventy-one contain texts in Latin and English, Anglo-Norman, or both, while thirty are monolingual in English, essentially a 70/30 percent breakdown within this subset. Another 16 were monolingual in Latin.

A preliminary tally of the manuscripts listed in Appendix B is even more strikingly multilingual than Voigts's sample: out of 222 manuscripts or booklets containing English uroscopy texts, no more than thirty-eight (17 percent) are monolingual in English, a figure that might be further reduced with closer reading of non-uroscopic materials in those manuscripts. At least 154 manuscripts or booklets contain both English works and Latin texts or portions of texts. (This figure includes the Latin prologues and epilogues of the *Liber Uricrisiarum*, the Latin components of the *Dome of Uryne*, and similar material, but not Latin structural markers or intrasentential switches.) Another twenty-seven manuscripts/booklets contain English, Latin, and French texts, though some of the French occurs only in synonym lists; one contains English and French. One manuscript contains Welsh medical material as well as Latin and English, and one booklet has English, a little Latin, and fragmentary bits of French and Welsh. The total number of originally discrete, multilingual manuscripts containing Middle English uroscopies is thus at least 184, or 83 percent of the whole.

The noticeably lower frequency of monolingual manuscripts containing English uroscopy texts than among Voigts's more diverse sample of medical and scientific manuscripts may have to to do with the likely value of uroscopy to medical practitioners who, even without the benefit of university education, were probably more likely to be literate in Latin than broader cross-sections of the reading public. However, the topic of audience(s) for vernacular uroscopy texts requires further exploration before definitive explanations can be offered.

[7] For more recent work on code-switching and multilingualism in English medical and other manuscripts, see the following: Herbert Schendl, "Text Types

4. Formulaic language

Some of the uroscopic subgenres or text types—most notably the token lists—are marked by a variety of repetitive syntactic structures that could bear studies analogous to work done on culinary, medical, and alchemical recipe collections.[8] At a minimum, statements of uroscopic signification can vary between "Urine X signifies/(be)tokens Diagnosis Y," "Diagnosis Y is signified/(be)tokened by Urine X" and "If the patient has Diagnosis Y, then the Urine will be X." Individual signs may go on to offer prognoses including long illness, improvement, or death, but prognosticatory signs are in a minority compared to diagnostic ones. Other features in the token lists that may be worth examining are the use of abbreviations (examples include "V." for "Vrine/Vrina," "s." and "s^t" for "signifies" [whether perceived as English or Latin], "b. t." for "betokeneth," patently perceived as English), inclusion of remedies, and the kinds of intrasentential glossing and other code-switching already noted above.

and Code-Switching in Medieval and Early Modern English," *Vienna English Working Papers* 5 (1996): 50–62, and "Linguistic Aspects of Code-Switching in Medieval English Texts," in David A. Trotter, ed., *Multilingualism in Later Medieval Britain* (Cambridge, 2000), 77–92; Tony Hunt, "Code-Switching in Medical Texts," in David A. Trotter, ed., *Multilingualism in Later Medieval Britain* (Cambridge, 2000), 131–48; Päivi Pahta, "Code-Switching in Medieval Medical Writing," in Irma Taavitsainen and Päivi Pahta, eds., *Medical and Scientific Writing in Late Medieval English* (Cambridge, 2004), 73–99; Ralph Hanna, "Lambeth Palace Library MS 260 and the Problem of English Vernacularity," *Studies in Medieval and Renaissance History* 20 (2008): 131–99; Herbert Schendl and Laura Wright, eds., *Code-Switching in Early English* (Berlin, 2011); Simon Meecham-Jones, "'Gadryng Togedre of Medecyne in the Partye of Cyrugie'": Strategies of Code-Switching in the Middle English Translations of Chauliac's *Chirurgia Magna*," in Herbert Schendl and Laura Wright, eds., *Code-Switching in Early English* (Berlin, 2011), 253–80.

   [8] E.g., Peter Grund, "The Golden Formulas: Genre Conventions of Alchemical Recipes in the Middle English Period," *Neuphilologische Mitteilungen* 104 (2003): 454–75; Claire Jones, "Formula and Formulation: 'Efficacy Phrases' in Medieval English Medical Manuscripts," *Neuphilologische Mitteilungen* 99 (1998): 199–209. A different approach to recurrent phrases and other linguistic structures is presented in Irma Taavitsainen and Päivi Pahta, "Vernacularisation of Medical Writing in English: A Corpus-Based Study of Scholasticism," *Early Science and Medicine* 3 (1998): 157–85.

PARIS TO ROME AND BACK AGAIN: THE NUNS OF LONGCHAMP AND LEO X'S 1521 BULL *PIIS OMNIUM*

Sean L. Field
University of Vermont

ON 21 DECEMBER 1521 the Franciscan sisters of Longchamp received final ecclesiastical approval to celebrate a solemn office in honor of Isabelle of France (1225–70), the Capetian princess who had founded their community in 1260.[1] This approval had been a long time in coming.

I thank Elizabeth A. R. Brown, David J. Collins S.J., Jacques Dalarun, Larry F. Field, M. Cecilia Gaposchkin, Mark Jurdjevic, Henry Ansgar Kelly, Janet Whatley, and the journal's editors and anonymous readers for their criticisms and suggestions.

 [1] On Isabelle the most important recent works are William Chester Jordan, "Isabelle of France and Religious Devotion at the Court of Louis IX," in Kathleen Nolan, ed., *Capetian Women* (New York, 2003), 209–23; Sean L. Field, *Isabelle of France: Capetian Sanctity and Franciscan Identity in the Thirteenth Century* (Notre Dame, IN, 2006); Anne-Hélène Allirot, *Filles de roy de France: Princesses royales, mémoire de saint Louis et conscience dynastique (de 1270 à la fin du XIVe siècle)* (Turnhout, 2010), ch. 8; and Sean L. Field, *The Rules of Isabelle of France: An English Translation with Introductory Study* (additional documents trans. Larry F. Field) (St. Bonaventure, NY, 2014). A major collection of French translations of the sources for Isabelle's life is forthcoming from Les éditions franciscaines as *Isabelle de France, soeur de Saint Louis. Une princesse mineure*, by Jacques Dalarun,

Indeed, in one sense it had taken nearly 240 years, since the first steps toward an envisioned recognition of Isabelle's sanctity went back to at least 1282–83, when the third abbess of Longchamp, Agnes of Harcourt, had composed a French *Vie* of Louis IX's only sister.[2] More recently, this goal had been revived in the mid fifteenth century at Longchamp, which stood just west of Paris (more or less on the site of the modern eponymous hippodrome) and where Isabelle's tomb could be found. This tomb was opened around 1461 to the accompaniment of several miraculous cures, a new narrative epitaph for Isabelle was created and displayed there, and further miracles were recorded over the next decades.[3] New

---

Sean L. Field, Jean-Baptiste Lebigue, and Anne-Françoise Leurquin-Labie. On Longchamp, see Gaston Duchesne, *Histoire de l'abbaye royale de Longchamp* (1255–1789), 2nd ed. (Paris, 1906); Gertrud Młynarczyk, *Ein Franziskanerinnenkloster im 15. Jahrhundert: Edition und Analyse von Besitzinventaren aus der Abtei Longchamp* (Bonn, 1987); Sean L. Field, "The Abbesses of Longchamp up to the Black Death," *Archivum franciscanum historicum* 96 (2003): 237–44; Gabrielle Joudiou, *Isabelle de France et l'abbaye de Longchamp* (Paris, 2006); Sean L.. Field, "The Abbesses of Longchamp in the Sixteenth Century," *Archivum franciscanum historicum* 100 (2007): 553–59; Anne-Hélène Allirot, "Longchamp and Lourcine: The Role of Female Abbeys in the Construction of Capetian Memory (Late Thirteenth Century to Mid-Fourteenth Century)," in Elma Brenner, Meredith Cohen, and Mary Franklin-Brown, eds. *Memory and Commemoration in Medieval Culture* (Farnham, 2013): 243–60; Fabien Guilloux, "*La Regle et la Vie des Sereurs meneurs enclose*: Un traduction en langue romane de la règle d'Isabelle de France (ca. 1315–1325)," *Archivum franciscanum historicum* 106 (2013): 5–39; and Linda Barney Burke, " 'She is the Second St. Clare': The Exemplum of Jehanne de Neuville, Abbess of Longchamp, in a Fourteenth-Century Defense of Women by Jehan Le Fèvre," *Franciscan Studies* 71 (2013): 325–60.

    [2] Sean L. Field, *The Writings of Agnes of Harcourt: The Life of Isabelle of France and the Letter on Louis IX and Longchamp* (Notre Dame, IN, 2003) (hereafter *Writings of AH*); Anne-Hélène Allirot, "Isabelle de France, soeur de saint Louis: La vierge savante. Étude de la *Vie d'Isabelle de France* écrite par Agnès d'Harcourt," *Médiévales* 48 (2005): 55–98. A modern French translation by Jean-François Kost-Théfaine has also recently appeared as *La vie et les miracles de la Bienheureuse Isabelle de France, soeur de Saint Louis* (Paris, 2012); Anne-François Leurquin-Labie's forthcoming translation in *Isabelle de France, soeur de Saint Louis. Une princesse mineure* will be a significant advance, incorporating the important findings of Levente Seláf, 'Párhuzamos Életrajzok: Szent Erzsébet és Isabelle de France Legendái', in *Árpád-házi Szent Erzsébet kultusza a 13–16. Században* (Budapest, 2009), 141–50.

    [3] Sean L. Field, "Imagining Isabelle: Isabelle of France's Fifteenth-Century Epitaph at Longchamp," *Franciscan Studies* 66 (2007): 371–403. For further evidence of interest in Isabelle in the later fifteenth century, see Sarah Elizabeth Hoover,

evidence demonstrates that Agnes of Harcourt's early *Vie* was circulating more widely in this era than previously known.[4] The true push for recognition, however, began in 1517, after the spectacular cure of a novice at Longchamp named Jeanne Carphaude was attributed to Isabelle's miraculous intervention. The nuns recorded the story of this cure and displayed their account at the entry to the abbey church. Shortly afterward, a member of the community composed a new vernacular life of Isabelle that emphasized the importance of this modern miracle.[5] At the same time, one of the abbey's Franciscan confessors, the master of theology Robert Messier, set about composing an office.[6] Before such an office

---

"Gender and Dynastic Sanctity in Late Fifteenth-Century France: *Le livre des faiz monseigneur saint Loys* (Paris, Bibliothèque national de France ms. fr. 2829)" (M.A. Thesis, University of Illinois at Urbana-Champagne, 2012), which shows how this late-fifteenth-century manuscript (created for the Bourbon family and then owned by Charles VIII) emphasized the piety of Louis IX's female relatives, including Isabelle.

    [4] At the time of her death Marie de Bretagne (d. 1477), abbess of Fontevrault, daughter of Richard de Bretagne (count of Étampes) and Marguerite d'Orléans, owned a copy of "La *Vie de madame Ysabeau de France*, en pappier, couvert d'ung parchemin dur." See Marie-Françoise Damongeot-Bourdat, "Le Coffre aux livres de Marie de Bretagne (1424–1477), abbesse de Fontevraud," in Anne-Marie Legaré, ed., *Livres et lectures de femmes en Europe entre Moyen Âge et Renaissance* (Turnhout: Brepols, 2007), 81–99, at 94. Marie de Bretagne's younger sister Madeleine had taken the veil at Longchamp in 1461 (and died the following year; see Field, "Imagining Isabelle," 382), and so family ties clearly explain the appearance of this text at Fontevrault. This is an important addition to our knowledge of this text's circulation in this era, otherwise only recorded in inventories at Longchamp or the royal court.

    [5] Sean L. Field, "A New Life of Isabelle of France from the Early Sixteenth Century," *Studies in Medieval and Renaissance History*, 3rd series, 8 (2011): 27–80.

    [6] Study of the office itself is outside the scope of the present article. The earliest surviving version has been edited from Paris, Bibliothèque nationale de France (hereafter BnF) ms. lat. 912 (black and white digitization now available on Gallica) in Livier Oliger, "Le plus ancien office liturgique de la B.se Isabelle de France (†1270)," in *Miscellanea Giovanni Mercati*, vol. 2 (Vatican City, 1946), 484–508. Certainly Isabelle was commemorated at Longchamp long before the sixteenth century. For example, the fifteenth-century list of prayers for the abbey's patrons indicates that on February 22 "vespres de mors" would be chanted "pour ma dame Ysabel de France la quelle fonda ceste eglise" (BnF ms. fr. 11662, fol. 22ᵛ). But no trace of any earlier liturgical office survives, and almost certainly Oliger was correct to argue that ms. lat. 912 represents the newly composed office of 1521. Although a detailed new study of this manuscript and the Latin text is still needed, the analysis and French translation by Jacques Dalarun and Jean-Baptiste Lebigue included in the forthcoming

could be celebrated, however, permission was needed from the Medici Pope Leo X (r. 1513–21).

When that permission finally came, first in the form of a preliminary letter from Leo and then in a final promulgation by Cardinal Adrien de Boisy, the nuns took care not only to preserve the original Latin texts they received, but also to create their own vernacular narrative of events and translation of the letters. Under the leadership of abbess Catherine Le Picart, they drew up a triumphant record of their struggle to achieve Isabelle's formal recognition, to which they appended French translations of Leo's and Adrien's letters. The result was copied into one of the abbey's most treasured manuscripts (now Paris, BnF ms. fr. 11662), which also held copies of early privileges, essential liturgical texts, and the abbey's necrology. This manuscript, which in the later fifteenth century was kept "in the choir for the use of all,"[7] shaped the community's memory of these events for decades to come.

Yet the texts generated by Longchamp's campaign to see Isabelle recognized in Rome are little known to modern scholarship.[8] The papal bull and the cardinal's promulgation of it were last published in the seventeenth century, while the vernacular texts produced by the nuns have not previously been edited.[9] The dossier as a whole has received no serious modern study. Close examination of these texts, however, reveals the mechanisms through which a female Franciscan community sought to have its wishes recognized in Rome, and how it then shaped the textual memory of that process. Although Longchamp's early modern inhabitants remain little studied, they in fact produced their own distinctive "convent voices" as part of the wider flowering of nuns' writings visible in

---

collection *Isabelle de France, soeur de Saint Louis. Une princesse mineure* (see note 1 above) offers important advances, including an argument that the nuns of Longchamp should be seen as active collaborators with Messier in the composition of the office.

[7] Młynarczyk, *Ein Franziskanerinnenkloster im 15. Jahrhundert*, 298, 314, 333 (from inventories of 1447, 1467, and 1483).

[8] A confused version of these events was given in Duchesne, *Histoire de l'abbaye royale de Longchamp*, 8–9.

[9] The 1622 printing of the Latin texts is Aubertus Mireaus, *Isabellae sanctae: Elisabetha Ioannis bapt. mater, Elisabetha Andr. Regis Hung. Filia, Isabella regina Portugallix, Isabella, S. Lud. Galliae Regis soror* (Brussels, 1622). See Appendix A for a new edition and English translation of these texts, and Appendix B for the first edition and English translation of the relevant material in BnF ms. fr. 11662.

both French and Franciscan contexts in this period.[10] The present article articulates the networks of influence involved in the effort to obtain recognition for Isabelle's cult, and analyzes the rhetorical moves carried out as Longchamp crafted its translations and original narrative. Like other monastic "textual communities," the sixteenth-century nuns of Longchamp reimagined their collective past in ways that served the present. [11] The texts studied here offered both a reminder of Isabelle of France's importance and a retelling of the recent campaign to secure her recognition. In creating French translations of the official Latin documents, the sisters of Longchamp even subtly altered the pope's words in order to emphasize their own understanding of their founder's life and saintly status.

Paris to Rome

It must have been in late 1520 that a request from Longchamp reached the papal curia. According to the narrative later prepared by the nuns, the "supplication" was transmitted to the pope by "a noble man of Genoa staying in Paris, named Franc de Spinolle." This man was surely Lanfranc Spinola (d. 1528), who is refered to in royal documents from the 1520s as *conseillier et maitre de l'hôtel du roi* and was the father of Jeanne Spinola

---

[10]   For France see Thomas M. Carr, Jr., ed., *The Cloister and the World: Early Modern Convent Voices*, Studies in Early Modern France 11 (Charlottesville, 2007); for Franciscan examples, Lezlie S. Knox, *Creating Clare of Assisi: Female Franciscan Identities in Later Medieval Italy* (Leiden and Boston, 2008), esp. ch. 5, "Writing Female Franciscan Identity"; and Jeanne de Jussie, *The Short Chronicle*, ed. and trans. by Carrie F. Klaus (Chicago, 2006). More broadly see Anne Winston-Allen, *Convent Chronicles: Women Writing About Women and Reform in the Late Middle Ages* (University Park, PA, 2004), K. J. P. Lowe, *Nuns' Chronicles and Convent Culture in Renaissance and Counter-Reformation Italy* (Cambridge, 2003); and Charlotte Woodford, *Nuns as Historians in Early Modern Germany* (Oxford, 2002).

[11]   There is a rich literature analyzing the ways in which monastic communities used texts to shape memories of their founders and foundations. See for instance Amy G. Remensnyder, *Remembering Kings Past: Monastic Foundation Legends in Medieval Southern France* (Ithaca, 1995), and Sharon Farmer, *Communities of Saint Martin: Legend and Ritual in Medieval Tours* (Ithaca, 1991). For a more recent study of similar practices not limited to monastic communities, see Samantha Kahn Herrick, *Imagining the Sacred Past: Hagiography and Power in Early Normandy* (Cambridge, MA, 2007).

(Jehanne Le Spinelle), a nun who entered Longchamp in 1515 and lived until 1577.[12]

Lanfranc must have been selected not only because of his familial connection to Longchamp, but also because he was planning to cross the Alps and offered the promise of some level of access to the papal court. Indeed, just gaining papal acknowledgment of their request represented a significant challenge for the nuns of Longchamp; in Ronald Finucane's recent description of Rome in this period, "On any given day, usually in the morning, litigants, lobbyists and proctors, prelates and their clergy, the laity and their servants swarmed the streets of the City heading for cardinals' palaces or judges' and curial bureaucrats' homes or offices. . . . many of those lobbyists came armed with letters supplicating for canonizations."[13]

It is not clear what larger purposes might have brought Lanfranc

---

[12] An unpublished *Vie d'Isabelle de France* written by Pierre Perrier in 1699 (generally reliable in citing documents available at Longchamp at that time) preserved in Paris, Archives nationales de France (hereafter AN) L 1029 no. 37, noted that "L'obit du sieur Lanfranc de Spinoli ou de l'Espinole, avec ceux de Damoiselle Jacobinette Frigare sa femme et de Jean-Baptiste leur fils, est marqué le 22 septembre 1528. . . . Mais celui de seur Jeanne Spinole, fille du dit sieur Lanfranc et religieuse de cette abaïe, est le 29 juin 1577.» It seems certain then that the "Franc de Spinolle" referred to in the narrative was the father of the nun Jeanne Le Spinolle (who did indeed die in 1577, see Appendix C no. 48). And the date of death and indication of his wife and son's names prove that this is also the same Lanfranc (or Lucien) Spinola refered to in several royal documents as "conseiller et maître d'hôtel du roi." See Académie des Sciences Morales et Politiques, *Collection des Ordonnances des rois de France, Catalogue des actes de François Ier*, vol. 2 (Paris, 1888), p. 700, #7157 ; and vol. 7 (Paris, 1896), p. 784, #29043. These documents indicate that in March 1529 the king had ordered payment of 1,593 livres 18 sous 6 deniers, to "Jacqueline Sigalle" widow of Lanfranc Spinola, and to their children Jean-Baptiste, Florette, and Isabelle Spinola (Lanfranc had been owed this sum at the time of his death). The same Lanfranc Spinola is also presumably referred to in ibid., vol. 1 (Paris, 1887), p. 311, #1679, where "Espignolle, l'un des maitres d'hôtel du roi," is paid 288 livres tournois in October 1522 "pour avoir assuré les vivres de Briançon à Guillestre, organisé les étapes de troupes, et averti Bonnivet, amiral de France." This information suggests important connections, since the "amiral de France" was Guillaume de Bonnivet, brother of Adrien de Boisy (see below). And if Lanfrance may have served as *maître de l'hôtel* as early as 1519, he would have been associated with a third brother, Artus, *Grand maître de l'hôtel du roi* until the latter's death in that year.

[13] Ronald C. Finucane, *Contested Canonizations: The Last Medieval Saints, 1482–1523* (Washington, D.C., 2011), 6.

Spinola to Rome, but once there his position at the French court would have facilitated entry to the papal curia, particularly if he traveled on the king's business. Family connections, however, might have been useful as well, since the Spinola had long been among the most powerful clans in Genoa. In addition to a tradition of military and political leadership, the Spinola held powerful positions in the Church. Most immediately, Agostino Spinola had been secretary to his cousin Pope Julius II, by whom he was made bishop of Perugia in 1509 (he would later be created cardinal by another Medici pope, Clement VII, in 1527). After Julius's death (February 1513), Agostino may not have been as close to the new pope Leo X, but he did accompany Leo to his meeting with the French King Francis I in Bologna in 1515 and participated in the Fifth Lateran Council.[14] Unfortunately it has not been possible to establish the exact relationship between Lanfranc Spinola and various branches of the larger Spinola clan.[15] But if the nuns of Longchamp saw him as a *noble homme* "of Genoa" (merely residing [*demourant*] in Paris), then it seems likely that he would have maintained contacts with family still based in Italy. He thus might well have had some relation to the future cardinal Agostino Spinola and hence additional access to circles close to the papal curia.

In any case, Lanfranc Spinola must have done his work well, because Leo X's *Piis omnium*, dated 11 January 1521 from Rome, gave a cautiously favorable response.[16] The *narratio* of the papal rescript related that a petition had been presented on behalf of the abbess and nuns of Longchamp,[17] which claimed that God was performing miracles through the intercession of the "blessed" Isabelle at Longchamp where her body

---

[14] Lorenzo Cardella, *Memorie storiche de' cardinali della Santa Romana Chiesa* (Rome, 1793), vol. 4, 83–84. I thank Signora Costanza Orsi at the Fondazione Spinola for a kind if inconclusive response to my query on Spinola family genealogy.

[15] Agostino did in fact have a brother named Francesco. See Armando Schiavo, "Un personaggio della 'Messa di Bolsena': Agostino Spinola," *Studi romani* 12 (1964): 289–95, at 290. I was able to securely identify "Franc de Spinolle" as Lanfranc Spinola only just as this article was going to press. I thank the editors for their patience in allowing me to make last minute revisions, and I regret that I have not been able to draw out fully all the possible connections of Lanfranc Spinola to the royal court and to the Italian context.

[16] This is the date in the surviving printed version (see Appendix A); the nuns' translation in BnF ms. fr. 11662 gives the date as 19 January.

[17] The *narratio* is the part of the bull that relates events that have led to the present document; "rescript" is the technical name for a papal response to a petition.

lay. The nuns and abbess were therefore seeking papal permission for the annual celebration of Isabelle's solemn office.

On some level, the nuns of Longchamp may have hoped that this request would ultimately provide a first step toward a true canonization inquiry. This idea is hinted at by the way Leo's text seems to echo the nuns' remark that Isabelle was performing miracles even though she was not enrolled in the catalogue of saints; the unstated implication by the nuns is "even though she deserves to be." In fact, Longchamp's actions over the last few decades bore all the hallmarks of a wider campaign with canonization in view: a translation of relics (albeit a generation earlier in 1461), a new office, and a new *vita*.

Leo, however, was besieged with requests for canonizations from powerful quarters all over Europe, and wary of encouraging them too warmly. Canonizations had become quite rare by the later Middle Ages, with only five in the period 1482–1523 (and then none during what Peter Burke famously labeled a "crisis of canonization" lasting to 1588).[18] The few successful canonizations demanded elaborate hearings, time-consuming gathering of testimony, and sustained monetary support—none of which was forthcoming for Isabelle in 1521. But although only one candidate was in fact canonized during Leo's pontificate (Francis of Paola, discussed below), the Medici pope did grant limited approval for offices to at least eight others besides Isabelle.[19] Since the formal category

---

[18]   On canonization processes in the fifteenth century see Thomas Wetzstein, *Heilige vor Gericht: Das Kanonisationsverfahren im europäischen Spätmittelalter* (Cologne, 2004), convenient appendix listing eighteen processes (515–32); for canonizations 1482–1523, Finucane, *Contested Canonizations*; for the idea of a "crisis of canonization" and then a brief survey of saint-making in the period 1588–1767, see Peter Burke's classic article "How to Be a Counter-Reformation Saint," in *Religion and Society in Early Modern Europe, 1500–1800*, ed. Kaspar Von Greyerz (London, 1984), 45–55.

[19]   Finucane, *Contested Canonizations*, 151–52. Processes for Antoninus of Florence and Benno of Meissen were also ongoing at the time of Leo's death and resulted in canonizations in 1523. Ibid., 184–97 and 213–19. Benno's cause was supported by, among others, the emperor elect and then emperor Charles V in 1520–21, and can be seen as in some fashion a German and imperial counter to Francis I's successful petition for Francis of Paola. For the wider context of Benno's canonization see David J. Collins, *Reforming Saints: Saints Lives and their Authors in Germany, 1470–1530* (Oxford, 2008). Of the more limited offices approved by Leo, perhaps most relevant is that in 1516 of the Franciscan-affiliated laywoman Margaret of

of "beatification" as opposed to "canonization" had not yet been articulated in the early sixteenth century,[20] Leo had significant leeway to allow local recognition for a *beata* such as Isabelle. Thus offices could sometimes be approved for local celebration as something of a consolation prize when formal canonizations were denied; for example Dominican attempts to see Isabelle's contemporary Albert the Great (d. 1280) canonized in the 1480s led only to the approval of his office in 1484. Yet they could also—sometimes many years later—prove to have been the first step toward eventual canonization; Albert, in fact, was finally raised to the altar in 1931.[21]

In any case, Leo's bull actually gives evidence of only very limited knowledge about Isabelle's life and miracles. The text refers to her as "sister of the most glorious saint Louis, former king of France," calls her a "lover of eternal blessedness," and alludes to a story that dates back to Agnes of Harcourt about a Psalm-singing voice heard at Isabelle's death that proclaimed *Factus est ejus in pace locus*. But Leo also seems to have mistakenly believed that Isabelle had been a professed nun at Longchamp (we shall return to this confusion), and he does not mention any of the more recent miracles attributed to her. His tone expresses no great reverence, but rather seems more to suggest that there can be no harm in the nuns' celebration of such an office. Indeed, when one considers that *Piis omnium* was issued only eight days after Leo's bull *Decet Romanum Pontificem* had excommunicated Martin Luther, one suspects that the papal curia would have been preoccupied with larger issues at this moment.[22]

Cortona (d. 1297; canonized 1728). See Fra Giunta Bevegnati, *The Life and Miracles of Saint Margaret of Cortona (1247–1297)*, trans. by Thomas Renna, ed. by Shannon Larson (St. Bonaventure, NY, 2012).

[20] The distinct category of *beatus/beata* was not fully articulated until the pontificate of Urban VIII (1625–34), when "beatification" was defined as local (not universal) permission to celebrate a revered individual with specifically approved liturgical rituals. It is in this anachronistic (but retroactively accurate enough) sense that Isabelle of France is often said to have been "beatified" in 1521.

[21] See David J. Collins, "Albertus, *Magnus* or *Magus*? Magic, Natural Philosophy, and Religious Reform in the Late Middle Ages," *Renaissance Quarterly* 63 (2010): 1–44, esp. 3–4. The Dominicans translated Albert's relics in 1483, formally sought canonization in 1484, and composed his first two *vitae* in 1483 and 1490.

[22] The practically completed canonization process of Antoninus of Florence was put on hold at just this time due to Leo's preoccupation. Finucane, *Contested Canonizations*, 196.

On some level, however, Leo must have viewed the question of Isabelle's proposed office as intersecting with French and Franciscan political contexts. Particularly if Longchamp's petition was known to have been transmitted by a man associated with the court of Francis I,[23] Leo X may have assumed that this gesture regarding a holy French princess would be well received by King Francis I. The pope had ample reason to make such a gesture (particularly since it cost him nothing) as he balanced papal relations with Francis I and the new emperor Charles V in 1521. From 1516 into 1519 Franco-papal relations had been largely harmonious. Francis and Leo had of course reached agreement on the famous Concordat of Bologna, following Francis's dramatic victory at the battle of Marignano and their face to face meeting in Bologna in December 1515. The Concordat was signed by Leo in August 1516 and ratified by the Fifth Lateran Council in December, but not finally registered by the reluctant Parlement de Paris until March 1518.[24] In Paris, Francis's extended battle to secure adherence to the new Concordat was driven not only by his satisfaction at having his control of episcopal nominations confirmed, but by his need for Leo X's support for his claims to Milan and Naples.[25] Leo in turn was counting on Francis in his calls for a new crusade against the Turks.[26] The election of Charles V as Holy Roman Emperor—a title Francis had avidly sought for himself—in June 1519, however, changed the political landscape. In early 1521 Leo and Charles were negotiating the terms of Charles's entry into Italy for his imperial coronation, with a treaty signed in May. In this political context, although Leo's response

---

[23] Aside from Lanfranc Spinola's status as *maître de l'hôtel*, there is no further evidence for direct royal involvment in Longchamp's campaign to secure recognition for Isabelle. There is no mention of Isabelle, for instance, in Giovanni Rucellai, *Lettere dalla nunziatura di Franci (1520–1521)*, ed. Giovanni Falaschi (Rome, [1983]), or Angelo Mercati, "Frammenti di una corrispondenza di Giovanni Rucellai nunzio in Francia (1521)," *Archivio della Società romana di Storia patria* 71 (1948): 1–47.

[24] Summary in R. J. Knecht, *Renaissance Warrior and Patron: The Reign of Francis I* (Cambridge, 1994), 90–103.

[25] R. J. Knecht, "The Concordat of 1516: A Reassessment," *University of Birmingham Historical Journal* 9 (1963): 16–32.

[26] Good relations between pope and king were then cemented by the marriage of Leo's nephew Lorenzo to a cousin of King Francis, Madeleine de la Tour d'Auvergne, in May 1518, although both the bride and groom died in spring 1519, just weeks after the birth of Catherine de Medici.

to Longchamp in January 1521 can hardly be seen as a grand diplomatic gesture, it might have served as a small signal of goodwill toward the royal house of France, even as the pope was maneuvering to pull his support out from under Francis.[27]

Leo also had good reason to consider Longchamp's request through the lens of his relationship to the ever-fractious Franciscan Order. Leo was in fact a decisive figure in Franciscan history. Most famously, on 29 May 1517 he issued *Ite vos*, which attempted to settle the deep, long-standing divisions in the order by treating only the reformed (Observant and Colettine) branches as henceforth constituting the *Ordo Fratrum Minorum*.[28] Moreover, on 20 January 1521 (barely a week after *Piis omnium*) Leo issued *Inter cetera nostro regimini*, a revised rule in ten chapters for "the Brothers and Sisters of the Third Order of Blessed Francis, living in congregations under the three essential vows."[29] Though these measures were not so specifically directed at Franciscan nuns, questions of proper Franciscan comportment for men and women, professed and secular, were certainly on his mind.

These factors—French political concerns and ongoing interventions in Franciscan regulation and sanctity—had blended most fully in Leo's

---

[27] On the relationship between Leo X and France see Götz-Rüdiger Tewes, "Die Medici und Frankreich im Pontifikat Leos X.: Ursachen, Formen und Folgen einer Europa polarisierenden Allianz," in Tewes and Michael Rohlmann, eds., *Der Medici-Papst Leo X. und Frankreich: Politik, Kultur und Familiengeschäfte in der europäischen Renaissance* (Tübingen, 2002), 11–116; for a wider picture Marc H. Smith, "Les Médicis et la France de 1450 à 1600," unpublished paper given at the colloquium *Les Médicis et la France*, Château de Blois, 25 September 1999 (made available by the author at http://sorbonne.academia.edu/MarcHSmith/Papers). On Leo X's diplomatic objectives in these years more broadly see Maurizio Gattoni, *Leone X e la geo-politica dello stato pontificio (1513–1521)* (Vatican City, 2000), 225–48; and Francesco Saverio Nitti, *Leone X et la sua politica secondo documenti e carteggi inediti* (Florence, 1892).

[28] Pacifico Sella, *Leone X e la definitiva divisione dell'Ordine dei Minori (O.min.): La bolla* Ite vos *(29 Maggio 1517)* (Grottaferrata, 2001); John Moorman, *A History of the Franciscan Order, from its Origins to the Year 1517* (Chicago, 1968), 581–85.

[29] See Margaret Carney, Jean François Godet-Calogeras, and Suzanne M. Kush, eds., *History of the Third Order Regular Rule: A Source Book* (St. Bonaventure, NY, 2008), 86–95 for Latin and English texts; more generally Ingrid Peterson, "The Third Order of Francis," in *The Cambridge Companion to Francis of Assisi*, ed. Michael J. P. Robson (Cambridge, 2012), 193–207.

recent canonization of Francis of Paola (c. 1416–1507) on 1 May 1519.[30] This wonder-working hermit had moved from southern Italy to near Tours in 1483 at the invitation of the ailing Louis XI. Francis was also founder of the Minims, a Franciscan offshoot for whom four versions of a new rule were approved between 1493 and 1506. Even after Louis XI's death, he was particularly venerated by the immediate family of the future Francis I. Among those seeking his miraculous aid had been Louise of Savoy, who in 1491 sought his intercession with God to grant her a son. Francis of Paola famously promised her that not only would she have a male child, but that he would someday be king of France. Thus, when her prayers were answered, she named the boy (the eventual Francis I) after this relocated Italian saint. Francis I's wife Claude (daughter of Louis XII and Anne of Brittany) had also been healed by Francis of Paola in her girlhood,[31] and in turn prayed to him for a son of her own. When the royal couple's first son was born in 1518 they named him Francis as well, with Leo X serving as godfather.

Given this history, it is no surprise that Leo X held his canonization hearings for Francis of Paola at the express request of the king of France, his wife, and his mother. The resulting canonization clearly had a political dimension in the context of Leo X's attempts to placate Francis I while dealing with the imperial election in the months immediately following the death of Maximilian I.[32] To a less dramatic extent, the approval two years later of a local cult for Isabelle of France—in some ways a similar figure as a miracle-working Franciscan-inspired rule giver—fitted into this kind of political dynamic as well.

Back to Paris

Once Leo had issued *Piis omnium*, it was again Lanfranc Spinola—according to the nuns' account—who received it from the papal curia. He in turn entrusted it to "a certain banker named Fristobaldi," presumably because this man could arrange the immediate physical transport

---

[30] See Finucane, *Contested Canonizations*, 117–66; and Klaus Pietschmann, "*Opus Leone decimo dignum*. Die Heiligsprechung des Francesco di Paola und die Frankreich-Politik Leos X.," in Tewes and Rohlmann, eds., *Der Medici-Papst Leo X. und Frankreich*, 151–70.

[31] Finucane, *Contested Canonizations*, 147.

[32] Finucane, *Contested Canonizations*, 147; Pietschmann, "*Opus Leone decimo dignum*," 162, 164.

of the letter from Italy back to Paris. As with the Spinola, here again we encounter one of the most established and influential families in Italy, the Frescobaldi.[33] From its original Florentine base, the family banking business opened branches all across Europe, with particular ties to England, Flanders, and Portugal, but certainly doing business in Paris as well. This bull was thus making its return journey to Paris via a tour of powerful Italian clans, from Medici pope to Spinola noble to Frescobaldi banker.

In fact, this Frescobaldi banker must almost certainly have been Filippo (Philippe) Frescobaldi,[34] who had been resident in Paris since at least 1518 and shows up in notarial records as facilitating financial transactions and correspondence between Paris and the papal court at just this time.[35] For instance, on 28 January 1523 "Philippe de Frescobaldis" and Jean d'Aqua, dean of Courpalay-en-Brie, paid Jean de Salazar, archdeacon of Sens, 1,017 *écus d'or* in exchange for the credit of that sum that he held from Gabriel de Grammont, papal protonotary. Evidently the point of the transaction was to use the Frescobaldi banking network as a way to obtain payment from Italy. More directly relevant to understanding his involvement with Longchamp, on 28 February the same Philippe and Jean recognized that because of the plague in Rome and other manifest impediments, they had not yet been able to obtain bulls from the papal curia which they had promised to Pierre Cordier, doctor of canon law and counselor to the Grand Counsel, in favor of the Cistercian abbey of Notre-Dame de Fontaine-Daneil. And on 8 April (at the request of Nicolas Simon, acting for Michel le Fèvre, cleric of the diocese of Autun), "Bernarde de Caruyson" and "Philippe de Friscobaldis, *marchans fleurentins et banquiers*," declared that they could not send and receive bulls to and from Rome as before, due to wars, plague, and the vacancy of the papal throne.

---

[33] See generally Dino Frescobaldi and Francesco Solinas, *I Frescobaldi: Una famiglia fiorentina* (Florence, 2004).

[34] Émile Picot, *Les Italiens en France au XVIe siècle*, Extrait du *Bulletin italien* de 1901 (Bordeaux, 1901), 125. Fillippo's seal, along with seals of Leonardo, Alessandro, Antonio, Girolamo, Francesco, and Gian Frescobaldi, survives in documents dated 1516 and now found in the Archives nationales in Paris. See Camille Piton, *Les Lombards en France et à Paris* (Paris, 1892), 72–74 (citing documents in AN J 919).

[35] He seems to have been in Paris from at least 1518 since letters of naturalization accorded to Philippe and Jean-Baptiste de Friscobaldi in March 1528 indicate they had been established there "depuis dix ans." *Collection des Ordonnances des rois de France, Catalogue des actes de François Ier*, vol. 6, #19770.

A final notice does not involve Italian traffic but does localize Filippo's operation in Paris, since on 9 June an inventory was registered of two coffers "deposited in a chamber of the house of Philippe de Friscobaldis, *marchand florentin, bourgeois de Paris, rue Saint-Jacques, à l'enseigne de la Croix verte*."[36] Evidently Filippo Frescobaldi had been handling the Parisian end of an active business that included transporting papal documents in January 1521. Lanfranc Spinola must have put *Piis omnium* in the hands of some representative of the Frescobaldi house, who carried the bull across the Alps to Filippo on the rue Saint-Jacques in Paris, at the sign of the Green Cross.

The "Fristobaldi banker," however, did not do this work out of the goodness of his heart. He demanded (according to the nuns) the hefty sum of 244 *écus d'or* before he would deliver *Piis omnium*. At this point one of Longchamp's Franciscan confessors, Robert Messier, intervened. Originally based in Amiens, this doctor of theology had been guardian of that house in 1497, of Troyes in 1504, and a confessor at Longchamp since at least 1512.[37] He was a reformer,[38] preacher,[39] author,[40] and (shortly after

---

[36] Ernest Coyecque, "Inventaire sommaire d'un minutier parisien pendant le cours du XVIᵉ siècle (1498–1600)," *Bulletin de la Société de l'histoire de Paris et de l'Ile de France* (1893): 40–58, 114–36, at 118–21 (from two paper and parchment registers of the notary Pierre Crozon); more formally described in idem, *Recueil d'actes notariés relatifs à l'histoire de Paris et de ses environs au XVIᵉ siècle*, vol. 1 (Paris, 1905), #361–62, 375, 385, 415. (#381 also relates that Oudoin de Houlmieres [*licencié en lois*] and Jean du Buisson [*écuyer, seigneur de Mirabel*] borrowed twenty *écus d'or soleil* from Philippe de Frescobaldis in March, to be paid back to his agent in Toulouse by April.)

[37] He is called confessor of Longchamp in AN L 1028 no. 10, an inventory of Longchamp's accounts and possessions dated 22 October 1513, but referring to a donation of 1512.

[38] Clément Schmitt, "Lettres des ministres généraux conservées aux archives franciscaines de Saint-Trond," *Archivum franciscanum historicum* 69 (1976): 107–85 and 401–22, at 118–20.

[39] One collection of *Super epistolas et evangelia totius quadragesimae sermones* is known, in printings of 1525 (Paris, Cl. Chevallon) and 1531 (Paris, J. Petit). The only study I know of that considers these sermons is Larissa Taylor, *Soldiers of Christ: Preaching in Late Medieval and Reformation France* (New York, 1992) (brief biographical note on Messier at 240).

[40] BnF ms. fr. 1888 is a copy of Messier's work entitled *L'address de salut*, composed for Marie de Livres, sister of Longchamp. It is dated 1523 and copied by François le Herice, identified as confessor of Longchamp. Brief summary in Hugues

this period) provincial minister for France (1523–26 and 1529–32) and guardian of Paris (1526–29) in a long administrative career that ended with his death and burial at Longchamp in 1546.[41] Messier was credited in the nuns' narrative as the driving force behind the campaign to secure approval for Isabelle's office. He had apparently already prepared the office itself, and so obviously had a strong interest in expediting the process. In the end, he was able to talk the banker down to a price of 100 *écus d'or*,[42] which was lent to the abbey by "a certain friend" at Robert's request. The bull was thus liberated from the hands of its courier, and on 23 August 1521, Robert along with his fellow confessor Adam Falconis and "master" Pierre du Puys, Longchamp's procurator,[43] was able to carry the bull to Longchamp and present it to the community. The reception took place after Compline, with the bells sounding and the nuns singing *Te Deum laudamus.*

A Detour to Berry

Since the proposed day of Isabelle's feast, 31 August, was only a week away, perhaps the nuns and their confessors might have hoped to be able to celebrate the new office immediately.[44] If so, it must have been anticlimactic to realize that the pope had stipulated that an additional process of review would be necessary. Leo's letter was addressed to Adrien

---

Dedieu, "Messier (Le Messier; Robert)," *Dictionnaire de spiritualité,* vol. 10:1092–93; and Bert Roest, *Franciscan Literature of Religious Instruction before the Council of Trent* (Leiden, 2004), 410–11; Messier may perhaps also have been the author of a life of Isabelle of France found in BnF nouv. acq. fr. 10871 (see Field, "A New Life of Isabelle of France from the Early Sixteenth Century," 41–43). Both these texts remain to be edited and studied.

[41] Antoine Béguit (de Sérent), "Nécrologe des frères mineurs d'Auxerre," *Archivum franciscanum historicum* 3 (1910): 115–38, 310–32, 530–50, 716–78, at 535.

[42] This seems to have been closer to the going rate. See an example from 1496 cited by Jacqueline Boucher, "Les Italiens à Lyons," in Jean Balsamo, ed., *Passer les monts: Français en Italie – l'Italie en France (1494–1525). X^e colloque de la Société française d'étude du Seizième Siècle* (Paris, 1998), 39–46, at 40.

[43] Doubtless some information on these two men could be gleaned from Longchamp's surviving archives from this period, but I have not been able to carry out such a search.

[44] At least, the date of 31 August was approved by Adrien de Boisy, most likely because it had been proposed by Longchamp. This date made Isabelle's feast fall six days after that of her brother.

Gouffier de Boisy, bishop of Albi, Cardinal-Priest of Saint Sabina, and papal legate *a latere* to France, instructing the cardinal to carry out his own investigation before authorizing the office on behalf of the pope. Only if the legate found that the claims being made on Isabelle's behalf were accurate, and the new office acceptable, should he then give final permission to Longchamp for the celebration of Isabelle's feast.

Adrien was from a powerful family close to Francis I.[45] His brothers Artus (d. 1519) and Guillaume (de Bonnivet, d. 1525) were grand master and admiral of France (respectively) and among Francis's most trusted and influential advisors (Artus had been the king's tutor and Guillaume his boyhood friend). Adrien himself had been named bishop of Coutances in 1511, grand almoner of France upon Francis's ascension to the throne, cardinal in December 1515 at the time of Francis I's meeting with Leo X, bishop of Albi in 1519, and titular abbot of several monasteries. At the urging of Francis I (who referred to Adrien as his "cousin"), Leo X had named the cardinal de Boisy as his legate *a latere* to the kingdom of France 23 March 1519, with a particular mission to preach the crusade against the Turks. The term of this legation was set for one year beginning 1 September 1519.[46]

---

[45]   P. Carouge, "Gouffier, famille," in *La France de la Renaissance: histoire et dictionnaire* (2001): 851–54; idem, "Artus (1474–1519) et Guillaume (1482–1525) Gouffier à l'emergence de nouvelles modalités de gouvernement," in *Les Conseillers de François Ier*, ed. Cédric Michon (Rennes, 2011), 229–53. Adrien's reputation may not have been above reproach in Roman circles, since P. Richard, "Origines de la nonciature de France: débuts de la représentation permanente sous Léon X, 1513–1521," *Revue des questions historiques* 35 (1906): 112–80, cites (169 n2) Paris de Grassis's statement that after Adrien received the cardinal's hat he was heard singing a French drinking song. Moreover, in a widely-circulated satirical last will of Leo X's elephant Hanno composed in 1516, Adrien is called "protector of drunkards in hypocrisy and ignorance of all France." Quoted in Silvio A. Bedini, *The Pope's Elephant* (New York, 1997), 156. Some evidence of this "hypocrisy" may be seen in the legitimization of his daughter, *Collection des Ordonnances des rois de France, Catalogue des actes de François Ier*, vol. 8, #33119. See note 12 above for Lanfranc Spinola's association with this family.

[46]   Bernard Barbiche and Ségolène de Dainville-Barbiche, "Les légats *a latere* en France et leurs facultés aux XVIe et XVIIe siècles," *Archivum historiae pontificiae* 23 (1985): 93–165, at 151. See also Bernard Jacqueline, "Trois évêques de Coutances légats 'a latere': Giuliano della Rovere, Bernardo Dovizi da Bibbiena, Adrien Gouffier de Boisy," *Revue du département de la Manche* 31 (1989): 3–10; Richard, "Origines de la nonciature," 169–72; C. Guasti, ed., "I Manoscritti Torrigiani donati al R. Archivio

This chronological delimitation presents a puzzle, since it would seem that by January 1521 Adrien should no longer have held his official status as legate *a latere*,[47] and yet *Piis omnium* still refers to him as *in regno Franciae nostro et apostolicae sedis legato de latere*. The explanation for this apparent inconsistency would seem to lie in ongoing negotiations between Francis and Leo over whether Adrien's legation would be extended for another year after 1 September 1520. Leo had in fact promised the king that this extension would be granted.[48] According to two letters written by Francis I, in October 1520 papal nuncios were refusing to hand over the bulls confirming this extension, in violation of the papal promise, because of a jurisdictional dispute over the relative powers of the legates to France and to the Dauphiné.[49] Although in the event the dispute dragged on and the prolongation never did occur, the question was evidently still being negotiated in early 1521 (indeed no legate *a latere* for France took Adrien's place until June 1522, after Leo's death).[50] Thus although by January 1521 Leo must have been aware that his original intention to prolong Adrien's legature had hit a snag, he may have assumed that this was a temporary matter and that his original directive would eventually be implemented as the king wished, particularly since the relevant papal bulls may already have been issued, only

Centrale di Stato di Firenze," *Archivio Storico Italiano*, 3rd series, 26 (1877): 177–203, at 178; *Collection des Ordonnances*, vol. 1, #977, #1079, #1102; Giovanni Rucellai, *Letture dalla nunziatura di Franci (1520–1521)*, 49, 61–63, 70–72, 84–85, 90.

[47] Two registers of Adrien's official acts as legate were entrusted by the Parlement de Paris to the abbot of Saint-Denis in 1524 and survive as AN LL 1A and LL 1B. Because (according to Barbiche and Dainville-Barbiche, p. 142) these 478 acts cover only the year from 4 September 1519 to 31 August 1520, one would not expect to find there a copy of any correspondence concerning Isabelle's office.

[48] Richard, "Origines de la nonciature," 170, cites a now lost letter of 22 July 1519 where Leo promised this extension. Richard further states (without citation) that Leo sent the the the letter authorizing the prologation 22 August 1520.

[49] Barbiche and Dainville-Barbiche, "Les légats *a latere*," 103, 131. For the letters see P. Dupuy, *Preuves des libertez de l'Eglise gallicane*, 3rd ed. (Paris, 1731), 2:79–80.

[50] Richard, "Origines de la nonciature de France," 172, refers to a "bulle du renouvellement" of 18 March 1521 that was never put into effect (citing "*Secreta Leonis X*, dans *Regesta Vaticana*, t. 1202, fol. 78, renouvellement *ad annum*, xv kal. Junii"). Richard, however, incorrectly believed that Cardinal Adrien died shortly thereafter, in June 1521; he in fact lived until July 1523. For the appointment of the next legate, see Barbiche and Dainville-Barbiche, "Les légats *a latere*," 151.

to be held back at the last moment. But as the question languished, by December 1521 Adrien in his own letter called himself only *in hac parte a sede apostolica delegatus*, acknowledging by default that his powers were no longer officially those of a legate *a latere*, but merely that of a cardinal who had been asked to deal with a particular matter.

According to the nuns' recounting, Robert Messier himself then carried the bull to Adrien in Berry. Adrien was too busy to tend to the matter himself, and so sent "master" Antoine Chabanier as his commissioner to Longchamp to investigate Isabelle's miracles, the nature of her life, and the text of her new office.[51] Antoine brought his report back to Adrien, who at last approved the bull and the office. The text of Adrien's own letter provides further details, and his own perspective, on this process. He received Longchamp's representative and Leo's letter 27 September at the château of Vatan (west of Bourges). He then sent his vicar, *magister* Antoine, to Longchamp, where he examined "many witnesses. . . concerning the exhibited articles," made copies "from the ancient books" and other documents found at Longchamp, and had them signed by a notary before carrying his results back to Adrien. Thus Antoine (who would go on to be deacon of Clermont in 1528 and *conseiller* to the Parlement de Paris in 1535 before resigning by 1543)[52] evidently carried out a serious inquiry. The witnesses he interviewed presumably would have included Jeanne Carphaude and other contemporary nuns. His consultation of Longchamp's "ancient books" must have included at least one of the several copies of Agnes of Harcourt's *Vie d'Isabelle* held at Longchamp. And he took care to turn the extracts from this and other texts into notarized documents before submitting them to the cardinal de Boisy.

Adrien duly read the records of his vicar's investigation and took counsel with several learned professors in law and theology. Then, on 11 December 1521, near Amboise, the "procurator" for Longchamp (presumably Robert Messier, though perhaps Pierre du Puy) appeared again

---

[51]   Adrien, as legate, had apparently promised not to appoint a vicar or substitute to act with his own full powers. Dupuy, *Preuves des libertez*, 2:79. Presumably in 1521, no longer bearing the full powers of legate *a latere*, the cardinal felt himself absolved of this promise.

[52]   Michel Popoff, *Prosopographie des gens du Parlement de Paris (1266–1753): d'après les ms Fr. 7553, 7554, 7555, 7555 bis conservés au Cabinet des manuscrits de la Bibliothèque nationale de France* (Saint-Nazaire-le-Désert, 1996), 412; *Collection des Ordonnances*, vol. 2 #7036; vol. 5, #15189; vol. 7, #26091.

in Adrien's presence and asked that the papal bull now be promulgated, since a diligent inquiry had been completed. Adrien acquiesced, convinced, and thus approved the celebration at Longchamp of the new office, signed and corrected with his own hand,[53] for the last day of August, while noting that this approval of a local office fell short of canonization. It took ten days for this joyous news to make its way back to Paris, since according to the nuns' narrative it was on 21 December that at long last the document granting final approval was received at Longchamp.

Did this new recognition of the *beata* virgin "sister of *divus* Louis, former king of the Franks," make any impression on the court of Francis I? Nothing proves that it did.[54] It is likely, though, that the bare facts were at least known, given the cardinal de Boisy's close ties to the king, as well as the positions at court held by members of the Spinola and Le Picart (see below) families. If so, Isabelle's image might have struck a contemporary chord. For one thing, Francis's own sister Marguerite of Navarre was by this time already widely recognized as a devout monastic patron and reformer, and as a charismatic and literate presence in the royal family with a close relationship to her brother. In broad strokes, this is a description that could have applied equally well to Isabelle of France (though in 1521 Marguerite was a married woman, in sharp distinction to Isabelle's life of holy celibacy, and she was the king's older sister whereas Isabelle had been some eleven years Louis's junior). In retrospect, we know that Marguerite's piety was perceived by some as veering in dangerous directions by the 1530s; and modern readers of the *Heptaméron* might be hard pressed to envision its author as a saintly figure. Nevertheless any reference to "the sister of the king of the Franks" might have conjured up associations with Marguerite, and, in the context of 1521, Francis's pious, learned sister might well have appeared in some sense as an "Isabelle" to the Francis's "Louis."[55] The implications of this comparison would have

---

[53] "... quod correctum, manuque propria nostra signatum." There is no indication of what kind of "corrections" the cardinal felt were necessary.

[54] Francis I was not unaware of Longchamp's existence, since he did apparently issue "lettres de sauvegarde" to Longchamp in 1538. Duchesne, *Histoire de l'abbaye royale de Longchamp*, 80, citing AN K 87 no. 8 (I have not examined this document myself).

[55] A recent biography (in the large body of literature devoted to Marguerite) is Patricia F. Cholakian and Rouben C. Cholakian, *Marguerite de Navarre: Mother of the Renaissance* (New York, 2006). The cardinal de Boisy may not have been entirely

been flattering to Francis, particularly to the extent that he was being encouraged to imagine himself as a new crusader against the Turks, following in the mold of the great crusader king Louis IX.

Perhaps more directly, contemporaries might have thought of Jeanne de France (1464–1505), the daughter of Louis XI and wife of Louis XII, who after the annulment of that marriage (1498) administered the duchy of Berry and founded a new Franciscan-associated order for women, based at her new house of the Annonciade in Bourges. She composed a rule (approved by Alexander VI in 1502) and herself took vows at the end of her life. Miracles were recorded there, though she was not beatified until 1742 and canonized only in 1950. Isabelle had never been married and never took formal monastic vows (though she was buried in a Franciscan habit), but otherwise the parallels are striking between these two women, who both wrote Franciscan rules and took strong directing interests in the new orders and houses they created.[56] Jeanne's location in Bourges would have made her, and perhaps her miracles, particularly known to Adrien de Boisy and the royal court as well.

Writing and Re-Writing at Longchamp

By 21 December 1521, Leo X had in fact been dead for nearly three weeks, though his demise does not seem to have yet become known at Longchamp. But now that his bull could take full effect, the nuns could rejoice and prepare for the first celebration of the office the following

---

in Marguerite's good graces in 1521, if indeed the fourth story in her *Heptaméron* is a veiled reference to Adrien's brother, Guillaume Gouffier (with whom Marguerite had a long and complex relationship, focused on by Cholakian and Cholakian), and his attempt to sexually assault Marguerite in 1520. See ibid., 1–3. And considering Jeanne de France, the annulment of her marriage to Louis XII for a time raised the possibility that Louis might have a son through his second marriage to Anne of Brittany, which would have stood in the way of Francis's ascent to the throne. Thus the admittedly speculative reflections suggested here would hardly have been one-dimensional.

[56] See Dominique Dinet, Pierre Moracchini, and Marie-Emmanuel Portebos, eds., *Jeanne de France et l'Annonciade, Actes du colloque international de l'Institut catholique de Paris (13–14 mars 2002)* (Paris, 2004). Another interesting parallel is that lives of both "saints" were written by nuns, Agnes of Harcourt in the case of Isabelle, Françoise Guyard in the case of Jeanne. For the latter, see Jean-Fr. Bonnefoy, *Chronique de l'annonciade. Vies de la bienheureuse Jeanne de France et du bienheureux Gabriel-Maria, O. F. M.* (Paris, 1937).

August. More immediately, however, they had record-keeping to do. They not only preserved Leo's bull and Adrien's letter of promulgation, but recounted events from their own perspective and prepared French translations of the documents. These texts were then copied into a six-folio quire of parchment that was at some point bound into what is now BnF ms. fr. 11662. This copy was made with great care (see Appendix B) with the names of seventy-three sisters of Longchamp appended, including the abbess, Catherine Le Picart. The production of this record must have been something of a group effort, with Robert Messier most likely playing some role along with the abbess herself.

Catherine Le Picart had entered Longchamp at age thirteen in 1474 (along with her short-lived sister Anne), and was elected abbess in 1514, serving in that capacity until her death in 1532.[57] Thus by 1521 she was a mature woman of approximately sixty years, with nearly a half century at Longchamp and seven years as abbess behind her. She was from a prosperous Parisian family, well-established in royal service and part of the new "financial aristocracy." Her parents were the royal secretary Martin Le Picart (d. 1490) and his wife Jeanne de Marle. Hence Catherine was sister to Jean Le Picart, seigneur of Villeron and Atilly, who was currently secretary to Francis I. She was aunt to Jean's many children, including Francis, who was a master of theology and important preacher in Paris. Jean subsequently inherited his father's post with the king.[58] One would

---

[57] Field, "Abbesses of Longchamp in the Sixteenth Century," 557.

[58] See Młynarczyk, *Ein Franziskanerinnenkloster*, 208, for clear evidence from the archives of Longchamp. On this family in the next generation see Larissa Juliet Taylor, *Heresy and Orthodoxy in Sixteenth-Century Paris: François Le Picart and the Beginnings of the Catholic Reformation* (Leiden, 1999), 25–27, but Taylor mistakenly stated that Catherine was a daughter of Jean Le Picart and Jacquette de Champagne, and thus sister of the university master François. This error resulted from reliance on Hilarion de Coste, *Le parfait ecclesiastique ou l'histoire de la vie et de la mort de François Le Picart. . .* (Paris, 1658), 21–22, who in turn was simply relying on Sébastian Roulliard's 1619 biography of Isabelle of France. Another Catherine Picard, born in 1516, entered Longchamp in 1524 and lived until 1590. This may be the source of the confusion (cf. Duchesne, *Histoire de l'abbaye royale de Longchamp*, 124). BnF ms. fr. 11662, fol. 64ʳ: "Seur Katherine Picard fut vestue le xxiᵉ iour de aoust lan mil. cinq cens xxiiii. de laage de viii. ans. Et trespassa *Le xixᵉ Jour de Juillet m vᶜ iiii.ˣˣ dix*." It is interesting to note that although this second Catherine took her vows on Isabelle's new feast day (August 31) the entry in the necrology did not draw attention to this fact.

expect a daughter of this family to be well-educated (Guillaume Budé, for instance, was her first cousin). Catherine's family connections also suggest another conduit by which figures close to the court might have become aware of the approval of Isabelle's new office.

The concise French narrative tells a triumphant story of the nuns' quest to have Isabelle's claims recognized. The narrative's structure deftly balances interest-generating suspense with a reassuring certainty of success. The ultimate result is made a foregone conclusion by the way the narrative commences: In accordance with God's benevolence, demonstrated by Isabelle's miracles at Longchamp and particularly the cure of Jeanne Carphaude, Leo X conceded "to the nuns of the said monastery the permission to perform the divine office and solemn celebration of the said saintly lady (*saincte dame*) Isabelle on the last day of August, to sing a proper office with the solemn celebration of a major duplex (*grand double*)." The reality of Isabelle's miracle-working is thus already treated as proven, and the pope's approval is stated unambiguously so as to leave no question about the validity of the new office for *madame saincte* Isabelle. Only then does the narrative double back to recount the role of *Franc de Spinolle*, the greed of the *bancquier nommé Fristobaldi*, the successful negotiation by Robert Messier, who "had composed the proper office of the said *saincte*," and the joyous reception of the bull at Longchamp. After this first narrative highpoint, the introduction of the whole quest to gain ratification by the cardinal de Boisy creates a new tension. Linguistic hints, however, again tip off the fact that this delay will surely be resolved with final approval. The cardinal's deputy Antoine, for instance, comes not to investigate an open question, but "to inform himself of the truth of the miracles of the said *saincte*." This truth is reinforced by the internal logic of the text repeatedly referring to *la dicte saincte*. Interestingly, the nuns' narrative suggests that Antoine consulted with other learned men and presented the results to the cardinal, whereas Adrien's own letter makes clear it was he who showed Antoine's information to learned advisors to get their opinions. Still, the diligence of this inquiry and the involvement of "several doctors of theology and canon law" put beyond doubt the cardinal's judgment that the new office was *catholicque et veritable*. Concluding the narrative, Messier is constructed as its true hero, with the final remark that it was all due "to the efforts, care, and nearly inconceivable labor of the said Brother Robert Messier."

It would seem that this narrative was written almost immediately,[59] and copied into the surviving version quite soon. The solemn nature of the recording in BnF ms. fr. 11662 is emphasized by the appending of the name of abbess Catherine and all "*les religieuses et dames discrettes*" of the abbey, in two carefully-ruled columns.[60] Comparison of this list of seventy-two sisters with the abbey's necrology (also found in ms. fr. 11662) reveals that the next sixty-one names are those of fully professed nuns, listed by loose order of seniority. Thus after the abbess, the first name was that of the most senior nun, Jeanne la Duchesse. Born in 1459, Jeanne had entered Longchamp in May 1470 and so had been there for fifty-one years at the time this document was created. The next two women, Marguerite Queulu and Marie de Rubspré, had entered Longchamp only a few months after Jeanne. The fourth woman on the list, Marguerite de Mailly, professed slightly later (in 1478), but because she was already twenty-four when she entered (much older than average), she was in fact the oldest living nun at Longchamp in 1521, aged sixty-seven. From here, although the names do not follow an absolutely rigorous chronological order, in a general sense the list moves from the more senior to the more junior. The most recent nun to have professed was Sister Etienne Le Gay, on 8 December 1521, only three days before the date of Adrien de Boisy's final approval for the new office. Indeed, she was part of a surge of professions in 1521, along with Madeleine de Marle (21 April; probably related to Catherine Le Picart's mother's family) and Anne Senesme (1 September).[61] It seems, moreover, that the list was meant to include all the nuns who had been part of the process, even if they died during 1521. Thus sister Catherine Fourmont (or Fromont) died 1 October 1521, yet her name is still appended. On the other hand, living memory of these events among these sisters would eventually have stretched almost to the end of the century, since the last of the named nuns, Jeanne de Mailly

---

[59] Certainly before August 1522 (since after that point one would expect some mention of the first celebration of the office) and probably very early in 1522 (since there is no indicate that the nuns yet knew of Leo X's death 1 December 1521).

[60] The names themselves were printed in Duchesne, *Histoire de l'abbaye royale de Longchamp*, 134–35.

[61] The next sister to enter Longchamp, lay sister Jeanne Prunier, did not do so until 18 October 1522, and so does not appear on the list. BnF ms. fr. 11662, fol. 63ᵛ: "Seur Jehanne Prunier fut vestue le iour sainct Luc lan mi cinq cens xxii. Aagee de xvii ans pour estre seur laye. Et trespassa *le x. Jour de Juillet Lan mil .v.ᶜ xxxvi.*"

(abbess 1580–85), lived until September 1590.

At the end of the list, following the abbess and sixty-one nuns (one of whom was already deceased),[62] are eleven lay sisters. Interestingly, this list of lay sisters proceeds by absolutely strict chronological order, suggesting that within this group seniority carried closely-guarded privileges. Thus the first lay sister on the list (no. 63 overall) is Jeanne le Fèvre, who at age 57 and with 42 years at Longchamp was a senior presence indeed. Very last on the list is Isabeau Brodon, who had become a lay sister in 1515 to act as barber to the abbey.[63]

The French translation of Adrien's letter (with Leo's letter embedded) which immediately follows these names is faithful enough to the original in substance, although in a few places the flowery papal periods are only awkwardly rendered into French, and in other spots some information (such as the cardinal's full honors and titles) is slightly abbreviated. Several more significant shifts, however, reveal interesting aspects of the nuns' perspective, demonstrating how they wished to interpret what had been approved. Two points are particularly notable.

First, the nuns corrected Leo X's apparent assertion that Isabelle had herself been a nun. The residents of Longchamp were well aware that this was not the case. Althoughy Isabelle had been buried in a Franciscan habit,[64] no *vie* or account produced at Longchamp had ever claimed that

    [62] Longchamp was limited to sixty nuns by Clement IV's bull *Licet cultum divini* of 20 April 1268, preserved in AN L 262 nos. 112 and 112*bis*. See Sean L. Field, "The Princess, the Abbess, and the Friars: Isabelle of France (1225–1270) and the Course of Thirteenth-Century Religious History," (Ph.D. Diss., Northwestern University, 2002), 408. If the abbess is excluded, it can be seen that the nuns were still keeping strictly to this limit, with Etienne Le Gay not becoming the sixtieth nun until after Catherine Fourmont's death. Lay sisters were evidently regarded as legitimate additions to the statutory number of sixty nuns.

    [63] The last lay barber, Massee Berum, had died 1 September 1515 after twenty-two years in that office. BnF ms. fr. 11662, fol. 60ᵛ: "Seur Massee Berum laye de lage de xvi ans pour loffice de barbiere fut vestue lan mil iiii.ᶜᶜ iiii.ˣˣ et xiii et trespassa *le premier Jour de septembre lan mil vc et quinze*." Interestingly, this entry did not bother to record the exact date of her entry. For records of earlier barbers (that is, trained bloodletters), see Ernest Wickersheimer, *Dictionnaire biographique des médecins en France au moyen âge*, vol. 2 (1936; reprint, Geneva: Droz, 1979), 505, 532. I thank Professor Monica Green for this reference.

    [64] *Writings of AH*, 48. For more detailed discussion of the question of whether Isabelle ever took formal vows at Longchamp, see Field, *Isabelle of France*, 122–25.

Isabelle had been a professed sister,[65] and in fact she lived to the end of her life as Longchamp's non-professed, royal/lay patron—the abbey's *saincte mère*. Leo, however, had written about her as though one of her actual claims to quasi-sanctity resided in her fulfilling the vows of a professed nun. This passage thus presented an obvious dilemma: How to memorialize the pope's words, when they contained a statement such as this that the internal audience at Longchamp would have recognized as false and contradicting their own shared memories of their founder? Compare Leo's Latin with the nuns' translation:

Piis omnium	BnF ms. fr. 11662, fol. 18rb
Quae etiam dum in humanis ageret tanquam aeternae beatitudinis amatrix, et propulsato fragilis viri thoro ac abjectis mundanis illecebris, ipsi Altissimo vota sua in pacis amoenitudine exsolvere cupiens, monasterium ingressa et ordinem hujusmodi expresse professa, sub religionis jugo inibi famulatum praestare, et vitam sanctimonialis ducere quoad universae carnis viam, prout Altissimo placuit, ingrederetur, indefesse non desiit. . .	Laquelle en son vivant comme amateresse de eternelle beatitude, en propos de virginité, en abjection des charnelles voluptés, desirant en amenité de paix rendre ses veulx et desires a Dieu, au dict monastere est entrée et la a faict residence comme se elle eust faict expresse profession soubz la charge de religion, faisant service a Dieu en menant vie de parfaicte religion et sanctimonie. . .

---

[65] The new *Vie* composed c. 1520 (now found in Princeton University Liberary ms. 188; see Field, "A New Life of Isabelle"), says absolutely nothing about Isabelle taking vows, portraying her always as a holy presence apart from the nuns. Thus it seems certain that thirteenth-century historical fact had not grown confused in the minds of the sixteenth-century inhabitants of Longchamp. In circles near the French royal court, however, the idea that Isabelle had been a professed nun may have become prevalent. See for example the illumination in BnF ms fr. 2829, *Le livre des faiz monseigneur saint Loys* (made c. 1480, owned by Charles VIII by 1488) that represented Isabelle taking the veil with her brother the king looking on. Studied in Hoover, "Gender and Dynastic Sanctity in Late Fifteenth-Century France" (see her figures 10 and 11), with a color facsimile available in Marie-Thérèse Gousset, François Avril, and Jean Richard, eds., *Saint Louis, roi de France: Livre des faits de Monseigneur Saint Louis* (Paris, 1990), 69.

Leo first described Isabelle generally as having rejected "marriage to a frail man," which the nuns shifted subtly to a more positive assertion of her "purpose of virginity." Then where Leo had written "having entered the monastery and expressly professed this order, [she] tirelessly did not cease to perform service there under the yoke of religion, and to lead the life of a nun. . .", the Longchamp vernacular narrative asserted that Isabelle "entered the said monastery and resided there *as if* she had expressly professed under the charge of religion, doing service to God by leading a life of perfect religion and piety." The *ordinem hujusmodi expresse professa* ("expressly professed this order" or "an order of this kind") becomes *la a faict residence comme se elle eust faict expresse profession* ("and there made her residence as if she had made an express profession of religion"). A true profession and entrance into "this" order, presumably referring back to the Order of Saint Clare, becomes a statement merely about where Isabelle chose to make her residence and how she had lived "as if" she had made an explicit profession. And the *vitam sanctimonialis*, meaning the "life of a nun," becomes the French *vie de parfaicte religion et sanctimonie*, "life of perfect religion and holiness." Visually *sanctimonialis* has only shifted slightly to *sanctimonie*, perhaps creating the illusion of a quite literal translation for eyes merely skimming the text. But in fact the meaning has been entirely changed.[66]

Even more directly, at the end of his letter of promulgation, Adrien de Boisy approved the office of the woman he referred to as "the blessed Isabelle, the aforementioned virgin, sister of *divus* Louis former king of the Franks, nun of the same monastery [Longchamp] while she was in life." The cardinal, even more clearly than the pope, revealed here that he

---

[66] Moreover, this semantic shift may not have been simply a case of the nuns correcting Leo's honest mistake. For Leo surely based his *narratio* on the supplication he was sent. It may well be, therefore, that Robert Messier, Catherine Le Picart, and the nuns of Longchamp had found language in their original communication that allowed the pope to assume Isabelle had been a nun—a less problematic position than that of the resident royal lay patron which she had been in reality. I regret that I have not been able to undertake a search of the Vatican archives to determine whether Longchamp's original supplication might by chance survive there. Only if such an original document were discovered could we be sure of the exact language used in the nuns' request, and therefore of how closely Leo's *narratio* mirrored that specific language; even then we would need to be certain that no additional "supporting documentation" helped shape the pope's perception.

believed Isabelle to have been a nun of Longchamp. But when the current nuns translated this passage into French, they simple omitted the clause "*vita comite praedicti monasterii moniali*" altogether![67] So far as the abbey's internal textual memory would record, this historically incorrect representation of their foundress never existed.

The second interesting point is the way the word *saincte* bleeds over from the prefatory narrative into the translation of the two letters. Leo's first use of the phrase *beata Elisabetha* is translated as *bienheureuse Ysabel*, but as the same phrase *beata Elisabetha* is repeated, it quickly becomes *saincte Ysabel*. Leo's bull does itself use the phrase *sancta Elisabetha* once (translated of course as *saincte*), but it occurs in Leo's *narratio* (recounting of the abbey's request) and may thus actually reflect the language the nuns included in their petition. But then the same operation is also performed on Cardinal Adrien's words. In his closing clauses, where he agreed that indeed miracles of *ipsa Elisabetha beata* had been occurring, and approved the *proprium officium de beata Elisabetha*, in both instances the translation reads *saincte Ysabel*. The narrative had already set up the expectation that the woman under consideration was a saint, and even though the nuns were aware that no canonization had taken place, the term irresistibly eclipses the more restrained *beata/ bienheureuse*.[68]

In sum, the nuns wished to make it clear that their founder had lived 'like a nun" but had never been one, and that she was, in their eyes not merely the "blessed Isabelle" but "saint Isabelle." The delayed slippage, as the very first use of *beata* is more accurately translated but every subsequent use of the word becomes *saincte*, is perhaps a subtle strategy to suggest adherence to wording when in fact significant change is being

---

[67] I particularly thank Prof. H. A. Kelly for drawing my attention to this omission.

[68] It is true that in French (then and now) *saincte Ysabel* could mean "the holy woman Isabelle" as well as the more specific "Saint Isabelle," and thus the use of this adjective is perhaps not as definitive as it appears in English translation. Nevertheless, the initial choice of *bienheureuse* indicates that the translators were aware of this available equivalent for *beata*, and thus the systematic rejection of that term throughout the rest of the texts seems significant. For instance, Isabelle's canonized brother is always *sainct Loys* here, never *bienheureux* (though sometimes the more humanistic *divus* in the Latin). Thus the repeated invocation of Saint Isabelle creates an apparent pair of true, royal saints.

made. Although Leo X had been careful to state that his approval of Isabelle's local cult was short of canonization, in Longchamp's retelling she nevertheless was transformed into *saincte Isabelle*.

Similarly creative, "loose" translations of authoritative Latin texts by nuns for their own internal use were hardly unheard of. For instance, Lezlie Knox has recently analyzed the way Italian Franciscan women at the end of the fifteenth century, such as Sister Battista Alfani of Monteluce, recast the thirteenth-century Latin *vita* of Clare of Assisi in new translations where "the author might add to, subtract from, or even rearrange incidents in the traditional narrative according to the interests of the expected audience."[69] But the nuns of Longchamp seem to have been particularly subtle in their re-shading of more recent texts, issued directly to them by a pope and a cardinal. By crafting their vernacular version and binding it into one of Longchamp's most important commemorative manuscripts, the sisters of Longchamp controlled the terms on which readers at the abbey would remember Pope Leo's and Cardinal Adrien's praise of their foundress.

Conclusion

The sixteenth-century nuns of Longchamp might be pleased to know that Longchamp's foundress is still sometimes referred to as "Saint Isabelle" by the modern faithful, even though she has never formally been canonized by the Catholic Church. It is also often written that Leo X "beatified" her in 1521; technically this assertion is neither entirely true nor false, since the formal category of beatification would not be articulated in canon law until a century later. This was, however, the moment when the Church first granted some level of formal recognition to the idea that not only Louis IX but also his sister could intercede with God on behalf of those devoted to her cult. Beyond individual prayers and offerings, there would now be an annual ritual and an office with its own set of rhetorical claims to serve as recurring reminders that the pope himself had recognized Isabelle's efficacy as a miracle worker. Although the effects of the office's implementation have not yet been closely studied, they clearly did have an impact, if not perhaps as quickly as Robert Messier, Catherine Le Picart, and the other inhabitants of Longchamp might have wished in 1521. A century later Isabelle's cult was flourishing alongside renewed

---

[69] Knox, *Creating Clare of Assisi*, 172.

devotion to her brother, with the first printed biographies of her appearing in 1619 and 1644, and an illustrious gathering of French ecclesiastical dignitaries assembling for a translation of her relics in 1637.[70] Although the events of 1521 may have been only a dim memory by that point, these later successes owed a great deal to Longchamp's earlier struggles to get the nuns' petition and Leo X's response from Paris to Rome and back again.

---

[70] For the printed biographies by Roulliard and Caussin, see Appendix A, note 3. The translation of 1637 is described in a short pamphlet entitled *L'abrégé de la vie et miracle fait à l'abbaye de Long-champ sur le tombeau de la bienheureuse Isabel de France, fille du roy Louys VIII et soeur du bon roy S. Louys* (Longchamp, 1637).

Appendix A

Leo X's bull *Piis omnium* (11 January 1521) and its Promulgation by Cardinal Adrien de Boisy (11 December 1521)

NO ORIGINAL OF either of these letters is known to survive.[1] A sealed original of *Piis omnium*, however, was certainly preserved at Longchamp for centuries, as was the original of the confirmation letter from Cardinal Adrien de Boisy. These originals were consulted there and described in 1699 by Isabelle of France's would-be biographer, the Parisian priest Pierre Perrier; his inventory of the documents held at Longchamp and used for his (never published) biography included "La bulle de Léon X,

---

[1] In a well-informed 1946 publication, the Franciscan scholar Livier Oliger wrote concerning *Piis omnium* that "On l'a cherchée en vain dans les Archives du Vatican." See "Le plus ancien office liturgique de la B.se Isabelle de France," in *Miscellana Giovanni Mercati*, vol. 2 (Vatican City, 1946): 484–508, at 490 n13. No copy seems to have been known to Guy Trouillard when he compiled his 1896 École des chartes thesis, *Études sur la discipline et l'état intérieur des abbayes de l'ordre des Urbanistes et principalement de l'abbaye de Longchamp du XIII*ᵉ *siècle au XVIII*ᵉ (I have consulted the copy held as ms. 1530 of the Bibliothèque franciscaine provinciale in Paris) or to Gaston Duchesne, *Histoire de l'abbaye royale de Longchamp (1255 à 1789),* 2ⁿᵈ ed. (Paris, 1906), although both scholars combed the holdings of the Archives nationales.

pour la béatification de s^te Isabelle, avec le seau de plomb sur lacs de corde, et l'ordre du cardinal de s^te Sabine, qui contient aussi la dite bule [*sic*], mais qui n'a point le sceau, quoi qu'il soit percée pour le mettre."[2]

While Perrier provided the clearest description, he was not the first scholar to use or copy these original documents held at Longchamp. When Sébastian Roulliard published the first printed biography of Isabelle in 1619 (based on documents preserved at Longchamp as well as a large dose of his imagination), he gave his own French translation of Leo's bull and then a summary of Adrian's confirmation.[3] By around 1680 Le Nain de Tillemont possessed two copies; both are extant though one is now incomplete. Since his notebooks demonstrably contained copies made at Longchamp, it seems very likely that these copies were also made from the Longchamp originals.[4]

The best complete version of the texts known to me is that printed in

---

    [2] This biography in manuscript is now AN L 1029 no. 37. For a brief description see Sean L. Field, "Imagining Isabelle: The Fifteenth-Century Epitaph of Isabelle of France at Longchamp," *Franciscan Studies* 65 (2007): 371–403, at 402–3. In its current state, the manuscript has been rebound with folios out of their original order, and many folios have been lost. A second copy of this biography is found in BnF ms. fr. 24950 (now available digitally through Gallica) but without this list of sources.
    [3] Sébastian Roulliard [*sic*], *La saincte mère, ou vie, de M. saincte Isabel de France* (Paris, 1619), 482–85, followed by summary. The other important printed biography from this era is Nicolas Caussin, *La Vie de sainte Isabelle, soeur du Roy Saint Loy et fondatrice du monastère royal de Long-champ, qui a donné un parfait exemple de la vie neutre des personnes non mariées ny religieuses* (Paris, 1644). Caussin, Jesuit confessor to Louis XIII, wrote at the instigation of Abbess Isabel Mortier of Longchamp, and was overtly disdainful of Roulliard while neverthless drawing freely on his work. It is not clear that he used the abbey's archives, however, and he probably did not have independent access to Longchamp's copy of the documents under consideration here. On this work see Thomas Worcester, "Neither Married nor Cloistered: Blessed Isabelle in Catholic Reformation France," *The Sixteenth Century Journal* 30 (1999): 457–72, and more recently Véronique Desnian, "The Origins of *La vie neutre*: Nicolas Caussin's Influence on the Writings of Gabrielle Suchon," *French Studies* 63 (2009): 148–60.
    [4] One copy was in his "cahier B," now BnF ms. fr. 13747, fols. 120–123^v; the other is in BnF nouv. acq. fr. 10407, fols. 141^r–142^r (small changes in punctuation and orthography, as well as a very few variant readings, indicate that at least the latter copy was probably not made from Mireaus' printed edition, even though this edition was available by Tillemont's day). On Tillement and his manuscripts see Sean L. Field, "The Missing Sister: Sébastien le Nain de Tillemont's Life of Isabelle of France," *Revue Mabillon* n.s. 19 (2008): 243–70.

Brussels by Aubertus Mireaus (Aubert Le Mire) in 1622 as part of a short work on "Saintly Isabelles."[5] Le Mire (1573–1640), canon and then dean of the cathedral of Antwerp, librarian to Archduke Albert of Austria, and prolific author of works on various aspects of ecclesiastical history,[6] dedicated this book to Albert's wife (and co-ruler of the Netherlands) Isabella Clara Eugenia (1566–1633). Writing just after Albert's death in 1621, this work was meant to honor and console his widow by pointing out the examples of pious "Isabelles" of the past.[7] Presumably Le Mire's choice of topic was based not only on Isabella Clara Eugenia's given name, but on the fact that she was the daughter of Elisabeth/Isabelle of Valois and granddaughter of Isabella of Portugal. Le Mire began his dedicatory preface, however, with particular reference to Isabelle of France, noting how little-known she seemed to be in her native region:[8] "For Isabella Clara Eugenia, Infanta of Spain, I am bringing forth, as in a threater, most

---

[5] Aubertus Mireaus, *Isabellae sanctae: Elisabetha Ioannis bapt. mater, Elisabetha Andr. Regis Hung. Filia, Isabella regina Portugallix, Isabella, S. Lud. Galliae Regis soror* (Brussels, 1622). The booklet is unpaginated, but fols. 7^r–12^v, and 13^v–14^v concern Isabelle of France (the latter folios are a short summary of the foundation of Longchamp, written in French and referring the reader to Roulliard).

[6] See C.-B. De Ridder, "Aubert Le Mire, sa vie, ses écrits: Mémoire historique et critique," in *Mémoires couronnés et mémoires des savants étrangers, publiés par l'Académie royale des sciences, des lettres et des beaux-arts de Belgique* 31 (1862–63): 1–112 (separate pagination within the larger volume; the author's initials are given as "C.-B." on the volume title page, but "B.-C." on the interior title page of the article itself), p. 81 for entry on *Isabellae sanctae*. De Ridder indicated that Le Mire referred to the discovery of Isabelle of France's incorrupt body in 1612. In fact, this was a careless error by De Ridder, since Le Mire (on the page before Isabelle of France's biography begins) was actually referring to the body of Isabel of Portugal in this passage.

[7] The contents (following the dedication) are (ch. 1, fol. 3^r) "S. Elisabetha Ioannis Baptistae mater"; (ch. 2, fol. 3^v) "S. Elisabetha Andrae Hungariae Regis filia"; (ch. 3, fol. 5^v) "S. Isabella Portugalliae Regina"; (ch. 4, fol. 7^r) "S. Isabella S. Ludovici Galliae Regis soror"; (ch. 5, fol. 13^r) "Isabellae ex varius ordinibus Beatae." A shortened version of his treatment of Elizabeth of Hungary, Isabella of Portugal, and Isabelle of France was appended to Le Mire's *Serenissimae principis Isabellae Clarae Eugeniae Hispaniarum infantis laudatio funebris* (Antwerp, 1634), 44–50, but this version did not include a printing of Leo X's bull or Cardinal Adrien's promulgation.

[8] Fol. 1^r: "SERENISSIMAE ISABELLAE CLARAE EVGENIAE, HISPANIARVM INFANTI, Isabellas coelo insertas, SERENISSIMA PRINCEPS, velut in theatrum produco, vel ISABELLAE FRANCIAE caussa. Latuit illa diu intra Longi-Campi monasterij, à se fundati septa quodammodo conclusa: adeò vt vicina Parisiensi aula, illa inquam Tripolis, omnium scientiarum altrix, tantum sidus poenè ignoraret."

serene princess, the Isabellas introduced into heaven, or even in the cause of Isabelle of France. She has lain hidden for a long time within the walls of the monastery of Longchamp which she founded, concealed to such an extent that the court near Paris. . . nourisher of all knowledge, knew almost nothing of such a star." Mireaus did not indicate where he found his copies of Leo X's bull and Cardinal Adrien's promulgation. But he had visited Paris in 1609–1610 and toured various churches and monasteries there,[9] so it is not impossible that he came in contact with Longchamp's copy directly. Alternatively, he may have received a copy from one of his erudite correspondents.[10]

In 1638, the *Martyrologium Franciscanum* edited by Arturus a Monasterio (Arthur du Moustier, O.F.M.) included the opening sections of Leo's bull and Adrien's confirmation.[11] Again, it is not clear what the source was, but the *Martyrologium* was published in Paris, and as a French Franciscan du Moustier would have had ample opportunity to visit Longchamp, so again it is possible or perhaps likely that the abbey's copies were directly or indirectly the source (small differences would seem to indicate that this printing was not based directly on Le Mire). These passages were then reprinted and discussed by J. Stilting in the relevant volume of the *Acta sanctorum* printed at Antwerp in 1743.[12] Since

---

[9] For Le Mire's own (partially preserved) "Discours de notre voiaige de France," and letters from the trip of 1609–10 see Léon de Burbure, "Lettres inédites de Aubert le Mire," *Messager des sciences historiques et archives des arts de Belgique* (1849): 318–35 (describing Le Mire's visits to various Parisian churches and monasteries in October 1609, but with no mention of Longchamp in the extant portion), and 433–53 (letters to family members, with no directly relevant material).

[10] See De Ridder, "Aubert Le Mire, sa vie, ses écrits," 23.

[11] *Martyrologium Franciscanum, in quo sancti beati, aliique servi Dei, martyres, pontifices, confessores, ac virgines, qui tum vitae sanctitate, tum miraculorum gloria, claruere; in universo Ordine FF. Minorum toto orbe terrarum cunctis usque nunc saeculis.* . . (Paris, 1638), 400–2.

[12] J. Stilting, "Commentarius praevius" to "De. B. Elisabetha seu Isabella virgine regia, fundatrice monasterii Longi-Campi prope fanum S. Clodoaldi in Agro Parisiensi," in *Acta Sanctorum, Augusti tomus VI* (Antwerp, 1743): 787–98, at 796. The text of the bull may have been printed an additional time. Among his list of sources found at Longchamp in 1699, Perrier (see note 2 above) included "L'indult d'Urbain VIII pour la translation des reliques de sainte Isabelle, avec la requête des religieuses à M. l'archevêque de Paris, le procès verbal des députés du dit archevêque, et l'acte de la translation des reliques de la sainte faite par le même archevêque, et plusieurs lettres touchant cette affaire et sur les miracles de la sainte, qui se sont

then, the few references to Leo X's bull of 1521 have generally relied on the latter volume.[13]

The edition that follows is based on the text printed by Aubert le Mire in 1622 in his *Isabellae sanctae*, fols. 8ʳ–12ᵛ. I have noted (and occasionally preferred) variants in the partial versions printed in the *Martyrologium Franciscanum* and reprinted in the *Acta sanctorum* [*MF* and *AS* in the notes below], and with a partial copy in manuscript owned by Sébastien Le Nain de Tillemont around 1680, BnF ms. nouv. acq. Fr. 10407, fols. 141ʳ–142ʳ (*T* in the notes below) I regret that I have not been able to include variants from his second copy in BnF ms. fr. 13747, fols. 120–123ᵛ (I made notes on this copy in 1999/2000, but several more recent requests to consult the manuscript have been denied on the grounds of its fragile state). I have standardized capitalization and punctuation, differentiated u from v and i from j, replaced the sign "&" with "et," and removed accents employed by early modern editors of Latin.

For the English translation, I thank Larry F. Field, Henry Ansgar Kelly, and Jacques Dalarun for their criticisms and suggestions (though I am responsible for all errors and infelicities). Because one of the goals of the present article is to allow comparison between the Latin documents and the French translations, my English has stayed close to the literal meaning and word order of the Latin, even where this produces long and somewhat unwieldy sentences.

* * * * *

Leo episcopus, servus servorum Dei, dilecto filio Adriano, tituli Sanctae Sabinae presbytero cardinali, in regno Franciae nostro et apostolicae sedis legato de latere, salutem et apostolicam benedictionem.

Piis omnium praesertim devoti feminei //[fol. 8ᵛ] sexus personarum sub suavi religionis jugu Altissimo famulantium votis, illis praesertim

---

faits depuis, comme aussi le decret de la Congrégation des Rites, accordé par le Pape Innocent XII, qu'on a fait imprimer l'année passée 1698, avec l'ordre du Cardinal de Sainte Sabine qui contient la bulle de Léon X." I know of no extant copies of this 1699 printing concerning events around the translation of Isabelle's relics.

[13] Oliger, for instance, mistakenly concluded that no full text had ever been printed (see the first note to this appendix). Albert Garreau, *Bienheureuse Isabelle de France, soeur de saint Louis* (Paris, 1955), 94, showed no evidence of having seen it.

per quae[14] propheta docente *in suis sanctis*[15] Deus laudari valeat ac divinus[16] cultus cum personarum earumdem spirituali consolatione augmentum suscipiat, libenter annuimus, et ad id nostrae sollicitudinis partes impartimur.

Exhibita siquidem nobis nuper pro parte dilectarum in Christo filiarum, abbatissae modernae et conventus monasterii monialium de Longo Campo ordinis sanctae Clarae Parisiensis dioecesis, petitio continebat quod cum in ecclesia dicti monasterii beatae Elisabethae, gloriosissimi sancti Ludovici quondam regis Franciae sororis (quae etiam dum in humanis ageret tanquam aeternae beatitudinis amatrix, et propulsato fragilis viri thoro ac abjectis mundanis illecebris, ipsi Altissimo vota sua in pacis amoenitudine exsolvere cupiens, monasterium ingressa et //[fol. 9ʳ] ordinem hujusmodi expresse professa, sub religionis jugo inibi famulatum praestare et vitam sanctimonialis[17] ducere quoad universae carnis viam, prout Altissimo placuit, ingrederetur, indefesse non desiit)[18] corpus reconditum honorifice existat, et ejusdem beatae Elisabethae (post cujus ab hac luce transitum, voce e coelo ut pie creditur emissa,[19] auribus tunc dicti monasterii monialium versiculus, "Factus est ejus in pace locus"[20] innotuit) intercessione crebra inibi ipse Altissimus miracula operetur, propterea abbatissa et conventus praefatae, pia devotione ductae, ipsi Christo de operibus hujusmodi gratias condignas reddere et in ejusdem beatae Elisabethae honorem, licet aliorum sanctorum et sanctarum catalogo solemni hominum ministerio aggregata non existat, officium solemne annis singulis recitare cupiant, si eis ad hoc sedis apostolicae licentia suffragaretur. Quare pro parte abbatissae et conventus //[fol. 9ᵛ] praedictarum nobis fuit humiliter supplicatum, ut eidem moderne et pro

---

[14] Le Mire actually reads "quos," but "quae" as found in *AS/MF* must be correct.

[15] Psalms 67:36; 2 Thessalonians 1:10.

[16] divinus] divini *AS/MF* (this variant would make God the active subject of both clauses).

[17] sanctimonialis] sanctimonialium *AS/MF* (with this variant the passage would mean "the life of the nuns" rather than "the life of a nun").

[18] desiit] desivit *AS/MF*

[19] *AS/MF* ends here with "etc." and then gives only the dating clause. The partial copy in *T* picks up one word later, with "tunc dicti monasterii." This may be an odd coincidence, but more likely indicates that the copyist already had access to the sections included in *MF* and only needed to copy out the rest.

[20] Cf. Psalms 75:3; *Writings of AH*, 72.

tempore existenti dicti monasterii abbatissae ac conventui praefatis, offi-cum proprium solemne de dicta sancta Elisabetha annis singulis reci-tandi licentiam et facultatem concedere, aliasque in praemissis oportune providere de benignitate apostolica dignaremur.

Nos igitur, qui Christi fidelium quorumlibet praesertim feminei sexus sub suavi religionis jugo militantium devotas preces ad exauditionis gra-tiam, quantum cum Deo possumus, libenter admittimus, abbatissam modernam et conventum praefatas ac conventus hujusmodi singulares personas a quibusvis excommunicationis suspensionis et interdicti aliisque ecclesiasticis sententiis censuris et poenis a jure vel ab homine quavis occasione vel caussa latis, si quibus quomodolibet innodatae exis-tunt, ad effectum praesentium dumtaxat consequendum, harum //[fol. 10ʳ] serie absolventes et absolutas fore censentes, hujusmodi supplicatio-nibus inclinati, circumspectioni tuae per apostolica scripta mandamus, quatenus de praemissis te diligenter informes, ut[21] si per informationem eamdem ita esse repereris, modernae hujusmodi et pro tempore existenti dicti monasterii abbatissae et conventui praedictis, officium solemne pro-prium de dicta beata Elisabetha, illo prius per te inspecto, annis singulis tempore quo tibi videbitur, recitandi et decantandi (sine[22] tamen illius canonizatione) licentiam et facultatem auctoritate nostra concedas,[23] non obstantibus apostolicis ac in provincialibus et synodalibus conciliis editis generalibus vel specialibus constitutionibus et ordinationibus ceterisque contrariis quibuscumque.

Datum Romae apud Sanctum Petrum, anno incarnationis Domini-cae millesimo quingentesimo vicesimo, III. idus Jenuarii, pontificatus nostri anno octavo.[24]

---

[21] ut] et *T*

[22] sine] pro *T*

[23] concedas] concedere *T*

[24] The date is 11 January 1521 in modern reckoning, since Leo's eighth regnal year ran from March 1520 to March 1521 (for example the bull excommunicating Martin Luther, *Decet Romanum Pontificem*, 3 January 1521, is also dated to Leo's eighth regnal year).

//[fol. 10ᵛ]:

Adrianus, miseratione divina tituli sanctae Sabinae sanctae Romanae ecclesiae presbyter cardinalis, de Boisii vulgariter nuncupatus, Albiensis episcopus ac abbas commendatarius inclytorum monasteriorum beatae Mariae Burgidolensis et sanctissimae Trinitatis Fiscanensis ordinis Sancti Benedicti Bituricensis et Rotomagensis dioecesis ad Romanam ecclesiam nullo medio pertinentium, in hac parte a sede apostolica delegatus, notum facimus omnibus quibus interest aut interesse poterit, quod die vicesima VII. mensis Septembris, anno Domini millesimo, quingentesimo vicesimo primo, in Castro de Batan[25] ejusdem Bituricensis dioecesis, pro parte procuratoris *//*[fol. 11ʳ] modernae abbatissae et conventus monialium de Longo Campo ordinis sanctae Clarae Parisiensis dioecesis, fuit nobis praesentatum et exhibitum rescriptum apostolicum instantibus abbatissa et conventu praefatis impetratum, tenoris subsequentis: *Leo episcopus, servus servorum Dei,*[26] *dilecto filio Adriano tituli sanctae Sabinae presbytero cardinali in regno Franciae nostro et apostoicae sedis legato de latere, salutem et apostolicam benedictionem etc.,* et instantissime supplicatum, quatenus ad executionem memorati rescripti processusque fulminationem procedere dignaremur, juxta tributam per summum pontificem Leonem nobis potestatem.

Et quia justa postulantibus non est denegandus assensus, rescripti praefati tenore perpenso, cum quadam detentus infirmitate aliisque arduis occupatus negotiis, personaliter si preces veritate niterentur *//* [f. 11ᵛ] inquirere non valeremus, ad inquirendum et informandum an narrata in eodem rescripto vera forent, dilectum nostrum magistrum Antonium Chabavier jurium licentiatum, ecclesiarum Albiensis et Claromontensis canonicum, vicarium nostrum in spiritualibus et temporalibus generalem, subdelegavimus et expresse deputavimus. Qui quidem Chabavier vicarius et subdelegatus praedictus, precibus dicti procuratoris, plures testes examinavit super articulis eidem exhibitis, exemplaria etiam ab antiquis libris et aliquibus tabulariis in eodem monasterio existentibus fecit et extraxit. Demum informationem et exemplaria suo et alterius notarii apostolici signis signata apud nos retulit et fideliter reportavit, quam legimus et palpavimus, pluribus etiam viris doctis et litteratis

---

[25]   Baten] Vaten *MF*
[26]   *MF* ends here.

in jure et sancta theologia professoribus videndam et palpandam tradidimus //[fol. 12ʳ]. Tandem die undecima mensis Decembris, anno quo supra, in suburbiis villae Ambasiae, Turonensis dioecesis, procurator praefatae modernae abbatissae et conventus de Longo Campo iterum et secundo coram nobis comparuit et requisivit ut ad executionem ejusdem rescripti apostolici, cum satis de contentis in illo informati essemus per inquisitionem et exemplaria ab eodem vicario et subdelegato nostro facta, procedere dignaremur.

Nos vero Adrianus, cardinalis praefatus, plurium peritorum habito consilio, mandatis apostolicis tamquam filius obedientiae inhaerendo, considerans cultus divini augmentum, informatus luculenter et clare tam testium depositionibus quam exemplaribus sive extractis antiquorum librorum dicti monasterii de Longo Campo de veritate contentorum in eodem rescripto, quodque ipsa Elisabetha beata pluribus coruscat in dies miraculis, eidem //[f. 12ᵛ] modernae et pro tempore existenti abbatissae et conventui dicti monasterii de Longo Campo, ut possint et valeant anno quolibet die ultima mensis Augusti solemne et proprium officium de beata Elisabetha, virgine praefata, divi Ludovici quondam Francorum regis sorore, vita comite praedicti monasterii moniali, quod correctum manuque propria nostra signatum eis transmittimus, cantare et recitare (citra tamen illius canonizationem), auctoritate apostolica qua fungimur in hac parte concedimus licentiam et facultatem.

In quorum fidem praesentes litteras fieri et per secretarium nostrum subsignari sigillique camerae nostrae jussimus et fecimus appensione communiri. Datum et actum loco, anno, die, et mense quibus supra.

* * * *

Leo, bishop, servant of the servants of God, to his beloved son Adrien, titular Cardinal-Priest of Saint Sabina, legate *de latere* in the kingdom of France on our behalf and on behalf of the Apostolic See, greetings and apostolic blessing.

We willingly assent to the pious supplications of all persons, especially those of the devout female sex serving the Most High under the sweet yoke of religion, and especially to those supplications by which, as the prophet teaches, God may be praised *in his saints*, and divine worship may receive augmentation with the spiritual consolation of these same people; and for this purpose we bestow a measure of our care.

Accordingly, a petition recently presented to us on behalf of our beloved daughters in Christ, the current abbess and convent of the monastery of nuns of Longchamp of the Order of Saint Clare in the diocese of Paris, related that since the body of the blessed Isabelle, sister of the most glorious Saint Louis former king of France (who even while she acted in human affairs like a lover of eternal blessedness, and with marriage to a frail man rejected and worldly enticements cast down, desiring to discharge her vows to this same Most High in the tranquility of peace, having entered the monastery and expressly professed this order, tirelessly did not cease to perform service there under the yoke of religion, and to lead the life of a nun, until she went the way of all flesh as it pleased the Most High) lies honorably interred in the church of this monastery, and since through the frequent intercession of this same Isabelle (after whose departure from the light the verse "Her place has been made in peace," was made known to the ears of the nuns then in the said monastery, sent by a voice from heaven as it is piously believed) this same Most High is there performing miracles; therefore the aforementioned abbess and convent, led by pious devotion, wish to recite each year a solemn office, if permission for this will be granted by the Apostolic See, to render fitting thanks to Christ for these works and in honor of this same Isabelle, even though she is not added to the catalogue of the other male and female saints by the solemn ministry of men. Wherefore, it has been humbly requested of us on behalf of the aforesaid abbess and convent that to this same abbess and convent of this said monastery existing at the present time we might deign out of apostolic kindness to concede the right and permission to recite each year a proper solemn office for the said Saint Isabelle, and to suitably provide for other things in the foregoing.

We, therefore, who, as far as we are able with God, listen willingly to devout prayers for the favor of approval from all the faithful in Christ, especially from the female sex doing service under the sweet yoke of religion, do solemnly absolve and judge absolved the aforestated current abbess and convent and every single inhabitant of this convent from whatever excommunication, suspension, interdict, and other ecclesiastic sentences, censures, and punishments brought for whatever reason or cause by law or by man, if they are bound in any way by these, to take effect with the present letter. Moved by these entreaties, with these apostolic writings we entrust to your careful consideration that, as far as you may diligently inform yourself about the foregoing things, if you will find through this inquiry that the case is indeed thus, then by our authority you may concede to the current abbess of the said monastery existing at the present time and the aforementioned convent the right and permission of reciting and singing each year, at the time that will seem appropriate to you, a solemn proper office for the said blessed Isabelle (without, however, her canonization), once [this office] has been examined by you, any general or specific constitutions or regulations published by apostolic authority or in provincial or synodal councils or anything else to the contrary notwithstanding.

Given at Saint Peter's in Rome, in the year of the Lord's incarnation 1520, three days before the Ides of January, in the eighth year of our pontificate.

Adrien, by divine mercy titular Cardinal-Priest of Saint Sabina of the Holy Roman Church, commonly called "de Boisy," bishop of Albi and commendatory abbot of the celebrated monasteries of the blessed Mary of Châteauroux and the Most Holy Trinity of Fécamp of the Order of Saint Benedict in the dioceses of Bourges and Rouen subject directly to the Roman Church, delegated by the Apostolic See in this matter, makes known to all whom it concerns or will concern that on the twenty-seventh day of September in the year of our Lord 1521, at the Castle of Vaten in this same diocese of Bourges, on behalf of the procurator of the current abbess and convent of nuns of Longchamp of the Order of Saint Clare in the diocese of Paris, an apostolic rescript, obtained at the petition of the aforesaid abbess and convent, was presented and shown to us, the tenor of which was the following: *Leo, bishop, servant of the servants of God, to his beloved son Adrien, titular Cardinal-Priest of Saint Sabina, legate de latere in the kingdom of France on our behalf and on behalf of the Apostolic See, greetings and apostolic blessing, etc.*, and it was most insistently asked of us that we might deign to proceed to the execution of the above-mentioned rescript and the formal publication of the process,[27] in accordance with the power granted to us by the Supreme Pontiff Leo.

---

[27] The Latin *fulminatio* (literally "lightning strike") was traditionally used only in a negative metaphorical sense, for instance with the imposition of an excommunication. Ecclesiastical French of the period, however, used *fulmination* more generally for formal publication of a bull or other Church sentence (compare the usage in

And because assent is not to be denied to those asking justly, after carefully considering the aforesaid rescript, because we were detained by a certain infirmity and were occupied with other arduous tasks and not able personally to conduct an inquiry into whether these entreaties were in full accord with the truth, we sub-delegated and deputed our beloved master Antoine Chabanier, licentiate in both laws, canon of the churches of Albi and Clermont, our general vicar in spiritual and temporal matters, to inquire and inform himself as to whether what was narrated in this rescript was true. Accordingly, the aforesaid vicar and sub-delegate Chabanier, at the request of the said procurator, examined many witnesses concerning the articles shown to him, and even made extracts of exemplary passages from ancient books and various records[28] preserved in this monastery. At last he brought back and faithfully reported to us this information and these copies, signed with his sign and the sign of another apostolic notary, which we read and examined and also handed over to be seen and examined by several learned and literate men, professors in law and holy theology. Finally, on the eleventh day of the month of December, in the year indicated above, in the suburbs of the town of Amboise in the diocese of Tours, the procurator of the abovementioned current abbess and convent of Longchamp again appeared in our presence for a second time, and asked that we deign to proceed to the execution of this same apostolic rescript, since we were sufficiently informed as to its contents through inquiry and copies made for us by this same vicar and delegate.

Therefore we, Adrien, the aforesaid cardinal, having received the counsel of several experts, as a son of obedience in adherence to apostolic commands, considering the increase of divine worship, completely and clearly informed both by depositions of witnesses and by copies or extracts of ancient books from the said monastery of Longchamp as to the truth of the contents in the said rescript and to the fact that this same blessed Isabelle shines forth with many miracles from day to day, do by

---

the French translation of this text in Appendix B), which is clearly the sense invoked here.

[28] The French translation (Appendix B) has *tableaux*; possibly what is being referred to are several texts known to have been hanging on the walls of Longchamp's church—specifically Isabelle's lengthy fifteenth-century epitaph and the account of the healing of Jeanne Carphaude that the nuns had hung at the church's entrance after 1517.

the apostolic authority which we discharge in this matter concede permission and right to this same current abbess and convent of Longchamp existing at this time that each year on the last day of August they may and can sing and recite (short, however, of her canonization) the solemn and proper office—which we have sent to them corrected and signed with our own hand—of the blessed Isabelle the aforementioned virgin, sister of Saint Louis former king of the Franks, nun of the aforesaid monastery while she was in life.

In witness of these things we have ordered and caused the present letter to be written and to be signed below by our secretary and secured with the appending of the seal of our chamber. Given and done in the place, year, day and month as above.

Appendix B

Longchamp's Narrative of the Approval of Isabelle's Office, and Translation of Cardinal Adrien de Boisy's Promulgation of *Piis omnium*

BY EARLY 1522 the nuns of Longchamp had written up a French narrative describing their successful efforts to secure permission to celebrate their founder's office, followed by a French translation of the letter from Cardinal Adrien that granted final approval for such a celebration (with Leo X's original letter embedded and translated within). Two manuscripts created at Longchamp in the sixteenth century preserve this narrative and translation. The earlier version is in BnF ms. fr. 11662, fols. 15^r–20^r, which then must have served as the examplar for the copy in BnF ms. nouv. acq. fr. 10871, where it is inserted in a life of Isabelle of France.

BnF ms. fr. 11662 is a manuscript containing Longchamp's calendar, French and Latin versions of important texts about the foundation and privileges of the abbey, and a continuation of the abbey's necrology.[1] Some sections were begun in the mid fifteenth century, and the necrology was continued up through the eighteenth, but the folios (15–20) under

---

[1] For a brief description see *Writings of AH,* 33–34. A black and white digitization of this manuscript is now available through Gallica.

Studies in Medieval and Renaissance History, 3rd Series, Vol. 11 (2014)

consideration here form a discrete block, in a single hand, copied some-
time after early 1522.[2] The initial narrative is subscribed with the names
of abbess Catherine Le Picart and 72 nuns (all the names were written
by a single hand, rather than being individual signatures; see Appendix
C on the nuns). This copy was almost certainly made before Catherine's
death in 1532. It is not clear who prepared the translation of the letter,
but it seems likely that Robert Messier, the Franciscan confessor given so
much credit in the initial narrative, might have played a part.

The narrative is in a one-column format, but then beginning with
the subscription of the names of all the nuns, and continuing with the
translation of Adrien de Boisy's letter, the text is in two columns carefully
ruled in red. Fol. 20[v] is also ruled in this manner, but otherwise blank.
The initial "A" in the narrative is a large capital decorated in blue and red.
Subsequent capital letters are lightly shaded with gold. "T" in *Te Deum
laudamus* is in red. For the witnesses' names, the "S" in "Suer" alternates
red and blue for each entry, and line endings are filled in with red and
blue designs. In the translation of Adrien de Boisy's text, the initial "S"
and the "A" in Adrien are also capitals decorated in blue and red.

The second copy is found in BnF ms. nouv. acq. fr. 10871, a book given
by Sister Jeanne de Mailly to Longchamp in 1569. It contains (fols. 1[v]–67[r])
a French life of Isabelle, which may be a copy of that known to have been
written by Robert Messier soon after 1521.[3] The manuscript also has the
"Passion of the Five Martyr Brothers," lives of saints Anthony of Padua,
Bonaventure, and Louis of Toulouse, and an addition relating a later
miracle attributed to Isabelle. This practically unstudied manuscript is
generally of interest as a compilation of Franciscan saints' lives in the vernacular (all texts are in French, all copied in the same hand) for an early
modern, female audience. But here it is relevant because the narrative
(fols. 47[r]–49[r]) and then Cardinal Adrien's letter (fols. 49[r]-53[v]) are inserted
into the text, taken directly from the translation found in ms. fr. 11662.
The only significant difference is that in this manuscript the list of nuns

---

[2] This portion of the manuscript bears both a pagination in roman numerals
(crossed out) and foliation in arabic numerals. My references follow the latter; in the
pagination the texts under consideration here would be found on xxv–xxxvii (with
fol. 20[v] or page xxxviii ruled but otherwise blank).

[3] For a brief treatment of this manuscript, see Sean L. Field, "A New Life of Isabelle of France from the Early Sixteenth Century," *Studies in Medieval and Renaissance History*, 3rd series, 8 (2011): 27–80, at 41–43.

is replaced by a single sentence referring to Abbess Catherine Le Picard and seventy-two sisters.

Neither the nuns' narrative nor the French translation of Cardinal Adrien's letter has ever appeared in print, but they were cited by early modern scholars who had access to one or both of the manuscripts described above, and thus some of the information they convey has made its way (with greater or lesser accuracy) into scholarship on Longchamp and Isabelle of France. Roulliard, for example, had access to the narrative, which he summarized and referred to as the "procès verbal qui en fut dressé" (the translation of Leo's bull which he gave, however, was not the same as the one found in 11662, indicating he prepared his own translation).[4] His comments (translated into Latin!) were reported in the *Acta sanctorum*, and thus became more widely available to later scholars.[5]

The edition that follows is based on BnF ms. fr. 11662. No accents appear in the manuscript. I have added acute accents and cedillas in keeping with standard practice in editing Middle French texts, but used the dieresis only in cases where true confusion might arise. I have combined or separated words, employed capitalization, punctuation, and apostrophes, and differentiated u/v and i/j in keeping with modern French practice as well. Since the copy in nouv. ac. fr. 10871 is nearly identical and depends directly on fr. 11662, I have not noted shifts in orthography, or minor changes that seem to have been inadvertent, but it has seemed worth noting several small changes where presumably the perspective of the nuns a half century later suggested rephrasing.

I thank Janet Whatley for her suggestions and corrections on the English translation that follows (though I am uniquely responsible for errors and infelicities). In order to facililate comparison with the Latin, my translation is quite literal and respects word and phrase order where possible. At times, the French translation did not quite make smooth sense out of the Latin; in those cases I have not sought to hide those difficulties.

---

[4] Roulliard, *La saincte mère*, 487.

[5] Duchesne, *Histoire de l'abbaye royale de Longchamp*, 8, gives a thoroughly garbled version of events.

*　*　*　*　*

Aprés la bonté de Dieu, demoustree par plusieurs miracles au monastere de Longchamp, pour declarer et approuver les dignes et excellens merites de madame saincte Ysabel de France seur de monsieur sainct Loys et fondateresse et mere du dict monastere, et singulierement aprés le miracle faict sur une religieuse du dict monastere nommee seur Jehenne Charphaude, lequel fut faict l'an mil cinq cens et saize, donc le dict miracle est recité et mys par escript en ung tableau pendant a l'entree de[6] l'eglise du dict monastere, du sainct siege apostolique a esté emanee une bulle concedee de nostre sainct pere le pape Leon X.ᵉ de ce nom seant en la chaire de sainct Pierre, par laquelle est concedee l'auctorité aux religieuses du dict monastere grace de faire l'office divin et solempnité de la dicte saincte dame Ysabel le dernier jour d'aoust pour chanter l'office propre en solempnité de grand double. Et fut la suplication de la dicte bulle presentee par ung noble homme de Jennes demourant a Paris, nommé de Franc de Spinolle, et concedé par le dict sainct pere en l'an mil cinq cens et xxi, le xix.ᵉ jour de janvier.[7] Et la bulle fut envoyé a Paris par le dict Spinolle, mist aux mains de quelque bancquier //[15ᵛ] nommé Fristobaldi. Et n'ont peu les dictes religieuses tirer la dicte bulle des mains du dict banquier pour la somme d'argent qu'il demandoit, qui estoit la somme de deux cens quarante quatre escus d'or. Mais par la solicitude d'ung religieulx nommé frere Robert Messier, docteur en theologie et confesseur des dictes religieuses, lequel avoit composé l'office propre de la dicte saincte, ont esté les dictes bulles delivrés en baillant cent escus d'or, lesquelz ont estés prestés au dict monastere de quelque amy a la requeste du dicte frere Robert. Et fut la bulle receue et aportee en nostre monastere par le dict frere Robert, acompaigné de frere Adam Falconis, confesseur du dict lieu, et de maistre Pierre du Puys, procureur de la maison. Et receue moult solempnellement le dict an le xxiiiᵉ jour d'aoust, la veille sainct Barthelemy, aprés complie. Lors sonnoient les cloches a

---

[6] Nouv. ac. fr. 10871 omits "l'entrée de," perhaps indicating that this *tableau* no longer hung at this spot by 1569 (though the omission may simply have been accidental).

[7] The date of Leo's bull (at least as edited by Le Mire) was actually "III Idus Jenuarii," or 11 January 1521 in modern reckoning. Perhaps the scribe inadvertantly changed "xi" to "xix" here.

quarrelon, et les religieuses chanterent[8] *Te Deum laudamus* en rendant graces a Dieu le createur de leur desir qui estoit acompli. Et pour tant que la dicte bulle adrechoit a monsieur le cardinal Adrien de Bouesy, legat en France et evesque de Albi, le dict frere Robert c'est [*sic*] transporté envers luy jusques en Berri et luy a presenté //[16ʳ] la dicte bulle. Pour quoy le dict seigneur a envoyé ung commissaire au dict monastere de Longchamp pour soy informer de la verité des miracles de la dicte saincte, et de sa vie, et pour faire visiter l'office propre. Et le dict commissaire, nommé maistre Anthoene Basennier, doyen de Bougival, aprés deue information faicte a toute diligence, par le conseil et determination de plusieurs docteurs en theologie et en decret, a porté le dict commissaire son information au dict seigneur legat. Lequel a decerné[9] et approuvé et fulminé la dicte bulle, et approuvé le dict office estre catholicque et veritable. Et avons receu en nostre[10] monastere la dicte fulmination et approbation au dict an, le xxiᵉ jour de decembre, jour de sainct Thomas.[11] Et tout cecy a la solicitude, paine et labeur qui ne sont point a penser du dict frere Robert Messier. Dieu luy veulle tout rendre a l'utilité de son salut.[12] Amen.

---

[8]   Lors sonnoient les cloches a quarrelon et les religieuses chanterent] nouv. ac. fr. 10871 reads "en grande iubilation de tout le couvent sonnet les cloches a quarrillon chantant devottement."

[9]   "a decerne et" is added in another ink, with space apparently having been left for it.

[10]   Et avons receu en nostre] nouv. ac. fr. 10871 reads "Et fut receu au dict."

[11]   Nouv. ac. fr. 10871 adds here "et mise entre les mains de Seur Katherine le Picard abbesse de soixante et douze seurs" and then omits the entire list of sisters.

[12]   Dieu luy veulle tout rendre a l'utilité de son salut] nouv. ac. fr. 10871 reads "dieu luy ensoit loyer et la sainte dame."

Alors estoit abbesse
Seur Katherine Picarde.
Et les religieuses
 et dames discrettes estoient:
Seur Jehenne la Duchesse.
Seur Marguerite Querlu.
Seur Marie de Rubenpre.
Seur Marguerite de Mailly.

// [fol. 16^v]
Seur Loyse de Hangest.
Seur Jehenne la Mye.
Seur Loyse Aveline.
Seur Françoyse de Nouvion.
Seur Marie Lotin.
Seur Katherine Pimorine.
Seur Marguerite la Fevre.
Seur Katherine de Sainctz.
Seur Katherine Fourmont.
Seur Marie de Livre.
Seur Anne de Chouvreux.
Seur Katherine de Landres.
Seur Jacqueline Baudequin.
Seur Geneviefve Richevillain.
Seur Anthonette du Boys.

//[fol. 17^r]
Seur Anthoenette Le Picard.
Seur Jehenne le Spinolle.
Seur Katherine le Mercier.
Seur Ragonde de Longueil.
Seur Valentine Prevost.
Seur Geneviefve Laurens.
Seur Germaine Godin.
Seur Jehenne Charphaude.
Seur Jehenne de Mailly.
Seur Helie de Malignac.
Seur Jehenne du Boc.
Seur Marie Bignet.
Seur Ethienette Le Gue.
Seur Magdalene de Marle.
Seur Guionne de Caules.

Seur Marthe Mychon.
Seur Françoyse de la Preuse.
Seur Jehenne Dangue.
Seur Georgette Cueur.
Seur Anne de Cambray.
Seur Perrette Darragon.
Seur Loyse Senesine.
Seur Prette de Nully.

Seur Marie Picard.
Seur Marie Boliard.
Seur Charlotte de St Laurens.
Seur Clere de Varlusel.
Seur Regnee Luylier.
Seur Anne de Rochebaron.
Seur Marguerite du Buc.
Seur Ysabeau du Harlay.
Seur Guionne Coignet.
Seur Denise Sevin.
Seur Gillette Brinum.
Seur Anthoenette Buraude.
Seur Magadalene Lombart.
Seur Magdalene Gallet.
Seur Katherine Agnes.
Seur Jehenne Paulmier.
Seur Jehenne Dauvet.
Seur Katherine Bret.

Seur Anne Senesme.
Seur Jehenne la Fevre.
Seur Lyenarde Pastee.
Seur Yvonnette Malice.
Seur Jehenne Quotine.
Seur Françoyse Boyleau.
Seur Françoyse de Laistre.
Seur Collette Buferelle.
Seur Jehenne Boulengiere.
Seur Charlotte Guernyer.
Seur Cecille Grignon.
Seur Ysabeau Brodon.

// [fol. 17ᵛ][13] S'ensuit la fulmination de la bulle en laquelle est inseree et contenue la dicte bulle translatee de Latin en François.

Adrian, par la miseration divine presbytere[14] cardinal de l'eglise de saincte Sabine de Romme, vulgarement appellé de Boysy, evesque d'Albi et abbé commendataire des monasteres renommés de saincte Marie au diocese de Bourges et de saincte Trinité au diocese de Rouen, delegué en ceste partie du sainct siege apostolicque, faisons asçavoir a tous ceulx a qui il appartient ou pourroit appartenir, que le xxvij.ᵉ jour du moys de septembre en l'an mil v.ᶜᶜ et xxi., au chasteau de Vaten au dict diocese de Bourges, de la partie du procureur moderne de l'abbesse et convent des religieuses de Longchamp de l'ordre de saincte Clare au diocese de Paris nous fut presenté et exibé ung rescript apostolicque impetré a l'instance de l'abbesse et du dict couvent de subsequente teneur:

> Leon evesque, serviteur des serviteurs de Dieu, a nostre filz bien aymé Adrian cardinal presbytere de saincte Sabine, legat en France de nostre siege apostolicque, salut et apostolicque benediction.
>
> Condescendant aux veux et desirs piteux de toutes personnes, et particulierement au devot sexe feminin servant a Dieu soubz //[fol. 18ʳ] la doulce charge de religion, et singulierement es choses par quoy, selon le tesmongnage du prophete, Dieu peult estre loué et le service divin avec la consolation espirituelle des dictes personnes prengne augmentation, voulentiers nous concedons et a ce nous elargissons partie de nostre solicicitude [*sic*].
>
> Retentement [*sic*] nous a esté exibee une peticion de la partie de noz filles bien aymees en Jesu Crist l'abbesse moderne et convent du monastere des religieuses de Longchamp de l'ordre de saincte Clare au diocese de Paris et contenoit come il soit ainsi que en l'eglise du dict monastere[15] soit reposant le corps de bienheureuse Ysabel, seur de sainct Loys jadis roy de France, laquelle en son vivant comme amateresse de eternelle beatitude en propos de virginité en abjection des charnelles voluptés desirant en amenité de paix rendre ses

---

[13] In ms. fr. 11662 the text continues to be in two columns from this point. My inclusion of paragraph breaks and the use of indented text to mark out Leo's original text are editorial decisions.

[14] The abbreviation here and elsewhere is "pbre."

[15] Nouv. ac. fr. 10871 omitted this word, then added "couvent" above the line.

veulx et desirs a Dieu, au dict monastere est entree et la a faict residence comme se elle eust faict expresse profession soubz la charge
de religion, faisant service a Dieu en menant vie de parfaicte religion
et sanctimonie, aprés le trespas de laquelle aux auÿes des manans au
dict monastere comme piteusement on peult croire a esté auÿe une
voix du ciel sounant ce verset du psalmiste: *In pace factus est locus
eius.* Et a l'intercession d'icelle par //[fol. 18ᵛ] l'operation du souverain Dieu, la et alieurs, operations miraculeuses sont faictes. Pour
icelle cause la dicte abbesse et convent incitees de piteuse devotion
en Jesu Crist de vouloir pour les dictes oeuvres miraculeuses rendre
condignes graces a Dieu, et a l'honneur d'icelle saincte Ysabel, combien que au cathologue des sainctz ne soit point nombree, demand-
ent de faire et reciter en l'eglise solempnel office par chascun an, se
le sainct siege apostolicque leur concede. Par quoy de la partie de
l'abbesse et du dict convent nous a esté humblement suplié de faire
le dict service annuellement de la dicte saincte Ysabel et reciter la
propre office par l'auctorité de nous et du sainct siege apostolicque.

Par quoy nous, qui de tous les fideles Crestiens singulierement de devotes religieuses autant que avec Dieu nous povons a
l'exaudition de grace, promettons et voulons la dicte abbesse et le
convent. Et aussi du dict convent singulieres personnes absolvons
de toutes excommunications suspensions et interdictz, et de toutes autres sentences ecclesiasticques censures et peines encourues
de quelques causes ou occasions qui pourroit estre inferees, par
lesquelles tu serois innodés ou empesché a l'execution de l'effect des
choses icy declarees, // [fol. 19ʳ] et par la[16] teneur de ceste [bulle][17] te
declarons absoubz et ydone.[18]

Nous doncques, enclins aux dictes supplications, par escriptz
apostolicques mandons a ta circumspection affin que des choses
premises tu te informe diligentement; et si par icelle information tu
trouves qu'il soit ainsi, a l'abbesse et au dict convent tu confereras
de nostre auctorité faculté de reciter solennellement l'office propre,
pourveu que tu l'aye preveu et regardé, sans la canonisation d'icelle,
non obstant les constitutions apostolicques tant aux sinodalles

---

[16] "la" is added above the line.
[17] This word only in nouv. ac. fr. 10871.
[18] *Sic.* "idione" is found in nouv. ac. fr. 10871, presumably for "idoine."

provintiaux comme aux consilles generaulx ordonnés et d'aultres choses qui seroyent au contraire.

Daté a Romme, au lieu de sainct Pierre, l'an de l'incarnation domincque mil v.ᶜᶜ et xx, iij[19] aux ides de janvier et l'an viijᵉ de nostre pontificat.

Et instamment nous a esté suplié, affin que nous veullons proceder au proces et a la fulmination du dict rescript selon la puissance et auctorité qui nous est baillee par le souverain prelat Leon X.ᵉ Et pourtant que on ne doibt point denier conscentement a ceulx qui postulent justement, combien que soyons detenues de quelque infirmité et occupé es autres negoces ardues tellement que personellement ne povons enquerir se le prieres sont conformes a verité, tout //[fol. 19ᵛ] bien pensé a la teneur du dict rescript pour enquerir et se informer se les choses en icelluy rescript narrees sont veritables, nous avons subdelegué et expressement deputé nostre bien aymé maistre Anthoine Chabanier, licentié en droit, chanoine des eglises de Albi et de Cleremont, nostre vicaire general tant en spirituel comme temporel. Lequel Chabanier vicaire et subdelegué, aux prieres et procuration du dict procureur, a examiné plusieurs tesmoingz des articles qui luy ont esté exibés, et a faict et extrait les exemplaires prins aux livres anciens et en aulcuns tableaux estans au dict monastere, derechef a referé et rapporté par devers nous les informations et les dictes exemplaires, signés de luy et d'autre notaire apostolicque, lesquelz nous avons leuz, veuz, et traictiés, et l'avons faict voir a plusieurs hommes doctes et litterés, docteurs en droit de la[20] saincte theologie. Finablement le procureur de la dicte abbesse moderne et du dict convent de Longchamp derechef et secondement est comparu devant nous, le xi.ᵉ jour de decembre de l'an dessus dict, es faubors de la ville d'Amboise du diocese de Tours, et nous a requis que nous veullons proceder a l'execution du dict rescript apostolicque consideré que des choses contenues en icelluy nous //[fol. 20ʳ] estoyons assez informez par les inquisitions et exenplaires faiz par nostre dict vicaire subdelegué.

---

[19] The manuscript actually appears to read "et xxiij aux ides de ianvier," indicating a scribal confusion about the date being copied.

[20] "la" is added above the line. It seems likely that "et" was inadvertently omitted before "de la".

Nous doncques, Adrien cardinal, par le conseil de plusieurs doctes sages et expers, adherant aux mandemens apostoliques comme filz de obedience, considerant l'augmentation du divin service, informé luculentement et clerement par les depositions des tesmoingz et par les exemplaires antiques et les livres du dict monastere, selon la verité contenue au dict rescript, et comme il soit ainsi que la dicte saincte Ysabel de jour en jour est chorustante par plusieurs miracles, de l'auctorite apostolicque a nous concedee, concedons licence et faculté a l'abbesse et convent du dict monastere de Longchamp de faire solennité tous les ans le dernier jour d'aoust et chanter solennellement l'office propre de la dicte saincte Ysabel, vierge, seur de jadis sainct Loys roy de France, lequel office est veu et corrigé et de nostre propre main signé,[21] sans la canonization d'icelle.

En la foy desquelles choses avons faict faire les lettres presentes et subsigner par nostre secretaire et avons commandé et si avons faict munir icelles par l'appension du seau de nostre chambre. Daté au lieu et l'an et le moys et le jour dessus dictz.

* * * *

In accordance with God's benevolence, demonstrated by several miracles at the monastery of Longchamp, to declare and confirm the worthy and excellent merits of Madame Saint Isabelle of France, sister of Monsieur Saint Louis and foundress and mother of the said monastery—and especially following the miracle done for a nun of the said monastery named Sister Jeanne Carphaude, which was done in the year 1516, of which said miracle [the story] was told and put into writing on a *tableau* hanging at the entrance of the said monastery—from the Holy Apostolic See was sent a bull conceded by our Holy Father Pope Leo, tenth of this name to occupy the chair of Saint Peter, by whose authority was conceded to the nuns of the said monastery permission to perform the divine office and solemn celebration of the said saintly lady Isabelle on the last day of August, to sing a proper office with the solemn celebration of a major duplex. And the request for the said bull was presented by a nobleman from Genoa staying in Paris, named Franc de Spinolle, and was conceded by the said Holy Father in the year 1521 on the nineteenth [*sic*] day of

---

[21] This word omitted in nouv. ac. fr. 10871.

January. And the bull was sent to Paris by the said Spinolle, [and] put into the hands of a certain banker named Fristobaldi. And the said nuns were not able to get the said bull out of the hands of the said banker for the sum of money that he was demanding, which was the sum of 244 gold *écus*. But by the efforts of a monk named Brother Robert Messier, doctor of theology and confessor to the said nuns, who had composed the proper office of the said saint, the said bulls[22] were secured by handing over 100 gold *écus*, which had been lent to the said monastery by a certain friend at the request of the said Brother Robert. And the bull was received and brought to our monastery by the said Brother Robert, accompanied by Brother Adam Falconis, confessor of the said place, and Master Pierre du Puys, procurator of the house. And it was received most solemnly in the same year on the twenty-third day of August, the vigil of the feast of Saint Bartholomew, after Compline. Then the carillon was rung, and the nuns said a *Te Deum laudamus*, giving thanks to God the Creator for the accomplishment of their desire. And because the said bull was addressed to Monsieur Cardinal Adrien de Boisy, legate in France and bishop of Albi, the said Brother Robert traveled to him in Berry and presented the said bull to him. For which reason the said lord sent a commissioner to the said monastery of Longchamp to inform himself of the truth of the miracles of the said saint, and of her life, and to have the proper office reviewed. And the said commissioner, named Master Antoine Basennier, dean of Bougival, after diligently gathering the appropriate information, by the counsel and determination of several doctors of theology and canon law, the said commissioner[23] brought his information to the said lord legate, who decided and approved and formally published the said bull and approved the said office as catholic and true. And we received the said publication and approval in our monastery in the said year on the twenty-first day of December, the feast of Saint Thomas. And all of this due to the efforts, care, and nearly inconceivable labor of the said Brother Robert Messier. May God turn it all to the service of his salvation!

[names omitted]

Here follows the formal publication of the bull, in which is inserted and contained the said bull, translated from Latin into French:

---

[22] The single "bull" has unexpectedly become plural here.
[23] The repetition of "the said commissioner" is in the text.

Adrien, by divine mercy Cardinal-Priest of the Church of Saint Sabina of Rome, commonly called de Boisy, bishop of Albi and commendatory abbot of the renowned abbeys of Saint Mary in the diocese of Bourges and the Holy Trinity in the diocese of Rouen, delegated in this matter by the Holy Apostolic See, makes known to all those whom it concerns or to whom it may concern, that the twenty-seventh day of the month of September in the year 1521, at the castle of Vaten in the said diocese of Bourges, on behalf of the current procurator of the abbess and convent of nuns of Longchamp of the Order of Saint Clare in the diocese of Paris, was presented and exhibited to us an apostolic rescript obtained at the request of the abbess and of the said convent, the tenor of which was the following:

Leo, bishop, servant of the servants of God, to our beloved son Adrien, Cardinal-Priest of Saint Sabina, legate in France from our Holy See, greetings and apostolic benediction.

Assenting to the wishes and pious desires of all people, and particularly to the devout female sex serving God under the sweet charge of religion, and especially in things through which, according to the witness of the prophet, God can be praised and the divine service with the spiritual consolation of the said people can be augmented, we willingly concede and extend a measure of our care for this.

Recently we were shown a petition on behalf of our beloved daughters in Jesus Christ, the current abbess and convent of the monastery of nuns of Longchamp of the Order of Saint Clare in the diocese of Paris, relating how it would seem that in the church of the said monastery was reposing the body of the blessed Isabelle, sister of Saint Louis former king of France (who, during her life, like a lover of eternal blessedness, in [her] purpose of virginity, in rejection of carnal pleasures, desiring in the service of peace to render her wishes and desires to God, entered in the said monastery and there made her residence as if she had made an express profession under the charge of religion, doing service to God while living a life of perfect religion and holiness), after whose death by the ears of those staying in the said monastery (as one may piously believe) was heard a voice from heaven sounding this verse of the psalmist, *In pace factus est locus ejus,* and at whose intercession by the work of sovereign God, there and elsewhere, miraculous works are done. For this reason the said abbess and convent, moved by pious devotion in Jesus Christ to want to give due thanks to God for the said works, and in honor of the same Saint Isabelle, although she is not numbered in the catalogue of the saints, requested to [be able to] perform and recite in church a solemn office each year, if the Holy Apostolic See concedes it to them. For this reason, on behalf of the abbess and said convent, we were humbly asked that the said service of the said Saint Isabelle and the proper office be annually recited, by our authority and that of the Holy Apostolic See.

For this reason we, who, as far as God permits, [incline to the] granting of prayers of faithful Christians [and] especially of devout nuns, promise and wish [this for] the said abbess and convent. And also we absolve each person of the said convent of all excommunications, suspensions, and interdicts, and of all other ecclesiastical sentences, censures, and punishments, incurred through whatever cause or occasion, which might be imposed, by which you may be bound or stopped from the execution of the effect of the things declared here, and by the tenor of this bull we declare you absolved and competent. We, therefore, inclining to the said entreaties, by apostolic writing, entrust to your careful consideration to inform yourself diligently as to the foregoing things; and if by this informing you find that it is thus, by apostolic authority you will confer on the abbess and the said convent the right to recite solemnly the proper office, provided that you have reviewed and seen it, without her canonization, with apostolic constitutions—whether ordered by provincial synods or general councils—and any other things to the contrary not withstanding.

Dated at Rome, at Saint Peter's, in the year of the Lord's Incarnation 1520, three before the Ides of January.

And we were urgently entreated that we might proceed to the process and formal publication of the said rescript in accordance with the power and authority granted to us by the sovereign prelate Leo X.

And because one should not deny consent to those who request justly, since we were detained by a certain infirmity and occupied with other arduous duties so that we could not personally inquire into whether the requests were in accordance with truth, considering the tenor of the said rescript to inquire and be informed as to whether the things narrated in this rescript were true, we have sub-delegated and expressly deputed our beloved master Antoine Chabanier, licentiate in law, canon of the churches of Albi and Clermont, our general vicar in matters spiritual as well as temporal. This Chabanier, vicar and sub-delegate, at the entreaties and request of the said procurator, examined several witnesses on the articles that were shown to him, and made and extracted examples taken from ancient books and certain *tableaux* that are at the said monastery, and further carried and reported to us the information and the said copies, signed by him and another apostolic notary, which we have read, seen, and dealt with, and have caused to be seen by several learned and literate men, doctors in law [and] of holy theology. Finally, the procurator of the said current abbess and of the said convent of Longchamp yet again came before us, the eleventh day of December in the aforesaid year, in the suburbs of the town of Amboise in the diocese of Tours, and asked of us that we might proceed to the execution of the said apostolic rescript, considering that we were sufficiently informed about the things contained in it by the inquiries and copies made by our said delegated vicar.

Therefore we, Cardinal Adrien, by the council of several learned, wise, and expert men, adhering to apostolic commands like a son of obedience, considering the augmentation of divine service, informed completely and clearly by the depositions of witnesses and by the ancient copies and books of the said monastery, following the truth contained in the said rescript, and since it seems that the said Saint Isabelle from day to day shines forth through many miracles, by the apostolic authority conceded to us, do concede permission and right to the abbess and convent of the said monastery of Longchamp to hold the solemn celebration each year the last day of August and to solemnly sing the proper office of the said Saint Isabelle, virgin, sister of the former Saint Louis king of France, which office has been seen and corrected and signed by our own hand, without her canonization.

In witness of which things we have caused and commanded this letter to be written and signed below by our secretary, and secured with the appending of the seal of our chamber. Dated in the place and year and month and day said above.

Appendix C
Identification of Nuns' Names Appended to the French Narrative

THE NAMES OF seventy-three inhabitants of Longchamp, including the abbess and lay sisters, are appended to the end of the narrative found in BnF ms. fr. 11662. The simple list of names (with some modernized spellings) was printed by Duchesne, with brief references to lands and rents received by Perette d'Arragon and Loyse de Hangest.[1]

The information given below comes, where not otherwise noted, from the necrology found later in this same ms. fr. 11662, beginning fol. 44^v. Picking up from the early fourteenth-century necrology preserved in AN L 1027 no. 22, this list was begun in 1446 and continued to the abbey's dissolution at the time of the Revolution. The early portions of this list were partially edited by Auguste Molinier, in principle up to the year 1500.[2] Some of the sisters below are therefore included in his edition. But in fact Molinier did not include all names from the last years before 1500, and his criteria for inclusion or omission are unclear (ellipses in his edition indicate one or more sisters have been passed over). Thus the basic information for the vast majority of the sisters here has never been published.

---

[1] Duchesne, *Histoire de l'abbaye royale de Longchamp*, 134–35.
[2] Auguste Molinier, *Obituaires de la province de Sens*, vol. 1 part 2 (Paris, 1902), 669–83.

As the list in BnF ms. fr. 11662 was constructed, each sister's name, age, and date of profession was entered, and then, when that sister eventually died, that information would be added at that time (the label "necrology" is thus slightly misleading, since in fact the list proceeds chronologically by date of entry).[3] Text in italics below indicates the later additions. In the case of sisters who served as abbesses, some indication of the length of their term in office was included. For the women designated below as abbesses (Catherine Le Picard, Georgette Coeur, Loyse Senesme, and Marie Lotin), additional information from AN L 1028 nos. 10 and 11 and LL 1604 is edited elsewhere[4] and I have not repeated it here. Sisters Jeanne Carphaude, Georgette Coeur, Magdalene de Marle, and Valentine Prevost also appear in relation to miracles recorded in Princeton University Library ms. 188, the *Vie* of Isabelle of France composed just before 1521 and added to in 1530.[5]

Before the 1560s, practice in Paris was to date the new year from Easter. Where necessary, dates before the 1560s have thus been rendered according to modern reckoning. In 1564 Charles IX decreed that January 1 would be considered the beginning of the new year, but not all French institutions adopted the practice immediately. There is thus some potential confusion for dates in the four or five years following this decree. Where ambiguity arises for this or other reasons, I have explained the possible confusion in a note.

Where possible, feast days for saints have been checked against Longchamp's contemporary calendar, conveniently enough bound into the same manuscript, fr. 11662.

---

[3]   In fact, for most entries the phrase "et trespassa/trepassa" was added in the original hand, at the time of profession. It must have been sobering (and was perhaps meant to be) for a young girl taking the veil to have her death written about in the past tense.

[4]   Field, "The Abbesses of Longchamp in the Sixteenth Century."

[5]   Field, "A New Life of Isabelle of France from the Early Sixteenth Century." Unfortunately at 78 n130 of that article I mistranscribed the date of sister Jeanne Massiot/Macieux's entrance to Longchamp as "mil cinq cens xvi" when it in fact reads "mil cinq cens xxvi." Thus her name does not appear on the present list, since she did not enter Longchamp until 1526, and my comment in ibid., 42, about Jeanne entering Longchamp just after the miraculous cure of Jeanne Carphaude was incorrect.

* * * * *

1) Seur Katherine Picarde: born ca. 1461, entered 19 June 1474, died 22 April 1532.
   [fol. 59^r: Seur Katherine Lapicarde agee de xiii ans fut vestue le xix^e iour de Juing lan M iiii^c lxxiiii Et trespassa le xxii^e Jour davril . Lan mil. v^c xxxii. Et fut abbesse environ xviii ans.]

2) Seur Jehenne la Duchesse: born ca. 1459, entered 6 May 1470, died 24 June 1528.
   [fol. 58^v: Seur Jehanne la Duchesse dicte Hagueuyne fut vestue le vi^e iour de may feste de saint Iehan porte Latine lan mil iiii^c lxx de laage de unze ans et demy. *Et trespassa le Jour de sainct Jehan baptiste. Lan mil. v.^{c} et xxviii*]

3) Seur Marguerite Queulu: born ca. 1459, entered 7 October 1470, died 16 December 1523.
   [fol. 58^v: Seur Marguerite Queuleu fut vestue le dimenche vii^e iour doctobre lan mil iiii^c lxx de laage de unze ans et trespassa le *xvi^e jour de decembre lan mil cinq cens vingt et troys*]

4) Seur Marie de Rubenpre: born ca. 1460, entered 19 June 1470, died 30 May 1546.
   [fol. 58^v: Seur Marie de Rubenpre fut vestue le mardi xixme iour de iuing lan mil iiii^c lxx, de laage de dix ans, et trespassa le *xxx^e de may mil cinq cens quarente six*]

5) Seur Marguerite de Mailly: born ca. 1454, entered 28 July 1478, died 27 April 1535.
   [fol. 59^v: Seur Marguerite de Mailly fut vestue le iour saint Leon xxviii^e de iuillet lan mil iiii^{c}lxxviii, de lage de xxiiii ans, et trespassa *le xvii^e iour davril mil v^c xxxv*]

6) Seur Marthe Mychon: born ca. 1466, entered 26 June 1474, died 8 October 1524.
   [fol. 59^r: Seur Marthe Michon agee de huyt ans our environs fut vestue la dimenche xxvi^e iour de Juing lan mil iiii^c lxxiiii Et trespassa le *viii^e Jour doctobre lan mil v^{cc} xxiiii*]

7) Seur Francoyse de la Perreuse: born ca. 1467, entered 12 December 1473, died 29 March 1524 or 1525.[6]
   [fol. 59^r: Seur Francoize de la Perreuse fut vestue le dimenche xii^e iour de decembre lan m iiii^c lxxiii de la age de six ans Et trespassa *le xxixe de mars lan mil v.^{c} xxiiii*]

8) Seur Jehanne Dangue: born ca. 1464, entered 20 June 1473, died 10 March 1541.
   [fol. 59^r: Seur Jehanne Dangue niepce de seur Jehanne Dangue fut

---

   [6] "29 March 1524" could refer to either 1524 or 1525 in modern reckoning, because Easter fell on March 27 in 1524, and on April 16 in 1525, so by the Parisian method of reckoning two 29 Marchs fell between these dates.

vestue le xxᵉ jour de Juing lan m iiiiᶜ lxxiii agee dentre huyt et nuef ans Et trespassa *le xᵉ de mars mil vᶜ xl*]

9) Seur Georgette Cueur: born ca. 1470, entered 25 August 1482, died 2 May 1550.

[59ᵛ: Seur Georgette Cueur fut vestue le xxvᵉ iour daoust lan mil iiiiᶜ iiiiˣˣ et deux de lage de xii ans *et trespassa le second iour de may lan mil vᶜ cinqᵗᵉ et a este abbesse environ xvii ans*]

10) Seur Anne de Cambray. born ca. 1476, entered 25 November 1486, died 9 August 1555.

[fol. 60ʳ: Seur Anne de Cambray fut vestue le xxvᵉ de novembre mil iiiiᶜ iiiiˣˣ et vi de laage de dix ans Et trespassa *le ixᵉ jour daoust. m. vᶜ cinquente cinq*]

11) Seur Perette d'Arragon: born ca. 1476, entered 23 May 1490, died 12 September 1539.

[fol. 60ᵛ: Seur Perrette Darragon fut vestue le xxiiiᵉ de may lan mil iiiiᶜ iiiiˣˣ et dix aaggee de xiiii ans Et trespassa *le xii Jour de septembre. mil. v.ᶜ xxxix*]

12) Seur Loyse Senesme: born ca. 1478, entered 14 September 1488, died 11 January 1553.

[fol. 60ʳ: Seur Loys Senesme fut vestue le xiiiiᵉ iour de septembre mil iiiiᶜ iiiiˣˣ et viii de laage de dix ans Et trespassa *En loffice dabbesse le onsiesme iour de janvier mil vᶜ cinquentte deulx Et fust audict office trois ans et cinq mois*]

13) Seur Perrette de Milly: born ca. 1478, entered 9 May 1490, died 12 December 1548.

[fol. 60ᵛ: Seur Perrette de Mylly fut vestue le ixᵉ de may lan mil iiiiᶜ iiiiˣˣ et x de laage de xii ans Et trespassa *le xiiᵉ Jour de decembre mil vᶜ xlviii*]

14) Seur Loyse de Hangest: born ca. 1478, entered 12 December 1486, died 27 December 1536.

[fol. 60ʳ: Seur Loyse de Hangest fut vestue le xiiᵉ iour de decembre mil iiiiᶜ iiiiˣˣ et six de laage de huit ans Et trespassa *le iour sainct Iehan levangeliste. Lan mil. v.ᶜ xxxvi*]

15) Seur Jehenne Lamye: born ca. 1474, entered 12 February 1492, died 20 May 1538.

[fol. 60ᵛ: Seur Iehanne Amys fut vestue le xiiᵉ de fevrier mil iiiiᶜ iiiiˣˣ xi de laage de xviii ans et trespassa *le xxᵉ Jour de may. Lan mil. v.ᶜ xxxviii.*][7]

16) Seur Loyse Aveline: born ca. 1482 entered 29 July 1499, died 20 April 1548.

[fol. 60ᵛ: Seur Loyse Aveline fut vestue le xxixᵉ de iullet mil iiiiᶜ iiiiˣˣ xii de laage de xvii ans et trespassa *le xxᵉ dabvril mil cinq cens quarente*

---

[7] The indication of age, "xviii," was first omitted with space left, and then filled in later with different ink.

huit]

17) Seur Francoyse de Nouvion: born ca. 1483, entered 12 October 1494, died 19 March 1523.

[fol. 61ʳ: Seur Francoise de Novion fut vestue de lage de xi ans le xiiᵉ doctobre lan mil iiiiᶜᶜ iiiiˣˣ et xiiii et trespassa *le xixᵉ jour de mars lan mil vᶜ vingt et deux.*]

18) Seur Marie Lotin: born ca. 1485, entered 19 February 1498, died 20 April 1569.[8]

[fol. 61ʳ: Seur Marie Lotin fut vestue en lage de xiii ans le xix.ᵉ de frevier lan mil iiii.ᶜᶜ iiii.ˣˣ et xvii. Et trespassa *le xxᵉ davril 1569 ayant este abbess de ceans 14 ans*]

19) Seur Katherine Pimorine: born ca. 1481, entered 23 June 1497, died 16 May 1552.

[fol. 61ʳ: Seur Katherine Pymosin fut vestue en lage de xvi ans le iour sainct audry lan mil iiiiᶜᶜ. iiiiˣˣ et xvii Et trespassa *le xviᵉ jour de may mil cinq cens cinquante deulx*]

20) Seur Marguerite la Fevre: born ca. 1487, entered 24 august 1494, 1 November 1551.

[fol. 61ʳ: Seur Marguerite La Fevre fut vestue en lage de vii ans et demy le xxiiiiᵉ daust lan mil iiiiᶜᶜ. iiii.ˣˣ et xiiii Et trespassa *le Jour des mors lan mil v cens cinquante et ung*]

21) Seur Katherine de Sainctz: born ca. 1488, entered 3 August 1495, died 28 October 1543.

[fol. 61ʳ: Seur Katherine de Sains fut vestue en lage de vii ans le iiiᵉ daust lan mil iiiiᶜᶜ iiiiˣˣ et xv. Et trespassa *Le xxviiᵉ de octobre lan mil vᶜ xliii*]

22) Seur Katherine Fourmont: born ca. 1484, entered 31 January 1502, died 1 October 1521.

[fol. 61ᵛ: Seur Katherine Fromont de laage de xviii ans fust vestue le derrenier iour de Janvier lan mil v.ᶜᶜ et ung Et trespassa *le jour saint Remy lan mil cinq cens vingt et ung*]

23) Seur Marie de Livre: born ca. 1490, entered 13 May 1498, died 12 April 1540.

[fol. 61ʳ: Seur Marie de Livres fut vestue de lage de viii ans et demy le xiiiᵉ de may lan mil iiii.ᶜᶜ iiii.ˣˣ et xviii. Et trespassa *le xiiᵉ davril mil v.ᶜᶜ quarante*]

24) Seur Anne de Chouvreux: born ca. 1488, entered 11 September 1502, died 21 August 1555.

[fol. 61ᵛ: Seur Anne Chauvereux de laage de xiiii ans fust vestue le xi.ᵉ iour de septembre lan mil vᶜᶜ et deux Et trepassa *le xxie jour daoust*[9]

---

[8] In "Abbesses of Longchamp in the Sixteenth Century," 558, I inadvertently gave her year of entry as 1497 (without correcting to new style).

[9] "de may" is crossed out, and "daoust" is added in the margin.

mil cinq cens cinquante]

25) Seur Katherine de Landres: born ca. 1490, entered 15 September 1499, died 1547.

[fols. 61^{r-v}: Seur Katherine de Landres fut vestue en lage de ix ans le xv.^{e} de septembre lan mil iiii.^{cc} iiii.^{xx} et xix // *Et trespassa le xv^e de Juillet mil v^{c}xlvii*]

26) Seur Jacqueline Baudequin: born ca. 1490, entered 25 November 1501, died 9 September 1556.

[fol. 61^v: Seur Jaqueline Baudequin fut vestue en lage de xi. ans et demy le iour saincte Katherine lan mil. v.^{cc} et ung Et trespassa *le ix^e septembre .m. v^c l. vi*]

27) Seur Geneviefve Richevillain: born ca. 1487, entered 21 March 1505, died 24 May 1546.

[fol. 62^r: Seur Gennevieve Richevillain fust vestue le iour sainct benoyst lan mil v.^{cc} et iiii aagee de xviii ans et trespassa *le xxiiii^e Jour de may mil cinq cens quarente six*]

28) Seur Anthonette du Boys: born ca. 1491, entered 21 November 1501, died 31 December 1549.

[fol. 61^v: Seur Anthoinette du Bois fut vestue en lage de x ans le xxi.^{e} de novembre lan mil .v.^{cc} et ung Et trespassa *le darnier jour de december .m. v^c xlix*]

29) Seur Marie Picard: born ca. 1491, entered 5 August 1503, died 27 April 1532.

[fols. 61^v-62^r: Seur Marie Picart fust vestue le ve iour daoust lan mil v.^{cc} // et trois de laage de xii ans et trespassa *le xxvii^e jour davril lan mil. v.^{c} et xxxii*]

30) Seur Marie Boliard: born ca. 1492, entered 14 September 1505, died 28 September 1556.

[fol. 62^r: Seur Marie Bouliarde fut vestue le xiiii^e de septembre v.^{cc} v aagee de xiii ans et trespassa *le xxviii^e Septembre m. v^c.l. vi*]

31) Seur Charlotte de St Laurens: born ca. 1493, entered 26 February 1506, died 20 June 1536.

[fol. 62^r: Seur Charlotte de Sainct Laurens fut vestue le xxvi^e de frevier v.^{cc} et sinq de laage de xiii ans et trespassa *le xx^e jour de Juin lan mil .v.^{c} xxxvi*]

32) Seur Clere de Varlusel: born ca. 1497, entered 29 September 1504, died 24 January 1568.[10]

[fol. 62^r: Seur Claire de Valusel fust vestue le iour sainct michel lan mil v.^{cc} et iiii aagee de vii ans et demy et trespassa *Le 24 de Janvier 1568*]

33) Seur Regnee Luylier: born, ca. 1496, entered 19 February 1503, died 16 November 1564.

[fol. 61^v: Seur Regnee Luylier fut vestue le xix^e Jour de fevrier lan mil

---

[10] I have assumed here that by 1568 Longchamp was beginning the new year with 1 January.

v.ᶜᶜ et deux de laage de sept ans et trespassa *le xviᵉ de Novembre Mil vᶜ lxiiii*]

34) Seur Anne de Rochebaron: born ca. 1496, entered 9 July 1503, died 9 September 1537.
   [fol. 61ᵛ: Seur Anne de Rochebaron fut vestue le ixᵉ iour de Juillet lan .m. v.ᶜᶜ et trois de laage de vii ans et demy et trespassa *le ix.ᵉ iour de septembre lan mil v.ᶜ et xxxvii*]

35) Seur Marguerite du Buc: born ca. 1496, entered 5 July 1506, died 25 August 1565.
   [fol. 62ʳ: Seur Marguerite du buc fut vestue le v.ᵉ de Juillet vᶜᶜ et vi aagee de x ans et trespassa *le iour de saint Loys de france mil vᶜᶜ lxv*]

36) Seur Ysabeau du Harlay: born ca. 1496, entered 15 April 1509, died 22 February 1579.
   [Fol. 62ᵛ: Seur Ysabiau de Herlay fust vestue le xvᵉ davril v.ᶜᶜ et ix. aagee de xiii ans et trespassa *le xxiiᵉ febvrier m vᶜ lxxix*]

37) Seur Guionne Coignet: born ca. 1490, entered 18 January 1511, died 18 July 1562.
   [fol. 62ᵛ: Seur Guionne Coignet fut vestue le xviiiᵉ Jour de Janvier lan mil et x agee de xxi an et trespassa *le xviiiᵉ Juillet m vᶜ lxii*]

38) Seur Denise Sevin: born ca. 1498, entered 26 July 1507, died 21 August 1556.
   [fol. 62ʳ: Seur Denise Sevin fut vestue le Jour sainct anne vᶜᶜ et vii aagee de ix ans *et trespassa le xxiᵉ aoust .m. vᶜ .l. vi*]

39) Seur Gillette Brinum: born ca. 1498, entered 21 September 1507, died 25 March 1538.
   [fols. 62ʳ⁻ᵛ: Seur Gillette Brinum fut vestue le Jour sainct mathieu vᶜᶜ et vii // aagee de .ix. ans et trespassa *le xxv. de mars. Lan mil v.ᶜ xxxvii*]

40) Seur Anthoenette Buraude: born ca. 1497, entered 17 August 1511, died 28 March 1535.
   [fol. 62ᵛ: Seur Anthoinette Buraude fut vestue le xviiᵉ Jour daust lan mil v.ᶜᶜ et xi agee de xiiii ans et trespassa le *xxviiiᵉ de mars mil vᶜ xxxiiii*]

41) Seur Magadalene Lombart: born ca. 1498, entered 29 September 1511,[11] died 20 April 1533.
   [fol. 62ᵛ: Seur Madelaine Lombert fut vestue le Jour des anges lan mil v.ᶜᶜ et xi agee de xiii ans et trespassa le *xxᵉ dapvril lan mil v.ᶜᶜ xxxiii*]

42) Seur Magdalene Gallet:born ca. 1500(?), entered 11 January 1512, died 4 August 1560.
   [fol. 62ᵛ: Seur Madelaine Gallet fut vestue le xi.ᵉ de Janvier lan mil .v.ᶜᶜ

---

[11] This date assumes that "le jour des anges" refers to the feast of saints Michael, Gabriel, and Raphael (the "jour des anges gardiens" has also been celebrated 2 October). In any case, given her position in the profession list, Magdalene had to have entered Longchamp between 21 September 1511 and 11 January 1512.

et xi. agee de xii[12] ans et trespassa *le iiii^e daoust m v.^c lx*]

43) Seur Katherine Agnes: born ca. 1498, entered 30 May 1512, died 15 September 1559.

 [fol. 62^v: Seur Katherine Agnes fut vestue le Jour de la trinite lan mil v.^cc et xii agee de xiiii ans et trespassa *le xv^e septembre m v^e lix*]

44) Seur Jehenne Paulmier:born ca. 1500, entered 29 June 1511, died 3 October 1560.

 [fol. 62^v: Seur Jehanne Paulmier fut vestue le Jour sainct pierre et sainct paul lan mil. v^cc et xi agee de xi ans Et tepassa *le iii^e octobre m v^e lx*]

45) Seur Jehenne Dauvet: born ca. 1500, entered 22 May 1513, died 14 September 1564.

 [fol. 62^v: Seur Jehanne Dauvette fust vestu le jour de la trinite lan mil v.^cc et xiii agee de xiii ans et trespassa *le xiiii.^e de Septembre. m. v.^c lxiiii*]

46) Seur Katherine Bret: born ca. 1500, entered 21 September 1511, died 27 April 1569.

 [fol. 62^v: Seur Katherine Bret fut vestue le Jour sainct mathieu lan mil v^cc et xi agee de xi ans et trepassa *le 27 d'avril 1569*]

47) Seur Anthoenette Le Picard: born ca. 1501, entered 10 September 1514, died 14 July 1572.

 [fol. 63^r: Seur Anthoinette Le Picard fut vestue le xe jour de Septembre lan mil .v.^cc et xiiii agee de xiii ans et trespassa *Le xiiii.^e Juillet m v^e lxxii*]

48) Seur Jehenne le Spinolle: born ca. 1504, entered 4 February 1515, died 29 June 1577.

[fol. 63^r: Seur Jehanne le Spinolle fut vetue le iiii^e jour de frevier lan mil v^cc et xiiii, agee de xi ans et trespassa *le xxix^e jour de Juing m v^e soixante dix sept.*]

49) Seur Katherine le Mercier: born ca. 1502(?), entered 30 September 1515, died 20 October 1576.

 [fol. 63^r: Seur Katherine Mercier fut vestue le Jour sainct Jherome lan mil v^cc et xv agee de xiii[13] ans et trespassa *le xx doctobre mil v lxxvi*]

50) Seur Ragonde de Longueil: born ca. 1504, entered 25 June 1514, died 5 March 1572.

 [fol. 62^v: Seur Ragonde de Longueil fut vestue landemain sainct Jehan Baptiste lan mil v.^cc et xiiii agee de x ans et trepassa *Le ve Jour de mars m v^e soixante douze*]

51) Seur Valentine Prevost: born ca. 1504, entered 9 September 1515, died 19 March 1558.

 [fol. 63^r: Seur Valantine Prevost fut vetue le ix^e Jour de septembre lan

---

 [12] This number has been partly obscured, but whether in an attempt to change the "xii" or by later accident is impossible to tell.

 [13] This number is difficult to decipher. The "x" is clear but then the following digits have been partly effaced, whether purposely or not is impossible to say.

mil v^cc et xv agee de xi ans et trespassa *le xix^e14 Iour de mars m v^c cinquante sept*]

52) Seur Geneviefve Laurens: born ca. 1504, entered 10 August 1516, died 24 August 1570.

[fol. 63^r: Seur Gennevieve Laurence fut vestue le Jour sainct Lorens lan mil v^cc et xvi agee de xii ans Et trespassa *Le xxiiii^e aoust m v^c lxx*]

53) Seur Germaine Godin: born ca. 1502, entered 9 November 1516, died 13 April 1560.

[fol. 63^r: Seur Germaine Godin fut vestue le ix.^e Jour de Novembre lan mil v^cc et xvi agee de xiiii ans et trespassa *la veuille de pasques qui fut le xiii^e davril m vc lix*]

54) Seur Jehenne Charphaude: Born ca. 1499, entered 4 November 1515, died 17 July 1526.

[fol. 63^r: Seur Jehanne Cafaut fut vestue le iiii.^e Jour de novembre lan mil v^cc et xv agee de xvi ans Et trespassa *Le xxvii^e de Juillet v^c xxvi*]

55) Seur Jehenne de Mailly: born ca. 1507, entered 15 July 1515, died 29 September 1590.

[fol. 63^r: Seur Jehanne de Mailli fut vestue le xv^e Jour de Juillet lan mil v^cc et xv agee de viii ans Et trespassa *Le Jour des anges v^c iiii^xx dix. A este abbesse quatre ans neuf moys*]

56) Seur Helie de Malignac: born ca. 1501, entered 27 July 1519, died 8 August 1559.

[fol. 63^v: Seur Helye de Malignace fut vestue le xxvii Jour de Juillet lan mil cinq cens xix aagee de xviii ans Et trespassa *le viii^e aoust m vc cinquante neuf*]

57) Seur Jehenne du Boc: born c. 1508, entered 18 May 1516, died 27 April 1575.

[fol. 63^r: Seur Jehanne du Boc fut vetue le Jour de la trinite xviii^e de may lan mil v.^cc et xvi agee de viii ans et trespassa *Le xxvii.^e apvril mil v^c lxxv*]

58) Seur Marie Bignet: born ca. 1510(?), entered 9 September 1520, died 25 August, 1550.

[fol. 63^v: Seur Marie Bignet fut vestue le ix Jour de septembre mil cinq cens et vingt aagee de x^15 ans et trepassa *Le xxv^e Jour daoust mil cinq^c cinquante*]

59) Seur Ethienette Le Gue: born ca. 1510, entered 8 December 1521, died 10 July 1567.

[fol. 63^v: Seur Estiennette le Gay fut vestue le iour de la concepcion de la vierge marie. Lan mil v.^cc xxi aagee de xi ans et demi Et trespassa *le xe Jour de Juillet mil v^c soixante dix*]

60) Seur Magdalene de Marle: born ca. 1511, entered 21 April 1521, died 19 August 1551]

An original number was crossed out here, and replaced with "xix."
This number may be "xi."

[fol. 63ᵛ:¹⁶ Seur Magdelaine de Marle fut vestue le xxi Jour davril lan
mil cinq cens xxi apres pasques agee de x ans Et trespassa *le xixᵉ Jour
daoust mil vᶜ cinquante et ung*]

61) Seur Guionne de Caules: born ca. 1513, entered 10 June 1520, died 2¹⁷
March 1562.

[fol. 63ᵛ: Seur Guyonne de Caulez fut vestue Le x.ᵉ Jour de Juing mil
cinq cens et vingt aagee de vii ans. Et trepassa *le 2ᵐᵉ Jour de mars m vᶜ
soixante et ung*]

62) Seur Anne Senesme: born ca. 1512, entered 1 September 1521, died 27
octobre 1557.

[fol. 63ᵛ: Seur Anne Cenesme fut vestue le premier iour de septembre
agee de ix ans lan mil v.ᶜᶜ xxi et trespassa *a Luzarches durent la fuite et
peur des gueres Lan m. vᶜ cinquante sept le xxviiᵉ octobre*]¹⁸

63) Seur Jehenne la Fevre: born ca. 1464, entered 22 August 1479 (lay sister),
died 27 may 1532.

[fol. 59ᵛ: Seur Iehanne la Fevre laye fut vestue le xxiiᵉ daoust lan mil iiiiᶜ
soixante disneuf de laage de xv ans et trespassa *le xvii iour de may. lan
mil. vᶜ. xxxii.*]

64) Seur Lyenarde Pastee: born ca. 1464, entered 28 October 1482 (lay sister), died 10 November 1532.

[fol. 59ᵛ: Seur Lyenarde Pastee fut vestue le xxviiiᵉ iour doctobre lan mil
iiiiᶜ iiiixx et deux seur laye de lage de xviii ans *et trespasa le xᵉ jour de
novembre mil vᶜ xxxii*]

65) Seur Yvonnette Malice: born ca. 1470, entered 29 May 1485 (lay sister),
died 10 August 1524.

[Fol. 59ᵛ: Seur Yvonette Malice fut vestue le iour de la trinite iiiixx et
cinq laye de lage de xv ans *Et trespassa lan mil v.ᶜᶜ vint et quatre le x.ᵉ
jour daust*]

66) Seur Jehenne Quotine: born ca. 1477, entered 28 October 1492 (lay sister), died 4 December 1537.

[fol. 60ᵛ: Seur Iehanne Cotine fut vestue seur laye le iour saint simon

---

¹⁶ I incorrectly gave this location as fol. 64ᵛ in "A New Life of Isabelle of France,"
76 n127.

¹⁷ The nun or scribe entering this date wrote what looks like a modern "z"
(zᵐᵉ). No reading, however, other than a "2" seems possible. I thank an illustrious
group of specialists (Elizabeth A. R. Brown, Marc H. Smith, Marie-Noëlle Baud-
ouin-Matuszek, Françoise Hildesheimer, Monique Bonnet) for weighing in on this
small problem.

¹⁸ The nuns of Longchamp repeatedly had to leave their abbey in the face of
threats from various armed bands in the second half of the sixteenth century. See
Duchesne, *Histoire de l'abbaye royale de Longchamp*, 80–81 (though without information specific to 1557). Luzarches is in the Ile-de-France north of Paris (department of Val-d'Oise). Presumably Anne found refuge with family there.

et saint iude lan mil iiii^c iiii^{xx} xii[19] de laage de xv ans et trespassa *le iiii^e Jour decembre mil. v.^c xxxvii*]

67) Seur Francoyse Boyleau: born ca. 1486, entered 12 March 1500 (lay sister), died 15 January 1522.

[fol. 61^v: Seur Francoise Boyleaue[20] laye fut vestue en lage de xiiii ans le iour sainct gregoire lan mil iiii.^{cc} iiii.^{xx} et xix. Et trespassa *le xv^e iour de janvier lan mil v^c ving et ung*]

68) Seur Francoyse de Laistre: born ca. 1485, entered 25 August 1504 (lay sister), died 8 December 1566.

[fol. 62^r: Seur Francoise de Lastre fust vestue seur laye le Jour sainct Loys de France lan mil v.^{cc} et iiii^e de laage de xix ans et trespassa *le viii^e de decembre mil cinz cens soixante six*]

69) Seur Collette Buferelle: born ca. 1488, entered 13 July 1505 (lay sister), died 19 December 1561.

[fol. 62^r: Seur Collette Bufetelle fut vestue seur laye le xiii^e de iuillet lan mil v.^{cc} et v[21] de laage de xvii ans et trespassa *le xix decembre m v^c soixante et ung*]

70) Seur Jehenne Boulengiere: born ca. 1490, entered 29 September 1507 (lay sister), died 24 August 1550.

[fol. 62^v: Seur Jehenne Boulengere fut vestue seur laye le Jour sainct michel v^{cc} et vii aagee de xvii ans *Et trespassa le jour st. Barthelemi mil v^c l*]

71) Seur Charlotte Guernyer: born ca. 1491, entered 25 January 1510 (lay sister) died 7 January 1554.

[fol. 62^v: Seur Charlotte Guernier fut vestue seur laye le Jour de la convercion sainct paul lan mil. v.^{cc} et ix agee de xix ans Et trepassa *le vii^e Jour de jenvier m v^c cinq^{te} troys*]

72) Seur Cecille Grignon: born ca. 1492, entered 25 January 1510 (lay sister), died 17 July 1559.

[fol. 62^v: Seur Cecille Grignon fut vetue sueur laye le xxv^e de genvier lan mil v^{cc} et ix agee de xviii ans et trespassa *le xvii juliet m v^c lix*]

73) Seur Ysabeau Brodon: born ca. 1500, entered 28 October 1516 (lay sister; barber), died 7 January 1546.

[Fol. 63^r: Seur Ysabeau Bradon fut vestue pour estre barbiere le Jour sainct simon sainct iude lan mil v^{cc} et xvi agee de xvi ans Et trespassa *le vii^e Jour de jenvier mil cinq cens quarente cinq*]

---

[19] "xii" is added above the line.

[20] First written as "Boyeleaue" but then the "e" effaced.

[21] "et v" is added above the line.

Between Aristotle and Augustine: Peter Martyr Vermigli and the Development of Protestant Ethics

Simon J. G. Burton
University of Warsaw

1. Introduction

PETER MARTYR VERMIGLI (1499–1562) was one of the most important second-generation Protestant Reformers. From around 1542 to his
death in 1562 he occupied important teaching chairs in Strasbourg,
Oxford, and Zürich, including the Regius Professorship of Divinity at
Oxford. A colleague and friend of Martin Bucer, John Calvin, Thomas
Cranmer, and Heinrich Bullinger, Vermigli helped to secure the progress
of Swiss and Alsatian Reform and had a lasting impact on the nascent
English Reformation. Through his voluminous biblical commentaries and his posthumous *Commonplaces* (*Loci Communes*) he exerted a
profound influence on subsequent Reformed thought, especially in the

The research for this article has been kindly funded by DFAIT as part of a
Canadian Commonwealth Fellowship. This paper is a much expanded and modified
version of a short conference paper given at Prague in March 2012 and published in
electronic proceedings as "Sin and Virtue in the Ethics of Peter Martyr Vermigli," in
Sins, Vices and Virtues: Dialectical Tensions in Moral Concepts, ed. Andrzej Danczak
and Joshua Farris.

areas of hermeneutics and eucharistic theology.[1] Before his conversion to Protestantism and his dramatic flight over the Alps in 1542, Vermigli had been one of the leading Augustinian Abbots and a prominent voice in favor of Catholic reform in Italy. He therefore came to his Protestant convictions having benefitted from a thorough scholastic, and indeed humanist, education, received both at the University of Padua and from his own order of the Lateran Canons. As is clear from his writings, the influence of this stayed with him throughout his life and contributed to his becoming one of the most important pioneers of the developing Protestant scholastic movement.[2]

While he has gone underappreciated for a long time, Vermigli's reputation as one of the most important Reformed theologians of the sixteenth century, second perhaps only to Calvin himself, now seems assured. Less well known, however—although the work of Luca Baschera and Stephen Grabill has done much to change this—is his important role in the birth of Protestant ethics.[3] While Luther had famously blamed Aristotle's ethics, and especially his concept of virtue as an acquired *habitus*, for the degeneration of scholastic theology, his successors quickly recognized the need for a more sensitive engagement with Aristotelian thought. In particular, both internal pressures of confessionalization, especially the

---

[1] For a recent comprehensive assessment of Vermigli and his influence, see Torrance Kirby, Emidio Campi, and Frank James III, eds., *A Companion to Peter Martyr Vermigli* (Leiden, 2009). The classic work on Vermigli's eucharistic theology remains Joseph McLelland, *The Visible Words of God: An Exposition of the Sacramental Theology of Peter Martyr Vermigli, AD 1500–1562* (Grand Rapids, MI, 1957).

[2] The most detailed discussion of Vermigli's involvement in Catholic Reform and the Augustinian Order is still to be found in Philip McNair, *Peter Martyr in Italy: An Anatomy of Apostasy* (Oxford, 1967), although see also the collection of essays in Joseph McLelland, ed., *Peter Martyr Vermigli and Italian Reform* (Waterloo, Ontario, 1980). For discussion of Vermigli's influence on the development of Reformed scholasticism see John Patrick Donnelly, "Calvinist Thomism," *Viator* 7 (1976): 441–55; "Italian Influences on the Development of Calvinist Scholasticism," *Sixteenth Century Journal* 7 (1976): 81–101, and Richard Muller, *Post-Reformation Reformed Dogmatics: The Rise and Development of Reformed Orthodoxy, ca. 1520 to ca. 1725* (Grand Rapids, MI, 2003), passim.

[3] See Luca Baschera, *Tugend und Rechtfertigung: Peter Martyr Vermiglis Kommentar zur Nikomachischen Ethik im Spannungsfeld von Philosophie und Theologie* (Zürich, 2008), and Stephen Grabill, *Rediscovering the Natural Law in Reformed Theological Ethics* (Grand Rapids, MI, 2006), 98–121.

pressing need to develop curricula and textbooks for the new Protestant schools and universities, and external pressures of polemic rendered wholesale abandonment of the traditional, scholastic model of education out of the question. Instead, Melanchthon and others began the long and arduous process of molding Aristotle to fit their Protestant sensibilities. Vermigli's unfinished 1563 *Commentary on Aristotle's Nicomachean Ethics*, originally presented between 1554 and 1556 as lectures to his students in Strasbourg, belongs to the first humanist wave of this process, which took up the Aristotelian texts most beloved of the Renaissance humanists, especially Aristotle's moral and psychological works, and repackaged them for the Protestant classroom.[4]

2. The Sources

The *Commentary* itself therefore bears all the hallmarks of Vermigli's scholastic and humanist education, as well as his Protestant convictions. His method combined a careful analysis and exegesis of Aristotle's text, including due attention to the interpretation of critical Greek terms, a syllogistic analysis of its content, and a detailed probing of its philosophical and theological implications.[5] In his convergence of systematic and philological interests Vermigli is hardly unusual. Indeed, as David Lines suggests, this was very much the norm for Renaissance commentators.[6] Vermigli's sources are also fairly typical for the Italian Renaissance milieu in which he was educated. Thus, as well as making extensive use of classical authors, Byzantine scholarship, and the new translations of the fifteenth and sixteenth century, he also draws on older writers such as Eustratius of Nicaea, one of the most popular medieval commentators. While it is

---

[4] For Vermigli's place in this broader context see Baschera, *Tugend und Rechtfertigung*, 31–60.

[5] Vermigli, *In Primum, Secundum et Tertii Libri Ethicorum Aristotelis ad Nicomachum* (Zürich, 1563), 7 (see also Emidio Campi and Joseph McLelland, eds., *Commentary on the Nicomachean Ethics. Peter Martyr Library Vol. 9* [hereafter *PML* 9] (Kirksville, MO, 2006), 13). Baschera, *Tugend und Rechtfertigung*, 44–53 argues for the combination of humanist and scholastic elements in Vermigli's hermeneutics. He also notes important parallels between Vermigli's commentary and that of the fifteenth-century humanist Donato Acciaiuoli.

[6] David Lines, "Aristotle's *Ethics* in the Renaissance," in *The Reception of Aristotle's Ethics*, ed. Jon Miller (Cambridge, 2012), 191–92.

surprising that Vermigli does not cite other conventional sources, such as the medieval commentaries of Albertus Magnus or Thomas Aquinas, there is some evidence that he made use of these.[7] More distinctive is Vermigli's concern throughout his *Commentary* to weigh Aristotle's pronouncements according to the testimony of Scripture.[8] However, even this was not at all unprecedented. Renaissance commentaries on the *Nicomachean Ethics* often had definite theological concerns. That these were only heightened by the Reformation is manifest from the clear confessional overtones of many commentaries of this period.[9]

While the context, method, and sources of Vermigli's *Commentary* do not much distinguish it from other Renaissance commentaries, its philosophical and theological content undoubtedly do. As one of the earliest Protestant commentaries on the *Nicomachean Ethics* it was also one of the first attempts to truly engage Aristotelian moral philosophy with Reformational theology. In doing so it both offered a truly distinctive ethics, both Reformed and scholastic in character, and helped to pave the way for future Protestant ethical reflection. As mentioned above, in recent years the signal importance of Vermigli's ethics has begun to be recognized by scholars. Thus Baschera has not only demonstrated the important synergy between Aristotelian virtue ethics and the theological concept of inherent righteousness in Vermigli's thought but also the way in which this shaped discussion from Theodore Beza and Lambert Daneau to Richard Hooker.[10] In a similar vein Stephen Grabill has offered a fascinating, and, in light of the current Barthian climate, much needed discussion of Vermigli's theological ethics and its place in a developing trajectory of Protestant reflection on the natural law.[11]

What is particularly refreshing about both of these scholars is the way in which they insightfully draw on both the *Commentary* and the *Commonplaces* and biblical commentaries to offer a well-rounded view of

---

[7] A comprehensive discussion of Vermigli's sources is to be found in Baschera, *Tugend und Rechtfertigung*, 60–84.

[8] Vermigli, *Ethicorum*, 7 (*PML* 9:13). Vermigli concludes his discussion of each chapter of the *Ethics* with a comparison with Scripture.

[9] Lines, "Aristotle's *Ethics*," 188–93, discusses this in a general Renaissance context. Baschera, *Tugend und Rechtfertigung*, 49–50 highlights the theological and polemical valence of the *Ethicorum*.

[10] Baschera, *Tugend und Rechtfertigung*, 143–241.

[11] Grabill, *Rediscovering the Natural Law*, 98–121.

Vermigli's ethics and its theological motivations. In doing so they offer an important perspective on its Aristotelian and Thomist elements, as well as their interaction with humanist strains in his thought. Yet, arguably, where they fall short is in failing to realize the full-extent of the Augustinian, and indeed late medieval Augustinian, influence on Vermigli's moral philosophy and theology.[12] This is not to say that they do not acknowledge Augustinian elements in Vermigli—for they undoubtedly do. Rather, in line with a general tendency of Vermigli scholarship, they tend to see these as mere modifiers of a basically Thomist or Aristotelian framework.[13] The result is that their treatments of his discussion of virtue, natural law, and free will, like the earlier discussions of John Patrick Donnelly, are markedly one-sided. Yet, this is to neglect not only the important work of Frank James III on Vermigli's soteriology, which demonstrated a profound influence of the fourteenth-century Augustinian Gregory of Rimini on his predestinarian thought, but also the wider research of Adolar Zumkeller, Heiko Oberman, and Manfred Schulze into late medieval Augustinian theology and ethics and its influence on the Reformation.[14]

There is a need, therefore, which this paper addresses, for a discussion of Vermigli's scholastic ethics which probes *both* its Thomist and Augustinian elements in detail and their subtle interaction. Only when this is done will we fully understand either his relation to late medieval and Renaissance ethics or to developed Protestant moral theology. For Vermigli stands at an important cross-roads in the development of

---

[12] For a discussion of Vermigli's Thomism, see John Patrick Donnelly, *Calvinism and Scholasticism in Vermigli's Doctrine of Man and Grace* (Leiden, 1976). For an account of late medieval Augustinian influence on Vermigli, see Frank James III, *Peter Martyr Vermigli and Predestination: The Augustinian Heritage of an Italian Reformer* (Oxford, 1998). Joseph McLelland, "Italy: Religious and Intellectual Ferment," in *Companion*, ed. Kirby, Campi, and James, 26–27, highlights the need for a detailed study of the influence of Thomist and Augustinian scholasticism on Vermigli.

[13] See, for example, Muller, *Post-Reformation Reformed Dogmatics*, 1:343. Luca Baschera, "Aristotle and Scholasticism," in *Companion*, ed. Kirby, Campi, and James, 151–59, argues for the eclectic nature of Vermigli's scholasticism, but this fails to do justice to the carefully woven Thomist and Augustinian strands in his thought.

[14] James, *Vermigli and Predestination*, 106–50. The literature on late medieval Augustinianism and its connection to the Reformation is extensive. For bibliographical discussion see Eric Saak, *High Way to Heaven: The Augustinian Platform Between Reform and Reformation, 1292–1524* (Leiden, 2002), 683–710.

Christian ethics. Thus when we read the *Commentary* we see Vermigli not only reaching for a new synthesis of Augustine and Aristotle—parallel to the older synthesis of Aquinas and the High Scholastics—but also, with his fellow Reformers, continuing to grapple with a new awareness of the transcendence of God and the depths of human depravity. This, as we shall see, on the one hand leaves little space for traditional Aristotelian accounts of virtue and happiness, while on the other hand opens out onto a new, transfigured understanding of virtue in many important respects true to its Aristotelian original.

3. Original Sin and Fallen Nature

In accounting for virtue it is important to give consideration to its contrary, vice—an Aristotelian principle certainly, but also a scriptural one given the predicament of fallen man. As Donnelly remarks, sin is one of the principal themes of Vermigli's theology.[15] For him it serves the purpose of demonstrating man's inability to save himself and his consequent need for the grace of God in Christ. It also (as we shall discuss below), relativizes the relation of virtue to happiness, giving his ethics its characteristic shape. Following a long Christian tradition, which he traced back both to Scripture and the earliest Fathers of the Church, Vermigli made an important two-fold distinction between sin as original and sin as actual—that is between the sinful nature and the sinful act.[16] While no one opposed the notion of actual sin, the situation with regard to original sin was quite different. In particular, Vermigli held this doctrine to be threatened both by Anabaptists and a number of prominent Catholics. These he viewed as reviving the Pelagian heresy, holding that their watered down account of original sin went hand-in-hand with their stress on human merit and unwarranted optimism concerning unaided human potential.[17]

In his *scholium* on Romans 5, his most extensive treatment of original sin, Vermigli singled out especially for attack Albert Pighius, the

---

[15] Donnelly, *Calvinism and Scholasticism*, 101.

[16] Peter Martyr Vermigli, *Commonplaces*, trans. Anthony Marten (London, 1583), 2:229.

[17] Vermigli, *Commonplaces*, 2:213–14.

prominent Dutch Catholic theologian and polemicist, whom he viewed as a kind of *Pelagius redivivus*. In his 1542 *De Libero Hominis Arbitrio et Divina Gratia*, which was one of the most important Catholic responses to developed Reformation theology, Pighius had launched a scorching attack on Luther and Calvin, castigating them for their account of the "bondage of the will" and their distorted understanding of human nature. In another earlier work, the *Controversarium* of 1541, Pighius set out his own understanding of original sin. According to Vermigli this was basically identical to the erroneous doctrine, cited by Peter Lombard in his *Sentences*, that original sin is "onelie a guilt, trespasse or bond, whereunto we are tied by the sinne of Adam." In line with this, Pighius regarded original sin as merely the imputing of Adam's sin to his posterity and not as entailing actual sin or corruption, despite the fact that it incurred damnation. He defended this claim, arguing that since original sin is neither voluntary nor an actual transgressing of the law it cannot be counted as sin.[18] While Pighius's doctrine was his own, he drew, implicitly, on a number of important late medieval concepts in articulating it. As many scholars have noted, from Duns Scotus onwards the doctrine of "acceptance" (*acceptatio*) became prominent in expounding the theology of justification. According to this God wills to accept the faith and works of fallen man as worthy of eternal life despite their intrinsic deficiency. In this covenantal framework the value of human action becomes determined solely by divine will, whereby God imputes a value to human actions that they do not intrinsically possess.[19] In effect, Pighius inverted this logic, arguing that although Adam's descendants are not guilty, God decrees to impute Adam's own guilt to them. For him, this had the advantage of retaining a traditional Catholic doctrine of the condemnation of all in Adam—albeit mitigating some of its severer aspects—while avoiding the notion of human nature itself as corrupted by the fall. Instead of holding the traditional Augustinian doctrine that the fall

---

[18] Vermigli, *Commonplaces*, 2:216–17; cf. Albert Pighius, *Controversarium Praecipuarum in Comitiis Ratisponensibus Tractatarus* (Paris, 1549), 5^r–5^v, 30^r–33^v.

[19] Acceptance became especially prominent in soteriology after Scotus, but Adolar Zumkeller, *Erbsünde, Gnade, Rechtfertigung und Verdienst nach der Lehre der Erfurter Augustinertheologen des Spätmittelalters* (Würzburg, 1983), 2–3, notes its Augustinian roots. The covenantal character of late medieval thought is brought out in William Courtenay, *Covenant and Causality in Medieval Thought: Studies in Philosophy, Theology and Economic Practice* (London, 1984).

plunged human nature into a state of depravity and bondage, Pighius thus argued that it simply returned man to a state of "pure nature." In a move redolent of late medieval theologians like William of Ockham and Gabriel Biel, he therefore sharply distinguished between man's natural state and the extrinsic gift of grace superadded to it.[20] Following something of a Scotist tendency, Pighius also naturalized concupiscence and, going beyond Scotus, he even went so far as to espouse the Pelagian position that death itself proceeded from the "wellsprings of nature."[21] In his understanding death was a natural state which followed only upon the deprivation of original, preserving righteousness to Adam and his descendants. For Adam's descendants, at least, it was not therefore to be considered as penal but simply as a reversion to humanity's natural mortal and bestial state.[22]

For Vermigli Pighius's doctrine was not only an affront to divine justice and human dignity but an outright denial of the scriptural testimonies that death and concupiscence entered the world through sin.[23] Significantly, in countering what he viewed as Pighius's revived Pelagianism, Vermigli had particular recourse to the later works of Augustine, especially his *De Peccatorum Meritis et Remissione* and his *Contra Iulianum*, in which Augustine laid out his most robust account of original sin and human bondage. Indeed, a close inspection of the *scholium* on Romans 5 reveals just how much he is indebted to these works of Augustine for his own position.[24] In this he appears very similar to Gregory of Rimini whose own anthropology and soteriology also derived from the mature Augustine. While it is very difficult to prove a direct influence of late medieval Augustinianism on Vermigli's account of original sin, especially as elements of the Augustinian doctrine were common to all medieval theologians, we shall see there are some suggestive indications.

---

[20]   Pighius, *Controversarium*, 16^r-18^v. For a discussion of the late medieval concept of "pure nature," see Heiko Oberman, *The Harvest of Medieval Theology: Gabriel Biel and Late Medieval Nominalism* (Cambridge, MA, 1963), 47–50.

[21]   Oberman, *Harvest*, 125, points out that for Scotus concupiscence belonged to man's nature and even in Paradise needed to be restrained by natural justice.

[22]   Pighius, *Controversarium*, 15^r-16^v; cf. Vermigli, *Commonplaces*, 2:216–17.

[23]   Vermigli, *Commonplaces*, 2:216–17.

[24]   For Vermigli's explicit citations of these works of Augustine, see *Commonplaces*, 2:215, 219, 224–25, 227–29. There are also numerous other citations of Augustine in this section.

At the very least these serve to underscore the intensified Augustinian character of Vermigli's own doctrine and its marked affinity with that of Rimini. To follow in detail all of Vermigli's arguments against Pighius (and Pelagius) would take us too far afield. Yet in order to understand Vermigli's Augustinian view of sin and its ethical ramifications, it is important to get at least a flavor of them.

The heart of Pighius's objection to the traditional doctrine lay in his understanding that sin must be a voluntary action arising from human election.[25] In these terms involuntary sin, which everyone agreed that original sin must be, made no sense at all. Vermigli's response to this was to upbraid Pighius for making a "lesse and lighter matter of sin than he ought to do." Following a scriptural and Augustinian understanding he argued that sin was properly to be understood as transgression of the divine law, whether voluntary or involuntary.[26] Elsewhere he reverted to an important Augustinian distinction, also found prominently in Rimini, between voluntary sin as fault and involuntary sin as both fault and punishment. Using this he argued that the necessity of sinning incurred by all Adam's descendants was a punishment for the original fault of their forebear.[27] Nevertheless, Vermigli vehemently denied Pighius's position that humans were punished simply for the sin of Adam and not for their own sin. Rather, like Rimini, he upheld the Augustinian line that everyone is punished only for their own fault—the corruption of their nature originally contracted in Adam. For anything else would be flatly contrary to divine justice.[28]

For Vermigli, Pighius's understanding of sin was therefore much too narrow. This became particularly apparent in their different treatment of unbaptized infants. According to Pighius while infants who die without baptism cannot enter heaven they will not be subject to hell either. Instead they will exist in a kind of state of natural blessedness in which they are

---

[25] Pighius, *Controversarium*, 5ʳ–5ᵛ; cf. Vermigli, *Commonplaces*, 2:217, 219–20. In fact both Pighius and Vermigli held that sin was essentially iniquity. The difference was that Pighius insisted that this entailed sin's voluntary character.

[26] Vermigli, *Commonplaces*, 2:217, 220, 271.

[27] Vermigli, *Commonplaces*, 2:219, 273–74; cf. Gregory of Rimini, *Lectura super Primum et Secundum Sententiarium*, ed. Damasus Trapp and Venicio Marcolino (Berlin, 1980–81), 2 d. 30–33 q. 1 art. 1, 4 (6:174–82, 196).

[28] Vermigli, *Commonplaces*, 2:222, 234; cf. Rimini, *Lectura*, 2 d. 30–33 q. 1 art. 1 (6:179).

able to praise God and even love him wholeheartedly. Indeed, he ada-
mantly maintains their fundamental innocence, arguing that they cannot be subject to sin from conception since they have not done anything
wrong.[29] Such a position is for Vermigli worse than that of the Pelagians
who, he says, denied only the propagation of sin through Adam and not
either the sinfulness of infants or the condemnation of the unbaptized to
hell.[30] By contrast his own position is starkly Augustinian. He holds that
children contract sin from their conception and that because of this are
worthy of eternal punishment. While Pighius held this to be unjust Vermigli pointed him to the famous image in Romans 9 of God as a potter
who is entitled to do what he will with his human clay. In this he arguably
goes beyond even Rimini, who despite his famous moniker "torturer of
children" (*tortor infantium*) finally stopped short of a positive affirmation
of this harsh doctrine.[31] This aside, Vermigli, like Rimini, clearly sees the
sacrament of baptism as a key argument in favor of an Augustinian doctrine of original sin. For if there were no corruption of nature then the
need for baptism and regeneration in Christ would be obviated. Instead,
following Augustine precisely, Vermigli held that baptism removes the
guilt of original sin but not the stain of the sin itself.[32]

Unsurprisingly, given the Augustinian tenor of his response to
Pighius, Vermigli's own discussion of original sin follows closely that
found in the works of the great Church Father. This we have already seen
in his claim that Adam's fall corrupted not only his own nature but that
of all his descendants, namely the entire human race. However, in his
Commonplaces Vermigli also takes up the strident doctrine of Augustine's later anti-Pelagian works that original sin is itself the concupiscence of the flesh.[33] In this he goes considerably further than many of the
medieval scholastics, who, as we shall see, tended to view concupiscence

---

[29]   Pighius, *Controversarium*, 34^r–35^r; cf. Vermigli, *Commonplaces*, 2:213, 233.

[30]   Vermigli, *Commonplaces*, 2:229.

[31]   Vermigli, *Commonplaces*, 2:220, 233–34; cf. Rimini, *Lectura*, 2 d. 30–33 q. 3
(6:218). Following Augustine, Vermigli does suggest that the punishments of those
dying only in original sin will most likely be less than those dying with actual sin
as well.

[32]   Vermigli, *Commonplaces*, 2:214, 233, 274; cf. Rimini, *Lectura*, 2 d. 30–33 q.
1 art. 4 (6:175, 194–96).

[33]   Vermigli, *Commonplaces*, 2:219. This opinion is found prominently in
Augustine, *De Peccatorum Meritis et Remissione*, 1:29.57, 39.70, 2:4.4 in *Patrologia*

as consequential on original sin rather than strictly identical with it. In espousing such a view Vermigli may well have been influenced by his reading of Rimini's *Lectura*. For the doctrine features prominently there and was, as Zumkeller remarks, one of the hallmarks of the late medieval Augustinian school.[34] Whether or not this is the case, as we shall see below, the deep affinity between Vermigli and Rimini led them both to make very similar ethical claims. With the scholastic mainstream Vermigli interpreted concupiscence not only as the rebellion of the "grosser parts of the mind"—the senses and affections—but as the revolt of the highest reaches of the soul against the law of God. Against Pighius, who held that concupiscence resided only in the "flesh and members," he held that concupiscence was comprehensive of all human faculties, blinding the intellect and dragging the will away from the things of God.[35] He therefore cited with approval Hugh of St. Victor's definition of original sin as that "which we from our nativitie drawe into our mind through ignorance, and into our flesh through concupiscence."[36] Following Augustine, Vermigli was clear, however, that it was not the act itself of concupiscence which should be considered as original sin but rather the "ableness, proanesse and readie disposition unto ill doing." In this sense Vermigli would surely have concurred with both Aquinas's description of original sin as an "inordinate disposition" and Rimini's of it as a "habitual fault or quasi-habitual vice."[37] Nevertheless, as we shall discuss below, the similarity of language may well mask an important difference between the two Augustinians and Aquinas.

In explaining the transmission of original sin Vermigli holds to the standard Augustinian understanding, affirmed by both Aquinas and Rimini, of seminal transmission. According to this original sin exists as an evil quality in human seed (sperm) which acts as an instrument for conveying this quality from parent to child. The soul itself acquires

---

Latina Cursus Completus [hereafter *PL*], ed. Jacques-Paul Migne, 221 vols. (Paris, 1844–55), 44:0142, 0150, 0152–3.

[34] Zumkeller, *Erbsünde*, 6. Rimini offers an in-depth discussion of this in *Lectura*, 2 d. 30–33 q. 1 art. 2 (6:182–92).

[35] Vermigli, *Commonplaces*, 2:219; cf. Pighius, *Controversarium*, 6ʳ.

[36] Hugh of St. Victor, *De Sacramentis Christianae Fidei*, 7:34 (*PL* 176:0302D) cited in Vermigli, *Commonplaces*, 2:219.

[37] Vermigli, *Commonplaces*, 2:219; cf. Aquinas, *Summa Theologiae*, 1a2ae 82.1; Rimini, *Lectura*, 2 d. 30–33 q. 1 art. 1 (6:180).

original sin when it is conjoined, at the moment of its creation by God, with a corrupt body derived from the affected seed. In this way the sin of Adam, existing in him as the quality of concupiscence, spread like an infection throughout the entirety of the human race.[38] With Augustine, Vermigli held that in children sin lies dormant until the coming of reason, when it awakes and becomes manifest for all to see.[39] There is a sense then, although doubtless one in need of careful construal, in which every soul undergoes its own fall. Vermigli describes this in the graphic language of Bernard of Clairvaux and William of Paris as similar to toppling onto a heap of potsherds or sinking into the mire, leaving us "plunged into darkness of ignorance . . . defiled with lusts . . . and wounded in our powers."[40]

Clearly, Vermigli's understanding of original sin is steeped in the Augustinianism of the scholastics. However, he does stop short of the notorious claim of Augustine, echoed by many of the medievals including Rimini himself, that original sin is conveyed by the lust of the sexual act "imprinting" itself on the seed.[41] For Vermigli this both degrades marriage, by implicitly suggesting that procreation is a kind of necessary evil, and associates original sin as concupiscence too narrowly with the "foul affection of lust." Instead he affirms the doctrine of the "wiser schoolmen"—of whom Aquinas surely represents the chief—that original sin is propagated by generation alone. In this way Vermigli reiterates his fundamental claim that original sin represents the "whole corrupting of nature."[42]

While Vermigli's Augustinian doctrine of concupiscence is undoubtedly at the heart of his doctrine of original sin, to focus on this alone is to miss the full scope of his understanding. For, as Donnelly rightly suggests, he is deeply concerned with harmonizing his understanding of original sin as a corruption of human nature with an alternative scholastic understanding of it, derived from Anselm, as a loss, or privation, of

---

[38] Vermigli, *Commonplaces*, 2:219, 229–30; cf. Aquinas, *Summa Theologiae*, 1a2ae 81.1; 82.4 ad. 3; Rimini, *Lectura*, 2 d. 30–33 q. 1 art. 2 (6:184–92). For this see Augustine, *De Peccatorum Meritis et Remissione*, 1:29.57, 39.70 (*PL* 44:0142, 0150).

[39] Vermigli, *Commonplaces*, 2:224.

[40] Vermigli, *Commonplaces*, 2:230.

[41] Augustine expounds this doctrine in *Contra Iulianum*, 4:3.33–4.34 (*PL* 44:0756). It is also to be found in Rimini, *Lectura*, 2 d. 30–33 q. 1 art. 2 (6:185).

[42] Vermigli, *Commonplaces*, 2:219; cf. Aquinas, *Summa Theologiae*, 1a2ae 82.4 ad. 3.

original righteousness.[43] Such an understanding might seem perilously close to that of Pighius, who also affirmed that original sin was a privation of God's gifts, but Vermigli recognized a crucial distinction. For Pighius original sin was a mere privation (as well as an extrinsic imputation), whereas for Anselm the privation was inextricably bound to a corruption of nature.[44] This in itself points to a much deeper underlying difference—a gulf in their conception of human nature. Pighius, as we have seen, operates with a conception of "pure nature," most likely derived from late medieval scholasticism. Divine grace comes to such a nature only from outside and its removal therefore simply returns it to its original created state. For Vermigli, however, who follows an older scholastic conception of nature, man was created not in a state of neutrality but in the image of God.[45]

Distancing himself from the usual medieval preoccupation with an Augustinian psychological account of the *imago Trinitatis,* Vermigli redefined the understanding of image Christologically, in terms of likeness to Christ and the mirroring of his divine properties.[46] The original righteousness of Adam therefore consisted in the ordering of all his faculties towards God, with his reason subject to God and his law and his lower, sensitive powers, restrained by his reason. Moreover, Vermigli held that as created in a state of grace Adam possessed all the natural and supernatural virtues.[47] This explains why Adam's fall was so catastrophic. For it not only stripped him of this original righteousness, but in so doing wounded human nature to its very core, disrupting its

---

[43] Donnelly, *Calvinism and Scholasticism*, 106.

[44] Vermigli, *Commonplaces*, 2:222; cf. Anselm of Canterbury, *De Conceptu Virginali et Originali Peccato*, 2–3 (*PL* 158:0435A–0436C).

[45] Vermigli, *Commonplaces*, 2:222–3. For an important discussion of nature in scholasticism and the debate over "pure nature" see Henri de Lubac, *The Mystery of the Supernatural* (New York, 1967).

[46] Vermigli, *Commonplaces*, 2:223. It should be noted that Vermigli by no means denied a trinitarian aspect to the soul rooted in memory, understanding, and will. Indeed, in *Commonplaces*, 1:123 and 2:223 he explicitly affirmed this. Rather, he simply did not see this as the essential meaning of the image of God. Aquinas in *Summa Theologiae*, 1a 93.8 and Rimini in *Lectura*, 2 d. 16–17 q. 3 art. 2; d. 29 q. 1 art. 2 (5:368–73; 6:140–1) also relativize this natural image. Augustine himself in *De Trinitate*, 14:15.21 (*PL* 42:1051–2) affirmed the true image to lie in the soul's remembering, understanding and loving God.

[47] Vermigli, *Ethicorum*, 353 (*PML* 9:337).

intrinsic orientation to God and causing it to become curved or "bent" in on itself—the state which Augustine called concupiscence. Moreover, following Anselm, Vermigli held that all humans must be considered as "debtors" to this original righteousness. Thus, through the institution and restitution of humanity in Christ, a law is given obliging all. It is by this universal law, manifest in the natural law, human conscience, and the Ten Commandments, that all are worthily condemned for falling short not only of the divine command but of their very own nature and purpose.[48]

Weaving together these Augustinian and Anselmic strands Vermigli offered his own definition of original sin as "a corrupting of the whole nature of man, derived by generation from the fall of our first parent into his posteritie; which (were it not for the benefit of Christ) adjudgeth all that are borne therein in a manner to infinite miseries, and eternall damnation." Significantly, he held this to comprehend the Aristotelian causal order, with the material cause the powers of man, the formal cause the corruption of these powers, the efficient cause the sinful will of Adam, the instrumental cause human generation, and the final cause eternal damnation.[49] In offering such a definition Vermigli puts his own distinctive twist on the scholastic tradition. For, as he recognizes, he is not the first to attempt this project of reconciliation. Indeed, he cites Aquinas, Scotus, and especially Bonaventure as attempting to combine Augustine and Anselm by assigning the material cause of original sin to concupiscence and the (more important) formal cause to the loss of original righteousness.[50] Likewise, Rimini, for all his strident Augustinianism, at times seemed perfectly willing to equate original sin with the loss of original righteousness. More precisely, he held that this privation was an inseparable effect of original

---

[48] Vermigli, *Commonplaces*, 2:223–24.

[49] Vermigli, *Commonplaces*, 2:224.

[50] Vermigli, *Commonplaces*, 2:226. See Aquinas, *Summa Theologiae*, 1a2ae 82.3, Duns Scotus, *Lectura*, 2 d. 30–32 q. 4 n. 48–49, in *Doctoris Subtilis et Mariania B. Ioannis Duns Scoti Opera Omnia*, ed. Carolus Balic (Vatican City, 1993), 19:305–6 and Bonaventure of Bagnoregio, *Commentaria in Quatuor Libros Sententiarum*, 2 d. 30 q. 1 art. 2, in *Doctoris Seraphici S. Bonaventurae Opera Omnia* (Florence, 1885), 2:722. Oberman, *Harvest*, 122–23 argues for three main medieval views on original sin. Broadly speaking, these are the Augustinians, the Anselmians, and those who tried to reconcile the two.

sin as concupiscence.[51] Now Vermigli, who clearly intends to comprehend both privation of original righteousness *and* concupiscence in the formal cause of original sin, shows important similarities and differences with both these approaches. On the one hand he affirms with Anselm and his thirteenth-century followers the vital importance of recognizing original sin as the loss of man's original rectitude, on the other hand he is at one with Rimini and the late medieval Augustinians in refusing to downgrade concupiscence to a merely material aspect of original sin. Rather, for Vermigli as a convinced Augustinian, concupiscence as the rebellion against divine law represents the very heart of sin.

4. Actual Sin and the "Splendid Vices"

As Vermigli argued frequently in his *Commentary*, the effects of original sin on man's ethical life were nothing short of catastrophic. For it meant that the human heart was habitually inclined towards evil from birth. All of its actions, habits, and affections, even those which Aristotle would class as naturally good, must therefore be considered as tainted by sin. In his discussion of free will in his *Commonplaces* Vermigli offers an important discussion of actual sin and its relation to original sin, which helps to clarify some of these points. Bracketing the unforgivable sin for discussion elsewhere, he distinguishes three different degrees of sin. The first degree is original sin itself, which he characterizes as lust ingrafted into human nature (concupiscence). The second degree consists of the first motions of concupiscence in the soul. The third and highest degree is the consent of the will to these first motions which, he says, "perfects" the sin and makes it actual. As Vermigli recognized, the status of these "first motions" was somewhat ambiguous. In particular it was not clear whether they should be taken as belonging to original sin or actual sin. His own solution is to argue that the first motions participate in and have the characteristics of both. As they desire or lust for things contrary to God's will they belong to actual sin, but since they do this in an involuntary manner, even at times against human will, they belong to original sin.[52]

---

[51]   Rimini, *Lectura*, 2 d. 30–33 q. 1 art. 2 (6:183).

[52]   Vermigli, *Commonplaces*, 2:272–73. It is true that in *Ethicorum*, 352 (*PML* 9:336) Vermigli subsumes the first motions under choice, but the context suggests

In arguing that the first motions themselves were sins, Vermigli departs markedly from what Risto Saarinen has called the "commonplace Augustinianism" of the medieval mainstream. According to this, while the first motions of concupiscence themselves undoubtedly stemmed from the soul's disorder; they were not in themselves sinful. Rather, voluntary consent was held to be required in order to constitute something a sin.[53] For Vermigli, as we have already seen, sin was broadly defined as striving against the divine law, a definition which clearly included within its scope even involuntary motions of concupiscence. In holding this position he recognized himself to be following the late Augustine's own uncompromising assertion that all concupiscence is sin.[54] This also marks a subtle but important difference with Aquinas. For while there are passages in his work which hold that the first movements of concupiscence should be classed as venial sins, the broader context suggests that he is referring to *unchecked* movements. Thus, although Aquinas holds that the will cannot prevent such movements, he is clear that it can either forestall them by preventing their occurrence in the first place or check them by turning the mind to think of other things.[55] Indeed, Aquinas explicitly states that "even the first movement of the sensuality has nothing sinful in it, except in so far as it can be suppressed by reason."[56] Thus, as Charles Raith comments on Aquinas's reading of Romans 7, "the rise of perverse concupiscence per se does not constitute a sin, but it is

---

that this respects previous choice and especially the choice of Adam which plunged human nature into sin.

[53] Risto Saarinen, *Weakness of Will in Renaissance and Reformation Thought* (Oxford, 2011), 23–26, 38–41, 106–08. The best recent discussion of the first motions in medieval ethics is to be found in Simo Knuuttila, *Emotions in Ancient and Medieval Philosophy* (Oxford, 2004), 178–95.

[54] Vermigli, *Commonplaces*, 2:219; cf. Augustine, *Contra Iulianum Opus Imperfectum*, 5:50 (*PL* 45:1485). Saarinen, *Weakness of Will*, 24–25, helpfully charts the evolution of Augustine's discussion of concupiscence away from the "commonplace Augustinianism" of his *Confessions* and early works.

[55] Aquinas affirms that the first motions are venial sins in *Summa Theologiae*, 1a2ae 89.5. However, in *Summa Theologiae*, 1a2ae 10.3, 17.7, 74.3, and 77.7 and 2a2ae 122.6 he qualifies this significantly. Knuuttila, *Emotions*, 191–92 points out that Aquinas holds the first motions to be indirectly voluntary and venial sins through a kind of consent.

[56] Aquinas, *Summa Theologiae*, 2a2ae 154.5. This is in the context of "nocturnal pollutions" which since they occur in sleep without any judgment of reason cannot be considered sins.

Paul's failure to prevent the rise of the desires that renders Paul sinful insofar as he falls short of doing the good of preventing these desires."[57]

Vermigli's implicit disagreement with Aquinas over the first motions signals a deeper underlying difference between their understanding of sin and man's natural capacity for virtue. For while it is undoubtedly true that Aquinas's moral theology was profoundly shaped by his engagement with Augustine, it also seems clear that he sought to avoid, or at least moderate, some of Augustine's more radical claims. In particular he was concerned to offer as sympathetic an account as possible of man's natural capacities within the constraints of his overarching Augustinian moral framework. The roots of this lie in the distinction, outlined above, between a positive and privative account of original sin. For in holding to a privative account Aquinas is adamant that original sin, although a habit, does not incline directly to actual sin. Rather, he holds that it only inclines indirectly through the removal of original righteousness.[58] This is significant, as it implies a disconnect between original sin and actual sins committed, equivalent to the moral gap between the first motions of concupiscence and intentional consent. Significantly it was within this space that Aquinas was able to develop a positive, if restricted, account of fallen humanity's moral aspirations and accomplishments.

Aquinas's discussion of natural morality is highly complex and has been for centuries the subject of considerable dispute. For our purposes, however, it can be summarized in two central theses. The first is his overarching claim that man through his own unaided powers is able to accomplish moral good. For, while Aquinas undoubtedly believed human nature to be deeply wounded through original sin, he was nevertheless adamant that not every unaided human action should be considered as tainted by sin. In particular, he held that fallen nature retains important moral resources—like conscience and the natural law—which enable true, if imperfect, moral knowledge and action. While concupiscence frequently tugs us away from higher things, all humans retain a natural desire for God and for the good, which implicitly structures and

[57] Charles Raith, "Portraits of Paul," in *Reading Romans with St Thomas Aquinas*, ed. Matthew Levering and Michael Dauphinais (Washington, DC, 2012), 245.

[58] Aquinas, *Summa Theologiae*, 1a2ae 82.1 ad. 3.

motivates their moral actions.[59] What this meant for Aquinas was that without the aid of grace man could achieve provisional but significant ordering to his moral life. Although perfect fulfilment of the law and avoidance of sin remain far beyond him, Aquinas is clear that unaided he is both able to fulfil individual precepts of the law and avoid particular sins, including the majority of mortal sins against his neighbor.[60] He thus explicitly denies the claim, typical of a robust Augustinianism, that unbelievers sin in everything they do, holding that while they sin whenever they do anything out of their unbelief, it is possible for them to do good deeds which do not relate to the end of unbelief.[61]

From this follows Aquinas's second thesis, that man is naturally able to achieve genuine virtue. Now interpretation of this claim has been the cause of considerable contention among scholars. Some, like Alasdair MacIntyre, have held that for Aquinas virtue must be shaped by charity, while others, like Bonnie Kent, have argued that Aquinas held a highly positive and robust understanding of virtue independent of the order of grace.[62] The solution, as Brian Shanley insightfully suggests, is a *via media* between the extremes. For it is clear from Aquinas's writings that he did believe it possible for non-Christians to have *genuine* virtue without charity, but not *true* virtue taken in a strict and proper sense.[63] In particular, Aquinas is clear that inasmuch as natural virtue directs man to a proximate end which is a true good and not incompatible with man's final end, then it may be considered authentic. In his *Summa Theologiae* he therefore specifically rejects the stark Augustinian understanding of these acquired virtues as counterfeit virtues and actual sins in the non-Christian.[64] Also, while it is certainly true that Aquinas holds the

---

[59] Thomas Aquinas, *Commentary on the Nicomachean Ethics*, trans. C. I. Litzinger (Chicago, 1964), 1:11, p. 9; *Summa Theologiae*, 1a2ae 85.4.

[60] Aquinas, *Summa Theologiae*, 1a2ae 63.2 ad. 2; 109.8; cf. Brian Shanley, "Aquinas on Pagan Virtue," *The Thomist* 63 (1999): 558.

[61] Aquinas, *Summa Theologiae*, 2a2ae 10.4.

[62] See Alasdair MacIntyre, *Whose Justice? Which Rationality?* (Notre Dame, IN, 1988), 181–82, and Bonnie Kent, "Moral Provincialism," *Religious Studies* 30 (1994): 274–77.

[63] Shanley, "Aquinas on Pagan Virtue," 556–67.

[64] Aquinas, *Summa Theologiae*, 1a2ae 65.2; 2a2ae 23.7. For detailed discussion of this see Shanley, "Aquinas on Pagan Virtue," 553–77; Jennifer Herdt, *Putting on Virtue: The Legacy of the Splendid Vices* (Chicago, IL, 2008), 72–97; and T. H. Irwin,

primary purpose of acquired virtues to be the directing of human society towards the common good—hence his general characterization of them as political or civil virtues,[65]—as Jennifer Herdt suggests, they also clearly relate to the perfection of the individual.[66] They are therefore not only good in themselves but they are also good for the one who possesses them, implying an important continuity between the sphere of nature and the sphere of grace.

Vermigli's account of natural morality departs markedly from that of Aquinas on both accounts. For Vermigli, like Rimini, original sin is not only a privation but also a positive habit. It is therefore connected directly, and not only indirectly, to actual sin. In Vermigli the critical gap between the first motions and the response of the human will, which for Aquinas is determinative of their moral character, has thus effectively been closed off. From its fountainhead of concupiscence sin flows into and corrupts every human action. On its own he held that human nature is powerless to stem the floodtide of sinful desire. This led him to espouse the famous—or perhaps notorious—position of the late medieval Augustinians, that without the "special help of God" (*auxilium speciale Dei*)—God's immediate moving and determining of the human will towards the good—it is impossible for humans to achieve any moral good.[67] Moreover, again following an Augustinian trajectory, Vermigli argued that true virtue must be grounded on actions carried out for the sake of the love of God, something requiring faith to direct intention and charity to impel the will. Where Aquinas had stopped short of Augustine's strident claim in *Contra Iulianum* that all the virtues of the pagans are but "splendid vices," Vermigli, like Rimini, explicitly affirms it.[68] This is not

---

"Splendid Vices? Augustine for and against Pagan Virtues," *Medieval Philosophy and Theology* 8 (1999): 119–27.

[65] Aquinas, *Summa Theologiae*, 1a2ae 63.4; 2a2ae 23.7.

[66] Herdt, *Putting on Virtue*, 76.

[67] Peter Martyr Vermigli, *In Selectissimam D. Pauli Priorem ad Corinthios* (Zürich, 1572 [2nd ed.]), 29r-v. A thorough discussion of Rimini's doctrine of the *auxilium speciale* is to be found in Manuel Santos Noya, *Die Sünden- und Gnadenlehre des Gregor von Rimini* (Frankfurt, 1990), 67–89.

[68] Vermigli, *Romanos*, 542–43; *Ethicorum*, 21-22 (*PML* 9:26–7); cf. Rimini, *Lectura*, 2 d. 26–28 q. 1 art. 3 (6:74, 85). For the Augustinian texts that Vermigli cites, see Augustine, *Contra Julianum*, 4:3.25–6.32 (*PL* 44:750–1, 755); *Ad Simplicianum*, 1:2 (*PL* 40:126); and *Enarrationes in Psalmos*, 30 (*PL* 36:226).

to say that he recognized nothing good about the naturally acquired virtues. For Vermigli affirms, like Aquinas, that they are important both for the ordering of the individual moral life and for society as a whole.[69] Yet, while in themselves the virtues may be considered good, when instantiated in the human moral life they become poisoned with concupiscence. They are therefore a snare and Vermigli holds that it is because of these moral and civic virtues that men "are accustomed to become proud, to rely on themselves and judge themselves to have no need of the covenant, grace or help of God."[70] For Aquinas the natural virtues constituted an implicit ordering towards grace. By contrast Vermigli holds that God's employment of human virtues as a means for saving his elect is an abuse, and not a use, of their proper nature. On their own they are not more preparatory for salvation than damnation.[71]

5. The Character of True Virtue and Happiness

Vermigli's strident Augustinianism clearly challenges the very foundation of Aristotelian ethics. Nevertheless, it would be entirely wrong to conclude that the Aristotelian concept of virtue has no place in his ethical system. In fact, reconfigured in a Christian manner, it remains at the very heart of his ethics. For both in his *Commentary* and in his theological works Vermigli clearly sought to fuse an Augustinian understanding of virtue as gifted by and oriented towards God with an Aristotelian emphasis on the connection of virtue with moderate human action. In doing so he notably remained within the broad parameters of a eudaemonistic ethics, asserting the intimate connection between his renewed, Christian understanding of virtue and human flourishing and happiness in both this life and the life to come.

In order to understand this we need to retrace our steps to consider Vermigli's understanding of human aspiration and action and its relation to an Aristotelian and scholastic paradigm. The starting point of ethics for both Vermigli and Aristotle is the principle that all things desire the good. In arguing this Vermigli was careful to affirm that by "the good"

---

[69] Vermigli, *Ethicorum*, 21–22 (*PML* 9:26–7).
[70] Vermigli, *Corinthios*, 30ᵛ.
[71] Vermigli, *Corinthios*, 30ʳ⁻ᵛ.

was not meant God, as some Renaissance commentators like Leonardo Bruni and George of Trebizond had argued.[72] Indeed, Aquinas himself had suggested that since nothing is good except by participation in the highest good, this itself is in some way desired in every particular good.[73] However, Vermigli rejected this line of argument, denying even an implicit desire for God except where taken in a purely accidental sense. Instead, following Cardinal Bessarion and Johannes Argyropoulos, he argued that by the good should be understood not its highest manifestation but rather the reason and common form underlying all of its individual instantiations.[74] Vermigli rooted this desire in a Platonic dynamic of poverty and plenty, holding that every nature must be considered as having its own particular good, which completes it and supplies its lack.[75] As a rational animal man must therefore be considered as moved by a rational desire, his will, towards the good which constitutes his own fulfilment. This highest good he understood as that which is complete and sufficient in itself and sought after for its own intrinsic value and not for the sake of anything else.[76] For man this is happiness, defined by Aristotle as that which "alone makes life desirable and lacking in nothing."[77] For Aristotle happiness lay in the perfection of man's characteristic activity and function—his reason. In his *Nicomachean Ethics* he argued that the virtues were indispensable for this, defining happiness itself as "a whole life lived in accordance with virtue."[78]

Vermigli, however, regarded Aristotelian virtue as counterfeit, which meant that the happiness it brought must be illusory. Instead, he argued that true happiness lay in reconciliation and union with God—something

---

[72] Vermigli, *Ethicorum*, 14–15 (*PML* 9:20); cf. Leonardo Bruni, "Aristotelis Ethica Aretino Interprete," 1, in Jacques Lefèvre d'Étaples, *Decem Librorum Moralium Aristotelis Tres Conversiones* (Paris, 1535), and George of Trebizond, *Comparatio Philosophorum Aristotelis et Platonis* (Venice, 1523), F8ʳ.

[73] Aquinas, *Commentary on the Nicomachean Ethics*, 1:11, p. 9.

[74] Vermigli, *Ethicorum*, 14–21 (*PML* 9:20–7); cf. Basilius Bessarion, *In Calumniatorem Platonis* (Venice, 1503), 3:19.6.

[75] Vermigli, *Ethicorum*, 17 (*PML* 9:22–3). He derives this understanding from Plato, *Symposium*, 203c.

[76] Vermigli, *Ethicorum*, 11–17, 32–8, 178–84 (*PML* 9:17–23, 37–42, 177–81).

[77] Vermigli, *Ethicorum*, 182–83 (*PML* 9:180); cf. Aristotle, *Nicomachean Ethics*, 1:7 (1097b14–20).

[78] Aristotle, *Nicomachean Ethics*, 1:7 (1097b24–1098a20); cf. Vermigli, *Ethicorum*, 184–91 (*PML* 9:182–7).

he reckoned, unlike some Renaissance commentators, as completely beyond Aristotle's ken.[79] Following his Protestant convictions Vermigli therefore distinguished between the primary happiness of justification and the secondary happiness of justification, with predestination and grace undergirding both of these. The first happiness, foundational to all the others, consists in the forgiveness of sins and the reconciliation with God through Christ, while the second comes from acting rightly, acquiring virtue, conquering our sinful nature, and contemplating God. Significantly, as we shall discover below, this happiness of sanctification corresponds closely to Aristotle's own account of happiness, with the crucial difference that this is a happiness which flows from the Holy Spirit and is not attained by human effort or striving. Like in kind to this double blessing of earthly happiness, although far exceeding it in perfection, is the culminating form of Christian happiness, which, with the patristic and medieval tradition, Vermigli identified as the eternal, beatific vision of God.[80]

Despite certain qualifications, which we shall come to below, Vermigli was also in fundamental agreement with Aristotle that the virtues were intended for the perfection of the human life of reason. He therefore concurred in their crucial role in moderating and restraining the passions. Against the Stoics Vermigli held that moderate passions were essential for right action. For it is not enough to know the right thing to do if one does not take delight in doing it. He argued that used correctly the passions are therefore to be regarded as a vital incentive for moral action. Following the scholastics he defined passion very simply as "a power or faculty by which we either pursue or shun objects set before us." While rejecting the Stoic claim that passions were thoughts and opinions Vermigli held that most passions in animate creatures, except very primitive ones like hunger and thirst, followed cognition. As motions of the sensitive soul they are therefore triggered through mentally apprehending or anticipating a particular object. In doing so, pleasant passions like joy and hope draw the soul towards good objects, whereas the unpleasant, contrary passions of sorrow and fear repel the soul from evil objects.

---

[79] Vermigli, *Ethicorum*, 16, 200 (*PML* 9:22, 197). In *Ethicorum*, 15 (*PML* 9:20) Vermigli opposes George of Trebizond for his view that Aristotle had some knowledge of the Trinity.

[80] Vermigli, *Ethicorum*, 76–77, 200–201, 257–58 (*PML* 9:78–79, 197–98, 250–51).

While Vermigli held that in sinful man the passions remained outside of complete control he was clear that as sensitive qualities they at least came under the sway of reason. Moreover, with Aristotle, he held that this control could only be exercised through virtue. For it is virtue that prevents them from reaching harmful excess and harnesses their power to impel the soul towards moral action. In this way, to extend Vermigli's own evocative analogy, the virtuous person resembles a sailor who skilfully trims the sails of his boat to the winds of the passions, avoiding harmful cross winds and using the right wind to drive him towards his desired harbour.[81]

In perfecting man's function and moderating the passions, Vermigli followed an Aristotelian consensus in assigning the virtues to the higher parts of the human soul, both in its rational and appetitive aspects. However, while all were agreed on the location of the intellectual virtues in the intellect, from the scholastic period onwards there had been considerable debate over the location of the moral, appetitive, virtues.[82] One position, often broadly characterized as intellectualism,[83] held that since the will necessarily followed reason, it had little, or no, need for virtues to perfect its action. The moral virtues, however, were understood to be required for the correct disposition of the sense appetite, which in sinful humans was not disposed to follow reason because of concupiscence, and were thus located in the sensitive soul.[84] A moderate version of this view was espoused by Aquinas.[85] The contrasting, voluntarist, position certainly acknowledged

---

[81]   Vermigli, *Ethicorum*, 328–35 (*PML* 9:314–20). Aquinas's treatise on passions in *Summa Theologiae*, 1a2ae 22–48 is clearly an important source for Vermigli's discussion here. For an extensive discussion of the passions in Aquinas, see Knuuttila, *Emotions*, 239–55.

[82]   For the context of this debate see Bonnie Kent, *Virtues of the Will: The Transformation of Ethics in the Late Thirteenth Century* (Washington, DC, 1995), 199–245.

[83]   The labels intellectualism and voluntarism have fallen into some disrepute in scholarship on later medieval thought. Here they are used advisedly in full awareness of the complexity of the issues at stake. A helpful discussion of these positions is to be found in Tobias Hoffmann, "Intellectualism and Voluntarism," in *The Cambridge History of Medieval Philosophy*, ed. Robert Pasnau and Christina van Dyke (Cambridge, 2010), 1:414–27.

[84]   Kent, *Virtues of the Will*, 222–23, 236. Kent notes that a good example of this (extreme) intellectualism is to be found in the *Quodlibet* of Godfrey of Fontaines.

[85]   Aquinas, *Summa Theologiae*, 1a2ae 56.4 ad. 4.

the power of passions to distort reason, but its own emphasis was on the necessity of virtue for the will's correct moral action. For voluntarists like Scotus it was axiomatic that the will must be free from determination by the intellect and even from any necessary connection with happiness. For this reason virtues were considered necessary in order to help determine the will's action towards the moral good. Since the passions were believed to be under the command of the will, the need for separate virtues in the sensitive soul was either deemphasized or denied.[86]

While Vermigli was always careful to argue for a nuanced and subtle relation of intellect and will he was certainly not a voluntarist. As a rational appetite he was emphatic that the will was necessarily determined towards its own happiness. Indeed, in his *Commonplaces* he rejects emphatically the position of those "crabbed sophisters"—presumably he has Scotus and Ockham in mind—who argue that the "blessed may understand the chiefest good thing and yet withhold their will from the love and embracing of the same."[87] However, his own position was also markedly different from the extreme intellectualists, whose tendency was sometimes to regard the will as a mere appendage of intellect. Rather, like Aquinas and Rimini, he presented the relation between intellect and will as a delicate feedback-loop in which both faculties played a vital role in the act of choice. In this way while he placed the root of freedom in the intellect, as judging and discerning, he still emphasized the integrity of the will's own self-motion.[88] Significantly, Vermigli's moderate stance is also reflected in his treatment of the moral virtues, which, while broadly Thomist, has important voluntarist accents. Thus, although against the voluntarists, he affirmed the usual location of the moral virtues to be in

---

[86] Kent, *Virtues of the Will*, 229–45. For Scotus's influential account of virtue and its relation to the will, see John Duns Scotus, *Duns Scotus on the Will and Morality*, ed. and trans. Allan Wolter (Washington, DC, 1986), 319–46.

[87] Vermigli, *Commonplaces*, 3:72. The view that the human will is not necessarily determined towards its own happiness is found in Scotus and Ockham. This is generally assumed to be the foundation of anti-eudaemonistic ethics (Terence Irwin, *The Development of Ethics: A Historical and Critical Study. Volume 1: From Socrates to the Reformation* (Oxford, 2007), 653–78, 702–05).

[88] Vermigli, *Ethicorum*, 426–35 (*PML* 9:400–10); *Corinthios*, 27ᵛ–28ʳ; *Commonplaces*, Appendix 101; cf. Aquinas, *Summa Theologiae*, 2a2ae 9.1 and Rimini, *Lectura*, 2 d.24–5 q. 1 (6:1–16). The complex, reciprocal relationship of intellect and will in Aquinas is discussed briefly in Hoffmann, "Intellectualism and Voluntarism," 416–17.

the upper parts of the sensitive soul, he clearly recognized the crucial role of the will in governing and commanding the sense appetite. For this reason he located at least some moral virtues in the will itself.[89]

Aristotle had argued that the virtues are neither present to us by nature nor contrary to nature but are engendered through constant, repeated action and therefore acquired through practice and training. He understood them as habits perfecting man's intellectual and moral faculties and allowing him to do the good both freely and easily. This led him to claim that moral virtues were composed of three essential ingredients: knowledge, choice, and constancy, and that they thus stemmed from the threefold root of reason, will, and action.[90] Leaving aside for the moment the order of grace, Vermigli by no means dissented from this basic description, although he did offer two important caveats. Firstly, although he agreed that action, reason, and will are crucial to the formation and constitution of moral virtues, he insisted that God must still be seen as their primary cause. For, as we have seen, Vermigli's Augustinianism committed him to the position that right moral action, and thus virtue, were impossible without divine help. Thus, while he could affirm that the repeated actions of the human will were the cause of acquiring virtue, he insisted that this was only as the will was moved by God.[91] Secondly, due to the corruption of original sin, Vermigli held that in order to achieve true virtue the human intellect and will must be reoriented towards God. This not only implied an intimate connection between ordinary virtue and the theological virtues of faith, hope, and charity, which we shall come to below, but it also entailed that human reason must be formed by the Word of God in pursuit of virtue.[92]

Significantly, however, although Vermigli insisted in Augustinian fashion that true virtue required a transcendent reference and cause, he remained in full agreement with the classic Aristotelian doctrine that virtue exists as a mean between two opposing vices. With Aristotle he clarified that this is not to be understood as an objective mean with regard

---

[89] Vermigli, *Ethicorum*, 203, 292, 335–36, 345 (*PML* 9:199, 283, 320–21, 330).

[90] Aristotle, *Nicomachean Ethics*, 2:4 (1105a27–b4); cf. Vermigli, *Ethicorum*, 307–08, 341 (*PML* 9:295–96, 326).

[91] Vermigli, *Ethicorum*, 308 (*PML* 9:296). As noted above, this connection between virtue and the *auxilium speciale Dei* is prominent in Rimini as well.

[92] Vermigli, *Ethicorum*, 297–309 (*PML* 9:287–96, 305–06, 327–30).

to the things themselves, but rather as a mean relative to the person in question. Their reasoning is that in every passion and action we may find excess and defect, which correspond to the two opposing vices, but in between these is always the right passion and action which corresponds to the mean virtue.[93] Thus, for example, with regard to boldness it is possible to be rash and overly bold—the vice of excess—or cowardly and not bold enough—the vice of defect. The true virtue of courage therefore must be that which occupies the mean between the two.[94] Yet, although in regard to its substance and essential definition virtue occupies a mean, both Vermigli and Aristotle argued that as it is the perfection of action virtue must be considered an extreme.[95] Importantly, Vermigli insisted that the essentials of this perspective were borne out by Scripture. As he says, "the royal way tells us not to deviate either to the left or the right" and thus commands us to hold to the mean. Yet the Bible also commands us to be perfect as God is perfect and to always seek the best, and so in this way virtue is clearly an extreme. Where he differs from Aristotle, as we remarked above, is in holding that this mean cannot be located by reason alone but only through the testimony of the Holy Spirit and Scripture.[96]

Unfortunately, due to the incomplete character of Vermigli's *Commentary*, his discussion of the different intellectual and moral virtues and their connection is fragmentary at best. However, what it is possible to glean from this does serve to further confirm the basically Thomist orientation of his account of the virtues. Following a long tradition, which received increasing systematic reflection over the course of the Middle Ages, Vermigli gave a special place to the four "famous virtues" of prudence, justice, courage, and temperance, often called the cardinal virtues, which he viewed as encompassing in their scope "almost all the activities of human life."[97] Of these he assigned priority to prudence as

---

[93]   Vermigli, *Ethicorum*, 353–67 (*PML* 9:338–49). Aristotle's complex doctrine of the relative mean is found in *Nicomachean Ethics*, 2:6 (1106a14–b28). It became a standard feature of medieval scholasticism as can be seen in Aquinas, *Summa Theologiae*, 1a2ae 64.1–2.

[94]   Vermigli, *Ethicorum*, 370–71 (*PML* 9:352).

[95]   Vermigli, *Ethicorum*, 362–63 (*PML* 9:345–6); cf. Aristotle, *Nicomachean Ethics*, 2:6 (1107a6–8).

[96]   Vermigli, *Ethicorum*, 318, 368 (*PML* 9:306, 50).

[97]   Vermigli, *Ethicorum*, 247 (*PML* 9:240). For a concise discussion of the evolution of the cardinal virtues in scholastic thought see Istvan Bejczy, "The

the "beginning of virtues and the one on which they all depend." This he explained in terms of its twofold function of deliberating about ends and commanding the appetite and its actions. While he followed a general consensus in describing prudence as an intellectual virtue, he also, following Aquinas, Albert the Great, and ultimately Eustratius, emphasized its intimate relation to both the higher and lower appetites of the soul, ascribing it a significant volitional component.[98] Like Aquinas, Vermigli also located the cardinal virtues of courage and temperance in the irascible and concupiscible parts of the sensitive soul respectively. In Thomist fashion he clearly perceived these as working in tandem, the one restraining harmful desire and the other restraining fear.[99] Unfortunately, Vermigli offered no detailed description of justice, but given his location of the other moral virtues in the sensitive appetite it is plausible to claim that he would have followed Aquinas in recognizing in justice a virtue of the will.[100] What is more important to note is the reciprocity or—to use Vermigli's own term—harmony of the principal virtues. Against a late medieval voluntarist trend he refused to atomize the virtues but rather affirmed their mutual participation in each other's actions.[101] For like Aquinas he argued, at least implicitly, that courage, temperance, and justice all work together through prudence, "harmonising with reason," in order to ensure correct moral action.

Cardinal Virtues in Medieval Commentaries on the *Nicomachean Ethics*, 1250–1350," in *Virtue Ethics in the Middle Ages: Commentaries on Aristotle's Nicomachean Ethics, 1200–1500*, ed. Istvan Bejczy (Leiden, 2008), 199–221.

[98] Vermigli, *Ethicorum*, 298, 312, 345–46 (*PML* 9:287, 299, 330); cf. Bejczy, "Cardinal Virtues," 203.

[99] Vermigli, *Ethicorum*, 278–79, 288–89 (*PML* 9:270–71, 279–80); cf. Aquinas, *Summa Theologiae*, 1a2ae 61.2.

[100] Aquinas, *Summa Theologiae*, 1a2ae 61.2. Kent, *Virtues of the Will*, 219–22 points out that Aquinas placed justice in the will as a moderator of action and choice.

[101] Vermigli, *Commonplaces*, 3:86. For the standard view that late medieval thinkers, like Scotus and Ockham, atomized the virtues, see Irwin, *Development of Ethics*, 684–85, 711–13. Marilyn McCord Adams, "Scotus and Ockham on the Connection of the Virtues," in *John Duns Scotus: Metaphysics and Ethics*, ed. Ludger Honnefelder, Rega Wood, and Mechtild Dreyer (Leiden, 1996), 499–523 argues that in the case of Ockham this has been overstated. She concedes, however, that both Scotus and Ockham deny the unity of prudence and the necessary co-dependence of the virtues.

6. The Theological Virtues

Vermigli's general paradigm of virtue was clearly profoundly shaped by Aristotle. However, departing from Aristotle, he also followed a long medieval Christian, and indeed Augustinian, tradition in arguing the need for supernatural, infused virtues and gifts in order to ensure perfect moral action:

> Now we must see how these words of Aristotle agree or disagree with Holy Scripture. He has located three things in the soul pertaining to virtue: passion, natural power, and habit. Nevertheless, he passes over the gifts of the Holy Spirit, namely, the spirit of fortitude, the spirit of fear, and the inspirations of God by which we are moved to act rightly. Because these things surpass nature, Aristotle did not recognise them. Since we, however, have been instructed in them, let us ask God for them in prayer. Virtue is not one of those two things, I mean passion and natural power. Therefore, as Aristotle understands it, virtue is a habit acquired by good actions when these are frequently repeated. This inference is not sound. For faith, hope, and charity, and many other virtues are not habits of this sort, but are inspired suddenly by God in those who have been reborn.[102]

Beyond the acquired intellectual and moral virtues, Vermigli therefore posited three further classes of infused moral principles: the gifts of the Holy Spirit, infused moral virtues, and the theological virtues of faith, hope, and charity.

In his *Commentary* Vermigli only refers to both the gifts of the Spirit and the infused moral virtues in passing. Unfortunately, it is therefore impossible to say anything extensive about their relation to his wider ethics. Nevertheless, what is apparent is that in holding to such a threefold division of the supernatural moral sphere Vermigli is drawing on Thomist moral theory. In particular, the positing of both acquired and infused moral virtues is something distinctive to Aquinas. For to later medieval theologians, like Scotus, the infused moral virtues seemed superfluous, especially when compared to the more important theological virtues.

---

[102] Vermigli, *Ethicorum*, 352 (*PML* 9:336).

Aquinas, however, argued for the indispensable nature of both the gifts and the infused moral virtues. In his understanding the gifts and infused virtues worked together, with the gifts disposing man to be moved by God and the virtues disposing him to be moved by reason towards God.[103] We can only presume that Vermigli would have held to a similar understanding. Certainly, his affirmation of the infused gifts and virtues fits into his wider theology of grace. With the scholastics this assumes the need not only for the perfection of action—the work of the *auxilium speciale*—but also for the perfection of disposition. Before it is possible to cooperate with grace and acquire the virtues it is therefore necessary for the whole of the soul to be reoriented to God. While Vermigli affirms that this happens primarily through the higher, theological virtues, it seems entirely consistent with his overall anthropology to posit other infused virtues to work in conjunction with these to help quell the passions of the sensitive soul.[104]

In offering his account of the theological virtues Vermigli follows the scholastics in locating them in the highest faculties of the human soul. As he wrote "we restore the mind by ornating the intellect with faith and the will with hope and charity."[105] For Vermigli faith perfects the intellect according to its knowledge of the divine truth of Scripture. It is a habit infused by God which enables the soul to give assent to his Word and have infallible certainty of its truth. Its chief object is the promise of God to be merciful to us in Christ. Echoing a famous definition in Hugh of St. Victor he held that it was to be placed between opinion and science in character.[106] While the majority of medieval theologians classed faith as an intellectual virtue they generally insisted that it included within it

---

[103] Aquinas, *Summa Theologiae*, 1a2ae 63.3, 68.1. For discussion of the role of the infused moral virtues in Aquinas's ethics see Bonnie Kent, "Habits and Virtues," in *The Ethics of Aquinas*, ed. Stephen Pope (Washington, DC, 2002), 124–27. For Scotus's rejection of infused moral virtues see *Duns Scotus on the Will and Morality*, 414–17.

[104] This is implicit in Vermigli, *Ethicorum*, 353 (*PML* 9:337). Vermigli discusses the need for perfection of disposition in *Commonplaces*, Appendix 118–19.

[105] Vermigli, *Corinthios*, 12ʳ.

[106] Vermigli, *Commonplaces*, 3:56–59; cf. Hugh of St Victor, *De Sacramentis*, 1:10.2 (*PL* 176:330D–331A).

an act of will commanding the intellect to give assent.[107] Significantly, Vermigli departs from this consensus, holding that the divine illumination offered by faith to the intellect is sufficient by itself to move the will to delight in this truth and to command all the other faculties of the soul to reorient themselves in conformity with it. In this Augustinian fashion, faith is therefore held to direct the intention of the soul.[108]

As an intellectual virtue Vermigli held that faith naturally precedes the volitional virtues of hope and charity, constituting the source from which they flow. In connecting hope to faith he understood it as an anticipation of divine reward, arguing that "by faith we admit and embrace the promises offered unto us by God: but by the helpe of hope, we doo patientlie wait to have those promises at the length to be performed unto us." Many of the scholastics had connected hope to merits, at least consequently, but Vermigli held that it was infused by the Holy Spirit to enable us to pursue that good thing which we can by no means obtain on our own.[109] In this way he argued that hope perfected the rational aspect of desire. It therefore helped to ensure the correct affective stance towards God, thereby enabling us to transcend awareness of our own unworthiness and to press on to attain the promises of God.[110] Significantly, such a description of hope finds many echoes in medieval, and perhaps especially later medieval, theology.[111] However, it is important to note one crucial difference: as a Protestant Vermigli held that hope brought perfect assurance of salvation. He therefore attacked the scholastic theologians in no uncertain terms for holding that hope only brought a conjectural

---

[107]   For a good example of this see Aquinas, *Summa Theologiae*, 2a2ae 4.1. An important partial exception can be found in Duns Scotus, *Lectura*, 3 d. 24 q. 1 n. 40–51, in *Opera Omnia*, ed. Carolus Balic (Vatican City, 2004), 21:171–75. He argues that an act of the will is only necessary for acquired faith and not for infused faith.

[108]   Vermigli, *Commonplaces*, 3:59–60. Vermigli's discussion here bears comparison with Scotus's account of infused faith.

[109]   Vermigli, *Commonplaces*, 3:81–83, 86–87. For the classic definition connecting hope to merit see Peter Lombard, *Sententiae in IV Libris Distinctae* (Grottaferrata, 1981), 3 d. 26.

[110]   Vermigli, *Commonplaces*, 3:84–86. For Vermigli's discussion of natural hope and desire see *Ethicorum*, 336 (*PML* 9:321).

[111]   Berndt Hamm, *The Reformation of Faith in the Context of Late Medieval Theology and Piety: Essays by Berndt Hamm*, ed. Robert Bast (Leiden, 2004), 157–63, discusses the late medieval transition to a theology of hope and notes especially the instrumental role of Jean Gerson in effecting this.

or objective, and not a subjective, kind of certainty. For Vermigli this was not only to debase the dignity of hope but also to corrode its certainty through doubt.[112]

For the medieval scholastics, charity was the chief theological virtue and the "form" of all the virtues. It was charity's special role to ensure union with God and they held that in order to be of salvific value faith must be informed by charity. As a Protestant Vermigli had to dissent from these conclusions. Famously, Luther had said that where the scholastics speak of charity we speak of faith. Precisely this same inversion is evident in Vermigli's discussion.[113] Thus, although he certainly linked charity to the indwelling of God in the soul he did not give it any special role in securing union with God, reserving this role for faith, which in intellectualist fashion he held to make God truly present to the soul.[114] Likewise, he utterly rejected the scholastic notion of charity as the form of the virtues. The medieval theologians had argued this as they believed charity to be the end at which all the virtues aimed and according to which all their actions were coordinated. Vermigli, however, held that it was only through faith that the will was able to apprehend and love the good, and thus it was properly faith, and not charity, that governed the virtues (although not as their form).[115] Charity's role was simply to "provoke and drive the will" to express that which the mind has received. In this way—again echoing Luther—charity could be seen as the overflow of faith, communicating to others what faith had received from God.[116] Yet, despite these significant departures, in one important respect Vermigli continued to follow the medieval tradition. For he was clear that faith

---

[112]   Vermigli, *Commonplaces*, 3:83–84. A classic discussion of the certainty offered by hope compared to that offered by faith can be found in Aquinas, *Summa Theologiae*, 2a2ae 18.4.

[113]   Martin Luther, *Commentary on Galatians*, 2.16, in *D. Martin Luthers Werke*, ed. Joachim Knaake (Weimar, 1908), 40/1:228–29; cf. Jaroslav Pelikan, *The Christian Tradition: History of the Development of Doctrine. Growth of Medieval Theology, 600–1300* (London, 1978), 153–54.

[114]   Vermigli, *Commonplaces*, 3:77; cf. Donnelly, *Calvinism and Scholasticism*, 87 n.

[115]   Vermigli, *Commonplaces*, 3:73–75. In his *Treatise on Good Works* (Wittenberg, 1520), 1.7 Martin Luther effectively makes faith the form of all the virtues.

[116]   Vermigli, *Commonplaces*, 3:76. This is the principal theme of Luther's *Treatise on Good Works*.

and hope were only virtues of the wayfarer, ceasing with the attainment of the blessed vision. Charity alone endures forever.[117]

For Aristotle, as we have seen, virtues were by nature moderate in character. Any virtue was therefore considered as poised delicately between the vices of excess and defect. For the majority of the medieval scholastics it seemed entirely wrong to constrain the theological virtues in this manner. Following a much cited axiom, taken from Bernard of Clairvaux, they held that the measure of the theological virtues was to have no measure, for God was infinite in truth and goodness and so there could be no excess in human knowledge or desire with respect to him.[118] While Vermigli doubtless agreed with this sentiment, for him it entirely missed the point at issue. Indeed, we have already noted his adherence to the Aristotelian principle that the mean of virtue is with respect to substance and essential definition and not the perfection of its action—in this case its degree. For this reason he had no problem in claiming that the theological virtues must also conform to the "golden mean," albeit with the important caveat that this must be determined according to Scripture and not reason alone. Thus, for example, faith must observe a mean in content, believing neither more nor less than Scripture. Likewise hope represents a mean virtue between despair and presumption, and even charity cannot run untrammelled but must be confined by the precepts of Scripture.[119] In this way the Aristotelian understanding of virtue was enshrined at the very heart of Vermigli's theology.

It is clear then that, for Vermigli, faith, hope, and charity are not only gifts of the Holy Spirit, as they were for other Protestants, but also gracious *virtues*. They are in fact the preeminent virtues, for as he says, the actions of the faithful could not be counted right and pleasing to God unless they are seeds of faith, hope, and love.[120] The theological virtues are thus of ethical as well as soteriological value. In fact it is clear that they act in a variety of interconnected ways to coordinate the entirety of the ethical field. Above we remarked in passing on the role of faith in directing

---

[117] Vermigli, *Commonplaces*, 3:76.

[118] This principle is elaborated in Thomas Aquinas, *Disputed Questions on the Virtues*, ed. E. M. Atkins and Thomas Williams (Cambridge, 2005), q. 2.2 ad. 13; 4.1 ad. 7.

[119] Vermigli, *Ethicorum*, 367–68, 392–94 (*PML* 9:349–50, 371–72).

[120] Vermigli, *Ethicorum*, 200–201 (*PML* 9:197–98).

intention and governing the other virtues. In his *Commonplaces* Vermigli clarifies this role with an analogy drawn ultimately from Chrysostom. According to this, faith relates to hope and charity as wisdom relates to the intellectual virtues and prudence to the moral virtues.[121] In an Aristotelian paradigm, also upheld by Vermigli, the role of prudence was to determine the mean of the other virtues and order them towards their proper end.[122] Analogously, therefore, the role of faith is to determine the mean from Scripture. Once it has done this, prudence is able to apply it to the cardinal virtues and through these to all the virtues in turn.

Ultimately, therefore, it is through faith, hope, and charity that the diverse ends of the Christian life attain their definite hierarchical order. As he says: "For the stronger the faith, and the better God is perceived through it, the more love is inflamed towards its goal; so that the end and, as they say, the object of faith prescribes love, and love of your neighbour is as deep as your faith in God. Therefore, the end of love that is your neighbour's good is contained in the goal of faith." Faith therefore governs not only love of God but also love of neighbor, comprehending both the vertical and horizontal dimensions of human relationship. Moreover, Vermigli argued it is through the three virtues together that we attain the strength to conquer our sinful nature. Here they act as a virtuous, reinforcing circle so that as faith deepens, charity becomes more active and hope more constant. In turn, as we expect the fulfilment of God's promises more through a stronger hope, we perceive them with a deeper faith and work more effectively towards them through charity.[123]

Finally, it is through faith, hope, and charity that the passive happiness of justification is bound inextricably to the active happiness of sanctification and both together to the assured happiness of the beatific vision. As a Protestant theologian Vermigli was, of course, insistent that justification was through faith alone. Against the medieval scholastics he therefore held that true faith and love were inseparable.[124] Indeed, Vermigli seems to have recognized a necessary connection between faith,

---

[121] Vermigli, *Commonplaces*, 3:74.

[122] Vermigli, *Commonplaces*, 3:86.

[123] Vermigli, *Ethicorum*, 31–32 (*PML* 9:35–6).

[124] Vermigli makes this point forcefully in *Commonplaces*, 3:71–72. Here he attacks especially the prominent scholastic distinction between formed and unformed faith, singling out Aquinas for particular criticism.

hope, and love, holding that hope was included in faith and that love was united to faith as the light to the Sun.[125] In both his *Commentary* and his *Commonplaces* Vermigli therefore emphasized the Augustinian dynamic of faith working through love, arguing that we could only be justified by such an efficacious faith.[126] Through faith working by love and expectant in hope man is both justified and sanctified and finally brought to the beatific vision. The theological virtues therefore cross not only the chasm of divine acceptance, in the process uniting the imparted and inherent aspects of human virtue, but also bridge the gap between the temporal and eternal, securing ultimate union with God.[127]

Yet we must remember that while for Vermigli happiness might be defined in quasi-Aristotelian terms as life lived in accordance with the theological virtues, it also rests entirely in God and not the intrinsic nature of the virtues themselves. Even the theological virtues are ultimately means used by God to secure his own ends.[128] With the late medieval theologians as well as the Protestant Reformers he thus insists that grace is not primarily a quality but rather an attitude of God. As he puts it God finds nothing in us worthy of love, but rather through his love bestows on us all that makes us acceptable to him.[129] Ultimately then Vermigli's understanding of sin and virtue is best summed up in the words of a beloved English hymn: "Love to the loveless shown that they might lovely be."[130]

---

[125] Vermigli, *Commonplaces*, 3:69–75.

[126] Vermigli, *Ethicorum*, 346–47 (*PML* 9:330–1); *Commonplaces*, 3:69–75. Saak, *High Way to Heaven*, 348–50, 362–68 points to an important affective turn in late medieval Augustinian theology. Hamm, *Reformation of Faith*, 128–63 argues for a wider affective current in late medieval thought, pointing out that in the fifteenth century it became increasingly common to focus on faith as it was intrinsically oriented towards love.

[127] For a detailed discussion of the controverted issue of Vermigli's theology of justification and its relation to sanctification and inherent righteousness, see Baschera, *Tugend und Rechtfertigung*, 157–99.

[128] Vermigli, *Ethicorum*, 367–68 (*PML* 9:349–50).

[129] Vermigli, *Commonplaces*, 3:47–52.

[130] Samuel Crossman, *My Song is Love Unknown* (1664).

7. Conclusion

We have said above that Vermigli stands at the crossroads of a number of important intellectual and theological movements. The question remains of his place in the wider ethical landscape of his age. Here, we can only attempt the briefest possible answer, for further discussion would not only require another article in itself but also a clearer picture than we currently have of the relationship between medieval, Renaissance, and Reformation ethics. The late Middle Ages and Renaissance has sometimes been characterized as an age of virtue. Thus Istjvan Bejczy, for one, contrasts the pessimism of the earlier medieval period with the optimism of the later medieval period.[131] Such a picture, however, not only neglects what social historians have told us about the crisis of the fourteenth and fifteenth centuries, but also focusses rather one-sidedly on just one aspect, albeit an important one, of late medieval ethics.[132] For although theologians like Ockham or Biel may indeed have had a remarkably optimistic, even Pelagian, view of human potential, others shared to the full Augustine's negative assessment of the same. Currently our understanding of this late medieval Augustinian stream—for want of a better term—remains in considerable flux. Yet, as the scholarship of William Bouwsma, Eric Saak, and Risto Saarinen suggests, it exercised a

---

[131] See Istvan Bejczy, *The Cardinal Virtues in the Middle Ages: A Study in Moral Thought from the Fourth to the Fourteenth Century* (Leiden, 2011). Bejczy clearly sees the twelfth century as marking the breakthrough from a pessimistic theology centered on sin, in which virtue was almost wholly subsumed under grace, to a more optimistic theology centered on the acquisition of virtue. Ample testimony to the continuing late medieval and Renaissance fascination with sin as well as the pervasive presence of vice in the social and political culture of the time is found in Richard Newhauser, "These Seven Devils: The Capital Vices on the Way to Modernity," in *Sin in Medieval and Early Modern Culture*, ed. Richard Newhauser and Susan Ridyard (York, 2012), 157–88.

[132] While dated, the classic study of this is Johan Huizinga, *The Waning of the Middle Ages: A Study of the Forms of Life, Thought and Art in France and the Netherlands in the XIVth and XVth Centuries* (New York, 1954). Although Huizinga's portrayal of the late Middle Ages as an age of crisis is at times excessive and one-sided he does draw attention to an important aspect of the era and a darker side of the nascent Renaissance.

profound influence on the developing Renaissance and its psychological and ethical consciousness.[133]

As we have sought to argue, Vermigli is very much the inheritor of this Augustinian mantle. Thus, in his debate with Pighius we see a close reprisal of these important late medieval and Renaissance debates. This in itself reveals the extent to which an Augustinian theology of depravity cast a long shadow over conventional, optimistic accounts of human virtue. Yet at the same time the scholarship that speaks of the death of virtue ethics, in the Reformation is surely premature.[134] Rather, the example of Vermigli suggests that it is better to think of a transposing, or even transfiguring, of Aristotelian notions of virtue. Moreover, while we have noted important parallels between this process and the medieval transposition of Aristotelian ethics it is apparent that this led him to a thoroughly Protestant reconfiguration of the theological virtues, marking a complete inversion of the scholastic relation between faith and charity. Whether or not Vermigli should ultimately be taken as representative of wider trends, his complex thought points to the need—urged also by Saarinen—for a thorough and careful evaluation of early modern Protestant ethics, able to do full justice to the complex interweaving of its Aristotelian and Augustinian strands.[135]

---

[133]   See William Bouwsma, "The Two Faces of Humanism: Stoicism and Augustinianism in Renaissance Thought," in *Itinerarium Italicum: The Profile of the Italian Renaissance in the Mirror of its European Transformations*, ed. Thomas Brady and Heiko Oberman (Leiden, 1975), 3–60; Eric Saak, *Creating Augustine: Interpreting Augustine and Augustinianism in the Later Middle Ages* (Oxford, 2012) and Saarinen, *Weakness of Will*, 43–54, 115–32, 164–74.

[134]   Irwin, *Development of Ethics*, 744–74 tends to view the Reformation as repudiating scholastic accounts of virtue, even while allowing its retention of other important aspects of scholastic moral theory.

[135]   Saarinen, *Weakness of Will*, 210–32 emphasises the necessity of viewing the Renaissance and Reformation as a complex age of transition in which traditional scholastic Aristotelian accounts of ethics were combined with rediscovered classical and Augustinian currents to attain new, delicately poised, syntheses.

"AND OPENLY I PROFES MYSELF/ OF THE *ARMINIAN* SECT": ARMINIANISM IN *SIR JOHN VAN OLDENBARNAVELT* (1619) AND TWO SEVENTEENTH CENTURY ENGLISH POLITICAL PRINTS, CA. 1628–41

Christina M. Carlson,
Emerson College

> To this cursed end,
> In humane shape, *Arminius* they send;
> Got by *Pelagius*, and in *Rome* nurst up;
> Whence, drunke with superstitious errours cup,
> He's sent to *Leyden* by the *Popes* direction
> To blast the world with's heresyes infection,
> Nor rests th'ambiguous craft monster there;
> But spewes the poyson of false doctrine here:
> Comes, like a protestant, in shew, before;
> And vowes he hates the *Antichristian* whore . . .
>
> — I. R. [i.e., John Russell],
> *The Spy: Discovering the*
> *Danger of Arminian Heresie*
> *and Spanish Trecherie* (1628)

I.

IN THIS ESSAY I discuss the appropriation of polemical discourse concerning Arminianism in John Fletcher and Philip Massinger's *Sir John van Oldenbarnavelt* (1619) and two political cartoons, "Arminius between Truth and Heresie" (1628; 1641) and the fold-out illustration accompanying John Russell's controversial pamphlet *The Spy* (1628).[1] Coinciding with the opening of the two Caroline parliaments of 1628 and 1641 the dates of these prints frame the period of Charles I's personal rule and suggest the importance of parliamentary debate over Arminianism to the publication of popular and controversial materials on the subject. Seventeenth-century political plays and prints tend to follow the public's saturation with contemporary debate, and such materials respond to the emergence of consensus views on certain highly controversial issues over months, years, and even decades of discussion in the popular public sphere. The texts therefore function less as "oppositonal" documents than as historical efforts to comment upon current events, often at a point removed in time.[2] The lag between contemporary events of mid-seventeenth-century England and their popular representation changes the focus of debates about Arminianism from strictly theological speculation to an engagement with its polemic and political effects.

In other contexts, the opposite is true. At Cambridge and Oxford, emphasis fell on doctrinal debate. Free will, divine grace, good works, and election emerge as central concerns in university pamphlets and

---

[1] A note on terminology: the term political cartoon was not used until the nineteenth century. Art historians who discuss visual satires from the sixteenth and seventeenth centuries tend to describe these materials either in terms of the method by which they were circulated or copied (prints) or the means by which they were created by the artist (woodcut or engraving). The present paper only deals with engravings, so I either refer to these materials as prints or engravings.

[2] For studies of political prints of this period, see Arthur M. Hind, *Engraving in England in the Sixteenth and Seventeenth Centuries: A Descriptive Catalogue with Introductions.* 3 vols. (Cambridge, 1952–64); Mary Dorothy George, *English Political Caricature to 1792: A Study of Opinion and Propaganda* (Oxford, 1959); Antony Griffiths, *The Print in Stuart Britain, 1603–1689. Exhibition Catalogue* (London: British Museum, 1998); Alexandra Walsham, *Providence in Early Modern England* (Oxford, 1999); Helen Pierce, *Unseemly Pictures: Graphic Satire and Politics in Early Modern England* (New Haven, 2008); and Malcolm Jones, *The Print in Early Modern England: an Historical Oversight* (New Haven, 2012).

commonplace books of the period.[3] In the 1628 and 1641 parliaments, religious and political aspects of Arminianism receive equal attention, and Charles and Archbishop Laud appear to have preferred Arminian clergymen over their Calvinist brethren.[4] But in anti-Arminian plays and political cartoons theological questions are relatively unimportant. These materials stress the importance of Arminianism to a host of international problems, from the crisis over the Spanish Match to the Thirty Years' War. They focus on state censorship, and decry the government's suppression of anti-Arminian positions while apparently allowing pro-Arminian beliefs free rein. Although theological discussion is not absent, religion is almost always represented as a feature of Arminian heresy and double-dealing. Arminians "profess" contradictory doctrinal positions, and resemble religious factions that deny the importance of grace and election. Arminianism is also often conflated with Catholicism. It becomes a catch-all term of abuse, as in the case of anti-popery.[5]

In *Sir John van Oldenbarnavelt*, Fletcher and Massinger draw on contemporary pamphlets and political prints, both English and Dutch, which describe Barnavelt's trial and execution.[6] They treat the material in

---

   [3] See David Hoyle, *Reformation and Religious Identity in Cambridge. 1590–1644* (Woodbridge, 2007); and Anthony Milton, *Catholic and Reformed: The Roman and Protestant Churches in English Protestant Thought, 1600–1640* (Cambridge, 1995).

   [4] See Conrad Russell, *The Fall of the British Monarchies, 1637–1642* (Oxford, 1991). What counted as Arminianism appears to have better clarified in the 1630s and 40s, and became even more explicit after 1641.

   [5] See Peter Lake, "Anti-popery."

   [6] Fletcher and Massinger call the character in their play "Barnavelt." The historical figure on which this character was based is almost always referred to as "Oldenbarnavelt." I have maintained this distinction throughout the paper. Arthur Henry Bullen, John Lothrop Motley, and Wilhelmina Frijlinck describe the pamphlet sources of *Sir John van Oldenbarnavelt* in detail. See Bullen, ed., *A Collection of Old English Plays* (London, 1882–85); Motley, *The Life and Death of John of Barnaveld Advocate of Holland* (New York, 1874), in 2 vols.; and Frijlinck, *The Tragedy of Sir John Van Olden Barnavelt: Anonymous Elizabethan Play. Edited from the Manuscript with Introduction and Notes by Wilhelmina P. Frijlinck* (Amsterdam, 1922), esp. xxiv–lviii. For further discussion of the response to Arminianism in print see Peter Milward, *Religious Controversies of the Jacobean Age: A Survey of Printed Sources* (London, 1978), esp. 33–44. For a more recent argument that shows the important impact of Dutch propaganda upon English polemicists, see Debra

a way that is both retrospective and divergent. Earlier pamphlets on Barnavelt stress the links between religious and political Arminianism. By contrast, Fletcher and Massinger tend to ignore religious concerns. They elaborate the connection between Barnavelt's supposed "Arminianism" and his avowed republican political stance and argue that Barnavelt's Arminianism is simply an extension of his Machiavellian political views. It is of a piece with his hypocrisy and duplicity and says more about Barnavelt's ethics and politics than his Arminian belief.

In the political prints of the late 1620s and early 1640s, Arminianism is similarly politicized. By "political," I refer to the whole range of polemic, satiric, and oppositional concerns that stand outside of strictly theological speculation—and often work to suppress such discussion. Although "religious" issues having to do with defining Arminianism polemically and in opposition to mainstream English Protestantism fall under this category, strictly theological debates about doctrine and belief do not. The engravings I discuss in this essay emphasize the problematic nature of state censorship and urge an "active and free Parliament" in the line of Puritan "oppositional" political sentiment that David Colclough traces.[7] In a way that mirrors the stance of Thomas Scott in responding to the crisis over the Spanish Match, such polemical works idealize Parliament as the most effective means of redressing the subjects' grievances. They see Parliament as an important system of checks and balances over Charles and his counselors. Anti-Arminian political cartoons do not ignore theological debate. But their concerns are almost always with translating theology into politics.[8]

Shuger, *Censorship and Cultural Sensibility: The Regulation of Language in Tudor-Stuart England* (Philadelphia, 2006): 46–47.

[7] In making this assessment, I draw upon the arguments of David Colclough, Andrew McCrae, and Cyndia Clegg, particularly in their analysis of John Russell's *The Spy* (London, 1628). These authors focus only on the text of this pamphlet, not the image that accompanies it. See David Colclough, *Freedom of Speech in Early Stuart England* (Cambridge, 2005), 118–19; Andrew McCrae, *Literature, Satire, and the Early Stuart State* (Cambridge, 2004): 194–95; and Cyndia Clegg, *Press Censorship in Caroline England* (Cambridge, 2001): 44–67.

[8] By "political" Arminianism, I refer specifically to the effort to translate concerns about theological Arminianism into a context in which doctrine is subordinated to questions about political effects. My point is that theology is less relevant to these popular representations of Arminianism than one might assume. What these anti-Arminian materials specifically object to is the proliferation of Arminian

In making these claims, this essay draws on past and current historiography about the "rise" of Arminianism in seventeenth-century England. According to Nicholas Tyacke, during the reigns of Elizabeth I and
James I, England was doctrinally Calvinist. Under Bishop Neile (as well
as Andrewes, Buckeridge, Overall, and others), and later, following the
installation of Laud as archbishop in 1633, the Church of England became
increasingly Arminian. As Tyacke argues, the tension between Calvinism and Arminianism was one of the central reasons for the breakdown
in religious and political harmony that led to the English Civil Wars.[9]

In response to Tyacke, Peter White, Kevin Sharpe, and Julian Davies
questioned the degree of "Calvinist consensus" in the sixteenth and
seventeenth centuries and contested Tyacke's assertion that Laud and
Charles espoused any clear-cut Arminian theology.[10] Although Charles

---

polemic, in the popular sphere. As a result, the true Protestant Church has been
subjected to assault, and the marketplace of print has been dominated by one faction—the "Arminian" one.

[9] See Nicholas Tyacke, "Puritanism, Arminianism, and Counter-Revolution,"
in Conrad Russell, ed., *The Origins of the English Civil War* (London, 1973): 119–43;
and Tyacke, *Anti-Calvinists: The Rise of English Arminianism, c. 1590–1640* (Oxford,
1987). For an extension of Tyacke's view that argues for the increasingly virulent
nature of the Arminian ascendency during the reign of Charles, see the introduction to: Russell, *Origins*, 23–31. Russell subsequently published a book length study
that extended these claims, as: *Parliaments and English Politics, 1621–1629* (Oxford,
1979). For other authors who support Tyacke's thesis, see Dewy D. Wallace, *Puritans
and Predestination: Grace in English Protestant Theology, 1525–1695* (Chapel Hill,
1982): 3–111; and Patrick Collinson, *The Religion of Protestants: the Church in English Society, 1559–1625* (Oxford, 1982): 39–91.

[10] For historical revisions of Tyacke's original thesis concerning the "rise" of
Arminianism, including Tyacke's own rejoinders, and historical responses that seek
to chart a middle ground between Tyacke and his opponents, see Peter White, "The
Rise of Arminianism Reconsidered," *Past and Present* (Nov. 1983): 34–54; William
M. Lamont, "The Rise of Arminianism Reconsidered," ibid. (May 1985): 227–31;
Nicholas Tyacke and Peter White, "Debate: The Rise of Arminianism Reconsidered,"
ibid. (May 1987), 201–29; Peter Lake, "Calvinism and the English Church, 1570–
1635," ibid. (February 1987): 32–76; Kenneth Fincham and Lake, "The Ecclesiastical Policy of King James I," *Journal of British Studies* (April 1985): 169–207; White,
"The Rise of Arminianism Reconsidered: A Rejoinder," *Past and Present* (May 1987):
217–29; Sheila Lambert, "Richard Montagu, Arminianism, and Censorship," *Past
and Present* (August 1989): 36–68; Anthony Milton, "Licensing, Censorship, and
Religious Orthodoxy in Early Stuart England," *Historical Journal* (September 1998):
625–51; Kevin Sharpe, *The Personal Rule of Charles I* (New Haven, 1992), esp. 284–92;

may have promoted Arminian bishops over Calvinists in the early years of his reign, the motivation was, they surmise, more political than religious. While Laud appears to have held special animosity for Puritan dissenters, he is less hostile towards Arminianism. But the anti-Tyacke group goes further. They contend that Laud's suppression of Calvinist views was far less systematic and repressive than Tyacke implies. Rather than see Laud as the instigator of an Arminian vs. Calvinist divide, the revisionists argued for a more balanced politics. They suggest that Laud's primary concern was to maintain peace, harmony, and unity within the English body politic, as well as to sustain order and discipline in the English Church. Laud was, they maintain, wholly uninterested in the "minutiae of theological dispute."[11] Insofar as religious texts were censored, this occurred as a result of particularly flagrant cases of abuse, and, more important, was not simply anti-Calvinist but anti-Arminian as well.[12]

Finally, and in a way that reflects the political and satiric interests of this essay, the anti-Tyacke group stresses the important polemic construction of Arminianism. They argue that the debate over Arminianism in England was largely shaped by nonconformist Protestants such as William Prynne in an effort to define Arminianism negatively. According to Sharpe, "As often with fears and phobias, the spectre of doctrinal Arminianism was out of all proportion to the reality."[13] For Puritan polemicists, and Calvinist members of Parliament, the problem of Arminianism

---

Julian Davies, *The Caroline Captivity of the Church: Charles I and the Remoulding of Anglicanism, 1625–1641* (Oxford, 1992), esp. 87–125; White, *Predestination, Policy, and Polemic: Conflict and Consensus in the English Church from the Reformation to the English Civil War* (Cambridge, 1993); White, "The *Via Media* in the Early Stuart Church," in *The Early Stuart Church, 1603–1642*, ed. Kenneth Fincham (London, 1993), 211–30; George Bernard, "The Church of England c. 1529–c. 1642," *History* (June 1990): 183–206; David R. Como, "Puritans, Predestination and the Construction of Orthodoxy in Seventeenth-Century England" in *Conformity and Orthodoxy in the Early Stuart Church*, ed. Peter Lake and Michael Questier (Woodbridge, 2000): 64–87; and Como, "Predestination and Political Conflict in Laud's London," *The Historical Journal* (June 2003): 263–94.

[11] For the local parishes and their basic disregard and/or non-interest in Arminian controversy, see Sharpe, esp. 300ff. and 388ff.

[12] See Sharpe, *The Personal Rule*, 644–54. For a rebuttal to Sharpe, see Como, "Predestination and Political Conflict in Laud's London."

[13] Sharpe, *The Personal Rule*, 296.

had less to do with theology than with the general religious and political ramifications of the Arminian threat to the English nation.[14]

Not surprisingly, White, Sharpe, and Davies have in turn been criticized. William Lamont, Peter Lake, Kenneth Fincham, and, most recently, David Como, have all, in one way or another, asserted the importance of English Arminian theology and argued for the continued viability of Tyacke's initial hypothesis.[15] Many of the anti-revisionist (pro-Tyacke) historians have focused on the evidence of Charles's promotion of "Arminian" bishops (including Laud). They have discerned a pattern of censorship of Calvinist and Arminian printed texts and sermons which is confirmed by Charles's official proclamations against "predestinarian preaching," issued in 1626, 1628, and 1629.[16] Such anti-Tyacke historians use this evidence to suggest an important shift in official court policy beginning in the 1620s and in direct opposition to a previously dominant form of English Calvinism. Tyacke's supporters contend that until the 1620s Calvinism was the dominant discourse in England. Subsequently, Arminianism was. Following this line of inquiry, David Como has presented new archival evidence in support of Laud's anti-Calvinist policies. Como sees Laud as pursuing this end in a much more indirect way than Tyacke had suggested. He presents an important account of the anti-Calvinist bias that motivated Laud and Charles. He argues that Charles and Laud's motivations were theological as well as political: both men espoused Arminianism *and* prosecuted Calvinists and did so for both religious and political reasons.[17]

---

[14] See esp. White, "The Rise of Arminianism Reconsidered"; White, *Predestination, Policy, and Polemic*; and Sharpe, *The Personal Rule of Charles I.*

[15] See Lamont, "The Rise of Arminianism Reconsidered"; Lake, "Calvinism and the English Church"; Fincham and Lake, "The Ecclesiastical Policy of King James I"; Fincham, "Prelacy and Politics: Archbishop Abbot's Defence of Protestant Orthodoxy," *Historical Research* (February 1988): 36–69; Como, "Puritans, Predestination and the Construction of Orthodoxy in Seventeenth-Century England"; and Como, "Predestination and Political Conflict in Laud's London."

[16] For a more in-depth analysis of these royal proclamations dealing with predestination see Como, "Predestination and Political Conflict in Laud's London," 264, n2.3; 220–22; and *Articles Agreed Upon by the Archbishops and Bishops of both Provinces, and the Whole Cleargie* (London, 1628), sigs. A3ʳ–Bᵛ. Other authors who discuss these are Lambert, "Richard Montagu, Arminianism, and Censorship"; Milton, "Licensing, Censorship, and Religious Orthodoxy in Early Stuart England"; and Bernard, "The Church of England c. 1529–c. 1642."

[17] See Como, "Predestination and Political Conflict in Laud's London."

Without attempting to resolve the debates over Arminianism, I wish
to engage these questions more specifically and show that in the popular
representation of the Arminian conflict the political and not the theolog-
ical/ doctrinal aspect of the debates mattered most. In seventeenth-century England politics and theology intertwine, and it is often difficult to
separate the various strands. Certainly political prints and plays evince
an understanding of the theological questions. But when it comes to representing Arminianism to a popular audience, it is the political rather
than the theological aspect that receives emphasis.[18]

II.

Examination of Fletcher and Massinger's use of the pamphlet materials in *Sir John van Oldenbarnavelt* reveals that the authors drew on the
political arguments of the tracts but tended to ignore their discussion
of Arminian theology. Similarly, as I shall discuss in Part III, the two
anti-Arminian political prints make use of the theological materials but
refashion them into visual images for distinctly satirical purposes. Janet
Clare and Thomas H. Howard-Hill have addressed the censorship of *Sir
John van Oldenbarnavelt* at length.[19] Written between 14 May (Barnavelt's

---

[18]   Both Sharpe and White emphasize the politicized nature of Arminianism—
how it was shaped, in large part, by polemic debates. See Sharpe, *The Personal Rule*;
White, "The Rise of Arminianism Reconsidered"; and White, *Predestination, Policy,
and Polemic*.

[19]   Janet Clare, "Chapter VI: 'Too sawcie in censuring princes': drama and censorship, 1608–1624," in *"Art made tongue-tied by authority": Elizabethan and Jacobean Censorship* (Manchester, 1999): 173–231; and Thomas H. Howard-Hill, "Buc
and the Censorship of *Sir John van Oldenbarnavelt* in 1619," *The Review of English
Studies* (February 1988): 39–63. Ivo Kamps discusses the importance of the pamphlet accounts of Barnavelt's trial to the descriptions in *Sir John van Oldenbarnavelt*,
but less critically than does this essay. Kamps focuses on the tension in the play
between providentialist and Machiavellian (humanist) rhetoric and finds the play
an "ideologically charged work with distinct republican and anti-authoritarian connotations." See Kamps, *Historiography and Ideology in Stuart Drama* (Cambridge,
1996), esp. ch. 5: "'No meete matters to be wrytten or treated vpon': The Tragedy
of *Sir John Van Olden Barnavelt*": 140–67. Finally, Fritz Levy has argued for the
relationship of the play to contemporary news culture. See Levy, "The Decorum of
News," in *News, Newspapers, and Society in Early Modern Britain*, ed. Joad Raymond
(London, 1999): 12–38.

execution) and 14 August 1619 (the first performance date), the play was censored by the Master of the Revels, Sir George Buc, with "deletions, annotations, and comments."[20] The final manuscript of the play, British Library Additional 18653, includes these changes, along with the scribe's amendments, those of Ralph Crane.[21] According to Clare, the reasons for the censorship were multiple and included concern that the "dignity of the Prince of Orange should not be violated and that he should not be represented . . . in an unfavourable light."[22] With respect to the subject of Arminianism in the play, however, Clare sees the censorship as more the province of the bishop of London, John King, who would have "reacted against an account of events which showed the Arminian sect in a treacherous light."[23] Clare believes that Massinger and Fletcher touch only briefly on religious issues and contends that the playwrights present "the Advocate's espousal of Arminianism purely as a form of political opportunism to extend his influence in the States."[24] Howard-Hill argues that "*The Tragedy of Sir John Van Olden Barnavelt* was primarily a play to test the censor's sensitivity to issues which might provoke his master's censure against him."[25] He focuses on Buc's influence upon the manuscript and provides thorough assessment of the censor's role in the final version of the text as performed. Regarding the play's topical description of Arminianism, it was Buc's "responsibility to ensure that the play did not inflame the religious sensitivities of the audience."[26] Howard-Hill sees most of the references to Arminianism in the play as being "in the main . . . neutral." Although Fletcher and Massinger refer to a number of "'secular' Arminianians," such as Hugo Grotius and Rombout Hogerbouts, "the Arminian leader in Leiden," the parts of Arminian divines were "deleted" from the play, presumably because such treatment would have been too controversial.[27]

Here I wish to shift the emphasis and highlight the difference between the play of *Sir John van Oldenbarnavelt* and its pamphlet and political

---

[20] Clare, 195.
[21] Clare, 227 n44; and Howard-Hill, 40.
[22] Clare, 200.
[23] Clare, 204.
[24] Clare, 203.
[25] Howard-Hill, 43.
[26] Howard-Hill, 56.
[27] Howard-Hill, 59.

cartoon sources. In describing the play's appropriation of this discourse, I focus on its translation of religious questions into the domain of politics and international affairs. In this connection, I agree with Clare and Howard-Hill in their views that the censorship of the play was primarily political in nature and I attempt to show the ways in which the play's treatment of Arminianism follows a similar emphasis on political as opposed to religious implications.

Sir John van Oldenbarnavelt responded to the political and religious crisis in the Netherlands. In May of 1619, Oldenbarnavelt, the advocate general to the United Provinces, was tried and executed for treason against the state.[28] The play centers on the last days of the Advocate's life and dramatizes the power struggles that developed between Oldenbarnavelt, who represented the fledgling Dutch Republic, and Prince Maurice of Nassau, the heir to the hereditary dynasty of the House of Orange.[29] Following the Union of Utrecht in 1579, the northerly provinces of the Netherlands became a unified state, though much of Flanders and Brabant were later repossessed by Spain in the 1580s. The survival of the Northern Provinces depended upon the deflection of Spanish interests away from the United Provinces and towards England and France.[30] As a result of Spain's decreased involvement in the United Provinces, new political leadership became necessary, and Oldenbarnavelt stepped in. As advocate general he brought "purpose and consistency" to both national and international policy in the Netherlands.[31] "Within less than a decade," writes J. L. Price, "Barnavelt had secured the effective recognition of Dutch independence by England and France and had transformed the Republic into an equal, and indeed formidable, player in the game of international politics."[32]

---

[28] J. Leslie Price, *The Dutch Republic in the Seventeenth Century* (New York, 1998). Price situates the downfall of Oldenbarnavelt within the context of the political and religious tensions that emerged in the Netherlands in the years after the Revolt of the Provinces (1568–1609). For other historical accounts of the religious and political situation in the United Provinces, see Pieter Geyl, *The Netherlands Divided (1609–1648)* trans. Stanley Thomas Bindoff (London, 1936); and Jan den Tex, *Oldenbarnevelt* (Cambridge, 1973), vol. 1.
[29] Price, ibid.
[30] Price, *The Dutch Republic*, 2.
[31] Price, *The Dutch Republic*, 11.
[32] Price, *The Dutch Republic*, 12.

Oldenbarnavelt helped to solidify the Dutch Provinces both politically and economically, and his popularity became a source of resentment for Prince Maurice, who regarded Oldenbarnavelt's successes as a threat to his own sovereignty. Fletcher and Massinger's play dramatizes Maurice's coup in 1618 which led to Oldenbarnavelt's defeat, reestablished the monarchy, and resulted in the princes of Orange becoming the de facto political leaders of the United Provinces.[33] In the play, Maurice appears as a providential hero in contrast to the "villain" Barnavelt. It describes Barnavelt's "profession" of Arminianism as a hypocritical "cloak" to conceal Machiavellian political motives.[34]

At the beginning of the play, Maurice is ascendant and Barnavelt has lost much of the people's favor and support. Presented as a *de casibus* tragedy of sorts, in the tradition of the *Mirror for Magistrates, Sir John van Oldenbarnavelt* seeks to explain the reasons for Barnavelt's fall.[35] In the opening scenes, Barnavelt's loss of authority gives rise to naked and ruthless ambition. His efforts to secure the rights and freedoms of the United Provinces over the past thirty years appear both selfish and politically expedient. Barnavelt resolves to revenge himself on the "ingratefull" multitude who have rejected him in favor of Maurice. He will create a political alliance with Spain and bring the now independent United Provinces back under the yoke of Spanish tyranny:

> . . . this ingratefull Cuntry, [and this bold] this base people
> know he that could defeat the Spanish counsailes,
> and countermyne their darck works, he that made
> the State what 'tis, will change it once againe
> ere fall with dishonor. (I.i.50–55)

If Barnavelt has "made" the Dutch Republic, he can unmake it—and the "base people" will have to accept Barnavelt's authoritarian rule. Barnavelt will stop "defeating" the "Spanish counsailes" and pursue a policy of

---

[33] Price, *The Dutch Republic,* 62.

[34] For an excellent analysis of the political ramifications of the religious controversy between Remonstrants and Counter-Remonstrants in the United Provinces, including the effect of this conflict on James I himself, see White, "The Rise of Arminianism Reconsidered"; and White, *Predestination, Policy, and Polemic,* 159–66.

[35] See William Baldwin, *A Myrroure for Magistrates* (London, 1559).

diplomacy and détente. He will use Spain to solidify his own power even if it means destroying his people's political and economic freedoms.

For Modesbargen, one of Barnavelt's advisors, the decision is not simply rash and self-destructive, but tyrannical and absolutist. If Barnavelt succeeds, the Netherlands will depend entirely upon the Spanish Empire. Modesbargen is skeptical about whether such a course will bring Barnavelt the power that he desires. He speculates that all Barnavelt will accomplish is to substitute one rival leader (Maurice) for another (Spain):

> ... Shoulde you bring in
> (as heaven avert the purpose, or the thought
> of such a mischeif) the old Tirrany
> that *Spaine* hath practisd, do you thinck you should be
> or greater than you are, or more secure
> from danger? would you change the government,
> make it a Monarchie? suppose this don,
> and any man you favord most, set up,
> shall your authoritie by him encrease? (I.i.85–93)

Modesbargen asks Barnavelt why he would want to "ruyn whatsoever/ the good succes of forty yeeres employment/ in the most serious affaires of State" (I.i.75–77) for nothing more than "glory" and "the popular applause" (I.i.79). He urges Barnavelt to remember his past successes and triumphs, and not to focus on the relatively minor, and perhaps only temporary, loss of power that Barnavelt feels that he has suffered as a result of Maurice's rise.

For "thirtie yeeres," Modesbargen continues, the only thing that Barnavelt has lacked is the "name of King" (I.i.100):

> I know not what You ayme at:
> for thirtie yeeres (onely the name of King
> you have not had, and yet your absolute powre
> hath ben as ample) who hath ben employd
> in office, government, or Embassie,
> who raisd to wealth or honor that was not
> brought in by your allowaunce? who hath held
> his place without your lycence? your Estate is
> beyond a privat mans: your Brothers, Sonnes,

Frends, Famylies made rich, in trust & honors;
Nay; this Grave *Maurice*, this now Prince of *Orange*
who popularitie you weakely envy
was still by you commaunded: for when did he
enter the Field, but 'twas by your allowance?
what service undertake, which you approu'd not?
what victory was won, in which you shard not?
what Action of his renownd, in which
your Counsaile was forgotten? yf all theis then
suffice not your Ambition, but you must
extend it further, I am sorry that
you give me cause to feare, that when You move next
you move to your destruction. (I.i.99–120)

According to Modesbargen, Barnavelt's secret alliance with Spain may achieve its intended effect, in the short term, by undermining Maurice's influence. But it will have one of two consequences. Such action will either turn Barnavelt into a Spanish pawn or lead to charges of treason (as it did). The only reason why Barnavelt would want to ally himself with Spain is to hurt Maurice. Such reckless action can only backfire. In pursuing his own political ambitions, Barnavelt has opposed the republican political ideals of the United Provinces and actions approach the tyrannical.

The opening scenes emphasize Barnavelt's ambition, arrogance, and seeming disregard for the Dutch Republic. He aims to enter into an alliance with Spain after years of working to secure independence from Spanish imperial rule, and his "monarchical" motives are everywhere manifest. In such a depiction, the playwrights repeat many of the accusations leveled against Barnavelt in their sources. As Arthur H. Bullen, John Lothrup Motley, and Wilhemina Frijlinck have shown, *Sir John van Oldenbarnavelt* is a tissue of illusions to a series of contemporary pamphlets, both Dutch and English. These materials describe the religious and political tensions between Oldenbarnavelt and Maurice in a way that highlights the close connection between Arminian theology and the contemporary politics of the Dutch Republic.

One principal source for the play of *Sir John van Oldenbarnavelt* is *Newes Out of Holland: Concerning Barnavelt and his fellow-Prisoners their Conspiracy against their Native Country with the Enemies therof*

(London, 1619). It appears in the form of an "oration" and "proposition" by the French king's ambassadors to the General Estates of the United Provinces on behalf of Barnavelt and his fellow prisoners.[36] It includes the "Generall States answere." In the first half of the text, the ambassadors caution against breeding "enmity" and "dissention" among the citizens by the "changing of magistrates and counsellors."[37] They concede that Barnavelt may be "capable" of "disloyalty," but ask that the Estates exercise "favour and clemency" towards him, nonetheless.[38] They describe the "good and notable" services of Barnavelt to the Netherlandish states, and they counsel that exercising mercy towards Barnavelt will be the most effective means of winning "the hearts of the people" and reuniting "your subjects who are divided."[39] In the second part, the Estates General speak of administering "good and speedie justice" and of using the prisoners favorably "*if* they have not conspired the ruine of their state, with their enemyes."[40] They strongly imply that Barnavelt is guilty of treason and that he and his compatriots have "aspired to novelties by alteration of Religion, Justice, and fundamentall laws and all politicke orders."[41]

The True Description of the Execution of Justice done in the Graven-hage, by the Counsell of the Generall States holden for the same purpose, upon Sir John van Olden Barnavelt (London, 1619) reprints the entirety of *Newes Out of Holland*, in its latter pages, essentially pirating the earlier text. It adds several preliminary pages that detail Oldenbarnavelt's trial and execution in front of some "two thousand men and women."[42] The pamphlet includes a dedication to "the Christian Reader" which suggests the moral that "all busie-headed plotters, of treacherous and dangerous designes, would take warning by this example, and be deterred from interprising against their Soveraigne and their native Country, or against God and true Religion." Both pamphlets emphasize Oldenbarnavelt's Machiavellian actions. They describe the public's response to Oldenbarnavelt's trial as divided over whether he should be celebrated as a hero or condemned as a villain. Neither text focuses on the problem of Arminian

---

[36]   *Newes Out of Holland*, sig. A2.

[37]   Sig. A2ᵛ.

[38]   Sig. A3, sig. A4.

[39]   Sig. A4.

[40]   Sig. B3ᵛ. Emphasis mine.

[41]   Sig. B3ᵛ.

[42]   *The True Description*, sig. A1.

vs. Calvinist theology. Although both tracts refer to the Sinode (of Dort), they do so mainly to stress the importance of bringing peace and concord to a country rent by religious and political faction. In *Sir John van Oldenbarnavelt*, however, even such passing references to the theological controversy between the Arminians and the Calvinists are omitted. The language is distinctly political, and religion appears as a tactic of Machiavellian subterfuge and political scheming.

Important to my discussion of the play's relationship to political prints is Wilhelmina Frijlinck's study of several satirical engravings on the conflict between Maurice and Oldenbarnavelt. The most striking of these includes verses by Joost van den Vondel that commemorate "the victory of the Contra-Remonstrants." Frijlinck describes the print in this way:

> In a hall hangs an enormous pair of scales; in the right scale, which is higher than the other, the gown of the Advocate and the cushion of the council lie; by the side of this Barnaveld and the others stand, probably Grotius and Hogerbeets. Through the open window the square in Utrecht is seen, with the picture of the Prince disbanding the mercenaries. Maurice comes, and puts his sword in the left scale, so that it goes down."[43]

The religious and political conflicts between the Remonstrants (i.e., the Arminians) and the Counter-Remonstrants (i.e., the Calvinists) take center stage. The common emblematic device of scales to weigh down the two men makes the contrast clear. The engraving highlights Oldenbarnavelt's association with Hugo Grotius, the philosopher, theologian, and jurist, and Rombout Hogerbeets, a statesmen and jurist. All three were tried and executed for treason during the political conflict in the Dutch Republic, ca. 1617–1619. The print also indicates Maurice's political triumph over Oldenbarnavelt, depicting the temporal power of Maurice's sword working to pull down the scales in his favor.

Newes Out of Holland has the "General States" criticizing Barnavelt's efforts to subvert religion, justice, and law. *The True Description* equates the advocate general's transgressions against his "soveraigne," his "country," "God" and "true religion." "The Victory of the Contra-Remonstrants" shows Maurice, the proponent of Calvinism, as victorious.

---

[43] Frijlinck, lvii–lviii.

Fletcher and Massinger downplay the religious aspects of the power dynamic between Barnavelt and Maurice. As with these pamphlets and the discussed engraving, *Sir John van Oldenbarnavelt* presents "Arminianism" as explicitly politicized. In the play, Arminianism functions as a Machiavellian tactic of deception and subterfuge by which Barnavelt will use religion as a "cloak" for political rebellion and treason in his efforts to carry out his ambitious political designs. In Act I, scene ii, Barnavelt says to Hugo Grotius: "I am of your belief in every point you hold touching religion, and openly I profes myself of the *Arminian* sect" (I.ii.234–37). Modesbargen sees through the ruse and advises Barnavelt that:

> where Religion
> is made a cloke to our bad purposes
> they seldom have succes. (I.ii.269–71)

Barnavelt replies:

> you are too holly:
> we live not now with Saincts, but wicked men,
> and any thriving way, we can make use of
> what shape soere it weares, to crosse their arts
> we must embrace, and cherish: and this course
> (carrying a zealous face) will countenance
> our other actions; make the Burgers ours,
> raise Soldiers for our guard; strengthen our side
> against the now unequall opposition
> of this prowd prince of Orange; that Contemns us at the worst
> when he shall know there are some Regiments
> we may call ours, and that have no dependaunce
> upon his favour, 'twill take from his pride
> and make us more respected. (I.ii.272–85)

For Barnavelt, the current age is hypocritical and not religious. Political designs require a creative response to present circumstances, and Machiavellian deception is essential in political engagement. The outward "profession" of Arminianism will help secure a truce with Spain and will lead to the overthrow of Maurice as a political rival. Barnavelt's pretended

Arminianism will bring the "Burgers" to his aid. It will assist in raising "Soldiers" to fight against Maurice.

In this way, Fletcher and Massinger thematize Arminianism as a political issue, rehearsing the arguments against Barnavelt that had been circulating in print for months. They also highlight the play's own extra-textual nature by invoking the very "libels" that had sought to slander Barnavelt in the press, and that serve as the play's primary source material. Fletcher and Massinger call further attention to the polemical nature of Arminianism by bringing one of the authors of these pamphlets, Robert Holderus, onstage, in order to satirize him for his supposed "Arminian" beliefs. The portrayal underscores the contingency of religious faith since Holderus was not an Arminian but rather a committed Calvinist.[44] The allusion to Holderus appears to raise the subject of theology. But the the context in which Fletcher and Massinger do so is purely satiric, and the doctrinal aspect of Arminianism is subordinated to the comedy. Further, the playwrights' use of Holderus specifically omits any of the religious discussion that Holderus describes in his own polemic works.

In the scene described above, Barnavelt "professes" his Arminian faith. But he follows his statement of "genuine" belief with a highly self-conscious acknowledgement of the political meaning that "Arminianism" had come to have in the various libels written against him. According to Barnavelt:

> Reverend men
> your loves I am ambitious of: Alreadie
> 'tis known I favor you, and that hath drawne
> Libells against me: but the stinglesse hate
> of those that wryte them, I contempne. (I.ii.240–46)

These words echo a letter, written on 26 May 1618, from Oldenbarna-velt to Nöel de Caron, the States's ambassador to England, in which he laments that "we are tortured more and more with religious differences; the factious libels become daily more numerous and more impudent, and no man comes undamaged from the field. I, as a reward for all my troubles, labours, and sorrows, have three double portions of them."[45]

---

[44] See Howard-Hill, "Buc and the Censorship."
[45] See Frijlinck, xxv. The reference is to: The Hague Archives, Manuscript.

The differences between these two statements are revealing. In the play, Barnavelt dismisses the polemic impact of libels. He suggests that they have no real "sting" and they cannot hurt him either personally or politically. In the letter, the opposite is true, and Barnavelt stresses the "damage" that public opinion can have on individual reputations. The move to reject the impact of the libels makes sense, however, given its context in the play: it confirms Barnavelt's ultimate purpose of using religion in order to achieve his political ends. If Barnavelt has been defined as an Arminian by his enemies, he will employ this false assignation to his own political advantage.

Barnavelt acknowledges that, if he has "become" an "Arminian," it is as a result of his enemies' attempt to brand him as such publicly. He concedes that Arminianism can be used as a term of opprobrium, as in the scandalous accounts of his character that had been circulating in both English and Dutch pamphlets and political prints. But instead of attempting to defend himself straightforwardly against the charge, Barnavelt resolves on the opposite tact. He determines that the best way to counter the slander is to adopt the slander as one's own, with the full force of both belief and conviction—even if such a posture is fundamentally duplicitous and misleading. To this end, Barnavelt attempts to transform the "libelous" characterization of his Arminianism in the pamphlets into a personal strength, an integral part of his own political identity.[46]

The pamphlets that "libeled" Oldenbarnavelt sought to use his supposed Arminianism to undermine him politically. But in the play, Fletcher and Massinger stress the religious hypocrisy of Holderus. This intention reveals itself most clearly in the difference between the manuscript and printed versions of the play. In the original manuscript version of the scene with the "upstart" Dutch women (II.ii), Fletcher and Massinger introduce "Holderus" by having him referred to, falsely, by the Second Dutch Woman as an "Arminian" preacher. She describes him as:

---

[46] Both Howard-Hill and Price comment on the polemic construction of Oldenbarnavelt's "Arminianism," by his detractors, as well as by himself, for politically expedient reasons. However, neither author sees this as impacting the general perception of Oldenbarnavelt's religious faith. See Howard-Hill, "Buc and the Censorship," 54; and Price, *The Dutch Republic*, 103.

a fine talker, and a zealous talker,
we can make him thinck what we list, preach what we list,
print what we list, and whom we list, abuse in't
Eng-gent'W. and a Preacher do you say?
2 Dutch.w. a singular Preacher. (800–804)

She then connects Holderus's "preaching" and "printing" with the lack of "modestie" of "this [i.e these] new Arminians" who engage in "hissing tosts" (II.ii.805–807). By contrast, in the final print version of the text, all of the references to preaching have been omitted (by Buc), and substituted with less religiously-inflected terms, such as "teacher" for "preacher" in lines 803 and 804: "Teacher do you say?"; "a singular Teacher." The connection of the single word "preaching" to the Arminian and Calvinist controversy was clearly enough to bring about the censorship of these few lines.

The move to transform the Calvinist Holderus into an Arminian (in the manuscript version) is clearly satiric. According to Trevor H. Howard-Hill, "There is some irony in identifying Arminians—who were all but Catholics—with their opposites among the dissenters within the established religion. The general effect is [thus] to deny the Arminians any colour of theological validity" and to associate them with troublemakers "besides dissenters, the unruly Dutch women."[47] In the case of Holderus, his doctrinal Arminianism makes him the perfect scapegoat for the upstart Dutch women.[48] But the fact that Holderus was one of the principal writers of anti-Barnavelt pamphlets creates yet another level of parody. It shows the very real difference between, on the one hand, the pamphlets sources on the conflict between Barnavelt and Maurice upon which Fletcher and Massinger drew, and, on the other, the play of *Sir John van Oldenbarnavelt*.

Holderus's pamphlet is entitled *Barnavel's Apology: or Holland Mysterie. With Marginall Castigations* (London, 1618).[49] It is prefaced by a

---

[47] Howard-Hill, "Buc and the Censorship," 61.

[48] Howard-Hill, "Buc and the Censorship," 62. See also Janet Clare's discussion of these two scenes in: *Art Made Tongue-Tied by Authority*, 204. Clare makes essentially the same points as Howard-Hill, but also stresses Crane's desire to "differentiate between Arminian and Calvinist clergy and to ensure that it was the Arminians who suffered the opprobrium."

[49] Howard-Hill refers to the pamphlet on page 59 of "Buc and the Censorship."

letter, written by Holderus, to "David Pareus," a doctor of divinity at the University of Heidelberg. Holderus argues that he has written this tract in order to acquaint his friend, and ostensibly a larger reading public, with the "profitable proceeding of the sincere Gospel in Holland, as also the tottering and extreme ruine of the new upstart Arminians."[50] According to Holderus, Barnavelt's chief offenses lie in his Arminian faith. But he has also transgressed by affirming the "secular authoritie to be above the Ecclesiasticall."[51]

More troublingly, Oldenbarnavelt has interfered with Prince Maurice's efforts to suppress Arminian discussion in the public sphere. According to Holderus, Arminians are "false brethren, false teachers, even farre worse then the Papists," whose primary misdeed has been their advocacy of a "pestilent doctrine concerning Predestination and Justification."[52] According to Holderus, the problem with Arminianism is threefold: (1) it represents an attack on Calvinist ideas concerning predestination; (2) it has the potential to generate religious conflict in a way that resembles the threat posed by Catholicism; and (3) it seeks to extend "liberty of conscience," i.e., religious toleration, and thus to further undermine the religious uniformity of the Protestant Netherlands. [53]

The fact that Holderus's principal argument against Oldenbarnavelt emphasizes his Arminian theology is important—especially since none of this material appears in Fletcher and Massinger's play. Howard-Hill argues that the play sought to avoid all discussion of religious controversy since it was the main reason for censoring dramatic texts.[54] But, if the point of using Dutch and English pamphlets from the period was to create an accurate historical picture of the conflict between Maurice and Barnavelt, the choice of the playwright's to omit discussion of theology must have to do with more than just censorship restrictions. Arminianism needed to be discussed since it was critical to the perception of Barnavelt's defeat, in both Dutch and English accounts of the issue. But in *Sir John van Oldenbarnavelt*, Barnavelt's "Arminianism" is never presented as an aspect of religious belief. It is instead portrayed as

---

[50] Holderus, sig. A2.
[51] Holderus, sig. A2ᵛ.
[52] Holderus, sig. A2ᵛ.
[53] Holderus, sig. A2ᵛ.
[54] See Howard Hill, "Buc and the Censorship."

hypocritical and self-serving, an expedient use of religion for political ends. This is true both for Barnavelt and for the anti-Barnavelt polemicists, such as Holderus, who sought to use Arminianism for their own political ends.

In 1619, Fletcher and Massinger's decision to write a play about Oldenbarnavelt in which Arminianism becomes a cloak for political deception makes historical sense. The play connects Dutch Arminianism, the conflict in the United Provinces involving Oldenbarnavelt and Maurice, and the developing crisis in England over the Spanish Match.[55] James was beginning to propose a form of Catholic toleration as part of the negotiations with Spain for the marriage of Prince Charles and the Infanta.[56] Barnavelt's interest in Spain, along with his clear-cut republican ambitions, may have provided the playwrights with a useful cautionary tale for James. At the time the king appeared to be following Barnavelt in his pro-Catholic and pro-Spanish foreign and domestic policies. By omitting most of the references to Arminian theology in the pamphlet sources, and by creating a figure in Barnavelt whose interest in Arminianism served to disguise political ambition, the playwrights offer an implicit critique of James's pro-Catholic foreign and domestic policies. They conflate Arminianism and Catholicism and stress the political implications of Dutch Arminianism for the spread of Catholicism, both in England and abroad. The point is that while Arminianism was understood in its manifold theological complexity by popular polemicists and playwrights of the early seventeenth century, it was the broader influence of Arminianism on English politics and foreign policy that concerned these writers most.

---

[55] See White, "The Rise of Arminianism Reconsidered." For a further argument in favor of the importance of the political situation in the United Provinces, and of the importance of the Spanish Match in determining James I's decision to promote "Arminian" bishops, see Fincham and Lake, "The Ecclesiastical Policy of James I."

[56] See Tyacke, *Anti-Calvinists*, 183.

III.

In much the same vein as *Sir John van Oldenbarnavelt*, the print by Hendrick Laurensz and the fold-out plate in John Russell's *The Spy* exploit the political potential of Arminianism in mid-seventeenth-century England.[57] Both prints create a personification of Arminianism by evoking the specter of the dead Arminius. They do so in order to illustrate the dangers posed by what they regard as an increasingly influential "Arminian" faction at Court and by Jacobean and Caroline censors. The political engravings deplore the restraints on public criticism of the King's foreign and domestic policies, particularly with respect to his seeming pro-Catholic leanings. They reflect views of individuals who believe that their "Arminian" enemies are bent on branding them radical "Puritans" intent on the subversion of the Caroline Church and State. In an effort to appeal to the people, and to a possibly more sympathetic political authority than the king, both prints petition the Parliament directly. They conceive of this legislative body as the voice of reason and neutrality, and as the most effective arbiter of political and religious conflict in the realm. Both prints stress the importance of free speech as the guarantor of religious

---

[57] Frederick G. Stephens, *Catalogue of Prints and Drawings in the British Museum: Satirical and Personal Subjects*, vol. I (London, 1870–1873) does not include references to either of the Arminian prints discussed in this essay. I have found them both through archival research. Neither Pierce, Griffiths, or Jones mentions these prints in their studies of seventeenth-century political engravings. Stephens includes only the 1641 print, discussed on 180–181. A copy of the 1628 print is in the Bodleian Library and is STC 5028. It is engraved by Hendrick Laurensz, a Dutch engraver working in Amsterdam between 1610 and 1648. The later print is contained in the Thomason Collection (669.f.4[14]) and in the general British Library collection of rare books. The fold-out plate to *The Spy* is mentioned in *Early English Books Online*, but the archives where this can be found are incorrect. The fold-out plate does not exist in the Huntington Library copy of *The Spy* (as *EEBO* suggests). From what I have been able to find, the plate only exists in three extant copies of the book: at The Folger Shakespeare Library, the University of Illinois Rare Books Room, and the Trinity College Library in Cambridge University. For a later, post-1641, anti-Arminian print, see the title page illustration to Thomas Harbie's *Divi Arminii Mactorum Renata, et Renovata Petitio. Or the Arminian Priests Last Petition for their former formalitie, and ancient Innovation, both in Church and Common-weale* (London, 1642).

and political liberty and they argue that open and unrestrained discussion is the most effective means of preventing tyranny.[58]

The political prints on Arminianism contend that censorship in England has tended to favor Arminian polemic (but not necessarily theology). They insist that Arminians have gained preferment in Church and State. While such an insistence might seem to confirm the Tyacke thesis concerning the rise of Arminianism in England, it is important to note that nowhere do these prints suggest that the opposition is between Arminians and Calvinists. Instead, both cartoons stress the negative effects that Arminianism has had on the true English Protestant Church more generally defined.[59] Further, while the engraving that accompanies *The Spy* discusses questions of election, merit, and good works (all theological points of contention between Arminians and Calvinists), it does so not to present a clear-cut Arminian theological position but to suggest that Arminians espouse contradictory theological views, some pro-Catholic, others anti-*Arminian*. The point is the inconsistent and hypocritical nature of Arminianism in England. Russell argues that the Arminians are more concerned with achieving political influence than with advancing a systematically integrated program of doctrine and belief. The Arminians have gained great authority through preferment in court and Church, and that dominance has resulted in the overflow in print with pro-Arminian views.

Both engravings oppose the dominance, but Russell takes the opposition a step further. He suggests that Arminianism be confined to the theological speculation of the schools where it would be readily confuted. Russell distinguishes sharply between theological questions of predestination, the polemic construction of Arminianism, and the political consequences of the public debate about religion. He contends that Arminianism

---

[58]　See Colclough, *Freedom of Speech in Early Stuart England*; McCrae, *Literature, Satire, and the Early Stuart State*; and Clegg, *Press Censorship in Caroline England*.

[59]　Many historians have argued for a "Calvinist consensus" during the early seventeenth century in England. My point is that the kind of theological disputation that one gets in the religious tracts of the period (especially at the universities) is largely absent from these more "popular" materials. If Calvinism is presumed as the dominant religion, nothing in the language of these political prints suggests that the problem (with Arminianism in England) has anything to do with debates about predestination *per se*. For the argument about a "Calvinist consensus," see Tyacke, *Anti-Calvinists*; and Patrick Collinson, *The Religion of the Protestants* (Oxford, 1982).

has become a threat in England as a result of the effectiveness of religious propaganda – especially against the "true" Protestants. He wishes an end to the public debate about Arminianism and a return to the *status quo*. To achieve this end both Russell and the anonymous author of "Arminius Between Truth and Heresie" appeal directly to the king and Parliament.

IV.

Figure 1.

"Arminius Between Truth and Heresie" [fig. 1] presents a caricatured depiction of Jacobus Arminius. Stephens describes it in this way:

> Arminius [is] standing on a pedestal in front of an architectural screen. His right hand is raised as if rejecting "*Veritas*," who holds out the Bible, "*Biblia*," in her hand, and tramples upon the symbols of Popery. On the other side, "*Heresia*," holds him by the hand. She wears a tiara, carries a chalice, and stands upon and is enveloped by a seven-headed dragon [the Beast of the Apocalypse]. He has a windmill on his head; a Jesuit is whispering into one ear, and a monk is speaking through a trumpet. Below is a sculptured frieze, representing a battle.[60]

---

[60] Stephens, *Catalogue of Prints and Drawings*, 180.

Beneath the image appears the following text:

> Great King protect us with thy gratious hand
> Or else *Armenius* will o're spread this Land:
> For if in *England* th'enemy doth appeare,
> This is the shape of him we need to feare.
> He raiseth Factions, and that brings in jarres
> Which broacheth Errors, and upholds the wars
> The *Netherlands* ruine he sought to bring,
> In England now he doth the self same thing
> To raile, to write, to publish bitter gall,
> To change Religion and subvert us all
> His squint-ey'd looks & *Linsie-Wolsie* gowne;
> Shewes how Religion he wil soone throw downe
> His grinding pate with weather-Cocks turn'd brain
> Seeketh the *Churches* tenets for to staine:
> The Christal streams of truth he shuns most pure,
> The tryall of *Gods* word he'le not endure:
> But unto *Error* cast his blinking eye,
> Presuming *Truth* doth not the same espie.
> *Heresie* upon a stately *Beast* doth stand.
> *Armenius* bids him welcome holds his hand,
> *Truth* by her brightnesse and her sincere heart,
> Shewes that with *Heresie* she takes no part;
> Treades on their *Mountebanke* & *Cozning* tricks,
> Blowne in his eares by *Pelagius* and *Jesuites*.
> Which makes his *Wind-mil* for promotions grace,
> Publish his bookes abroad in everie place:
> And begs protection for his workes of wonder,
> Which against *Truth* he bellowes forth like thunder.
> Thus doth *Armenius* to preferment rise,
> By Equivocating and his Cheverill lies;
> And *Truth* to all appeales to open view,
> Bidding all heresies for ere adew.
> Desiring our great CHARLES to take to hart,
> And by the Parliament make *Armenius* smart,
> Which being done, *England* shall ever blesse
> The *King*, the *State*, the *Churches* happinesse.

And if for telling truth I burne or frye,
What then deserves he that tells a lye?[61]

In the 1641 edition, the following title is added, below the image, and above the lines of verse:

Englands petition, to her gratious king,
That he, Arminius would to ruine bring
Who, by his doctrine, privie plots, and hate
To Verity, doth ruine Church and State.

Print and text are directed to the king, who is not only "great," the source of all power in the nation, but also the visible instrument of the nation's "protection." As such, "Arminius Between Truth and Heresie" sees the stability of the kingdom depending on the maintenance of a balanced and harmonious relationship between the "King," the "State," and the "Church." It petitions Charles and the Parliament to address themselves to the religious and political problems it raises. It does so by depicting the founder of Arminianism, Jacobus Arminius, in both satiric and fantastic form.

The design of the engraving highlights the interconnectedness of its iconography. It follows a kind of snakelike path from (1) the monk at the top right, who speaks into Arminius's ear through a trumpet; into (2) the crouched Jesuit, to the left, depicted in an animalistic pose, holding himself up with his arms, and speaking into Arminius' other ear; across (3) the body of "Veritas," whose draped garments continue the winding path; over (4) Truth's extended arm to the open Bible that she extends to Arminius; following (5) the clasped hand of "Heresia," and down through her tartan-like, or "linsie-wolsie" garments, crossed in a kind of visual parallel with the flowing cloth draped over "Veritas; and (6) ending in the figure of the seven-headed Hydra, whose tail completes the chain, from Heresy's hand to her feet. So the viewer's eye moves over the picture-plane, winding like an Archimedean screw across the various figures and symbols. In the face of gossip and Jesuitical influence, Truth, the Bible, and Heresy assume apocalyptic connotations. The reference to the seven-headed Hydra (Beast

---

[61] See Stephens, *Catalogue of Prints and Drawings*, 180-81. The figures of Truth and Heresy, along with the general iconography of this print, were copied, at a later date, in BM Sat #697, "Truth flatters not," dated 1647 in Stephens.

of the Apocalypse) brings in an apocalyptic dimension to the print. Along with the sculptured frieze depicting a battle scene upon which the whole print sits, the implication is that the battle between Truth and Heresy follows a model of apocalyptic judgments that were central to the early seventeenth century rhetoric of religious conflict.[62]

For the author of these verses, appearance and moral character are one. It is those who appear most outlandish and strange who are to be most distrusted, and the audience must read and interpret the visual ensemble correctly. The capacity to recognize the charlatan, the Machiavel, and the madman, will expose Arminius as a force of Error and Heresy, and a serious threat to Church and State. The precept emerges from the satirical imagery of "Linsie-Wolsie gowne[s]," "*Mountebanks*," and windmills which caricature and render fantastical both Arminius and the Arminian faith. "Linsey woolsey" was originally "a textile material, woven from a mixture of wool and flax" and distinguished by its lightness and thinness. Its figurative sense, especially in relationship to the deceptive nature of the papacy, appears as early as 1522. In "Why come ye not to Court" John Skelton writes that the "Pope of Rome" shall "weve all in one lome A Webbe of lylse wulse." Later texts viewed the tartan cloth as a "signe of inconstancie." "Linsie-wolsie" also meant "a strange medley in talk or action; confusion."[63] The engraving appears to invoke all of these contexts, simultaneously. Mountebanks were "itinerant charlatan[s] who sold supposed medicines and remedies, freq[uently] using various entertainments to attract a crowd of potential customers."[64] A mountebank "falsely claims knowledge of or skill in some matter, esp. for personal gain; a person who pretends to be something he or she is not, in order to gain prestige, fame, etc." In the sixteenth and seventeenth centuries, the term "mountebank" was often employed in order to describe the "corrupt

---

[62] The model for this was John Foxe's *Actes and Monuments* (London, 1563), which depicted the battle between Protestant and Catholic in providential and apocalyptic terms—both in the work itself and in its famous, and graphic, title page.

[63] "linsey-woolsey, n." OED Online. March 2014. Oxford University Press. http://www.oed.com/view/Entry/108778?redirectedFrom=linsey-woolsey (accessed May 06, 2014).

[64] "mountebank, n." OED Online. March 2014. Oxford University Press. http://www.oed.com/view/Entry/122915?rskey=y5B8uD&result=1&isAdvanced=false (accessed May 06, 2014).

clergy and others assuming false piety or religiosity."[65] And windmills were traditionally viewed as emblems of insanity, frivolity, and fantasy. In Richard Brome's *The Court Beggar* (1640), the character of Mendicant arrives from Hell "attir'd all in Patents; A Windmill on his head." "Thus, attended by his projectors," writes Martin Butler, "he is established as a caricature of the generic type, the Monopolist; his windmill is the satirical badge of mad or fanciful enterprises."[66]

In addition to ridicule, the imaginative satire challenges the Arminian threat to the English Church and State. The author underscores the threat of English Arminianism through the organization of the engraving. His decision to place Arminius in an architectural space signals authority: Arminius stands upon an engraved frieze, in a kind of triptych with Heresie and Truth on either side. He is granted visual precedence over the two others by his position atop a pedestal. The power is undermined, in part, by the image of the windmill and the whispering Jesuit, but the sense of Arminius's baleful influence predominates.

The accompanying verses extend this view and call attention to the negative effects of "Arminius" upon the English nation and people. The author writes of Arminius's capacity to "raise Factions," and "bring in jarres," to "broach" Errors and "uphold" wars. He suggests as well that the "ruine" that Arminius has brought to the Netherlands will soon undermine English Protestantism ("The *Netherlands* ruine, he sought to bring,/ In *England* now he doth the selfe same thing"). The author expresses concern that Arminius has "stained" the Church's "tenets." He connects Arminianism to Pelagianism, "the denial of the transmission of original sin, and... the principle that human will is capable of good without the assistance of divine grace," and Catholicism, a common polemic linkage in anti-Arminian pamphlets of the period. [67]

Most importantly, if the Arminians constitute one side of the ideological divide implied by "Arminius Between Truth and Heresie," the opposite position is not Calvinism but rather mainstream English Protestantism. The author of "Arminius Between Truth and Heresie"

---

[65] *Ibid.*

[66] See Butler, *Theatre and Crisis*, 226. Butler discusses the play on 220-27.

[67] "Pelagian, n.1 and adj.1." OED Online. March 2014. Oxford University Press. http://www.oed.com/view/Entry/139815?rskey=bFYpy1&result=1&isAdvanced=false (accessed May 06, 2014).

describes the negative effects that Arminianism has wrought upon the English Protestant Church. But the particularity of this assault is omitted. Arminianism is no different than Catholicism, or any other religious sect that seeks to undermine the English Church and State. Within England Arminianism increases faction, instigates wars, and "stain[s]" the Church's true beliefs. The emphasis falls on civil strife, and the creation of generalized chaos, from within the body politic.

The main issue that the text of the print addresses is the alleged capacity of the Arminian faction to use the press and pulpit in order to freely "raile," "write," and "publish bitter gall." The engraving thus potentially alludes to the controversy over "predestinarian preaching" and the series of royal proclamations issued by Charles in 1626, 1628, and 1629.[68] But rather than make the issue about predestination, or Arminian vs. Calvinist theology, the author argues against the dominance of the marketplace of print by any one party. The print suggests that Arminians have engaged in the distortion of "Truth" and the promotion of "Heresie." It implies that the ultimate effect of such public discussion will be the undermining of true Religion, and the upending of the existing order ("To change Religion and subvert us all"). For the author of "Arminius Between Truth and Heresie," the fact that the Arminians have been able to publish their books (though, interestingly, "abroad," and not at home), has led to the general proliferation of Arminian ideas in England. As a result, Arminianism has entered the English public sphere, and has led to the subversion of the true Protestant faith. Further, "Arminians" have been able to secure "preferment," "protection," and "promotion" in the Church. In this respect, "Arminius Between Truth and Heresie" appears to confirm the Tyacke thesis concerning the rise of Arminianism. But what is objected to most is not the theological difference between Arminian and Calvinist but the political influence of the Arminian faction.

"Arminius Between Truth and Heresie" confirms the political and polemic representation of Arminianism in the public sphere and evokes the stereotype of Arminius in order to underscore the problematic nature

---

[68] For a further discussion of the controversy surrounding Montagu's publication of two, allegedly pro-Arminian, pamphlets, including *A Gagg for the New Gospell* (London, 1624) and *Appello Caesarem* (London, 1625), see Tyacke, *Anti-Calvinists*; Lambert, "Richard Montagu, Arminianism, and Censorship," and Como, "Predestination and Political Conflict in Laud's London."

of Arminius's political motivations. But it also proposes that the only solution to growing influence of Arminianism lies in political action by the king and Parliament. The engraving's response to the problem of censorship, and to religious and political grievances more generally, is consequently both polemic and ameliorative. It aims to redress grievances through the direct involvement of the king, acting in concert with Parliament ("Desiring our great CHARLES to take to heart/ And by the *Parliament* make *Armenius* smart").

In the face of Arminius's attempts to "change" and "transform" religion, "subverting" the traditional institutions of the established Church of England, it is the king ("Charles") and Parliament who will prevail. The dates of publication for this print (1628 and 1641) underscore the point, as they mark the two parliaments, namely 1628–9 and 1640–42— "The Long Parliament"—that flank the eleven years of "personal rule" of Charles.[69] It is these political and temporal institutions of the English nation which are most suited to confront the Arminian threat.

The Parliament of 1628–29 was much concerned with the problem of Arminianism, a point on which both the pro-Tyacke and anti-Tyacke groups concur. However, they differ in their interpretation of the source of the problem—did the threat of Arminianism issue from a genuine theological and political reality (the Tyacke view)? Or did it follow from the super-saturation of the public with polemic concerns about Puritan opposition and the Arminian counter-attack (the anti-Tyacke view)?[70] The print appears to confirm the latter view. But it is also important because it raises the question of Charles's commitment to theological Arminianism. Tyacke sees this as confirmed, while the anti-Tyacke camp wonders whether

---

[69]   See Sharpe, *The Personal Rule*.

[70]   See, for instance, Tyacke, "The Rise of Arminianism Reconsidered," 214; Tyacke, *Anti-Calvinists*; and (for the opposite perspective) White, "The Rise of Arminianism Reconsidered," 51–53. White quotes Conrad Russell's view that the 1629 Parliament showed the Commons for the "first time as a whole," regarding the "growth of Arminianism as a conspiracy to alter the doctrine of the Church of England." See Russell, *Parliaments and English Politics*, 404. However, according to White, "it is clear from the debates that the attempt to prove that contention . . . ended in failure." Further, "for most members the real significance of Arminianism consisted in its connotations with 'Jesuits', 'Romish tyranny', and 'Spanish monarchy'." As the example of John Russell's *The Spy* suggests, it is precisely these nondoctrinal associations of English Arminianism that were most important to Russell. See White, "The Rise of Arminianism Reconsidered," 52.

there is any clear evidence for Charles's religious preferences. "Arminius Between Truth and Heresie" emphasizes the need for unity and harmony in Church and State. It affirms an optimistic belief that Charles and Parliament will be able to confront the problem of Arminianism together. Far from conceiving of Charles as the enemy of Calvinism, or as a proponent of Arminian theology, the print strongly suggests that the power to resist Arminianism lies with the Parliament and the King. This may be more wishful than realistic. But the fact that "Arminius Between Truth and Heresie" can imagine Charles's capacity to work with Parliament in order to defeat "Arminius" is significant. It suggests the potential for flexibility on Charles's part in the case of Arminian religion and politics.

V.

Figure 2.

In a similar manner to "Arminius Between Truth and Heresie," the political print that accompanies *The Spy* [fig. 2] stresses both the threat of English "Arminianism" and the need for parliamentary action to halt

the proliferation of Arminian polemic. [71] It should be read in conjunction with the pamphlet itself, which serves as a verse "explanation" and
"description" of the engraving. *The Spy* is specifically dedicated to "All
Zealous Professors and true hearted Patriots in Great Britaine" (sig. +2ʳ).
In the fold-out engraving, Russell depicts a procession of "*Cardinalls,*"
"fat *Bishops,*" and "a whole *Legion* of *Ignatius Priests*" (sig. Bᵛ). Looming
large, the Pope appears with his "standardbearer[s]," noted in the margin as "*The Divel,*" the "*Divells Duke,* great *Lucifer,* " and "*Beelzebub*"
(sig. B3ᵛ) who, in order to betray "*Truth,*" "enlarge" the Popish/ Spanish
"empire" and "bring it nigher/ To universall greatnes" (sig. B4ʳ). The print
invokes the common trappings of heraldry. There are flags with the coat
of arms of Castile and Leon (the castle and lion *rampant*), the three fleur-
de-lis—which appear on the coat of arms of the king of France, evoking
sovereignty, and the Holy Trinity—and other heraldic animals. These
include the cock (the Gallic rooster), the double-headed eagle (representing the Byzantine Empire, or, in this case, the Holy Roman Empire), and
a horse. The last most probably refers to the Trojan Horse of antiquity,
as implied by the wheeled platform it stands on. However, a single white
horse was also used on the coat-of-arms of Lower Saxony, the kingdom of
Hanover, and the kingdom of Prussia. [72]

In addition to representing the flags of international Catholic nations,
the coats of arms register the fraudulent nature of these states, through
Latin inscriptions testifying to their deceit and dishonesty. The allusions
include a series of interconnected mythological, fabulous, religious, and
political references. One flag, depicting a fox leading a lion by a string
tied to the lion's nose, reads: "Fraude non vi captum duco in exilium"
("By fraud not by strength I lead him captive into exile"). [73] The reference
may be to Aesop's fable of "The Ass, the Fox, and the Lion," the moral of
which is "Traitors must expect treachery." [74] It also could refer to the fox
and the lion of Classical and Renaissance political philosophy. In Cicero
and Machiavelli, the fox was traditionally the representative of fraud; the

---

[71] On sig. +2ᵛ, Russell writes that "the whole book is but an explanation of the
Frontis-piece."
[72] See Thomas Woodcock and John Martin Robinson, *The Oxford Guide to
Heraldry* (Oxford, 1988).
[73] Thank you to Robert Dulgarian for help with identifying many of these references, and for aid in translating the Latin.
[74] See *Aesop's Fables,* trans. Laura Gibbs (Oxford, 2002).

lion of force.[75] A second flag, depicting another fox, reinforces the asso-ciation of the fox with deception. It states: "Falleris You are cozened," including both the Latin and the English translation. A third flag pos-sibly alludes to Aesop's fable of Mercury and the Woodman, the moral of which is "honesty is the best policy."[76] It quotes Ovid's *Ars Amato-ria* in a way that undercuts the meaning: "Tuta frequensque via est per amici fallere nomen" ("It is a safe and often trodden path to deceive under the name of friend").[77] A fourth flag, reading "Nil prodire tenus si datur ultra," adapts a quotation from Horace—"Est quadam prodire tenus, si non datur ultra" ("one can always reach a certain point even if one can-not go further")—to its opposite: "you can't reach any point unless you can go further."[78] The picture that accompanies this quotation portrays a soldier cutting off his right hand. The image recalls the common bibli-cal trope of cutting off one's hand to remove sin. It may also refer to the punishments meted out to conquered enemies by Roman emperors, and, in early modern England, to legal retribution for stealing. [79]

The bearers of the flags represent a religious and political fifth column of sorts. Positioned from within the castle gates, they are distinguished from the Catholic forces that are organizing outside of the castle walls. These are, most probably, meant to represent the Arminians themselves: neither Catholic nor Protestant, they have infiltrated the Protestant cas-tle, and represent falsity and deception in opposition to the "true" Protes-tant faith. The ambivalence of this relationship is underscored by the fact that the Arminians are not, however, in the older Medieval keep itself, but rather in the outworks. They are outside of the center of power, and separate from it. At the top appears the tetragrammaton, encircled with clouds, and three letters, X, Y, and Z, labeled "Potentia" (power), "Provi-dentia" (providence), and "protectio" (protection). These materialize atop an architectural edifice, described as "Castello della verita" (The Castle of Truth). At the entrance of the castle stands an armed figure, with a raised sword in one hand and an outstretched shield in the other. Above the

---

[75]   See Niccolo Machiavelli, *The Prince*, Anthony Grafton, ed., William Bull, trans., (Penguin, 2003); and Marcus Tullius Cicero, *De Officiis. English and Latin* (Cambridge, 1947).

[76]   See Aesop, *Fables.*

[77]   Ovid, *Ars Amatoria*, trans. B. P. Moore (London, 1965).

[78]   *The Epistles of Horace*, trans. David Ferry (New York, 2001). Bk. 1, Epistle 1.

[79]   See Deuteronomy 25:12; Matthew 5:30; and Mark 9:43.

entrance is written: "defensor fidei" (the defender of the faith). Inscribed in the stone walls are names of the evangelists, Matthew, Mark, Luke, and John, of Protestant divines, Calvin and Luther, and of biblical figures, Josiah, Daniel, Jeremiah, Isaiah, Moses. A flag representing the Old and New Testaments reads: "Tandem splendescet" ("Both will shine forth"). These suggest the beliefs of the true English Protestant Church, as well as their basis in scripture and more recent religious history. Two gates to the castle, one to the left and one to the right, are labeled "Port[a?] della fidelita" (the gate of loyalty) and "Port or=/thodosso" [sic] (the gate [of] orthodoxy). To the left is the pope and his forces, accompanied by a devil. The pope carries a paper, labeled "Bulla" (a pun on the Medieval Latin for a "sealed document" and "child's toy"). He holds a thunderbolt ("Anathema"), used to damn people. The pope also bears a flag, with a cross key and sword, labeled "Arte Marte" ("the Art of War"). He is satirized as one whose authority is childlike. But he is also depicted as a potential threat, with his Jove-like weapons and his investment in military solutions. At the bottom of the print appear the popish forces themselves, divided into groups, including cardinals holding the triple cross and papal insignia, bishops with miters, friars with pick-axes, monks with powder kegs, and soldiers with guns. The imagery suggests the martial allegiance of Catholic armies. They conspire together in order to attack the "True" Church of England, while divine providence looks on, protecting the Church from violence.

In the verses that describe this emblem in the text of *The Spy*, Russell expands the allegory of Spanish, French, and Catholic treachery that appears in the fold-out engraving to incorporate the parallel deceptions of Arminius (though Arminius does not appear in the print itself):

> To this cursed end,
> In humane shape, *Arminius* they send;
> Got by *Pelagius*, and in *Rome* nurst up;
> Whence, drunke with superstitious errours cup,
> He's sent to *Leyden* by the *Popes* direction
> To blast the world with's heresyes infection,
> Nor rests th'ambiguous craft monster there;
> But spewes the poyson of false doctrine here:
> Comes, like a protestant, in shew, before;
> And vowes he hates the *Antichristian* whore;

Disclaimes her tenents: nay none seemes to be
More zealous, in the gospells cause, then he,
. . .
Tell him the doctrine of the *Pope* is' true
Concerning merits, he will censure you
For errours straight. Say that we may attaine
By nature, power salvation to gaine,
By working it our selves: he will reply
These doctrines are condemnd for heresy:
And yet (what positively he thus denyes)
By necessary consequence implyes.
So that observe him well: within you'le find
A friers hat, as here his coule behind.
Behold, now, sathans masterpiece, t or'e spread
The *Church* with *Popery,* so long banished.
. . .
Yet though *Arminius, Holland* had infected,
Since we, his poysonous doctrine had detected,
And that blest King [i.e. James I], most learnedly refelled [sic]
Those false positions seduc'd *Vorstius* held:
What madness was't, for us, to foster here,
Those errours, that our Church condemned there? (sigs. B4^{r-v})

While Russell's pamphlet is significantly longer, and more complex in its arguments, than are the verses that accompany "Arminius Between Truth and Heresie," there are striking similarities between the two. Both tracts personify and allegorize Arminius; both stress the "heretical" nature of Arminianism; both rehearse the Arminian/ Catholic connection; both imply that Arminianism will lead to Pelagianism; and both situate the origin of the Arminian controversy in the political and religious circumstances of the United Provinces which led to the conflict between Oldenbarnavelt and Maurice. But Russell goes further than "Arminius Between Truth and Heresie." He calls attention to the theological nature of the "Arminian" controversy, and, as with Fletcher and Massinger in *Sir John van Oldenbarnavelt,* reconceptualizes Arminianism in distinctly political terms. For Russell, as for Fletcher and Massinger, "Arminianism" is synonymous with religious hypocrisy. It is dangerous insofar as it has the capacity to falsify religious claims for political ends. Arminianism pretends "truth" while simultaneously promoting the twin "heresies" of "Rome" and "atheism."

Russell begins by describing "Arminius" as a "protestant, in shew." The phrase echoes "Arminius Between Truth and Heresie." In both engravings, Arminius supposedly professes orthodox Protestant views, such as the idea that the pope is Antichrist. But the addition of the term "in shew," as with the earlier print, suggests duplicity and pretense. Although "Arminius" says that he believes that the pope is Antichrist, the implication is that "he" is only expressing this opinion in order to maintain the disguise of being a "true" Protestant. Russell also presents "Arminius" as an anti-Catholic theologian who, to Arminian beliefs, rejects the "Pope's" ideas regarding "merit" and good works. The claim opposes the religious tenets of "true" Arminians, who assert the importance of merit and good works in opposition to strict Calvinist views about election. "Arminius," according to Russell, does not believe even the most fundamental of "Arminian" theological tenets, namely their critique of predestinarian perspectives.

Russell depicts "Arminius" as rejecting the (anti-Calvinist) views that "merit" can influence election and that good works can similarly change our "predestined" fate. For "Arminius," it is not possible that "we may attaine . . . power salvation to gaine, / By working it our selves." This confusing set of seemingly contradictory religious beliefs is shown, however, to be simply another aspect of what Russell sees as the double-dealing and false nature of Arminianism in general, i.e., saying one thing while meaning another. As Russell writes: "And yet (what positively he thus denyes)/ By necessary consequence implyes" (sig. B4ᵛ).

Although Russell clearly alludes to questions of Arminian theology, he undercuts the seriousness of the religious issue by showing the insincerity of the Arminian pretense to Protestant religious beliefs. He continually stresses the political motives that animate this theological Arminianism. The references to theology in *The Spy* confuse rather than clarify the religious differences between Arminians and Calvinists. As with "Arminius Between Truth and Heresie," Russell's point seems to be that Arminianism is important not because it threatens Calvinist religion, but because it is aligned with Catholicism and other more general anti-Protestant beliefs. Arminianism is a danger because its over-arching position involves heresy, duplicity, and deception. As with Catholicism, Arminianism represents falseness and deceit. It stands in opposition to the true Protestant faith and cannot be trusted. But Russell goes further than this. In the rest of the pamphlet, he situates the Arminian crisis in the context of both national and international political concerns. In the lines quoted above, Russell looks back over the decades from the Vorstius controversy to the present. He desires an end to religious controversy, which in his view can only lead to civil unrest. He locates the origins of English Arminianism (as does the author of "Arminius Between Truth and Heresie") in the disputes over Arminianism in the Netherlands. Later, Russell specifically refers to Oldenbarnavelt and to his "treacherous designes" and asks why England does not appear to have learned the lesson of Barnavelt's sedition (sig. C4^r).

Finally, Russell conceives of the Arminian threat in England as emerging from the international situation. He sees this as being related to the continued menace, throughout the reigns of James and Charles, of Catholic Spain ("To Spanish thraldome upon Spanish wheeles?," sig. A^v).[80] For Russell, Arminianism is, as it was in the propaganda against Oldenbarnavelt, linked to "popery" and to Spanish power. He describes his intentions in writing *The Spy* as being motivated by "hate of Spanish treason, and true zeale / Unto the good of Church and Commonweale" (sig. A2^r).

What Russell sees is the political consequences of the discussion of Arminianism in the public sphere. The worry is that Arminianism will undermine both the Church and State, but the problem has to do less with theology or doctrine than with concerns about influence and interference. The effect of Arminianism in England has been mainly caused by Charles's religious views, specifically his censorship of anti-Arminian works and his preferment of Arminian clergy. Unlike his father, James I, whose policy was to "welcome a plurality of religious opinion within the broad framework of a national church,"[81] Charles consistently sought to "define" his own position (making others need to define theirs).[82] If James preferred some "high church clerics" Charles I promoted only such members. Rather than embrace plurality, Charles's insistence on defini-

---

[80]   See White, "The Rise of Arminianism Reconsidered"; and Fincham, "The Ecclesiastical Policy of James I."

[81]   David Smith, *Constitutional Royalism and the Search for Settlement, c. 1640–1649* (Cambridge, 1994), 24.

[82]   Smith, 26.

tion has led to a situation in which Arminians have gained the king's ear, and those who object to this party's dominance have been labeled "Puritan" subversives, intent on destroying the nation from within. The foldout plate to *The Spy*, with its warlike imagery and its representation of the Arminian party as a political fifth-column of sorts, attempts to reverse the terms of this assault. Rather than see the "Puritans" as the "opposition," the print suggests that it is the Arminians who occupy this role.

Russell's solution to the infiltration of Arminianism in England is to restrict the religious debate to the universities. This will lead to the cessation of all public discussion of Arminianism:

> Nor were these tenents in the schooles discust
> (Fit places where such paradoxes must
> Be controverted) but in publiq[ue] print
> (To make unlearned vulgar eyes to squint
> From truth on falsehood) all the land about
> These dang'rous books are cast, to make men doubt
> The truth receiv'd: and not resolving where
> Safely to stand, or to what side t'adhere,
> To fall as fast to *Rome* or atheisme . . . . (sig. C4ᵛ)

For Russell, Arminianism has achieved political currency and recognition through its constant circulation in pamphlet debates—and other places of public consumption, such as the pulpit. The overall effect of this has been to confuse dangerously "unlearned" and "vulgar" people who are incapable of distinguishing between "truth" and "falsehood," or between the reality of religious conflict and the polemic use of it for other than strictly religious ends. According to Russell, the "danger" of Arminianism lies in its capacity to mislead the common people, transforming the "true" religion into extremes of popery or atheism. When Arminianism enters the public sphere it distorts the "Truth" and promotes "Error." It creates civil unrest by the promulgation of religious falsehoods—that disguise true political motives.

In their various studies of *The Spy*, David Colclough, Andrew McCrae, and Cyndia Clegg similarly stress the political interpretation of Russell's pamphlet.[83] They collectively view the text of *The Spy* (none of them directly comment on the engraving) as presenting an argument: against the "political" uses of Arminianism; in favor of free speech; and for the resisting the negative characterization of Calvinists as Puritans. According to Colclough, the issue at the heart of the Puritan opposition in the 1620s was the debate over "when and for whom truly free speech was appropriate."[84] Colclough sees Russell's pamphlet as opposing the "increasing encroachment upon the liberties of the people and the security of the commonwealth." He argues that Russell's primary concern was to link the continued dominance of Spanish and Catholic influences at court with the "rise of the anti-Calvinist faction in the Church of England."[85] For Russell, Colclough contends, Arminianism was simply another form of popery and the solution to the problem of confessional strife lay in open debate in which criticism of the monarch and his policies could be freely expressed.

McCrae describes Puritan writers in the Caroline era as willfully conflating "religious and political threats." The Puritans in particular attempted to "stigmatize" their opponents, "as they insistently suggest[ed] the interrelated religious and political dangers associated with the spectre of Arminianism." In the 1630s, Puritans used the "structures of antipopery" to argue against their "opponents *within* the English Church."[86] McCrae finds that those who were negatively labeled as Puritans were especially willing to "label Laud and the episcopate as Arminians, and to dismiss the doctrine as 'in truth meere Popery.'" Such a strategy was, however, primarily about political "opportunism." According to John Selden, "we charge the prelatical clergie with popery to make them odious though wee know they are guilty of no such thing."[87] McCrae views the

---

[83]   See Colclough, *Freedom of Speech in Early Stuart England*; McCrae, *Literature, Satire, and the Early Stuart State*; and Clegg, *Press Censorship in Caroline England*.

[84]   Colclough, *Freedom of Speech*, 118. Colclough's discussion of Russell's pamphlet occurs in the context of a longer chapter on freedom of speech, the bulk of which focuses on the Puritan polemicist and radical pamphleteer, Thomas Scott.

[85]   Colclough, ibid, 118.

[86]   McCrae, *Literature, Satire, and the Early Stuart State*, 195.

[87]   McCrae, ibid, 195. The reference is to: John Selden, *Table Talk of John Selden*, Sir Frederick Pollock, ed., (London, 1927): 99. It is quoted in John Sommerville, *Royalists and Patriots: Politics and Ideology in England 1603–1640* (London, 1999).

"political charge" of such attacks as interweaving "anti-court discourse" with "ecclesiastical polemic." He suggests that the problem of Arminianism had as much (if not more) to do with the "subjects liberties" as with anything specific to Church reform.[88]

Finally, for Clegg, *The Spy* is best seen as the "epitome of the kind of 'schismaticall and hereticall books' that the London Stationers saw fit not to "meddle with."[89] It was clearly "intended for the English market since it addresses Parliament," but was "printed abroad to avoid the ecclesiastical licensers, certainly necessary since it openly made scandalous claims about the Durham House clerics and libeled the Duke of Buckingham."[90] The purpose of *The Spy*, Clegg surmises, was to "provide Parliament and the Crown with the knowledge requisite for good government." It connects "anti-Catholic, anti-Arminian, anti-Durham House, anti-Spanish, and anti-Buckingham sentiments."[91]

The version of Arminianism that *The Spy* offers, Clegg suggests, is a "popular one." It is grounded in the "central difference between Protestant and Roman soeteriology articulated first by Luther—that salvation came by faith rather than works (merit)—and refined by John Calvin and Theodore Beza—that salvation was effected not by man's choice of faith but by God's will."[92] For Clegg, however, *The Spy* is less concerned with "theological disputation" than with the ways that Arminianism has infected "silly soules" as it has spread from the continent into England.[93] The "real" objection to the "rise of English Arminianism is that its political divisiveness makes way for a Spanish conquest." "From this perspective," Clegg continues, "the English agents of Arminianism, dangerous though they may be on their own account, threaten England because their political ambitions unwittingly make them tools of the devil's agents—the Pope and Spain. That the Pope, the King of Spain, and the Arminians have succeeded in weakening England, the poem claims, is evidenced in the Duke of Buckingham's failed military campaign on the French Isle of Ré."[94]

---

[88] McCrae, ibid, 195.
[89] Clegg, *Press Censorship in Caroline England*, 49. The reference is to: SP 16/142 art. 22, *PRO*.
[90] Clegg, 49.
[91] Clegg, 49.
[92] Clegg, 50–51.
[93] Clegg, 51.
[94] Clegg, 51.

What these authors confirm is the continued dominance of anti-popish discourse in Puritan "oppositional" writing. They specifically connect the "rise" of Arminianism to concerns about James's and Charles's seemingly pro-Catholic foreign and domestic policies. They suggest that, far from caring about the intricacies of theological debates over predestination, Russell's motive in writing *The Spy* was much more involved in the continued problem of international conflict, throughout the 1620s, and with Spain and France in particular. Russell worried that the Caroline authorities were bent on suppressing Calvinist "opposition" and that Charles's anti-predestinarian proclamations were designed to suppress all criticism in the public sphere.

VI.

In the foregoing examination of the representation of Arminianism in *Sir John van Oldenbarnavelt* and two anti-Arminian political prints from the late 1620s, I have argued that the problem of Arminianism had less to do with theological doctrine than its political consequences. I find the play and prints express the way that Arminianism was understood outside of the narrower circles of the Caroline authorities and in the popular imagination. In such contexts, Arminianism was associated with a whole range of social, political, and religious ills. These included the continued problem of popery, both at home and abroad, a general concern about James's and Charles's pro-Catholic and pro-Spanish foreign and domestic policies, anxieties about freedom of speech, and worries about religious and political censorship.

Although it is difficult to generalize from this evidence, what these materials suggest is the *possibility* that, for most English men and women, the issue of Arminianism in England was mainly political. Or at least that matters of theology were always secondary to political concerns. As Russell stresses, Arminian theology should be discussed in the "schools" (i.e., at Oxford and Cambridge) and in the schools alone. The debate about Arminianism in the public sphere is, Russell intimates, confusing to the general English populace because it has collapsed distinctions between theology on the one hand and politics and satire on the other. In the process, a difference over theology (Arminian vs. Calvinist) has been transformed into a difference over politics. The effect has been to make "Arminianism" stand in for a whole host of political and satirical consequences that have little to do with theological speculation. What the political plays and prints on the subject of Arminianism that this essay has surveyed implicitly suggest is that, Arminianism has become a problem in England precisely *because* it has been so polemicized and politicized.

For Fletcher and Massinger, the problem lay outside of England, though the analogy between Oldenbarnavelt's pro-Spanish sympathies and those of James I was present as well. For the authors that this essay examines, and especially for Russell, the problem had become a specifically English one, but not, again, for primarily theological reasons. Arminianism was a concern because it had led to Arminian prominence in the religious establishment and in the public sphere. The only solution to this issue lay in the suppression of Arminian (and anti-Calvinist) polemic, and in the joint workings of the king and Parliament to promote unity and harmony in Church and State. That none of this occurred, and that, if anything, the debate about Arminianism and its polemic corollary Laudianism continued and intensified in the 1630s and 40s, is testament to the importance of popular polemic in shaping the religious and political conflicts of the decades leading up to, and including, the era of the English Civil Wars.

"It's good to talk: conversations between gods, men and beasts in Early Modern English versions of Lucian's 'Dialogues'"

Paul Hartle
St Catharine's College, University of Cambridge

THE "very *Proteus* of Wit"; thus Ferrand Spence, in the "Epistle Dedicatory" to his five-volume complete translation of Lucian, published in 1684–1685.[1] While the phrase may sound merely conventional, in Lucian's case it has a peculiar appropriateness, because, pre-eminently among classical writers, the Greek satirist, so popular in the long Renaissance, so almost unread since, is—to adapt Falstaff's account of Mistress Quickly—"neither fish nor flesh; a man knows not where to have [him]."[2] Janus-faced, Lucian provokes a combination of admiration and revulsion from the moment when his works first enter the marketplace of print (in Latin translation) in about 1470; between 1496 and 1550, the original Greek text was printed more than sixty times, while the number of

---

[1] *Lucian's Works, Translated from the Greek . . . by Ferrand Spence*, 5 Vols. (1684–85), Vol. 1, sig. C3ᵛ.

[2] *1 Henry 4*, 3.iii.127–28 (eds. S. Wells and G. Taylor, William Shakespeare, *The Complete Works*, (Oxford, 1988), 472).

Studies in Medieval and Renaissance History, 3rd Series, Vol. 11 (2014)

Latin versions exceeded two hundred by the same date:[3] Lucian was hot. For the humanists of the early sixteenth century, his witty and elegant prose offered a welcome model for young scholars: carefully expurgated selections were on the syllabus of the grammar schools of Winchester, Canterbury, Westminster, Eton, and St. Paul's,[4] but while Thomas Linacre (who taught Greek to Thomas More) encouraged students of the language to "read a little Lucian every day,"[5] in his *A New Catechism* (c.1560) Thomas Becon advised his exclusion from the curriculum as "wicked and ungodly."[6] In *The Boke Named the Governour* (1531), Sir Thomas Elyot (the probable translator of the first English version of the Dialogue *Cynicus*),[7] aimed to strike a balance:

> The next lesson wolde be some quicke and mery dialogues, elect out of Luciane, whiche be without ribawdry, or to moche skorning, for either of them is exactly to be eschewed, specially for a noble man, the one anoyeng the soule, the other his estimation concerning his gravitie . . . thus moche dare I say, that it were better that a childe shuld never rede any parte of Luciane than all Luciane.[8]

The problem was simple: not only did Lucian scoff directly at Christianity itself, but his scabrous mockery of both pagan religions and moral philosophy might be seen to offend against all sense of religious or ethical value. In Dryden's words (borrowed without acknowledgement from one of Lucian's editors, Gilbert Cousin),[9] "he doubted of every thing; weigh'd all Opinions, and adher'd to none of them; only us'd them, as they serv'd his occasion for the present Dialogue; and perhaps rejected

---

[3] See Christopher Robinson, *Lucian and His Influence in Europe* (Chapel Hill, 1979); C. R. Thompson, *The Translations of Lucian by Erasmus and St. Thomas More* (Ithaca, 1940), 3.

[4] Brenda M. Hosington, "'Compluria Opuscula Longe Festivissima': Translations of Lucian in Renaissance England," in Dirk Sacre and Jan Papy, eds. *Syntagmatia: Essays on Neo-Latin Literature in Honour of Monique Mund-Dopchie and Gilbert Tournoy* (Leuven, 2009), 187–205, at 194.

[5] Douglas Duncan, *Ben Jonson and the Lucianic Tradition* (Cambridge, 1979), 26.

[6] Duncan, *Ben Jonson and the Lucianic Tradition*, 82.

[7] See C. R. Thompson, ed., *Works of St. Thomas More* (New Haven, 1963–), vol. 3 Part 1 (1974), 140–41.

[8] Foster Watson, ed., *The Governour* (London, 1907), 36.

[9] See Duncan, *Ben Jonson and the Lucianic Tradition*, 50.

them in the next."[10] Whilst one admirer might write of him, "deos . . . et ridet et lacerat,"[11] that too readily transmuted into "[Deum] et ridet et lacerat." That particular admirer was Erasmus, and it is in him and his friend Thomas More that Lucian found his greatest humanist advocates. Each translated several dialogues, working in tandem, and their Latin versions were among the most often reprinted of their works in their lifetimes. For More, dedicating his *Cynicus* (and it was More's Latin that Elyot rendered English) to Thomas Ruthall, Henry VII's Royal Secretary, Lucian ranks among the foremost of those "qui Horatianum praeceptum impleuerit, uoluptatemque cum utilitate coniunxerit."[12] In *Utopia*, Hythloday assures us, the natives are "delyted wyth Lucianes mery conceytes and jestes."[13]

For Erasmus and More, Lucian offered a model of a space for independent thinking that might be opened by the form of dialogue, together with a brilliance in the deployment of irony which Dryden (no mean exponent himself) later acknowledged: "[N]o Man is so great a Master of Irony, as our Author: That Figure is not only a keen, but a shining Weapon in his Hand; it glitters in the Eyes of those it kills, his own God's his greatest Enemies, are not butchered by him, but fairly slain: they must acknowledge the Heroe in the stroke."[14] Lucian's influence on *Utopia* and *The Praise of Folly* is profound, not in local detail alone, but in the protean quality of those works, which dare to trifle with both secular and sacred authority in challenges whose humor disarms censure. In the ecclesiastical and monarchical context of the time, such challenges were dangerous—"circa Regna tonat," as Wyatt wrote, quoting Seneca's *Phaedra*—thunder surrounds the throne.[15]

Later sixteenth- and early seventeenth-century writers manifest the same divided response as their predecessors, although (as Gabriel Harvey

---

[10] *The Works of Lucian, translated from the Greek, by several eminent hands* (1711), 4 Vols., "The Life of Lucian," 1:26.

[11] Thompson, *The Translations of Lucian*, 21. Thompson gives the fullest account available of the two humanists' engagement with Lucian.

[12] More, *Works*, 3, 1:2.

[13] John O'Hagan, ed., and Raphe Robinson, trans., (1551), *Utopia* (London, 1910), 82.

[14] "The Life of Lucien," 42–43.

[15] The refrain of 'Who lyst his welthe and eas Retayne', in Kenneth Muir and Patricia Thomson, eds., *Collected Poems of Sir Thomas Wyatt* (Liverpool, 1969), 187–88.

commented in 1580), *"Lucian* [is] never so much" "studyed, as [he was] wonte"[16]—perhaps being placed on the first *Index Librorum Prohibitorum* in 1559 might have discouraged some.[17] Thomas Nashe finds him "admirably blest in the abundant giftes of art and nature [and yet an] abhominable Atheiste;"[18] In 1621 Richard Brathwaite casts *"Lucian* a professed enemy to Christ" as addressee of his "Third Satyre. Of Atheisme," condemning "thy lascivious works" in a tone more of sorrow than anger, since *"Ingenious* Lucian" is *"in all Morall knowledge excellent."*[19] Even the fiercely virtuous Samuel Sheppard, whose *"Lucians memoriall"* consigns Lucian to a Hades where "fishes worrie / Thy Ravens Soule" while "all the deathlesse Dieties [sic] / Laugh at thy dolor," in another epigram acknowledges "thy wilie hand" and "applaud[s] thy wit."[20]

---

[16] Duncan, *Ben Jonson and the Lucianic Tradition,* 84. Stern records Harvey's copy of Lucian, in the four-volume edition (Basle, 1563) by Gilbert Cousin [Gilbertus Cognatus], books which Harvey was to forfeit to Edmund Spenser, should Harvey fail to read several comical works in English (including Skelton) lent to him by the poet, on condition that he completed reading them over the last twelve days of 1578 (Virginia F. Stern, *Gabriel Harvey: A Study of His Life, Marginalia, and Library* [Oxford, 1979], 226, 228).   Harvey was nonetheless keen to use Lucian's atheism as a stick with which to beat his own pamphleteering enemies, Robert Greene and Thomas Nashe.   Greene he castigates as "a derider of all religions: a contemner of God, and man: a desperate Lucianist: an abhominable Aretinist: an Arch-Athiest [sic]:" (G. B. Harrison, ed., *Foure Letters and certeine Sonnets* [London, 1922], 40); Harvey's term "Lucianist" had been in use from 1573 (John Bridges, *The supremacie of Christian princes,* 354) and was still current in 1655 (Alexander Ross, *Pansebeia, or, A view of all religions in the world,* 234).   Nashe's writings "sauour whotly of the same Lucianicall breath" (*Pierces Supererogation* (1593),135–36); this second adjective (which may be Harvey's coinage) is also found in Robert Parsons, *A manifestation of the great folly and bad spirit of certayne in England* (1602), 92.   The notorious charge of atheism levelled against Marlowe is also expressed in terms of Harvey's glancing identification with the Greek writer: "Though *Greene* were a Iulian, and *Marlow* a Lucian: yet I would be loth, *He* [Nashe] should be an Aretin" (*A New Letter of Notable Contents* [1593], sig. D[r]).

[17] Hosington, "Compluria Opuscula Longe Festivissima," 188. Harvey himself characterized Lucian in 1592 as one of "that whole venemous and viperous brood, of old & new Raylers" (*Foure Letters,* 15).

[18] R. B. McKerrow, ed., revised by F. P. Wilson, *The Works of Thomas Nashe* (Oxford, 1966), 5 vols., 1:285.

[19] *Natures Embassie* (Boston, Lincs., 1877), 86, 93, 87.

[20] Samuel Sheppard, *Epigrams theological, philosophical, and romantick* (1651), "The Third Book: Epig. 23" (52); "The Fourth Book: Epig. 5," *"On* Lucians *true History,"* 72.

However, these are for the most part passing remarks. What I want to focus on now is the major task of bringing Lucian to an English readership.[21] This was work barely begun until the second quarter of the seventeenth century saw the posthumously published selections penned by Francis Hickes (eight dialogues and the *True Historie*),[22] and by Thomas Heywood (fifteen dialogues).[23] Only *Timon, or the Man-hater* is common to both writers. Heywood, a veritable factory of Early Modern literary production, concentrates on the *Dialogues of the Gods* (nine, including *The Judgment of Paris*) and is careful to exclude scatology and too much bawdry, while affixing a moralistic "Argument" to each; the two dialogues dealing with Jupiter's abduction of Ganymede, teasingly erotic in Lucian, are decisively labelled *"Joves Masculine love this Fable reprehends"* and *"Base sordid lust in man [this Fable] reprehends."*[24] Like many before him, Heywood regrets that Lucian's atheism damns his talent, offering this elegy in *The Hierarchie of the Blessed Angells* in 1635:

> Yet for the love I to his learning owe,
> This funerall Farewell I on him bestow.
> Unhappy *Lucian*, what sad passionate Verse
> Shall I bestow upon the marble stone
> That covers thee? How shall I deck thy Herse?[25]

Francis Hickes was brought up as an arras-maker, and the family held supervisory office to maintain the royal tapestries. But he appears to have spent his later years in *"a countrie retirement,"* translating Thucydides and Herodian in addition to Lucian out of *"a true love[r] of Schollers,*

---

[21]   See Hosington, "Compluria Opuscula Longe Festivissima," 193–99. For more general surveys of Lucian's influence in Britain, see Gilbert Highet, *The Classical Tradition* (Oxford, 1949), esp. 123–24, 304–5; J. A. K. Thomson, *The Classical Background of English Literature* (London, 1948), 129–30, 139–41, and *Classical Influences on English Prose* (London, 1956), 193–206, 273–74); Peter France, ed., *The Oxford Guide to Literature in English Translation* (Oxford, 2000), 390.

[22]   *Certaine Select Dialogues of Lucian: Together with his True Historie, Translated from the Greeke into English* (Oxford, 1634).

[23]   *Pleasant Dialogues and Dramma's, Selected out of Lucian, Erasmus, Textor, Ovid, &c* (1637).

[24]   Heywood, *Pleasant Dialogues*, 96, 101.

[25]   *The Hierarchie of the Blessed Angells* (1635), 1:506–10 (14).

and Learning," albeit *"indeed no profest scholler"* himself.[26] In his prefatory "Life," Hickes proclaims his aim that Lucian be "in some sort vindicated from certaine grosse Aspersions, heretofore cast upon him" (sig. Bʳ); while he cannot deny Lucian's blasphemy, *"that his whole workes so much admired and approv'd of by the most learned in all ages, both for wit and language should be therefore utterly banisht from the world, and condemn'd to a perpetuall obscurity, or those parts of him denyed the light in which there is no such impietie found, but on the contrary, many rules and documents both of vertue and good learning . . . seemes unto mee a most unjust, and partiall censure"* (sig. [B3]ʳ/ᵛ). Therefore, he concludes, *"it is no such impious thing, as some of the rigid censurers of these times would persuade us, to make a good use even of the worst Writers, yea and that if occasion serve, in matter of divinity"* (sig. [B3]ᵛ). Improbably, Lucian the skeptic steps into the pulpit.

Hickes's versions were reissued in 1663 and 1664 accompanying Jasper Mayne's more substantial and complementary *Part of Lucian Made English*, translations actually completed, according to Mayne whose word there is no cause to doubt, a quarter of a century earlier at Christ Church Oxford, forming a composite volume which can for the first time claim to be an English Lucian, the dignity of which is attested both by its publication at Oxford, bearing the University's arms on its title page, and by William Faithorne's serene bust of the satirist, who gazes directly at the reader, presented without embarrassment as *"sharpe* Lucian *who reform'd yᵉ Times."*[27] Mayne dedicated his work to the duke of Newcastle, a royalist peer whose sufferings for the Stuarts were recognized at the Restoration, but even in the looser moral climate of the time, his long and careful "Epistle Dedicatory" bears witness to his sense of the risk incurred in publishing his Lucian, now that he is no longer an Oxford student but archdeacon of Chichester and chaplain to Charles II:

> *For if I be thus* censured *for turning a* few pieces *of him into* English
> *. . . your* Excellency *knowes, I was no* Divine, *but a* young Student *of*

---

[26] See *ODNB*; [Thomas] Hickes, "To the Honest and Judicious Reader," sig. A3ʳ.

[27] *Part of Lucian made English from the Originall. In the Yeare 1638* (Oxford, 1663), Plate facing title page. Faithorne's bust became the model for the plate in the two editions of Cotton's *Burlesque upon Burlesque* of 1675 and 1686/7 (see below); the 1675 version is plate 1 in this article.

this Colledge, when these Sheets *past through my* Pen. . . . *How am I to be* accused . , .? . . . *[H]e Wrote . . .* Obscœne *. . . and* Meretricious Dilaogues [sic], *not fit for the* Eyes *or* Eares *of a* Chaste, *or* Christian Reader. These *. . . I have left with their* owne Curtaine *drawne before them* [i.e. untranslated], *and have not held a* Candle *to the* mysterious *doings of a* Stewes (sig. [A7]ᵛ).

Arguing, with even more hyperbole than Hickes, that we may "*owe our* Christianity, *where the* true God *hath succeeded such a* multitude *of false, . . . to his* facetious wit" (sig. [A6]ʳ), Mayne positions himself and his Lucian not only in opposition to the critical "Vineger *men, at whose* Births *sure* Saturne *raign'd, and convey'd his* leaden Influence *into their* Morosity *and* Manners" (sig. [A5]ᵛ), but specifically to the manners and language of the now abolished English Republic:

[A] canting Generation *of men, whose* Rhetorick *was as* rude, & mechanick *as their persons, [did]* defile *the English Tongue with their* Republick *words, which are most* immusicall *to the* Eare, *and* scarce significant *to a* Monarchicall *understanding. Words which are the meer* Excrements *of Language; which proceeded from the late* Body politick *of this* Vncivilized Nation, *and were not allowed their legitimate* concoxion, *but broke forth into the World with* Brutishness, *and* Rebellion. Coyned, & *minted by those* Seditious, Rump Grammarians, *who did put their own* impressions *to the Kings* Silver, *and so committed* Treason *against their* Prince, *and their own* rude stamp *and* sense *to their* Goth *and* Vandall *words; and so committed* Treason *against His* good people (sig. A4ʳ).

For Mayne, good language (including good translated language) is authenticated, like the national coinage, only by the king's head, and it needs to be a king whose head is still on his shoulders; without this guarantee, words are not only inelegantly unmusical, but "scarce significant," signs without referents.

Mayne's work is succeeded a decade later by Charles Cotton's *Burlesque upon Burlesque: OR, THE Scoffer Scoft. Being some of LUCIANS DIALOGUES Newly put into ENGLISH FUSTIAN* (1675), a burlesque version of the "Dialogues of the Gods," trading on Cotton's commercially successful travesty of Virgil, *Scarronides* (1664–65), but based not on the original but on Nicolas Perrot's very popular French version of Lucian's works;[28] these knockabout comic transvestings of Lucian have an energetic Bakhtinian physicality about them, but proved less popular than *Scarronides*,[29] although an anonymous but acknowledged imitation, *The Scoffer Scoft. The Second Part*, appeared in 1684, printed for Edward Goldin and Charles Corbet, initially in the form of travesties of individual Dialogues "*Publish'd every* Tuesday *and* Friday" in January and February.[30]

Two declared "compleat" Lucians round out the century: Ferrand Spence's five-volume *Lucian's Works, Translated from the Greek* (1684–85) and John Dryden's edited collaborative four-volume *The Works of Lucian, Translated from the Greek, by several Eminent Hands*, which, although not printed until 1711, was begun, according to the publisher, "*before and in the Year* 1696, *and* [completed] *in the subsequent Years*" (sig. [A3ʳ]). Spence's version has been much overlooked, partly because its piecemeal printing leads to an extremely messy bibliographic status, and it is far from a common book.[31] The two copies in institutional Cambridge, in St. John's College and the University Library, are both defective, while my own three assorted bound-up tomes, although between them containing all but a single leaf of the five volumes issued, are severally mispaginated and misbound.

Spence was unlucky. The publication of his version coincided with the death of Charles II and the far from straightforward or fortunate succession of his hapless brother James. His publisher piously hoped to

---

[28]   *Lucien. De la Traduction de N. Perrot Sᴿ D'Ablancourt,* first published at Paris in 1654, with further editions in 1655, 1659 (Leiden), 1674 and 1683 (Amsterdam).

[29]   Only one further edition was issued in Cotton's lifetime (in 1686/7), in contrast with the six editions of the collected *Scarronides* (1666, 1667, 1670, 1672, 1678, 1682).

[30]   In the same year, printed for William Bateman, appeared *Lucians Dialogues (Not) from the Greek: Done Into English Burlesque,* in two Parts issued together. With the exception of the two title pages, the sheets of this volume are identical with those of *The Scoffer Scoffed, The Second Part,* except that the 'Epistle to the Reader' is sewn in not at the beginning but before 'The Second Part', preceding the Dialogue between Menippus and Cerberus rather than that between Mercury and the Sun. It is impossible to ascertain priority between the two issues.

[31]   Hosington, for example, observing ("Compluria Opuscula Longe Festivissima," 203–4) that "the *Dialogues of the Courtesans* . . . never saw the light of day before the 1711 translation," has missed Spence's version in Volume 5:293–335.

> have no reason to doubt of my satisfaction in the business, especially,
> when I consider, how kindly Lucian has been entertain'd in all Ages
> and Countreys in the very Disguises of his Translatours, and that the
> greater and better part of him, was never yet turn'd into our Mother
> Tongue, and how this present time is more than ordinary prone to
> and fond of Satyr, his Company will certainly be sought after by all
> sorts of Persons. . . . I am so publick a spirited person [sic], that I am
> willing to communicate him to the Age (sig. [x2]ᵛ).

But Spence's racy prose had perhaps missed its historical moment, and the
"Epistle Dedicatory" to his friend Brian Turner comments sharply on the
contemporary hypocrisy of "the *Grand Reformers* of our Age, who whilst
in *Publick* they Exclaim against the *Lewdness of the Times*, yet at the same
Instant are Contriving to *Act* and *Improve* in *Private* all the *Enormities* of
the Ancients" (sigs. A4ᵛ–[A5]ʳ). Spence has, he acknowledges, rehabited
Lucian in the fashions of the day, fitted him "to be entertain'd in any
Civil Company" (sig. [A5]ᵛ); "he is (as it were) born again, and *Baptiz'd*
into our *Language*, that he may be able to pass *Safely* and *Handsomly* in a
Christian Commonwealth" (sig. [A5]ʳ).

Like Mayne before him, Spence is a conservative royalist, and by the
mid-1680s we can probably call him a Tory, since one of the prefatory
eulogies to Volume 3 pauses to lambast "*the* Whiggs *unequall'd Crimes.*"[32]
Spence's own "Epistle Dedicatory" launches a savage attack upon "Our
Preaching *Fanatical* Gang [who] think because they are *Familiar* with
God *Almighty* in their *prayers*, they may top upon him too in their
Actions, Especially on Princes, his *Vicegerents*" (sig. B3ʳ/ᵛ); this "Gang"
turns out to be the Earl of Shaftesbury and the nonconformist ministers Richard Baxter and Stephen Lobb (sigs. B4ᵛ-[B6]ᵛ), leaders of Whig
thought. Dryden too will later use his preface as an opportunity to attack
"*Calvinists* or *Quakers*," whom he sees as heirs to Lucian's earliest detractors, "the first *Christians*, with their cropt Hair, their whining Voices,
melancholy Faces, mournful Discourses, [and] nasty Habits" (20), sharing the same "*want of Charity*, . . . *presumption of meddling with God's
Government, and . . . Spirit of Calumny*" (14), quite unlike the admirably
robust "*Roman Catholicks*, or *Church of* England-Men" (20).

---

[32] D. M., "To his Worthy Friend Mr. *FERRAND SPENCE*, On His Excellent
Translation of Lucian," sig. [A6]ʳ.

Given their similar affiliations, one might have expected that Dryden would have treated Spence with some courtesy, but publishing rivalry proved the stronger motive, and Dryden's "Life of Lucian" viciously impugns Spence's abilities in both Greek and English:

> *Lucian*, that is the sincere Example of *Attique* Eloquence . . . is only a mass of *Solecism*, and mere Vulgarisms in Mr. *Spence.* I do not think it worth my while, to rake into the filth of so scandalous a Version; nor had I vouchsaf'd so much as to take notice of it, had it not been so gross an Affront to the Memory of *Lucian*, and so great a scandal to our Nation . . . he makes him speak in the Stile and Language of a *Jack-Pudding*, not a Master of Eloquence . . . for the fine Raillery, and *Attique* Salt of *Lucian*, we find the gross Expressions of *Billings-Gate*, or *More-Fields* and *Bartholomew* Fair (53–61).

Snobbish and commercially motivated as this transparently is, Dryden is right to claim that Spence's Lucian speaks in the voice of a contemporary Londoner. In this ventriloquial act, Spence is building upon foundations laid by his predecessors; Heywood's Mercury complains about having to clerk not only for the Gods' "Consistorie," but also "at the Bar" of Pluto's "generall Sessions," ecclesiastical and legal assemblies of seventeenth-century England (115); Hickes dresses one pompous Pooh-Bah in a "ruffe" and "purple cassock" (99), while his Jupiter has become so unintimidating that even a "knight of the post" (151)—a professional perjurer—contemns him; in Jasper Mayne's world, meanwhile, Bacchus "is the Leader of a Morris [dance]," and the Colossus of Rhodes is so amply-buttocked as to "take up the whole wooll-sacke" (274), traditional parliamentary seat of the English Lord Chancellor.

But Spence goes well beyond these occasional allusions, immersing his Lucian into the same world of seventeenth-century idiom and social context as that of his several burlesquers; figures are variously and colourfully berated as "Buffle-Head" (1:113), "swinging Bully-Rock" (3:221) and "but a Taper'd Scull'd Gallant, . . . an Effeminate Doodle" (1:177). In a brilliant exchange between Bacchus and Apollo, the former advises the latter to beware of that "strange Belswagger" Priapus:

> *Bacchus.* Nay, and thou'rt a good plumpt, bonny *Sawny* too: Wherefore if he comes near you, have a care he does not fall to Gambetting.

Apollo. To Gambetting! Faith, I would not advise him to rummage in my Quarters; for notwithstanding my white Wigg, I carry a Bow and Arrows, and as I look out very sharp, he will find it a hard matter, to surprize my Back-Door. (1:102)

A "sawny" is a fool, first recorded in *OED* in 1699, while "gambetting" seems likeliest to be from chess "gambit," the opening play (*OED* from 1656 as a noun only)—this is the latest 'street'.

While Spence's comedy probably owes something to Wycherley's famous 'China Scene'—"Wife, he is coming into you the back way." "Let him come, and welcome, which way he will"[33]—the influence of Cotton's burlesque version of Lucian's Dialogue (76-85) is also evident:

Apol. Well! well! but he were best take heed
How he attaques my *Maiden-head.*
His mighty *Trap-stick* cannot scare-us;
For we have good Yew-bow, and Arrows,
As well as a white Wig to tempt him,
And if he draw, he will repent him.
Besides, I'me so set round with light,
And am withal so quick of sight,
That much I do not need to fear,
To be surprized in my Rear.[34]

One can see why Dryden may have felt that Spence fell short of "that Nice and *Delicate Raillery*" which he claimed to embody in his English version (Vol. 1, C3ᵛ). But what Spence grasped as essential was that satire find its mark, and that refinement and decorum were not the way to attain it. As 'J.P.' wrote in his pointedly entitled '*To Mr.* Spence *on his Accurate Translation of* Lucian', prefacing Volume 4, "For Satyr must be still allow'd / To speak the Language of the Vice corrected: / The Crime would else be not the Crime detected: / And thus our Ladies all despise / The Mirror that resemblance falsifies." In the dying decadence of Charles

---

[33] *The Country-Wife* (1675), 4.i.533–35 (M. Summers, ed., *The Complete Works* [Soho, 1924], 4 Vols., 2:62).

[34] "Dialogue. *Apollo* and *Bacchus*," 76–85 (*Burlesque upon Burlesque* [1675], 183).

II's "Obscæne Rout/Of English Whores" (Vol. 4, [A7]ᵛ), there was no place for the mealy-mouthed. In the diarist Evelyn's powerful evocation:

> I am never to forget the unexpressable luxury, & prophanesse, gaming, & all dissolution, and as it were total forgetfullnesse of God (it being Sunday Evening) which this day sennight, I was witnesse of; the King, sitting & toying with his Concubines Portsmouth, Cleaveland, & Mazarine: &c: A french boy singing love songs, in that glorious Gallery, . . . a sceane of uttmost vanity; and surely as they thought would never have an End: six days after was all in the dust.[35]

Lucian had always offered a model for political and social iconoclasm, in his attacks on both earthly and heavenly hierarchies, on the vanities of wealth and of desire, in his relentless emphasis on death's democracy. Even his admirers saw the dangers in this, while his detractors swiftly moved to align him with the Renaissance bugbear, Machiavelli; the early seventeenth-century Divine Thomas Adams proclaimed that "*Sinnes* text is from Hels *Scriptum est*: taken out of the Devils *Spell*; either *Lucian* his old *Testament*, or *Machiavell* his new."[36] In his *Religio Medici*, Thomas Browne picks up Adams's idea and runs with it a little further: "I confess every Countrey hath its *Machiavell*, every Age its *Lucian*, whereof common heads must not heare, nor more advanced judgements too rashly venture on: 'tis the Rhetorick of Satan, and may pervert a loose or prejudicate beleefe."[37] Less soberly, Nathaniel Lee in his tragedy of *Cæsar Borgia* (1680) has Machiavel breathlessly celebrate the triply and generationally incestuous Borgias, "Such a triumvirate of Lawless Lovers, / Such Rivals as out-do even *Lucian*'s Gods!"[38] In the world of Early Modern England, Lucian's spokesman Menippus could be used to expose the ills of a whole social hierarchy: ". . . in the Courts of their Kings, adulteries, murthers, treacheries, rapines, perjuries, feares, and false-heartednesse towards their friends . . . what should I tell you of other men, of whom some were breakers up of houses, some wranglers in law-suits, some

---

[35] Ed. E. S. De Beer, *The Diary* (Oxford, 1955), 6 Vols., 4:413–14.
[36] "The Fatall Banket" (*Workes* [1629], 167).
[37] Geoffrey Keynes, ed., *The Works of Sir Thomas Browne* (London, 1928), 4 Vols.,1:31.
[38] 1.i.277–78 (7).

usurers, some exactors" (Hickes, 19). In the context of its first printing (in 1634), Hickes's more detailed account of the life of rulers (in the zoomorphic voice of Lucian's Cockerel) would read uncomfortably like an account of the "Personal Rule" of Charles I:[39]

> What should I rehearse unto you . . . their feares, griefes, and suspicions; the hatred and conspiracies of those that are nearest to them, their short and unsound sleepes; their fearefull dreames, their variable thoughts, and ever evill hopes, their troubles and vexations, their collections of money [1634 was the year of Ship Money], and judgment of controversies [the Court of Star Chamber was the principal instrument of the Personal Rule from 1629], their militarie affaires, and warlike expeditions, their edicts and proclamations, their leagues and treaties [Charles's military and diplomatic failures from 1625-1630 in the Thirty Years War], their reckonings and accounts, which suffer them not once to enjoy a quiet dreame, but they are compel'd alone to have an eye in all things, & a thousand businesses to trouble them (Hickes, 65).

It is then unsurprising that the cobbler Micyllus lists among the benefits of Hades, "no calling for debts, no paying of subsidies" (Hickes, 81).

Remarkably, one case of the impact of Hickes's Lucian on a reader at the dawn of the English Republic survives, in the figure of William Walwyn, renowned as a leading Leveller thinker and writer.[40] In John Price's *Walwins Wiles* (1649), the following story is told of Walwyn and a companion (9):

> Having once upon a Fast day (as his usual manner was both upon those, and the Lords days) gone from place to place, hearing here a

---

[39] See Kevin Sharpe, *The Personal Rule of Charles I* (New Haven, 1992).

[40] See Nigel Smith, "The Charge of Atheism and the Language of Radical Speculation, 1640–1660", in Michael Hunter and David Wootton, eds., *Atheism from the Reformation to the Enlightenment* (Oxford, 1992), 131–58. For other work on influences (including Lucian's) on what might (cautiously) be described as atheism in the period, see George T. Buckley, *Atheism in the English Renaissance* (Chicago, 1932), 5–8; Michael Hunter, "The Problem of 'Atheism' in Early Modern England," *Transactions of the Royal Historical Society*, 5th ser., (1985), 135–57, at 144; M. J. Buckley, *At the Origins of Modern Atheism* (New Haven, 1987), 46.

little, and there a little what the Ministers said, making it the subject
matter of his prophane scorning and jeering, came at last to his own
house with one of his supposed Fast disciples, (though even at that
time his heart did rise against *Walwins* wickedness, but having got
within him, he did resolve, though with much reluctance of spirit, to
fathom the deep devout hypocrisie of this man for a through detec-
tion of him,) being at home, he fetcht out that prophane scurrilous
Lucians Dialogue, come (said he) let us go read that which hath
something in it, *Here is more wit in this* (saith he) *then in all the Bible.*

This very circumstantial attack drew a defensive salvo from Humphrey Brooke (*The Charity of Church-Men* [1649], 334–35):

'Tis true, that *Lucian* was taken off a shelf either by me, or Mr *Walwyn,* I can't say which, and that we read one of his Dialogues, which
was the Tyrant, or Megapenthes; and afterwards commended it as
very usefull in the time he lived; when by setting forth the foul-
nesse and deformity of Tyrannie in a third person, he informed the
people of the wickednesse of such under whom they lived: but that
any comparison was made between that and the Bible, is as false
as in it self ridiculous . . . Besides, Mr *Walwyn* prefer'd *Lucian* (as
the Pamphlet saies) for wit, before the Bible: 'Tis well known, that
Mr *Walwyn* hath the lowest esteem of wit that may be, counting
it the lightest, volatile and superficiall part of a man; whence his
observation is, that commonly those that have most wit, have most
wickednesse. . . . What ground is there for the least supposall that
he should for that prefer *Lucian* before the Bible?

Brooke's barely convincing casuistry carries less weight than Walwyn's
direct denial of the allegation in *Walwins Wiles,* in his own *Walwyns Just
Defence* (1649):

So in short time, we came to my house, where we went on dis-
coursing, from one thing to another, and amongst other things, of
the wisdom of the heathen, how wise and able they were in those
things, unto which their knowledge did extend; and what pains they
took to make men wise, vertuous, and good common-wealths men .
. . with which kinde of discourse, he was very much affected, though

it did not appear he had been accustomed to the reading of humane authors; which for twenty yeers before I had been, but I used them alwayes in their due place . . . and truly, I do not see I have cause to repent me of taking liberty in this kinde, having never in my life, I blesse God; made an ill use thereof, amongst which *Lucian* for his good ends, in dis[c]overing the vanity of things in worldly esteem, I like very well, whereof I can read only such as are translated into *English;* such a wise Jesuite I am, that withall [sic] my skill, I cannot construe three lines of any *Latin* author, nor do understand any, except such common proverbs, as are more familiar in *Latine* then in *English,* which sometimes I use not to dignifie my selfe, but because of the pertinency of them in some occasions . . . I am certain most of the university men in England, and most of the liberaries are not without all *Lucians* works, some whereof, as I am informed, are much more offencive to Christianity then these in *English.*

And why then I might not without blemish read one of his dialogues to this, Mr. *Richard Price,* I cannot yet perceive? as I take it we read that which is called his tyrant; a discourse, though possibly not in all things justifiable, yet such as he might have made a better use of, being so pointed against ambition, pride and coveteousnesse as he might have been the better for it whilst he lived . . . I was far from any such thought of impious blasphemy, as to say, here is more wit in this (meaning *Lucian)* then in all the bible: all our discourse was before my wife and children, and my friend, and a maid servant . . . *I* dare appeale to them all if ever they heard me value, any, or all the Books, or Sermons either, in the world Comparable to the Bible . . . (9–10)

Since Walwyn confesses that he could read in English alone, the only version of Lucian's dialogue he could have known was Francis Hickes's 'The Infernall Ferrie, or, the Tyrant,'[41] and as Nigel Smith observes, Walwyn's use of translations "thus justif[ies] the perennial fear of the privileged that the vulgar should not be permitted to have ideas that they might use to a subversive end . . . [ideas] which were introduced into a radical religious context where they were largely unknown and could be employed in a radically critical way."[42]

---

[41] Hickes, *Certaine Select Dialogues*, 71–88.
[42] Smith, "Atheism and the Language of Radical Speculation," 147.

Jasper Mayne's loyalist attack on the language of early republican-ism has already been cited; more dazzling is Alexander Brome's 1661 ver-sion of *Cynicus*, where the ragged Philosopher denounces the wealthy for their lack of social responsibility:

> . . . poor Men,
> . . . your fellow Creatures, [who] have been
> Made of the self same matter, and inspir'd
> With the same soul, and form, and have acquir'd
> The same perfections too, and by their birth,
> Have as good interest in what's here on Earth,
> As the Great'st He[43]

That last instantly recognizable phrase is from Colonel Rainsbor-ough's famous plea for universal suffrage in the *Putney Debates* of the Army in 1647: "For really I think that the poorest he that is in England hath a life to live, as the greatest he; and therefore truly, sir, I think it's clear, that every man that is to live under a government ought first by his own consent to put himself under that government."[44]

By the later seventeenth century, the two sides of British politics, as we have already seen from the language of Whigs and Tories in Spence, have metamorphosed into a new sense of "party," and Spence evenhandedly deplores on the one hand a Jupiter in an "outragious Passion, . . . [fear-ing] he had lost a great deal of Prerogative [a royal power hotly debated in Charles II's reign]" (1:53) and on the other "those great Parliaments . . . [where] one takes delight in undoing what another does" (3:187). Struggling to order their affairs, the Olympian Gods engage in a flurry of bureaucratic activity: ". . . it seems good to the Council, and present Assembly, to convene a Parliament against the next Winter-solstice . . . to Elect a Committee . . . [to] exercise their Commission . . ." (Spence, 4:128). Aficionados of both British and American politics will estimate the likelihood of effective governmental action.

Translating the same passage as Hickes on the woes of monarchs, Spence goes further, to develop a brilliant argument on the theatricality of power:

---

[43] *"An Essay of the Contempt of Greatnesse, being a Dialogue of* Lucian *made English,"* 296–302 (R. R. Dubinski, ed., *Poems* [Toronto, 1982], 2 Vols., 1:329).

[44] A. S. P. Woodhouse, ed., *Puritanism and Liberty* (London, 1938), 53.

Add hereto the Spight of a Mistress [remember Evelyn's "Portsmouth, Cleaveland, & Mazarine &c"], . . . The Jealousy of a Favourite, that has been rais'd too high: The fear of a Sedition of the People, or of the conspiracy of Grandees [the Exclusion Crisis 1678-1681]; the fatal Example of Princes de-/thron'd, Assassinated [Charles I] . . . and other Tragical Histories, which Ring and Eccho upon the Theatres. . . . they are only *Comedians*, who under a Royal Cloak hide the Soul of a Skip-Jack, & shew the smalness of their Foot in the greatness of their Buskin (3:227–28).

In the same year, the anonymous author of *The Scoffer Scoffed. The Second Part* has Menippus accuse Trophonius of having "like a true Dissenter, strove / To break th' Allegiance, sworn to *Jove*" (5), whereas Achilles praises Antilochus as an "honest Tory" (9). For this writer, "Monsieur *Mors* [Death] . . . Was always known, to be a Leveller [the once-dominant Republican political faction]" (8), and in Hades (15–16):

Here's no Ambition, no great places,
No haughty looks, nor bold Menaces.
No striving to be Rich, or great
But all's Hail-fellow here, well met.
'Tis like a Pop'lar-state,[45] for here
No one must huff or domineer;
Where ev'ry Cobler is as free
And of as high Nobility,
As any man dare shew his face,
Or live, in such a Govern'd place. . . .

It is particularly telling that even translators who can be loosely described as conservative and sometimes even as passionate monarchists nonetheless expose through Lucian a powerful vision of "the World turn'd topsy turvy" (*The Scoffer Scoffed. The Second Part*, 1). What is more, instead of simply deploying this familiar image as a satirical strategy to argue for the reestablishment of conventional norms and hierarchies, they respond to its deeper, darker fears of a world without order, without government terrestrial or celestial, a world without guidance. In

---

[45] Democracy (*OED* dating from 1546).

Lucian's merciless analysis, the models of excellence bestowed by culture are mere fables: "neither was *Ajax* so mighty, nor *Helen* so faire as [the *Iliad*] would have them to be," the Cockerel tells his human interlocutor Micyllus, since, due to the universality of Pythagorean metempsychosis, "[Homer] in the time of those warres, . . . was a camell in *Bactria*" (Hickes, [5]8). Heywood, whose *Troia Britanica* of 1609 had rendered the Trojan war in heroic *ottava rima*, a quarter-century later gives us Menippus's gloating encomium:

> O thou ingenious *Homer*, see how bare,
> How groveling and how dejected lie,
> How low the heads of thy great Rapsodie:
> Ignoble and obscure they now are all,
> Ashes and dust, trifles in value small (134)

Homer is now "a meer Dunderhead" (Spence, 3:214), and Lucian, according to Samuel Sheppard, "*Homers Momus*":[46] Momus the son of Night, "*[t]he carping god.*"[47]

In *Icaromenippus*, "like *Homers Jupiter*," Menippus looks down upon the Earth, "and fixing mine eyes more stedfastly on it, the whole life of man was made apparent to mee, not by Nations and Cities, but all particular sort of persons, Marriners, Souldiers, plough-men, Lawyers, Women, Beasts, and whatsoever feedeth upon the face of the Earth" (Hickes, 16). In that deliberately archaic final clause the echo of the 1611 Bible resonates, but—unlike God—Menippus does *not* see that it is good, and the hierarchy of the social orders is deliberately jumbled—plough-men above lawyers (although we might all sympathise with that)—"I thought I might compare the life of man to nothing so well, as to a long shew or pageant, in which fortune was the setter out, . . . and fitted every person with sundry and different habites . . . but when the time comes that the triumph must have an end, then every man unclothes himselfe, and puts off his proportion together with his bodie . . . when the play is ended, every man must be disrob'd of his gorgeous garments, lay aside his vizard, step out of his buskins, and walke aloofe of[f] like a forlorne fellow . . . (Hickes, 39–40).

---

46 "The Socratick Session," 236, in *Epigrams* (1651), 198.
47 Francis Gouldman, *A Copious Dictionary* (1664), sig. 4Kᵛ.

Three of the four engraved plates in Spence's translation display the reach of Lucian's radicalism: a satyr unceremoniously heaves Jupiter from his Olympian throne (plate 2); another tumbles a king from his triumphal chariot (plate 3) while a third offers a mask to the eulogist who awaits him—and who no doubt will turn the disaster into good journalistic copy (in *Timon*, Lucian adumbrates the spin doctor's dark art);[48] while in the third plate (plate 4), although the ostensible focus is the bestial head of the unmasked struggling figure in the lawyer's gown, his discarded headgear lies beside a laurel wreath. The satirist undoes his own profession as well as all others. Because "he doubted of every thing," Lucian blurs the distinction between divine, human and animal kingdoms; the form of dialogue, "that great and pow'rful art," as Mulgrave calls it,[49] "the best and surest *Vehicle*, to Convey and Insinuate [his Design] into Men's Minds" (Spence, Vol. 1, sig. C3ᵛ), allows his gods, men and beasts to debate on a levelled footing (and it is characteristic of his wit that, in "The Double Accusation," Dialogue herself takes Lucian to task for misusing her "grave and serious" nature, "speaking only of God and of Principles" (Spence, 3:271). Occupying the same spaces, there is no room for deference to species.

Lucian's espousal of metempsychosis as literary trope creates a metamorphic world surpassing Ovid's, in which a cockerel (who was once Pythagoras himself) can chatter away to both gods and men, shape-shifting not only between human and animal forms (Hickes, 55), but across genders too (60). And the disparate orders of being are subjected to the same sharp-eyed assessment; Jupiter's revenge on Prometheus "is unworthy, I say not of a God, or of the King of Gods, but of a meer private Gentleman" (Spence, 1:51); "Mortall men deal much discreetlier in the like cases" (Mayne, 27). The unstable body of Greek myth enables Lucian to question not only the nature but the quality of the divine, especially in "The Councell of the Gods," summoned by Jupiter (with Momus as secretary) to define the essence of "any perfect God" in a context where heaven is invaded by "forraigners . . . who are not themselves content of men to be made Gods," but also wish to deify "their followers and servants"

---

[48]   A. M. Harmon and M. D. MacLeod, eds. and trans., *Lucian* (Cambridge, Mass., 1913–67), 8 Vols., 2:382–85; for Hickes's version, see 172–74.

[49]   John Sheffield, "An Essay on Poetry (1682)," 212 (*Miscellanea* [Halifax, 1933], 48).

(Mayne, 238). As Momus complains, "wee have need of mysteries, *Jupiter*, by which wee may know Gods to be Gods, and Dogs to be Dogs" (242); not so easy, though, when: ". . . the *Memphites* have an Oxe for their God; the *Pelusiots* an Onion; some a Storke, or Crockodile; others a Dogge, or Catt, or Ape. . . . Some adore an earthen cup, others a dish. Are not these Gods to be laught at . . .?" (Mayne, 289).

In the absence of a stable order ("Take but degree away, untune that string . . ."),[50] atheism becomes a logical stance; as Jupiter acknowledges, "it stands upon the edge of a rasour whether we shall hereafter be worshipt, and receive sacrifice, or be utterly neglected, and held in contempt . . . when [men] see such an unequall disposition of thinges, they may dispute whether there bee such thinges as Gods" (Mayne, 270, 278). Trapped in a predestiny anticipating Calvin, "wee men do nothing voluntarily, but as wee are moved by an inevitable necessity" (Mayne, 310). Whereas for More and Erasmus, Lucian's atheism did not seriously threaten their own Christian Humanism, in the later seventeenth-century, Lucian's challenge to any kind of belief was more potent; in Bacon's shrewd analysis, Lucian was the more dangerous because he might be characterised as a "Contemplative *Atheist*":[51]

> *Merchant.* What are Men?
> *Heraclitus.* Mortall Gods.
> *Merchant.* What are Gods?
> *Heraclitus.* Immortall men. (Mayne, 186)

> *Micyllus.* But let's now proceed to Brute Animals, what think ye of their Condition?
> *Cock.* . . . I'le only say, it's more Calm and Sedate than ours, because its confin'd within the bounds of Nature; and is not disturb'd by so many Evils, and so many Crimes. (Spence, 3:228)

Inferior to the beasts, then—one is reminded of Rochester's shame, ending his visit to 'Tunbridge Wells', when he "us'd the insolence to

---

[50]   *Troilus and Cressida*, 1.iii.109 (Shakespeare, *The Complete Works*, 721).
[51]   See Michael Kiernan, ed., *The Essayes or Counsels* (Oxford, 1985), 'Of Atheisme', 52.

mount my horse,"[52]—driven by inescapable necessity in a godless universe, where even if there is something after death, it is indeed to be dreaded:

> When you are faln to Dust and Ashes;
> And Threed-bare Vicar going first,
> Cries here's the hole, and in you must.
> And tell the Smock-fac't *Megibus,*
> And the Wrestler *Damoxenus,*
> That here strong Back, nor able Thighs,
> Nor curled Hair, nor sparkling Eyes,
> Nor all the Charms adorn'd by Art,
> In this place signifie a Fart.[53]

In that indecorous emission resounds the collapse of the unchallenged social, political, ecclesiastical, and cultural authority of tradition—*all* laurels in the dust—and the birth of the Royal Society. Job done, Lucian: job done.

---

[52] 'Tunbridge Wells', 185 (Harold Love, ed., *The Works of John Wilmot Earl of Rochester* [Oxford, 1999], 54).

[53] *The Scoffer Scoft. Part Two,* 8.

Peter Heylyn's Seventeenth-Century English Worldview

Peter Craft
Felician College

EVEN THOUGH PETER Heylyn's *Cosmographie* (1652) is better organized and larger in scope than similar works, it has received little attention from scholars of the seventeenth century.[1] While the names of other

---

[1] Research for this essay was conducted with the generous support of a Summer Research Stipend from Felician College. The librarians at Felician College, Harvard University, and the University of Illinois were especially helpful, and I am indebted to the National Portrait Gallery for permission to reproduce the Francis Hayman painting. I would also like to thank Robert Markley, Anthony Pollock, and the editor and anonymous readers at *Studies in Medieval and Renaissance History* for helpful comments on earlier versions of this essay.
There were eight editions of *Microcosmus* between 1621 and 1639, and *Cosmographie* went through nine editions between 1652 and 1703. Heylyn significantly expanded *Microcosmus* between the first and second editions, from 417 pages in 1621 to 812 pages in 1625. The remaining editions of *Microcosmus* remained fairly consistent lengthwise, ranging from 807 to 808 pages. Heylyn had expanded *Microcosmus* into *Cosmographie* by 1652, and by 1703 the work had reached 1,132 pages. The first edition of *Microcosmus* in 1621 had Latin characters in the title, whereas subsequent editions in the seventeenth century had the title spelled with Greek letters. Different combinations of these languages, in addition to the generally nonstandardized spelling practices in England prior to the publication

---

voyage collection editors such as Richard Hakluyt and Samuel Purchas remain well known, Heylyn has slipped through the cracks of history, despite his being one of the best-selling authors of the seventeenth century. In this essay I should like to recur to the *Cosmographie* and explore its depiction of non-European cultures. I suggest that the depiction is central to Heylyn's conception of England's place in the world during the 1640s and 1650s.

Moreover, the large gap between the desperate circumstances that Heylyn as an English Royalist found himself in during this period and the consolatory, self-aggrandizing rhetoric that he employed in reaction to these conditions makes him a kind of paradigm for the understanding of English ideas of warfare, trade, and "Indians" in the second half of the seventeenth century. Whereas Purchas edited Hakluyt's voyage collection, Heylyn rewrote it and provided a comprehensive description of the "entire" world. In other words, Heylyn offered general, authoritative principles based on specific voyage accounts and observations. By sifting through, categorizing, and summarizing Hakluyt and Purchas's massive tomes, Heylyn prioritized those elements of each country's descriptions that merited the attention of his English readers and, to a greater extent than his predecessors, contextualized voyage narratives in relation to contemporary concerns about military might, wealth, and trade.

While publication records reveal the popularity of voyage collections with English readers, it is more difficult to gauge who exactly purchased these works. Sailors and merchants would certainly have been a primary audience, since the commodities and geographic descriptions of various countries in voyage collections were highly relevant to international trade. Common sailors and especially officers had both the money and

---

of Samuel Johnson's *A Dictionary of the English Language* in 1755, account for the many variant spellings one finds in articles, books, and bibliographic records of this work today: *Microcosmus, Microcosmos, Mikrocosmos, Mikrokosmos, Mikrókosmos,* and *Micrócosmos.* For a chart that displays the publication history of Heylyn's geographies, see Adrian Johns, "Natural History as Print Culture," in *Cultures of Natural History,* ed. N. Jardine, J. A. Secord, and E. C. Spary (Cambridge, 1996), 109. This chart is a helpful starting point for determining the number of editions of Heylyn's works. With help from the former senior bibliographer of the ESTC, I compared the chart to the ESTC's records and the original manuscripts to weed out imprint variants, ghosts, bad records, reissues, and stop-press alterations. My calculations therefore differ from both the ESTC's data and Johns' chart.

the reading skills to buy and consume these volumes. Money was one of the few perks of the grim life at sea. A sailor or merchant could save by engaging for long voyages on which room and board (hard, sometimes weevil-filled biscuits) were included, and the outlets for spending wages were few. If the seaman finally did reach land, he generally had sufficient funds to purchase books for the next journey. The length of voyages, which could span months or even years, provided men at sea with time for reading, and an impressive number of them were literate. Estimates are that between 1700 and 1750, eighty percent or more of the highest ranking officers (captains; first, second, and third mates; and surgeons) could read. Even among the unskilled common seamen, apprentices, and quartermasters, the literacy rate ranged between 62.5 and 100 percent, with a total merchant shipping industry average of 75.4 percent.[2] These numbers suggest why merchants appear to have been the primary targets for the consumption of secondhand voyage collections such as Heylyn's *Cosmographie*. Even though voyage collections were primarily by, for, and about sailors and merchants, a relatively larger audience must have included the general reading public for a work such as Heylyn's *Cosmographie* to have gone through eight editions in half a century.

Because some voyage collections such as *Cosmographie* stretched to over a thousand pages, it is more likely that they were read sporadically rather than cover to cover. Heylyn's *Microcosmus* (1621) and *Cosmographie*, unlike Hakluyt's *Principal Navigations, Voyages and Discoveries of the English Nation* (1589) or Purchas's *Hakluytus Posthumus* (1625), facilitated this approach by providing synopses of countries that authors of fiction and others could refer to with relative ease. Heylyn's cosmographies were not the first to provide concise summaries of the cultures, resources, history, inhabitants, wildlife, wealth, religious practices, and armies of various countries. Other roughly contemporaneous books similarly organized through the use of country names for their category headings, such as Botero's *Travellers Breviat* and d'Avity's *Estates, Empires, and Principallities of the World*, were only translated once into English, which suggests that they were less popular and less widely consulted in England than Heylyn's work. Heylyn's works not only reached the public at large, but they also found their way into the hands of at least

---

2 Marcus Rediker, *Between the Devil and the Deep Blue Sea: Merchant Seamen, Pirates, and the Anglo-American Maritime World, 1700-1750* (Cambridge, 1987), 307.

three English monarchs. Heylyn presented Prince Charles with a copy of *Microcosmus* in person in 1621, and Robert Markley argues that a 1657 edition of *Cosmographie* with hand-colored maps in the British Library may have been a presentation copy that Heylyn gave to Charles II during his Restoration. Markley's theory seems especially plausible considering the fact that Heylyn carried the scepter to the altar during the coronation ceremony. Gilbert Burnet has stated that Heylyn's *Ecclesia Restaurata* converted James II to Roman Catholicism, a claim that makes sense when one considers that Heylyn's Laudian beliefs were envisioned in such a way that he once referred to himself as a Catholic.[3] With a combined total of sixteen editions between 1621 and 1700, Heylyn's two major works were virtually ubiquitous both at court and beyond.

As a result, when writers such as Richard Head or John Dryden needed information on India or the Americas for their prose fiction and plays, they would have naturally turned to Heylyn's *Microcosmus* or *Cosmographie*. However, even if such authors did not directly consult Heylyn's work, the ideas about "Indians," warfare, and trade in the Americas and India helped to form the popular conceptions that inspired fictional representations. Heylyn therefore not only reflected but also shaped and refined seventeenth-century English literary tastes. In the pages that follow, I argue that the commercial success of Heylyn's *Cosmographie* was partially the result of specific historical circumstances and his corresponding interpretation of them. He included potentially unsettling

---

[3]   Peter Heylyn, "Heylyn's Own Memoranda," in *Memorials of Bishop Waynflete*, ed. John R. Bloxam (London, 1851), xvi; Robert Markley, *The Far East and the English Imagination 1660–1730* (Cambridge, 2006), 140; Sir Edward Walker, *A Circumstantial Account of the Preparations for the Coronation of His Majesty King Charles the Second* (London, 1820), 85; Robert J. Mayhew, introduction to *Cosmographie*, by Peter Heylyn, ed. Robert J. Mayhew (1652; repr., Bristol, 2003), xxi. Heylyn was not alone since geographers from William Camden on tended to employ variations of an Anglo-Catholic perspective. Like Camden, Heylyn used geography and history to support British patriotism. See Robert J. Mayhew, *Enlightenment Geography: The Political Languages of British Geography, 1650–1850* (New York, 2000), 54, 173. Heylyn's zeal in researching information that would support his viewpoints led early biographers to believe that excessive reading directly caused his blindness. In keeping with the book culture of the seventeenth century, in which reading could cause all manner of ailments, an overheating of Heylyn's brain allegedly damaged the crystalline humor of his eyes. See Adrian Johns, *The Nature of the Book: Print and Knowledge in the Making* (Chicago, 1997), 383.

contemporary information within his book, such as the inferiority of England's military in relation to India's, within not only a cyclical view of history, but also a spiritual and nationalistic rhetoric that later English authors would borrow and adapt.

In order to gain a sense of Heylyn's intention in expanding his *Microcosmos* (1621) into the *Cosmographie* (1652) and a contemporary audience's reactions to the revised work, it is helpful to recall the historical context. Heylyn's early associations were more with Puritanism than the Laudian movement, but by 1629 he actively sought William Laud's patronage. Laud strengthened Heylyn's ties with Charles I by presenting Heylyn's *The History of Saint George* (1631) to the king. In the 1630s Heylyn dedicated his poems to both Charles I and Laud. Since Laud firmly supported Charles I and opposed Puritanism, which led to the former's execution in 1645, Heylyn's Royalist politics and Laudian theology complemented and reinforced one another. These values also led to Heylyn's sequestration in 1644. Although no source appears to exist for the exact dates when Heylyn began and finished *Cosmographie*, a seventeenth-century biographer, John Barnard, claims that the book was begun around 1648 and was finished by its date of publication in 1652.[4] Barnard was in a position to make such a claim with some accuracy since he was married to Heylyn's daughter. Evidently Heylyn was working on the "General Introduction" in 1648, since he includes that date in a discussion of the age of the earth. While he wrote *Cosmographie*, the House of Commons tried and executed his patron Charles I, to whom he dedicated *Microcosmus*. For Heylyn, this was yet another tragic incident in a long string of misfortunes. A few years earlier, Heylyn joined Charles at Oxford and acted as his "historian of the war," which led to Parliament's decision to strip Heylyn's house at Alresford of its contents and reduce him to destitution.[5]

---

[4] *Oxford Dictionary of National Biography,* s.v. "Heylyn, Peter"; John Barnard, *The True Life of the Most Reverend Divine and Excellent Historian, Peter Heylyn* (London, 1683), 214–15.

[5] *Oxford Dictionary of National Biography,* s.v. "Heylyn, Peter." Heylyn envisioned his role as Charles's "historian of war" as a corrector of misleading or inaccurate information that previous historians had published. Royce MacGillivray argues that Heylyn had a "formidable talent for proving a set historical thesis," a "wide knowledge of contemporary English history," and a "more realistic" view than most of his fellow Royalist historians. According to MacGillivray, Heylyn's perspective

Indeed, Heylyn refers to his bleak situation in the preface to *Cosmographie*:

> For being, by the unhappiness of my Destiny, or the infelicity of the Times, deprived of my Preferments, and divested of my Ministerial Function, (as to the ordinary and public exercise thereof) I cannot chuse but say, I have leisure enough; the opportunity of spending more idle hours (if I were so minded) than I ever expected or desired.[6]

No immediate relief appeared within view. The New Model Army, led by Cromwell, was the biggest and most expensive in English history up to that point. If viewed from an Old Testament perspective in which God rewarded His "chosen people" with military victories and economic prosperity, Heylyn seemed to be on the losing, punished, or "sinful" side. One way around this conclusion, as Heylyn realized, was to regard the apparent wrath of God at the English Royalist party in terms of a Job-like test. In the Old Testament, Job's divinely approved behavior in the midst of afflictions eventually restores him to even greater wealth and prosperity than he had before, which in turn signifies an even higher degree of favor with God.[7]

In the "To The Reader" section that prefaces *Comographie*, Heylyn casts himself in this Job-like role and explains the "wants and difficulties" that he "struggle[d]" with while composing this work. He advertises his own learning by posing the following indirect question: "Books I had few to help my self with of mine own" and "it rather may be wondred at by an equall Reader, how I could write so much, with so little help?" The reason Heylyn lacked books was that Parliament confiscated his possessions in his Alresford home. While he does not denounce Parliament in so many words, which would have been dangerous, he implicitly casts its members in the role of Satan. After all, Satan, like the Puritans in Heylyn's life, was the agent of deprivation in Job's trials.[8]

---

on ecclesiastical history is strictly Laudian and Heylyn's vision of political history is Royalist extremist, though he occasionally critiques individual monarchs for displays of weakness. See Royce MacGillivray, *Restoration Historians and the English Civil War* (The Hague, 1974), 30, 32–35, 39.

  [6]   Peter Heylyn, *Cosmographie in Four Books . . .* (London, 1652), 1:A3.

  [7]   Job 42:10–12 (AV).

  [8]   Job 2:6-7 (AV).

Moreover, just as Job's suffering forged a closer bond between himself and God, Heylyn claims the same process took place during the writing of *Cosmographie*: "And to say truth, the work so prospered in my hand, and swelled so much above my thought and expectation, that I hope I may with modesty enough [say that] . . . The Lord God brought it to me."[9] Far from being forsaken, Heylyn claims to be the medium through which God speaks. By making this claim, Heylyn defines himself, his work, and the destiny of the English nation in terms of Old Testament typology.

With a need to reaffirm his place in the cosmos and with time on his hands because he had lost his "Ministerial Function," Heylyn decided to revise and expand one of his earlier works. The prospect of successful publication promised much-needed money. But also the decision to enlarge *Microcosmus* into his *Cosmographie* appears to have been motivated by a desire to place recent events in England within a larger biblical narrative of providential history and cast himself and his fellow Royalists in the role of God's chosen people in the midst of a temporarily painful test that would eventually lead them to unprecedented prosperity. The example of India was especially relevant since its vast military forces dwarfed the Commonwealth government's seemingly unlimited power and revealed the New Model Army's relative vulnerability. In fact, India's armies serve as a kind of metaphor for nearly absolute power that Heylyn believed he and his loyal English followers would attain once they passed their divine test and the cycle of history put them in a position appropriate to their supposed merits in the eyes of the Judeo-Christian God. Shah Jahan (ruled 1628-1658) and the Indian emperors who preceded him served as apt models for the type of power and wealth that Heylyn and other Englishmen aspired to.

Given the near constant war-footing condition of England during the seventeenth and eighteenth centuries, it is not surprising that Heylyn should devote a significant portion of his *Cosmographie* to the relative military strengths of other countries. His assessment of Mughal India, however, is far more thorough and respectful than his discussion of the Americas. If a relatively well-informed English reader of the mid-seventeenth century were to peruse this work, he or she would be struck by Heylyn's repeated emphasis on the enormous size of India's armies.

---

[9] This section of Heylyn's *Cosmographie* is not paginated.

Heylyn concerned himself with this aspect of India in his *Microcosmus*, but it loomed far larger in *Cosmographie*. Whereas *Microcosmus* contains six references to the size of armies, *Cosmographie* has twenty-seven.[10] One might assume that he simply followed Purchas's lead. After all, five of the six references to the size of Indian armies in *Microcosmus* come from *Purchas his Pilgrimage*, and many of the military statistics in *Cosmographie* are also taken directly from that work. Of Purchas's collections, *his Pilgrimage* (1613) would have been a most convenient source for India's army counts because it is organized by country and contains summaries of voyagers' letters rather than the actual letters. Yet *Purchas his Pilgrimage* only has twelve references to India's troops, which leaves fifteen unaccounted for in Heylyn's *Cosmographie*. Heylyn therefore must have drawn the remaining figures from other sources.

Heylyn's use of *Purchas his Pilgrimes* (1625), which is more than four thousand pages and fills twenty volumes in the 1905 edition, reveals a significant degree of selectivity and prioritizing. While *his Pilgrimes*, much longer than *Purchas his Pilgrimage*, had not been published when Heylyn wrote the first edition of *Microcosmus* (1621), it had been in print for decades by the time he composed *Cosmographie* (1652). Moreover, none of Purchas's indices and prefaces contain easy reference points such as "Indian Armies" or "Military Statistics" which might have facilitated Heylyn's intensive labor.

The figures Heylyn records can scarcely be accurate since the sheer task of counting troops in that quantity would be difficult, especially under the duress of an impending battle. Moreover, the rounded sums, usually to the hundred or even thousand, which Heylyn consistently gives, suggest estimation rather than exact counts. The few precise numbers that Heylyn gives tend to be smaller than one thousand and easily countable. For instance, at one point Heylyn mentions that an army had 537 elephants, animals whose size would make them readily distinguishable from the rest of the troops with little difficulty.[11] By uncharacteristically using a nonrounded number for elephants, Heylyn also draws his English readers' attention to this part of the military description and so strengthens its rhetorical power.

---

[10]   Heylyn, *Cosmographie*, 3:213–46; Heylyn, *Microcosmos* (Oxford, 1621), 348–56.

[11]   Heylyn, *Cosmographie*, 3:227, 233.

Heylyn's source for this unusually precise number appears to be Giovanni Botero. Although Heylyn does not cite sources frequently in *Cosmographie*, the 1621 edition of *Microcosmus* features extensive marginal citations. In one of them, Heylyn cites Boterus, the Latinized name, Botero's, as the source for the number of elephants that an army brought to battle against Prince Idalcan in the Narsinga province of India. Interestingly, the number changes between Botero's *Traveller's Breviat*, Heylyn's *Microcosmus*, and again in *Cosmographie*: 557, 558, and 537, respectively. Botero lists the numbers of foot soldiers, cavalry, and elephants in nine separate battalions of troops, but he does not provide a total for the entire army. One can only assume that Heylyn added these figures. The one-elephant discrepancy between Botero's *Breviat* and Heylyn's *Microcosmus* was most likely a typographical or mathematical error. Heylyn does not list his sources in *Cosmographie*, however, and it is possible that he found the 537 figure from someone other than Botero. Yet Botero lists two battalions that contain twenty elephants so another possibility is that Heylyn forgot to add in the second regiment. Thus the figures Heylyn listed were not perfectly consistent with either his sources or his own later work, but they nonetheless gave readers a general idea about the huge forces India was capable of fielding.

The fact that Heylyn counted Botero's nine separate battalions (with three different troop subdivisions and hundreds of thousands of foot soldiers) reveals the importance that he attached to sum totals for Indian armies. Heylyn combined these numbers and, in doing so, presented an overwhelming integrated force rather than individual regiments. The rhetorical effect that the idea of over 500 elephants in one place had on a reader's mind would be far greater than listing twenty or so at a time as Botero does. Cromwell's entire army, by contrast, enlisted roughly 34,000 soldiers in England alone in 1652 and 70,000 troops in England, Ireland, and Scotland combined that same year.[12]

Even if numbers had been painstakingly counted, the temptation to exaggerate would have been great. From a victorious army's standpoint, a greater number of enemy troops meant more glory for those who won and, from a voyage writer's perspective, larger armies created a more wondrous, unusual, and therefore marketable work. Daniel Defoe

---

[12] Lois G. Schwoerer, *No Standing Armies!: The Antiarmy Ideology in Seventeenth Century England* (Baltimore, 1979), 52.

emphasizes this idea in his *New Voyage Round the World* by saying that an account of a routine voyage "in it self" has "no Value," but that the story of an unusual journey "may be worth publishing."[13] Even with exaggerations taken into consideration, numeric trends are fairly consistent by country in Heylyn's work. Of his twenty-seven references to India's army sizes, only eight have fewer than 100,000 troops. The largest of these armies exceeds 3,000,000 troops. In all of the Americas, however, the biggest army had 300,000 troops, and that was *before* the Spanish invaded and diseases decimated the population. Moreover, this army of 300,000 is the only one of the five references in all of the sections on the Americas to exceed 100,000 troops, and that army had been disbanded well before the arrival of the Spanish conquistadors. The oral nature of much pre-European American history and the inherent possibility of miscommunication that translation presents further cast doubt on the accuracy of this number. In spite of these potential inaccuracies, Heylyn's *Cosmographie* provided seventeenth-century English readers with a clear sense of the overwhelming differences in the sizes of Amerindian as opposed to South Asian armies.

In the section on the Americas in *Cosmographie*, Heylyn scarcely mentions armies composed of native peoples. The omission is especially significant considering that the section on the Americas is about three times as long as the one on India. In the 1652 edition of *Cosmographie*, Heylyn devotes thirty-three pages to India and ninety-five to the Americas. For the relatively short section on India, Heylyn crams in twenty-seven numerical references to the size of India's armies, nearly one per page. The sections on the New World only list five numerical allusions to indigenous armies, which is about one reference for every twenty pages.

By the time Heylyn produced his *Cosmographie*, then, it seems clear that he thought these numbers were important for India. At one point, he claims that King Badurius of Cambaia had an army that consisted of "150000 Horses, 500000 foot, 2000 Elephants armed, 200 Pieces of brass Ordnance, of which were 4 *Basilisks*, each of them drawn with 100 yoke of Oxen: and 500 Carts loaded with Powder and Shot."[14] The references in this passage to "Ordnance," "Basilisks," and "Carts loaded with Powder and Shot" are important because India's armies had more than just

---

[13]   Daniel Defoe, *A New Voyage Round the World*. . . . (London, 1725), 2.

[14]   Peter Heylyn, *Cosmographie*, 3:237.

numbers; they were also equipped with gunpowder and cannons. In fact, the first recorded reference to the use of gunpowder in India dates from 1290, and the earliest known records of artillery use in battle were in 1368. England's first known use and description of cannons in battle, by contrast, is 1327.[15] India's armies had therefore been using gunpowder-based projectiles for approximately as long as Europeans and were at no technological disadvantage with their Western adversaries. Many of the armies Heylyn described also had "Horse," or cavalry, and war elephants. The depiction of Indian armies that Heylyn presents, complete with cavalry, war elephants, hundreds of thousands of troops, gunpowder, and cannons, would have been highly impressive to contemporary English readers, especially since their own military had no war elephants and only a small fraction of India's soldiers (see fig. 1).

For Heylyn, cavalry and "ordnance," both of which Amerindians lacked in the fifteenth century, were the hallmarks of an advanced nation and could compensate for overwhelming odds. When Heylyn describes a combined European and South American army, he distinguishes the "Savages" or Aztecs from the Spanish cavalry.[16] He repeats the word "savages" when referring to an indigenous army of New Spain. In 1518 at the town of Potonchon, Heylyn writes that 550 Spaniards led by Cortez were able, "by the help of . . . Horse and Ordinance . . . [to] discomfit . . . 40000 of the naked savages."[17] Heylyn's emphasis on the "naked" nature of the Amerindians reveals his small regard for armies that lacked armor and ordinance, and his reliance on the word "savages" to describe Amerindian troops marks a distinct contrast to his respectful descriptions of India's armies.

While the "Indian" armies of the New World were largely overlooked or trivialized by Heylyn, the forces of India proper were a different story. He states that King Badurius of Cambaia's army, which was approximately nine times the size of the Commonwealth government's combined forces in all of England, Ireland, and Scotland, was still insufficient to defeat the soldiers of another Indian king named Merhamed.[18] Heylyn then tells his

---

[15] Iqtidar Khan, *Gunpowder and Firearms: Warfare in Medieval India* (Oxford, 2004), 18; S.K. Chatterji, *Vintage Guns of India* (New Delhi, 2001), 20–21.

[16] Heylyn, *Cosmographie*, 4:134.

[17] Heylyn, *Cosmographie*, 4:134.

[18] Heylyn, *Cosmographie*, 3:237.

readers that even this victorious empire, which for a time ruled a huge portion of India, began to stagnate within a relatively brief period and was soon overrun by "puissant Rebels."[19] From the cycle of victory and defeat on a massive scale, Heylyn concludes that "Nature or Divine providence have given to Empires, as to men, a determinate growth, beyond which there is no exceeding."[20] For English Royalists such as Heylyn who opposed the reigning Puritan government, the idea of a

natural or divinely ordained "determinate growth, beyond which there is no exceeding," which pertained even in the case of the largest armies and strongest empires, would have been appealing and comforting precisely because it could be applied to Cromwell's regime, whose fall or at least decline would appear inevitable. The view would also explain the defeat of the Royalists which, to some extent, would have exonerated them from charges of mismanagement and tyranny. After all, if the decline of all nations is unavoidable, Charles I's specific policy decisions do not seem to be solely responsible for the collapse of his government.

Heylyn's decision to expand the scope of *Microcosmus* into the *Cosmographie* and to add a religio-historical "General Introduction" assumes added significance when one views it in light of his personal situation in the middle of the seventeenth century. On the local level in England, Cromwell's army must have seemed large and powerful, much to the Royalist Heylyn's chagrin. From the grander perspective that Heylyn offers, however, the situation was not so bleak. If Indian empires with hundreds of thousands of troops and seemingly infinite wealth could be subsumed into a biblical master narrative of "determinate growth," then the Cromwellian government's relatively smaller forces and finances, which had existed for less than a decade, appeared far less threatening. From Heylyn's Royalist perspective, the cycle of history would eventually restore the Stuarts to their rightful throne.

As one of the most influential works of its kind in England in the seventeenth century, then, *Cosmographie* demonstrates at least one Englishman's recognition of the real-life limitations of his own country. It also reflects an effort to transcend those limitations by appropriating non-European histories to serve as a kind of consolation fantasy. Heylyn finds consolation in his account of the wealth and might of Indian rulers

---

[19]   Heylyn, *Cosmographie*, 3:237.
[20]   Heylyn, *Cosmographie*, 3:237.

whose thriving monarchical governments seem to validate Royalist ideology. When he reached the parts of Indian history in which the empire began to decline, he enjoyed vindication of a different sort. The ultimate failure of the pagan rulers would confirm the belief that the Judeo-Christian biblical histories and prophecies in which non-Christians could not survive indefinitely still governed the fates of countries with other religions or "idolatries." In the unpaginated "To the Reader" section of the 1652 edition of *Cosmographie*, Heylyn makes the connection between morality and long-term national survival: "If now we look into the causes of that desolation which hath hapned in the Civill State of those mighty Empires; to what can we impute it but their crying sins?" If the "crying sins" of such "mighty Empires" have led to their decline, what will befall the Commonwealth government?

Moreover, Heylyn was not above graphically recounting the "crying sins" for his readers, which provides a sensational aspect to his writing and doubtless accounts for some of its popularity. In one of the more gruesome descriptions, Heylyn tells of an Indian village where "Fathers devoured their Children, the stronger preyed on the weaker; not only devouring their more fleshly parts, but their entrails also: nay, they broke up the skuls of such as they had slain, and sucked out their brains."[21] The image of fathers eating their own children is horrifying enough, but Heylyn heightens the shock value by including lurid details that likely both repulsed and fascinated readers. In another passage, Heylyn describes a regional Indian king who "cutteth off his nose, ears, lips, and other parts."[22] In addition to the accounts of self-mutilation and cannibalism, other sections of the *Cosmographie* detail self-immolations, live burials, euthanasia, torture, polygamy, public nudity, bloody rituals, and defilement of virgins. Such sensational descriptions fit naturally into the exotic adventure fiction of the next few decades and may have inspired them.

---

[21] Heylyn, *Cosmographie*, 3:245. Descriptions such as this one support Robert Markley's argument that Heylyn carefully or even obsessively anatomizes civilizations' "crying sins" in order to reinforce the idea of humankind's perpetual fall from Edenic grace into postlapsarian history. Markley contends that Heylyn's fascination with the fall of empires is part of a larger seventeenth-century trend. See Robert Markley, "Newton, Corruption, and the Tradition of Universal History," in *Newton and Religion: Context, Nature, and Influence*, ed. James E. Force and Richard H. Popkin (Dordrecht, 1999), 131.

[22] Heylyn, *Cosmographie*, 3:232.

In Aphra Behn's *Oroonoko*, published in 1688, the narrator provides a similar description of native self-mutilation. A competition for leadership among Surinamese natives requires physical displays of valor that include cutting off their "nose," "lips," and "eye."[23] The line between voyage narratives and exotic adventure fiction was so thin that an authentic version of the former, *Madagascar, or Robert Drury's Journal* (1729), was attributed to Defoe by some critics until 1945.[24]

While Behn may or may not have directly consulted Heylyn's work, there is no question that Richard Head plagiarized *Cosmographie* for the section of *The English Rogue* (1665) where Meriton Latroon travels to India. Heylyn provides the following: "The people are of coal-black colour (differing therein from the rest of the *Indians,* swarth and complexioned like the *Olive*) well limbed, and wearing their hair long and curled: about their heads an hankerchief wrought with gold and silver, and about their middle a cloth, which hangeth down to conceal their nakedness."[25]

Head has: "These Malabars are coal-black, well limb'd, their hair long and curled; about their heads they only tye a small piece of linen, but about their bodies nothing but a little cloth which covers their secrets."[26]

---

[23] Aphra Behn, *Oroonoko, the Rover and Other Works,* ed. Janet Todd (New York, 1992), 124.

[24] Philip Edwards, *The Story of the Voyage: Sea-Narratives in Eighteenth-Century England* (Cambridge, 1994), 169–70.

[25] Heylyn, *Cosmographie*, 3:227.

[26] Richard Head, *The English Rogue: Being a Complete History of the Most Eminent Cheats of Both Sexes* (1665; repr., London, 1996), 267. Other authors who directly took material from   Heylyn's works were: John Newton, *Cosmographia* (London, 1679); Edmund Bohun, *Geographical Dictionary* (London, 1688); Laurence Echard, *A Most Compleat Compendium of Geography* (London, 1691). Later historians, such as E. G. R. Taylor and Margarita Bowen, criticize Heylyn himself for what would today be called plagiarism. While modern scholars might expect original research or personal travel from a geographer, Robert J. Mayhew points out that in Heylyn's time there would have been nothing unethical or unusual about his practice since he saw his original authorial contribution in his method, the way that he collected, organized, and presented information from a variety of sources that he put into a spatial framework by country. Heylyn's clear organizational method was especially valuable during the Renaissance as the English received a flood of new information from the Americas and the rediscovery of classical texts. See E. G. R. Taylor, *Late Tudor and Early Stuart Geography, 1583–1650* (Cambridge, 1934), 140; Margarita Bowen, *Empiricism and Geographical Thought: from Francis Bacon to Alexander*

Phrases such as "coal-black," "well-limb[e]d," and "hair long and curled" are identical. These passages not only suggest *Cosmographie*'s direct influence on popular seventeenth-century fiction but also reveal Heylyn's distinction between the "coal-black" skin color of Malabar natives on the southern coast of India and "the rest of the *Indians*" under Mughal rule, who are "complexioned like the *Olive*." The inhabitants of central and northern India generally looked more like Europeans, and more important from Heylyn's perspective shared more of their religious beliefs than the Hindi natives of southern India and its surrounding islands.

This distinction between English perceptions of Mughal Indians in the north and Hindi natives in the south is important because it helps to contextualize later authors' depictions of East Indian characters. In Balachandra Rajan's book *Under Western Eyes*, he says that "Mughal history is treated by Dryden with a disrespect that no writer would have thought of bringing to bear on the Greek and Roman past. Such a disrespect points to a stubbornly resident devaluation of the Orient."[27] In the context of the relative economic and military positions of England and India in the 1670s, however, there would have been few reasons for Dryden to disrespect or devalue the latter country, especially since it was an ally. As Heylyn's 1674 edition of *Cosmographie* and other contemporary voyage collections make clear, India and its surrounding islands provided valuable spices, cloth, precious metals, and stones for the English market, and the Mughal Empire was far more powerful than England at this time. Since these voyage collections were enormously popular, almost all English men and women in the seventeenth century knew that their country was weaker than India. Under Aurangzeb's rule, the Mughal Empire achieved its largest territorial size ever, and his military forces dwarfed England's.[28]

Far from treating Mughal history with disrespect, Dryden compares it to the venerable Romans of antiquity and even elevates an East Indian

---

von Humboldt (New York, 1981), 92–93; Mayhew, introduction to *Cosmographie*, xv. Authors of fiction such as Richard Head looked to *Cosmographie* for inspiration, and Heylyn himself, who also wrote poetry, quoted works of literature such as Sir Philip Sidney's *Arcadia* and Sir Thomas More's *Utopia*, which created a reciprocal relationship between genres. See Heylyn, *Cosmographie*, 1:20, 1:259.

[27] Balachandra Rajan, *Under Western Eyes: India from Milton to Macaulay* (Durham, 1999), 76.

[28] John Keay, *India: A History* (New York, 2000), 314.

character above some Englishwomen of his own time. Jack Armistead argues that the Mughal prince Morat in *Aureng-Zebe* (1676) resembles the Roman character Sempronius in Joseph Addison's *Cato*, and Dryden himself makes the following comparisons in his unpaginated Epistle Dedicatory: "I have made my *Melesinda*, in opposition to *Nourmahal*, a Woman passionately loving of her Husband, patient of injuries and contempt, and constant in her kindness, to the last: and in that, perhaps, I may have err'd, because it is not a Virtue much in use. Those *Indian* Wives are loving Fools, and may do well to keep themselves in their own Countrey, or, at least, to keep company with the *Arria's* and *Portia's* of old *Rome:* some of our Ladies know better things." [29] Although Dryden refers to Indian wives as "fools," a word that was less harsh in the seventeenth century than it is today, he actually praises their devotion with words such as "patient," "constant," and "Virtue." The true targets of Dryden's mockery are some of his contemporary English women who do not exhibit the admirable characteristics of their East Indian and Roman counterparts. Dryden therefore reinforces the respectful attitude toward the Mughal Empire that Heylyn displays in his *Cosmographie*, a book that remained current and went through a new edition two years before the first publication of *Aureng-Zebe*.

Heylyn's moralistic approach to his subject matter encouraged and entertained English readers who shared his views because it enabled him to invoke biblical origins and rationalize apparent historical contradictions (such as the seemingly infinite number of inhabitants of India and the relatively short time since Noah's flood). Moreover, because Heylyn provided a lengthy biblical explanation of history in his "General Introduction," a section that did not appear in *Microcosmus*, the shift between the historical claims of his sources and the ways in which they could be reconciled with Judeo-Christian historiography often led him to reiterate and expand upon points he had made in the earlier work. For instance, Heylyn used this rhetorical strategy to explain a potentially unsettling disparity between the reported size of one Indian army and biblical history: how could King Staurobates of India have a "greater force made up of natural *Indians* only" than Queen Semiramis, whose own army was

[29] J. M. Armistead, "Drama of Renewal: Cato and Moral Empiricism," *Papers on Language & Literature* 17, No. 3 (1981): 276–77; John Dryden, *Aureng-Zebe* (London, 1676).

"three Millions of men and upwards," within "four hundred years" of the great flood's destruction of all human beings except Noah and his family?[30] The presence of this enormous population in a single area of the world posed a direct challenge to the Mosaic narrative.

Heylyn further complicated the question by noting that the descendants of Noah were said to be scattered to the far corners of the earth after the Tower of Babel or "*Confusion of Tongues*," described in Gen. 11.[31] In order to resolve the apparent disparities between his sources and the biblical account, Heylyn used about three double-columned pages of small print in his "General Introduction" and another column in his section on India.[32] The argument that Heylyn begins in the "General Introduction" and continues in the India section is too lengthy to deal with here. The gist is that people lived longer in those days and therefore had more opportunities to have children; he also specifies Noah's Ark as landing "on the top of Mount *Caucasus* in the Countries of *Tartary, Persia*, and *India*" and claims that the people in these countries started reproducing rapidly before the Tower of Babel dispersal.[33] Heylyn's constant shifting between a specific country's description and the way that it fits into the biblical view of history enabled him to impose a rigorous master narrative on individual events that might have seemed chaotic or threatening if viewed in isolation.

Heylyn derives satisfaction in returning to what he calls the "Real" or "True" version of interpreting world affairs, which suggests a macrocosmic divine perspective. However, this perspective encompasses more traditionally secular elements such as lists of army sizes and currency exchange rates (see fig. 2). The association between wealth and military size would have been natural to the English in the seventeenth century for several reasons. On a practical level, India would have to be incredibly spacious and endowed with an abundance of natural resources to support a population capable of producing armies of that magnitude.

More specifically, English government was structured in the seventeenth century so as to link money and army size since revenues went almost entirely to military expenditures. Between 1689 and 1697, for

---

[30] Heylyn, *Cosmographie*, 1:6.
[31] Heylyn, *Cosmographie*, 1:7.
[32] Heylyn, *Cosmographie*, 1:6–8; 3:218.
[33] Heylyn, *Cosmographie*, 1:7.

instance, seventy-four percent of England's overall government expenditure was devoted to the military.[34] No large-scale social programs existed and specific tolls rather than general income taxes paid for necessary public works like roads and bridges. Heylyn makes the connection between wealth and armies explicit:

> if *Badurius*, which was King of *Cambaia* only, could bring into the field at once 500 Tun of Gold and Silver to pay his Army; and after the loss of all that treasure, advanced upon the sudden the sum of 600000 Crowns, which he sent to *Solyman* . . . What infinite *Treasures* must we think this Prince to be Master of, who hath more than four times the estate of the King of *Cambaia*?[35]

As this passage suggests, the size of India's armies reveals a complex network of associations that connect the size of the army to the cost of its maintenance and thence to the wealth of the ruler.

By repeatedly listing these figures in an almost incantatory way, Heylyn excites his readers' appetites for a revival of the East India trade, a project that both Charles I and Cromwell endorsed. Each of these rulers used the East India Company as a creditor, or more accurately as a benefactor since neither of the two men repaid their loans.[36] Consequently, Heylyn's promotion of trade to the East Indies testified to loyalty to Charles I which could be safely made in print without endangering Heylyn further with the Commonwealth government. With such broad support in place, Heylyn was free to dwell on the trade benefits that India could offer England. He exclaims, "Only we may conjecture by the great wealth of those several Princes, and the vast Armies by them raised in their several Territories; that his *Annual Revenues, Casualties*, and united Forces must be almost infinite."[37] The phrase "almost infinite" indicates one of his main points about the Mughal Empire. By constantly emphasizing the numbers of Mughal troops, and the wealth that the maintenance of those soldiers suggested, Heylyn expresses his envy of India's power. A strong army also provided rulers with the ability to seize and defend strategic

---

[34] John Childs, *Warfare in the Seventeenth Century* (London, 2001), 88.

[35] Heylyn, *Cosmographie*, 3:237.

[36] Markley, *Far East*, 64.

[37] Heylyn, *Cosmographie*, 3:246.

ports. Thus, wealth led to the equipment and provision of armies, which in turn captured and protected wealth. The large forces could guarantee, at least in theory, safe trade with the English. India's vast military would also require a steady supply of gunpowder, so England's saltpetre merchants could have a ready market. Appropriately enough, the sentence about the infinite nature of Mughal military might and wealth is the last line that Heylyn writes about India before closing with his stock phrase: "And so much for" India.[38]

What they could not take by force, then, Englishmen might gain through trade. Yet trade was not favorably balanced in the seventeenth century. England's main export, wool, was not especially valuable on the European market, and the English were running out of natural resources. Timber, which was crucial for the production of ships, buildings, and heat during England's cold winters, serves as a case in point. In Andrew Marvell's 1653 poem "Bermudas," a crew in an "English boat" describes the island as "far kinder than [their] own" with pineapple trees and "cedars," and Aphra Behn's narrator in *Oroonoko* says "The very wood" in Surinam has "an intrinsic value above common timber . . . and bear[s] a price considerable."[39] By 1732, according to Oliver Goldsmith, a dispute over England's right of "cutting logwood in the bay of Campeachy" led directly to war with Spain.[40]

Heylyn follows Purchas by attempting to provide an ideological justification for the trade imbalance through theological rhetoric:

> But nothing more sets forth the Power and Wisdom of Almighty God, as it relates to these particulars, than that most admirable intermixture of Want with Plenty, whereby he hath united all the parts of the World in a continual Traffique and Commerce with one another: some Countries being destitute of those Commodities, with which others abound; and being plentiful in those, which the others want.[41]

---

[38]   Heylyn, *Cosmographie*, 3:246.

[39]   Behn, *Oroonoko*, 116; Andrew Marvell, *The Complete Poems*, ed. George de Forest Lord (New York, 1984), 10-11.

[40]   Oliver Goldsmith, *Pinnock's Improved Edition of Dr. Goldsmith's History of England: From the Invasion of Julius Caesar to the Death of George II. . . .* [1771] (Philadelphia, 1846), 321.

[41]   Heylyn, *Cosmographie*, 1:5.

In this passage, which idealistically posits that nations will "Traffique and Commerce with one another" rather than forcibly taking the things they need by warfare, Heylyn argues that the Judeo-Christian God created a world in which the intermingling and interdependence of all His people was not just encouraged but actually required. In practice, Englishmen were forced to trade with "Indians" in India if they wanted to gain access to valuable spices and commodities since a military takeover of the Mughal Empire was out of the question. By framing the weakness as obedience to divine mandate, Heylyn furnished his countrymen a sense of dignity and importance in global affairs.

Voyage collection editors such as Heylyn had a determinative impact on the popular fiction and worldviews of the ensuing decades. Heylyn is especially significant since he was not just an isolated bestselling author; he summarized firsthand accounts by English travelers such as William Hawkins, Ralph Fitch, and dozens of others. Heylyn's religiously saturated *Cosmographie* reveals a good deal about the ways in which the English saw themselves in relation to the rest of the world and performs the cultural work of national identity formation which the more secular and fictionalized literary forms would increasingly share.

Diamond Jubilee: A History of the New England Renaissance Conference, 1939–2014

Christopher Carlsmith
University of Massachusetts Lowell

Introduction

FOUNDED IN THE spring of 1939, the New England Renaissance Conference (NERC) is the oldest scholarly association in the U.S. dedicated to the study of the Renaissance. Given NERC's lack of institutional structure—it has no constitution, no membership fees, no secretary, no publications, and no fixed location—one may marvel that

I wish to thank Peter Fergusson, Ann Moyer, and Kenneth Gouwens for their willingness to read an early draft of this article, as well as Touba Ghadessi and the anonymous reader for the American Philosophical Society for substantive comments on the full manuscript. I am grateful to Tara Nummedal for early encouragement and temporary possession of the NERC Archive. I thank John Gilmore for permission to consult the Myron Gilmore Papers at Harvard University Archives. I also wish to acknowledge the assistance of students Meghan Chapman and Derek Winslow, who worked hard to digitize the conference programs and to write preliminary studies of several NERC presidents, and of Emily Jarmolowicz who reorganized the NERC Archive in Spring 2014 and assisted with editing this article. At the annual meeting of the Renaissance Society of America (RSA) in New York in March 2014, Kristin Bezio, Paul Budra, Martine Van Elk, and Tara Nummedal shared their impressions of the different regional Renaissance societies, for which I am very grateful.

it has survived seventy-five years. Despite such limitations, NERC has played a significant role in promoting and disseminating scholarship about the Renaissance, particularly in the region between Boston and New York, and its history is one that deserves closer scrutiny.[1] This essay provides an analytical summary of the history of NERC, with particular focus upon important developments and transitions under each of the conference's leaders from 1939 to 2014. Some of those developments, such as the rise of social history or the advent of computer-aided analysis, are evident across the broader field of Renaissance Studies, but others seem more limited to Renaissance scholars of the Northeast.[2] Comparisons are also drawn with other regional Renaissance societies in the United States. This essay is based chiefly upon conference programs and professional correspondence within NERC's own archive, as well as material from the American Council of Learned Societies (ACLS), the Renaissance Society of America (RSA), and other scholarly societies devoted to Renaissance Studies, supplemented by oral interviews, published accounts, and personal papers.[3]

---

[1]   The only account of NERC's history is F. Edward Cranz, "Fifty Years of the New England Renaissance Conference," *Renaissance Quarterly*, 42 (1989): 749–59, an amusing, quite brief overview first written as a talk for the 50th anniversary of NERC at Harvard in March 1989. A year-by-year "Chronology" of NERC conferences is available at the NERC website: <http://nercblog.wordpress.com/nerc-archive-project/history-of-nerc>.

[2]   The historiography of the Renaissance in the USA is a vast topic. For an introduction, see Anthony Molho, "The Italian Renaissance: Made in the USA," in *Imagined Histories: American Historians Interpret the Past*, ed. Molho and Gordon S. Wood (Princeton, 1998), 264–94; Edward Muir, "The Italian Renaissance in America," *American Historical Review*, 100 (1995): 1095–1118; John Jeffries Martin, "The Renaissance: A World in Motion," in *The Renaissance World*, ed. Martin (New York, 2007): 3–27; on earlier interpretations, see DeLamar Jensen, "The 'Renaissance' in Recent Thought: Fifteen Years of Interpretation," *Brigham Young University Studies*, 6 (1964): 1–23. Of course, some changes in Renaissance Studies are also reflected across the entire field of historical study, but that topic is too vast to be considered here.

[3]   NERC has had no formal archive; some mailing lists and correspondence were passed from one president to another but not in any methodical way. Edward Cranz gathered some material together in 1989; Kenneth Gouwens organized the extant conference programs ca. 2005 during his term as president of NERC. The current "archive" consists primarily of correspondence, conference programs, and related documents; all references in this article, unless indicated otherwise, refer to

The New England Renaissance Conference can be viewed as a case-study of the changing roles of learned societies in the USA, and of the challenges now facing them. In this sense, the example of NERC speaks to major issues in the history of education, institutional history, and intellectual history. Among these issues are those of elitism, and the "opening" of what had been private preserves of certain elite schools, to include wider representation of the profession. The divergent missions of small colleges and large research universities, the rise of state institutions, and the shifting balance between regional and national organizations, are considered here. Also evident are the shifting emphases in geographical, political, and methodological priorities of Renaissance scholars across multiple disciplinary fields. Lastly, analysis of NERC illustrates issues of organizational structure and sustainability, as well as recent attempts at the democratization of scholarship through both technological and traditional means.

Like most academic organizations and scholarly societies, the New England Renaissance Conference was founded by scholars who shared a common intellectual interest and who wished to promote their field of chosen study. Such scholarly societies date back to the "academies" of early modern Europe, or even to the *universitates* of the late Middle Ages. The roots of NERC are similar, albeit a decade or more antecedent, to its sister organizations in other regions, such as the South-Central Renaissance Conference (SCRC, founded 1952), the Pacific Northwest Renaissance Society (PNRS, founded 1956), the Renaissance Conference of Southern California (RCSC, founded ca. 1956–59) or the Rocky Mountain Medieval and Renaissance Association (RMRRA, founded 1968).[4]

---

documents within this NERC archive, which was thoroughly reorganized by Emily Jarmolowicz in Spring 2014. The current archive consists of a total of three boxes. The first two boxes contain the majority of the correspondence, and are organized as a single chronological series separated into folders based primarily on conference year and secondarily by subject. The third box consists of a binder containing available conference programs beginning in 1943. Documents from this archive are identified as "NERCA" followed by the box, folder, and document number(s), e.g., NERCA 1.2.3. Multiple documents in the same folder are identified by letter (e.g., NERCA 1.2.3-B); where necessary, page numbers of individual documents are listed at the end of the citation (e.g., NERCA 1.2.3, 3).

[4] To the best of my knowledge, none of the other regional scholarly societies of the Renaissance in the USA possesses a comprehensive and documented written history. The PNRS does have a chronology on its website that offers a brief synopsis

Each of these regional scholarly societies, including NERC, is dwarfed by the Renaissance Society of America (founded 1954), the leading organization in North America for the study of the Renaissance. With membership currently numbering about 5,000 scholars, the RSA engages in an array of activities: it publishes the journal *Renaissance Quarterly* and the newsletter *Renaissance News and Notes*; it organizes a major annual meeting each spring for several thousand scholars; it collaborates with libraries and international organizations; and it sponsors book prizes, research grants, and electronic publishing of important primary texts.[5] It was long believed that NERC (f. 1939) was the original parent of the RSA (f. 1954). As Paul Oskar Kristeller firmly pointed out, however, while there existed a common purpose, and some overlap in the identity of early members, the two organizations were independent of each other from the very beginning.[6] Nevertheless, NERC can take pride in being a pioneer of

---

of each conference from 1956–1996, written by Jean MacIntyre, at <http://www.pnrs.org>; this will be superseded by the forthcoming article by Paul Budra and Jean MacIntyre, "The Pacific Northwest Renaissance Society," *Renaissance and Reformation*, published by the Canadian Society for Renaissance Studies, which Paul Budra graciously shared with me in advance of publication. The SCRC has an excellent online archive of minutes and programs at <http://www.scrc.us.com/archives.shtml>, but no narrative history.

[5] See the RSA's website: <http://www.rsa.org>. As this article went to press, the RSA office began to digitize many of its own documents from the 1930s–1950s, including executive board minutes, bound ledgers with membership information, and extensive correspondence related to the Society. As one might expect, the paper record is particularly strong during and after the RSA's founding in 1954. The RSA is also digitizing some papers pertaining to Leicester Bradner and the ACLS Committee on Renaissance Studies, donated by Paul Oskar Kristeller. The documents do not shed any additional light on the history of NERC but they are a treasure trove for the intellectual history of Renaissance Studies, as well as offering insight into the contributions of major scholars such as Josephine Waters Bennett, W.G. Constable, Paul Oskar Kristeller, and others.

[6] The original title for Edward Cranz's 1989 talk (n. 1 above) was "Fifty Years of NERC: Parent of the RSA" but this changed upon receipt of Kristeller's stern reproof to Cranz. See Letter from Edward Cranz to Samuel Edgerton (24 Dec. 1988), NERCA 1.25.2: "[Kristeller] says categorically that the NERC is not the parent of the RSA and [he] indicated, kindly but firmly, that the phrase should be omitted from the title." Letter from Edward Cranz to Richard Douglas (8 Feb. 1989), NERCA 1.25.10: "Paul Kristeller, who insisted that the NERC is not the parent of the RSA, sent me some valuable material on the RSA and a little on the NERC." See also Letter from Edward Cranz to Richard Douglas (4 March 1989), NERCA 1.25.12, referring to

Renaissance Studies in the period just before World War II, and in maintaining its (admittedly nebulous) identity for three-quarters of a century.

Foundation and Early Years (1939–1959)

The origins of NERC can be traced to 1937, when the American Council of Learned Societies (ACLS) convened a group of Renaissance scholars interested in establishing a more formal association.[7] Leicester Bradner of Brown University was at the heart of this correspondence, and he would remain the leader of NERC for decades to come.[8] Inspired in part by an address offered to the MLA in December 1936 by Don Cameron Allen on "Desiderata for Further Study of the Renaissance," this small group of scholars declared that "some form of inclusive organization for Renaissance Studies was desirable."[9] Bradner and his colleagues rejected the idea of a new national society modeled upon the Medieval Academy of America (f. 1925), recommending instead a larger, more representative committee as well as a small executive committee to execute plans and make final decisions.[10] As their report observed, "What is wanted is a body of some sort that will keep track of everything useful that is being

---

"stern pronouncements from Kristeller making it quite clear that we are not the parent of the RSA." The relationship between NERC and RSA is briefly sketched in the following paragraphs but deserves a more thorough treatment that would include the documents cited in the previous note

[7] Report on the Conference of Renaissance Studies (Oct. 1937), NERCA 1.25.26-M; the conference occurred 9–10 Oct. 1937 in Chicago with representatives from eight disciplines, after which the report was submitted to the ACLS. See Leicester Bradner's admirably clear summary of this early history from 1936–52: Leicester Bradner, "Renaissance Scholarship in America," *Renaissance News*, 7 (1954): 1–6. See also Letter from Paul Kristeller to Andrew Sabol (29 May 1988), NERCA 1.25.23-C, in which Kristeller summarized the relevant points pertaining to Bradner and to NERC from 1938 to 1947. Kristeller included his original typescript summary and later sent the photocopied pages from the ACLS *Bulletin*; all of this material (in the NERC Archive) is in an envelope addressed to Edward Cranz from Kristeller dated 23 Dec. 1988.

[8] On Bradner, see n. 18 below.

[9] Report of the Conference on Renaissance Studies (Oct. 1937), NERCA 1.25.26-M, 1.

[10] Report of the Conference on Renaissance Studies (Oct. 1937), NERCA 1.25.26.M, 2: "a major enterprise like the Medieval Academy is not in this case

done in Renaissance scholarship, and that will determine what more needs to be done and seek to find ways of doing it."[11] In 1938 the ACLS created a five-member Committee on Renaissance Studies, which pursued two long-term projects: "(1) a review of the present state of Renaissance scholarship, to be done as a cooperative project, each chapter being written by an expert, and (2) a survey of the resources for the study of the Renaissance in America."[12] In 1944 Bradner succeeded to the position of chairman and held the post for another three years. After several name changes and reformulations, this Committee on Renaissance Studies would ultimately become the RSA in 1954.[13]

In the spring of 1939, Bradner and his committee established the New England Renaissance Conference. According to William G. Constable, who had become the director of the Museum of Fine Arts in Boston the previous year, "The basic idea of this [conference] was the importance of bringing together scholars of the Renaissance within a limited area for informal and frank discussion."[14] Constable explained

---

desirable." Cranz, "Fifty Years," 751–52 (n. 1 above), also summarizes the early history of NERC, utilizing Bradner, "Renaissance Scholarship" as a principal source.

[11] Report of the Conference on Renaissance Studies (Oct. 1937), NERCA 1.25.26-M, 1.

[12] Report of the Conference on Renaissance Studies (Oct. 1937), NERCA 1.25.26-M, 2; see also the ACLS *Bulletin*, 27 (1938). The ACLS Committee was very productive: a volume entitled *Surveys of Recent Scholarship in the Field of the Renaissance* was issued in 1945; *Studies in Philology* included an annual bibliography of Renaissance Studies with the committee's support; *Renaissance News* was founded in 1948; and what would become the 8-volume *Catalogus Translationum et Commentariorum: Medieval and Renaissance Latin Translations and Commentaries* (Washington, DC, 1960–2011), ed. Paul Oskar Kristeller, Edward Cranz, and Virginia Brown, was begun in 1946.

[13] "The Renaissance Society of America. An Account by the Executive Board," *Renaissance News*, 7 (1954): 7–11; Cranz, "Fifty Years," 751–52. See also Letter from Catherine Rauchenberger to Paul Kristeller (23 Aug. 1988), NERCA 1.25.26-K: "Margaret King asked me to look up the history of Leicester Bradner. He was never on the Executive Board of the Society nor did he serve as President. However, it seems that he was instrumental in the formation of the [Renaissance] Society [of America]."

[14] Letter from William Constable to David Berkowitz (19 April 1966), NERCA 1.1.8. Constable (b. 1887) studied for the bar at Cambridge University but later pursued his studies at the Bartlett School of Architecture. He joined the [British] National Gallery in 1923 as an art historian, became the founding Director of the

that NERC responded to the exigencies of the time period in choosing its format:

> To do this [informal, local discussion about the Renaissance] was all the more important since conditions made establishment of a national body practically impossible, and meetings pretty well out of the question. Moreover, the times did not favor elaborate and widespread organization. The note [*sic*] of the NE Conference was that it had no rules, and that each annual meeting was organized exactly as the institution acting as host considered the most practical. Naturally, a certain element of standardization has developed; but from the beginning we insisted on elasticity.[15]

From its inception, NERC eschewed most of the trappings of bureaucracy: it charged no membership fee, it published no journal, it maintained no minutes, it kept no archive, and it had only one officer. Its sole goal appears to have been the organization of an annual conference, so that members could share their most recent research with one other. Particularly in recent decades, NERC's commitment to academic minimalism stands in contrast to the impressive achievements of other Renaissance societies, which have established peer-reviewed journals, scholarships, annual awards, regular newsletters, and attractive websites. But NERC was determined to stay simple: as Richard Douglas of MIT phrased it in his 1989 letter to Edward Cranz:

> The New England Renaissance Conference has flourished through years of graceful disarray, to the point at times when it has almost denied itself a coherent past. One organization in Modern America that manages without constitution or structure of any kind, but it turns out to be very durable.[16]

Courtauld Institute in 1930, and left the Courtauld in 1937, whereupon he became Curator of Paintings at the Boston MFA in 1938 until his retirement in 1957.

[15] Letter from Constable to Berkowitz (19 April 1966), NERCA 1.1.8.

[16] Letter from Richard Douglas to Edward Cranz (15 March 1989), NERCA 1.25.13.

The New England Renaissance Conference was the only local conference group to be directly sponsored by the ACLS committee, but it served as an example for similar societies in North Carolina (1943), New York (1944), Middle West (1945), Philadelphia (1948), and South-Central (1952). In his brief memoir of this early history, Leicester Bradner observed that these annual regional conferences "exhibit a healthy variety of organization and constitute the most important Renaissance activity now going on in America."[17]

Leicester Bradner (1939-1959)

As noted above, Leicester Bradner was the guiding force behind the establishment of NERC in the late 1930s.[18] In addition to his seminal role within NERC, he led the ACLS Committee on Renaissance Studies as well as the Brown Renaissance Colloquium. A professor of literature with wide-ranging interests, his most important work was the *Musae Anglicanae: A History of Anglo-Latin Poetry, 1500–1925*, published in 1940; he also wrote on Spencer's *Faerie Queene* and on Renaissance theatre, as well as co-authoring a book on the epigrams of Thomas More. According to an obituary penned by Bradner's son, shortly after Leicester Bradner's retirement in 1968 one of his former students referred to him as "our Renaissance Man"—a fitting title for the man who created NERC. This admiration for Bradner as a scholar who was conversant in many different fields was echoed by his Brown colleague, Elmer Blistein, in the foreword to a Festschrift in honor of Bradner: "[he was] that rare type,

---

[17]   Bradner, "Renaissance Scholarship," 4 (n. 7 above).
[18]   On Bradner's career and personality, see Paul Oskar Kristeller's memorial in *Renaissance Quarterly*, 41 (1988): 777-78, a draft of which was sent by Kristeller to Cranz (23 Dec. 1988), NERCA 1.25.26-J. See also the obituaries sent to Cranz on 3 March 1989 by Andrew Sobol: a "Memorial Minute" offered to the Brown Faculty Senate by Elmer M. Blistein (3 May 1988), NERCA 1.25.23-E; a brief anonymous obituary published in the [Providence?] *Evening Bulletin* (13 April 1988), NERCA 1.25.23-B; and an obituary authored by son Rev. Lawrence Bradner (undated), NERCA 1.25.23-F. See also the draft of Robert "Sparks" Sorlien's remembrance, mailed to Edward Cranz by Sorlien (14 Feb. 1989), NERCA 1.25.18-B, intended for publication in the biannual international journal *Moreana*.

the specialist who is, at the same time the genuinely competent utility infielder."[19]

Bradner and his colleague Harcourt Brown of the French Department organized NERC's first conference at Brown University in April 1940. The speakers were Harcourt Brown on science, William G. Constable on art, Wallace Ferguson on history, and Paul Oskar Kristeller on letters. One could hardly ask for a more impressive roster of scholars for an inaugural conference! Ferguson published his first views on the Renaissance in a monograph that same year and amplified them eight years later in a historiographical classic.[20] Kristeller's contribution, "The Study of the Philosophies of the Renaissance," appeared in the *Journal of the History of Ideas* the following year,[21] while Harcourt Brown later looked back to 1940–41 as a watershed moment in his own career and in the history of science.[22] No extant program exists for this event but it seems likely that it followed the two-day, four-paper format so popular at subsequent NERC events.[23] The ACLS Committee on Renaissance

---

[19] Elmer Blistein, foreword to *The Drama of the Renaissance: Essays for Leicester Bradner* (Providence, 1971), viii.

[20] Wallace K. Ferguson, *The Renaissance* (New York, 1940); idem, *The Renaissance in Historical Thought: Five Centuries of Interpretation* (Boston, 1948).

[21] Letter from Paul Kristeller to Edward Cranz (20 March 1989), NERCA 1.25.27: "I have a list of the lectures given by me. It lists two papers for the New England Renaissance Conference at Brown University on April 13, 1940: Manuscript materials for Italian humanism, and (with J[ohn H.] Randall) a survey of the present state of scholarship on Renaissance philosophy. I suppose this was the first New England Renaissance Conference. Apart from Bradner himself, [Roland] Bainton and Randall were surely active in getting me on the program. I was far too new to have had any influence at that stage....Harcourt Brown probably was active in advising Bradner and in making local arrangements at Brown, but he was not a member of the ACLS committee....I am sure Bradner organized the first conference in 1940 and had it sponsored and perhaps partly financed by the committee of which he was then the secretary [i.e., the ACLS Committee on Renaissance Studies]. I am not able to say more."

[22] Paul O. Kristeller and John H. Randall, Jr. "The Study of the Philosophies of the Renaissance," *Journal of the History of Ideas*, 2 (1941): 449–496, as cited in *Philosophy and Humanism: Renaissance Essays in Honor of Paul Oskar Kristeller*, ed. Edward P. Mahoney (Leiden, 1976), 547. Harcourt Brown, "The Renaissance and Historians of Science," *Studies in the Renaissance*, 7 (1960): 27–42, esp. 27–28.

[23] In preparing his remarks for the 50th anniversary of NERC in 1989 (see n. 1 above), Edward Cranz sent at least a dozen letters to colleagues asking for information and documents about the early history of NERC, and especially for the 1940 program; he received quite a bit of material but not the 1940 program. As he put it in

Studies noted in its 1941 annual report that "The Committee has stimulated an interest in conferences on the problems of Renaissance Studies in various parts of the country....[A] very successful conference was held at Brown University in April. Several members of the Committee participated in this conference, and the interest and active cooperation of scholars in several fields can be reported."[24] The report pointed out that conferences on Renaissance Studies were also planned in Chicago and at the Huntington Library, and proclaimed "These conferences...are, we think, very effective means of furthering the ends for which the Committee was appointed."

The second meeting of NERC was at Connecticut College in 1941, with reported attendance of fifty scholars. Leicester Bradner deemed this conference to be "very successful," although his annual report to the ACLS noted that "Attempts to stimulate conferences in other regions have not as yet been successful. For the present, in view of the national emergency [i.e., WW II], they are not being pushed any further."[25] The NERC soldiered on: the third conference was at Yale in 1942, the fourth at Harvard in 1943, and the fifth at Brown in 1944.[26]

Immediately apparent is the limited academic circle in which Renaissance studies was conducted in this era: with the exception of Connecticut College as noted above, it was the Ivy League institutions that dominated the opening decades of the New England Renaissance Conference. For example, of the twenty-one conferences sponsored by NERC between 1950 and 1970, just under half (9/21) were held at Ivy League institutions (Harvard, Yale, Brown, Dartmouth). By contrast, during the 1970s and most of the 1980s no Ivy League institution hosted NERC; it only returned

---

a letter of 5 April 1989 to Samuel Edgerton, NERCA 1.25.5, "I beat the bushes far and wide, and the result was very encouraging." Cranz promised to return material gathered from Jane Ruby, Dick Douglas, Paul Kristeller, Andy Sabol, Bill Dinneen, and other early participants in NERC, to Sam Edgerton (NERC's president, 1985–90); Cranz added parenthetically "You might as well put them into the archivall [sic] file, so someone can puzzle over them for the hundredth anniversary."

[24] Archer Taylor, "Committee on Renaissance Studies, Report of Activities, 1940" [Annex 8], ACLS *Bulletin*, 33 (1941): 88–89 (also paginated as 536–37).

[25] Leicester Bradner, "Committee on Renaissance Studies, Report of Activities, 1941" [Annex 11], ACLS *Bulletin*, 35 (1942): 86–87 (also paginated as 756-57).

[26] ACLS *Bulletin*, 33 (1941): 88–89; ibid, 35 (1942): 86–87 (also paginated as 756–57); ibid, 36 (1944): 21, 80; ibid, 38 (1945): 82–83.

to Harvard in 1989 on account of the fiftieth anniversary of the organization and the desire to have a grand celebration.[27] This trend has continued to the present day; Yale was the only Ivy League institution to host in the 1990s (1991) while Brown hosted twice (2002, 2007) in the following decade. The tendency has clearly been for other New England colleges and universities to host the conference during the past thirty years, from major research universities (Boston University, University of Connecticut, UMass Amherst) to liberal arts colleges (Wheaton College, Wesleyan University). Such a trend has been explicitly encouraged by the immediate past presidents of NERC, Tara Nummedal and Kenneth Gouwens, respectively. Both expressed support for pushing NERC out to other institutions that have not traditionally hosted, as a means to "democratize" the study of the Renaissance, and also to encourage those scholars more likely to be working without a group of like-minded colleagues.[28] In other parts of the country, where no cadre of schools equivalent to the Ivy League exists, it has chiefly been the major state universities and colleges that have hosted the regional Renaissance societies.

It is also worth noting that NERC's perennial lack of a budget requires the host institution to bear all costs associated with the conference; thus sharing the conference among a wider swath of institutions makes financial sense by reducing the burden upon a small group of repeat hosts. The other regional Renaissance societies, with one notable exception, have followed a similar pattern of rotating hosts. The SCRC has moved its meeting virtually every year since 1953, as has the RMRRA and the PNRS (the latter stipulates that its annual meeting must alternate between Canada and the USA each year). The lone exception is the Renaissance Conference of Southern California (RCSC), which has for years met at the Huntington Library in San Marino.

To return to the early history of NERC: the 1943 program specifies that the conference, held at Harvard's Houghton Library, "is designed to bring

---

[27] The 1989 conference was originally to be at Brown but was transferred to Harvard somewhat abruptly; see the collection of 6 letters from 10 May 1984 to 2 Sept. 1985 sent by Jane Ruby to Edward Cranz on 17 Feb. 1989, which document how the conference was unexpectedly moved from Providence to Cambridge, NERCA 1.25.

[28] Oral interviews conducted with Kenneth Gouwens (14 Jan. 2013) in Cambridge, and with Tara Nummedal (15 Jan. 2013) in Providence; summaries are at the NERC Archive, NERCA 2.28.1–2.

together workers in varied disciplines in the period of the late fifteenth and sixteenth centuries."[29] A group dinner at the Harvard Faculty Club was followed by two talks: Theodore Spencer of Harvard on "Shakespeare and Intellectual History," and Howard Mumford Jones of Harvard on the topic "American Origins and the Renaissance." Accommodation was offered at the Hotel Statler in Boston for the princely sum of $4.40 per person. Saturday morning witnessed another pair of talks: Harry Levin of Harvard spoke on "Jonson's Metempsychosis" while book collector and investor Imrie de Vegh of Washington, D.C. described the career of the sixteenth-century Hungarian humanist and book collector Johannes Sambucus.[30] Following the morning talks, the entire group adjourned to a buffet luncheon at a private house on Garden Street, and then reconvened at Houghton Library in mid-afternoon for a concert of Renaissance music given by Erwin Bodky and musicians from the Boston Symphony Orchestra.

The 1943 program has been described in some detail because it encapsulates several important themes for the early history of NERC, some of

---

[29] Conference Program (1943), NERCA 3.1. Given the rarefied nature of this NERC meeting, the choice of the word "workers" here, rather than "scholars" or "researchers," is an interesting one.

[30] It is not possible to document all of those who presented at NERC but I include here a brief description of Imrie de Vegh as he was a most unusual participant, coming from outside the academy and outside New England. As cited in James E. Walsh, *A Catalogue of the Fifteenth-Century Printed Books in the Harvard University Library*, vol. 5 (Tempe, AZ, 1997), 46: "Born in Budapest in 1906, Imrie de Vegh (as he preferred to spell his name, the Hungarian form being Imre) earned an LL.D. at the University of Budapest in 1928 and then spent two years of further study at Trinity College, Cambridge. Moving to the United States, he worked as an economist with the New York firm of Scudder, Stevens & Clark for ten years. During World War II he was a member of the War Production Board. After the war he founded his own firm, de Vegh & Co., and was president and director of the de Vegh Mutual Fund until his premature death from lung cancer in 1962. He was a discriminating book collector and concentrated on works illustrating the history of ideas in all periods and parts of the world. One of his special interests was Johannes Sambucus (Janos Samboky), a fellow Hungarian (1531–1584), a humanist, and an important collector of books and manuscripts, whose collection on his death passed to what is now the Nationalbibliothek in Vienna. De Vegh assembled an impressive number of Sambucus's works, which he gave to the Harvard Library. His gifts of thirty-four incunabula might seem a miscellaneous lot, but looked at closely they will reveal his concern to bring together books that illustrate unusual and sometimes fantastic workings of the human mind."

which would later by echoed by other regional learned societies. First, both the location (in Cambridge) and the affiliation of the speakers (3/4 from Harvard) testify to the dominance of the Ivy League in the opening decades of NERC. Second, the speakers in these early decades were always established professors; graduate students were never invited to speak. Third, the inclusion of an afternoon concert of Renaissance music foreshadows a trend in these NERC conferences to include a poetry reading, a theatrical production, or a musical ensemble to entertain and edify conference participants about high Renaissance culture. Such cultural entertainment has continued to be featured in more recent NERC gatherings, as well as in those of its sister societies. For example, the RMRRA routinely holds its meetings in conjunction with the Utah Shakespeare Festival, and the PNRS annual meeting has long had a tradition of performing a fully-staged play or else a community reading of a play.

Virtually all NERC conferences from 1943–1983 were two-day affairs on a Friday and Saturday, with plenty of time for socializing and cultural attractions. The Renaissance societies elsewhere in the USA have always hosted two-day conferences, and continue to do so today. By contrast, the past decade or so (2000–2013) has seen a decided preference for NERC to host a one-day Saturday conference, presumably to better accommodate the reality of increased professional pressure and domestic demands upon conference participants. It may be that the regional conferences in less densely-populated areas, such as the West, have continued to be two-day events both because the travel distances are substantially greater and because there is less competition from other events or institutions with similar foci.

It is worth noting, too, that there were only four papers offered at this 1943 NERC conference, which seems a low number for a regional conference extending over two days. It suggests—but we cannot easily verify such a hypothesis—that conference papers of the mid-twentieth century were perhaps more weighty and required more preparation by the speakers (or more digestion by the listeners) than is the norm today.[31] NERC has almost always limited the number of papers to the single digits; other

---

[31] The comments of Myron Gilmore and other NERC presidents support the interpretation that conference papers were more substantial—in the 1950s and 1960s the papers were often 40–45 minutes in length, and scholars routinely spent years investigating a particular topic before being invited to speak.

Renaissance conferences (e.g., PNRS, RMRRA) have in recent decades often solicited more papers and run concurrent panels, with more recent conferences featuring 45–70 papers in a single weekend.[32]

We have no record of the NERC conferences held in the immediate post-war period from 1945 to 1947; the next few were held at Dartmouth (1949), Mt. Holyoke (1950), Brown (1951), Harvard (1952), and Yale (1953).[33] Nor do we have extant copies of the program again until 1954 when the annual meeting convened at Wellesley College in mid-November under the direction of M. Ruth Michael. At Wellesley, three of the five speakers were from Harvard, including art historian Millard Meiss and literary scholar Herbert Dieckmann, as well as Latin professor Dorothy Robathan of Wellesley who spoke about "Renaissance Reactions to a Literary Forgery of the Thirteenth Century." An exhibition of various editions of English Renaissance poetry in the college library, and a chamber music concert in the evening by Hubert Lamb, provided entertainment for the conference attendees.[34]

In 1955 the conference moved to nearby Tufts University under the direction of Harold Blanchard. The program was similar, featuring three talks on Friday afternoon followed by cocktails, an exhibition of Renaissance paintings, a group dinner at the faculty club, and a theater performance. An undergraduate theater group called Pen, Paint, and Pretzels offered a "Jacobean comedy burlesque" in three acts, described in the playbill as "a pastiche of current popular romantic plays and fiction . . .

---

[32] One should notice also that the RSA has steadily ballooned in size in recent years, with the 2014 conference registering nearly 3,000 scholars in New York. Thus it may well be NERC that is anomalous here in maintaining what John Paoletti later referred to as NERC's "small-town quality".

[33] The conference at Mt. Holyoke occurred 5–6 May 1950 (*Renaissance News*, 2 [1950]: 78). The 27–28 April 1951 Brown conference included papers by Cranz, Kristeller, and Bradner (*Renaissance News*, 4 [1951]: 10–11); in addition, "At the business meeting Leicester Bradner (Brown) was appointed a one-man clearing house for future annual meetings" (*Renaissance News*, 4 [1951], 20). The conference on 9–10 May 1952 was organized by John Coolidge (Art) and Myron Gilmore (History); in honor of the quincentenary of Leonardo da Vinci's birth, the theme was "Science in the Civilization of the Renaissance" with papers on Paracelsus, Claudius Ptolemy, and Renaissance theories of generation (*Renaissance News*, 5 [1952]: 18). The 1953 conference was held 30–31 October at Yale.

[34] In addition to the conference program in the NERC Archive (1954), NERCA 3.1, see *Renaissance News*, 7 (1954): 111.

[that] also pokes fun at the playgoing tastes and manners of London's rising merchant class."[35] The conference struck a more serious note on Saturday morning with a talk by Paul Oskar Kristeller about apocryphal sources of Renaissance Platonism, and a report from Myron Gilmore (who would assume the presidency of NERC in 1959) on the Sept. 1955 meeting of the International Congress of Historical Sciences and on the proposal to create an edition of the Medici correspondence in Florence (the eventual Medici Archive Project).[36]

The 1956 conference moved west to Amherst College for a mid-October meeting. The focus remained on the traditional fields of Italian history and art, as well as English literature, with talks by Leona Gabel (Smith), Raymond de Roover (Boston College), Frederick Lane (Johns Hopkins), Leicester Bradner (Brown), and Caesar Barber (Amherst College). The Amherst Glee Club offered a brief program of Renaissance choral music. Connecticut College hosted the 1957 conference in New London, with a program organized by Edward Cranz that turned toward religion and humanism: Richard Douglas (Amherst College, subsequently at MIT) spoke about the humanist and religious reformer Jacopo Sadoleto, and Wilhelm Pauck of the Union Theological Seminary presented his findings about Martin Luther's biblical exegesis. The Palestrina Society of Connecticut College sang the "Quaeramus cum pastoribus" Mass by Cristòbal Morales after an evening visit to view Renaissance drawings in the college's own collection.[37]

Dartmouth College hosted NERC for second time in 1958 with an interdisciplinary panel of medieval and Renaissance topics. Vernon Hall Jr. of Dartmouth opened the Friday session with an exhibition of Renaissance medals, followed by a lecture on Trecento music by his colleague Royal MacDonald and then a talk on "The Genesis of 'Barocco,' a German Style" by S. Lane Faison Jr. (Williams College). The following morning

---

[35] In addition to the conference program and playbill (1955), NERCA 3.1, see *Renaissance News*, 8 (1955): 222–23.

[36] Letters from Harold Blanchard to Myron Gilmore (4 May 1955), NERCA 1.2.1; (9 June 1955), NERCA 1.2.2.; and (13 Aug. 1955), NERCA 1.2.4; replies from Myron Gilmore to Harold Blanchard (3 Aug. 1955), NERCA 1.2.3. and (23 Aug. 1955), NERCA 1.2.5.

[37] A thorough summary of the 1957 meeting was recorded in *Renaissance News*, 10 (1957): 223–24; the typescript program is in the NERC Archive (1957), NERCA 3.1.

witnessed another contribution from Paul Oskar Kristeller, this time on Renaissance Manuscripts in Eastern Europe, and a talk by Stephen Gilman (Harvard) about the metamorphosis of medieval death imagery in the *Coplas* of fifteenth-century Spaniard Jorge Manrique.[38]

These conferences of the 1950s thus confirm the picture that was first sketched out at Brown, Harvard, and elsewhere in the prior decade: a relatively small conference with important professors from elite institutions, focused on topics of high Renaissance culture. Socializing and entertainment were just as important as the papers themselves. Italy and England remained the preferred locales of study, with lesser attention to Spain, France, and the rest of Europe. Conferences alternated between fall and spring; the choice of dates, subjects, speakers, and entertainment was largely at the discretion of the conference host each year. As noted previously, several Renaissance societies were founded in the 1950s but the absence of conference programs in those early years makes it difficult to compare them with NERC.

The decision to limit NERC membership was a conscious one by Leicester Bradner, in which he was supported by the members of a small *ad hoc* committee.[39] As noted by Brown history professor William F. Church in a letter to Myron Gilmore of Harvard, "Leicester and the committee apparently feel that it is decidedly preferable to keep the group a small, informal one, with emphasis on selectivity, and discussions at the meetings, rather than permitting the organization to grow in size to the point of being something that anyone can join merely by paying dues and securing automatic membership."[40] As noted below, this issue of membership would soon become a "red hot potato"[41] and would remain a contentious issue for decades.

Leicester Bradner remained the tireless, behind-the-scenes organizer of NERC from 1939 to 1959. In his final year (1959), he organized a twentieth-anniversary conference at Brown, featuring the original

---

[38]   Conference Program (1958), NERCA 3.1.

[39]   The committee included William Dinneen (Brown), Richard Douglas (Amherst), and Grace Hawks (Wellesley); see Letter from William Church to Myron Gilmore (8 Nov. 1958), NERCA 1.1.1, 1.

[40]   Letter from Church to Gilmore, (8 Nov. 1958), NERCA 1.1.1, 1.

[41]   The phrase "red hot potato" was used in a letter from William Dinneen to Myron Gilmore (24 April 1959), NERCA 1.1.5 to refer to the debate over membership size.

four speakers from the 1940 conference. At this commemoration of two decades of NERC, all four scholars—Harcourt Brown, William Constable, Paul Oskar Kristeller, Wallace Ferguson—spoke on the theme of "Progress in Renaissance Scholarship in the Last Twenty Years."[42] A "Concert of Renaissance Music" at Manning Chapel, arranged by organist and professor of music William Dinneen, occurred on Friday evening.[43]

The fall 1959 conference was a watershed in several ways. First, NERC had survived two decades and was now flanked by both the RSA and other regional Renaissance societies in the South and the West. Second, this conference marked the last time that Leicester Bradner would be at the helm of NERC. Third, archival records after 1959 are more numerous and provide greater insight into how the organization developed. Lastly, the 1960s witnessed the diffusion of Renaissance Studies to a wider array of colleges and universities, as the graduate students of Ivy League schools fanned out to state universities and liberal arts colleges across the country. Of course, the 1960s was a decade marked by radical social upheaval, and some of those changes spilled over into how the Renaissance was conceived, studied, and taught. Such changes become more evident in the presidencies of those who succeeded Leicester Bradner: they include Myron Gilmore, David Berkowitz, Jane Ruby, and Samuel Edgerton.

The Middle Years (1959–1989)

Myron P. Gilmore (1959–1964)

Historian Myron Gilmore of Harvard University was Leicester Bradner's hand-picked successor to lead the New England Renaissance Conference. William Church described Gilmore as "a man of stature . . . [with] contacts in the field" who had already established a formidable reputation

---

[42] Harcourt Brown, "The Renaissance and Historians of Science" (n. 23 above); Wallace K. Ferguson, "The Reinterpretation of the Renaissance" in *Facets of the Renaissance*, ed. Ferguson and W. H. Werkmeister (Los Angeles, 1959), 1–18; Kristeller contributed an essay on Renaissance Platonism to *Facets of the Renaissance* but it's not clear if it was the paper presented at NERC in 1959.

[43] Conference Program (1959), NERCA 3.1, 1–2.

in early modern European history.[44] In offering the position of chairman to Myron Gilmore in early November 1958, Church wrote that the new chairman "would merely be required to keep the *ad hoc* committee alive (if necessary), write a letter or two…, and keep track of the list of members."[45] Church soft-pedaled the extent of the Chairman's responsibilities, writing that the conference "seems to be quite self-perpetuating" and that "there seems to be very little in the way of specific work."[46] Gilmore was not so easily fooled, however, and he responded directly to Bradner with a pointed question about precisely how much work would be involved.[47] Gilmore also made clear his reservations about the exclusivity of Bradner's membership list for NERC.[48] Nevertheless, with some reluctance, Gilmore agreed to take on the office in the winter of 1959.

It soon became clear that Gilmore would seek continuity with some of Bradner's policies while establishing decisively different approaches in other areas. For example, Gilmore noted that Bradner had "always very sensibly followed a principle of decentralization" in terms of delegating work to the individual conference hosts.[49] Gilmore too believed that the program chairman should have great latitude in determining the

---

[44] Letter from Church to Gilmore (8 Nov. 1958), NERCA 1.1.1, 1. Gilmore earned both an M.A. (1933) and a Ph.D. (1937) from Harvard, where he continued to teach except for three years of military service during WW II. He served as Chair of the Harvard History Department (1955–56, 1957–60), and subsequently as director of Harvard's Villa I Tatti (1964–73). He published five books on humanism and political thought in the Renaissance. Although his leadership of NERC lasted only five years, there is a remarkably good collection of correspondence for the heart of his tenure there (1960–62).

[45] Letter from Church to Gilmore (8 Nov. 1958), NERCA 1.1.1, 1.

[46] Letter from Church to Gilmore (8 Nov. 1958), NERCA 1.1.1, 1–2.

[47] Letter from Myron Gilmore to Leicester Bradner, with copy to W. F. Church (26 Nov. 1958), NERCA 1.1.2. "I should like to have some frank discussion with you before I agree to take on this additional responsibility. In the first place, I would naturally want to know more precisely how much work is involved."

[48] Letter from Myron Gilmore to Leicester Bradner (26 Nov. 1958), NERCA 1.1.2: "I sympathize with the desire to keep the group small and informal, and to limit the meetings to those actively interested. On the other hand, I do see some force in the argument that those who have paid dues to the large organization [i.e., the RSA] feel that they should be on the mailing list of the New England group, and I am not sure that I should wish to assume the chairmanship with any understanding of a commitment to adhere to the former policy."

[49] Letter from Gilmore to Bradner (26 Nov. 1958), NERCA 1.1.2.

conference schedule each year. Gilmore also favored Bradner's practice of a small *ad hoc* committee to provide advice, and asked to keep the same members in place.[50] Furthermore, Gilmore continued Bradner's efforts to make NERC an interdisciplinary group rather than privileging one discipline or another. Like Bradner, Gilmore seemed reluctant to rule by fiat, proposing that any changes to the term or the role of the chairman and his advisory group should be voted upon by the entire membership, not decided unilaterally by the NERC chairman.

On the other hand, the issues of "exclusivity" and "formality" were ones about which Gilmore felt quite differently than Bradner. As noted above, Gilmore had expressed reservations about continuing to follow Bradner's elitist approach to the mailing list.[51] In April 1959—just a few weeks after Gilmore had agreed to serve as NERC Chairman—Bradner circulated for review by Gilmore and others of the inner circle a policy statement that summarized Bradner's view of the relationship between the RSA and NERC.[52] Bradner saw the two organizations as distinct, and argued that dues paid to one did not automatically entitle one to benefits (such as one's name on the mailing list) from the other. The subtext here was Bradner's effort to limit those who could be on NERC's mailing list; Bradner routinely removed the names of those who had not attended the conference in the previous three to four years. Bradner referred to these non-participants as "deadheads who never come, [who] ought to be cut off."[53] Gilmore disagreed; in his reply to Bradner about the policy statement, Gilmore gently suggested that all interested persons should be allowed to submit their names.[54] In subsequent years, Gilmore regularly sought to expand the mailing list to include young faculty or recent arrivals in New England.

---

[50] Letter from Gilmore to Bradner (6 May 1959), NERCA 1.1.7; Letter from Myron Gilmore to William Dinneen (6 May 1959), NERCA 1.1.6.

[51] Letter from Myron Gilmore to Leicester Bradner, with copy to W. F. Church (26 Nov. 1958), NERCA 1.1.2.

[52] "The New England Conference on the Renaissance and The Renaissance Society of America: An Explanation" (n.d.), NERCA 1.1.3-B, n.a., but internal references (e.g., "this is the way it has operated for the last twenty years") make clear it is by Bradner. This policy statement was accompanied by a pair of brief letters from Bradner to Gilmore (9 April 1959), NERCA 1.1.3-A and (20 April 1959), NERCA 1.1.4, in which Bradner sought to justify the necessity of such a statement.

[53] Letter from Bradner to Gilmore (20 April 1959), NERCA 1.1.4.

[54] Letter from Gilmore to Bradner (6 May 1959), NERCA 1.1.7: "As I said to you when we last met, I think the notice you propose to publish in the Bulletin [i.e.,

The October 1959 conference at Brown had already been organized by the time Gilmore took office, so he focused on organizing the next meeting at Harvard in the spring of 1961. He hoped to have one session on the fifteenth century, another on the sixteenth century, and a third on Church Fathers in the Renaissance. In late September 1960, he wrote to a group of Harvard colleagues, including Reformation historian Heiko Oberman, literary scholar Douglas Bush, curator Philip Hofer, librarian William Jackson, art historian Sydney Freedberg, and literary critic Harry Levin, to solicit recommendations for speakers.[55] The suggestions that he received indicate who was already considered a senior figure (e.g., Erwin Panofsky) and who was considered to be a "rising star" in 1960 (e.g., W. R. Rearick, Walter Kaiser, Dante Della Terza). The letters also demonstrate that Gilmore was indeed the "man of stature" that the *ad hoc* committee had sought in its new chairman, with connections across multiple academic disciplines. Gilmore encountered several obstacles in recruiting speakers; art historian Frederick Hartt suffered a "severe accident to [his] right arm" necessitating an operation just three months before the conference, for example, and art historian James Holderbaum simultaneously withdrew due to a scheduling conflict.[56] Nevertheless, Gilmore was able to draw upon his extensive list of contacts to put together an impressive roster of speakers.[57]

It is clear that Gilmore had firm ideas about the content of the 1961 program. For an opening session on the humanist idea of Christian antiquity, he asked historian Hanna Holborn Gray at the University

---

Renaissance News] might contain an additional invitation to all interested persons to send in their names."

[55] Letter from Myron Gilmore to "Dear Colleagues" (28 Sept. 1960), NERCA 1.3.1. His colleagues responded promptly: see Letter from Douglas Bush to Myron Gilmore (25 Oct. 1960), NERCA 1.3.10; Letter from Heiko Oberman to Myron Gilmore (13 Oct. 1960), NERCA 1.3.8; Letter from Sydney Freedberg to Myron Gilmore (4 Oct. 1960), NERCA 1.3.4; Letter from Philip Hofer to Myron Gilmore (4 Oct. 1960), NERCA 1.3.3; Letter from Harry Levin to Myron Gilmore (5 Oct. 1960), NERCA 1.3.9.

[56] Letter from Frederick Hartt to Myron Gilmore (24 Jan. 1961), NERCA 1.3.35; and Gilmore's reply (2 Feb. 1961), NERCA 1.3.34. See also the letter from James Holderbaum to Myron Gilmore (31 Dec. 1960), NERCA 1.3.21, and Gilmore's reply (9 Jan. 1961), NERCA 1.3.25.

[57] Conference Program (1961), NERCA 3.1.

of Chicago to give a paper on "Lorenzo Valla and his Circle."[58] Gray responded that such a title was "misleading" because of the difficulty of identifying exactly who was (and was not) a member of Valla's circle; she proposed "Lorenzo Valla and his Contemporaries" instead.[59] Gilmore paired this topic with a paper by Cornell historian Eugene Rice, Jr. (later Executive Director of the RSA) on "Lefevre D'Etaples and his Circle."[60] The correspondence makes clear that Gilmore shared a deep friendship with each of these scholars. It is also clear that the traditional view of the Renaissance, with an emphasis upon humanism and the "great men" of the period, remained a dominant view in 1961, even as Gilmore and others were beginning to conceptualize a new idea of how to study the Renaissance.[61] Gilmore next convinced his Harvard colleague Walter Kaiser to give a paper related to that evening's theatrical production of *The Alchemist*, entitled "The Alembic of Satire."[62] Attendance was estimated at 100 to 150 people for each of the sessions and for the show. Three additional papers on the later Italian Renaissance, and an exhibition about Ariosto at the Houghton Library, rounded out the weekend.

Gilmore's correspondence demonstrates skill at identifying future conference hosts for NERC, and at mediating between them when

---

[58] Letters from Myron Gilmore to Hanna Gray (15 Nov. 1960), NERCA 1.3.12, and (7 March 1961), NERCA 1.3.47.

[59] Letters from Hanna Gray to Myron Gilmore (28 Nov. 1960), NERCA 1.3.17, and (8 March 1961), NERCA 1.3.49.

[60] Letters from Myron Gilmore to Eugene Rice (15 Nov. 1960), NERCA 1.3.13, (5 Jan. 1961), NERCA 1.3.23, and (7 March 1961), NERCA 1.3.48; reply from Eugene Rice to Myron Gilmore (undated but likely Dec. 1960), NERCA 1.3.14, notes that Rice would be "very happy" to return to Cambridge.

[61] See the comments of John O'Malley about Gilmore's teaching in 1961: "Paul Grendler and the Triumph of the Renaissance: A Reminiscence and Some Thoughts," in *The Renaissance in the Streets, Schools, and Studios: Essays in Honor of Paul F. Grendler*, ed. Nicholas Terpstra and Konrad Eisenbichler (Toronto, 2008), 323–44, esp. 324.

[62] Letter from Walter Kaiser to Myron Gilmore (18 Jan. 1961), NERCA 1.3.32; Kaiser noted that in trying to define a topic about alchemy, he had already read Petrarch, Chaucer, Bruno, Agrippa, Flamel, Cardanus, Arnoldus of Villa Nova, Paracelsus, Delrio, and even Jung; he observed wryly that "If all else fails, I can always perform an alchemical experiment and transmute a base metal or two for the edification of the assembled company!"

conflicts arose.[63] For the spring of 1962 Gilmore convinced a young
Charles Nauert to organize a conference at Williams College.[64] Visiting
professor of art John Pope-Hennessy anchored that conference with a
talk on Renaissance bronze statuettes. The Chapin Library at Williams
hosted a session on Renaissance books, which complemented another
session on historical manuscripts; there was also a session on the *siglo
de oro* in Spain. The location of the 1962 conference in Western Massachusetts extended (albeit only slightly) the Harvard-Yale-Brown triangle
that had recently dominated NERC. Although half of the speakers were
from Harvard and Brown, speakers from the University of Missouri, the
University of Toronto, and UMass Amherst were also present.

In 1963 NERC landed at Brandeis, where an ambitious conference
hosted by David Berkowitz foreshadowed his elevation to the presidency
of NERC in the following year (on which see more below). The surviving archival evidence suggests that Myron Gilmore was a forceful and
strong-minded leader, but one who was unfailingly courteous. Gilmore's
correspondence demonstrates that he sometimes instructed his colleagues about an appropriate title for a NERC conference paper rather
than asking for suggestions from them. His statements about the independence of NERC from the RSA reflect similarly strong opinions about
what was best for the organization. Gilmore did not share with Bradner the view that NERC should be just an elite organization of scholars.
Gilmore continued to participate in NERC until shortly before his death
in 1978.[65] Myron Gilmore thus provided direction and strong leadership
to NERC at a time when both were necessary; his term of five years has

[63] E.g., Gilmore's correspondence with Ruth Kennedy of Smith College (15
Dec. 1962), NERCA 1.5.4, (28 Dec. 1962) NERCA 1.5.5, (21 Feb. 1961), NERCA 1.4.3,
(2 March 1961), NERCA 1.4.5, and (1 June 1962), NERCA 1.5.7, who moved the date
of the conference three times; Gilmore observed to Charles Garside on 4 Jan. 1963
that he was "rather irritated" with the "Smith ladies" who could not make up their
minds, NERCA 1.5.8.
[64] Nauert left for the Univ. of Missouri in Fall 1961, but did much of the preparatory work and returned to chair a session at Williams. See the collegial correspondence (8 letters) between Gilmore and Nauert (4 March 1961 through 19 Apr. 1962),
NERCA 1.4.6-7; 1.4.9–10; 1.4.14–15; and 1.4.17.
[65] Gilmore gave a paper at the 1973 NERC entitled "Erasmus on Images and
the Council of Trent"; he moderated a panel discussion at the 1975 NERC on the
question of "What Was the Renaissance?"; Harvard University Archive, Myron P.
Gilmore Papers, HUGFP 32.45, "Professional and Research Papers," Box 2, Folder

perhaps been overshadowed as a result of his chairmanship occurring between two of the longest-serving leaders in NERC's history.

David S. Berkowitz (1964–1983)

With Myron Gilmore's departure to Italy as Director of Harvard University's Villa I Tatti in 1964, the responsibility to lead NERC fell to David Berkowitz. Like Gilmore, Berkowitz obtained his Ph.D. in History at Harvard (1946); in that same year he became Chairman of Social Sciences at Emerson College. In 1948 he was one of thirteen original faculty at Brandeis University, where he taught history and political science for more than three decades. Berkowitz had substantial administrative experience from his post as Executive Officer of the Association of Colleges and Universities of New York, and as Director of University Planning and Assistant to the President at Brandeis; he was also deeply involved with Brandeis' library and particularly its Special Collections.[66]

NERC did not have (and still does not have) any formal mechanism for choosing a leader. The typical method, as established by Leicester Bradner and his *ad hoc* committee, was for the outgoing executive to consult with various senior scholars within the organization in order to settle upon a worthy candidate. In a memorial note of 8 March 1983, Richard Douglas of MIT described how David Berkowitz took a different path to lead the New England Renaissance Conference in the early 1960s:

> Many of us came to know David during his term as President of the New England Renaissance Conference. Although he held this office for twenty-one years, until the end of his life, he was never formally appointed, elected, or re-elected to it. He simply occupied it by the silent consensus of Renaissance scholars all over the

---

"New England Renaissance Conference," contains correspondence and programs for the 1973 and 1975 conferences.

[66] On Berkowitz's career, see Richard M. Douglas, "A Memorial Note on David Sandler Berkowitz" (8 March 1983), NERCA 1.25.11-B; see also the brief biography of him in the finding aid to David S. Berkowitz Papers, Robert D. Farber University Archives and Special Collections, Brandeis University Library; available online at <http://lts.brandeis.edu/research/archives-speccoll/findingguides/archives/faculty/berkowitz.html> [accessed 28 April 2013]. My thanks to Brandeis Special Collections Librarian Maggie McNeely for her assistance.

Northeast. And year after year, like obedient nomads, we followed
David from meeting to meeting, a permanent tribal patriarch, uni-
versally loved and respected....[67]

Berkowitz's tenure of two decades was equivalent to that of Leicester
Bradner, and his impact upon NERC was equally important. Berkowitz
maintained the tradition of an annual two-day conference that included
both erudite talks and festive entertainment. He continued to promote a
multidisciplinary approach to the Renaissance as had his predecessors.
Yet he introduced important changes too, such as broadening the membership of NERC, moving beyond the Ivy League for conference hosts,
and granting more freedom to the program chairs.

    Together with nine of his faculty colleagues, Berkowitz organized
the May 1963 conference at Brandeis. It featured an unusually ambitious program, with multiple exhibitions and a stronger emphasis upon
exchange of ideas among conference participants.[68] The Brandeis conference opened on Friday afternoon with a symposium on early Italian Renaissance art, followed by an exhibition at the Rose Art Museum
called "Major Masters of the Renaissance." Curated by Creighton Gilbert,
that exhibition included fifteen paintings, thirty-nine prints, and three
drawings from major artists of the period: Tintoretto, Lorenzo Lotto,
Giorgione, Pieter Brueghel the Elder, Sebastiano del Piombo, Albrecht
Dürer, Parmigianino, Giovan Battista Moroni, Hans Holbein the Elder,
and Andrea Schiavone. The evening featured "Music and Dances of the
Renaissance" with a particular focus on sixteenth-century Spanish compositions.[69] Berkowitz also organized two exhibitions at the Brandeis

---

    [67]   Richard M. Douglas, "A Memorial Note on David Sandler Berkowitz" (8
March 1983), NERCA 1.25.11-B. See also the 1966 Newsletter, as in n. 85 below, which
observes that Berkowitz was elected by the 1965 annual conference, but clearly this
election was ex post facto.

    [68]   Among David Berkowitz's papers at Brandeis are 8 folders that contain
memos, letters, press releases, notes, budgets, biographies, and other miscellanea
related to the 1963 conference. These provide an unusually detailed look at how
Berkowitz organized this conference, and complement the full record preserved by
Myron Gilmore for the 1961 conference. David S. Berkowitz Papers, Box 42, Folders 1–8, Brandeis University Library. The NERC Archive also contains a copy of the
1963 conference program and some ancillary materials.

    [69]   David S. Berkowitz Papers, Box 42, Folder 3, "Exhibits" includes a pre-
liminary catalogue list of the artist, title of work, brief description, and loaning

Library. The first, drawing upon materials from Brandeis' own collection as well as loans from Hebrew Union College in Cincinnati, featured illuminated manuscripts, incunabulae, and early Aldine editions in Hebrew, Latin, and Italian. This exhibition included a recently-discovered manuscript that contained early fragments of *Amadis de Gaul*; Berkowitz's correspondence shows that he worked closely with the donor and with the American consulate to ship the manuscript in a diplomatic pouch! The second exhibition included sixteenth-century armor and weapons from the Higgins Armory in Worcester. All three of the exhibitions included significant loans from other institutions, and required extensive advance planning.

The heart of the conference on Saturday included four panels on the broad theme of "New—and Old—Currents in the Renaissance," to which four scholars contributed thirty-minute papers on the history of medicine, humanism, art history, and philosophy, followed by the briefer observations of six "discussants." Berkowitz consciously changed the program in two ways: first, he adopted a theme to unite the papers, and secondly he introduced the practice of using commentators in order to spur discussion. He outlined these ideas three weeks prior to the conference in a letter to Leicester Bradner:

> As an experiment we are asking two people to serve as discussants of the first three papers to be presented. I do not know whether it will work out well or not. The past conference discussions' level has, in my opinion, been lamentably low. This is, of course, understandable with a highly technical paper. In this case I felt that at least two members of the audience will have had the advantage of weighing the writer's words at leisure. The possibility of thoughtful and informed comment, I felt, would be very welcome to the writers.[70]

Two of the discussants were Berkowitz's colleagues while the rest came from other New England schools. Berkowitz had originally hoped to lure Hans Baron or Federico Zeri, two of the most important names in

institutions. Folder 7, "Press Releases" includes additional information about the exhibition and about the Friday evening concert.

[70] Letter from David Berkowitz to Leicester Bradner (19 April 1963) David S. Berkowitz Papers, Box 42, Folder 2.

Renaissance Studies, but in the end he enticed Harry Berger (Yale), Ray-mond Klibansky (McGill), George Mora (Yale), and Richard Douglas (MIT) to speak.[71] Berkowitz adapted a technique from Myron Gilmore when he hinted to at least one of the potential speakers that "Many of these papers have subsequently appeared in learned journals, most nota-bly in *Studies of the Renaissance*."[72] The most unusual topic was that of George Mora, a medical doctor who spoke on the figure of Johann Weyer (Wier) as a precursor of modern psychiatry on the occasion of the 400th anniversary of the publication of *De Praestigiis Daemonum*.[73]

As should be clear by now, this 1963 gathering was unusually ambi-tious in the range of activities offered to conference participants. The 1963 conference benefited greatly from Berkowitz's administrative expe-rience. It may well have been this same administrative savvy that led him to include with the conference invitation a questionnaire to be completed by NERC members, about their respective interests, publications, and projects. The goal of the questionnaire was twofold: to update the mail-ing list and to assist planners of future conferences. In reflecting upon the conference to his colleague Sam Hunter several weeks later, Berkowitz observed that it had been "the most successful of the conferences held in

---

[71] Minutes from David Berkowitz to Coordinating Committee (2 Nov. 1962), NERCA 1.5.1, listing scholars who might be available in the Boston area in 1963. The full list was: Hans Baron, Federico Zeri, Joseph Schulwath, Jacob Katz, Cecil Roth. David S. Berkowitz Papers, Brandeis University, Box 42, Folder 6, "Minutes of the Coordinating Committee."

[72] Letter from David Berkowitz to Raymond Klibansky (9 Nov. 1962), David S. Berkowitz Papers, Brandeis University, Box 42, Folder 2, "Correspondence." In the same collection, in a letter of 27 April 1961, just after the conference had concluded at Harvard, Myron Gilmore had encouraged both Hanna Gray and Eugene Rice to publish their papers in *Renaissance Studies*; Gilmore observed that the editor, [Lisa?] Sheeber, "is always glad to get papers which were offered at these conferences." Gilm-ore added "As long as Mrs. [Phyllis Goodhart] Gordan continues to be an angel to the Society, I think that we can print almost as much that is good as we want or as we have available."

[73] Later that same day, Mora gave a similar address "for a meeting of the His-tory of Medicine" in Boston; it was published as George Mora, "On the 400th anni-versary of Johann Weyer's De praestigiis daemonum--Its significance for today's psychiatry," *The American Journal of Psychiatry*, 120 (1963): 417–428. Berkowitz's correspondence (Box 42, Folder 2) shows repeated negotiations to ensure that Mora could speak at both events on the same day. The original copy of Mora's talk to NERC remains in David Berkowitz's papers, Box 42, Folder 4.

the last dozen years."[74] Nevertheless, he was not eager to do it again, and indeed the conference did not return to Brandeis for thirty years.[75]

Subsequent conferences at Yale (1965), MIT (1966), Brown (1967), Vassar (1968), and University of Rhode Island (1969) followed the traditional pattern of a two-day, four-paper conference with an evening concert or exhibition at a local museum. The speakers included many of the leading scholars of the day: H. W. Janson, Roland Bainton, Lewis Lockwood, Ronald Witt, Anthony Molho, Marvin Becker, Raymond de Roover, and Charles Trinkaus. Most of these speakers were local to New England, but some traveled considerable distances to participate. Italian topics—especially history, humanism, and art—remained the most common, but other regions of Europe received substantial coverage as well. With the exception of the 1963 gathering at Brandeis, none of the conferences in the 1960s offered a comprehensive theme to bring all papers together; this practice would emerge only in the 1980s and later.

What of the other academic societies founded to promote Renaissance Studies during the 1950s and 1960s? To what extent did their mission, hierarchy, size, hosts, or membership parallel that of NERC?

The South-Central Renaissance Conference (SCRC) was the first regional association to follow NERC; the SCRC initially met in 1952 as an interdisciplinary association of Renaissance scholars whose membership was largely concentrated across the southeastern United States. No documentation of the first meeting is extant, but typescript minutes of the SCRC Executive Committee meeting at Austin, Texas were recorded in April 1953.[76] Under the leadership of Albert Howard Carter of the

---

[74] Letter from David Berkowitz to Sam Hunter (20 May 1963), David S. Berkowitz Papers, Box 42, Folder 2. Hunter was the director of the Poses Institute of Fine Arts, and had collaborated in the preparation of the symposium and the art exhibition.

[75] Letter from David Berkowitz to Paul Brainard (15 May 1963), David S. Berkowitz Papers, Box 42, Folder 2: "I don't ever want to do another conference...." Brainard was the chair of the Brandeis Music Department, and had collaborated in the Friday evening program of music and dance. NERC returned to Brandeis in 1993 and again in 2013.

[76] South-Central Renaissance Conference Archives, at <http://www.scrc.us.com/archives.shtml> [accessed 30 March 2014]; for the years beginning in 1953, all of the minutes are posted; and beginning in 1999, all of the conference programs, abstracts, and some photos are posted. The minutes are recorded in typescript in some years, and in manuscript in other years.

University of Arkansas, the committee approved a constitution, elected by acclamation a slate of new officers, and planned the next year's meeting at the University of Arkansas. In Fayetteville the following year, the minutes of May 1954 acknowledge the creation of the RSA in New York, and the decision of the SCRC to elect a pair of representatives to serve on the RSA Advisory Council.[77] The minutes in this and following years largely document routine business, such as acceptance of the prior year's minutes, selection of a nominating committee, approval of constitutional amendments, and the like. Subsequent meetings in this decade occurred at Tulane University (Nov. 1954), UC Berkeley (1955), Louisiana State University (1956), University of Mississippi (1957), Texas Christian University (1958), and Rice University (1959).[78] William Peery was the first President of the SCRC, and Willis H. Bowem faithfully recorded the minutes as Secretary. The minutes document the regular turnover of the SCRC officers each year as new members moved onto the Board.

During the 1960s the SCRC continued to meet every year, with more than half of those meetings occurring in the state of Texas. The 1963 program (at the University of Houston) and that of 1965 (at Texas A&M) demonstrate that about a dozen papers were offered at each conference, as well as a dinner with a lecture and entertainment. The topics were similar to those proposed at NERC, with a preponderance of Italian history and art, as well as English theater and literature.[79] The conferences always lasted two days, and were occasionally held in conjunction with the meetings of the Modern Language Association, the Southern Humanities Conference, or even (as in 1964 in Austin) with a Renaissance Faire. The 1964 minutes, from a meeting at UT-Austin, are the first to include a budget, and show that membership dues collected as of April 1964 totaled $92, with total disbursements of $58.82. It is worth noting also the report of Robert G. Collmer, SCRC representative to the

---

[77]   SCRC Archives, at: <http://www.scrc.us.com/archives/minutes/minutes1954_may_exec.pdf>

[78]   SCRC Archives, at <http://www.scrc.us.com/archives.shtml> [accessed 30 March 2014]. Berkeley is clearly an anomaly on this list; it was decided in 1954 that no meeting would be planned for Spring 1955, and the minutes of March 1955 suggest that the "meeting" of the Executive Committee took place by post, as President Howard Carter was on leave in CA. See: <http://www.scrc.us.com/archives/minutes/minutes1955.pdf.> Rice University was known as The Rice Institute in 1958.

[79]   There are only transcriptions of these two programs, not the originals.

Advisory Council of the RSA, who reported his impression after the Jan. 1964 meeting at Columbia University that "the national meeting does not seem to know what it is doing."[80]

Almost simultaneously with the foundation of the SCRC in the South, the Pacific Northwest Renaissance Conference (PNRS) was organized in 1956 by historian Quirinus Breen (University of Oregon), classicist Paul Pascal (University of Washington), and literary scholar G. P. V. Akrigg (University of British Columbia). The program of the following year's conference, in April 1957 at the University of Washington, shows that the PNRS met jointly with the local chapters of the American Musicological Society and of the Classical Association.[81] Seventeen papers and two plenary lectures confirm an auspicious start for this fledgling organization. The PNRS continued to meet annually, at the University of British Columbia (1958), Gonzaga University (1959), the University of Oregon (1960), the University of Washington (1961), Western Washington State College (1963), University of Oregon again (1964), Central Washington State College (1965), University of Victoria (1966), Washington State University (1967), the University of Alberta (1968), and Lewis & Clark College (1969). Paul Oskar Kristeller was to have spoken at the 1960 meeting but an automobile accident prevented his attendance.

One unique feature of the PNRS is its distinctly bi-national character; beginning in 1971, the annual meeting formally alternated between the USA and Canada, just as the presidency also had to alternate between an American and a Canadian scholar. The PNRS struggled in its early years with the problem of hosting the conference at schools remote from a major airport, with resultant declines in attendance. In reflecting upon the history of the PNRS and the RSA, Jean MacIntyre and Paul Budra have written:

> In the early years of both societies, distance, cost, and surface travel militated against any close association. When the PNRC began, the Pacific Northwest was remote and inaccessible to most of North America. This remoteness, along with the easy

---

[80] See SCRC Archives, at: <http://www.scrc.us.com/archives/minutes/minutes1964_exec.pdf.>

[81] Here I am indebted to the history of the PNRS compiled by Jean MacIntyre and Paul Budra (see n. 4 above).

communication between British Columbia and the American states to the south, has meant that the PNRC has always been an international association....As air travel has grown cheaper and more convenient, the isolation of the region from scholars from east of the Cascades and the Rockies has almost disappeared, and it is usual to find at least one or two presenters from as far east as Halifax and Boston on every PNRC programme.[82]

Also in the late 1950s, the Renaissance Conference of Southern California (RCSC) was formed as a "scholarly association dedicated to the advancement of learning in Renaissance Studies."[83] It has always been centered in the Los Angeles Basin, anchored by UCLA and USC as well as the plethora of other colleges and universities in that area. Similar to NERC, SCRC, and PNRS, the RCSC has consciously promoted an interdisciplinary approach to Renaissance Studies, and has for decades been an affiliate of the Renaissance Society of America. Also similar to NERC, the RCSC has maintained a "minimalist" approach by focusing on an annual conference but eschewing a journal and membership dues. Unlike its sister societies, however, the RCSC does not typically migrate from one university host to another; instead, it has been able to meet regularly at the Huntington Library in San Marino, CA, a locale which offers not only exceptional natural beauty but also a fine collection of Renaissance books and manuscripts. The RCSC also developed a different system of leadership than NERC. The Southern California Conference has a ladder of officers, ranging from Treasurer to Second Vice-President to Vice-President to President; each consists of a one-year term and one moves up the hierarchy over the course of four years. Such a system offers the benefits and disadvantages of frequent turnover at the top; it is quite different than the long-serving presidents that have characterized NERC.

The isolation of Western scholars may also have prompted, at least in part, the formation of the Rocky Mountain Medieval and Renaissance

---

[82]   See <http://www.pnrs.org/about.html> [accessed 30 March 2014].
[83]   See <http://rcsconline.org/about-us.html> [accessed 31 March 2014]. To the best of my knowledge, no archive exists for the RCSC; I am grateful to current President Martine Van Elk (CSU-Long Beach) for this information.

Association (RMRRA) in 1968.[84] The RMRRA had its inaugural meeting at the University of Denver under the leadership of its first President, historian Allen D. Breck, with an Advisory Board that consisted of Charles P. Carlson, Boyd H. Hill, Harry Rosenberg, and Edith C. Tatnall. Its original intention was to be an informal group, rather than an official society, whose purpose was to provide a gathering-place to promote "sharing of knowledge and experiences." The initial board was composed entirely of historians, and the association has met annually since 1968, in cities both large (e.g., Denver, Salt Lake City) and small (e.g., Pocatello, Idaho), but always "within sight of the Rocky Mountains." More recently it has established a journal *Quidditas*, a Facebook page, a Doodle poll, and scholarship and ride-sharing opportunities for younger scholars who wish to attend the conference.

Returning to NERC, David Berkowitz introduced a short-lived "Occasional Newsletter" in the mid-1960s with the goal of providing updates to conference members. In contrast to the memos and letters authored by Berkowitz, the two newsletters are full of amusing anecdotes, jokes, and clever word plays. For example, in summarizing the 1965 conference at Yale, Berkowitz wrote "one veteran conference-goer was heard to murmur that the new Beinecke rare book library made an even more impressive cocktail lounge than the (then new) Brandeis art gallery"; and in announcing the 1967 conference at Brown University, Berkowitz referred to it as a "return to the womb," with *pater academicus* Leicester Bradner serving as mid-wife.[85] A declaration that the University of Rhode Island would serve as host in 1969 was announced as follows:

> Giving validity (and another first) to its motto "Join NERC and see New England first," we take great pride, etc. in announcing that our 1969 host will be the University of Rhode Island. The University impartially holds up its lamp of learning for those who do and those

---

[84] For information on the RMRRA, I am grateful to Kristin Bezio (Univ. of Richmond), who with assistance from Ginger Smoak compiled a four-page history of the RMRRA for the meeting at the RSA in 2014. The RMRRA website, currently at http://rowdy.msudenver.edu/~tayljeff/RMMRA/Index.html [accessed 31 March 2014], includes links to newsletters dating back to 1996 but no additional information about the formative years.

[85] An Occasional Newsletter of the New England Renaissance Conference, No. 1 (March 1966), NERCA 1.7.1, 1 [hereafter "1966 Newsletter"].

who do not require alcoholic stimulation as a prelude to learning, eating, or sleeping. But Kingston itself is one of those interesting survivals of the "noble experiment," a "dry town." However, there is no need to fortify oneself in advance for the next two years; an ingenious dean knows how to solve the problem of our presence with all due regard for the niceties of obedience to the law.[86]

The newsletters also included regular pleas from Berkowitz to his colleagues to consider hosting NERC in a future year, and ruminations about how the mailing list each year vastly exceeded the actual turnout. In addition, Berkowitz reminded his readers that NERC had survived, and even prospered, without the services of a treasurer or a secretary, but instead relied upon each program's chairman: "sometimes self-designated and sometimes coerced, he (or she) may be accurately characterised as one with enough nerve, confidence, influence or skill to convince a college administration to play host to our conference."[87] Berkowitz also poked fun at his own nebulous role in a short piece entitled "The Invisible Organization; or, how to be a fifth wheel." He characterized himself as "a functionary, variously described as a president, a general secretary, or a permanent chairman, apparently designated to serve 'without limit of time'. He is described as 'a sort of secretary' charged with the task 'to keep it alive' by seeing to it that an annual conference [is] in actuality held, as it should be every year."[88]

On a more serious note, Berkowitz made clear to members of his own program committee for the 1963 conference that faculty from the host institution were not expected to participate as principal speakers, although they were welcome to serve in secondary roles (i.e., chairs or discussants).[89] He repeated this injunction in a 1974 letter, noting that "Program participants are recruited from all over the country; the only rule I enforce is that the program chairman avoid invitations to local, i.e.

---

[86] An Occasional Newsletter of the New England Renaissance Conference, No. 2 (February 1967), NERCA 1.7.2, 1 [hereafter "1967 Newsletter"].

[87] 1966 Newsletter, NERCA 1.7.1, 1.

[88] 1966 Newsletter, NERCA 1.7.1, 1.

[89] Memo from David Berkowitz to "Messrs. [Edgar] Johnson, [James] Cunningham, [James] Duffy . . .," [members of the Program Committee for the 1963 conference at Brandeis] (23 May 1962) NERCA 1.5.1, 1; this is in the NERC Archive, and also in Box 42, Folder 1, David S. Berkowitz Papers, Brandeis Special Collections.

campus, talent."[90] He elaborated a bit further on this idea in another letter to Yale President A. Bartlett Giamatti, noting that NERC enforced an
"absolute ban on 'local' talent" so that young program chairs could say
no to their senior colleagues.[91]

In a letter to John Tedeschi early in 1974, Berkowitz elaborated his views
on NERC's informal organizational structure. Coming almost exactly at the
midpoint of Berkowitz's administration, the letter serves both as a description of past practice and as a guide to future policy. Berkowitz pointed
out that the New England Renaissance Conference "is less formal than
elsewhere; it has only one permanent officer and in succession they have
been Leicester Bradner, Myron Gilmore, and myself." Berkowitz explained
that the leader of NERC was responsible "to provide for continuity of the
annual meetings by recruiting and encouraging local institutions." Upon
receipt of a formal invitation, he continued, "the President's function is
discharged and full responsibility for the organization and conduct of the
program devolves on the local program chairman."[92] Berkowitz underscored this latter point by emphasizing yet again that "The local program
chairman has a free hand in fashioning both the program and the nature of
the organization he or she thinks necessary for the occasion." Berkowitz's
correspondence during the 1970s with various program chairs provides
additional evidence of his willingness to let the chairs make virtually all of
the decisions about the shape and scope of the conference program.[93]

Berkowitz's letter to Tedeschi also offers rough estimates about attendance, cost, and program quality. He noted that the number of participants varied widely, running from a minimum of 60 to a maximum of

---

[90]   Letter from David Berkowitz to John Tedeschi (15 Jan. 1974), NERCA 1.9.1,
1. See the following two paragraphs for further explanation of this correspondence
with Tedeschi.

[91]   Letter from David Berkowitz to A. Bartlett Giamatti (2 Oct. 1979), NERCA
1.15.1.

[92]   Letter from David Berkowitz to John Tedeschi (15 Jan. 1974), NERCA 1.9.1,
1. In this letter Berkowitz sometimes uses the term "President" although elsewhere
in his correspondence and memos he is careful to avoid using this term, preferring
"coordinator" or "permanent officer." Only with the appointment of Samuel Y. Edgerton in 1995 did the title of "President" come into regular usage, as discussed below.

[93]   For example, correspondence between Berkowitz and Karen F. Wiley
who organized the 1976 conference at University of Vermont, NERCA 1.11.1–4; or
between Berkowitz and Elizabeth H. Hageman who organized the 1974 conference
at UNH, NERCA 1.9.2.

200. Interestingly, he commented that "in recent years there has been an extraordinary out-migration of Renaissance scholars from New England," which reflects the growth of state universities in the rest of the United States, and naturally is linked to the growth of Renaissance societies elsewhere in the nation too. Berkowitz was astute enough to recognize that other factors influenced NERC attendance too; he cited weather, population density of academics, transportation, and "competing attractions" among other factors. Budgets, too, varied significantly from a low of $500 to over $20,000, according to Berkowitz. Regardless of this variability, Berkowitz boasted, "the quality of the programs are uniformly high." It is difficult to test the veracity of Berkowitz's assertion about program quality, but certainly many of the speakers were well-known in the field. Perhaps the most illuminating excerpt from Berkowitz's letter to Tedeschi comes in the final paragraph, in which Berkowitz offers an overview of NERC. Here he lauded the lack of bureaucracy, the conscious efforts to mix academic disciplines, and the enthusiasm of the membership. He wrote "The New England Renaissance Conference remains stuanchly [sic] informal, staunchly interdisciplinary, and vigorous. Although efforts have been made from time to time to see if the membership has any interest in changing the format, no such interest has yet appeared.... The only 'business' [that] our members have is to enjoy the varied program which our two-day sessions offer."[94]

The conferences in the 1970s continued to follow the time-honored tradition of the previous three decades. Every conference followed the two-day format of panel sessions, a Renaissance concert or stage performance, and a formal dinner on Friday evening. Special events, such as the 500th anniversary of Michelangelo's birth in 1975, were commemorated with exhibitions or lectures. Dartmouth (1970) was the only Ivy League school to host, followed by Wheaton College (1971), UMass Amherst (1972), Southeastern Massachusetts University [today UMass Dartmouth] (1973), University of New Hampshire (1974), Boston University (1975), University of Vermont (1976), Rhode Island College (1977), Mount Holyoke College (1978), and Williams College (1979). It is worth noting the prevalence of "colleges" as opposed to "universities" in this list, which is yet one more sign of the move away from the major research universities.

---

[94] Letter from David Berkowitz to John Tedeschi (15 Jan. 1974), NERCA 1.9.1, 1–2.

Nearly all of these conferences appear to have run smoothly and without incident. Berkowitz wrote, and received, numerous letters of effusive praise and heartfelt thanks to (and from) program chairs, deans, and presidents. One notable exception, however, was the October 1977 conference at Rhode Island College. Preliminary letters between Berkowitz, program chair and art history professor Ronald Steinberg, and Dean Noel Richards in 1974–75, suggested good will and advance planning on all sides.[95] Yet angry words and accusations of bad faith (or worse) flew in the wake of the conference. On 31 October 1975, just two days after the conference, Rhode Island College professor of English Carolyn Ruth Swift Lenz lambasted Berkowitz for his failure to adequately publicize the conference:

> The lack of publicity that burdens NERC from my own personal experience reached the zenith of absurdity in its Rhode Island College meeting when the Renaissance faculty of Rhode Island College—including some of the NERC committee members—were uninformed of both the dates and the papers of the conference until the week of the conference. In spite of this silence, you tell me 100 people attended Friday's meeting, which seems to testify to the truth of Renaissance belief in the beneficence of God's Providence....The personal insult to scholars and teachers, ignored by an important scholarly organization, should not however be underestimated, even if it is borne in dignified silence.[96]

Lenz's complaint seems odd in several ways. First, if the estimate of one hundred participants is to be believed, clearly attendance had not suffered too dramatically.[97] Secondly, although Lenz was on the program committee, it appears that she herself did not attend the opening day of the conference. Third, all other archival sources indicate that David

---

[95]   Letter from Ronald M. Steinberg to David Berkowitz (4 Dec. 1975), NERCA 1.12.1; Letter from David Berkowitz to Ronald M. Steinberg (19 Dec. 1975), NERCA 1.12.2; Letter from Noel Richards to David Berkowitz (17 Feb. 1975), NERCA 1.12.3; Letter from David Berkowitz to Noel Richards (21 Feb. 1975), NERCA 1.12.4.

[96]   Letter from Carolyn Ruth Swift Lenz to David Berkowitz (31 Oct. 1977), NERCA 1.16.9.

[97]   But cf. Steinberg's observation about low attendance at Friday's dinner below (n. 101).

Berkowitz was a conscientious and meticulous administrator, who was unlikely to misjudge the size of the audience so dramatically. Lastly, her reference to "dignified silence" implies that nobody else had come forward to complain about the lack of notification. To her credit, Lenz offered to take on the herculean task of updating the NERC mailing list and of making it available to future host institutions.

Three weeks later Lenz received a letter from John Lemly at Mount Holyoke College, coordinator of the following year's NERC. Lemly acknowledged that he had heard from another scholar "of your talk and of the various disasters which beset the Rhode Island College meeting."[98] Lemly thanked Lenz for her "public-spirited offer" to compile a mailing list, and referred obliquely to "a most inadequate [mailing] list" prepared by program chair Ronald Steinberg at Rhode Island College. The next day Lemly informed Berkowitz of his intention to "send announcements to 5–6 relevant departments at 100–150 New England and New York colleges and universities," as well as a notice to two dozen journals.[99] Six months later Steinberg himself sent a hand-written letter to David Berkowitz, together with a copy of the mailing list. Steinberg claimed that "the finished one was never re-typed or copied, and has been lost."[100] Steinberg went on to describe more serious conflicts with his university's administration that stemmed from the NERC meeting in the fall. Steinberg's outrage is palpable, but his account does imply that attendance at the conference was in fact much lower than expected. According to Steinberg, university administrators

> claim over $800 is owed them by the NERC (or the RSA) for dinner the night of the conference. They prepared for 150 persons (!) & only c. 35 were there. I believe they have even billed RSA! They are demanding I pay them if RSA doesn't. And there is no reason, as I've told them, for RSA to do so. It is bizarre! I have had to engage an

---

[98] Letter from John Lemly to Carolyn Ruth Swift Lenz (21 Nov. 1977), NERCA 1.13.1-B. Note, however, that Lenz does not appear in the conference program as one of the speakers or respondents. Lemly's report of this incident came from English professor Andrea Sununu.

[99] Letter from John Lemly to David Berkowitz (22 Nov. 1977), NERCA 1.13.1-A. Clearly Lemly wanted the 1978 conference to be well-publicized.

[100] Letter from Ronald Steinberg to David Berkowitz (15 Mar. 1978), NERCA 1.12.5.

attorney for the administration is claiming they can take the money from my pay (which, according to my attorney, is not likely).[101]

No replies from David Berkowitz to Steinberg or to Lenz are extant in the NERC files or in his papers at Brandeis University, so we cannot speculate as to Berkowitz's position on these issues. Perhaps the issue simply represents petty complaints by a sole aggrieved faculty member or a penny-pinching administration. It is certainly true that the infamous NERC mailing list caused no end of headaches for Berkowitz and for individual program chairs who had to update it.[102] It is also true that at least two other letters in the NERC files complain of being ignored or dropped from the NERC mailing list under Berkowitz's supervision.[103] On the other hand, these are isolated complaints, and dwarfed by dozens of positive statements.

Returning to a broader perspective across two decades of NERC, from 1963 to 1983, one of David Berkowitz's most important accomplishments for NERC was to broaden the membership of the organization. Richard Douglas noted this legacy in his memorial statement about Berkowitz:

> From New Haven or New London, to Hanover or Burlington, David held us together for over two decades, turning what started

---

[101] Letter from Ronald Steinberg to David Berkowitz (15 Mar. 1978), NERCA 1.12.5.

[102] Problems with the mailing list is a perennial complaint in the correspondence; as one example among many, see the letter from Karen W. Sandler to David Berkowitz (30 June 1976), NERCA 1.11.3-A: "I tried to call you today to ask for your help in straightening out the mailing list. Quite frankly, when we finally received it, it was a mess! [emphasis in the original] I doubt that anything had been done on it all year and we had to start from scratch to update it." The usual practice was for the NERC President to pass the mailing list of 300-500 names and addresses from one program chair to the next. Each year the Program Chair and the President would (theoretically) update the list to reflect actual attendance, recent deaths, and the like. About a dozen copies of the mailing list are extant in the NERC Archive for different years of the conference.

[103] Letter from Pardon E. Tillinghast (Middlebury College) to RSA, (1 Dec. 1971), NERCA 1.16.7; and the reply from Miss M.A. Riley to Pardon Tillinghast (20 Dec. 1971), NERCA 1.16.7, with copy to Berkowitz. See also the spirited reply of David Berkowitz to Barbara Hardy (SUNY Oswego) (10 Feb. 1975) NERCA 1.10.5, re: her complaint about the mailing list and about regional dues.

out as an exclusive group of several dozen elders into an open society where all serious scholars—young ones and emeriti alike—were
made to feel welcome.[104]

Six years later, in a letter to Edward Cranz that accompanied a thick
folder of Berkowitz's correspondence as president of NERC, Douglas
restated his view on Berkowitz's legacy:

> One of his achievements as President was to open up the mem-
> bership beyond the tight little band of two dozen who represented
> Bradner's ideal. I remember one slightly contentious Saturday eve-
> ning when David confronted Leicester about his exclusive canons
> for membership. Leicester winced at the idea of inviting clergy from
> Holy Cross or assistant professors from Rhode Island. But none of
> this bothered David, who quietly undertook to compile a vastly
> enlarged mailing list.[105]

In his brief history of NERC, Cranz agreed, writing that "under
[Berkowitz's] aegis the conference was an open society where any serious scholar was welcome. The conference also became more of an all-
New England affair than it had been."[106] As noted previously, the early
dominance of the Ivy League disappeared during the 1960s and 1970s,
precisely the period when David Berkowitz served as NERC's executive.
Berkowitz's efforts to broaden the membership of NERC were surely
inspired by a volume that he published early in his administrative career
entitled *Inequality of Opportunity in Higher Education*, which was a

---

[104]   Richard M. Douglas, "A Memorial Note on David Sandler Berkowitz" (8
Mar. 1983), NERCA 1.25.11-B. Douglas never occupied a leadership role of NERC
but his name appears frequently in the correspondence of the organization, and
he was recognized by Edward Cranz, "Fifty Years," 757 "for the role he played in
guiding the consultations that provided successors to the nameless post created by
Leicester Bradner..." A letter of 17 Sept. 1985 from Samuel Edgerton to Richard
Douglas, NERCA 1.19.1, written just after Edgerton had been nominated as president of NERC, claims that Douglas really should have been the one to receive this
honor.

[105]   Letter from Richard M. Douglas to F. Edward Cranz (28 Feb. 1989), NERCA
1.25.11-A.

[106]   Cranz, "Fifty Years," 758.

significant forerunner to the first Fair Education Practices Act. Of course Berkowitz was writing about the study of barriers to college enrollment of minorities, not about elite academic societies comprised of professors, but the push for inclusiveness and greater opportunity is evident in both examples.

Ill health forced David Berkowitz to step away from his duties as the leader of NERC in 1983, and he died shortly thereafter.[107] Together with Leicester Bradner, he retains the distinction of being NERC's longest-serving executive. Berkowitz led the transformation of NERC from an elite group of Ivy League professors to a broader professional society that included scholars at all levels and from all types of institutions across New England.

Jane Ruby (1983–85)

The NERC membership seemed at a loss after the death of their beloved long-time leader in March 1983. No conference was held that year. Five months after Berkowitz's passing, Richard Douglas wrote to Edward Cranz that a successor must be found to follow David Berkowitz as president of NERC. However, wrote Douglas, "I feel terribly awkward about taking any kind of initiative in this melancholy matter and would prefer simply to ignore it." He continued, "It is especially delicate in an organization which has insistently denied that it has a material existence in the first place. But at a moment like this one can hear David say, with a bit of impatience, 'You all know what has to be done. Consult, get a consensus of the elders, and announce the result in a recommendation to the Conference in October.'"[108] Although there are occasional references to a nominating committee prior to 1983, including Bradner's *ad hoc* committee and a reference to one in Berkowitz's own letter to John Tedeschi, there is little indication that any such formal body ever existed. Instead, private consultation among the senior members of NERC was the standard practice for choosing a new leader. It was not by accident

---

[107] See Richard M. Douglas, "A Memorial Note on David Sandler Berkowitz" (8 Mar. 1983), NERCA 1.25-11-B, for more on Berkowitz's leadership of NERC, and on the circumstances of his death.

[108] Letter from Richard Douglas to Edward Cranz (8 Aug. 1983), NERCA 1.17-1-B.

that one of the senior members involved in the search for a successor to
David Berkowitz referred to himself, with tongue firmly in cheek, as a
member of the "college of cardinals" who participated in the "investi-
ture" of a new leader for NERC, and who closed his letter by exclaiming
"Habeamus Papam!"[109] Richard Douglas's letter of 8 August 1983 made
clear that both the initial brainstorming and the final selection of a new
executive were to be handled by "a small number of NERC regulars....
who have extended association with the Conference."[110] The result of this
rump parliament was the first woman leader in the history of NERC: Jane
Ruby, a professor of history at Wheaton College, who was proclaimed
"popess" in the fall of 1983.[111]

Jane Ruby taught medieval and Renaissance history at Wheaton College for twenty-four years (1954–1978), and served the last two years as
Provost. A specialist in fourteenth-century political thought and concepts
of nature, she (like her predecessors) earned a degree from Harvard.[112]
In describing the reasons for her selection, Richard Douglas wrote that
"the consensus points very clearly to Jane Ruby—for her knowledge of
the Conference and her long standing commitment to it, for her acquain-
tance with its members and traditions, for her professional qualifications
and her personal qualities."[113]

Ruby had organized a NERC conference at Wheaton in October 1971
that included two papers on the Fifth Lateran Council, two papers on the
theme of "Ideas Into Poetry," and one paper on Baroque Portraiture, as
well as the performance of a Hans Sachs pro-Lutheran Carnival play of
1551, "How to Hatch Calves" (*Das Kälberbrüten*).[114] In a letter from Ruby
to Berkowitz a few days after the 1971 conference, Ruby observed that

---

[109] Letter from Samuel Edgerton to Richard Douglas (13 Sept. 1983), NERCA
1.17.2. Emphasis in the original.
[110] Letter from Richard Douglas to Edward Cranz (8 Aug. 1983), NERCA
1.1.17.1-B.
[111] Letter from Samuel Edgerton to Richard Douglas (13 Sept. 1983), NERCA
1.17.1-B. Edgerton uses the term "popess."
[112] See Jane Ruby's obituary in *The Boston Globe*, 19 Feb. 1992. Technically, the
degree was awarded by Radcliffe.
[113] Letter from Richard Douglas to Edward Cranz (8 Aug. 1983), NERCA
1.17.1-B.
[114] No conference program is extant, but a brief notice appeared in *Renaissance
Quarterly*, 24 (1971): 429.

the conference had gone very well, with "good attendance" and enthusiastic reception by the audience. The cheery tone of the letter suggests a familiarity with Berkowitz (who was often quite formal in his correspondence) and with NERC, as Ruby offered suggestions about future conference hosts, observations on editing the mailing list, and condolences on Berkowitz's health.[115] Ruby also gave a paper at the 1973 conference that examined the use of the term "law" in scientific writing from Roger Bacon to Issac Newton.

The conferences held under Ruby's aegis included one at Wellesley (April 1984), another at Wheaton (November 1984), and a third at UMass Amherst (1985). The program at Wellesley featured three sessions with an almost entirely Italian focus, including papers by Samuel K. Cohn, Werner Gundersheimer, and Wendy Stedman Sheard, as well as a performance on Wellesley's new Late Renaissance organ built by Charles Fisk. It was very unusual to have two conferences in the same calendar year, as happened in 1984, but presumably this was an effort to make up for the missed conference during the prior year. The conference at Wheaton, held 2-3 November 1984, was brief: two papers on Friday afternoon and three more on Saturday morning, including yet another paper by Paul Oskar Kristeller, this time on the university curriculum in Late Medieval and Renaissance Italy. Ruby commented in a letter to Samuel Edgerton that she would have liked to include more thematic sessions but "gave up the idea for the Wheaton meeting only because the time for preparation was unusually brief, from late spring to fall."[116] No extant program survives for the 1985 conference at UMass Amherst, which was organized by Daniel Martin, but we can glean something from the appreciative letter sent by Jane Ruby in her last act as president of NERC: "We owe you many thanks for the impressive conference you staged at the University this past weekend—in fact a combination of the traditional New England conference with an international conference! Praiseworthy were its variety and its quality, and also the fine attendance. Like others, I appreciated not only the papers, but also the handsomely illustrated program and the delightful entertainment at dinner."[117]

[115] Letter from Jane Ruby to David Berkowitz (30 Oct. 1971), NERCA 1.16.6.
[116] Letter from Jane Ruby to Samuel Edgerton (24 Sept. 1985), NERCA 1.19.2-A.
[117] Letter from Jane Ruby to Daniel Martin (4 Nov. 1985), NERCA 1.19-4-B. The program included at least one session on Boccaccio, chaired by Angelo Mazzocco:

It is difficult to gauge the impact of Jane Ruby upon NERC. Few examples of her correspondence survive, and she served only a brief three years before stepping down. In addition to the three conferences that occurred on her watch, she was involved, albeit indirectly, in some discussions about the location of the 1989 conference celebrating NERC's fiftieth anniversary.[118] She provided some counsel to her successor, Samuel Edgerton, about the formation of a "more structured" advisory council, consisting of "some able younger scholars on the Conference mailing list who might ponder the future of the Conference with you."[119] It is tempting to say that she broke the glass ceiling of an otherwise male-dominated cabal of NERC leadership. Certainly it is true that the 1980s witnessed important gains by female academics but it is impossible to link such advances to Jane Ruby's presidency of NERC, nor can we point to this isolated example as in any way representative of broader changes within the academy.

Samuel Y. Edgerton (1985–1990)

During the summer of 1985 Jane Ruby stepped down, and once again the elders of NERC conferred to appoint a successor. They selected Samuel Y. Edgerton, Jr., an art historian from Williams College whose research interests began in Medieval and Renaissance Europe and later shifted to the arts of pre- and post-conquest America. Edgerton earned four degrees from the University of Pennsylvania, including the Ph.D. in 1965; he taught art history at Boston University for sixteen years (1964–1980) before moving to Williams College for twenty-seven years as the Amos Lawrence Professor of Art and director of the Graduate Program there (1980–2007).[120] Edgerton was deeply familiar with the New England Renaissance Conference, having organized the October 1975 conference

---

"Boccaccio Newsletter," at <http://www.umass.edu/italian/ABA/newsletters/1985-2.pdf> [accessed 30 April 2013], 4.

[118] See n. 27 above.

[119] Letter from Jane Ruby to Samuel Edgerton (24 Sept. 1985), NERCA 1.19.2-A.

[120] The American Historical Association cited his innovative and interdisciplinary work on the importance of linear perspective; he also won a Guggenheim Fellowship and was a fellow at Princeton's Institute for Advanced Study. See his Emeritus Citation from Williams College: <http://archives.williams.edu/williamshistory/commencement/2007/edgerton_cit.php> [accessed 30 April 2013], which

at Boston University, and more recently having participated in the elevation of Jane Ruby as president of NERC.

In responding to the news of his election as the leader of NERC, Edgerton described it as a "complete surprise" which left him "overwhelmed and slightly unsure as to how [to] respond."[121] He expressed concern about what he called "the means of my elevation," by which he clearly meant the informal way in which he had been selected. He specified that "While I always approved of this method regarding prior presidents, I am less secure when it is applied to me. Somehow I think I won't be as unanimously acceptable as Myron [Gilmore] or David [Berkowitz] or Jane [Ruby] or even you, Dick [Douglas], whom I think deserves this honor more than anyone else." Despite his trepidation, Edgerton agreed to serve, and promised to outline "a few principles I have been cogitating."[122]

Within a week Jane Ruby had sent him a congratulatory letter and a list of eleven "able younger scholars" who could serve on an advisory committee.[123] Ruby noted that she and her (unnamed) colleagues had drawn up the list rapidly at the end of a long session devoted primarily to the presidency of NERC, and that it seemed to her flawed because it contained too many names from Wellesley and Brown. The list was "merely suggestive," she wrote, and he should feel free to add other names to it. She also sent Edgerton a mailing list of three hundred scholars, including their affiliation and (where known) their approximate age. Three weeks later Ruby reminded Edgerton of the importance of selecting his advisory committee in a prompt manner.[124] He responded immediately that he believed a committee of about five persons would be optimal. Although Edgerton may indeed have relied upon an inner circle of

---

notes his pre-academic pursuits as a meat salesman and as a wrestling opponent of Donald Rumsfeld(!), as well as later academic accomplishments.

[121] Letter from Samuel Edgerton to Jane Ruby and Richard Douglas (17 Sept. 1985), NERCA 1.19.1.

[122] Letter from Samuel Edgerton to Jane Ruby and Richard Douglas (17 Sept. 1985), NERCA 1.19.1.

[123] Letter from Jane Ruby to Samuel Edgerton (24 Sept. 1985), NERCA 1.19.2-A.

[124] Letter from Jane Ruby to Samuel Edgerton (4 Nov. 1985), NERCA 1.19.4-A: "I hope you will forgive me for observing also that I think it would be to the good if you could find time to select your advisory committee fairly soon. There is a certain momentum and interest created by the annual meeting. With that, I subside—for good. I shall, of course, be happy to help in any way I can; but henceforth our fate is in your hands!"

advisors, there is no extant evidence of a formal advisory group under his presidency.

Edgerton immediately began to organize the next year's conference; in keeping with the practice of his predecessors Bradner, Gilmore, and Ruby, he hosted it at his own institution. However, Edgerton introduced a twist by choosing a theme of "Three Current Controversies in Renaissance Studies." As he explained it to the members of NERC six months prior the conference:

> Two invited speakers with opposing opinions are planned for each 'controversy.' They are not necessarily to confront one another in adversary debate, however. Rather, the speakers will each present his or her side of the argument for about a half-hour to forty-five minutes. Then, the moderator of each session will invite NERC members in the audience to ask questions of the speakers and carry on their own discussion among themselves. In other words, NERC members should come to the 1986 meeting not just to hear lectures, but prepared to participate in three separate open forums."[125]

Edgerton's challenge to NERC members to participate more actively in the conference echoes the observation of David Berkowitz twenty years earlier that an absence of enthusiastic discussion had hampered the conference. Edgerton chose three contemporary subjects: the first was the dispute between artists and art historians concerning the on-going cleaning of Michelangelo's Sistine Chapel frescoes in Rome; the second was whether or not the differing texts in the Quarto and Folio editions of *King Lear* revealed something new about Shakespeare's working methods; and the third considered the relative merits of "micro-" and "macro-history" as currently practiced by Renaissance historians in light of recent interest in critical theory and 'methodology.'[126]

---

[125] Letter from Samuel Edgerton to 'Colleagues' (21 April 1986), NERCA 1.22.3 (emphasis in the original).

[126] Letter from Samuel Edgerton to 'Colleagues' (21 April 1986), NERCA 1.22.3. The description of the three controversies is taken verbatim from Edgerton's letter. The first "debate" involved Marcia Hall and Harold Bruder; the second featured Steven Urkowitz and George Hunter; and the third included Judith Brown and Vincent Ilardi.

In addition to organizing the inaugural conference at Williams, Edgerton immediately reached out to colleagues at Amherst College, Connecticut College, and Harvard University about hosting in future years.[127] In those letters he laid out a list of procedures that conference hosts should follow, and a timeline by which such tasks should be completed. He reiterated that the host institution should not invite its own faculty to be principal speakers; that "appropriate entertainment" should be arranged to follow the Friday night banquet; and that the provost or other academic officer should be prevailed upon to provide a budget of about $3,500. Edgerton also noted his own preference of a "themed" conference, but cautioned that "historically the hosts have preferred simply to have a meeting which represents all the constituencies of our organization."[128] Connecticut College did indeed host NERC in 1987; it remains unclear whether a conference was held in 1988.

1989 marked the fiftieth anniversary of NERC, and thus merited a particularly significant celebration. Planning had begun as far back as 1984, when Jane Ruby had initiated conversations with the administration at Brown University about hosting a "reunion" conference in Providence. Those plans changed somewhat unexpectedly, however, when Samuel Edgerton collaborated with Wallace MacCaffrey, the former chair of Harvard's History Department, and Eugene Rice, executive director of the RSA, to propose a joint NERC/RSA conference in the spring of 1989.[129] The result was the largest conference in the history of NERC. Prominent scholars from across the country as well as from Europe, flocked to Cambridge. Art historian Lilian Armstrong of Wellesley College was signaled out for special recognition for her work on the Program Committee; she received a fulsome letter of thanks from Samuel Edgerton for her "indispensable help" in organizing the 1989

---

[127] Letter from Samuel Edgerton to Joel Upton (Amherst College) (23 Oct. 1986), NERCA 1.23.1; Letter from Samuel Edgerton to Nancy Rash and Robert Proctor (Connecticut College) (10 Dec. 1986), NERCA 1.23.2; Letter from Samuel Edgerton to Eugene Rice (RSA executive director) [re: a joint meeting in Boston in 1989] (13 June 1986), NERCA 1.24.1.

[128] Ibid.

[129] Letter from Samuel Edgerton to Eugene Rice (13 June 1986), NERCA 1.24.1; see also n. 27 above re: previous correspondence on this matter. MacCaffrey was chair of the Harvard History Department from 1972–75 and 1979–82; Rice was executive director of the RSA from 1966–82 and 1985–87.

conference, in which he raved that the conference had suffered "not a hitch, not a balk, not an error."[130]

Like the conference organized by David Berkowitz at Brandeis twenty-five years earlier, the 1989 conference featured several exhibitions, including two at Harvard's Houghton Library and another at the Isabella Stewart Gardner Museum.[131] A companion symposium at the Boston Museum of Fine Arts, on "Power, Patronage, and Prestige: Art under the Medici in 15th century Florence" offered another venue for Renaissance scholars on Friday afternoon. To accommodate the large number of sessions, the conference stretched to three days. Following introductory remarks from Samuel Edgerton as both NERC president and Program chair, the conference opened with a talk by Edward Cranz entitled "Fifty Years of NERC." In an amusing and whimsical style, Cranz traced elements of NERC's early history, focusing in particular on the contributions of Leicester Bradner and of the Brown Renaissance Colloquium.[132] Cranz gathered reminiscences from more than a dozen early contributors to NERC, including Paul Oskar Kristeller who was then in ill health and unable to attend the meeting. Later that evening Anthony Molho moderated a round-table discussion on the provocative topic of "Is the Renaissance still what it used to be?" Friday witnessed twenty-eight sessions on all topics of Renaissance Studies, followed by a banquet and the annual Bennett Lecture, offered this time by Kathleen Weil-Garris Brandt of NYU on the recent discoveries in Michelangelo's Sistine Ceiling. Saturday witnessed another dozen concurrent sessions, and a plenary devoted to recent trends in Renaissance economic history, chaired by Richard Goldthwaite. The conference ended with a concert of Renaissance music and cocktails at the Isabella Stewart Gardner Museum.

Clearly the scale of this joint meeting was far grander than what NERC was used to, and it is unfair (even inaccurate) to compare attendance,

[130] Letter from Samuel Edgerton to Lilian Armstrong (6 April 1989), NERCA 1.24.12.

[131] At Houghton Library: "The First Roman Printers and the Idioms of Humanism" and "Italian Humanists in ten manuscripts from the Houghton Library" (with catalogue by James Hankins). At the ISGM: "Italian Etchers of the Renaissance and Baroque."

[132] Cranz, "Fifty Years" (n. 1 above), passim. Cranz cites a few documents, such as the 1966–67 Newsletter but he makes no reference to the specific correspondence of NERC presidents and members, nor to the conference programs.

budget, etc. for this joint effort with the more modest results of the traditional regional meeting. Nevertheless, the 1989 meeting provides an opportunity to take stock of how both NERC and RSA were changing. The RSA was entering a period of tremendous growth, which continues unabated today; NERC, by contrast, remained similar in size and scope to previous decades. In reflecting upon the changes that took place under his leadership, Samuel Edgerton observed recently that "It was a time of lessening interest in local organizations as the national Renaissance Conference (RSA) was becoming more important as the choicer venue for presenting papers—which pre-empted much of our membership."[133] This divergence between the national organization and the regional ones has only increased in recent years, as graduate students and assistant professors look to a national forum rather than a regional one for presentation of research and networking opportunities early in their careers.

The Spring 1989 conference marked the effective end of Samuel Edgerton's tenure as President of NERC. One more conference would take place at Wesleyan in October of 1989, under the coordination of John Paoletti. As had occurred with both Gilmore and Berkowitz, Paoletti's organization of that conference propelled him into a leadership position in the following year. The Wesleyan conference followed the traditional model in most respects: two papers on Friday afternoon by Peter Stallybrass (Penn) and Jonathan Goldberg (Johns Hopkins), and two more on Saturday morning by art historians Anne Rosalind Jones (Smith) and Margaret Carroll (Wellesley), chaired by John Paoletti. Anthony Grafton (Princeton) gave a talk after the banquet on Friday evening about the Renaissance astrologer, doctor, and mathematician Girolamo Cardano, which was expanded and published in 1999 as *Cardano's Cosmos: The Worlds and Works of a Renaissance Astrologer.*

One significant development during Samuel Edgerton's tenure concerns the title of the office that Edgerton assumed. As noted previously, there had never been a firm title for the person who led NERC. Leicester Bradner was christened the *pater academicus* of NERC[134]; Myron Gilmore had described the office as the "Secretaryship or Chairmanship or whatever it is to be called"[135]; and David Berkowitz portrayed his job as

---

[133] Email from Samuel Edgerton to the author, 12 April 2013.
[134] 1967 Newsletter, NERCA 1.7.2, 1.
[135] Letter from Myron Gilmore to Leicester Bradner (6 May 1959), NERCA 1.1.7.

"a functionary, variously described as a president, a general secretary, or a permanent chairman."[136] Jane Ruby actively resisted the title of "President," preferring instead to be referred to as the "coordinator" of NERC. Samuel Edgerton, however, firmly embraced the title of "President" and even had letterhead specially printed with this title on it. In the penultimate paragraph of his 1989 talk about the history of NERC, Edward Cranz commented that the question of "whether or not we should give our leader the formal title of president…[was] the closest that we ever came to a constitutional struggle."[137] Cranz then summarized the views of the victors: "As I remember it, the arguments in favor were that correspondence would be easier if one knew from whom one had heard and to whom one was replying, and further that less arm-twisting might be needed in arranging for the succession if the person knew to what post he was succeeding."[138] Cranz himself felt that the old-fashioned method had worked fine, and he pointed out his fear of "bureaucratic ossification" if the conference were to grow too large or too formal. Nevertheless, the transition to having a formal "President" of NERC was now in place and the executive officer of NERC retains that title today. Other Renaissance societies have been much less reticent to use the title of "President"; the SCRC, PNRS, and RMRRA have all used this honorific from their earliest days. NERC's reluctance to use such a title for nearly half a century thus stands out as an unusual characteristic among its peers.

The Last Twenty-Five Years (1989–2014)

John Paoletti (1990–1998)

With Samuel Edgerton's resignation as president announced at the 1990 NERC at Amherst College, there were immediately calls from the floor that a committee should be constituted to appoint the new president.[139] The members of this *ad hoc* committee included Lilian Armstrong (Wellesley), Kevin Dunn (Yale), Nicola Courtright (Amherst College),

---

[136] 1966 Newsletter, NERCA 1.7.1, 1.
[137] Cranz, "Fifty Years," 758.
[138] Cranz, "Fifty Years," 758.
[139] Daniel Martin, "Newsletter Number One" (3 Nov. 1990), NERCA 2.6.2, 1.

Vincent Ilardi (UMass Amherst), Daniel Martin (UMass Amherst), and John Paoletti (Wesleyan). This "First Appointed Board" was charged by the NERC membership with several tasks, including: (1) Appoint a president from themselves or from the membership at large; (2) Study possible name changes for NERC; (3) Seek affiliation with the MLA; (4) Investigate annual dues or a membership fee; (5) Create a permanent Governing Board, and possibly appoint a secretary-treasurer and a vice-president.[140] The informality and lack of bureaucracy that had long characterized NERC was clearly being challenged here, with the creation of new positions, a new name, new dues, and a permanent governing structure.

The group met on 11 Dec. 1990 at John Paoletti's house in Connecticut. Given Paoletti's success at hosting a conference the previous year, his stature within the field, and his willingness to host the inaugural meeting, it is not surprising that he was elected as president for a term of three years. At this same meeting Daniel Martin was elected as the first treasurer of NERC and Nicola Courtright agreed to create a newsletter and serve as its editor.[141] Per his own request, Samuel Edgerton was included ex officio.

With the 1990 conference behind him, Paoletti immediately focused upon the upcoming conference at Yale in early November 1991, which was significant in several ways. It marked the second time in three years that the conference was held at an Ivy League university, after an absence of nearly two decades. The topics also reflected the new currents of Renaissance Studies, including a strong interest in sexuality, alterity, and gender.[142] The conference was designed by English Department faculty Kevin Dunn and John Rogers, but executed by Yale Conference

---

[140] Memorandum from Daniel Martin to "First Appointed Board" (5 Nov. 1990), NERCA 2.6.3; the agenda is repeated in a follow-up memo (21 Nov. 1990), NERCA 2.6.4; the agenda is identical to that in "Newsletter Number One" as per the previous note.

[141] John Paoletti, "Notice for inclusion in Conference Notes of *Renaissance Quarterly*" (n.d. but probably Dec. 1990), NERCA 2.1.1; a second identical copy was sent to Michael Sappol of the RSA in summer 1991.

[142] For example, James Saslow, "Critical Orientations: The Homosexual Tradition in Renaissance Historiography from Winckelmann to Wilde"; Eugene Rice, "Sodomy in the European Criminal Law, c.1350–1700"; David Quint, "A Reconsideration of Montaigne's *Des cannibals*"; Maureen Quilligan, "Catherine de Medici and Elizabeth I: The Space of Female Performance": all were papers presented at Yale in 1991.

Services, thus lending a certain professionalism to the proceedings that had not always existed previously. John Paoletti instituted a new tradition of convening the Governing Board just prior to the opening of the conference in order to review the previous year's achievements and to anticipate problems.[143] Other elements remained largely unchanged, such as Paoletti's frustration with managing the mailing list and the way in which, as he put it, "NERC seems to be living up to its rather haphazard history."[144]

Despite the perennial difficulty of reconciling the mailing list, it is clear from extant documents that a new level of professionalism was evident in NERC under Paoletti's leadership. He called regular meetings of the Governing Board to solicit advice and to share the burden of choosing conference hosts, as well as to gain assistance in identifying new (and deceased) participants in NERC.[145] His memo of September 1992 posed important questions to his colleagues on the Governing Board:

> As I look at other conferences across the country we seem to be anomalous in our size and in the character of our meetings. Do we want to maintain the small town quality of our meetings or should we look to change their intensity? Do you have any sense about whether our universities and colleges will continue to support NERC operations in times of financial retrenchment? The dollar squeeze may force us to change our operations considerably for the short term. I look forward to your ideas.[146]

---

[143]   Memo from John Paoletti to Governing Board (22 Sept. 1991), NERCA 2.6.5; one month later, a more extended version of the memo was sent (22 Oct. 1991), NERCA 2.6.6.

[144]   Letter from John Paoletti to John Rogers (n.d. but likely July/Aug. 1991), NERCA 2.7.3.

[145]   In addition to the memos of 21 Nov. 1990 and 22 Oct. 1991 (see nn. 140, 143), see also the Memo from John Paoletti to Governing Board (24 Sept. 1992), NERCA 2.6.7.

[146]   Memo from John Paoletti to Governing Board (24 Sept. 1992), NERCA 2.6.7. A full list of the Governing Board, including addresses and phone numbers, is included with this memo. In addition to the six members noted previously, the list included the conference hosts for 1992 (Patricia Emison) and 1993 (Jessie Ann Owens), as well as Samuel Y. Edgerton as *ex officio*.

Paoletti circulated a similar memo to the Governing Board exactly one year later, calling for a Board meeting just prior to the October 1993 NERC conference at Brandeis. The questions raised previously about the size and funding of NERC must have been addressed satisfactorily, because Paoletti's 1993 memo raises a series of new questions for his *consiglieri* to consider. These included "strong sentiment that we should have more sessions during the two days of the Conference, thus necessitating concurrent sessions," as well as a desire to maintain the plenary session and a move to adopt a call for papers to widen participation. The Board was also interested in eliminating honoraria (thus partially addressing the "dollar squeeze" noted above), and in identifying ways to involve more graduate students.[147]

In the same memo, Paoletti pointed out to his board that he had agreed to serve only a three-year term, and that it was time "to begin discussions about who should succeed to the office of chief convener of meetings." Paoletti urged his colleagues to consider "a slate of possibilities" in identifying a replacement. He specified further that in his view it was critically important that the new president be "someone in a major urban area who might have the personnel resources to implement the changes in conference structure that we discussed last year but which I simply have not had the time to pursue."[148] Paoletti was unsuccessful in his bid to step down, however, and subsequently agreed to serve another three-year term. Nor do subsequent programs in the 1990s indicate concurrent sessions, wider participation, a plenary session, or the presence of graduate students as speakers.

The 1993 conference at Brandeis, organized by Jessie Ann Owens of the Music Department, adopted as its theme "Power and Illusion in the Renaissance City," with one session on civic pageantry in London and Germany, and another on urban space that focused on Florence. There were only four papers, plus the usual evening concert, in this case of fifteenth-century chamber music from the Capella Alamire Hampshire Consort. The 1995 conference, organized at Vassar by Benjamin Kohl and Nicholas Adams, chose the theme of "The Material City in the Renaissance." The program was expanded to ten speakers spread over four sessions, and—in a departure from past practice—focused exclusively upon

---

[147] Memo from John Paoletti to Governing Board (29 Sept. 1993), NERCA 2.6.8.
[148] Memo from John Paoletti to Governing Board (29 Sept. 1993), NERCA 2.6.8.

Italian topics. Doubtless that limited geographical range was in part the result of the Italianate research interests of the conference hosts. The conference also covered topics only in History and Art History, although a performance by the Vassar College Madrigals provided some musical content. In a letter of thanks to Vassar's president days later, John Paoletti praised the "imaginative planning and extraordinary efforts" of Kohl and Adams in organizing the conference, and further noted the large number of Vassar alumnae who were specialists in Renaissance art history.[149]

No conference was held in 1994 or 1996 or 1998. These gaps suggest that administration of the conference was indeed becoming too much of a burden for Paoletti. In March 1997 Virginia Reinburg and Elizabeth Rhodes of Boston College hosted a conference on the theme of "Prayer: Situation, Representation, Enactment." For the first time in the history of NERC, the conference took place on only one day, although it still included ten speakers organized into three sessions. Case studies and examples from Spain, Italy, and Germany were included, as well as "final remarks" from Robert Scribner and Clarissa Atkinson of the Harvard Divinity School. Despite the fact that the conference lasted only one day, the speakers came from across the continent: North Carolina, Minnesota, New York, California, and even Ontario, Canada. In 1999, the conference returned to Boston College, this time under the aegis of art historians Pamela Jones and Gauvin Alexander Bailey. Given their respective interests, it is no surprise that the theme was again quite narrowly defined, as "Caravaggio's Culture in Renaissance Italy." The focus was again largely Italian, and again privileged the fields of history and art history. Interestingly, only one paper dealt explicitly with Caravaggio; all of the others examined aspects of early modern Italian culture. As the conference was a one-day event, no evening concert was organized, but a concurrent exhibition and catalogue edited by Franco Mormando, *Saints & Sinners: Caravaggio and the Baroque Image* were available to conference participants.

In addition to heralding the end of the millennium and a definitive turn toward both themed conferences and a one-day duration, the 1999 conference marked the beginning of Kenneth Gouwens' term as president of NERC. He would hold this position for nearly a decade, during which NERC returned to its prior tradition of a regular annual conference. John

---

[149]   Letter from John Paoletti to Frances D. Fergusson (5 Nov. 1995), NERCA 2.5.3.

Paoletti, who had initially volunteered for just a single three-year term, ended up serving eight years as NERC president. His chief contribution was to create an active governing board and to introduce a stronger sense of professionalism. In reflecting upon his term of office, Paoletti observed that the numbers of Renaissance faculty in the 1990s were somewhat less than they are today, which made the process of recruiting both speakers and audience members more challenging.[150] Nevertheless, it is clear that he exceeded the stipulations laid down by Leicester Bradner and William Church in 1959, when they described the responsibilities of the NERC president in this way: "to keep the *ad hoc* committee alive (if necessary), write a letter or two…, and keep track of the list of members."[151]

Kenneth Gouwens (1998–2009)

Kenneth Gouwens assumed the presidency of NERC in 1998. A native Midwesterner who attended college in the South and graduate school in the West, Gouwens arrived at the University of Connecticut largely ignorant of NERC and its traditions. Following consultation with some of the senior scholars in the area, including members of his influential governing board, John Paoletti asked Gouwens to assume the mantle of president. Despite Gouwens' expertise in papal history, Gouwens notes that there was "no laying on of hands and no apostolic succession" for the transition, just an informal lunch in which Paoletti briefly summarized the responsibilities.[152]

---

[150] Email from John Paoletti to the author, 28 March 2013: "I recall that a good deal of our early history was a bit haphazard, having to rely on our own colleges to support the annual meetings. The numbers of Renaissance faculty were also somewhat smaller than they are now, so that attracting significant attendance to meetings and attracting challenging talks for the sessions was a challenge."

[151] Letter from William F. Church to Myron Gilmore (8 Nov. 1958), NERCA 1.1.1 offering Gilmore the chairmanship of NERC.

[152] Oral interview of K. Gouwens in Cambridge, MA (14 Jan. 2013), NERCA 2.28.1. Amidst Paoletti's file of correspondence is an undated typescript two-page document entitled "Organization of Annual Program," NERCA 2.6.11. It is possible that this document was written by Samuel Edgerton or even by David Berkowitz, but given Paoletti's penchant for organized memos, and its location in the middle of his NERC correspondence from the late 1990s, it seems more likely to have been authored by Paoletti, and thus to have served as the basis of his discussion with Ken Gouwens in 1998 about leading NERC.

Gouwens believed at the time that it was important for NERC not to become a preserve of either English literature or Italian Renaissance history and art, as these were subjects already well-represented at area institutions such as the UMass Center for Renaissance Studies. Rather, he wished to make NERC more broadly inclusive and more "democratic" in its outlook by appealing to scholars from a wide range of disciplines.[153] Gouwens insisted upon an interdisciplinary approach, and included this requirement in his "Guidelines for Organizers of the Annual Program": "It is mandatory that the topics and speakers represent a multi-disciplinary approach in the aggregate. Ideally, speakers should represent a range of geographical specializations and methodological approaches."[154] In an email to Dario Del Puppo of Trinity College about the 2004 NERC annual meeting, Gouwens warned that the proposed program on "Celebrating Petrarch" was too narrowly focused on Italian subjects. He wrote "While you and I may find things Italian most interesting of all, the NERC is by design and past practice not only interdisciplinary but also geographically wide-ranging."[155] In addition, wrote Gouwens, he "would not want the appearance of possibly steering the Conference toward my own special interests."[156] Gouwens made a similar point about the importance of interdisciplinarity in a letter to Arthur Kinney at UMass Amherst when planning the 2001 conference there.[157] As is evident from both correspondence

---

[153] Oral interview of K. Gouwens in Cambridge, MA (14 Jan. 2013), NERCA 2.28.1.

[154] Kenneth Gouwens, "Guidelines for Organizers of the Annual Program" (May 2001), NERCA 2.11.2-B.

[155] Email from Kenneth Gouwens to Dario Del Puppo (14 Aug. 2004), NERCA 2.12.3-A. See also the email of Dario Del Puppo to Kenneth Gouwens (16 Apr. 2002), NERCA 2.12.1, in which Del Puppo offered to host NERC as part of the celebration of the 700th anniversary of Petrarch's birth, and to coincide with a conference that Del Puppo and Eugenio Giusti were already planning at Trinity and at Vassar on successive days. Del Puppo had previously organized a NERC meeting at Trinity College in 2001, on the subject of "Emotion and Creativity in the Renaissance."

[156] Email from Kenneth Gouwens to Dario Del Puppo (14 Aug. 2004), NERCA 2.12.3-A. For the same reason, Gouwens declined Del Puppos's invitation of 16 July 2004 to give a paper at the conference on Petrarch in the 16th century.

[157] Email from Kenneth Gouwens to Arthur F. Kinney (10 Dec. 1999), NERCA 2.9.1.

and from the conference programs, Gouwens also emphasized the importance of an interdisciplinary approach in the two conferences held at his home institution in Storrs, Connecticut, in 2003 and again in 2006.[158]

Most of the conferences in Gouwens's term as president did indeed possess a distinct interdisciplinary theme, such as "Emotion and Creativity in the Renaissance" (2000), "Renaissance Courts" (2001), "Teaching, Learning, and the Transmission of Knowledge" (2002), "Piety and Plague" (2005), or "Nature's Disciplines" (2007). Some themes became increasingly abstract, such as the conference at Boston University called simply "Values and Judgments" (2009), or Yale University's choice of "The Immaterial Renaissance" the following year (2010). Such consciously interdisciplinary themes reflect the broader changes in Renaissance Studies in the 1990s and at the turn of the millennium, as scholars in history, art history, and literature deliberately borrowed methodologies from other disciplines such as anthropology or queer studies. Modern Renaissance Studies also has less certainty about the core texts and key subjects of the field than it did a generation or two ago; thus, conference papers encompass a much broader range of subjects than previously, a reality reflected in NERC's conference programs.

Virtually all of these conferences in the 1990s preserved the one-day format. Some issued a general call for papers while others preferred to follow the time-honored tradition of the program chair (or program committee) selecting speakers. The near-absolute freedom of the program chair to determine the theme and the structure of the conference remained as it had in the past. Although the conference continued to rely upon faculty from the New England area for a majority of presentations, the trend of inviting scholars from far away became increasingly common. For example, during the 2000 conference at Trinity College, speakers came from South Carolina, Texas, Spain, and Sweden; the 2006 conference included speakers from Duke, Michigan, and Johns Hopkins.

---

[158] Letter from Kenneth Gouwens to Francoise Dussart (28 June 2002), NERCA 2.11.2-A: this letter requested $4,000 in funding from the Univ. of Connecticut Humanities Institute (UCHI), and specified that "this conference explicitly promotes scholarly interchange across traditional academic boundaries, be they disciplinary or geographical," in accordance with the UCHI's mission. The 2006 conference lacked a theme but included papers ranging from anatomy and alchemy to humanism and subversive Renaissance music.

Gouwens also thought it important to continue the tradition of moving the conference to a new host each year, both to avoid wearing out the conference's welcome at the same institutions, and to encourage those institutions that had not traditionally hosted in the past. Reaching out to Renaissance scholars at colleges with small enrollments (or small travel budgets) was a way to broaden the impact of NERC across the region. Thus, the conference met at Trinity College (2000), Holy Cross (2005), and Wesleyan University (2008). Still, the conference often continued to rotate among those schools which had often hosted in the past, in part because they possessed the necessary funding and conference space, not to mention a cadre of Renaissance faculty to form the program committee: UMass Amherst (2001), Brown University (2002, 2007), University of Connecticut (2003, 2006), Boston University (2009), and Yale University (2010).

Gouwens did not continue the practice of having a formal governing board as Paoletti had, relying instead upon a network of colleagues, especially Evelyn Lincoln at Brown, who hosted a pair of conferences in 2002 and 2007. Gouwens's tenure from 1998 to 2009 also witnessed the transformation of communication from postal mail to email. The NERC mailing list increasingly became a file of email addresses, and Gouwens's own communication migrated toward the digital sphere. Such a transition is best captured in Gouwens's correspondence with Arthur Kinney on either side of the millennium. In mid-December 1999 Gouwens wrote to Kinney to ask if UMass Amherst would host NERC in 2001; he prefaced his request by saying "Please excuse the informality of e-mail, but I wanted to get a message to you sooner rather than later in this holiday mailing season." Kinney responded—with a hand-typed letter—on 11 December 1999, and again on 13 October 2001 with further information about the conference program and attendees.[159] Virtually all of Gouwens's subsequent communication from 2000 to 2009 was transmitted via email rather than "snail mail." Similar technological changes—the use of e-mail attachments to send the Call for Papers, the creation of websites to advertise the conference programs, and so forth—are evident throughout the NERC Archive for this period.

---

[159] Email from Kenneth Gouwens to Arthur F. Kinney (10 Dec. 1999), NERCA 2.9.1; Letters from Arthur F. Kinney to Kenneth Gouwens (11 Dec. 1999), NERCA 2.9.2 and (13 Oct. 2001), NERCA 2.9.6.

Tara Nummedal (2009-2013)

Historian Tara Nummedal of Brown University represented a distinct break from the past when she was selected to succeed Kenneth Gouwens as NERC president in 2009. A native Californian with a Stanford Ph.D., and a specialist in central Europe, alchemy, and the history of science, Nummedal was far removed from the traditional fields (both geographical and disciplinary) emphasized in Renaissance Studies generally and in NERC more specifically. This choice was not by accident. After consulting informally with longtime NERC participants, Ken Gouwens deliberately chose a successor who would bring a fresh perspective to the job and who would provide a challenge to the status quo of seventy years of tradition. Gouwens explained that he selected Nummedal for several reasons: (1) Nummedal would be the first female president of NERC[160]; (2) Nummedal's academic expertise represented new areas in Renaissance Studies; (3) Nummedal possessed both strong organizational skills and strong digital skills.[161] It helped, of course, that she was a tenured professor at Brown; not only did this appointment continue the legacy of Leicester Bradner, but it satisfied John Paoletti's earlier criterion that the president be "someone in a major urban area who might have the [necessary] personnel resources."[162]

Nummedal's vision for NERC was to preserve its historical character and traditions, while modernizing it in subtle ways. Thus she continued the tradition of an annual fall conference, with particular emphasis upon interdisciplinarity and a broad theme each year. She continued to support

---

[160] Obviously Gouwens was unfamiliar with the short term of Jane Ruby from 1983–85.

[161] Oral interviews conducted with Kenneth Gouwens (14 Jan. 2013) in Cambridge, and with Tara Nummedal (15 Jan. 2013) in Providence; summaries are at the NERC Archive, NERCA 2.28.1–2. See also the email from Ken Gouwens to Touba Ghadessi and Gen Liang (21 April 2013), NERCA 2.24.2, in which Gouwens wrote "When I consulted with my advisors about the selection of Tara, we all felt strongly that it was important to get someone whose focus was neither English Literature nor Italian history or art....While both John [Paoletti] and I sought a diversity of presenters, like everyone else we have our own bailiwicks. So, it was all the more beneficial for NERC to get Tara to serve: someone conversant in the Italian scholarship, but doing methodologically innovative work centered on Germany, traditionally underrepresented (when represented at all, which was rare) in the conference."

[162] Memo from John Paoletti to Governing Board (29 Sept. 1993), NERCA 2.6.8.

the idea of "democratizing" NERC by encouraging institutions that had not hosted in the past to do so. She also solved the age-old problem of the NERC mailing list by harnessing the power of the Internet to have scholars self-subscribe to a moderated list-serve; while it is true that some potential members of NERC thus fail to be notified, it saves the conference money on mailing and printing costs as well as putting the onus for being informed more directly upon members. Nummedal also created a hybrid website-blog where information of interest to members, including the digitization of some archival material about NERC, could be posted.[163] Nevertheless, NERC continues to lag in the digital revolution; by Nummedal's own admission, the website is updated infrequently and it offers little in terms of two-way communication or exchange among members. Perhaps it is not surprising that NERC continues to cling to its traditional view of what the conference has been: an annual gathering of like-minded scholars, whose interests evolve with the times, but not a great deal more.

The first conference under Nummedal's leadership, at Yale in 2010, was a major event with nearly 150 scholars and graduate students in attendance. Organized by Francesca Trivellato and Christopher Wood, and flawlessly managed by Yale Conference Services, the conference experimented with several new approaches. The conference opened with a two-hour round table discussion in the morning, and a series of inter-related papers in the afternoon; these were followed by a distinct keynote address. Many of the papers were highly theoretical and drew heavily from literary criticism, new historicism, and post-modern outlooks. The theme of "The Immaterial Renaissance" was deliberately opaque. The 2010 NERC took advantage of Yale's Art Gallery, Beinecke Library, and Center for British Art by organizing brief tours of each.

The 2011 conference broke new ground in several ways, and was a strong contrast with the previous conference at Yale. It was held at a small liberal arts college (Wheaton) in a rural location (Norton, MA) on a much more modest budget. The theme of "Family Relations in the Renaissance" was a familiar and accessible one to historians, art historians, and literary scholars. Undergraduate students were deliberately involved as conference staff, exhibition curators, and campus guides. According to Tara Nummedal, one of the goals of having the conference

---

[163] The NERC website is at <http://nercblog.wordpress.com>.

at Wheaton was to demonstrate that small liberal arts colleges could host NERC as successfully as major research universities. The 2012 conference traveled to a new venue at University of Massachusetts Lowell but returned to a traditional topic. The theme of "Classical Revival and Reception in the Renaissance" resulted in a program with one morning session on "Classical Authority" and a second afternoon session on "Classical Authors." Among the speakers solicited by an open call for papers were several advanced graduate students; there was also a keynote address at the end of the day by James Hankins on "Renaissance Views of the Roman Republic."

The 2013 NERC returned to Brandeis University exactly twenty years after its last appearance there. Art historian Jonathan Unglaub chose the theme "Thresholds of Faith and Fantasy: Spiritual Journeys and Real Spaces." This theme effectively combined literary, art historical, and historical perspectives on questions of religious history, especially the question of "sacred and profane geographies" and the issue of "body and spirit." Five of the six papers focused on Italian topics, although Leonard Barkan's keynote address offered something of a balance by considering three vignettes from across early modern Europe. The 2014 NERC, celebrating its 75th anniversary, was held in Durham, NH at the University of New Hampshire under the leadership of Liz Mellyn. The theme "Cultures of Credit and Debt in Medieval and Early Modern Europe" emphasized economic history, a focus not seen in recent years at the NERC. The 2015 conference is tentatively scheduled to be held at University of Massachusetts Boston, another new locale. Thus, the recent history of NERC conferences would seem to suggest a consistent pattern of blending traditional foci (e.g., sixteenth-century Italian topics) with new theoretical paradigms and new institutional hosts.

Touba Ghadessi and Yuan-Gen Liang (2013-)

The selection of art historian Touba Ghadessi and historian Yuan-Gen Liang as NERC co-presidents in 2013 signaled another milestone in the history of NERC. Although their respective disciplines of art history and history are traditional ones for NERC, several aspects of their leadership (like that of Tara Nummedal) represent new directions. The creation of a co-presidency is perhaps the most obvious innovation. It was instituted both to lessen the administrative burden on the recipients as well as to incorporate greater ethnic diversity in NERC's leadership. The geographical foci of Ghadessi and Liang are also new, as is the explicitly comparative and bi-national nature of their respective research agendas: Ghadessi has analyzed issues of anatomy and physical deformity in courts of Italy and France, while Liang has examined the "connected histories" of Spain and North Africa. Both scholars teach at Wheaton College, a small liberal-arts college far removed from the traditional locales of Providence, New Haven, or Cambridge. (Former NERC presidents Jane Ruby taught at Wheaton, and Samuel Edgerton taught at Williams, so the leaders of NERC have not always come from major research universities in urban centers).

Ghadessi and Liang were coorganizers of the 2011 NERC at Wheaton College, which emphasized inclusion of undergraduate students in conference planning and execution. Both Ghadessi and Liang strongly support interdisciplinary activities, an approach long associated with NERC and explicitly promoted by Gouwens and Nummedal as prior presidents.[164] In a letter to Ghadessi and Liang asking them to consider accepting the presidency of NERC, Tara Nummedal praised their "energy, creativity, professionalism, and commitment"; and she added "More importantly, though, your own expertise in French/Spanish, art history/history, etc. will ensure that NERC continues to represent a diverse intellectual agenda, rather than just the Italian Renaissance."[165] It is too soon to tell whether Ghadessi and Liang will move NERC in other new directions too. One of their first actions, at the 2013 meeting at Brandeis, was to convene an advisory board of a dozen Renaissance scholars to provide suggestions; topics included the possibility of a NERC workshop directed at graduate students, and of NERC-sponsored panels for the annual RSA conference. Nummedal also encouraged the new co-presidents to consider term limits, so that the position

---

[164]   Ghadessi and Liang co-founded the Wheaton Institute for Interdisciplinary Humanities in Fall 2012. Liang is co-founder and current president of the Spain-North Africa Project (SNAP), which seeks to bring together scholars traditionally divided by language and geography to find common interests around the Mediterranean.

[165]   Email from Tara Nummedal to Touba Ghadessi and Gen Liang (18 April 2013), NERCA 2.24.1. Ken Gouwens wrote a follow-up email explaining his perspective on the presidency (21 April 2013), NERCA 2.24.2. Ghadessi and Liang accepted the presidency in a letter to Tara Nummedal (13 June 2013), NERCA 2.24.3.

would become neither a sinecure nor an albatross, for themselves or their successors.[166]

Conclusion

The New England Renaissance Conference has played a significant role in the promotion and propagation of Renaissance Studies during the last three-quarters of a century, particularly for the Northeast. Through the vehicle of an annual conference that has rotated from school to school, the members of the Conference have been able to share their recent research and to discuss the significant issues in the profession. If we look back to the observation of William G. Constable about the purpose of NERC in 1939–40, which he defined as "bringing together scholars of the Renaissance within a limited area for informal and frank discussion," it seems that NERC has not evolved much at all.[167] Given the enormous changes that have occurred within the field of Renaissance Studies since World War II—including transatlantic air travel, the rise of quantitative and computer-aided analysis, the emergence of social history, the digitization of archival material, the growth of the RSA, the proliferation of academic sub-specialties, and the debate over nomenclature between "early modern" and "Renaissance," to name just a few—it is remarkable how little NERC has changed. The New England Renaissance Conference has remained true to its founder's vision of a minimalist academic organization that somehow survives "in graceful disarray" decade after decade. Despite its lack of a budget, a staff, or a mission statement, the Conference has managed to prosper through the good will and generosity of academics and institutions across New England. In one sense, then, the New England Renaissance Conference is firmly rooted in the past and even a bit antiquarian. However, this allegiance to the past, while appropriate for an organization that celebrates a historic era, is not to suggest that NERC has remained immobile. The leadership and the members of NERC have introduced substantial changes along the way, including the

---

[166] Email from Tara Nummedal to Touba Ghadessi and Gen Liang (18 April 2013), NERCA 2.24.1.

[167] Letter from W. G. Constable to David Berkowitz (19 April 1966), NERCA 1.1.8 (n. 14 above).

championing of interdisciplinarity, the expansion of NERC's constituency, and a growing diversity in conference themes. Such changes reflect broader transformations in the academy and in the field of Renaissance Studies. The New England Renaissance Conference can thus be viewed, with caution and in comparison with its sister organizations, as a case study of how academic societies evolve, and more specifically of how Renaissance Studies has developed in the northeastern United States over the past seventy-five years.

INDEX

NOTE: MANUSCRIPTS ARE indexed under "Manuscripts."

A

Adams, Thomas, 314

Adrian de Boisy, Cardinal, 158, 169–73, 174, 177–78, 180, 185–86, 188, 192–93, 195–96, 199–200, 205, 208, 210

Aesop's fables, 292–93

Agilon, Walter, 54, 67, 72, 92–95
  Craft of Urines, 73
  Summa medicinalis, 150

Agnes of Harcourt, 3rd Abbess of Long-champ, 156–57, 172

Akrigg, G. P. V., 373

Albertus Magnus, 228, 251

Alexander VI, Pope (1492–1503), 174

Allen, Don Cameron, 349

American Council of Learned Societies, 346, 349–50

Anne, Queen of England (d. 1394), 94

Anselm, Saint, 236–39

Aquinas, Saint Thomas, 228, 229–30, 235, 241, 242–45, 247–48, 251

Arderon, John, 76, 153

Aristotle, 225, 227, 228, 231, 234, 239, 244, 246–47, 248–49, 250, 252, 256, 260, Arminian vs. Calvinist theology, 289

Arminianism and Palagianism, 288

Arminianism in English politics, 262–65

Arminianism in 17th-century England, 261–302

"Arminius between Truth and Heresie," 284–86, 288–89, 291, 295–96

Augustine, Saint, 225, 231, 232–34, 235–36, 238, 242–44, 249, 252, 254, 258, 260

Avity, Pierre d', *Estates, Empires, and Principalities* (1615), 327

B

Badurius, King of Cambaia, 334, 335

Barnard, John, 329

Barton [Johannes?], 99
  Barton's Urines, 99

Baschera, Luca, 226, 228

Behn, Aphra, *Oroonoko* (1688), 338, 343

Bejczy, Istjvan, 259

Berkowitz, David S., 366, 362–83
  Inequality of Opportunity in Higher Education, 382–83

Bernard de Gordon, 97, 150

Bernard of Clairvaux, Saint, 236, 256

Beron, Thomas, 304

Beza, Theodore, 300

Blanchard, Harold, 358

Bouwsma, William, 259

Bradner, Leicester, 349, 350, 352–61, 362–63, 369

Submission Guidelines

For current submission guidelines and calls for papers, please visit the *Studies in Medieval and Renaissance History* website at http://acmrs.org/publications/journals/smrh/submissionguidelines.